© Hal Espen

CAROLINE FRASER is the editor of the Library of America edition of Laura Ingalls Wilder's Little House books, and the author of *Rewilding the World* and *God's Perfect Child*. Her writing has appeared in *The New York Review of Books*, *The New Yorker*, *The Atlantic*, the *Los Angeles Times*, and the *London Review of Books*, among other publications. She lives in New Mexico.

ALSO BY CAROLINE FRASER

God's Perfect Child

Rewilding the World

Prairie Fires represents a significant milestone in our understanding of Wilder's life, work, and legacy." —Wendy McClure, author of *The Wilder Life: My Adventures in the Lost World of "Little House on the Prairie"*

"Meticulously researched, feelingly told, *Prairie Fires* is the definitive biography of a major writer who did so much to mold public perceptions of the Western frontier. Once again, Caroline Fraser has shown that she is a master of the careful art of sifting a life, finding meaning in the large and small events that shaped an iconic American figure. *Prairie Fires* is a magnificent contribution to the literature of the West." —Hampton Sides, author of *Blood and Thunder: The Epic Story of Kit Carson and the Conquest of the American West*

"At last, an unsentimental examination of Laura Ingalls Wilder's real life on the frontier. Caroline Fraser rescues Wilder from frontier myth and gives us the gritty, passionate woman who endured the harshest experiences of homesteading, loved the Great Plains, and was devastated by their ultimate ruin and loss. Elegantly written and impeccably researched, *Prairie Fires* is a major contribution to environmental history and literary biography." —Linda Lear, author of *Beatrix Potter: A Life in Nature* and *Rachel Carson: Witness for Nature*

"In the twenty-first century, the tense and secret authorial partnership between Laura Ingalls Wilder and her daughter, Rose Wilder Lane, has emerged as the most complex and fascinating psychological saga of mother-daughter collaboration in American literary history. Caroline Fraser's deeply researched and stimulating biography analyzes their controversial relationship and places Wilder's influential fiction in the contexts of other myths of pioneer women and the frontier." —Elaine Showalter, author of *A Jury of Her Peers* and *The Civil Wars of Julia Ward Howe*

Additional Praise for *Prairie Fires*

"Magnificent . . . A remarkable, noteworthy biography of an American literary icon. It will captivate Little House fans as well as anyone looking to understand 'the perpetual hard winter' of life in frontier times." —*USA Today*

"Impressive . . . *Prairie Fires* could not have been published at a more propitious time in our national life." —*The New Republic*

"*Prairie Fires* honors the pristine beauty of Laura's fiction while sternly dismantling the frontier mythos her books shored up for generations. . . . Fraser places Laura's choices as a writer within the larger context of Americans' self-deception when it comes to the pioneer life and its legacy. This she manages to do without diminishing Laura herself, a woman Fraser clearly admires." —*Slate*

"Unforgettable . . . Wonderfully insightful . . . A magisterial biography, which surely must be called definitive. Richly documented, it is a compelling, beautifully written story." —*Booklist* (starred review)

"Engrossing . . . Exhilarating . . . Lovers of the series will delight in learning about real-life counterparts to classic fictional episodes, but, as Fraser emphasizes, the true story was often much harsher. Meticulously tracing the Ingalls and Wilder families' experiences through public records and private documents, Fraser discovers failed farm ventures and constant money problems, as well as natural disasters even more terrifying and devastating in real life than in Wilder's writing. She also helpfully puts Wilder's narrow world into larger historical context." —*Publishers Weekly*

"A fantastic book. We've long understood the Little House series to be a great American story, but Caroline Fraser brings it unprecedented new context, as she masterfully chronicles the life of Laura Ingalls Wilder and her family alongside the complicated history of our nation.

PRAIRIE FIRES

The American Dreams *of*
LAURA INGALLS WILDER

Caroline Fraser

PICADOR

METROPOLITAN BOOKS

Henry Holt and Company   New York

PRAIRIE FIRES. Copyright © 2017 by Caroline Fraser. All rights reserved.
Printed in the United States of America. For information, address
Picador, 175 Fifth Avenue, New York, N.Y. 10010.

picadorusa.com • instagram.com/picador
twitter.com/picadorusa • facebook.com/picadorusa

Picador® is a U.S. registered trademark and is used by Macmillan Publishing Group,
LLC, under license from Pan Books Limited.

For book club information, please visit facebook.com/picadorbookclub or email
marketing@picadorusa.com.

Parts of this book originally appeared, in somewhat different form, in essays in
The New York Review of Books, the *Los Angeles Review of Books*, and *Pioneer
Girl Perspectives: Exploring Laura Ingalls Wilder*, ed. Nancy Tystad Koupal
(Pierre: South Dakota Historical Society Press, 2017).

Map by Virginia Norey

Designed by Kelly S. Too

The Library of Congress has cataloged the Metropolitan Books edition as follows:

Names: Fraser, Caroline, author.
Title: Prairie fires : the American dreams of Laura Ingalls Wilder / Caroline Fraser.
Description: First edition. | New York : Metropolitan Books, 2017. | Includes index.
Identifiers: LCCN 2017028870 | ISBN 9781627792769 (hardcover) | ISBN
    9781627792776 (ebook)
Subjects: LCSH: Wilder, Laura Ingalls, 1867–1957. | Authors, American—20th
    century—Biography. | Women pioneers—United States—Biography. | Frontier
    and pioneer life—United States.
Classification: LCC PS3545.I342 Z6455 2017 | DDC 813'.52—dc23
LC record available at https://lccn.loc.gov/2017028870

Picador Paperback ISBN 978-1-250-18248-7

Our books may be purchased in bulk for promotional, educational, or business use.
Please contact your local bookseller or the Macmillan Corporate and Premium
Sales Department at 1-800-221-7945, extension 5442, or by email at
MacmillanSpecialMarkets@macmillan.com.

First published by Metropolitan Books, an imprint of Henry Holt and Company, LLC

First Picador Edition: August 2018

*In memory of my mother, Ruth Fraser,
and my grandmother Ruth Webb*

The prairies burning form some of the most beautiful scenes that are to be witnessed in this country.

—George Catlin

CONTENTS

PART III: THE DREAM

A NOTE ON QUOTATIONS

Unless otherwise indicated, in quotations from the letters, diaries, and manuscripts of Laura Ingalls Wilder, Rose Wilder Lane, and others, all spelling, grammar, and punctuation are reproduced as they appear in the original source.

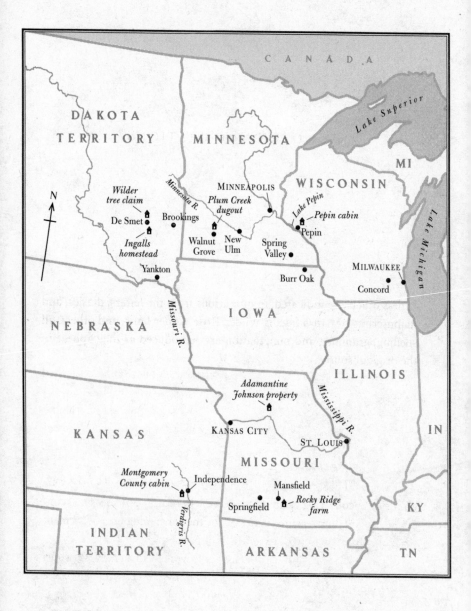

Introduction

On a spring day in April of 1924, Laura Ingalls Wilder, a fifty-seven-year-old farm wife in the Missouri Ozarks, received a telegram from South Dakota. Her mother, Caroline Ingalls, had just died. Wilder hadn't seen her for more than twenty years.

A few weeks later, still reeling, she wrote a brief note to be published in place of her regular column in a farm newspaper. Every woman in the world who has lost her mother will recognize the retrospective shadow of sorrow, regret, and crippling nostalgia that the news cast across her life. "Some of us have received such messages," she said flatly. "Those who have not, one day will."[1]

Then it all became too much to bear. "Memories!" she wrote. "We go thru life collecting them whether we will or not! Sometimes I wonder if they are our treasures in heaven or the consuming fires of torment when we carry them with us as we, too, pass on."[2]

It was a startling public outburst for a woman in a small Missouri town known to her neighbors as reserved, poised, even withdrawn. She seemed anguished by her memories, willed and unwilled. The realization that she would be visited for the rest of her life by images of people and places she could never forget was dismaying to her. "They are with us forever," she wrote, as if in disbelief.[3]

As children, we thought we knew her. She was the real-life pioneer girl who survived wildfires, tornadoes, malaria, blizzards, and near-starvation on the Great Plains in the late 1800s. She was the fierce, uncompromising tomboy who grew up to write famous books about her life: *Little House in the Big Woods*, *Farmer Boy*, *Little House on the Prairie*, *On the Banks of Plum Creek*, *By the Shores of Silver Lake*, *The Long Winter*, *Little Town on the Prairie*, and *These Happy Golden Years*. She was the woman whose true-life stories went on to sell over sixty million copies in forty-five languages and were reincarnated in the 1970s and 1980s as one of the longest-running, most popular shows in television history, still in syndication.

But as adults, we have come to see that her autobiographical novels were not only fictionalized but brilliantly edited, in a profound act of American myth-making and self-transformation. As unpublished manuscripts, letters, and documents have come to light, we have begun to apprehend the scope of her life, a story that needs to be fully told, in its historical context, as she lived it. That tale is different from the one she wrote. It is an adult story of poverty, struggle, and reinvention—a great American drama in three acts.

The third act was a long time in coming. At fifty-seven, Wilder was still far from becoming the emblematic figure of pioneer history. The woman whose life would become synonymous with the settlement of the West had spent most of her adult life living in the American South. She was not yet famous, had not yet written a book; the only writing she had published was her farm paper column. Anxious, she suffered from nerves and had a recurrent nightmare of walking down a "long, dark road" into obscure woods, the path of poverty.[4]

She prided herself on superior hen-raising skills and keeping an immaculate house. She worried about whether giving women the vote might lead to moral laxity. A product of rural life, she also stood outside it, questioning the iron drudgery of turn-of-the-century domestic expectations. She advised women to give up the exhausting ritual of spring cleaning.

She had a sharp temper and a dry humor, noting the resemblance of a yard full of swine to their owners. Judgmental of others, she could be humble, even self-excoriating. She was parsimonious to a fault, but when she went into town she dressed elegantly in full skirts, lace collars, and hats garlanded with feathers or flowers. She favored long, dangling earrings, fastening her blouses with a cameo brooch. She loved velvet.

She was not an intellectual, but she had an intellect. She had never graduated from high school, but had studied with passion and vigor the Independent Fifth Reader. She knew a song for every occasion and passages of Shakespeare, Longfellow, Tennyson, Scott, Swinburne, and the Brownings. Books took pride of place in her living room, on custom-built shelves beside a prized stone hearth.

As her fifties drew to a close, she stood at a turning point. The first act of her life was long over. Her childhood had been packed with drama and incident: Indian encounters, prairie fires, blizzards, a virtual compendium of American frontier life. Growing up, she could count her possessions on her fingers. One tin cup. One slate, for school. One hair ribbon. A doll her mother made her. Clothes and shoes were hand-me-downs: a good dress for Sundays, another for all the other days. She married at eighteen and was a mother a year later.

By the age of twenty-one, she knew that everything she had ever had, no matter how hard-won, held the capacity to be lost. After a series of disasters, she and her husband left the Dakotas to rebuild seven hundred miles south, a long climb out of poverty constituting her life's second act. She took in boarders and waited on tables. Her husband, crippled by a stroke in his twenties, recovered enough to drive a wagon, delivering fuel and freight. Their daughter, Rose, left home when still a teenager, eventually becoming a celebrity biographer in San Francisco. As soon as she saw the easy money to be made selling inspirational life stories of men as self-made as she was—Henry Ford, Jack London, Herbert Hoover—she began urging her mother to join her in the writing trade.

Wilder would become one of the self-made Americans her daughter so admired. In the third act of her life, in the midst of the Great Depression, she began recording, in soft pencil on tablets from the dime store, a memoir of her youth, the story of homesteaders who had unwittingly caused the Dust Bowl she was living through. Painfully casting her mind back to the previous century, she pressed on, kept awake all night by remembering her family's misfortunes and failed crops, her sister falling ill and going blind. What had been punishing to survive was heartbreaking to relive. "It's H—," she wrote to her daughter, taught never to swear.[5]

Rose once jotted down a quotation she attributed to her mother: "I don't know which is more heartbreaking, a dream un[ful]filled or a dream realized."[6] She would help her mother realize a dream, bringing her professional connections and polish to the work, adding touches of cozy security to the hard reality. But it was her mother's stoic vision of pioneer grit that prevailed.

Wilder's perseverance gave rise to one of the most astonishing rags-to-riches stories in American letters. On the brink of old age, fearing the loss of everything in the Depression, Wilder reimagined her frontier childhood as epic and uplifting. Her gently triumphal revision of home-steading would convince generations that the American farm was a model of self-sufficiency. At the same time, it would hint at the complex realities behind homesteading, suggesting that it broke more lives than it sustained.

Living most of her life in poverty, Wilder survived long enough to become a wealthy woman, a legend in children's literature, and a treasured incarnation of American tenacity. But fame obscures as it reveals. Swamped in pious sentimentality, dimmed and blurred by the marketing of the myth, Wilder has become a caricature, a brand, a commodity. In addition to the hit television show, the Little House series has given rise to scores of adaptations in print, on stage, and on screen—including a Japanese anime version—and a welter of songbooks, cookbooks, sequels, and chat sites. There are licensed dolls, clothes, fabrics, and, inevitably, sunbonnets.

The real woman was not a caricature. Her story, spanning ninety years, is broader, stranger, and darker than her books, containing whole chapters she could scarcely bear to examine. She hinted as much when she said, in a speech, "All I have told is true but it is not the whole truth."[7]

———

THE truth comes clear when we see Wilder as part of a wider history. Her story is the story of an era, which is present in her books but gets subsumed in their charm, their immersion in a child's world. When we set her life against epic movements—the Homestead Act, the spread of railroads, the closing of the frontier—we can see how economic depression and environmental disaster propelled settlers farther out on the Plains than they ever should have gone, how fear of massacre drove the squatters' rationale, how debt and drought kept farmers locked in recurrent waves of boom and bust.

Wilder made history. Sealing her themes inside an unassailably innocent vessel, a novelistic Trojan horse for complex and ambiguous reactions to manifest destiny, wilderness, self-reliance, and changing views of women's roles outside the home, her books have exercised more influence, across a wider segment of society, than the thesis of Frederick Jackson Turner, which held that American democracy was shaped by settlers conquering the frontier. Their place in our culture continues to evolve. Unfolding in the heartland of Indian removal, Wilder's life and her re-creation of it became a lasting expression and subterranean critique of America's harshest philosophies. She has become one of the national figures by which we take the measure of pioneer women.

"Often, if you want to write about women in history," the novelist Hilary Mantel has said, "you have to distort history to do it, or substitute fantasy for facts; you have to pretend that individual women were more important than they were or that we know more about them than we do."[8] But when it comes to Wilder, we don't have to pretend.

In the breadth of its impact, Wilder's work—even in its bowdlerized, co-opted versions—has few parallels. It has shaped and inspired politicians across the decades. The second heir to the Little House fortune, Roger MacBride, ran for president as a Libertarian. Ronald Reagan wept over his TV tray in the White House watching his friend Michael Landon enact a blow-dried Simi Valley version of Wilder's homespun pioneer values.[9] *Little House on the Prairie* is the one book Sarah Palin's family could remember her reading as a child.[10] Saddam Hussein is said to have been a fan.[11]

Greater than any such incidental endorsement has been Wilder's quieter influence on generations of schoolchildren. On *Publishers*

Weekly's list of the bestselling children's books of all time, *Little House in the Big Woods* and *Little House on the Prairie* are in the top twenty.[12] John Steinbeck would become America's lamenter of Dust Bowl destitution—and Woody Guthrie its anarchic troubadour—but Wilder staked out a place as champion of the simple life. She transformed poverty into pride, showing readers the heroism of endurance. With Shaker-like purity, she celebrated every day under shelter, every warm fire, and every mouthful of nourishment, no matter how modest. Not by accident are her books about "little" houses. They are also about making the best of little food and fewer choices.

If the fiction was gauzier than the reality, that was because it was inspired by her devotion to her parents. Every word Wilder wrote would be grounded in the satisfaction of simple pleasures she discovered through them: a song, a carpet of wildflowers, a floor swept clean. Showing American children how to be poor without shame, she herself grew rich. That too formed a powerful part of her mythology.

In 1856, a family came to far western Wisconsin, the edge of the frontier, in a covered wagon. As a descendant later recalled, they had heard from "friendly Indians" about an "Eden-like valley of great fertility" near the Mississippi. Their arrival was akin to something out of Genesis:

> In the morning they awoke to a very beautiful sight. Surely this was the Eden-like land the Indians had told them about. It was then just a little place in the wilderness, remote from any road and without buildings. There were plenty of trees, however; one, which stood in the farm yard until a few short years ago, was the same tree under which the family continued to camp until they could erect a log house.[13]

Their names were Eva and August, and they were my great-great-great-grandparents. They bought land in Buffalo County, about fifty miles as the crow flies from where the Ingalls family would settle a few years later. They arrived with four children and a cattle dog, but the dog ran all the way back to Muskego. Their land patent bore the name of President Andrew Johnson.

One of their daughters was named Caroline. I have her name and her quilt: appliqued flowers on a white field, pink and yellow calico blooming from curling green stems, all secured in thousands upon thousands of tiny, even stitches. She was sewing it around 1871, when Laura Ingalls was a youngster not far away.

There is a photograph of four generations of these Wisconsin women—Eva, Caroline, Della, and Marion—clinging to each other in front of a field of corn. A sepia flash of pale and distant faces. No one ever told the rest of the story. Who were they, really? What happened to the friendly Indians, and the wilderness, and the farm, and the family? What happened to the cattle dog? What happened to Eden?

The quilt keeps its mute counsel in a closet. But Laura Ingalls Wilder saved her quilts *and* her stories. In a heroic effort late in life, she gave those stories to the world. With the same exasperated patience that her mother instilled in her as a child, learning to sew a nine-patch quilt, she sat down and wrote—what she remembered, what she wanted to remember. For those of us seeking to understand the settlement of the frontier, she offers a path, perhaps our best path, to the past.

On the Frontier

"Once upon a time . . . a little girl lived in the Big Woods": the opening of the Little House series has the cadence of a fairy tale. The setting, too, feels like a place in a fable:

> The great, dark trees of the Big Woods stood all around . . . and beyond them were other trees and beyond them were more trees. As far as a man could go to the north in a day, or a week, or a whole month, there was nothing but woods. There were no houses. There were no roads. There were no people. There were only trees and the wild animals who had their homes among them.[1]

But the Big Woods was an actual name for a real place.[2] Dense forests stretched across northern Wisconsin and Minnesota, millions of acres of sugar maple, red oak, burr oak, basswood, and elm, shading into prairies to the south and west.[3] And this apparently unpeopled wilderness had a long history of human habitation.

The first whites to see the Big Woods were French trappers in the 1600s. They regarded the forests as a bank full of beaver and timber, a wealth of quality hardwood. But long before them, the Indians knew the land's value. "Mni Sota Makoce," the Dakota called it: "land where the waters are so clear they reflect the clouds."[4]

The Dakota included several separate bands, sharing language and customs but inhabiting different areas and known by different names. Each had their own relationship to the Big Woods and its lakes and rivers. There were the Wahpeton (meaning "the people who live in the forest") and the Yankton ("the people who live at the edge of the great forest"), the Mdewakanton ("the spiritual people who live by the water"), the Sisseton ("the medicine people who live by the water"), and the Wahpekute ("the warriors who protected the medicine people and could shoot from among the leaves").[5] Whites lumped them together as "Sioux," a name the Dakota found insulting. "Sioux" was what their enemies, the Ojibwe, called them. It meant "little snakes."[6]

Where were these Indians when Laura was growing up in the Big Woods? That was a story in its own right. It happened five years before she was born, but it reshaped the American landscape for centuries to come. The dispossession of the Dakota, the Homestead Act of 1862, and the war that they touched off set the stage for Laura Ingalls Wilder's life.

AT the beginning of the nineteenth century, the Dakota occupied a vast swath of forest and prairie west of the Mississippi River. Tied to the seasons, they lived by hunting, fishing, gathering wild produce, and growing crops. In fall and winter, deer-hunting parties set off in the north. Whole villages followed the hunt, tepees and other necessities heaped on sleds pulled by horses or dogs. By spring, as deer grew scarce and thin, the Dakota moved south, ice-fishing along the way for pike and bass. At the first thaw, women tapped maples in coveted groves to make sugar, while men hunted muskrat, geese, and ducks. Their summer villages along the Minnesota River had bark houses near meadows and marshes where they harvested chokecherries, wild turnips, potatoes, strawberries, and artichokes. Women and children raised corn, beating birds away from the crop.[7]

Even in the best of times their existence could be precarious, made more so by the disappearance of beaver and buffalo and white settlers' introduction of alcohol and smallpox. Sometimes the weather was bad, or the game sparse. Whatever the difficulties, however, it was their life and their country.

In the 1830s, the painter George Catlin was among the first whites struck by the land's wild beauty, calling it a paradise.[8] Its most terrifying spectacle—fires sweeping through the grass like "red buffaloes"—was, for him, an ecstatic vision. "The prairies burning form some of the most beautiful scenes that are to be witnessed in this country," he wrote.[9] He bemoaned the region's domestication by the "busy, talking, whistling, hopping, elated and exulting white man, with the first dip of the ploughshare, making sacrilegious trespass."[10]

The trespass had begun in 1803, when Thomas Jefferson bought the interior of North America from France, some 530 million acres between the Mississippi and the Rocky Mountains changing hands for fifteen million dollars. Over the following decades, a series of treaties were negotiated between the United States and the Dakota. Legally dubious, based on inaccurate translations of an oral language, the treaties steadily encroached on the Indians' land, confining them within ever-shrinking boundaries. In 1851, some six thousand Dakota were consigned to a cruelly narrow reservation, a strip of land one hundred and forty miles long and ten miles wide along each bank of the Upper Minnesota River.[11] There, they were expected to relinquish the immemorial pattern of their lives, give up hunting, settle down to farm, and become Christians. Few, however, chose to do so, the majority continuing to "live by the hunt."[12]

For settlers, the treaties set off a land rush. In the first wave, between 1854 and 1857, more than five million acres of public land were sold in Minnesota Territory, much of it for the rock-bottom price of $1.25 an acre.[13] Farmers raced to stake claims on land already broken for cultivation: the Indians' corn fields. Saw mills were set up, trees felled, and roads cut through the wilderness. In the 1840s, a few hundred whites were living among twenty-five to thirty thousand Indians of various tribes; by 1858, the year Minnesota became an American state, there were 150,000 whites.[14] By that time, squatters were encroaching on Dakota land north of the Minnesota River, finding a willing collaborator in the federal government. Less than a decade after creating the

Upper and Lower Sioux Reservations, the government took back half
the Dakota's land, the strip along the northern bank of the Minnesota,
after negotiations that were little more than veiled threats. Promised
$1.25 an acre, the Indians were paid thirty cents, a swindle that would
end up costing both sides dearly.[15]

For whites, free land was the original American dream. Inspired by
massive taxpayer-funded acquisitions such as the Louisiana Purchase,
the schemes to distribute such land were bitterly contested by well-
heeled congressional foes, especially those from the South.[16] Western
territories were a particular focus of the Free Soil movement of the
1840s and '50s, which joined farmers eager to colonize new lands with
abolitionists intent on keeping new states free from slavery. Their ral-
lying cry was, "Why not vote yourself a farm?," a goad to politicians
who abhorred giving land to the poor, arguing that such charity was
"demeaning."[17]

In the presidential campaign of 1860, Abraham Lincoln harnessed
and refined the Free Soiler argument, insisting that slavery was a stain
on the land, "a moral, a social, and a political wrong" that could not be
allowed to spread.[18] If elected, he promised "free land" for all Americans. And he was as good as his word. When his inaugural train passed
through Cincinnati on the way to the capital, he stepped out to speak
to a committee of industrialists. "I have to say that in so far as the
Government lands can be disposed of," he remarked, "I am in favor of
cutting up the wild lands into parcels, so that every poor man may
have a home."[19]

The Homestead Act that Lincoln signed into law in May 1862
promised 160 acres—a quarter of a square mile of land, or a "quarter
section"—to every citizen over twenty-one who wanted to stand up and
claim them. The offer was open to anyone who had never taken up arms
against the United States, including single women, immigrants, and
freed slaves. For a ten-dollar filing fee, potential homesteaders could
claim their acreage, and then had five years to "prove up" by cultivating
the land and building a structure on it. If these conditions were met, and
claimants could prove that they had lived at least six months of every
year on the property, they received a deed, or "patent," to the land.
There were also shortcuts: after six months in residence, those with

enough money could buy the land outright for $1.25 an acre. Altogether, a billion acres would be opened to homesteading when the Act went into effect the following year. Yet settlers were not content to wait: tens of thousands more began pouring into Minnesota when news of free land broke.[20]

Lincoln doubtless realized the consequences that the Homestead Act would have on the Union, and he had been warned about the Dakota's plight.[21] But he had never set foot in Minnesota. Distracted by the Civil War, he failed to foresee the havoc that a second wave of settlement would unleash among tribes still living on the lands America coveted.

In Minnesota, tensions were already running high long before Lincoln made free land a centerpiece of his campaign.

In 1853, a decade before the Homestead Act, a group calling itself the German Land Company placed an advertisement in a Chicago-based German-language newspaper, the *Illinois Staats-Zeitung*. It called for immigrants from Bohemia and Germany to stake their claims to riverfront acreage in Minnesota. Within a few years, the company had signed up eight hundred, at a few dollars a head. In a sentimental allusion to a city on the Danube, the seekers named their future home New Ulm. The town was to be built at the confluence of the Minnesota and Cottonwood Rivers, on land adjacent to the Dakota reservation. For immigrants' purposes, it was ideal: productive, naturally terraced bottomland, with steamboats running to the U.S. Army's Fort Snelling.

The first settlers arrived during the winter months of 1855, while the Indians were away, hunting. They moved into bark houses belonging to the Dakota. When the original inhabitants returned, the squatters refused to budge even as the natives continued to haunt the nascent town, arguing for their rights. Soon, smallpox broke out among the Indians.

The Germans and Bohemians who founded New Ulm preferred to live in ethnic enclaves where they could speak their own language and do business with their own kind. This was a common practice in Minnesota settlements. At New Ulm, the whites' encounters with Indians were made all the more thorny by the settlers' lack of interest in the history, culture, and language of the people they were displacing. Mutual incomprehension was compounded by the fact that the Dakota were disgusted by the newcomers, whom they called "bad talkers" (for their guttural, unfamiliar speech) or "Dutchmen," and whom they blamed for driving away game.

Among those incensed by New Ulm was a leader of the Mdewakanton band, a legendary chief named Little Crow. Renowned for his physical courage and spiritual acumen, he had been dealing with the whites for years. He had traveled twice by train to negotiations in Washington, D.C. He had signed treaties, only to watch white traders siphon away the money and white farmers continue to encroach on Indian land. He was particularly aggrieved about the land on which New Ulm sat: he'd believed he had negotiated its return in earlier talks, only to learn he had been outmaneuvered.

After their bark houses were seized by the New Ulm settlers, the Dakota began going from house to house, begging. Like many native groups, they held to a collective view of possessions, cherishing reciprocal hospitality. Those with more were expected to give to those with less. The Germans did not share that view. An 1859 article in the *New Ulm Pioneer* reported that laws had been enacted requiring the Dakota to present a pass before entering "the lands, claims, or settlement of the white inhabitants."[22]

Two years later, in 1861, Henry David Thoreau arrived in the Big Woods. Forty-three years old, suffering from the tuberculosis that would soon kill him, he recorded in his journal a brief but penetrating account. He started up the Minnesota River on the steamboat *Franklin Steele*, entranced by the tangle of wild grasses and roses along the banks. He saw "many large turtle-tracks on shore" and lagoons "fringed with willows."[23] At five o'clock in the morning, he wrote of his excitement at seeing "the big woods; the wood all alive with pigeons, and they flying across our course."[24] They were passenger pigeons, then common.

After the *Steele* docked at the Lower Sioux Agency, a compound housing the bureaucracy and trading posts at the south end of the reservation, Thoreau found himself listening to the Dakota, who had come on their ponies for a council with administrators.[25] The speechifying of white officials left him cold, but he was impressed by the Indians, who had "the advantage in point of truth and earnestness, and therefore of eloquence."[26]

Thoreau undertook the journey to Minnesota in a last bid to restore his health. But he had yearned all his life to escape tame New England. It had been "mutilated" and "emasculated," he wrote, left barren of "cougar, panther, lynx, wolverene, wolf, bear, moose, deer, the beaver, the turkey."[27] He had always wanted to see nature in its original profusion, a perfect whole.

Instead, he found himself standing on the riverbank of another diminished wilderness, witnessing the prologue to a violent confrontation. "The most prominent chief was named Little Crow," he wrote, and his people "were quite dissatisfied with the white man's treatment of them, and probably have reason to be so."[28]

By the following summer, Thoreau was dead, and the discord he had seen on the riverbank was about to explode. Little Crow did wield the point of truth, and he was about to engage in some mutilating of his own.

To the Dakota, the Homestead Act amounted to an act of war.

It immediately inflamed feelings in Minnesota. Minnie Buce Carrigan, a child of German immigrants who moved from Wisconsin to Minnesota in 1860, remembered the Indians as friendly at first. But "in the spring of 1862," she later recalled, "so many people came into the country that we did not know half of our neighbors." After that, she said, the Indians became "disagreeable and ill-natured."[29]

It was in this atmosphere that, in June 1862, around a thousand Dakota began gathering at the Upper Agency, some thirty miles north of the Lower Agency. Game scarce, hunting poor, they had no choice but to wait for the annuity payments owed in payment for the land they had sold. Many had traveled hundreds of miles. Expecting a brief stay—the payments were usually distributed at the beginning of July—most carried enough dried meat to last a week or so. The lone military fort in the region, Fort Ridgely, had sent word that they were not to come until notified, because the payment had been delayed, but the instructions seem not have reached the far-flung Dakota.

Their condition grew perilous as the weeks passed: the previous winter had been harsh, the corn harvest damaged by cutworm, and they were forced to eat unripe fruit and marsh grasses to survive. A white woman at the Upper Agency was pained by their desperation. "I remember distinctly . . . the agent giving them dry corn," she wrote, "and these poor creatures were so near starvation that they ate it raw, like cattle. They could not wait to cook it, and it affected them in such a manner that they were obliged to remove their camp to a clean spot of earth."[30]

By August, the money had still not arrived. Normally, the gold barely reached the palms of the recipients before it was snatched away by traders, who would have advanced food and other goods against it. But that summer, the Dakota could not buy on credit. Government agencies were taking a hard line, outraged that some Dakota, furious about the delay, had tried to break into a federal warehouse packed with provisions.[31]

The attempted break-in sparked a threatening exchange between Little Crow and Andrew Myrick, trader and storeowner at the Lower Agency. Typical of the notoriously corrupt cadre of Indian agents and traders, Myrick had a Dakota wife and had made tens of thousands of dollars off the treaties.[32] Little Crow told the trader that he should extend credit to the Dakota: that they were waiting for money that had not arrived, that Myrick's stores were full of food while people were starving. "When men are hungry they help themselves," Little Crow said, a remark so incendiary that the interpreter refused to translate it.[33]

When he found out what was said, Myrick blew up. He told Little Crow that if the Dakota were hungry, they could "eat grass or their own shit."[34] It was not the first time he had used such language. Translated for the crowd of Indians standing nearby, his taunt inspired angry cries.

On August 16, 1862, the annuity payment finally arrived at St. Paul. It was only a hundred miles away, but to the starving Dakota it might as well have been on the moon.

THE following day, August 17, a Sunday afternoon, four young Dakota men were returning on foot from an unsuccessful hunt in the Big Woods.

They were about forty miles from home and had found no game. They were hungry.

At a farm near the town of Acton, fifty miles west of Minneapolis, they found a hen's nest. They quarreled over taking the eggs. One warned against the theft, setting off a chorus of insults and dares. The exact sequence of events has crumbled into hearsay; the men may have been drunk, or simply past caring. What is clear is that the Indians went to the farmhouse, which also functioned as the town's general store and post office, and shot dead five people, among them the farmer, his wife, and their fifteen-year-old adopted daughter.[35]

The Dakota then fled on horses stolen from another farm, heading down a tributary of the Minnesota, gathering Mdewakanton elders as they went. In the middle of the night, they assembled at Little Crow's tepee, near the Lower Agency. They called him out in the traditional manner, by rasping their knives against the tepee's hides.[36]

The young men were not sorry for what they'd done. They argued that the killings were justified by years of treaty violations and the gross aggravation of being despised and mistreated. They recounted tales of being cheated by government agents and of Dakota women raped by white men. They aired their hatred of "half-breeds" and "cut-hairs," mixed-race Dakota who had chopped off their long hair, become farmers, and been rewarded for their treachery. The hunters noted that annuity payments had been delayed for months, and there were rumors that payments might arrive in the form of worthless paper. They had been pushed past the brink of endurance, they told Little Crow. They called for war.

Some of the other bands rejected the idea. The Sisseton and the Wahpeton wanted nothing to do with it; a Wahpeton leader said a few days later that "no one who fights with the white people ever becomes rich, or remains two days in one place, but is always fleeing and starving."[37] But chiefs of Lower Agency villages who had suffered under Myrick were eager to do battle.

Little Crow was reluctant but fatalistic. His Washington dealings had brought him benefits, including a frame house for the Minnesota winters. But they had cost him influence among his own people. Hearing their taunts—one of them called him a coward—stung him. And the

American betrayals, disappointments, and humiliations stung too. He had seen millions of whites covering the country between the Mississippi and the east; he had seen their armaments fired in the nation's capital, a display of irresistible force. Against it, he knew the Dakota could not prevail. But after the insult of New Ulm, he was ready to die.

According to one account, Little Crow turned to the warrior who denounced him and delivered an eloquent, contemptuous speech. The men who committed the murders, he said, were full of the white man's "devil-water," snapping at their own shadows like "dogs in the Hot Moon." He told them hard truths: that the murder of white women would call forth a terrible retribution, that they were outnumbered, that they did not stand a chance. Little Crow's son later set down his father's words:

> The white men are like the locusts when they fly so thick that the whole sky is a snowstorm. You may kill one—two—ten; yes, as many as the leaves in the forest yonder, and their brothers will not miss them . . . ten times ten will come to kill you. Count your fingers all day long and white men with guns in their hands will come faster than you can count. . . . Yes; they fight among themselves, but if you strike at them they will all turn on you and devour you and your women and little children just as the locusts in their time fall on the trees and devour all the leaves in one day. You are fools. You cannot see the face of your chief; your eyes are full of smoke. . . . Braves, you are little children—you are fools. You will die like little rabbits when the hungry wolves hunt them in the Hard Moon.[38]

Upon delivering these words, he is said to have blackened his face and "covered his head in sorrow."[39]

Then he and the Mdewakanton prepared to go to war.

THE morning of Monday, August 18, dawned hot. Rumors of the killings the night before had spread across the prairie, but no one knew what to believe. Just after first light, a hundred Dakota, walking in a silent line, massed at the trading center of the Lower Agency, led by Little Crow on a white horse.

First, they went to Andrew Myrick's house.

They shot the man who answered the door, an unpopular trader known for taking sexual advantage of Indian women. Myrick himself was hiding on the second floor. After hearing the shot, he jumped out of a window, making an ignominious run for the woods near the river. His body was found later, peppered with bullet holes, pierced by arrows, slashed with a knife. His mouth was stuffed with grass.

The Dakota attacked up and down the Minnesota River valley that day, taking settlers by surprise. Many were in the fields, beginning the harvest. Minnie Buce remembered every detail of "that dreadful Monday."[40] Seven years old, she was at the log cabin her father had built near Middle Creek, about fifty miles north of New Ulm, when her younger brother came in to say that he'd seen their neighbors "asleep" on the ground, with blood on their faces.[41] She ran with him to hide in a cornfield, then watched as her father, panicking, carrying three-month-old Bertha, tried to walk away from the approaching Indians, across the open prairie. He offered everything he had in exchange for his family's lives, but a Dakota warrior shot them both.

Her mother, behind him, sat down in shock, holding her two-year-old, Caroline. An Indian bullet passed through both their bodies, the child giving "one little scream and a gasp or two."[42] Another of Minnie's sisters lay dead nearby. "The birds were singing in the trees above," she wrote, "there was not a cloud in the sky. I have often wondered how there could be so much suffering . . . on such a perfect August day."[43] When she and her two remaining siblings tried to run, they were swept up and taken captive.

Their neighbors, the Boelters—two brothers and their parents, wives, and children, originally from Prussia—had filed claims on Beaver Creek. Breakfasting early, John Boelter and his family were startled when an Indian woman bearing an ax ran into the house and dashed out again. Shots were heard. Boelter rushed to protect his cattle and was never seen again. His wife, Justina, had been baking bread and was so rattled that she stuck a loaf just out of the oven on the nail meant for her oven mitt. With her baby in her arms, leading two younger children, she hurried to her brother-in-law's house. But when she saw Indians killing a neighbor, she dragged the children into the trees along the river bottom. They hid there for weeks, surviving on grape leaves, raw potatoes scavenged from root cellars, and cucumbers from abandoned gardens. In heavy rains, her eldest daughter died of exposure. Justina once ventured back to one of the family's houses, only to find her mother-in-law's body, beheaded, on the floor.[44]

On nearby Hawk Creek, the Ingalls family took flight.[45] Jedediah Hibbard Ingalls, a widower, heard the alarm when a settler from the Upper Agency tore past on horseback, yelling that Indians were attacking. He rushed his four children, Elizabeth Jane (fourteen), Amanda (twelve), George Washington (ten), and Lavina (eight), into a wagon and started for Fort Ridgely, the nearest U.S. Army outpost. But not fast enough. The family was overrun by Dakota soldiers.

The two older girls leapt from the wagon and dashed to a neighbor's house, only to be taken hostage by a fearsome warrior named Cut Nose.[46] As the younger children watched, Jedediah Ingalls was killed and scalped. Absorbed by another Indian band, Lavina wound up in Missouri, while George Washington Ingalls became one of Little Crow's hostages. His red hair was reportedly a source of fascination: on the medicine wheel of the Plains Indians, red represents north, denoting wisdom. The dramatic story of his captivity—he was taken so young and held for so long that he would forget the English language—would be widely publicized in coming years, in newspapers and at least one book, *Dakota War Whoop*.[47]

No one knows the relationship between Jedediah Ingalls and the clan that produced Laura's father, Charles Ingalls, and his family.[48] No gravestone marks the spot where Jedediah fell. So many were killed so quickly that bodies were left to lie in the fields.

WHEN news of the killings reached New Ulm, men erected barricades on the main street, ordering women and children into the basement of the brick building housing Frank Erd's Variety Store. Little Crow's men attacked on the afternoon of August 19, inflicting casualties in fierce fighting and burning outlying farms. A downpour provided temporary reprieve, but within a few days Little Crow was back, with a force of around 650.

Waged over twenty-four hours, the battle of New Ulm has no counterpart in the nineteenth-century frontier: it is the only occasion on which Indians surrounded and laid siege to a western town. Settlers would long remember the sound of the war cry of the Dakota leader Shakopee, though they could not understand the words. He was shouting: "The Dutch [Germans] have made me so angry, I will butcher them alive."[49]

Army reinforcements arrived just in time to keep New Ulm from being overrun. Thirty-four settlers had been killed, sixty wounded. The town was gutted. The following day, more than one hundred and fifty wagons loaded with women, children, and wounded men—some two thousand people in all, gathered from the entire region—were evacuated to the town of Mankato. One of the soldiers later wrote that "a more heart-rending procession was never witnessed in America."[50]

Sporadic and chaotic, the U.S.-Dakota War ground on for weeks, waged throughout the Minnesota River valley and across the state.[51] Henry Hastings Sibley, the former governor of Minnesota, was commissioned to lead untried volunteers against the Indians, since older, experienced men had already been deployed to fight in the Civil War. Those who were left were poorly supplied, having to melt down water pipes into bullets.[52]

During the hostilities, an estimated 650 to 800 white settlers were killed, some 265 of them on the first day alone. In casualties and in consequences, the conflict was historic. Since the founding of the country, the uprising marked the largest number of whites killed in a war with Indians, the largest attack on a fort and a town, the largest evacuation (of New Ulm), and the largest number of refugees, in the tens of thousands.[53] Survivors fled northeast to St. Paul and Minneapolis, north to St. Cloud, or out of the state entirely, emptying settlements throughout the southern part of Minnesota.[54]

After the attack on New Ulm, the Dakota continued fighting for over a month. But by the end of September, their own ammunition depleted, they were decisively defeated at the Battle of Wood Lake. Little Crow and other Dakota soldiers escaped to the north, leaving their prisoners near the ruins of the Upper Agency with Indian bands who had chosen not to fight. There, at what became known as Camp Release, 269 captives were turned over to Sibley, among them Minnie Buce and Elizabeth Jane and Amanda Ingalls.

The relentless Minnesota winter was setting in, and provisions were low. The combat was over, but for every Indian remaining in Minnesota—regardless of tribal identity, regardless of whether or not he had fought in Little Crow's war—the backlash was about to begin.

GRAPHIC, sensational accounts of killings carried out by the Dakota whipped survivors, city dwellers, and politicians into a frenzy of revenge. Minnesota newspapers published lurid reports of bodies hacked to pieces, of scalpings, and of children nailed to trees, walls, and fences. The national press took up the tale.

It took only days for Minnesota's governor, Alexander Ramsey, to seize upon the massacre as the pretext for doing what state and federal officials had wanted to do all along. On September 9, 1862, Ramsey declared that "the Sioux Indians of Minnesota must be exterminated or driven forever beyond the borders of the state."[55] After decades of hostilities with the Indians, it was not the first explicit call for extermination, but it was in deadly earnest.[56] It would soon be followed by an Interior Department report considering any means necessary for driving out the Dakota: "extermination, massacre, banishment, torture, huddling together, killing with small-pox, poison, and kindness."[57]

At Camp Release, a military commission was appointed to try, convict, and execute the Indians responsible. In little more than a month, calling few witnesses and marshaling little evidence, it pronounced death sentences on 303 Dakota prisoners. Sibley planned to execute them immediately, and only fear of stepping on presidential authority delayed the proceedings. When Lincoln's permission was sought by telegram, he called a halt, recognizing that many of the convicted were guilty only of fighting against American forces: they were prisoners of war, subject to release. He requested that a list be prepared of those who had committed rapes and murders of unarmed civilians. In the end, to near-universal outrage in Minnesota, he upheld thirty-nine of the death sentences but commuted the rest.

Carried out in the morning of December 26, 1862, the execution was one of the most grotesque public events in the nation's history, a triumphal display of race hatred. Mankato's carpenters and Sibley's soldiers had constructed an enormous scaffold, twenty-four feet square, designed to hang ten men on a side.[58] At the cutting of a single rope, the central platform would drop, hanging all at once. Several thousand spectators gathered to cheer on the ceremony. Captured in an elaborate drawing by *Leslie's Illustrated Newspaper*, it remains the largest mass execution in American history.[59]

But not even that extreme reprisal could stanch the local lust for revenge. Frustrated by Lincoln's clemency, Minnesota sought satisfaction through other means, killing, imprisoning, or banishing Indians found within its borders. Seventeen hundred women, children, elderly, and "friendly" villagers who refused to fight during the uprising were forced to march with a wagon train, in another heartrending procession, 150 miles from Camp Release to the Lower Agency to Fort Snelling, where they were held all winter, outside, in an internment camp.[60] Attacked on the journey by angry whites, as many as three hundred died of injuries, exposure, measles, and malnutrition. Survivors were forcibly removed, first to a harsh and distant reservation in Dakota Territory, then to Nebraska.[61]

The treaties were abrogated, the reservations seized, and the annuity money owed to the Dakota was redistributed to the settlers whose farms and crops had been destroyed.[62] The estate of Jedediah Ingalls was credited with $865 for "depredations committed by Sioux Indians," money that paid for clothing and feeding his orphaned children.

Reparations, and outright vengeance, did not stop there. Minnesota found ways to drive the Winnebago tribe—who took no part in the uprising—off their reservation south of Mankato, freeing up coveted farmland. After a spell at Fort Snelling, nearly two thousand were shipped off to share the Dakota's exile, first in Dakota Territory, then in Nebraska.[63]

During the summer of 1863, Sibley led an expedition of several

thousand men to drive all remaining Dakota from the state. More than
150 were taken prisoner; two hundred unarmed Yankton men, women,
and children camped in Dakota Territory were slaughtered. To ensure
the extirpation of all remaining Indians, Governor Ramsey declared a
bounty on male Dakota scalps, twenty-five dollars a head. Volunteer
scouts combed the Big Woods for any Dakota left alive. The order
would remain in effect until 1868. Among its victims was Little Crow,
shot in the back the year after the war, his scalp put on display in the
state capitol.[64]

LARGELY forgotten outside of Minnesota, the U.S.-Dakota War of 1862
was among the most pivotal in American history. More white Americans died that summer in Minnesota than were killed at the Battle of
the Little Bighorn or at any other military engagement in the Plains
Indian Wars. But in the end, the 1862 war was defined not by the ferocity of its battles or the number of its casualties (far eclipsed by those of
the Civil War), but by Dakota atrocities—some real, some imagined—
and the indignation they inflamed, inspiring retaliatory massacres of
Indians at Sand Creek, Washita River, and Wounded Knee.[65] In the eyes
of politicians, it was the atrocities that justified extermination as state
policy. They also gave rise to the ubiquitous slur, "The only good Indian
is a dead Indian."[66] As a result of the war, thousands of Indians would
be driven out of Minnesota, and white settlers would permanently take
their place.

The Homestead Act gave the settlers official permission and incen-
tive. But ultimately, it was not policy or legislation that opened the far
west. It was not reasoned debate. It was wrath and righteous retribution that did it, forever changing the contour and condition of the land,
pushing settlers farther west than they had ever gone before, flooding
the prairies with farms, towns, fields, grain elevators, and train stations. It was the massacre that cleared the way for thousands of white
families to seek their fortunes on the Great Plains.

By 1867, there were only fifty Dakota left in Minnesota.[67] That
year, a baby girl was born just across the Mississippi, in a little house
in the Big Woods.

PART I

THE
PIONEER

Chapter 1

Maiden Rock

The Legend

"I was born in a log house within . . . miles of legend-haunted Lake Pepin," Laura Ingalls Wilder would write.[1]

The lake was legendary before she was born. Where the Mississippi swallows the Chippewa, a wide tributary flowing sluggishly out of great Wisconsin pine forests to the north, the river swells at the delta, like a snake that has just devoured something. That swollen spot, widest on the Mississippi, is Lake Pepin.

Its dark waters are presided over by Maiden Rock, an immense four-hundred-foot limestone bluff so visually arresting that everyone had a story to tell about it. Like everything else, the story belonged to the Indians: Maiden Rock was a lover's leap, they said, where a Dakota girl in love with a young man leapt impetuously to her death rather than marry another. Those who passed at dusk were said to hear her sorrowful song.[2]

Whites would tell and retell the story until it had been rubbed smooth, playing up its romanticism, painting the scene in gloomy olives and mauves. George Catlin camped for days along Lake Pepin, hauling his canoe out of the water and gathering colorful pebbles by the handful,

"precious gems . . . rich agates."[3] Catlin told the story, and so did
Mark Twain and the poet William Cullen Bryant, who specialized in
brooding Indians.[4]

Maiden Rock captured the imagination of Charles Ingalls, who
told his daughters stories about the rock, the lake, and the Indians. On
one memorable occasion, he brought them to the beach bordering the
town of Pepin, just across the water from Minnesota, where they discovered the same pebbles, "pretty pebbles that had been rolled back
and forth by the waves until they were polished smooth."[5]

Like Catlin, Wilder as a tiny girl gathered them by the handful,
stuffing so many in her pocket that they tore her dress. Her mother
gently reproved her for being so greedy. But as Wilder chose to remember
it, her father just laughed, delighted.

She loved both her parents, but her primary, overwhelming identification was with her father. Charles had brown hair and blue eyes, just
as she did. Whenever she did something naughty, even as he punished
her he had a glint in his eye that told her it would be all right, that he
was moments away from holding her on his knee and telling her how
bad he himself had been as a boy. He was charming, cheerful, and
musical, playing by ear songs that would lift his family's spirits—and he
was an incomparable storyteller.

All of her stories begin with him, all of her memories. Her first, she
would say later, was "of my Father always," carrying her in his arms,
rocking her to sleep. "The feeling, the voice and the dim light over the
log wall make a picture that will never fade," she wrote.[6]

DISCOVERING how Charles Ingalls and his family came to find themselves a few miles from the shores of Lake Pepin, just a few years after
Pepin County was first marked on a map, is a detective story tracking
generations into the past. Pieces of the family portrait survive, but the
whole remains elusive, obscured under the soot of time. It may never
be complete.

That is always a problem, in writing about poor people. The
powerful, the rich and influential, tend to have a healthy sense of their
self-importance. They keep things: letters, portraits, and key documents,

such as the farm record of Thomas Jefferson, which preserved the number and identity of his slaves. No matter how far they may travel, people of high status and position are likely to be rooted by their very wealth, protecting fragile ephemera in a manse or great home. They have a Mount Vernon, a Monticello, a Montpelier.

But the Ingallses were not people of power or wealth. Generation after generation, they traveled light, leaving things behind. Looking for their ancestry is like looking through a glass darkly, images flickering in obscurity. As far as we can tell, from the moment they arrived on this continent they were poor, restless, struggling, constantly moving from one place to another in an attempt to find greater security from hunger and want. And as they moved, the traces of their existence were scattered and lost. Sometimes their lives vanish from view, as if in a puff of smoke.

So as we look back across the ages, trying to find what made Laura's parents who they were, imagine that we're on a prairie in a storm. The wind is whipping past and everything is obscured. But there are the occasional bright, blinding moments that illuminate a face here and there. Sometimes we hear a voice, a song snatched out of the air.

That Poverty Beat

Charles Ingalls was born at a crossroads. As if to fulfill the prophecy in that, he would always be a wanderer, propelled by hopes of a better future farther on.

But his rootlessness was not simply the sign of a "wandering foot," as his daughter would suggest.[7] It reflected generations of struggle, trying to break through, hoping to latch on to land. He would be among the first to make his way west, but he was not the first to know poverty. From the family's earliest beginnings in Puritan New England, that was all they would ever know. And the life of the previous generations had been even harder than Charles's own.

When Charles's father was a young boy, Charles told his daughters, he and his brothers labored for six days a week, Monday through Saturday.[8] During the winter, they got up in the dark, did their chores by lamplight, and worked until the sun went down, going to bed directly after supper. For play, they had a few hours off on Saturday afternoons. At sundown on Saturday, the "Puritan Sabbath" would begin.

On the Sabbath, all recreational pursuits, indeed all activities other than going to church or praying or studying a catechism, were strictly forbidden. There was no visiting, no sweeping, no gardening, no hunting, no haying, no fishing, no frivolous talk, no writing of notes or cutting of hair or kissing of children. Hot meals could not be prepared and horses could not be hitched to the wagon. To obey the Sabbath, the Ingalls family walked, reverently, to church. To break the Sabbath was a grave, even criminal offense, punishable by fines, public censure, or imprisonment.[9]

A flash of lightning in history's darkness gives us a glimpse of one such Sunday, more than two centuries before Laura's birth. Family lore has long maintained that the very first member of the Ingalls clan on this continent, Edmund Ingalls, arrived in Salem Harbor in 1628 with the expedition of John Endecott, first governor of the Massachusetts Bay Colony. We know little about the man; there isn't even a portrait of him. But we know that on April 20, 1646, he was fined for "bringing home sticks in both his arms on the Sabbath day," presumably for firewood.[10] Even worse, the sticks were stolen from somebody else's fence.

Another moment in bright relief: Edmund's last will and testament, sworn out two years after his theft. He bestowed upon his wife a house in Lynn and the lot it sat on, as well as "ye Stock of Cattle and Corne."[11] One daughter was left a "heifer Calf," another "two Ewes." A third, Mary, received "the heifer Calfe that formerly she enjoyed." Whatever Edmund possessed was in that livestock and small plots of land, perhaps poor plots, as in the "three acres of marsh ground" bequeathed to his son Henry. What his livestock may have been worth is hard to say. A large number of cattle were imported to the northern colonies from Virginia in the 1640s, depressing their price.[12]

There is one final discordant glimpse of the Ingalls family in the seventeenth century. One of Edmund's granddaughters would become notorious, victim of New England's most lurid hour. Martha Ingalls Allen Carrier, born to Edmund's daughter Faith, was dubbed the "Queen of Hell" during the Salem witchcraft trials by shrieking teenage accusers. She was said to have been seen riding a broomstick, to have caused neighbors' cows to sicken and die, to have started a smallpox epidemic. Cotton Mather called her "a rampant hag." In 1692, at the age of thirty-eight, the mother of several children, she was taken to Gallows Hill and hanged, having never wavered in proclaiming her innocence. Did her fate have anything to do with the family edging away from the country's Puritan heartland? We cannot know, but the intense impoverishment of a time when farmers "fought over ever-diminishing slivers of soil," as a historian put it, spurred neighbors to attack each other.[13]

Skip forward eighty years or so, and our most sustained flash of illumination catches Laura's great-grandfather, Samuel Ingalls, born in New Hampshire in 1770.[14] A self-lacerating individual, Samuel became a writer, in a family that would produce many of them. Devout and patriotic, he captured the suffering of yeoman farmers in a way that undermines Thomas Jefferson's golden vision of "those who labor in the earth" as "the chosen people of God, if ever he had a chosen people."[15]

As a young man, Samuel spent years living in Canada, perhaps exporting crops or other goods to America. There, in 1793, he married Margaret Delano, descendant of one of the passengers on the *Mayflower*. Generations later, the illustrious Delanos would produce an American president.

Like Edmund Ingalls, Samuel was a Puritan and may have been a Congregationalist.[16] The Massachusetts Bay Colony was strongly associated with the Congregationalist church, a Protestant denomination devoted to the precept that every parish should be self-governing. In a land in which independence and autonomy would become bywords, Congregationalists applied those principles with a will.

Unlike his stick-pilfering forebear, though, Samuel was unwavering in his rigid religiosity. On one occasion, his young sons, after a grueling week of chopping trees in midwinter, dared to sneak away for a forbidden sled ride on Sunday afternoon. As they shot past their house, their father's stern visage appeared in the doorway. On their return, they were greeted with silence. But the minute the sun went down, they were taken to the woodshed, one by one, and whipped.[17]

Religion suffused Samuel's politics. A vehement broadside that he published in 1809 against Thomas Jefferson's Embargo Act, denouncing the president's party as a "wicked club," summoned a vision of a carriage of angels, crowned in gold and armed with burnished scepters "about six or seven feet in length."[18] Descending on the town of Hartford, Connecticut, the angels shake the ground as if with an earthquake, arriving to deliver a partisan message against the president who had made trade with Canadian territories a crime. Hampering free trade was not simply an inconvenience or a bad decision. To Samuel, it was a sin.

In 1825, he published his *Rhymes of "The Unlearned Poet,"* the title humbly acknowledging his amateur status.[19] None of the original copies are known to survive, but from transcribed verses in the family papers his voice emerges impassioned and vital. He was an uncertain prosodist, his rhymes awkward and lines galloping. But what he lacked in finesse he made up for in sheer verve.

American exceptionalism was his great theme. Visions of the country's past rose before him in celestial glory, its heroes vanquishing the British "like lions," its pioneers withstanding the "savage whoops" and "scalping knives" of Indians.[20] The very land under their plows, he told his readers, had been purchased in blood. Other verses in the book showed Samuel transfixed by natural disasters, as later generations of the family would be. His "Lines . . . On The Great Hail and Wind Storm That Passed Through the Counties of Cattaraugus and Allegany in the Spring of 1834" exclaimed over eight-inch hail stones, and depicted a tornado—a column of air "filled / With the ruins of that day"—carrying away entire houses.[21]

To Puritans, every affliction—storms, pestilence, earthquakes—signaled God's judgment, and grappling with such calamities was the responsibility of the individual. The Ingallses' fixation on strict Sabbath observations would lapse as successive generations journeyed away from New England; one can even see the strictures relax over the course of Laura's memoir, as the family moves west. But one thing would never fade away: the belief in self-reliance as an absolute sacrament.

The most plaintive of Samuel's poems, "A Ditty on Poverty," acknowledged an invincible foe: hunger. "I've fought him for years in battle so strong, / But never could drive him an inch from the ground. / But many a time I had to retreat, / But scorn'd for to own that poverty beat."[22]

The poem echoed the Biblical warning against penury as a creeping evildoer waiting to strike the slothful.[23] Americans would later slough off the personification, but need still retains a whiff of shame.

Another piece in the book speaks of the melancholy of missing lost friends and family, of lying awake at night listening to "the midnight owl," hungry wolves, and screaming panthers. Samuel, in the seventh generation of Ingallses in America, translated that sorrow into song.[24] Unto the ninth and tenth generations, his descendants would sing it too.

By the time that *Rhymes of "The Unlearned Poet"* was published, Samuel and his family had returned from Canada to the United States, moving to Cuba Township in the far west of New York State. His youngest son, Lansford, born in 1812, would marry a woman named Laura. They raised a family of ten, their first, Peter, born near Cuba in 1833. A second died in infancy. The third, born January 10, 1836, was Charles Phillip Ingalls.

Cuba was a dark, dirty, and gloomy place, resting uneasily on swampy ground. Dotted with "unsightly stumps," the village hosted a tannery, an ashery producing lye, and lumber and stone mills. A railroad and canal were being constructed when Charles was a boy. As a child, he may have heard tales of the wolves and wildcats that had made life "pandemonium" for early settlers in the region. Bounties had thinned out the animals; the last wolf howl was heard around 1840, when Charles was four.

The town was a popular jumping-off point for the West, with families camping there in the winter to await spring passage. Cuba's Main Street served so many migrants wallowing across the town's primitive roads toward Lake Erie that an early history called it "one continuous mudhole . . . a mirehole in the center of a swamp."[25] Charles would have watched countless wagons heading westward. Safe to say, he yearned to join them.

Charles's childhood coincided with America's first great depression, the Panic of 1837, which lasted a Biblical seven years. A newspaper out of Albany, the *Knickerbocker*, reported in 1837 that "there never was a time like this," with "rumor after rumor of riot, insurrection, and tumult."[26] Banks collapsed, and unemployment climbed to 25 percent. Factories along the eastern seaboard were shuttered, and soup kitchens opened in major cities. Two out of three New Yorkers were said to be without means of support. Eight states defaulted on loans. In his literary magazine, Horace Greeley made the first of his famous entreaties to pull up stakes: "Fly, scatter through the country, go to the Great West, anything rather than remain here."[27]

Two of Charles's uncles quickly heeded that appeal, embarking for the West around 1838.[28] And when Charles was eight or nine, his family loaded up their own wagon and headed in the same direction, shaking off Cuba's mud forever.

The first railway connecting New York to Chicago lay several years in the future, so the family likely skirted below Lake Erie, picking up the Chicago Road. Formerly known to the Indians as the Great Sauk Trail, the road from Detroit and Fort Dearborn to Chicago—then a burgeoning town of a few thousand people—was traversed by thousands of pioneers during the 1830s and '40s. From there, the Ingallses headed forty miles west to Elgin, Illinois, a frontier outpost on the Fox River.

This was Charles Ingalls's first sight of the open plains. After the closed-in gloom of upstate New York, rolling western grasslands must have been a revelation. According to another settler, the Illinois prairies were still a thrilling "wolf-howling wilderness," packed with game and hopping with prairie chickens. Writing to a friend back in Kentucky, Daniel Pingree, who bought 160 acres of Kane County farmland not far from where the Ingallses settled, waxed lyrical over the rich productive soil, perfect for corn or wheat, and groves of oaks offering up raw material for cabins or fence rails: "In my opinion you could not find a better County in all the world for farming."[29]

At first the family thrived in Illinois, acquiring 164 acres of Kane County land themselves. But soon the land was gone—perhaps sold or lost on taxes—and Charles's father appeared on the 1850 census as a "laborer."[30] A local historian writes that the teenaged Charles, perhaps with his older brother and cousins, attended monthly Saturday dances upstairs at the Garfield House, a two-story brick inn and tavern near his uncles' land.[31] It may have been here that Charles picked up the violin, acquiring a taste for spirited music and dancing. Nearby, at Plato

Corners, a mile south of the family properties, was a "subscription school," taught in 1840 by a woman named Charlotte Griggs. Perhaps she was responsible for helping to instill Charles's lifelong dedication to books and his charming, literate style.[32]

Doubtless a laborer himself, Charles must also have honed hunting and trapping skills during those years. In addition to prairie chickens, the land teemed with geese, ducks, cranes (once a game bird), badgers, and foxes. But while his uncles kept working their farms in the area, his own family moved yet again around 1853, following the Fox River north to Wisconsin.[33]

This time they settled in Jefferson County, west of Milwaukee and near the village of Concord, buying eighty acres on the north banks of the Oconomowoc River. By this point the family included six children, with several more to follow in short order.[34] Households of this size were the norm: their neighbors across the stream had half a dozen children living with them as well. Among them, some four years Charles's junior, was a girl named Caroline.

Imagine a Ship on the Water in a Storm

Caroline Lake Quiner was born on December 12, 1839, in a rustic cabin near Brookfield, Wisconsin, about thirty miles from where she would later meet the Ingalls family. Like the Ingallses, her parents hailed from the east, in their case from Connecticut and Massachusetts. Wending their way west, Henry and Charlotte Quiner bore children as they traveled, stopping in Ohio and Indiana before arriving in Milwaukee—then "just a wilderness and Indians," as one of them would put it.[35] Caroline was the first to be born in Wisconsin.

Caroline's father had been a silversmith in New Haven, but turned to other work on the frontier. On November 10, 1845, he set sail as second mate of the *Ocean*, a two-masted schooner on Lake Michigan, planning to sell a load of lumber with his brother-in-law, the vessel's captain.[36] Caught in a storm, the ship capsized with the loss of all on board. The bodies were never found.

The disaster heralded a period of severe privation for five-year-old

Caroline and her family. Her mother was an intelligent and resourceful woman. But left on her own in the wild woods of Wisconsin to provide for six children under the age of eleven, she would find herself taxed nearly beyond endurance.

"Did your Mother ever tell you how we lived?" Caroline's sister Martha asked Laura, her niece, decades later. "Oh how I have tried to forget but never could."[37] As it turned out, Caroline had spared her daughter those stories. "I do not wonder that your Dear Mother and My Dear Sister did not like to talk about it," Martha said later. "It made ones heart ache."[38] She remembered cold bare feet in winter and days spent huddled in bed naked while their only clothes were washed.

The living conditions of frontier settlers were unimaginably primitive. Floors were dirt, and tiny cabins were uninsulated. Water was drunk directly out of rivers or rain barrels exposed to the elements. Cloth was at a premium: clothes and blankets had to be woven out of wool spun by hand, and undergarments hanging from clotheslines might bear the name of whatever flour company had sold the sack they were made from.[39] Feather ticks to sleep on were a rare luxury. Most mattresses were stuffed with corn shucks or straw.

The Quiners' brushes with starvation over the next few years permanently marked Caroline and her siblings. With no provider, the family ran out of flour and had nothing to eat but corn meal patties cooked on a griddle. Sometimes the children shared a bowl of water with bread crumbs broken into it. Eventually, a man on his way to Milwaukee with a load of flour let the family keep a barrel on credit. (Later, Laura would recall her mother as resistant to borrowing anything, even ashamed of it.) At times, the children scrounged for themselves, searching out berries and other wild foods.

Bears and mountain lions roamed the woods outside their door. Indians camping nearby materialized from time to time, on occasion bringing sides of venison for Caroline's mother to cook, then sharing them with the family.[40] At other times, the natives were less generous, slipping into the house to take food off the table. "They frighten us terrible," Martha wrote, "with the[ir] painted faces." She vividly recalled an Indian "all painted up" who was "on the war path," his brother having been killed by whites. He walked into their house, plucked a few peacock feathers from their looking glass, and stuck them in his hair, "proud as Lucifer." For a few hours, the family feared he had stolen baby Thomas, who had just learned to walk, only to find the child later, sitting peaceably in the corn patch.

Their mother moved them west again, to a farm next to the Oconomowoc River. Four years after her husband's death, she married a neighbor, Frederick Holbrook. Life improved, if only marginally, with the acquisition of a few chickens and sheep "rented" for their wool.[41] At one point, the couple fell ill with fever, and the children watched in horror, afraid they would both die. They recovered, however, and soon there were things to celebrate: Martha, Caroline, and their siblings welcomed a half sister, Lottie, the pet of the family.[42]

At sixteen, Caroline took over the job of teaching in the schoolhouse where she had been a pupil. All her life, she carefully saved her school books and a commendation from her teacher, Mary J. Moore: "Caroline L. Quiner for good behavior and attention to her studies merits my approbation and esteem."[43] She would name her first child Mary.

Caroline's brooding essay, "The Ocean," also survives, exhibiting a fluency and style surpassing the rough-and-ready letters of her brothers. Her father's fate preyed on her mind:

> Imagine a ship on the water in a storm. . . . All is hurry and confusion on board, for every hand must be at work, to save the ship if possible. And how often the ship, and its whole crew, find a grave in the bed of the ocean, and become the food of animals of the deep. Who can picture the sufferings of the survivors . . .[44]

Beginning in 1854, when Charles Ingalls's family bought the property nearby, the Quiners found enormous solace in their neighbors. "Your father's folks lived just across the Oconomowoc," Martha wrote to Laura. Even when the bridge washed out, the children were not deterred, simply walking across on logs called stringers.[45] Admitting that her own husband had never taken her to a dance during their courtship, Martha recalled Charles squiring her and Caroline to a corn husking party. They danced until they were exhausted, then hiked back through the snow.

In 1857, Charles Ingalls bought half of the family property, forty acres, from his father, who at the same time mortgaged the lots for five hundred dollars.[46] In February 1859, the first of several Quiner-Ingalls weddings took place, when Martha and Caroline's brother Henry married Polly Ingalls, Charles's younger sister.

Almost exactly a year later, on February 1, 1860, in the village of Concord, Charles and Caroline were married. The newlyweds' devotion still shines from their wedding photograph. Thin and bearded, Charles has wild hair, and his ebullient personality seems scarcely contained by a dark suit and bow tie. He tenderly embraces his bride with one arm, holding her hand on his knee. Her calm, grave face beams with the benevolence and resolve her daughter would describe years later. Rarely ruffled, Caroline had already known suffering, and her assent to the rigors of life appears not passive but quietly powerful. Through everything, she and Charles would honor and comfort each other.

Six months later, on July 24, 1860, there was another Concord wedding: Martha married a neighbor, Charles Carpenter, with Caroline and Charles Ingalls witnessing the ceremony. As a bachelor, Carpenter had bought property up north, land near Maiden Rock, and the newlyweds immediately embarked for Pepin County.

After the flurry of weddings, prosperity appeared to reign. In the summer of 1860, a federal census taker found Charles and Caroline apparently flourishing. Charles, twenty-four, was described as a farmer, with the value of his personal estate estimated at fifty dollars and his real estate at a thousand, a strong start.[47] The following year, Peter Ingalls, Charles's oldest brother, married Martha and Caroline's sister Eliza, further intertwining the Ingalls and Quiner families.

Still, the future was anything but secure. At that juncture, Wisconsin was a burgeoning young frontier state, with a population of more than 775,000, but a sterling reputation for high-quality dairy products was only a faint dream. Its inferior butter was sold in Chicago and points east as "western grease."[48] Its finances were shaky as well, and about to get worse.

Not long after Lincoln was elected in November 1860, Southern states began to secede. Many Wisconsin state banks were heavily invested in Southern bonds, whose value plummeted on the news; thirty-eight of the banks failed, setting off a riot outside one Milwaukee institution that June. Factories closed, and the unemployed marched through the city demanding bread. Crop prices fell to ruinous lows, while the freight rates charged to ship crops to market rose sharply. Some farmers ended up burning corn for fuel. "They are literally skinning the West alive," an angry newspaper columnist wrote of the railroads.[49]

The Ingallses' tenuous stability crumbled along with the state's. Caroline, writing to Martha up near Pepin, relayed the news from Concord. Charles was well, she said, but had worked hard throughout the summer and "is about tired out now."[50] With twenty laborers, he had picked, pressed, and sold $250 worth of hops, about half of what the couple had grown. "We do not expect to get as much for the remainder, as the price is reduced," she said. Failing to pay the mortgage and taxes, Charles and his father lost their land. In January 1862, the first Ingalls farm in Wisconsin was auctioned off.

The summer of 1862 saw Charles and Caroline still living within easy visiting distance of the village of Concord.[51] Since he owned no land, Charles may have been working as a hired hand, saving up money to buy property again. His parents had been traveling up north, perhaps scouting for land.[52] Sometime that fall or the following year, he and Caroline would pack up and move, following Martha and Charles Carpenter to Pepin County. Perhaps they traveled overland by wagon; perhaps, like the Carpenters, they took the train west to Prairie du Chien, then boarded a steamboat heading north on the Mississippi River.[53]

However they did it, their timing was propitious. At the very moment they decided to relocate, Wisconsin was embroiled in a deeply controversial drive to draft men into service in the Civil War.

A Soldier's Death

The interwoven clan of Ingallses, Carpenters, and Quiners had good reason to be wary of the military. In January 1862, Martha and Caroline's eldest brother, Joseph Quiner, had enlisted in Company B of Wisconsin's 16th Infantry Regiment. We know nothing of his motivation. Many men were inspired by patriotism, others by practicality: times were bad, and soldiers earned an enlistment bonus in addition to their pay and an allowance for their families.

Led by a Methodist minister, Company B was soon deployed to Tennessee. At home in Concord with two small boys, Joseph's wife, Nancy, grew frantic in mid-April after hearing news of the Battle of Shiloh on April 6. With no word from her husband for days, she wrote to Martha:

> I am all most crazy. I have hardly eat, drank or slept since I heard of the battle. I am so afraid that Joseph was hurt. It seems I could fly away to where he is. Oh I feel so bad. I would give worlds were they mine to give if he was at home with us. Were it not for our little ones I would go in one moment to him.[54]

Her fears were not misplaced. Private Quiner had been wounded at Shiloh, shot through the arm. After he was transferred to a hospital in Savannah, the wound reopened, and he bled to death on April 28.

Nancy was prostrate with grief. Two months later, Eliza Quiner Ingalls wrote to Martha to say that Caroline was caring for her sister-in-law and "thought it would kill her at first."[55] Caroline herself, in her flowing copperplate hand, recorded Joseph's fate with anguish on the reverse of the sheet on which she tallied vital records of her brothers and sisters:

> Died from his wounds—Joseph Quiner of Co B. . . . at the battle of Shiloh. . . . Thus have been left a wife and Children, mother, brothers, and sisters to mourn over his loss while in defen[s]e of his country against this cursed hell-born spirit of rebellion He died the soldier's death.[56]

It may have been the most vehement remark she ever made.

A few months later, in August 1862, Wisconsin initiated a draft, one of only two western states to do so.[57] The Secretary of War instructed the state to provide some 48,000 men. Every Wisconsin county was required to meet a quota, signing up volunteers if possible, or pressing men into service if not. Every able-bodied free white male between the ages of eighteen and forty-five was required to report to a county draft commissioner, who would be assisted by an examining physician in determining men's fitness to serve.[58]

The rolls of "Persons Liable for Military Duty" compiled that August reveal how deeply unpopular the war was among potential draftees. Farmers, carpenters, laborers, merchants, and cabinet makers, married and unmarried, all pleaded to be excused—because they were over-age, nervous, unable, disabled in their right hands, suffering from bad eyes, "troubled with bronchitis," or subjects of Great Britain.[59] The more stolid merely claimed to "have something the matter," while the fanciful developed lameness, epilepsy, ruptures of the skin, or weakness in the breast. Others confessed to being "completely broke down." A surprising number were said to be firemen, a class exempted from service.[60] In Milwaukee, "No Draft" marchers took to the streets, while in Sheboygan a draft commissioner was forced to draw a pistol to deter a mob threatening violence.[61]

Where Charles Ingalls found himself in all of this remains a mystery, but he did not enlist.[62] Between the summer of 1862 and autumn of the following year his whereabouts are unknown.[63] He may have been drifting around the state: as historians note, there was "no mechanism for keeping track of men who left to visit friends or relatives and never returned."[64] They also point out that 1862 saw a sudden, suspicious increase in the population of Wisconsin's northern and western counties, including Pepin. By the following year, so many men had fled to parts unknown that the exodus was characterized as a "stampede."[65]

THE toehold that Martha Quiner and Charles Carpenter had established on Maiden Rock in 1860—arriving as early pioneers in the area, with Indians as their "principal neighbors and frequent visitors"— would, within a few years, draw much of the clan near the Mississippi shores.[66] Along with Charles and Caroline, others in the extended family—Charles's parents, Peter Ingalls with Eliza Quiner, and Polly Ingalls with Henry Quiner—also decamped for Pepin County sometime between late 1862 and the summer of the following year.

It was in August 1862, just as the Ingallses and Quiners were about to set out toward the Big Woods, that the Dakota Indians launched their surprise attacks on New Ulm and other Minnesota settlements. Panic broke out along the Mississippi. Some forty thousand white settlers fled Minnesota, many crossing into Wisconsin and forming a vast wagon train stretching across the state into Milwaukee.

Many Wisconsin towns and settlements, too, were evacuated, with refugees abandoning homes and possessions. One man threw a sack of flour into the river so that Indians wouldn't get it, then took off for Pennsylvania.[67] In Pepin and neighboring counties near the Mississippi, hysterical midnight alarms sent people leaping from their beds, in anticipation of "bloody scenes of the Pioneer days of old."[68] Home Guards wielding pitchforks and scythes took to the streets of towns that had seen no bloodshed, ordering residents to sleep under guard inside defensive perimeters. Indians were prohibited from buying ammunition or whiskey. An Army captain, sent to investigate, reported that "the fear is mutual . . . whites are running in one direction the Indians are running in the other."[69]

Within weeks, terror had transfixed the entire state. In Sheboygan, on the western shores of Lake Michigan, hundreds of miles away from the fighting, townsfolk pulled up a drawbridge into town to keep out feared hordes.

As it turned out, the Dakota uprising would never cross the Mississippi. Compared to the brutality that would play out in Minnesota on both sides of the conflict, the panic in Wisconsin may have been, as one newspaper called it, a "ridiculous sight."[70] But the fear was real. Charles and Caroline would presumably remember it all their lives. So, indeed, would Laura, though the uprising happened five years before she was born. "I can't forget the Minnesota massacre," she would one day write.[71]

It was not enough to make the Ingallses and Quiners leave Wisconsin, though. In September 1863, Henry Quiner and Charles Ingalls found a promising piece of property about four miles from Martha's place. They pooled their money to buy it, a quarter section of land seven miles north of the town of Pepin. The land cost $335, but they could scrape together only thirty-five dollars in cash, arranging a mortgage for the rest.[72] Henry farmed the northern eighty acres while Charles worked the southern half. Each built a log cabin.

Shifting from place to place without a real home of their own, Charles and Caroline had been slow to start a family compared to their siblings. By 1865, Martha and Charles Carpenter, Eliza and Peter Ingalls, and Polly and Henry Quiner already had half a dozen children between them.[73]

But on January 10, 1865, Mary Amelia Ingalls was born to Charles and Caroline, on her father's twenty-ninth birthday. She was said to be a beautiful child, with blond hair and her father's blue eyes, cherished from her earliest days. Her parents hoped she would become a school-teacher, like her mother before her, and contribute to the family's welfare.

The Civil War was coming to an end. By April, Lincoln was dead. A month later, the fighting was over. Ninety-one thousand Wisconsin men had marched off to war, and more than twelve thousand never returned. The country settled into postwar recession, a time of bank collapses, falling prices, and stagnation. One of the bank failures cost the Ingallses their meager savings.[74]

It was during this inauspicious time, two years after Mary's birth, on February 7, 1867, that another daughter was born near legend-haunted Lake Pepin. Charles and Caroline named her Laura Elizabeth Ingalls.

Chapter 2

Indian Summers

The Wagon Was Home

Laura lived within the log walls of the Pepin cabin barely more than a year before Charles Ingalls entered into a dizzying series of financial maneuvers. He sold the property in April of 1868 for the astonishing sum of $1,012.50, receiving $100 in cash and a promissory note for the rest. At the same time, Henry Quiner sold his eighty acres to the same farmer, a Swede named Gustaf Gustafson.[1]

The increase in the value of the land, bought for a few hundred dollars only five years earlier, may be explained in part by the improvements the men had made. Both had built cabins and cleared acreage. Significantly more land seems to have been cleared on Henry Quiner's plot: agricultural schedules from 1870 reveal that his property boasted forty acres of plowed fields, producing eighty bushels of spring wheat, sixty bushels of Indian corn, and five tons of hay. Next door, Charles Ingalls had cleared only half as much.[2]

Later, Wilder would hint at the reasons, describing the "old place in the Big Woods" as hilly and brush-covered, "standing on edge and covered with stumps and sprouts."[3] Felling trees and pulling stumps in virgin forest was hazardous and difficult work. To clear an acre of forested land took 90 percent more labor than clearing an acre of prairie, demanding all the force that grown men and a team of oxen could bring to bear.

There could also have been other economic forces behind the increase in property values. Some decades later, the influential economist Thorstein Veblen—who grew up on a farm west of Milwaukee, not far from the Concord farms of the Quiner and Ingalls families—published an intensive examination of Number 2 spring wheat, the gold standard of agrarian commodities the world over. He found that wheat reached its peak value in 1867, the year Laura Ingalls was born, selling in Chicago for a giddy $1.43 a bushel.[4]

We have no way of knowing whether Charles Ingalls or Henry Quiner were able to bring their harvest to market and sell even a fraction of their crop at that price. There was as yet no railroad nearby, though ports south of Lake Pepin were already shipping Minnesota's wheat east. The two men may have found other ways to earn money—Charles always relied on trapping and carpentry to supplement the family income. But the news of high wheat prices may have spurred him to sell the farm while the selling was good, and search for more profitable land.

A month after the sale, Charles and Henry jumped on a Reconstruction bargain. Together with Henry and Caroline's younger brother, Tom Quiner, they bought land in the formerly slave-owning state of Missouri. It's likely that they purchased the property sight unseen. From our vantage point, the real estate transactions resemble a game of musical chairs, rushed and transitory.

The seller was a character who might well have sprung from the mind of Missouri's great fabulist, Mark Twain. His name was Adamantine Johnson; his siblings were Nova Zembla, Sylvetus, Italy, Sicily, and John.[5] Before the Civil War, Johnson had made a tidy fortune manufacturing chewing tobacco. The 1860 census shows him owning more than thirty thousand dollars' worth of real estate. He also owned three slaves in their twenties and four black children, ages sixteen, twelve, five, and three.[6]

In short order, however, the war dissolved that fortune and freed those slaves. The bank went bust, and Johnson set about selling off his

land. Charles Ingalls and Henry Quiner bought eighty acres each for
nine hundred dollars apiece, to be paid in five increasing installments.[7]
The lure: the land was a dollar down. The catch: a high interest rate of
10 percent.

At this point, the families' movements become hard to track. Charles
was still in Pepin County as of October 1868, when, as treasurer, he
signed a five-hundred-dollar bond for the local school district; he voted
in the general election a month later.[8] The following April, though, he
did not turn up at a town meeting to deal with the problem of swine
"running at large."[9]

Sometime in the spring or summer of 1869, Charles, Caroline, and
their two girls made the four-hundred-mile journey down to Missouri
by covered wagon. Emigrants typically left Wisconsin in late spring,
when there was grass on the ground to feed the horses. Slowly, making
ten to twenty miles per day, resting on Sundays, they trundled south,
passing through eastern Minnesota and Iowa on their way.

Having journeyed as a boy from New York State, Charles Ingalls
was an old hand at long-distance travel. Caroline, born in Wisconsin,
would not have been so accustomed. Her mother-in-law or other
family members, though, may have passed on the methods of preparing,
packing, and camping that generations of women had refined on the
overland western trails.

Weight was always a factor, and wagons were kept light to spare the
draft animals that pulled them. Commonly ten feet long, four feet
wide, and a couple of feet deep, the "prairie schooner" could hold only
essentials. Bedding, cookware, and food were packed within, protected
by a heavy canvas cover that was stretched over bows and rubbed with
linseed oil as waterproofing. Lashed to the outside were water barrels,
tools, spare wheels, and even furniture.[10]

"Put nothing in your wagon except provisions and clothing and
such articles as are indispensably necessary on the road," advised one
veteran of the California trail. She warned as well about the prevalence
of diarrhea and "gastric fever . . . produced by bad water and irregular
living."[11] Illness and accidents haunted travelers; children had to be
watched carefully to ensure they were not crushed by hooves or heavy

oak wheels. A grim pastime involved counting the crosses that marked the graves beside the trail.

Everything was a challenge: the wretched jolting of the wagon, the constant wind and dust, the search for water, cooking over an open campfire. "It is very trying on the patience to cook and bake on a little green fire with the smoke blowing in your eyes so as to blind you, and shivering with cold so as to make the teeth chatter," one young woman wrote.[12] She lacked the forbearance of Caroline Ingalls: the Ingalls girls recalled their mother brewing coffee and frying corn cakes with quiet competence, summoning comfort under the roughest conditions. "The wagon was home," Laura later recalled.[13]

Privacy was another concern on the trail. Traveling with a large company, Mormon women were said to have solved the problem by "walking out in a group, several standing with skirts spread wide to provide a screen for their sisters."[14] Generally, however, that topic, among other sensitive issues, was never addressed. Among "sanitary considerations" discussed in The Prairie Traveler, an 1859 handbook for westbound pioneers, human waste did not figure, merely the "noxious" airs believed to be emitted by swamps and rivers that were thought to cause malaria.[15]

Children were commonly born on the trail without siblings being any the wiser as to their mother's condition. A young girl recalled being awoken in the night by a crying baby. Asking whose it was, she was surprised to learn it was a new member of her own family. "I said not a word for some time," she wrote.[16] She already had nine brothers.

There were advantages to traveling in groups, especially security, but from what we know of them the Ingallses preferred to make their own way. We know they were in Missouri by the end of the summer: court records show that on August 26, 1869, "Charles P. Ingalls and Caroline, his wife, of Chariton County of the State of Missouri" signed a legal power of attorney authorizing Charles's father to manage their property in Wisconsin and collect all moneys owed from the sale to Gustafson.[17] The following week, on September 1, Caroline Ingalls appeared at a Missouri county courthouse to testify "apart from her husband" that she had been made aware of the contents of the legal instrument.[18]

Culturally, Missouri must have been a considerable shock. Before the Civil War, Chariton County, with a population of 12,562, had had 2,889 slaves working hemp and tobacco. In the 1860 presidential election, there was only a single vote cast for Abraham Lincoln in the entire county. Sterling "Old Pap" Price, a former governor of Missouri who then became a swashbuckling Confederate general, had his home in Chariton. The war was over by the time the Ingallses arrived, but deep wounds remained, the animus preserved by a "Record of Bloody Deeds" cataloguing robberies, hangings, drownings, and shootings said to have been perpetrated by Union troops during the conflict.[19]

And Adamantine Johnson's land, if not exactly a shock, was probably a disappointment. The Ingallses' plot lay near a tributary of Yellow Creek, an area of prairie and bottomland forest, and the creek was known for flooding.[20] Next door, Henry Quiner's plot had no access to the creek and no nearby water.

It's unclear whether Henry Quiner, Polly, and their four children made the trip down to Missouri with the Ingallses. If they did, at this point they must have turned around and returned to Pepin: Henry reappears in the voting record there in September.[21] The decision to return could not have been taken lightly. Travel was slow, hazardous, exhausting, and expensive. And if they were unable to raise a crop that year, missing it would have been a severe loss.

Whatever the Quiners did, Charles Ingalls did not return to Wisconsin. Nor did he stay in Missouri, however. He had other plans.

The Great, Flat Land Where No One Lived

Laura Ingalls came to consciousness gazing through the keyhole opening in the cinched canvas covering her family's wagon, swaying over an expanse of prairie grasses as they lurched slowly southwest from Missouri to Kansas.

It was one of her earliest specific memories and a sight she would never forget. Late in life, she would conjure it again and again, trying to recapture the stark beauty and isolation of that vista, seen through the eyes of her not-quite-three-year-old self. In her memory, the prairies represented a tabula rasa—wilderness as purity, free from human stain and experience. In her memoir, she recalled the scene: "I lay and looked through the opening in the wagon cover. . . . It was lonesome and so still with the stars shining down on the great, flat land where no one lived."[22]

As with her portrayal of the Big Woods as a place where "there were no people," there was a significant omission here. People did live in Kansas. And they fought over it, too.

The federal government originally planned to use Kansas as a dumping ground for the continent's original inhabitants. When Andrew Jackson signed the 1830 Indian Removal Act, maps were drawn up for an Indian Territory west of the Mississippi River. They showed strips of land stacked like cordwood, north to south, randomly assigned to Choctaws, Creeks, Cherokees, Osages, Shawnees, Pawnees, and so on.

Soon enough, however, whites decided they wanted the land for themselves after all. In the run-up to statehood, the free North and the slave-owning South fought over Kansas like wolves at a carcass. Kansas Territory became an early proxy battlefield in the Civil War, as free-soilers and pro-slavery posses attacked each other on the lawless frontier. Combatants on both sides rushed to seize land, establish towns, and publish newspapers that reflected their views, earning Kansas a reputation as the "Squatter State."

Winning statehood in 1861, Kansas had ultimately entered the war for the Union. But after the war, powerful interests were still scrapping over its fate. In order for the government to clear the way for farmers and the railroad lines to support them, the Indians who remained on their assigned lands would have to be permanently removed. For that, squatters were again the weapon of choice.

Charles Ingalls was one of them. There were rumors that Indian land in southeastern Kansas might soon be opened for claims under the 1841 Preemption Act, a forerunner of the Homestead Act that allowed settlers a one-time opportunity to acquire up to 160 acres of "public lands to which the Indian title had been at the time of such settlement extinguished."[23] Handbills and newspaper advertisements fueled a land rush to the region.[24] Charles, like others, doubtless expected the government to step in, move off the Indians, and let white farmers claim property for $1.25 an acre, the price specified in the act. Strange as it may seem today, eastern Kansas then lay on the frontier line, a conceptual boundary that was constantly shifting westward as the number of people per square mile ticked up.[25] Known for its cattle drives and the lawlessness that prevailed in cow towns such as Dodge City, Kansas was the West.

The Ingalls family, traveling on their own, probably arrived in Kansas in the fall of 1869, passing through a town just being built on the shores of the Verdigris River. Another early settler didn't think much of the outpost, writing to a friend that "some fly-by-nites started a village called hay-town . . . and gave it the high-toned name of Independence but it won't last long."[26] Thirteen miles southwest of the fledgling town, Charles Ingalls pulled up his wagon and camped on land he had not bought. He intended to make it his own.

He must have known that this was a dangerous game. The 1862 Dakota war was fresh in everyone's minds. Southeastern Kansas was home, by law, to the Osage Indians, a tribe that had been pushed west for decades and now found itself trapped in the same kind of shrinking box that the Dakota had tried to break out of just a few years earlier. The Osage had to decide: was it time to make their stand?

As a people, the Osage awed and astonished whites. Many of them stood over six feet tall, at a time when the average white male was a modest five-foot-six. Thomas Jefferson met a delegation of Osage in 1804 and described them as "certainly the most gigantic men we have ever seen."[27] An 1807 watercolor portrait of an Osage warrior shows his bald head sprouting a brilliant orange crest, like a mohawk, at the crown of his skull. His eyelids, cheeks, and torso are likewise colored a fierce orange, contrasting with a blue-green headdress bristling with the head of a small raptor, the beaks of waterfowl, and the skins of hummingbirds.[28]

The Osage were not shy about defending their land or their interests. Their clans organized posses, known as *Moh shon Ah ke ta*, Protectors of the Land, who hunted both whites and members of other tribes intruding on their territory, impaling their heads on stakes as a warning. According to early Spanish records, more than a thousand white and Indian trappers met such a fate.[29] In 1863, twenty-two Confederate soldiers had made the mistake of riding into southeastern

Kansas while looking for recruits. Less than twenty miles from where the Ingallses would build their cabin, Osage warriors led by a chief named Hard Rope surrounded the southerners at a creek. When the soldiers refused to identify themselves and fired on the Osage, killing a man, the warriors pinned them down on a gravel bar, dispatching twenty. As was the custom, the bodies were beheaded.[30]

By the late 1860s, the Osage had ample reason to be angry. They had signed multiple treaties, all to their disadvantage. They had been squeezed onto ever-smaller slivers of land, only to see settlers follow them even there, compromising their hunting grounds, corn crops, and their last vestiges of independence and solitude. In 1865, they had moved onto the Osage Diminished Reserve, a fifty-mile-wide strip where homesteading was prohibited. Within a few years, many were starving, newly impoverished as their annuity payments from the treaties ran out, and oppressed by settlers illegally squatting on the land.

Demoralized, the Osage decided to sign yet another agreement, known as the Sturges Treaty: a crooked deal that would have sold their reserve to the Leavenworth, Lawrence & Galveston Railroad for pennies an acre.[31] (William Sturges was the railroad's president.) But federal politicians were nervous after the Dakota War, reluctant to encourage another bloodbath. The proposed treaty blew up into a political scandal and was never ratified by Congress. Yet the damage had been done: months of debate and speculation had encouraged even more settlers to come to the area. Meanwhile, the Osage, unfamiliar with U.S. treaty ratification procedures, believed that the agreement they'd negotiated was now in force, and were furious at not receiving the money due to them under the treaty.

The land where Charles Ingalls began building a cabin lay well within the Osage Diminished Reserve.[32] Earlier in 1869 the Osage had posted the land, instructing all intruders to get out, but the settlers refused, asserting that only soldiers could dislodge them. A historian characterizes these settlers as the third surge of intruders, with each successive one setting up a "shock wave of pressure" on the Indians.[33] The first wave consisted of rabid pro- or anti-slavers in the 1850s. The second was Union veterans of the war, poverty-stricken and prone to violence; the Osage called them "sudden men," an apt description for

Indians' experience of settler incursions across the West, the whites showing up abruptly and demanding land for themselves.[34] The third wave—Charles Ingalls among them—was made up of farmers emboldened by the Civil War to call on federal troops to enforce what they saw as their rights, although they had none on Osage land.

By early 1870, seven thousand settlers had crowded into Montgomery County, camping within the Osage Diminished Reserve.[35] The Osage were off on their semiannual hunt, and Isaac Gibson, the U.S. Indian agent posted in the county, reported to his superior that "pioneer whites" had taken advantage of the Indians' absence. Pouring into the reserve, they were setting up saw mills, stealing fence rails, and dismantling or seizing cabins for themselves. They were setting fire to hay fields and looting or burning stores of Osage corn. A village that was home to nine hundred Osage was stripped of lumber and valuables.[36] According to one disgruntled settler, the Indians had already begun to retaliate for these incursions, planting corn next to his cabin and teaching their children "to spit in our rain barrel."[37]

Alarmed, Gibson reported that the Osage were near the breaking point. They had told him this:

> We sold our lands to the government nearly two years ago [in the Sturges Treaty], have received no pay, but the white man came at once and took our lodges and corn patches, and he has brought a great many cattle that eat our winter food. The commissioners said we should have a new country, but you won't let us go there nor protect us here. If government don't like that treaty why don't they let us make another. We have now no place to live. We want to live in peace with the white man, but we can't here; he robs us of our homes.[38]

Gibson urged his superiors to take action immediately, either by removing whites from the reserve or by moving the Osage to a new home. If something wasn't done, he feared that the Indians, numbering some 4,400, "could massacre the inhabitants of this valley in a few hours."[39]

Later that month, Gibson sent another dispatch. Two men had come to see him from the mouth of Walnut Creek (which flowed through the acreage where the Ingallses were perched), reporting that the Osage had assumed "a threatening attitude."[40] "Hard Rope will probably settle the disputes in the valley when he returns," Gibson wrote, "if something is not done."[41] As the Confederate recruiters had learned, disputes settled by Hard Rope stayed settled. Gibson's superiors lost no time in requesting that troops be sent to keep the peace, and some were duly dispatched. But the soldiers took no action to dispossess errant whites. They were merely stationed in case of Indian attack.

Historical reports left by Gibson and others suggest that when the Ingalls family arrived, the Osage were off hunting. The land seemed deserted. The family camped while Charles built a log house, felling trees in the nearby creek bottom and using the horses to drag them to the site. He left a raw opening in the wall for a window and hung a quilt across the open doorway. At night, Jack, the family's brindle bulldog, lay across the doorway to guard against the wolves howling outside.

The Ingallses did not engage in the overt provocations that Gibson described, but their presence in itself was illegal. The trees Charles Ingalls took to build his little house doubtless belonged to the Osage. One of them complained to Gibson of losing four hundred logs that winter.[42] The agent was so concerned that he consulted government lawyers about timber rights, but the lawyers—like the soldiers—did nothing.

VIRTUALLY everything known about the family's experience in Kansas derives from the first twenty pages of a memoir found among Wilder's papers, handwritten in 1930 on six dime-store tablets. Some of them bore the "Big Chief" brand name, with the profile of an Indian in a feathered headdress on their flimsy paper covers.

Recently published in an annotated edition as *Pioneer Girl*, the title Wilder scrawled across the cover of the first tablet, the memoir reveals much about the formation of the author's personality, her role in the family, and her ambition and craft. While it bears superficial similarities to diaries and letters left by women who crossed the plains on the California, Oregon, and Santa Fe trails, *Pioneer Girl* is a retrospective account, profoundly impressionistic, and its chronology is not always reliable.[43] Rather than an immediate response to events, the memoir is a casting back across decades, bringing to light memories buried under

the weight of adult experience. Those that were buried the deepest—
and yet emerged most vividly—were from Kansas.

As described, the nearly three-year-old Laura seemed initially bliss-
fully unaware of the tensions and acrimony that surrounded the settlers.
She was deeply impressed by the wildlife, which seemed to be their
closest neighbors. She remembered her father lifting her out of bed one
night and carrying her to the window so she could see a ring of wolves
circling the house, "with their noses pointed up at the big, bright moon,
howling as loud and long as they could, while Jack paced before the
door and growled."[44]

Aside from Charles's trip to town to buy a stove, a window pane,
and lumber for a door, that appeared to be all she could reconstruct of
the fall and winter of 1869. Her parents went to Independence again in
February 1870 to cancel the purchase of the Missouri land, signing it
back over to Adamantine Johnson; they had either decided not to make
payments or could not do so.[45] It was the third piece of property Charles
Ingalls had owned and the second relinquished for nonpayment.

The narrative picks up in the eventful summer of 1870, when "everyone was sick with chills and fever." Malaria was a mystery at the time,
though historians have described it as "the most prevalent disease on the
prairie frontier."[46] No one knew what caused it: Did it spring from the
virgin soil the first time it was turned by a plow? Did it seep through
the open window with the morning dew? The Ingalls family was convinced that eating ripe watermelons was somehow to blame. The whole
family lay prone in bed, Laura and her sister crying weakly for water.
She remembered her father, as sick as everyone else, staggering around
and waiting on them. She remembered his hand shaking as he held the
cup to her mouth.

Newspapers across the frontier invariably carried advertisements for
treatments for "fever and ague," as malaria was called. The Ingallses
were given quinine by a frontier doctor, George Tann, who lived less
than a mile from them. "One time I waked and there was a great, big
black man looking at me," Laura wrote.[47] He lifted her head and poured
bitter medicine down her throat with a spoon. She was afraid of him,
she admitted, "for I had never seen a colored person before."[48]

Tann had been born in Pennsylvania to free black tenant farmers who, like the Ingallses, joined the rush to Kansas in 1869. A Civil War veteran, he practiced "eclectic medicine," a nineteenth-century movement based on botanical treatments.[49] Like many physicians at the time, Tann had no formal training, but he served for years in the region, treating both whites and members of the Cherokee reservation nearby. Under his care, the Ingalls family recovered.

The Osage returned from their hunting trip sometime in the summer of 1870 and a couple of Indian men were seen near the barn, looking at the horses in a way that inspired Charles to tie his dog at the barn door. Jack was so fierce that even neighbors feared him.

One summer day, while Laura and Mary were playing with the dog in the barn, they saw two Indians walk into their cabin, clad in fresh skunk skins, their faces painted and heads shaved "except for a bunch of hair on top that was tied so it stood up straight."[50] The girls debated untying the dog but remembered their father's strict instructions to leave him chained. Though hesitant to leave his protection, they screwed up the courage to run to their mother, Mary clinging to her skirts while Laura hid behind the stove. The Indians examined everything in the house, telling Caroline to cook for them. After eating, they left, carrying away all the meat in the house as well as a pipe and tobacco.

Not long after, many Osage came and camped near the creek—perhaps Walnut Creek or Onion Creek, which fed into the Verdigris. All night, the family was kept awake by "shouting and screaming . . . much worse than the wolves."[51] Charles Ingalls dismissed it as Osage "war dances," urging his family not to worry. But Laura often saw her father up late, fully dressed, carrying his gun, until the Indians went away again.[52]

In early August, Charles led Mary and Laura, who was riding on Jack's back, down to the creek bed to spend the day picking over the remains of a deserted Osage camp. She remembered "finding a great many pretty beads that the Indian women had lost from their beadwork," white, blue, yellow, and "a great many red ones."[53] Returning home, the girls found their mother, tended by Dr. Tann and a woman who lived nearby, in bed with their new baby sister, Caroline Celestia Ingalls.

Born August 3, 1870, Carrie would always be slight and frail, perhaps due to her mother's exposure to malaria, associated with maternal anemia and low birth weight.

Ten days after Carrie was born, the federal census taker came through, listing the "Ingles" directly below the Tanns.[54] Charles Ingalls called himself a carpenter and gave the value of his personal property as two hundred dollars. The census taker left blank the column for property values, explaining that the "Lands belonged to the Osage Indians and settlers had no title to said Lands."[55]

In the fall of 1870 the weather turned dry, the creek shrank to a trickle, and the grass turned sere. Fire on the plains often comes in the spring, but one hot fall day smoke appeared on the horizon. Laura's father plowed a fire break around the house, and he and Caroline ran to fetch the horses, picketed on the grass. "Mary and I were very much excited," Wilder recalled, though they did not understand what was happening until a cloud of smoke swept past. "Then I saw the prairie fire coming," she wrote. "The flames came running across the prairie leaping high and the smoke rolled above them."[56] Her reaction to prairie fires, wolves, and Indians was matter-of-fact yet tinged with awe, reminiscent of others' encounters with near death on the open prairie.

The first Christmas Laura could remember was likewise strikingly dramatic. With the creek running high after days of rain, Charles warned his daughters that Santa Claus might not be able to reach them. The celebration was saved when a neighbor bravely swam across to deliver their gifts: a "bright shining new tin cup" for each of the older girls and a beautiful stick of striped peppermint candy.[57] Although no one, including the adult Wilder, could remember his name, his generosity would earn him a place in fictional history.[58]

Come spring, the Indians returned. Wilder's memoir tends to be terse, but she devoted a full page to re-creating the day she sat in the doorway watching the Osage file past, on their "spotted ponies and yellow ponies and red ponies."[59] The line extended clear to the horizon, first the men, then the women, with babies in baskets or tied to their backs.

Entranced by the "bright, black eyes" of a pair of infants in baskets, she begged her father to get them for her.[60] "I wanted those babies," she wrote. It was one of the few times when Charles Ingalls lost patience with Laura. He put her in the house when she cried, telling her they already had a baby. "I don't see what you [want] those papooses for," he said. She persisted. "I did want them," she said. "Their eyes were so bright."[61] This scene was so arresting that one day it would provide the climax of her most powerful work.

Almost immediately after the Indians left, she recalled, her father started putting the cover back on their wagon and hitching up the horses. They, too, were leaving. "Soldiers were taking all the white people off the Indian's land," she wrote.[62]

That was her recollection, at least. It was probably wrong: so much confusion surrounded the disposition of land within the Osage Diminished Reserve that settlers may have misinterpreted the presence and purpose of federal troops. Gibson's superior, the superintendent of Indian affairs for the region, had in fact decided that settlers who were not harassing the Osage "will be permitted quietly to remain."[63] But at least one local newspaper, the *Kansas Democrat*, contradicted him, reporting that troops would be removing squatters.[64]

Charles Ingalls also had another reason to return to Wisconsin. Sometime during 1870, he had received word that Gustaf Gustafson, the buyer of the farm in Pepin, was unable to make further payments. Perhaps to reclaim that property, Charles abruptly decided to quit Kansas, without attempting to make his squatter's claim legal by purchasing the land through the Preemption Act. Had he stayed only a few more weeks, it would have been possible: a federal survey was conducted in Montgomery County in the spring of 1871, and the first purchases were made in June. On the other hand, Charles may not have had the money. Forty acres would have cost fifty dollars.[65]

The trip out of Kansas proved hazardous, and it began with a bad omen. As the family traveled over the open prairie, they saw a covered wagon stalled beside the trail, adults and children sitting despondently in it, with no way to move on: their horses had been stolen in the night. Charles offered them a ride to Independence, but was refused, and the Ingallses left them sitting "stolidly" on the motionless wagon, looking off across the plains.

Swollen by spring rains to the north, rivers were nearly impassable. At one fording, Laura saw her mother hurriedly reach back into the

wagon to drop the baby on the mattress where she and Mary lay. She
pulled a blanket over their heads and told them sharply, "Lie still." Laura
could feel the wagon wheels lifting off the river bottom as her father
dove into the water, grabbing the swimming horses' bridles to lead them
to the other side. It was a terrifying moment. While the beds of expensive
Conestoga wagons, destined for the Oregon Trail, were built to be water-
tight, the Ingallses were probably using a rough farm wagon, which
would have started filling up like a leaky boat. Had the water gotten
high enough to top the sides, the whole family would have been lost.

Charles apparently thought better of crossing flooded creeks, and
they waited out the weather in Missouri, "in a log house with a big
fireplace," while he worked for the owner.[66] Caroline and her children
were alone in the house one day when the chimney—a mud-and-stick
affair—caught fire. As Caroline ran outside to knock burning pieces off
the house, Mary sat frozen with fear, holding the baby while blazing
sticks fell around her. Laura grabbed the back of her chair and jerked it
clear across the room. "Ma said I did well," she wrote later, "for a four
year old."[67] An early, abrupt emergence of her character, the incident
was stamped with the traits that would define her as a singularly
intrepid child, bent on action.

Before they left to complete the long, exhausting trip north, Charles
traded his horses, Pet and Patty, for a sturdier team. The troublesome
bulldog Jack, who wanted to stay with the ponies "as he always did,"
was traded as well.[68] By the spring of 1871, the family was in Wisconsin,
back where they had started out two years before.

In a brief and concentrated span of time, the Ingallses had experienced
virtually everything that would come to be seen as quintessentially
Western: encounters with wolves and Indians, angry disputes over open
range, prairie fires, neighbors coming to their aid. Although they would
retreat for a time to Wisconsin, an enduring impression had been made,
one that would strengthen over the years as the family moved. From
the open doorway of a tiny log cabin, Laura had watched as a parade
of Western iconography passed by. It was as if the spirit of manifest
destiny had been imprinted in her memory, leaving a series of stereo-
scopic images, each more dramatic than the one before, each intensely
experienced and utterly unique, yet emblematic of all of western

settlement. The family spent little more than a year on the Kansas prairie, but it shaped her temperament and outlook for the rest of her life. That year made her who she was.

But the Kansas adventure would inevitably push them closer to the edge of ruin. Charles Ingalls had labored to improve land that was not his own, felling trees, building a house and barn, digging a well, plowing fields. He gained nothing from it. In 1871, he was thirty-five, and he had seen his own father's strength sapped by the time he was in his forties. He had not yet produced a male child who could lend a hand. His daughter remembered their departure with puzzled sadness: "We drove away leaving our little house standing empty and lonely on the prairie."[69] They would never recover the economic ground lost in Kansas.

The image of Charles Ingalls that emerges from these unsettled early years contains elements of moral ambiguity missing from the portrait his daughter would one day so lovingly polish. Having avoided fighting in the Civil War, he was not above trying to profit from it. Like many in his time, he did not hesitate to put a young and growing family in harm's way. If he did not know Hard Rope's reputation, he should have. His dealings with Indians and implicit reliance on the government—to protect settlers from the consequences of their provocative actions and remove Indians from land he wanted—were self-serving. He was willing to press his advantage, to take something that did not belong to him if he thought he could get away with it. These were very different characteristics than the ones his daughter would choose to emphasize decades later. She would never refer to him in print as a "squatter." But she knew he was.[70]

Warm and Snug and Happy

May of 1871 found the Ingallses once more among their extended family of parents, siblings, and cousins. Waiting for the Gustafsons to vacate their log cabin, Charles and Caroline and their three girls stayed for a few weeks with Henry and Polly Quiner. Lansford and Laura Ingalls had sold their Pepin County land and moved to a farm twelve miles to the north, in neighboring Pierce County. Peter and Eliza Ingalls had joined them there, buying land nearby. Martha and Charles Carpenter and their growing brood were also within visiting distance.

Restored to the little house where Mary and Laura were born, the Ingallses enjoyed a happy and prosperous summer, feasting off venison, fish netted from Lake Pepin, and bounty from a prodigious garden planted by the Gustafsons, full of potatoes, carrots, beets, turnips, onions, cabbage, pumpkin, and squash. They were well provided with domestic livestock, the foundation of subsistence farming. Charles bought a pig from Henry, his brother-in-law, and the family acquired a cow named Sukey, a black-and-white spotted puppy named Wolf, and a cat named Black Susan.

Readers of Wilder's memoir will recognize this as the raw material out of which she crafted the cozy security of her first volume, *Little House in the Big Woods*, its attic packed with homemade cheeses and pumpkins, its barrels of salted meat, its horn of plenty. The girls created their own domestic havens in the yard, each choosing a tree where they kept their dolls and "housekeeping things," cracked teacups and play dishes.[71] "We were very warm and snug and happy in our little log house in the woods," she recalled in her memoir.

A busy social life and the tiny travails of a girl just finding her way drive the narrative over the next couple of years. After titanic effort, Laura produced the first of a pair of mittens for Carrie and was ready to abandon the job. But her mother told her that a task, once started, must be completed. Long and arduous struggle produced another mitten, but satisfaction was short-lived: the puppy Wolf had in the meantime stolen its mate and ripped it to shreds under the bed.

At the age of four, Laura attended the "Barry Corner School," intermittently, with her sister Mary and her uncle Henry's older children. Taught by Anna Barry, daughter of one of Pepin's town fathers and owner of its first flour mill, the school was less than half a mile from the Ingallses' cabin. Visitors admired Miss Barry's methods, praising the students' "orderly and good spellings."[72] These were probably not Laura's. She would joke all her life about her struggles with orthography.

She struggled, as well, with Mary. One day, her mother curled their hair specially before a visit by Aunt Lottie—Caroline Ingalls's twelve-year-old half sister, Charlotte—and Laura was peeved that everyone exclaimed over Mary's blond curls, ignoring her brown ones. Later that afternoon, the girls quarreled sharply, Mary telling her that golden curls were prettier. Laura slapped her. Their father saw the whole thing, and spanked Laura with a strap. Afterward, he took her on his knee and told her how he himself had been naughty as a boy, playing and forgetting to go for the cows until after dark. His father had "tanned my jacket," Charles recalled.[73]

But on this occasion, Laura was not soothed, and the minute drama of sibling rivalry and juvenile injustice would be etched in her mind. Forever after, she would compare herself to Mary—the good, blond, better-behaved daughter—in a manner suggesting her own mixed feelings of inferiority and defiance. In all her later writing, she would cast herself as the naughty one, whose darker hair and skin typified a contrary character: Mary would call her out for being "tanned brown as an Indian," for letting her sunbonnet hang down her back and her hair blow free.[74] Years later, Wilder would revisit the original quarrel as a defining moment, one that set the sisters in competition and engendered her fierce dedication to fairness.[75]

Glimpses of historical events can be seen in offhand references in Wilder's memoir, like blurry figures in the background of a photograph. A passage describing the family's first autumn back in Wisconsin, for instance, recounts how "one day the sun was nearly hidden by smoke all day and when dark came the sky was reddened by fire. We stood in the door watching it and soon we could see fire run up to the tops of some trees on a hill and then the trees stood there burning like great candles."[76] What they may have seen—without realizing it—was the firestorm that broke out across Wisconsin on the night of the great Chicago fire.

The summer of 1871 had been extraordinarily hot and dry across the upper Midwest. Decades of intensive logging of northern Wisconsin and Michigan had left behind thousands of acres of slash: stumps and piles of dead, discarded bark and branches. Railroad workers compounded the problem by clearing rights-of-way and leaving piles of brush to be ignited by sparks from passing locomotives.

Massive clear-cutting alters climate abruptly. It halts transpiration—the process by which leaves release moisture into the atmosphere—and can change the very reflectivity of the earth's surface. As shade vanishes, the ground absorbs heat and releases it back into the air. During the hot months of 1871, the wastelands left by logging exploded. Flames rose across the Midwest that summer, with Minnesota scorched by prairie fires. On October 8, 1871, came firestorms unprecedented in their ferocity.

Several hundred miles to the east of where the Ingallses lived, along the shores of Green Bay, winds from the south driven by a low-pressure system whipped several smaller fires together across a sixty-mile front. The flames swept toward the logging town of Peshtigo, built along the river of the same name. Its roads were covered in sawdust, its sidewalks built out of boards. Buildings, factories, and roof shingles, as well as a key bridge leading out of town, were wooden. The whole town burned that night, along with virtually everyone in it. There were so few survivors that hardly anyone remained to account for the dead. The fire left only bricks, stones, and molten metal. Somewhere between 1,200 and 2,400 people died. One and a half million acres burned that night. The fire would have been visible from space, and certainly from Pepin County.

To the south, in a separate event, Chicago burned, killing several hundred. Because newspapers were slow to learn of the horrific number of casualties in Peshtigo, the "Great Chicago Fire" overshadowed the far worse conflagration in neighboring Wisconsin. The Peshtigo fire remains one of the largest forest fires in North American history, and the most deadly.

As with so many of the disasters that the Ingallses lived through, there was nothing natural about it. The Midwest fires were human-caused, and their consequences would spread across the globe. The Ingallses could not know it, but the smoke they saw that October presaged a looming economic crisis, one that spun discrete disasters into a planetary event.

Laura was innocently unaware of these problems. And while her novels would stress the rugged isolation and independence of her nuclear family, her memoir's quotidian details reveal the closeness and interdependence of family and friends, geographically and emotionally. At Christmas their first year back, Peter and Eliza Ingalls came to visit with several of their children, Laura's "double cousins." Bedding down on the floor, the kids listened agog to Charles telling a thrilling story about their grandfather and a wild cat.

Fun-loving and endlessly engaging, Charles could always be relied upon to tell memorable stories. There were tales about bears, panthers, owls, and his own or his father's naughtiness as a youngster. When they weren't listening to him, his girls watched adoringly as he went about his day: making bullets, cleaning his gun, playing "Money Musk" and "The Red Heifer" on his fiddle, roughing up his hair and pretending to be a "mad dog."

There was constant visiting back and forth. Charles and Caroline loaded the children into the wagon for a dance at their grandparents' house, where the children met far-flung aunts and uncles. An even more elaborate affair took place at the house of their Irish neighbor, Thomas Huleatt, whose home was grandly known as "Summer Hill": "Everyone was proud to be invited."[77]

The whole family went to visit Aunt Martha and her brood. Laura played hard: at the schoolyard with Martha's older children, she bit the thumb of a big boy who tried to wash her face in snow. Upstairs, the children were raising an unholy din until Laura heard her aunt tell her mother, "You go up Caroline and spank them all. I'll go next time."[78]

Laura remembered her fifth birthday, in 1872, fondly. Her mother baked her five tiny cakes, one for each year, and her father gave her a little man whittled from wood, a friend for her doll. Adding to the fun, he played "Pop Goes the Weasel" on his violin. "A penny for a spool of thread, / Another for a needle, / That's the way the money goes—/ Pop! Goes the weasel."

"Pop" is exactly how the money was going. Ominous signs had been building since the turn of the decade. The price of gold had collapsed a few years before, on Black Friday, September 24, 1869; by 1872, inflation had reached dangerous levels. The Chicago fire—which destroyed 17,500 buildings and left a hundred thousand people homeless—further burdened the economy.

Globalization was already a major factor. After serfdom was abolished in Russia in 1861, millions of peasants shifted from subsistence to a market economy, raising and exporting wheat to Britain and

Europe.[79] With so many other countries entering the export market—
and the beginnings of technological mechanization enabling large-
scale agricultural production—the market was flooded. "The price of
wheat . . . tied the American West firmly into the world economy," a
historian notes.[80]

When demand for wheat slackened or its price fell, the railroads
built to carry it began to run into trouble. They were already weakened
by frenzied overinvestment: after the Civil War, subsidies had spurred
investors to support the laying of tens of thousands of miles of new
track, although the goods they would carry remained notional at best.
Foreshadowing modern-day pork barrel projects, railways were being
flung across clearly unprofitable areas: one desert crossing was characterized by a Bank of California official as "beginning nowhere and
ending nowhere."[81] Highly leveraged, borrowing more than their rev-
enues could supply, the great railroad corporations fudged their annual
reports, hiding oceans of debt.[82] By the fall of 1873, those debts were
about to be called in.

Meanwhile, throughout that year, the Ingallses were scrambling
again. In the spring, Charles and Caroline had borrowed two hundred
and fifty dollars against the value of their land from a Pepin storeowner.[83] Farmers commonly borrowed at that time of year to buy seed
or farm equipment, always planning to pay back the money from the
proceeds of the next crop. But that fall—at the very moment that the
Panic of 1873 began busting railroads, toppling banks, and seizing up
credit—the Ingallses sold their Wisconsin land yet again, accepting a
thousand dollars for their property from a Scandinavian couple named
Anderson.[84] Perhaps they were struggling to pay back their debt; perhaps
they simply received an offer too good to refuse. Perhaps Charles wanted
to live near a railroad, where grain could be shipped to market; railways
would not reach Pepin for over a decade.[85]

Years later, Wilder would attribute her father's decision to the disappearance of game and his distaste for the crowds piling into Wisconsin. From 1860 to 1870, the state's population had swelled from 775,881
to more than a million. Charles Ingalls never seemed to realize that
his ambition for a profitable farm was irreconcilable with a love of
untrammeled and unpopulated wilderness.

Whatever motivated them to sell a comfortable, established home with plowed fields and a productive garden, the decision appears in retrospect to have been yet another miscalculation, a leap into the unknown that would be repaid with disaster, heartbreak, and homelessness. This time, it was a cash deal; there was no mortgage. This time, there would be no going back to the little house in the Big Woods. The Ingallses were on their own, as the country and the world sank into a severe and seemingly interminable crisis. Like the financial crash that had propelled Charles's father and his uncles out of New York State, this slump too would be called—at least until the next one—"the Great Depression."

Chapter 3

Crying Hard Times

A Bad Dream

In February 1874, Charles Ingalls drove his family west across the frozen Mississippi into Minnesota. They stopped in a hotel in Lake City,
on the other side of Lake Pepin. Venturing out, Charles returned with
a present for Laura for her seventh birthday, a saddle-stitched book of
illustrated poems for children called *The Floweret: A Gift of Love*.[1]

Doubtless he could ill afford it, but he was always open-handed
and spontaneous, taking a lifelong joy in song and poetry, a gift he
bestowed on all his children. *The Floweret* contained "Over the brook
to Grandmamma's," as well as poems about little girls, playful dogs,
cats, mice, butterflies, and hummingbirds.

Like the rail-splitting, self-taught lawyer who had recently occupied
the White House, Charles may have been a poor farmer, but he was a
thoughtful and literate man. There is an unmistakable gulf between
his letters and the brief note that survives in his older brother Peter's
hand. In a brief postscript to a letter written by his wife, Eliza, in beautiful script, Peter struggled to put words on paper. "Eliza has ritten all
the news," he scratched out. "Crops are verry good our wheat is just

heading out . . . I cant think of much to write."[2] Eldest of ten, Peter had doubtless been needed in the fields from a very young age.

Through natural inclination or superior instruction, Charles wrote fluently, in a fair hand, and the few examples that survive of his writing carry his humor and humanity. Like Caroline, he treasured books. Among his possessions was one of the most magnificent tomes of the day, *The Polar and Tropical Worlds: A Description of Man and Nature* by Dr. G. Hartwig, "the whole splendidly embellished with nearly TWO HUNDRED BEAUTIFUL ILLUSTRATIONS." His daughter would call it "Pa's big green book," and it remains a fascinating compendium of nineteenth-century natural history, one that would enliven any blizzard-bound home. He also owned well-thumbed volumes of the *Poetical Works of Oliver Goldsmith* and *The Vicar of Wakefield*.[3] His children would all grow up to become writers of one kind or another.

Charles's family initially set out together with Peter, Eliza, and their offspring. Laura and the other children were suffering from what they called "scarlet fever." The illness left Laura with terrible earaches, her complaints so piteous that Mary and the cousins, standing beside her, were "almost crying from sympathy."[4] Finally, Aunt Eliza recalled a folk remedy: stuff the ears with warm wool freshly shorn from a black sheep. Laura's cousin Ella ran out, found a black sheep, pulled some wool off the struggling animal, and triumphantly produced the panacea.[5]

Leaving Peter and Eliza's family behind—they would eventually settle near the Zumbro River, south of the Mississippi—Charles, Caroline, and the girls crossed Minnesota, camping next to creeks and sleeping in the wagon bed. The children would fall asleep hearing the horses munching their oats, "with just the thin wagon cover between their heads and ours."[6] One hundred and fifty miles west of the Mississippi they came to New Ulm, newly rebuilt after the battle of 1862. Laura watched the American flag snapping over a beer garden and tasted beer herself for the first time, finding it bitter. She saw "grassy mounds that Pa said were ruins of houses where Indians had killed the settlers."[7]

West of New Ulm they entered Redwood County, source of the Dakota uprising, where Andrew Myrick's mouth was stuffed with grass that hot August day twelve years earlier.[8] Charles Ingalls found a quarter section of property in North Hero township, on Plum Creek, a tributary of the Cottonwood River. Paperwork on the land claim reveals the Ingallses settled there on May 24, 1874, moving into a dugout already on the property, a cavity scooped out of the creek's banks.[9]

In June, Charles filed a preemption claim on 172 acres. To get title to the land, he would have to stay at least six months, establish a residence, and eventually pay $2.50 an acre—twice the price for ordinary public land under the Preemption Act, because this property was near the railroad.[10] This time, unlike in Pepin, he would be able to ship his wheat to market.

The land was two miles north of a not-yet-incorporated town, then known as Walnut Station and later renamed Walnut Grove, for its black walnut trees. The town was platted, or mapped out, shortly after the family arrived. Sparsely settled before the Dakota uprising, it became even lonelier afterward: Lake Shetek, ten miles to the southwest, saw fifteen whites killed at "Slaughter Slough" in 1862. An early landmark in town was the "lookout pole" erected by American soldiers, shinnying up to search for Indians.[11]

In her memoir, Wilder recalled spending the first, fortunately mild winter in the dugout, "a funny little house" not much bigger than the wagon.[12] As was customary, the roof had been crafted from a lattice of willow branches with strips of sod laid across the top. As the grass grew together, its thatch formed a relatively sturdy ceiling, but one that could be pierced by an errant ox wandering across the top.

Dugouts and "soddies," their more elaborate cousins—freestanding houses built of sod squares stripped from the ground—were common across the treeless Great Plains during the "sod-house frontier" era, from the 1850s to the end of the century. They were cheap to build: in 1872, a Nebraska farmer itemized his costs as two dollars and seventy-eight and a half cents, mainly for lumber to build a door and a pipe to go through the roof.[13] They offered crude climate control, staying warm in winter and cool in summer.

But they were also damp and dirty. Dugouts were prone to flooding in the spring, and despite fabric hung overhead, or whitewash or newspapers slapped up as makeshift wallpaper, soil and spiders drifted down upon the occupants. A frontier cook recalled frying pancakes under an umbrella. They were so cramped that families routinely carried bedding outside during the day, just to have space to turn around. One pioneer wife objected to living in a hole in the ground "like a prairie dog."[14]

However primitive the accommodations, Plum Creek was a beautiful place. Along the creek bed, clear water meandered over a soft, silty bottom shaded by willows and plum thickets, perfect for wading. Tall-grass prairie spread to the horizon, waving with big bluestem and a riot of summer wildflowers: bergamot, butterfly weed, coreopsis, purple coneflower, black-eyed Susan. Butterflies, meadowlarks, and red-winged blackbirds flew among the grasses while badgers lay in their burrows. Beyond the east bank lay a vast flat tableland, the vista topped by a spectacular blue sky studded with distant white.

Laura and Mary were delighted with dugout living and had "wonderful times" playing in Plum Creek. They were proud of their new responsibilities: minding Carrie to make sure she didn't fall in the water and watching for the family cow, brought back each afternoon by a herd boy after a day grazing on the prairie. Like many of the neighbors, he was Scandinavian. On the neighboring property lived a Norwegian couple: Eleck C. Nelson, the first settler in the township, and his wife, Olena, who would become good friends of the family.

Their father was busy plowing and digging a well next to the site where he planned to build a house. Charles Ingalls was once again chasing a wheat crop that, he hoped, would put him in the black. Wheat was selling high at the moment, $1.02 a bushel.[15] As he had in Kansas, he was starting over, presumably laying out cash to buy seed and farm equipment.[16] He raised only a small crop that first year, possibly sown by a former occupant.

During the summer of 1874, Charles and Caroline met with a dozen townsfolk to organize a Congregational society in town. They helped raise money to build Walnut Grove's first house of worship, the Union Congregational Church of Christ, dedicated on December 20, 1874.[17] The local newspaper proclaimed it "the only church of any pretentions between Sleepy Eye lake and the Pacific ocean."[18]

Reverend Edwin H. Alden delivered the first sermon. He was thirty-eight, a soft-spoken, droopy-eyed graduate of Dartmouth who had been assigned by the American Home Missionary Society to establish churches in the godless reaches of Minnesota. He would become a familiar presence in the Ingallses' lives, beloved especially by Caroline.

He may have secured the family's affections that first winter by hosting the dedicatory celebration around a Christmas tree, the first the Ingalls girls had ever seen, decorated with candles, colored paper, and small bags of candy. Heaped around it were gifts the reverend helped distribute to the community: clothing, boots, dolls, sleds, and a barrel full of donated items sent from a wealthy eastern church. Laura had a fur collar bestowed on her, and was so awestruck by its soft magnificence she could barely speak.[19]

Charles and Caroline Ingalls demonstrated a lifelong fealty to the Congregationalists, perhaps reflecting family connections that predated Walnut Grove. The girls "loved to go to Sunday school," memorizing Bible verses and borrowing books from the church library.[20] That winter or the next, Charles delivered $26.15 to the treasurer, perhaps collected from members, and served as a church trustee, raising money for Alden's salary.[21] Wilder would recall that her father donated his own "boot money"—several dollars saved to replace footwear with holes in them—to buy a church bell.

But even as the Ingallses were finding a place for themselves in Walnut Grove society, there was trouble on the horizon. Ominously, two other men had previously filed claims on the same land, then relinquished it.[22] Neither one had "proved up" by completing the process and paying for the claim. Whether Charles knew it or not, the previous owners may have had good reason to leave the bucolic Plum Creek property.

In June 1873, a year before the Ingallses arrived, a mystifying cloud had darkened the clear sky of southwest Minnesota on "one of the finest days of the year."[23] Like a demonic visitation, it was flickering red, with silver edges, and appeared to be alive, arriving "at racehorse speed." Settlers were terrified to realize that it was composed of locusts, swarming grasshoppers that settled a foot thick over farms, breaking trees and shrubs under their weight. They sounded, according to one unnerved observer, like "thousands of scissors cutting and snipping."[24] A young Minnesota boy was in school with his brother when they heard the locusts coming, around two o'clock in the afternoon. As they started for home, cringing under a hail of falling insects, the boys had to "hold our hands over our faces to keep them from hitting us in our eyes."[25]

Farmers tried everything to get rid of them, firing guns, building barricades, starting fires, clubbing them off houses. Nothing worked. According to eyewitnesses, a month after they arrived, having eaten everything green, the grasshoppers formed a column and marched off to the east.

During that one month, the locust swarms destroyed more than three million dollars' worth of crops, including over half a million bushels of wheat. A dozen counties reported damages, including virtually all of Redwood County. Yet though it was a blow to the state's economy, the lost crops represented only 2 percent of that year's production.[26] The state wrote it off as a fluke, reveling in a banner year elsewhere.

Charles Ingalls must have heard of the grasshoppers; newspaper columns were full of them. Yet when the Ingallses settled on Plum Creek in 1874, the land was cloaked in spring green. They may have believed, as others did, that the grasshoppers had moved on. In fact, the previous year's swarm had laid their eggs before departing. While Charles Ingalls plowed his fields, grasshoppers flew and marched in columns again, leaving destitute farmers in their wake with no seed to plant the next season. As with tornadoes, however, devastation was spotty and localized, with locusts touching down like funnel clouds in one place only to leave a neighboring township untouched.[27] Perhaps a fluke of the wind spared Laura's family their first year.

Losses from the 1874 locust swarm were immense. Twenty-eight counties were affected, more than twice as many as in the previous year. Farmers lost a total of 4.5 million bushels of grain and potatoes, including 2.6 million bushels of wheat.[28] Many of them suffered crop failures two years in a row, leaving them wholly without food. An elderly farmer east of Walnut Grove pleaded with Minnesota's chief executive as if he were God himself: "Oh, most honorable governor, I hope you will help us poor old mortals."[29] A girl wrote to say that her family had seen all their crops destroyed by grasshoppers and were suffering from cold, "having but two quilts and two sheets in the house."[30]

But the governor was busy with other matters. As he saw it, the farmers' problems were primarily a matter for the private sector. That year, the state legislature appropriated only five thousand dollars in direct relief, with another twenty-five thousand to buy seed grain for affected farmers.[31] General Sibley, the state's renowned Indian killer, was brought out of retirement to coordinate charitable relief. St. Paul merchants proved generous, but need far exceeded supply.

Minnesota was far from the only state harmed by the locusts, with destitution also reported that winter in Kansas, Nebraska, Iowa, Colorado, and Dakota Territory. In Nebraska, soldiers were tasked with delivering surplus Army clothing, and found women and children surviving in a pitiable state, men having left to find work. One boy staggered into an army outpost with bare feet wrapped in cloth, saying that his mother and five siblings were at home, starving.[32]

Melanoplus spretus, the Rocky Mountain locust, was a stupendous force of nature. Individually, the grasshopper was scarcely noticeable: a dull olive green, just an inch and a half long. In the aggregate, however, it wielded immense power, as hinted at by the nomenclature. The word *locust* comes from the Latin phrase *locus ustus*, which means "burnt place."[33] *Spretus* means "despised." Reflecting the general feeling, one of the common names for the creature was "hateful grasshopper."

Ordinary grasshoppers never gather in immense clouds. Locusts, on the other hand, have the ability to become gregarious, form massive swarms, and fly astonishing distances. After settling, adults feed and lay eggs over a summer; their offspring hibernate during the winter and hatch out the following spring. It was these immature locusts that would march across the country, devouring foliage as they molted into adulthood.[34] Until recent times, every inhabited continent on earth had at least one locust species. Before modern pest control, Europe was plagued by them; Africa, Asia, and Australia still are. The U.S. had only a single species.[35] The Rocky Mountain locust could go for years without swarming, until the perfect conditions set it off.

Perfect conditions were created by drought. As Chicago and Peshtigo had discovered, drought was a major problem across the West and Midwest in the 1870s. Indeed, the entire planet was gripped that decade by a severe El Niño event, which disrupted climate around the globe.

It caused mass famines in China and India, triggering epidemics of disease; millions died. A study in *Nature* called it "the most destructive drought the world has ever known."[36]

In 1873, parts of Kansas had had their driest year on record. The following year, much of the Great Plains experienced a summer without rain.[37] A Kansas woman remembered eerie, oppressive heat, broken only by a cataclysmic hailstorm. "The grasses seemed to wither and the cattle bunched up near the creek and well and no air seemed to stir the leaves on the trees," she recalled. "All nature seemed still."[38] Then the clouds took on a "greenish hue" and hail fell, "devastating everything."[39]

Prolonged heat and aridity favored locusts by accelerating their growth and concentrating sugars in plants.[40] Then, as drought wasted wild vegetation, the invertebrates focused their attention on the densest, highest-quality source of nutrients: crops. In 1875, locust nymphs hatched from their eggs throughout the Great Plains. Billions upon billions matured in a flash.

Given the severity of damage the previous two years, some of the Ingallses' neighbors were simply sitting on their hands, refusing to plant until the danger had passed. Total acreage planted declined in 1875 and the following year by nearly 60 percent.[41] But there was a great deal of misinformation. An inveterate newspaper reader, Charles Ingalls may have taken the advice of farm papers such as the one in Red Wing, Minnesota, which confidently reported in late May 1875 that "there are no grasshoppers . . . in any part of Minnesota north, south, east or west . . . the conclusion is inevitable that their eggs have been entirely destroyed."[42]

That year, after the arid summer the year before and the mild winter that followed, Charles Ingalls had made a considerable financial outlay, building a spacious house, probably the finest the family had yet lived in. It stood twenty by twenty-four feet square and ten feet high, with a solid roof and floor, and three windows.[43] It was the pride of the family. Laura would later call it "the wonderful house."[44] Charles built two stables for oxen and horses, plowing and cultivating forty acres. He was feeling confident enough to take advantage of the Timber Culture Act, new legislation that allowed settlers to acquire 160 acres at no cost in exchange for planting a certain number of trees on that land.[45] In early June 1875, he filed on such a "tree claim" a few miles north of his Plum Creek property, expanding his holdings.[46] Meanwhile, he was raising a bumper crop of wheat.

Charles was gloating over the wheat as the family sat down to dinner one June day. Raising his arms, he showed them how tall it was, "with long beautiful heads and filling nicely."[47] Just as he pronounced it a "wonderful crop," they heard someone calling them outside. It was their neighbor Olena Nelson, and she was screaming, "The grasshoppers are coming! The grasshoppers are coming!"[48]

The Ingallses had no way of knowing it, but the locust swarm descending upon them was the largest in recorded human history. It would become known as "Albert's swarm": in Nebraska, a meteorologist named Albert Child measured its flight for ten days in June, telegraphing for further information from east and west, noting wind speed and carefully calculating the extent of the cloud of insects. He startled himself with his conclusions: the swarm appeared to be 110 miles wide, 1,800 miles long, and a quarter to a half mile in depth. The wind was blowing at ten miles an hour, but the locusts were moving even faster, at fifteen. They covered 198,000 square miles, Child concluded, an area equal to the states of Connecticut, Delaware, Maine, Maryland, Massachusetts, New Hampshire, New Jersey, New York, Pennsylvania, Rhode Island, and Vermont combined.[49] "This is utterly incredible," he wrote, "yet how can we put it aside?"[50] The cloud consisted of some 3.5 trillion insects.

The swarms swept from Saskatchewan to Texas, devouring everything in their path. The grasshoppers savored the sweat-stained handles of farm implements, chewed the wool off sheep, ate the leaves off trees. After flying, settling, consuming, and laying eggs, they began marching across the country, millions massing to form pontoons across creeks and rivers. Hoppers were said to "eat everything but the mortgage."[51]

Terrified, people reached for comparisons, likening the insectile clouds to other natural disasters: snow storms, hail storms, tornadoes, even wildfires. "The noise their myriad jaws make when engaged in their work of destruction can be realized by any one who has 'fought' a prairie fire . . . the low crackling and rasping," read a report from the

U.S. Entomological Commission, created by Congress to address the crisis.[52] Even modern scientists stretch for language to convey the swarm's ferocity, calling it a "metabolic wildfire." It consumed roughly a quarter of the country.[53]

Farmers ran frantically to cover tender garden plants with gunny sacks, quilts, shawls, and dresses, only to watch, stunned, as the insects chewed right through them. A Kansas woman found denuded pits hanging from her peach tree. She tried to save her garden by covering it with sacks but soon saw it was hopeless: "The hoppers regarded that as a huge joke, and enjoyed the awning . . . or if they could not get under, they ate their way through. The cabbage and lettuce disappeared the first afternoon."[54] She noticed the "neat way" they had of eating onions from the inside out, leaving the outer shell behind.

Grasshopper carcasses fouled wells, polluted creeks and rivers, and halted trains laboring up grades, the tracks greasy with crushed bodies. There were reports of children screaming in horror as insects alighted on them and of farmers' wives becoming hysterical, mad with fright.[55] A woman wearing a striped frock said insects settled on her and ate "every bit of green stripe in that dress."[56]

Technology was useless. Inventive farmers crafted "hopperdozers" out of sheet metal, contraptions drenched in coal tar and pulled across infested fields. These collected some pests, but their effectiveness was limited.[57] Grasshoppers could work faster than fields could be dragged.

When the Ingallses saw the locusts coming, Wilder recalled, her father put on his hat and "went out toward his beautiful wheat field."[58] He set fire to berms of straw and manure piled around the field, hoping to smoke out the locusts. But it was to no avail. By noon of the second day, he gave up and returned to the house exhausted, "his eyes all swollen and red from the smoke and lack of sleep."[59]

The dream of the perfect crop died that day. It was a nightmarish repetition of Caroline Ingalls's early privation, when she and her siblings had had nothing to eat but bread crumbs and water. Once again there was no money to buy food. The catastrophe could not have come at a worse time: Caroline was pregnant again, expecting a child in November.

On the third day, the insects began marching west, walking inexorably up the east side of the house, across the roof, and down the other side, coming in the window by the score until Caroline ran to close it. They were marching, Wilder wrote, "like an army," and the family looked around at each other "as though we were just waked from a bad dream."[60] Grasshopper bodies filled the creek and left fields pocked with holes, "like a honey comb." The holes were filled with eggs.

The locust plague constituted the worst and most widespread natural disaster the country had ever seen, causing an estimated $200 million in damage to western agriculture (the equivalent of $116 billion today) and threatening millions of farmers in remote locations—far from social services in the cities—with starvation.[61] In 1875, Minnesota once again lost more than two million bushels of wheat.[62] That January, the so-called Grasshopper Legislature appropriated a mere $20,000 in aid for the stricken, extending the deadline for property taxes but balking at doing more for those perceived as shirkers.[63] Miserly amounts of food aid were distributed in some counties, in amounts ranging from two to four dollars per family, while the minimum required by a family of four for a year was estimated at two hundred dollars.[64] Just like the locusts themselves, relief, such as it was, fell in haphazard fashion.[65]

As for the federal government, Congress appropriated $100,000 in aid for settlers on the western frontier. But the easterners were generally cavalier. Newspapers shrugged at the constant reports of "famine, suffering and misery" in the West. "It is humiliating to have them so constantly before us, passing round the hat," wrote one editorialist.[66]

Even as Minnesota distributed aid, it expressed contempt for the destitute, enacting punitive regulations that required farmers to prove they were completely bereft before applying for relief. In a cruel and counterproductive move, the state demanded that applicants sell any livestock they owned before receiving aid. Meanwhile, trying to empty the ocean a drop at a time, counties nailed flyers to town walls advertising a bounty for grasshoppers: five cents a quart, "caught and delivered dead."[67] An informational pamphlet distributed by a railroad urged farmers to get busy collecting the pests, since solving the problem was their responsibility. Newspapers advised their hungry readers to eat the bugs: "make it a 'hopper' feast."[68]

In desperation, Charles Ingalls sold his horses, leaving the money with his wife. With nothing left for train fare, he walked two hundred miles east to work the harvest, possibly near Peter Ingalls's farm in southeastern Minnesota, where the grasshoppers had not penetrated.[69] While he was gone, Eleck Nelson pitched in, cutting whatever hay had managed to grow on the family's land since the locusts' departure and plowing a fire break around the house. The prairie fires arrived that fall, heralded by a spate of burning tumbleweeds. Nelson came galloping on his horse when he saw them, but the fire break held.

Meanwhile, Charles sent money home to his family. When he returned, he moved them into town for the winter, where they rented a house behind the church. The children went to the Walnut Grove school, which, Wilder recalled, "we didn't think much of."[70] On November 1, 1875, they came home to find a newborn resting with their mother in bed. He was Charles Frederick Ingalls, the long-awaited boy, named for his father and his mother's beloved stepfather. He would be called Freddy.

On November 30, Charles Ingalls signed a sworn statement before county officials stating that he was "wholy without means," the humiliating requirement of the relief act passed earlier that year.[71] It made him eligible to receive two half-barrels of flour, worth five dollars and twenty-five cents. He may never have told his children where the flour came from.

The one thousand dollars he had received for the little house in the Big Woods was long gone. Wilder later recalled that her parents had hoped Plum Creek would restore their fortunes. "Prosperity was only just around the corner, just till that crop of wheat was raised," she wrote wistfully. "Plum Creek was safety and then look what happened."[72]

Back in Wisconsin, their relatives were concerned. Caroline's mother, Charlotte Holbrook, wrote to her daughter Martha, asking if she had any news of them. "They have had a hard time of it since they left Pepin," Charlotte said, "almost everyone we meet are crying hard times if they lived where the Grasshoppers are."[73]

Charles Ingalls and his family must have longed for their former

home. The locust swarm had never crossed the Mississippi River. It left
Wisconsin untouched.

WILDER'S memoir, written more than fifty years after the events it
described, is remarkable for the evenness of its tone, treating most
occurrences or anecdotes without retrospective judgment. Moments of
relief, joy, or sadness tend to be rendered without much emotional
freight. A notable exception is her recollection of people who wronged
her, and occasions on which she saw or experienced unfairness. Her
outrage at disgraceful or unkind behavior—her own and others'—
gives the memoir its vividness.

One such scene of injustice involved her mother, who had made
Laura a treasured rag doll back in Wisconsin. "Roxy was old but I had
kept her so carefully that she was still nice and I thought her beautiful," Wilder wrote, "with her curled black yarn hair, her red mouth and
her black bead eyes."[74] One day, as the girls were playing with their
neighbors, the Nelsons' toddler demanded Roxy for herself. Caroline
Ingalls scolded her daughter for not giving it up, telling her she was too
old for dolls. Laura relinquished her beloved companion, only to later
find the doll near the Nelsons' house, discarded in a mud puddle.

In her later novel about Plum Creek, the incident would be presented
as a wrenching moment, a keenly felt mother-daughter betrayal.[75] The
novel supplies a happy ending—the doll retrieved and repaired, restored
to its rightful owner, the mother apologetic—but the earlier memoir
suggests that there was no resolution along those lines. Such moments
of feeling ill-treated by those close to her would be inextricably tied to
Laura's hot temper, a trait she would lament in later life.

Wilder's fiercest disdain in all of her writing, though, was reserved
for the children of storekeepers in Walnut Grove, Nellie Owens and her
brother Willie. They flaunted their wealth before the impoverished
Ingalls girls: helping themselves to candy from the store and eating it
in front of them without offering them any, showing off a cornucopia
of "wonderful toys, tops and jumping jacks and beautiful picture books"
while refusing to let Mary and Laura play with them.[76] The treasures
included a doll so exquisite that it was kept wrapped in "soft paper,"

only to be taken out and held before the Ingalls girls, who were not permitted to touch it.

"We would not have been allowed to be so rude and selfish," Wilder said stoutly, and relished writing a long, lavishly detailed description of her revenge.[77] Without toys and picture books, Laura preferred to play and fish in Plum Creek, near the footbridge. A certain shady pool hosted "bloodsuckers"—rubbery, mud-colored leeches ready to fasten themselves on girls' legs—and a nearby stone concealed beneath it a "big old crab," a crawdad that would try to seize toes if teased. When the Owens children came to play, Laura deliberately terrorized Nellie with leeches and crawdads. Decades later, she still wasn't sorry.

Punctilious Mary was troubled by the game, arguing that "we ought not to frighten our company so."[78] But in Wilder's eyes, Nellie had it coming:

> I said, when we went to town to see them they wouldn't let us handle their toys, the wonderful doll that would open and shut it[s] eyes we were not allowed to hold and we could only look at their other things while they showed them to us; so I just would play my way when they came to see us.[79]

Eventually their mother forbade it, but Laura could see that her father was amused.

The contretemps with Nellie—perhaps the first time that Mary and Laura were made aware of their status as poor children of a failed farmer—ushered in a period of ever more severe economic insecurity and dependence on others. During the "spring freshet" of 1876, Caroline fell gravely ill out at Plum Creek. Charles, afraid to leave her, sent Laura to find Eleck Nelson and ask him to telegraph for a doctor, forty miles away. He forgot that the creek was in flood and uncrossable on foot. Passing by, Nelson saw Laura about to attempt the crossing and shouted to her to stay where she was, "You'll drown! You'll drown!" The telegram was sent, the doctor came, and the patient recovered. But the heavy medical bills added to the family's debt burden.

Wilder recalled that "Pa got some seed off the train," part of the relief supplies voted on by the state legislature.[80] Wary of grasshoppers, he sowed only a small crop that summer at his Plum Creek land. Indeed, the locusts' eggs soon hatched and the insects matured once more, with predictable results. "We smashed them when we walked," Wilder wrote. "They got up under our skirts when we walked to school and Sunday-school; they dropped down our necks and spit 'tobacco juice' on us making brown, ugly spots on our clothes."[81] Again, the locusts ate the crop.

And again, there was little help forthcoming. Minnesota had a new Republican governor, John Sargent Pillsbury, cofounder of the flour-milling enterprise that would eventually become one of the largest purveyors of foodstuffs in the world. Not above taking government assistance himself—as an official, he had his rent paid by the state—Pillsbury warned farmers against "weakening the habit of self-reliance."[82] To comfort the starving, he prescribed a day of prayer. Throughout his term, he would trivialize "poverty and deprivation" as "incidents of frontier life at its best."[83]

The *St. Paul Pioneer Press* praised Pillsbury's censure of grasshopper paupers, reasoning that any relief would have a "very demoralizing effect" on those known for their "suicidal indolence." The "better class of people," it argued, would not demean themselves by accepting aid. "If anybody chooses to lie down and be eaten up by grasshoppers," it remarked, "we don't care much if he is devoured body, boots, and breeches."[84]

Nearly devoured himself, Charles Ingalls had had enough, announcing emphatically that he "wouldn't stay in such a 'blasted country!' "[85] Characteristically, his daughter made it sound as if he had a choice. But in fact, he had to sell and move on. In July 1876 he completed his preemption claim, filing the paperwork and paying $431 for the land.[86] Three days later, he sold it for $400, and the family prepared to move some 200 miles east to Burr Oak, Iowa, where they would "partner" with a couple from Walnut Grove in running a hotel.

Laura was nine. For the rest of her childhood, she would work on and off in service, as a dishwasher, cook, maid, babysitter, waitress, seamstress, companion, and general dogsbody, often while going to school or studying on her own. She made light of it in her memoir, but she was becoming ever more essential to her family's very survival.

Dark and Dirty

On the way to Burr Oak, the Ingallses stopped to spend the rest of the summer with Peter Ingalls and his family in the township of South Troy, where Charles would work the harvest again until the fall. By this time Peter and Eliza had five children, including the toddler, Edith, whom they all called "Dolly Varden" after the flouncy costume popular in songs, dances, and a character in the Dickens novel *Barnaby Rudge*.

Laura loved the area, walking with her cousins down to the Zumbro River every afternoon to fetch the cows home to be milked, watching the river "running along in the sunshine and shade with trees and flowers on the banks." That summer, the children stuffed themselves with ripe plums. By fall, grazing the cows in meadows on cut hay, they were building small camp fires where they toasted bread and roasted wild crab apples. "We played even when we worked," she wrote.[87]

The idyll did not last. In August, baby Freddy suddenly took ill. Laura assumed he would get better after the doctor came, as her mother had the previous spring. But he did not. "One awful day he straightened out his little body and was dead," his sister wrote.[88] Charles Frederick Ingalls died on August 27, 1876, at nine months. No record confirms where he was buried, but another infant from the area, five-month-old Murtie Phelps, died on the same day or the day after and was buried in the Pleasant Prairie Cemetery. Residents of the South Troy area believe Freddy may be resting there as well.[89]

"We felt so badly to go on and leave Freddy," Wilder wrote, but the hotel job awaited them in Burr Oak. In the northeast corner of Iowa, a few miles south of the Minnesota border, Burr Oak was not a "new, clean little town like Walnut Grove," but instead "dark and dirty," a disturbing contrast to places they had lived before.[90] There the children were exposed to public drunkenness, wife-beating, corporal punishment, measles, and the strange behavior of a child termed an "idiot," in the harsh terminology of the day. Wilder left Burr Oak out of her books entirely.

The hotel job turned out to be a disappointment. Charles and Caroline Ingalls were not true partners in the venture but subordinate to a British couple, William and Mary Steadman, who bought the place from a man named William Masters. The Steadmans, who had lived in Walnut Grove and attended the Congregational Church with the Ingallses, had traded places with the Masterses, who moved to Walnut Grove and built a new hotel there. William Masters wanted to separate his wastrel son, Will, from the saloon next door to the Burr Oak hotel. The extended Masters clan would come to play an influential role in Laura's life, but during the fall of 1876, all Mary and Laura knew was that young Will Masters, firing at his wife in a drunken rage, had left his mark: several bullet holes in the door frame between the hotel dining room and kitchen. The girls were often frightened by rough characters coming and going from the saloon.

At home Mary and Laura helped in the kitchen, washing dishes and waiting on diners. They disliked the Steadmans' son, Johnny, who routinely pinched them and broke their playthings. At school, they watched in astonishment as the teacher, William Reed—a slim, sixteen-year-old farm boy who was taunted and threatened by pupils older and larger than himself—made an example of one miscreant by thrashing him with a homemade paddle. The boy never returned.

Living nearby, on a farm in Burr Oak township, was the Garland family. Their teenage son Hamlin, having had a taste of the high life at a private seminary, was beginning to realize how brutally monotonous farming could be. "All that we possessed seemed very cheap and deplorably commonplace," he wrote later in a classic memoir of Great Plains life. He wearily recalled "our ugly little farmhouse, with its rag carpets, its battered furniture, its barren attic, and its hard, rude beds."[91] The Ingallses no longer had even that.

Mrs. Steadman promised Mary and Laura "something nice for Christmas" if they minded her baby, but the holiday came and went with the promise unfulfilled. "Christmas was disappointing," Wilder wrote, in what would become a common refrain. Their father was busy, their mother seemed perpetually tired, and after the holiday the children came down with measles. Johnny Steadman would torment the bedridden girls by snatching their pillows. "I was glad when he had the measels himself and was awfully sick," Wilder wrote.[92] Whether the children knew it or not, Caroline Ingalls, at thirty-seven, was not simply "tired"—she was pregnant, expecting another child the following May.[93]

As with the babysitting, whatever promises the Steadmans had made to their father went unfulfilled. Wilder later conjectured that the couple cheated Charles Ingalls out of his "share" of the business.[94] Soon after, the family moved out of the hotel, into rooms over a grocery on the other side of the saloon, where the children once again had to run a gauntlet of drinkers. Charles found work running a feed mill.

Laura liked their rooms, which were "pleasant and sunny and clean," with a view across the street over the terraced lawn of one of Burr Oak's wealthier citizens. That winter, she and Mary, both studying out of the *Independent Fifth Reader*, were learning elocution, the art of reading with drama and feeling, practicing it on the popular poem "Tubal Cain" and on Longfellow's "The Village Blacksmith" and "Paul Revere's Ride." She learned later from her father that townsfolk gathered in the store below to listen to the girls' recitation.

But alarming incidents soon gave them cause to move. First, a fire broke out in the saloon: "Pa said if the darned saloon could have burned up without burning the town, he wouldn't have carried a drop of water."[95] Then, the whole family woke to screams one night: the store owner living on the first floor was discovered dragging his wife around by her hair while brandishing a kerosene lamp upside down, setting fire to his hand. Not long after, a tall, thin tippler dubbed "Hairpin," longtime beau of the hotel maid, awoke from a several days' drunk, swigged more alcohol, and then lit a cigar, inhaling the flames. He fell down dead. "Pa said we should not live near the saloon any longer," Wilder noted.[96]

By the spring of 1877, the family had taken up residence in a red-brick house on the outskirts of town. Laura resumed one of her favorite activities: leading the family cow to pasture, spending long afternoons wandering among meadow wildflowers. She waded in the creek and practiced multiplication tables by singing ditties. On May 23, the baby was born, and the family named her Grace Pearl Ingalls. She had Mary's golden hair and her father's bright blue eyes.

Laura enjoyed that summer, but at ten she was old enough to understand that her parents were "troubled." "Pa did not like an old settled place like Burr Oak," she wrote, hearing him call it "a dead town . . . without even a railroad."[97] Listening to her parents discuss financial matters, she also learned that they were worried about money and debts: they didn't have enough to pay their rent, the grocery bills, and the doctor who had attended at Grace's birth. Her father played "lonesome, longing" tunes on his violin: "There Is a Happy Land Far, Far Away" and "My Old Kentucky Home."

With these worries at the forefront of Laura's mind, another disturbing incident occurred. Mrs. Starr, wife of the family doctor to whom the Ingallses owed money, came to visit with a personal request: she wanted to adopt Laura. Her own daughters were grown, she explained, and she needed "a little girl to help her around the house and keep her from being lonesome."[98] Caroline Ingalls gently deflected the request, saying she "couldn't possibly spare" her daughter.

It was an era when the fear of "peonage"—debt slavery or servitude—still lingered in people's minds. The practice had been outlawed in 1867, the year Laura was born, but it survived in the South and many pockets of the country. Mrs. Starr's offer came at a time when the Ingallses must have felt particularly vulnerable, exposed to legal action for their debts. To Laura, the mere suggestion that she might be sold into servitude must have been profoundly unsettling. A later revision of the memoir made this plain: "Afterward, whenever I thought of her, the queer feeling came back. . . . Mrs. Starr might have taken me away from [my family]. It seemed strange and I always tried to forget about it as quickly as I could."[99]

Charles Ingalls soon arrived at a happier solution to his debt crisis. He had tried to negotiate with the landlord, a Mr. Bisby, asking him to allow the family to leave town and send payment later. Bisby would have none of it, threatening to seize their horses and sell them. Charles was furious, arguing that "he always had paid all he owed . . . but he'd 'be darned if he'd ever pay that rich old skinflint Bisbee a cent.'"[100] In the fall, he made good on that vow, waking the children in the dead of night and loading them into the covered wagon with all the family's goods. As Little Crow had said, "When men are hungry, they help themselves."

By dawn the next day, they were in a different county. Newly unburdened, Charles regaled them at their campfires with the rowdy, patriotic songs he loved: "Marching Through Georgia," "Yankee

Doodle," and "Buffalo Gals." Those songs, Wilder wrote, were "scattered on the air all the way from Burr Oak Iowa to Walnut Grove Minnesota."[101]

THE Ingallses may have left the seamy streets of Burr Oak, but when they returned to Walnut Grove they found the same kinds of problems waiting for them. The long depression of 1873 ground on, and times remained tough. Cities were plagued with widespread homelessness, joblessness, and hunger.

This drove emigrants west at a time when the frontier was least able to support them. Nearly two million flooded onto the Great Plains throughout the 1870s, at a time of pronounced food shortages there. While the locust plague began to taper off in 1877, grasshoppers were still ruining harvests, costing nearly five million bushels of wheat in Minnesota that year alone. When the governor announced his "day of fasting, humiliation, and prayer to deliver the people from the locusts and to comfort those afflicted," thousands were already fasting, whether they liked it or not.

Coming back to Walnut Grove, the Ingallses made do with a combination of charity and some odd jobs Charles was able to pick up. The two further years they would spend there were even more sordid and chaotic than their time in Iowa. With no more claim on the bucolic Plum Creek, the Ingalls family was essentially homeless. They stayed for a while with the Ensign family, friends from the Congregational Church. Charles then built a small house in a pasture belonging to William Masters, near the Masterses' new hotel, working for Masters over the winter as a carpenter. The following spring, he rented space in town and ran a temporary butcher shop.

In a revealing omission—in contrast to her emphasis on the coziness of their Wisconsin and Kansas cabins—Wilder did not provide any description of their quarters in the Masterses' pasture. Nor did she realize that her father never owned the property. She believed he had "paid for a lot," but no records support that view. Perhaps he was renting the pasture, or bartering with Masters for the use of the land.

At school, Mary and Laura were again thrown together with the hated Nellie Owens, as well as with new rivals. Their school was taught by William Masters's brother, Samuel Masters, whom the children called "Uncle Sam." He was a tall, thin, bald man with bad breath and a worrying habit of fondling girls' hands. Laura protected herself by concealing a pin in her fingers and stabbing him with it. After that, she said, he left her alone.

She was outraged by one of Samuel's daughters, Genevieve, who dressed in the latest styles, lisped, and cried pathetically when crossed. Born in New York, she sneered at the other girls for being "westerners." Laura secured a minor triumph over Nellie and Genevieve by dividing and conquering, throwing her allegiance from one to the other until they were both competing for her favor. "To my surprise I found myself the leader of them all."[102]

She chose to lead them in rowdy competitions, racing the boys (and beating them) and organizing rambunctious games of Anti-Over, Pull-away, and Prisoners Base, much to the scandal of her sister Mary. Eventually, the following winter, the conflict between the sisters turned rough, with Mary once pulling Laura into the house by her hair, away from her "gorgeous" snowball fights.[103] Laura yanked Mary back to the open door, where she was pelted with snow. After that, her mother forbade Laura to play with the boys.

As the eldest girls approached adolescence, the Ingallses found themselves at the periphery of a dizzying series of small-town scandals involving alcoholism, sexual jealousy, lying, and hypocrisy. The melodrama was heightened by an occasional religious tent revival at which neighbors confessed their sins.

Soon after they returned to Walnut Grove, a saloon opened in the former "temperance town," run by none other than their former neighbor, Eleck Nelson.[104] Nearby, a divorced woman set up shop as a milliner, selling hats trimmed with ribbons, lace, and flowers. She had such a gloomy air that Laura decided divorce must be an awful thing indeed.

During school vacations, Laura worked at the Masters hotel for fifty cents a week, washing dishes, waiting on tables, and watching "Little Nan," the baby of Will and Nancy Masters, the young couple behind the bullet holes in the Burr Oak hotel. Laura liked the work, she said, because "there were interesting things happening all the time."[105]

The interesting things included the courtship ploys of Will's sister, Mattie, who languished artfully in her bedroom, waited on by the rest of the household, until setting her cap for a boarder, Dr. Robert Hoyt. Laura watched avidly as Mattie was nearly frustrated in her pursuit of Hoyt by Fanny Starr, a daughter of the couple who had wanted to adopt Laura. Hoyt had studied with Dr. Starr, Fanny's father, in Burr Oak, and had possibly become engaged to Fanny during that time; now she was coming to visit Hoyt in Walnut Grove, much to Mattie's displeasure.[106]

The simpering Mattie eventually outmaneuvered Fanny, marrying the doctor. Wilder remembered hearing her mother hint that Mattie should have let Hoyt go rather than win him "that way."[107] But the intrigues weren't over. At the hotel, Laura heard Dr. Hoyt encouraging Will Masters to get drunk, and her father explained that Hoyt wanted the Masterses' heir to drink himself to death so that Hoyt and Mattie could inherit William Masters's property. But five months after her marriage, it was Mattie herself who took sick and died.

However much she gleaned from her mother's phrasing, Laura was becoming more sexually knowing and judgmental in any case. As a girl of eleven, she was more worldly than she would later let on, devouring the romantic serials published by the *New York Ledger*, a weekly "story paper" chock-full of "beautiful ladies and brave, handsome men; of dwarfs and villains of jewels and secret caverns."[108] She was privy to much gossip because she slept at the hotel, where she was paid to keep watch not only over Little Nan but over Nan's mother as well, who was prone to fainting. One night, Laura awoke to find Will Masters looming over her, smelling of whiskey and apparently intent on molesting her.[109] She threatened to scream, and he backed off.

There were other scandals, too. In 1879, Charles Ingalls was elected Walnut Grove's first justice of the peace, a position requiring literacy and negotiating skills but no legal education. He conducted business in the family's front room, and Laura raptly drank in the salacious scenes that played out there. She overheard, for instance, the incredible story of two sisters, Mrs. Welch, a local, and Mrs. Ray. In long-planned revenge on her sister for marrying the man she wanted, Mrs. Welch secretly became the owner of the mortgage on the Rays' property in New York.

Then, encouraging her sister to visit, Mrs. Welch inveigled the Rays to stay for months, imperiling their claim, which depended on their being in residence on the land. Triumphantly foreclosing on the mortgage and declaring her scheme, Mrs. Welch tore the deed out of her sister's hand in the Ingallses' front room, continuing to curse Mrs. Ray until she was pulled out the door, screaming and clawing.[110]

While all this was going on, it was becoming depressingly clear that the Ingallses' finances were again approaching a crisis. In the fall of 1878, Laura missed weeks of school while running errands for friends of the Masterses, undoubtedly for pay, and spending weeks with a couple in the countryside, cooking and caring for a sick woman. It was at this point that Laura recalled praying during a desperate bout of "home-sickness and worry . . . worse than usual." She wrote, "I knew things were not going well at home, because Pa could not get much work and we needed more money to live on."[111]

That winter, the Ingalls children stopped going to school because they lacked warm clothes. It was a sensible if dire precaution. Wilder remembered a horrific incident that took place at an isolated farm belonging to the Robbins family, out in the countryside. A blizzard blew up while the parents were in town. On their return, the Robbinses found the house cold and empty, the stovepipe fallen in. Charles Ingalls joined the search for the five children who had been home alone. Three were found dead in a snowdrift. The eldest girl, twelve years old, survived, along with the infant she was found clutching under her coat. The twelve-year-old eventually had to have a leg amputated for frostbite. Wilder heard a graphic description of the scene from her father: "Pa said it was terrible with the dead children lying there and this girl swearing horribly as her legs and arms hurt thawing out."[112]

Laura, too, was twelve in 1879, a child overwhelmed by responsibilities and anxieties that were almost too much to bear. Her memoir vividly exposes small-town life as a disordered spectacle of adults behaving badly, but it also conveys a sense of her family's indigence and lack of direction. While she would never stand back and analyze the period's effect on her, traits that would emerge in Laura's adolescence, forming her character, had their roots here: impulsivity, distrust of authority, an intense fear of destitution, and an equally powerful determination to resist it.

Then, that April, Mary got a headache that would not go away.

Struck by Lightening

Mary had been periodically ill all winter and seems to have stayed at home while Laura pursued her hectic circuit of odd jobs. The Ingallses' eldest had always been a homebody, fond of quiet, domestic pursuits, and markedly more religious than her sister. At a time when Laura was expressing impatience with public displays of piety, Mary was baptized and joined Walnut Grove's Union Congregational Church in 1878.[113]

The following spring, now fourteen, Mary was suddenly stricken with sharp pains in her head. She developed a high fever, and Caroline cut off her long hair to make her more comfortable.

The illness was so dire that the local newspapers tracked its progression. On April 10, 1879, the *Redwood Falls Gazette* reported that "Miss Mary Ingalls has been confined to her bed about ten days with severe head ache. It is feared that hemorrhage of the brain has set in . . . one side of her face became partially paralyzed. She is now slowly convalescing."[114]

A month later, she was still severely ill, "confined to her bed, and at times her sufferings are great."[115] By June 26, Mary's overall health had improved, but her vision was affected. "Her sight is so much impaired that she cannot distinguish one object from another," the *Gazette* reported. "She can discern day from night but even this slight vision is also failing."[116] Two physicians attended Mary and concurred that the illness—for which they had a "long name," Wilder recalled—had been brought on by Mary's earlier bout of the measles, from which she had not fully recovered.[117] Damaged by the stroke, the nerves in her eyes were failing, and nothing could be done.

Mary would later pen poems about family memories and religious devotion, but not a single word survives in her hand specifically regarding her illness.[118] That fell to her sister, and passages describing it are among the most affecting in Wilder's memoir:

> We feared for several days that she would not get well and one morning when I looked at her I saw one side of her face drawn out of shape. Ma said Mary had had a stroke and as I looked at her I remembered her oak tree away back in Wisconsin that had been struck by lightening all down one side.[119]

Laura's melancholy vigil continued throughout her sister's recovery, a catalyst in developing her unsentimental voice. She added this indelible depiction of Mary, now able to sit up, gradually losing her visual grasp on the family: "The last thing Mary ever saw was the bright blue of Grace's eyes as Grace stood holding by her chair, looking up at her."[120]

The family's lives would never be the same. Charles and Caroline Ingalls had invested great hopes in Mary's ability to help out the family. Some schools for the blind had opened in the east early in the 1800s, but nineteenth-century conceptions of disability meant that deaf or blind children were often kept at home, objects of pity and dismay. Mary would never be so neglected—one of Grace's earliest memories was hearing their mother reading the newspaper aloud to her—but the prospects for her future must have seemed unknowable.[121]

For the moment, the Ingallses were simply stunned. Whether on her own initiative or at her parents' urging, Laura would take on the responsibility for being her sister's eyes.[122] She was undoubtedly much more. In her newly vulnerable state, Mary would have to be accompanied everywhere, both in the house and outside, to go for a walk, to go to church, to go to the privy. At least at first, she would need assistance in eating, bathing, and dressing.

In July, the *Gazette* reported that the family intended to take Mary to a specialist in St. Paul, but that would have to wait. Charles Ingalls was out of town, having taken a job handling the payroll for a gang of railroad workers to the west, near Lake Benton.

He arrived at the job through family connections. His younger sister Docia had had a checkered history, divorcing her first husband after he was convicted of murdering a trespasser.[123] She had then married Hiram

Forbes, a contractor working for the Chicago & North Western Railway, which was laying a rail line west through Dakota Territory to Pierre. Managing 180 teams of horses and 480 men, Forbes hired his brother-in-law in June as bookkeeper and manager of the company store, selling goods to the graders. Likely making a higher wage than he ever had before—perhaps fifty dollars a month—Charles Ingalls immediately transferred the Walnut Grove house to William Masters, in payment for debts, and drove away with his sister. He made arrangements to send for the family later, after collecting his first paycheck.

Before leaving, Laura enjoyed a rare afternoon of leisure with school friends: "We had the day to ourselves with'. . . books and pictures and the sunshine and flowers." After an "extra good dinner," her friends walked her part of the way home. "I never saw them again," Wilder wrote.[124] Relationships on the prairie could end as abruptly as that.

On the morning of September 6, 1879, Caroline Ingalls and her daughters boarded the train for the seven-mile trip west to Tracy, Minnesota, then the last stop on the Chicago & North Western. "We were on our way again," Wilder wrote years later, "and going in the direction which always brought the happiest changes."[125] Throughout the brief rail journey—the first the girls had ever taken—she described everything she saw to Mary.

They spent a memorable day waiting for Charles in a "quiet and gloomy" hotel, where the innkeeper told them a remarkable tale. When he was on a Sunday drive on the prairie with his wife, his young twin sons, and other family members, the whole group was struck by lightning. The twins later staggered into town, frightened and alone, saying that their parents were "asleep" in the road. In fact, everyone in the party was dead except for their father, who survived with severe burns. He showed the visitors his gold watch, its works fused into a molten mass. A bookend to the terrible suddenness of Mary's ordeal, the story foreshadowed the dramatic events awaiting the Ingallses on the western prairie.

That afternoon Charles arrived to collect them in a lumber wagon, to take them to the railroad camp farther west in Minnesota. There they spent a few memorable weeks with Hiram and Docia Forbes, their rambunctious son Eugene, and their daughter Lena. In days of ecstatic freedom, Lena and Laura went riding bareback on the prairie; Wilder wrote that it was "hard to tell which enjoyed it most the ponies or Lena and I."[126] Delivering laundry to a washerwoman, they learned that her thirteen-year-old daughter had just gotten married. Lena and Laura decided they were too young for that.

Then the Ingallses packed up again and followed the railroad workers west, into Dakota Territory.

Chapter 4

God Hates a Coward

You Need a Farm

The Great Dakota Boom was on. California and Oregon each had had their land rush; so had Kansas, Nebraska, and Colorado. All eyes then turned to the last untrammeled tranche of undeveloped land in the West. Boosters called it the "sole remaining section of paradise in the western world."[1] In a country built on credulity—religious, economic, and agricultural—the Dakota Boom would be one of the biggest boondoggles of all.

Dakota Territory had remained undeveloped for good reason. First, Indian hostilities had given the region a fearsome reputation. After the 1862 Dakota uprising, successive Indian wars stretched into the 1870s, delaying the arrival of the railroad. In the western half of what is now South Dakota, Cheyenne and Lakota Sioux fought desperately to hold on to their lands, especially the striking ponderosa-studded mountains known as the Black Hills. The granite mountains and grassy meadows rich in wildlife were officially theirs, part of the "Great Sioux Reservation" granted to them by the U.S. government in 1868. But white prospectors impoverished by the economic crisis of 1873 began sneaking illegally into the Black Hills the following year, evading American troops whose forts ringed the reservation.

One of these gold diggers was Caroline Ingalls's little brother, Tom Quiner. In violation of the Sioux treaty, he penetrated the region in 1874 with a group of miners, the "Gordon Party," who then spent several winter months cowering behind a hastily built stockade in the Black Hills, fearing attack by "dreaded savages."[2] The group was eventually located and evicted by the U.S. Cavalry. But the gold rush they incited sparked the Black Hills War of 1876, pitting General George Crook and Lieutenant Colonel George Armstrong Custer against the superior forces of Crazy Horse, Sitting Bull, Little Wolf, and other Indian leaders in a series of epic battles. In their own small way, Tom Quiner and the rest of the Gordon Party shared responsibility for the Battle of the Little Big Horn, which left 270 American soldiers, including the vainglorious Custer, dead.

In addition to the Indian hostilities, grasshoppers were also a known peril in Dakota Territory, with locust swarms touching down in the 1850s, 1860s, and 1870s.[3] Early settlers reported hoppers making "a clean sweep of every growing thing," blown by the wind into piles four feet deep on the shores of local lakes.[4] Pursuing Indians, Brigadier General Alfred Sully thought the insects a worse foe. "The only thing spoken about here is the grasshopper," he wrote. "They are awful. They actually have eaten holes in my wagon covers and in the tarpaulins that cover my stores."[5] His horses died from want of grass, and he told of one hapless soldier falling asleep on the prairie at midday only to wake covered in a carpet of locusts, bleeding from tiny bites on his throat and wrist.

But the greatest deterrent to farming in the northern Great Plains was obvious: the place was parched. Well-watered areas south and farther west were snapped up, but farmers shied away from the Dakota plains. They knew they were too dry.

The Great Plains occupy the interior of the continent. Indeed, most of the world's great grasslands—in Siberia, East Africa, Brazil—lie far from the oceans, downwind of mountain ranges.[6] The air masses that reach the Great Plains—from the Arctic, the Pacific, and the Gulf of Mexico—have been stripped of moisture by the time they get there, leaving their payload of rain and snow miles behind, in the Coastal Range and the Rockies. Swept by powerful, desiccating winds, the plains routinely experience bizarrely variable weather. They receive precipitation at wildly shifting times and in varying ways. Out on the plains, there is no normal.[7]

Early on, aridity was recognized as a problem throughout the entire West, but particularly in the Great Plains. Thomas Jefferson had noted "immense and trackless deserts" in the West as early as 1803.[8] Two years later, Meriwether Lewis called the area that would become North Dakota "truly a desert barren country," and shortly thereafter Zebulon Pike compared the "destitute" western plains to "the sandy deserts of Africa."[9] In 1823, Stephen Long, the first government surveyor to journey by steamboat up the Missouri River, met with an Omaha Indian delegation, whose leader told him frankly: "I know that this land will not suit your farmers."[10] Long had the good sense to agree, labeling the central plains "the Great Desert." The most astonishing fact of the Dakota Boom is that it happened at all. Everyone knew better.

It took a scientist to make the definitive case. In 1877, Major John Wesley Powell, a war hero who had lost his right arm at the battle of Shiloh, gave a speech on "The Public Domain" to the National Academy of Sciences, arguing that the Great Plains should not be parceled out to homesteaders.[11] Powell, who had conducted major expeditions into the Rocky Mountains and the Grand Canyon and would soon become chief of the U.S. Geological Survey, illustrated his talk with maps, pointing out the country's "humid," "sub-humid," and "arid" lands. It was as if someone had taken a piece of chalk and drawn a line down the middle of the country, at the 100th meridian. Across the eastern half lay a dark shadow, the "humid area." A similarly dark band tinged the coast of the Pacific northwest.[12] But virtually everything in between was arid, bleached white on the map. The Great Plains, running from the eastern Dakotas down through Nebraska and Kansas to Texas, formed a transitional "sub-humid" area, but even there the average rainfall was far less than in the "humid" zone.

With his charts and maps, Powell was delivering a bombshell, the news that less than 3 percent of the arid west was suitable for farming.[13] Nothing could have been more consequential: he was warning that thousands of small farmers were due to be bankrupted. For the country, he predicted, this represented a major economic peril. As his biographer put it, it was "a danger looming for democracy."[14] Powell was lobbying for essential changes in the Homestead Act: most of the West, he argued, including the subhumid and arid regions, was fit only for grazing, not farming. The act should be modified to address the problem, he said, allowing farmers to claim far larger parcels than 160 acres. The *New York Tribune* took his point: "If it is true that there is scarcely any good land left fit for a poor man's farm, the sooner the fact is announced the better."[15]

In his *Report on the Lands of the Arid Region of the United States*, released in 1878—the year before the Ingalls family moved to Dakota Territory—Powell made the case again. As a solution, he suggested organizing agriculture and irrigation around watersheds, proposing a system based on the Mormon model he'd seen at his field camp near Kanab, Utah. Faced with extremely arid conditions there, the Mormons had studied the phenomenon of Hispanic communities around Santa Fe who maintained common irrigation ditches, or *acequias*. The land was so dry that individual water rights had been abandoned for a cooperative model, with each farmer apportioned a share.[16]

Powell argued that the West, likewise, could best be farmed cooperatively. He proposed the creation of "pasturage farms" of 2,560 acres (four square miles) apiece, to be tended by settlements organized around community-based irrigation and grazing schemes. Only a small fraction of Western lands, Powell said, were appropriate for immediate agricultural use; the rest would require drainage or irrigation "for their redemption."[17] Farmers alone, he added, lacked sufficient capital or labor to devise such complex, expensive solutions, as well as the engineering expertise to construct them.

Unfortunately for Powell, a model based on a competitive rather than cooperative design was already in place. It had a catchy name—the "bonanza farm"—and a reputation for producing extraordinary harvests in Dakota Territory. Bolstered by boosterish marketing, bonanza farms represented an early marriage between big business and agriculture. Outside of the South (where cotton was king and labor was supplied by slaves or sharecroppers), bonanza farms were among the first major agricultural projects in America promoting intensive cultivation of a single crop, now known as monoculture.

Bonanza farms originated in the Red River Valley, a floodplain formed at the bottom of an ancient glacial lake stretching south from Alberta, Canada, into northeastern Dakota Territory and Minnesota. In 1873, a farmer west of Fargo had raised 1,600 bushels of wheat on a mere forty acres. It was such a prodigious feat that investors sat up and took note. The Northern Pacific Railway had just gone bankrupt, helping to trigger the Panic of 1873; the railroad's bonds, however, could be exchanged for land, and several bondholders acquired enormous tracts in the Red River Valley. They would be the first to bring large-scale mechanized farming to the Midwest.

Bonanza farms benefited from the deep pockets of a few owners able to invest in advanced technology: plows, seeders, harvesters, and threshers. They hired experienced overseers to make critical decisions about where, when, and what to plant. Their results were spectacular. Of 2.8 million bushels of wheat grown in Dakota Territory in 1879, more than half came out of the Red River Valley. In 1879, *Harper's Magazine* touted the bonanza miracle, describing a railroad train rolling across "an ocean of grain." The following year, the *Atlantic Monthly* predicted a "revolution in the great economies of the farm."[18] Although Powell had remarked on the anomaly of its success, popular magazines failed to mention that the valley was strikingly more fertile than the rest of Dakota Territory. Soon, boosters were calling it the "Nile of the New World."[19]

Farmers' periodicals were more circumspect, cautioning readers that smaller, undercapitalized operators could not expect similar yields. One report estimated that a farmer cultivating several hundred acres could expect to invest $16,055 just to buy land and equipment, with additional expenses of nearly $50,000 over the first four years.[20] Farmers such as Charles Ingalls were more likely to have sixteen dollars than sixteen thousand.

Fundamentally, the question was whether national decisions of significant economic import, affecting thousands of citizens, would be governed by Enlightenment science or by huckster fantasy. The outcome was immediately clear to anyone reading the newspapers: fantasy

won. In a campaign comparable to modern-day corporate denial of
climate change, big business and the legislators in its pocket brushed
Powell's analysis aside. Railroads were not about to capitulate to the
geologist's limited vision, and his plans as director of the U.S. Geological Survey to limit western settlement would be undermined by
intense political attacks.[21] James B. Power, land agent for the Northern
Pacific—who had earlier admitted that Dakota was a "barren desert"—
dismissed Powell as an elite intellectual, lacking the experience of
"practical men." "No reliance can be placed upon any of his statements
as to the agricultural value of any country," Power said.[22] For good
measure, he called the geologist "an ass."[23]

Dependent on the business that railroads were driving, newspapers
on the Great Plains dismissed Powell too. In 1879, the *Fargo Times* lured
immigrants by distributing forty thousand copies of a special Red
River Valley issue. It was illustrated with mouth-watering illustrations
of bonanza farms, and a map showing the direct rail route for shipping
crops from Duluth to the Puget Sound via the Northern Pacific.[24] A
Nebraska reporter confidently asserted that "as the plains are settled
up we hear less and less of drouth, hot winds, alkali, and other bug-
bears that used to hold back the adventurous."[25]

Other promoters were more fanciful, pleading with farmers suffering in unbearably rainy climes, afflicted by mud and malaria, to join
them on the plains. "Come to God's country where the pure north wind
imparts vigor to the system and disease is scarcely known," one such
booster proclaimed. "Come where you can get land without money
and without price. Land that when you tickle it with the plow . . . laughs
with its abundance."[26] A more rational farmer, struggling behind his
plow in Kansas, found such hyperbole distasteful, suggesting it was
"little short of a crime" to urge the unwary to go west.[27]

Rain follows the plow: that was the spurious premise behind such
claims, put forward by successive presidents of the Union Pacific Railroad and at least one employee of Powell's own agency.[28] Powell's
report had refuted it, arguing that there was no scientific evidence for
it.[29] But climate falsifiers argued that a wet period during Dakota's
boom years proved the connection. Congress believed them, and the

quack theory supplied a rationale for the Timber Culture Act. By reducing wind, trees were supposed to produce rain.

If the railroads could not seed clouds in fact, they did so in fiction. The Chicago & North Western Railway, which employed Charles Ingalls through a subcontractor from 1879 to 1880, printed posters advertising two million farms: "Fertile Prairie Lands to be had Free of Cost!— YOU NEED A FARM!"[30] Profiting from planning towns, selling the land given them by the government, and shipping freight, the railroad had its press agents take rhetorical flights, painting the region as unfairly maligned. An 1875 broadside urged land seekers to "go and see for yourselves that the Grasshopper stories are false. That this is one of the best countries the sun ever shone upon, and a larger harvest per acre is already harvested and in the field, [than] you have in Wisconsin or Illinois—both small grains and corn—and for a Hog, Cattle and Sheep country it can best you all hollow!"[31]

The advertising worked. In 1860, around a thousand people lived in what is now South Dakota. Over the next decade, the population ticked slowly upward, to 11,776 residents, served by only six towns. Then, the deluge: in the 1880s, homesteaders filed on more than 41 million acres in Dakota Territory, an area bigger than the entire state of Iowa.[32] In 1890, nearly 329,000 people poured in, with more than three hundred towns springing up across the prairies virtually overnight. Trains packed with supplies, farm equipment, and personal possessions deposited people on the bare prairie; many camped in spare train cars parked on the sidings for the purpose.[33] The number of farms jumped from a paltry 1,700 to more than 50,000.[34]

The Ingalls family traveled only a hundred miles from Walnut Grove, Minnesota, to the land they would settle in Dakota Territory. Unwittingly, however, they were approaching Powell's 100th meridian, moving into the land that would inspire the tornado-scarred, wind-whipped plains of *The Wizard of Oz*. In Minnesota, while subject to locust swarms, the Ingallses had nonetheless inhabited a place where twenty-three to thirty-nine inches of precipitation fell reliably every year. In Dakota Territory, they entered a different world, where thirsty crops could expect only fifteen to twenty-three inches annually—if they were lucky.

Great, New Country

Having left behind the louche domestic squabbles and drunkenness of Walnut Grove, the Ingallses soon found themselves beyond established towns of any kind.

Swaying once again in the covered wagon, Laura drank in the hot, sweet scent of the sun-warmed prairie, reveling in the intoxicating, airy sense of unbounded freedom. They were crossing a sea of grass under open skies, leaving houses and roads behind, the trail marked only by bent and broken grasses. The wagon passed old buffalo wallows, wide shallow bowls in the earth, now grassed over. Above them flew flocks of geese and ducks in V formations. Years later, Wilder was moved to recall the setting sun, a "ball of pulsing, liquid light" sinking in "clouds of crimson and silver," leaving the wind whispering through the grasses and the earth "breathing softly under the summer night."[35]

The Ingallses may have been beyond towns, but they were not beyond society. When they reached their destination, the railroad camp on the north bank of Silver Lake, they found a cluster of raw shanties, as well as a bunkhouse, cooking shed, and company store. They also found family: Hiram and Docia Forbes were contractors, managing teams and running the company store, the hub of the camp. Henry Quiner was there with Charley and Louisa, last seen as children in Wisconsin, now grown. Louisa was cooking for the railroad crew. Charles Ingalls would be the camp's bookkeeper and paymaster, a position of some responsibility in what was essentially a temporary company town.

During the Dakota boom, the railroads ruled everything, maintaining a godlike power over those in their thrall. They brought the trappings of civilization, dropping down towns upon a map of raw land the way farmers dropped seeds in a furrow. Once the location of a town was set, it was then laid out, platted, and its lots sold. Arbitrarily mapped six to eight miles apart, many towns didn't "take" or were never built in the first place. In others, the railroad gave away lots to encourage development. The names of the towns were often as arbitrary, with many named for railroad officials or Civil War heroes or even postmasters' daughters.[36]

Once they arrived at the site where the railroad had determined a town was to be built, the Ingallses moved into a new shanty built by railroad workers, probably from a layer of boards and tar paper. There was a single room, with calico curtains—sewn by Caroline with fabric from the company store—separating the beds. A record of store prices in Charles's hand laid out the rates for goods hauled to the frontier by wagon: shirts selling for seventy cents, overalls a dollar, a hundred-pound sack of flour for three dollars and ten cents, a pair of boots for four dollars and forty cents.[37]

Laura set to work again as she had before, helping her mother cook for the crew and milking cows with her cousin Lena. They regaled the bovines with "Mary of the Wild Moor" and other popular songs. Glad to be out of Walnut Grove, Laura gloried in a "great, new country clean and fresh around us."[38] Forever after, she would associate the prairie with pristine and immaculate nature, a native purity.

The Chicago & North Western railroad camp was a rough place, ungoverned except by frontier justice. The Ingallses befriended several characters who might have leapt from a dime novel. There was Big Jerry, a powerfully built half-French, half-Indian man who frequented railroad camps up and down the line on his fast white pony, working, gambling, and starting fistfights. Jerry's pugnacious brother-in-law, Fred, reminded Laura of a Bantam rooster; he craved Caroline's cooking so much that he begged to board with the family. Jerry himself doted on an ancient, hunched-over Irishman named Johnny, who was too old to wield a shovel or swing a pickax. Ever generous, Charles gave Johnny a job delivering water to the crew.

The railroad workers provided nearly as much melodrama that fall as the *New York Ledgers* that Laura had devoured in the Masters hotel. There was excitement over a gang of horse thieves, with rumors flying that Big Jerry might be the gang's lookout; men lay in wait to catch him but never did. A prairie fire swept the tall marsh grasses south of Silver Lake one night, and the whole crew had to turn out to plow fire breaks and set backfires. And then there was the occasion when a high-handed, expensively dressed company man arrived to supervise work on the grade. Big Jerry took him down a notch, leading his horse through a trench where dirt rained down on his fine clothes. Derided by the crowd, the supervisor fled, never to return.

As often happened in itinerant camps, the workers grew restive under the railroad's payroll policy, which doled out money once a month while keeping men perpetually two weeks short of their full pay, to collect debts owed the company store. Strikes and labor unrest occurred throughout Dakota Territory in 1879.

One fall night, Charles faced down a mob of two hundred men crowding around the store and agitating for full pay. Firing guns, they threatened to break in and wreck the place. Hearing their "ugly" talk, Laura shook with rage, ready to run to her father's aid, and had to be physically restrained by her mother.[39] At Plum Creek, she had wreaked childish vengeance on Nellie; here she was ready to take on a gang of grown men, a teenage impetuosity that was to become ingrained. In the event, however, her father saved the day, talking down the men, telling them there was no money on-site and assuring them he would distribute it fairly when it arrived.

On December 1, 1879, the end of the season, the graders stopped work, packed up, and went back east. Charles was hired by the railroad to stay over the winter as caretaker for the surveyors' house, and he stocked up on food for the season. After dugouts and shanties, the house, roughly ten by twenty-two feet, seemed palatial, with a central room, a fully furnished pantry, a bedroom, and a lean-to that functioned as another bedroom and storage space. The girls slept upstairs, in a tiny space under the eaves. Released from their labors at the camp, Laura and her sisters were intoxicated by the sight and sound of flocks of geese, ducks, cranes, and swans massing on the lake before heading south for the winter.

Before he left, Hiram Forbes stayed with the Ingallses, settling accounts with the railroad and working a scam on his employer: contractors were not allowed to charge for their own horses, but Forbes listed his teams as the Ingallses', drew pay for their use, and pocketed the profit.[40] After several seasons coming out the loser on railroad contracts, Forbes rejoiced in taking advantage of a mighty company that he felt had taken advantage of him. Wilder called the scam "curiously satisfying."[41] As he bade them farewell, Uncle High, as the children called him, pressed a handful of money into Mary's hands.

The family was not entirely alone, boarding a young bachelor,

Walter Ogden, through the winter as caretaker for several yoke of oxen belonging to an absent homesteader.[42] But their isolation was nonetheless so profound—unearthly and reminiscent of the wild, melancholic nature so beloved by the Romantic poets Laura enjoyed—that virtually every member of the family would remark on it in years to come.[43] As Charles recalled, in a brief historical account:

> When I and my family were left alone for the winter on the prairie without neighbors we used to say we neighbored with Nelson, who lived on the Jim River 37 miles to the West of us. . . . We used to keep a lamp burning in the window for fear that some one might try to cross the prairie from the Sioux River to the Jim River and that light brought in some to shelter that must otherwise have perished on the prairie. The coyotes used to come to the door and pick up the crumbs that were scattered.[44]

Laura remembered the coyotes too, silently following as jackrabbits "drifted like shadows across the snow."[45]

Robert Boast, a thirty-year-old Canadian who had been working on the railroad, also stayed with the Ingallses for a few days, until leaving for Iowa to collect his wife, Ella. "About the last day of December on a bitter cold night . . . the coldest night during the winter," according to Charles, Boast returned, an apparition out of the night, leading Ella on horseback, and startled the family by calling out at the door.

The Boasts were soon followed by another known quantity, the Reverend Edwin Alden, the Ingallses' pastor from the Walnut Grove Congregational Church, sent out by the American Home Missionary Society to "plant churches" on a swing through the western territories.[46] Unbeknownst to the Ingallses, who remained fond of him, Alden had disgraced himself in the interim, embezzling funds while serving as an Indian agent in the northern part of Dakota Territory. Denounced as "a pious fraud" and swindler in the *New York Times*, Alden now returned to his previous calling.[47] He did not stay in town, however, being supplanted by the Reverend Edward Brown, a cousin of the notorious abolitionist. The Ingallses were dismayed to see Brown take over the congregation. "Rude and rough and unclean," with spit in his beard,

Brown disgusted the family, but having helped found the local church, the Ingallses had no alternative but to put up with him.[48]

To escape cabin fever, Laura and her younger sister Carrie occasionally went sliding on their shoes across the frozen surface of Silver Lake by moonlight. One memorable night, they slid far across the lake only to look up the embankment and see a wolf sitting silently above, watching them. They ran, terrified, but Laura looked back over her shoulder to catch a glimpse of the animal, its head raised, howling at the moon, "a black shadow against the moonlight . . . a sheet of silver glistening below him."[49] It was an indelible image, and also a propitious encounter. Ever the fur trapper, her father soon ventured out to hunt the wolves, and in the process stumbled across a promising piece of property south of Silver Lake.[50]

For Dakota Territory, it was a mild winter, which meant cold but without severe blizzards. The weather spurred land-hungry hordes to come early, eager to get a jump on the season, although they suffered for it. Charles Ingalls recalled how one of the first arrivals, after spending a night in a newly constructed claim shanty, woke to find the thermometer a crisp twelve below zero. "I well remember seeing him coming across the prairie toward the house," he wrote, "and you may be sure he did not come slow."[51]

Just as the birds returned to Silver Lake, would-be homesteaders flocked to the Ingallses. Occupying the only haven in the region, the family found themselves innkeepers, charging strangers fifty cents a night to sleep on their floor and twenty-five cents for a meal. "They covered the floor as thick as they could lay down," Charles wrote. Caroline, Laura, and Ella Boast cooked and washed dishes nearly every waking hour. Once, when her mother had a headache, Laura took on the whole job herself. That night she collapsed on the floor, too exhausted to eat.

Eighteen eighty got off to a hectic start. At the beginning of February, Charles published a newsy note in the *Brookings County Press* describing the dawning of the town of De Smet, "surrounded by as fine a country as can be found in the west." Hunters and trappers had been "on the go" to and from the Jim River all winter, he reported, finding the pickings slim out on the open plains. He himself had been more fortunate near Silver Lake: "The wolves, coyotes, foxes, and keeping warm have made lively times for your correspondent this winter; he has made a successful warfare and hopes to bring more stirring news when next he enters your sanctum."[52]

Soon enough he was off to Brookings himself. Fearing that he would lose his chance, he made the forty-mile trek east to the county seat, arriving on February 19, to file a claim on the homestead he had found while tracking the Silver Lake wolves. In March, the railroad surveyors returned to plat the town; it was laid out in a traditional T-shape, the main street dead-ending at the railroad tracks.[53] By the time town lots went on sale in April, Charles Ingalls had nearly completed a store building on a corner lot, and the family moved out of the surveyors' house and into the one-story structure on April 3. It was "a nice warm day," Wilder recalled, but the weather turned bitter overnight, snow drifting through cracks to cover their blankets. By morning, she could hear her father downstairs singing his warm-up song, "I am as happy as a big sun flower / That nods and bends in the breezes," and shouting to them to stay in bed.[54] He would be up in a minute to shovel them off.

De Smet's first train pulled into the station later that month, and Charles's building was soon sold at a profit, a welcome economic boon. Within a week he had framed another structure, diagonally across the street from the first: a two-story building with two rooms downstairs and two tiny attic rooms upstairs, separated only by a paper divider and reached by a ladder. The whole measured a little over fourteen feet wide, twenty-four feet deep, and around seventeen feet high.[55] It was in this building that the family would spend the next several winters.

The family camped out in the unfinished structure for a few weeks before heading to the homestead, planning to return during winter months while the girls attended school. Sixteen buildings sprang up that summer in all, another near-instantaneous town seeded by the railroad line.

The town was named for a Jesuit priest, Father Pierre-Jean De Smet (1801–1873), an indefatigable explorer for the Lord. De Smet spent his adult life traversing the Great Plains, founding missions and working to convert the Potawatomi, Dakota, and other "wild tribes." The Indians knew him by the name they reserved for all Jesuits, "Black Robe."

A Belgian, De Smet was often more baffled by white settlers than by the Indians. He described them as a "strange people," undeterred by lethal obstacles placed in their paths by climate, weather, or disease. "Nothing frightens them," he wrote wonderingly to his brother. "They will undertake anything. Sometimes they halt—stumble once in a while—but they get up again and march onward."[56]

Over his lifetime, De Smet amassed thousands of pages of maps, letters, and notes on terrain and weather conditions. Had any of the early founders of the town of De Smet perused them, they might have been chastened by a letter he received from a fellow missionary in Dakota. Dated December 11, 1850, it described a storm of such ferocity that the writer and his guide barely survived it:

> We had hardly encamped when the north wind began to blow with horrible violence; the snow fell so thick and fast, that you would have said the clouds had burst. . . . The snow and wind raged with unabated fury for two days and two nights. In some spots there were six, fifteen, and even twenty feet of snow. Conceive our position if you can, as we made our way along the valley of the James river.[57]

The town of De Smet lay between the James River to the west—the "Big Jim"—and the Big Sioux River to the east. Winter storms of "horrible violence" were commonplace in the area. Before the town was a year old, it would learn just how common.

Hard Winter

The Ingallses spent the summer of 1880 in a rudimentary shanty on their homestead claim, a mile south of town. They had hurriedly occupied their holding in May after alarming news broke that a nearby homesteader had been murdered by a claim jumper. To leave a claim standing empty in those days was to invite illegal possession, even violence. Already settlers were "too durned thick" for Charles Ingalls's taste.[58]

Around this time, a photograph of the three eldest Ingalls girls was taken, the only surviving group image of their childhood.[59] It subtly suggests their temperaments and the roles they assumed within the family. Carrie and Laura stand facing each other behind Mary, who is seated passively with a book in her lap, her gaze directed into the middle distance. Their poverty is apparent from their clothes, with Carrie swamped by a heavy and too-adult dress, doubtless a hand-me-down. Mary and Laura have lighter, well-worn dresses of checked gingham. An extra-long flounce has been sewn onto the hem of Laura's dress to cover her legs.

Their stance and expression speak to their characters. Mary strongly resembles her mother, bearing the grave resignation that can be seen in Caroline Ingalls's wedding portraits. Carrie's face appears thin, peaked, and anxious, a frailty she would carry throughout life.

But Laura is an entirely different animal. She leans slightly forward, as if into a strong prairie wind. Her arms are held stiffly at her sides, and her fists are clenched. She seems alert, vigilant, and ready to do battle.

With Charles still working on his buildings in town, the family was unable to clear much of the unbroken prairie and raise crops for cash, or even for sustaining themselves over the winter. That first season the family planted cottonwood trees around the shanty while Charles plowed a couple of acres of sod, planting turnips. On days when he didn't walk to town to do construction, he harvested wild hay, feed for their horses and cows during the winter, which Caroline and Laura helped load and stack. The money earned from selling the first building in town went to buy a mowing machine and hay rake, and Laura knew it must be running out. Later that summer she noticed her father leaving food for the rest of the family "when I knew he must still be hungry," snacking on raw turnips between meals.[60] She followed his example.

Fall rains began at the end of September. On the night of October 14, Laura fell asleep as water dripped on her blanket through a tear in the tar-paper roof. When she awoke the next morning—"we never paid any attention to so slight a discomfort"—she couldn't see out the window.[61] It was a whiteout. A blizzard had struck so early in the year that it caught many across the central plains unaware.

It lasted at least twenty-four hours. Trapped in the shanty, Laura and her parents did chores and prepared meals, while the other girls stayed in bed to keep warm. At Yankton, farther south, winds gusted at seventy miles an hour. Cattle trapped on exposed summer ranges, still in their summer coats, perished by the thousands.[62] Telegraph wires blew down, and snow and ice packed the railroad cuts, stalling hundreds of trains, so that food had be brought to those trapped onboard.

The storm eventually covered five hundred square miles of Nebraska, Dakota Territory, Minnesota, Iowa, Wisconsin, and northern Michigan, with gales blowing at 125 miles per hour across the Great Lakes, and snow ranging from a few inches to drifts as high as twenty feet. Virtually every ship on Lake Michigan at the time was lost, including the steamer *Alpena*, bound for Chicago with seventy-five souls on board.[63] The October Blizzard, as Wilder called it, remains one of the earliest on record for the region.[64]

Freakish incidents marked the disaster. Charles found cattle standing near the shanty blinded by ice that had formed over their faces, stunned by exhaustion. The family rescued unusual birds sheltering in the hay stacks, releasing them after the weather warmed. Charles decided to move his family to his building in De Smet, where they spent daylight hours in the single tiny room at the back, sleeping in attic rooms upstairs. For the time being, the front room was doing duty as the County Office, where Charles handled paperwork. Earlier that year, he had briefly served as clerk for Kingsbury County's first school district, then filled in as constable and justice of the peace, positions providing some small income.[65]

Earlier that spring, Caroline had acted as midwife at the birth of a baby in one of the upstairs attic rooms, the infant said to have been the first child born in De Smet.[66] Twenty-seven-year-old George Masters, eldest son of the Walnut Grove schoolmaster Uncle Sam, had hastily married a plump young woman of Scottish extraction, Margaret, who was pregnant. Ostracized for the shotgun marriage and with her husband off working for the railroad west of De Smet, Maggie Masters was befriended by Caroline and her neighbor Margaret Garland, a widow who had opened a boarding house behind the Ingallses' building. In the fall of 1880, when the Ingalls family moved back to town, Maggie and her baby took up residence in their attic; their stay was meant to be brief. Wilder later wrote, "We thought they were leaving but George put it off."[67]

With work on the railroad stopped by snow, George Masters joined Maggie and the baby in the attic. When the weather turned violent once again, the Ingalls and Masters families—not for the first time—found their lives uncomfortably entwined. Every house in town was full, and Laura's parents would not put a young couple and their baby out on the street. Their presence meant that the cramped building would be crowded with nine people (and nine mouths to feed) over the coming months. Charles Ingalls may well have felt a sense of obligation, having housed his family on William Masters's Walnut Grove property during their own perilous economic times. Laura, however, felt none of those finer impulses. For her, George Masters would make a hard winter infinitely harder, and she still hated him decades later.

On November 1, during a brief break in the severe weather, Laura and Carrie began attending school, taught by Margaret Garland's eighteen-year-old daughter. But the respite ended within days, when a sudden gust of wind struck the side of the school building "like a mighty sledge."[68] Led by their teacher and a man from town, the pupils tried to head back home. Immediately, their lives were in jeopardy: the school was several blocks west of the town center, with nothing "but bare prairie between."[69] Wilder later pointed out that the Garlands were from the east and had no knowledge of the dangers of a blizzard. As soon as they left the building, it was "a struggle to even breathe," she remembered.[70] Blinded by ferocious snow and wind, they nearly wandered out onto the open prairie, where they would have frozen to death. Fortuitously, the group struck the corner of the last building in town. A search party was already being organized, alerted by the teacher's brother, Cap Garland, an enterprising teenager two years older than Laura, who had boldly gone to fetch help. The blizzard blew for three days.

The near-disaster was only a taste of what was to come. Blizzard followed blizzard, packing the railroad tracks so that no plows were powerful enough to push through. When the weather cleared, all the men in De Smet turned out to shovel, but the snow piled up into enormous banks twenty-five feet deep; it took three men to hurl a shovelful clear. Virtually every night the winds would blow snow back onto the tracks, until fresh blizzards completed the rout. Back at Tracy, Minnesota, the snowbanks along the railroad sidings reached a hundred feet deep and railway officials called a halt to operations.[71] The last train to De Smet made it through on January 4, 1881.

Around a hundred people were trapped in town. Everyone kept hoping for a lull or a thaw, but it never happened. With no hope of food or fuel arriving by train, the severity of their situation began to sink in. Night after night, the Ingallses lay in their beds, listening to the howling of the blizzard gale, "the house rocked with the force of it."[72] The two small local stores were stripped of their goods, with the last bags of flour selling for fifty cents and finally a dollar a pound.

The quality of the housing was abysmal. Solid sod houses would have been more comfortable in the brutal wind, but that construction had been abandoned for cheap goods shipped by rail. Crude board-and-batten walls provided little insulation other than a layer of tar paper, and wind and snow whistled in through nail holes and around windows. Wilder described them as "shells at best."[73] Heated by a single wood stove, they were drafty and fearsomely cold.

Coal was quickly depleted, and townspeople fell back on a prairie staple: burning hay. This may have been the first time that the Ingallses were obliged to go to such lengths, but American settlers on the plains had been burning dried grass for decades, and entrepreneurs had even patented hay-twisting gadgets out of cranks and rollers.[74] But in De Smet, people were forced to twist hay by hand. "Sticks" or "cats" of hay burned so fast that it was said to take "two men and a boy to keep the hay fire going."[75] Laura helped her parents meet the need: Carrie was too small, and Mary too weak to be of assistance. As for George, Wilder said, he just sat.[76]

Kerosene ran out, and Caroline fashioned a button lamp, drawing on memories of her Wisconsin frontier childhood: wrapping a rag around a button, tying it off with thread, and setting the gathered rag in a saucer of axle grease. It made a "little light," Wilder wrote, "after a fashion."[77]

Otherwise, these were dark, dark days. There was no meat, no butter, no fruit, no coffee or tea. Sugar ran out, and the cow went dry. Before long, the family was grinding the seed wheat for next year's crop in their coffee mill, Mary patiently sitting in front of the fire and turning the handle. On the last train to get through, the Ingallses received a November letter from friends back east saying they had sent a barrel packed with warm winter clothing and a Christmas turkey. The letter got through; the barrel did not.

The family joked about that turkey, but when it came to George and Maggie Masters, Wilder's tone was scathing. The family and their unintended guests were surviving off a dwindling supply of potatoes, but George did not hold back, not even for the sake of his wife, nursing their child. Last to rise in the morning, he was the first to rush to the table, Wilder wrote, gobbling more than his share of potatoes so fast he burned himself. Maggie complacently sat in a prime spot by the fire, shirking other work.

By late January, the entire town was balanced on the edge of survival. By then, even De Smet's wealthiest man, the banker Thomas Ruth, who earlier had bought all the lumber left in town and burned it in his stove, was reduced to using hay for fuel and grinding seed wheat for bread. With stores of that seed dwindling and the last bags of flour gone, starvation loomed.

Rumor had it there was one farmer in the region, about twelve miles to the south, who had raised a crop of wheat in the spring of 1880. A De Smet storeowner offered to front the money to buy it. "If we were all to live until spring," Wilder wrote, "someone must go after it."[78] It was a risky proposition. Blizzards and whiteout conditions were occurring every few days; narrow windows of clear weather were often measured in hours. Getting caught on the prairie in a blizzard was a death sentence.

No one wanted to do it, but eventually two volunteers stepped forward. One was Cap Garland, Laura's teenage schoolmate and neighbor. The other was Almanzo Wilder.

BACHELOR brothers, Royal and Almanzo Wilder had arrived in the De Smet area in 1879, before the town was built, after filing on homesteads. Part of a prosperous farming family, the boys were born and raised near the town of Malone in upstate New York, north of the Adirondacks and a few miles from the Canadian border.

Their parents, James and Angeline Day Wilder, raised cash crops, fine horses, and a family of six: Laura, Royal, Eliza Jane, Alice, Almanzo, and Perley Day. Royal was named for an illustrious uncle, a graduate of Middlebury College and Andover Theological Seminary, who traveled to Kolapoor, India, to evangelize a city of "50,000 idolators," as mission propaganda had it.[79]

The origins of Almanzo's flamboyant name remain a mystery. Family lore suggests that it sprang from "El Mansur . . . brought into England from Asia during the Crusades" and thence to America.[80] Arabic for "one who is victorious," the name al-Mansur does indeed crop up across the Muslim world and in Seville, Spain, where caliph Yasuf al-Mansur built a famous mosque in the eleventh century. But "Almanzo" also might have arrived in upstate New York by a more prosaic route. In his mother's day, a vogue for exotic Moorish tales was launched by Washington Irving's *The Alhambra*, romantic sketches inspired by Irving's stay in a sultan's palace in Granada.[81] The book gave rise to a rash of Crusader fables, including a *Ladies Companion* serial about the Romeo-and-Juliet romance between Inez, a blushing Christian, and Almanzor, her fervid Moorish admirer.[82] Almanzo was born at the height of this vogue. His family just called him "Manzo."

On an 1860 agricultural census, James Wilder estimated the cash value of his farm at three thousand dollars, with several horses, eight milch cows, and a flock of nineteen sheep yielding seventy-six pounds of wool.[83] He grew more than forty bushels of wheat and two hundred and sixty of oats. His wife managed her own lucrative sideline, selling high-quality butter to buyers from New York City.[84] Compared to the Ingallses, they were rich.

But during the difficult years after the Panic of 1873, harvests in New York were damaged by the same drought causing havoc in the Midwest. Hearing that pockets of Minnesota were still viable, the Wilders decided to follow Angeline's brother to Spring Valley in the southeastern part of the state, not far from where Peter Ingalls had settled. There, Almanzo spent his teenage years.

In Spring Valley, he became friends with a boy he knew as Dick Sears.[85] Years later, Richard Sears would found Sears, Roebuck and Company, but he got his start in life by learning telegraphy and working for a railroad company in Minneapolis. It may have been from Sears that Almanzo Wilder heard intriguing information regarding the Dakota Boom. Rumor had it that the Chicago & North Western had designated the future town of De Smet as the end of its division line. With farmers from around the region poised to rely on its services and rail freight, it promised to become a hub.[86]

Royal and Almanzo embarked for Dakota Territory in August 1879. Royal was thirty-two, but questions surround Almanzo's true age. In later life, he would give February 13, 1857, as his date of birth, but early federal and New York State census records consistently identify the year as 1859.[87] The Homestead Act required claimants to be at least twenty-one, so if Almanzo was twenty years old in 1879 he might well have taken liberties with his age.[88]

Heading for the land office in the regional capitol of Yankton, in the far southeast corner of Dakota Territory, the Wilder brothers were driving a team of horses worth four hundred dollars. Almanzo had bought them with money saved from years of working harvests and cannily trading horseflesh. Their spirits were high, if subdued by the presence of another sibling: Almanzo's least favorite sister, Eliza Jane, resented for her high-handed ways. Unmarried at twenty-nine, Eliza Jane, known as E.J., also planned to homestead. It was not an unusual pursuit for women. One scholar has estimated that a third of Dakota homesteads were held by women a decade later.[89]

It was a hot day. In Almanzo's recollection, Eliza Jane kept urging him to hurry the horses: there was a land rush on, after all, and she was afraid they would arrive too late. They had covered most of the one hundred and fifty miles to Yankton when they met with disaster. One of the horses collapsed and within minutes was dead from colic. It was a terrible blow: Almanzo had been offered two hundred dollars for the animal just days before. For the rest of his life, he would blame E.J. for rushing them.

A few years later, Eliza Jane would write her own account, in which she spoke of Almanzo as if he were a hired hand:

The driver was urging his horses to do their best that we might reach
Yankton before stopping for the night when I noticed one horse
sweating profusely. I called his attention to the matter but he replied
twas only the heat of the day, which with the rapid driving caused the
horse to sweat profusely. I was not satisfied. I spoke again and the
same moment the horse became covered with foam. . . . She fell into
a convulsive agony and in less than an hour her sufferings were
ended.[90]

Eliza Jane complained of not being able to sleep that night, having
never, she said, witnessed the death of "even a chick"—unlikely for
someone who grew up on a farm eating beef, pork, and chicken raised
and slaughtered yards away. She could not bring herself to admit that
the person who suffered a loss that day was her brother.

Limping into town, the siblings each filed on homesteads and tree
claims at the Yankton office, apparently sight unseen, choosing sections neighboring the town site to the north.[91] A doctor friend of theirs
from St. Paul filed too, on a homestead meant for his son, violating
regulations that required the claimant to file in person. He then inveigled the Wilder brothers to help him, paying them twenty-five dollars
to build a sod shanty on his son's claim and strew some clothes around
to make it look inhabited. It was a common scam.

By November, while the Ingalls family was settling into the surveyors'
house near Silver Lake, the brothers were out at their new claims with
a wagon, lumber, and a breaking plow to cut sod. Camping on the open
prairie, they burned blue grass to cook their food. In three weeks, they
built four sod shanties, each with a door, a window, and a bunk bed.[92]
Then they left for the winter, reaching Spring Valley the day before
Christmas, where Almanzo worked hauling and selling cordwood at
four dollars a cord, hoping to earn enough to pay for a horse to replace
the one that died.[93]

The Wilder brothers returned in the spring of 1880, as De Smet was
becoming a town. Royal established a feed store on the main street, while
Almanzo worked his land. When the October 15 blizzard struck, Eliza
Jane recalled that one of the brothers was caught at her shanty. Shortly
thereafter, she left for the season, returning to her parents at Spring

Valley, while Royal and Almanzo moved into Royal's store building for the duration.

In her memoir, Laura Wilder wrote that her family was "shorter of food than anyone," probably due to their early arrival in the area, compounded by their poverty. Some settlers who traveled to De Smet in 1880 came by train, shipping a season's worth of provisions in freight cars; they would have been better positioned to last the winter. Royal and Almanzo appear to have been fairly comfortable, with an ample supply of seed wheat for the coming season, boarded up behind a false wall to keep it from prying eyes.

Charles Ingalls knew about their seed wheat, however, and when his family ran short he would pay the brothers a visit. Accommodatingly, the Wilder boys would pull a plug out of the wall and fill his bucket. They may have appreciated the plight of the Ingalls family, as well as Charles's bravery in hauling hay on the few clear days, as they did. The rest of the town, Wilder wrote, was "numbed and dumb" by storms, hunger, and extreme cold. "There were only a few who kept normal and very much alive. Pa and the Wilder boys did. . . . The others cowered."[94]

The brothers' wheat, however, could not feed the entire town. So on one cold, clear, calm day, Almanzo Wilder and Cap Garland drove south, each with a horse and a sled, stopping often to help the horses plow through drifts and climb out of sinkholes in the grassy sloughs. Miraculously, they found the farmer they sought. He was reluctant to part with his wheat, but with negotiation and some pressure they prevailed, paying him $1.50 a bushel. They returned to De Smet after dark. Another blizzard struck hours later. Having saved a hundred townspeople from acute privation, the two young men charged nothing for making the trip. They risked their lives, Wilder said, "cheerfully . . . for the sake of the community."[95]

The rest of the winter passed in an excruciating torpor. Month followed month with no respite from blizzards and no trains. Hope momentarily gripped the town one clear day when a herd of antelope was sighted, but the animals were frightened off by an overexcited hunter firing too soon. The shot also spooked one of Almanzo's horses, which ran with the herd for two hours before he could catch it.

A single antelope did get shot—by Charles, according to his daughter—but it proved to be starved itself.[96]

Finally, on April 1, after four months with no fresh supplies of food or fuel, the weather warmed. The first train got through on May 9, but the De Smet mob that greeted it found that it carried farm machinery, a shipment frozen on the line all winter. A riot was in the offing until the crowd found a freight car with provisions, which were broken open and rationed out. The next train carried telegraph poles. They were not for sale as firewood, railroad employees told them, but the townsfolk carried them away nonetheless, sawed them up, and burned them for fuel. No one who had lived through those months, Wilder wrote, could ever think kindly of a railroad again.

It was not until late spring that the train carrying the Ingallses' Christmas barrel arrived, and with it their long-awaited turkey, still frozen. The hard winter was over.

Ambition

Panic, depression, drought, and failure consumed the 1870s. But while De Smet was seeing out the hard winter, the national economy was beginning to stir, and the decade to follow saw an explosive rise in wealth, power, and ambition. For the first time in American history, the number of millionaires in the country topped one hundred.[97]

In 1879, Frank Woolworth opened his first successful Five and Dime. In 1880, George Pullman built his railway car factory. In 1882, John D. Rockefeller founded Standard Oil, and in 1885 Alexander Graham Bell launched American Telephone and Telegraph. In 1886, Almanzo Wilder's boyhood friend Dick Sears made a killing selling gold-filled pocket watches to farmers along the Minneapolis and St. Louis Railway line. The Gilded Age in all its gaudy glory was loosed upon the nation.

Sears's pocket watches, signs of prosperity, also signaled a new anxiety stalking the agricultural community, one engendered by increasingly intense competition. More than ever, farmers had to be able to tell time, keeping track of the arrival and departure of freight trains that hauled tools, seed, and harvests. Newfangled time zones had recently been instituted to sort out the mass confusion caused by each railroad setting its own time (in some places, competing clocks had been erected on a single platform). But coordinated schedules couldn't compensate for dramatically fluctuating shipping rates. Farmers who couldn't plan which crops to plant and when invariably felt they were falling behind.

As a result, waves of populist sentiment rolled across the land, and farmers began agitating for railroad regulation. First among the organizations formed to support them was the Grange, which attracted more than 750,000 members. Grange Halls, modeled after the fraternal organization of the Freemasons, sprang up in town after town. In the 1870s, the Grangers won a series of anti-corporate Supreme Court cases that classified railroads as companies operating in the public interest and subject to regulatory control.

The cases were later overturned, but such victories taught farmers that political power lay in numbers. Another organization, the Farmers' Alliance, built on the Grangers' momentum by promoting plans to nationalize railroads and regulate interest rates charged on bank loans.[98] During the last years of the 1880s, a thousand farmers a week were joining the Alliance.[99]

Such farmers' movements emphasized the growing divide between urban and rural America. In the 1870s, two-thirds of Americans still lived in rural areas, but that was down significantly from the 1820s, when 90 percent had been farmers. A great demographic shift was under way. More and more, homesteaders across the Plains—many as undercapitalized as Charles Ingalls—were washing out after struggling for years to turn wheat into cash. Exhausted and discouraged, they returned to towns or cities. Charles himself, throughout this period, found carpentering and other odd jobs in De Smet a more reliable source of income than homesteading.

WHEN it came to town and country, Laura Ingalls's allegiance was clear. Regarding De Smet, she wrote: "I didn't care much for all these people. I loved the prairie and the wild things that lived on it much better."[100]

For weeks during the summer of 1881, she sewed shirts in town for a Mrs. White for twenty-five cents a day, sleeping in the attic and eating with the family in the kitchen. She was astonished at their vehement prejudice against Catholics, which reached a fever pitch when the great comet of 1881 appeared, an occurrence that the White family took as a sure sign of the end times. She watched as the town tailor, a diminutive Irishman, marched up and down the sidewalk arm-in-arm with a tall, inebriated, bass-voiced friend, sonorously intoning: "I'm T. P. Power and I'm drunk." She laughed until she cried, she said, but she was glad to leave the sordid confines of town behind and "get away from all these people, funny and otherwise."[101]

Out on the homestead was where she wanted to be, roaming among birds and striped gophers and flowering native grasses, pausing in the buffalo wallow where violets blossomed in the spring, a bowl of color. Her rapturous passages about the prairie at dawn—the sun rising and "throwing streamers of light around the horizon and up across the sky"—contrast sharply with accounts of the social confusion she experienced in town.[102] She relaxed in solitary domestic pursuits—fetching water, milking cows, feeding calves, skimming milk, caring for hens and chicks—but chafed among crowds and under supervision.

She wasn't the only girl to fall in love with the Great Plains. In the spring of 1883, Virginia natives Charles and Jenny Cather stepped off a Burlington and Missouri River Railroad car at the depot at Red Cloud, Nebraska, three hundred and fifty miles due south of De Smet. Drawn by the land boom and by relatives who had settled out west a decade earlier, they were accompanied by their daughter, Wilella, known to the family as Willie. The nine-year-old was at first frightened by the blank inhuman expanse, "as if we had come to the end of everything . . . a kind of erasure of personality."[103] But by autumn it had a hold on her, gripping her with "a passion that I have never been able to shake." The Plains, Willa Cather wrote years later, are "the happiness and the curse of my life."[104]

CHARLES Ingalls was working as hard as ever but not getting ahead. During the summer of 1881, the family was living at the homestead, but he had to hire a local boy, Ernest Perry, to break ground for him while he continued working in De Smet. He planted a little corn, but apparently felt he could make more in the building trade. Both he and Laura were working for wages. Their dream now was that Mary could attend the Iowa College for the Blind, in Vinton, Iowa.

Since Dakota Territory had no such institution, Mary Ingalls qualified for state support for tuition and board, but the family had to cover transportation, clothing, and other expenses. With their limited means, it must have been an effort, but they sent Mary off in high hopes that November, her parents traveling with her to Vinton. "I had been slower and stupid at my books," Wilder wrote, as always judging herself against her elder sister. But she added that they were all happy that Mary would receive what amounted to a college education in the humanities, with additional training in Braille, music, sewing, and beadwork.[105]

Sometime that fall, Laura and Carrie took a circuitous route back to the homestead to avoid Thomas Ruth's frightening bull, who snorted at them and pawed the ground. Laura was convinced she could outrun it but worried that Carrie would fall. Making their way through the tall slough grass, they happened upon a man pitching hay onto a wagon while a younger fellow lolled atop the load, "kicking up his heels."[106] The man on the ground she recognized as Royal Wilder; the other one had to be his brother, Almanzo. Her father knew the Wilder boys well, but it was the first time she had laid eyes on the young man who had saved the town from starving.

The winter of 1881 was a mild one, but the family moved back to town so Laura and Carrie could return to school, a less happy and auspicious prospect than Mary's going off to college. Laura disliked the teacher, Willard Seelye, who had a disgusting habit of sucking on the end of his pointer and scratching his back with it as students recited. In retaliation, she and her fellow pupils tormented him by dunking the pointer in a bath of noxious substances. Laura contributed cayenne. As with Sam Masters, whom she stabbed with a pin for fondling her hand, she could be aggressive, however indirectly.

Like any teenager, Laura also suffered bouts of inferiority, despairing of her clothes ("nothing to speak of") and lamenting a fear of strangers: "It seemed some mornings as though I simply could not face the crowd on the school grounds and the palms of my hands would grow moist and sticky."[107] Grounded perhaps in her alarming experiences in the Masters Hotel, these feelings would prove transient. But her self-doubt recalled emotions that had deeper roots, too, extending back to the time as a young child when her brown hair seemed less attractive than Mary's blond curls. Judging herself against her sister, she had long questioned her own looks, intelligence, and innate goodness.

Years later, to her daughter, Wilder would admit to an adolescent conviction that she was "the homeliest girl ever." Concerns about her temperament, meanwhile, would find expression in a tale she told often, about an argument between the sisters over whether to put sage (Mary's favorite) or onions (Laura's preference) in the dressing for a much-anticipated roast goose.[108] Her father failed to bag the bird, so in the end there was no dressing at all, and the quarrel became her private parable for the importance of being thankful. But it was freighted with shame as well. "I wish I had let you have the sage," she recalled telling Mary, abashed at her own temper, not for the last time.[109]

In February 1882, Laura turned fifteen, and De Smet's social circles began to exert a greater attraction. A few days before her birthday, she had been delighted to attend her first grown-up party, for her classmate Ben Woodworth, the stationmaster's son, who lived above the railway depot. All her life she saved the invitation card, and remembered a menu doubtless made especially enjoyable by memories of the winter before: it featured fresh oranges peeled back to create the appearance of a flower, hot oyster soup and crackers, and birthday cake.[110]

But at school, she was horrified to discover that Genevieve Masters—her bête noire from Walnut Grove, daughter of Sam and sister of the loathsome George—would be one of her classmates. It was, she declared, "the last unbearable straw," hyperbole that contrasted oddly with her stoic account of real suffering of the year before.[111] Even worse, Seelye had been replaced by an even more problematic teacher: Eliza Jane Wilder.

Soon enough, Laura had it out with Genevieve, a typical teenage spat in which the other girl called her fat and made fun of her dowdy clothes, while she mocked Genevieve's big feet and pointed out that her fine dresses were castoffs from rich relations. The argument gave Laura a headache, but it was nothing compared to her battles with Eliza Jane, which eventually enveloped the entire school. Much of the difficulty arose from the teacher's uncertain and inconsistent discipline, but Laura felt that a particular animus was extended toward her and, by extension, Carrie.

At the time, she believed that the teacher's resentment stemmed from Charles Ingalls's position on the school board and E.J.'s assumption that Laura expected special treatment because of it. In her autobiography, however, Wilder acknowledged playing the ringleader among the students. As with her Walnut Grove days, when she expressed surprise at becoming a "leader," she again felt "strange"—a word repeated twice—to find herself at the head of her friends, and indeed of the student body as a whole.[112] But judging by her own description, Laura Ingalls at fifteen may have been an intimidating character, and she soon accepted her role.

Classroom decorum collapsed after weeks of Eliza Jane's mismanagement. Open insurrection ruled the aisles, with note-passing and spitballs perhaps the least of it. Wilder admitted to circulating a rhyme among her chums, a cruel twist on a taunt from E.J.'s own school days that the teacher had been imprudent enough to share:

> Going to school is lots of fun
> By laughter we have gained a ton
> For we laugh until we have a pain
> At lazy, lousey, Liza Jane.[113]

Decades later, Wilder ruefully acknowledged: "I should have been whipped."[114]

Matters came to a head one day when Carrie and her seatmate were punished for rocking the bench where they were sitting and studying. Laura, sitting behind them, recalled it as an unconscious movement, but the noise so irritated Eliza Jane that she ordered the two students to put away their books and just rock the heavy seat. The other girl simply moved away, leaving Carrie to do it alone. She turned white from the effort, and Laura leapt to the defense of her younger, weaker sibling: "Miss Wilder if Carrie isn't rocking that seat hard enough to suit you, let me do it!"[115]

Handing her tormentor a chance to disgrace herself, Eliza Jane assented. A contest of wills ensued, with Laura loudly rocking the bench and staring down the teacher for twenty minutes. Finally, Eliza Jane ordered her to stop and sent her and Carrie home. Their father shook his head over it but did not reprimand either one.

Shortly thereafter, the school board visited the school to see the chaos for themselves. Eliza Jane was soon dismissed, and the board hired another teacher to finish her term. (E.J. herself later denied that the events played out this way, saying instead that her fragile health, "failing slowly but surely," did not permit her to continue teaching.)[116]

The clash highlighted again Laura's fierceness and drive, her strong reaction to perceived injustice, and her impulsive behavior. It was perhaps a culmination of the years in Burr Oak and Walnut Grove, left on her own amid a hotel full of erratic adults, her parents desperate and distracted. If she cast herself as a leader, perhaps it was because no one else filled that role.

The rest of the winter passed in a whirlwind of sleigh rides and parties, a minstrel show starring the hardware store owners—brothers Charleton and Gerald Fuller—and a fund-raising New England Supper at the newly completed Congregational Church.

The "big boys," as she called them, were now paying attention to her. First she was squired around by Ernest Perry, the young man who had helped plow her father's land. He took her to parties where the young folk played kissing games such as "Post Office." But the more she attended such affairs, the less she liked them, dismissing "that country crowd" in her memoir, seeing herself apart.[117] She was a snob, she recalled, even at that age. For a time she admired Cap Garland, but one night after a revival meeting Almanzo Wilder asked to see her home. Startled, she wondered why he'd approached her; later she learned that he had done it on a dare. But what started as a lark became a habit, and he was soon seeing her home on a regular basis.

THE spring and summer of 1883 found the sixteen-year-old Laura once again working to support her family. First she was hired as companion and helpmate to Martha McKee, a seamstress, and her eleven-year-old daughter, Mary. She accompanied them to their homestead, west of De Smet, while Mr. McKee ran his lumberyard in town, visiting on the weekend. Having done odd sewing jobs for Martha before, Laura enjoyed her stay, but found her husband's Sabbath strictures against Sunday laughter or play exasperating. The wife was less straitlaced, freely advising Laura on her love life: "You'll marry that Wilder boy yet, because you'll be afraid you'll hurt his feelings if you say no. . . . A man of his age doesn't fool around with a girl so long for nothing."[118]

When she finished at the McKees', Laura went to work for Florence Bell, a fashionable new milliner and dressmaker in town, working alongside Laura Wilder Howard, Royal and Almanzo's eldest sibling, who was staying with Eliza Jane. There she sewed from seven in the morning to six in the evening, with only a few minutes' break for noon dinner, earning fifty cents a day for eleven hours' labor. She turned over all her earnings to her parents, for what she called "the home fund."[119]

The home definitely needed her. Charles Ingalls had spent the summer working as a carpenter, and had harvested his first real crops of wheat and oats at the homestead. But he could not afford any of the mechanical harvesters advertised in the pages of the *De Smet Leader*, and was forced to use a hand cradle instead, a physically punishing task. "Pa was very thin and tired from the hard work," Wilder wrote, and she knew that he was "not very happy" in De Smet, now "thickly settled." He wanted to go to Oregon, invited by an old friend who'd made the trip there after being driven out of Walnut Grove during the terrible grasshopper years. But for the first time, Caroline Ingalls balked at the idea of moving yet again. She refused to consider it, tired of "wandering around 'from pillar to post.'"[120]

The fall found Laura back at school with Carrie. But this time, De Smet had employed a gifted and dedicated instructor, Ven Owen, the first teacher to earn Laura's respect. Fondly remembered by students as "a builder of character," Owen set his older pupils to writing compositions.[121] Assigned to write on "Ambition," Laura drew from the definition in the heavy *Webster's Unabridged Dictionary* that sat in the schoolroom. She set out the merits of drive and determination as a spur to hard work, then examined ambition's dangers and follies, referring to Alexander the Great, who wept when he had no more worlds to conquer, and closed with a quotation from *Henry VIII*: "Cromwell, I charge thee fling away ambition, by that sin fell the angels."[122] She misspelled the conqueror's name as "Elaxander" but impressed her teacher, who offered high praise, urging her to write more. She kept that piece of paper for the rest of her life.

All through her teen years, Laura wrote poetry, cheering herself up and egging herself on. The essay on ambition might have brought forth the declarative lines in which she exhorted herself to "Do It with All Your Might."[123] Never brooding or introspective, she enjoyed strong swinging rhythm and the opportunity to try on emotions as if they were clothes, everything from exasperation and romantic melancholy to familial devotion.

In verse, she experimented with rousing patriotism in mourning the assassination of President Garfield—"for whom all hearts / Have bled"—and with mocking snooty schoolmates such as Genevieve: "I go to the school / Which she attends / In which I have 'chums' / And she has 'friends.' "[124] In a touching tribute, she honored her elder sister:

Who is it shakes me
Like a Child
When e'er my spirits
Grow too wild
Who gives reproof in accents mild?
My sister Mary.[125]

An amusing bit of doggerel inspired by the hard winter captured her pugnacious nature: "I will leave this frozen region / I will travel farther south / If you say one word against it / I will hit you in the mouth."[126] In such plainspoken exuberance, her adult personality began to emerge, shy at times but laced with an occasionally combative streak.

Soon she was called to become a teacher herself. Robert Boast, the old friend from the Ingallses' winter at Silver Lake, came to their door with a relative, Louis Bouchie, a homesteader looking for a teacher for a small school a half dozen miles out of town. Since the district could not afford to pay more than twenty dollars for a two-month contract, Boast recommended Laura. At sixteen, she was too young to get a certificate: Dakota Territory required that teachers be at least eighteen.[127] But superintendents could bend the rules a bit if needed.

When she sat for the exam, the presiding school superintendent, perhaps on purpose, neglected to ask her age. She passed, receiving a third-grade certificate dated December 10, 1883, allowing her to teach for a year. She was about to learn just how risky ambition could be.

FIVE children attended the Bouchie school, taught in a drafty, abandoned claim shanty where snow blew through the cracks in the walls. It should have been a simple two-month job, but Laura Ingalls was young and inexperienced, the conditions grim, the students difficult, and the Bouchie family, with whom Laura was boarding, a nightmare.

From the first, Oliv Bouchie, Louis's sullen wife, greeted her with silence and hostility. Laura was expected to sleep on a narrow couch separated from the couple and their children by a calico curtain. (Laura remembered them having one boy, but there may have been two, a three-year-old and an infant.) At night, behind the curtain, she listened as Liv Bouchie raged at her husband.

Certainly unpleasant, Mrs. Bouchie may also have been unhinged. Insanity was a common feature of life on the Great Plains, exacerbated by isolation and the dreary confines of tight spaces and bad weather. And these conditions were all too often accompanied by unbearable misfortune—bankruptcies, accidents, fires, suicides, deaths of children—aggravating any predisposition to mental illness. There was a word for it: "shack-wacky." At the time, it was said to happen "to an awful lot of women."[128]

Hamlin Garland, chronicler of prairie depression, would capture Liv Bouchie's type in a story when one of his luckless, exhausted characters lashes out:

"I hate farm life," she went on with a bitter inflection. "It's nothing but fret, fret and work the whole time, never going any place, never seeing anybody but a lot of neighbors just as big fools as you are.

I spend my time fighting flies and washing dishes and churning. I'm sick of it all."[129]

Shielded by her parents and safe in her happy home, Laura had seen something of such desperation with the Masterses, but never lived it so unrelievedly. She learned what hatred could be at the Bouchies'.

At school, Laura was intimidated, alarmed to discover that two of her pupils—fourteen-year-old Martha and sixteen-year-old Clarence—were taller than she.[130] Clarence, who was the same age as Laura, quickly made it clear that he had no intention of taking instruction from her. Martha and her brother Charles, while pleasant, seemed slow to learn, and the two youngest students, Ruby and Tommy Bouchie—half-siblings of Louis Bouchie from his father's second marriage—were tormented by Clarence's practical jokes, pinching, pin-sticking, and hair-pulling. Suddenly, Laura found herself in Eliza Jane's shoes.

Haunted by the prospect of spending an entire weekend stranded with the wretched Bouchies, Laura was thrilled when Almanzo Wilder drove up to the schoolroom door in a sleigh on her first Friday afternoon and offered to take her home. From then on, he never missed a weekend, coming even when the temperature dropped to forty-five below with a stiff north wind. On that occasion, Almanzo told her that he had been hesitating, standing beside his horses at a hitching post in De Smet, when Cap Garland passed by, gave him a glance, and said, "God hates a coward."[131] For her part, Laura was undeterred by the weather, telling Louis Bouchie that she would go "if I froze for it."[132] She was so stiff by the end of the drive that her mother had to pry her out of the sleigh.

Aside from the shenanigans at the Masterses' notorious hotel, this was perhaps the first opportunity Laura had ever had to measure her parents' calm and loving union against another kind of marriage, and her relief at escaping the Bouchies' grim home was palpable. But grateful as she was for the weekend reprieves, she finally warned Almanzo that her motives in accepting his services were purely selfish, not romantic, and that he need not return if he was expecting anything. In his laconic fashion, he acknowledged the caveat and kept on coming.

After coping with Eliza Jane's vapid manners, he may have found Laura refreshingly blunt.

When Laura consulted her father about the troublesome Clarence, he gave her good advice. "Better just manage!" he said, since she was too short to whip the boy.[133] And she did: her skills in juggling her school rivals served her well. She shamed Clarence into doing his school-work by pityingly assigning him easier lessons, asking if they were too long for him to handle. To prove her wrong, he was soon asking for more challenging fare. He began sharpening her pencils and helping her stoke the fire.

Back at the Bouchies', Laura was counting the days left in the school term when a sinister confrontation played out. Asleep on the couch one night, she was awoken by Liv Bouchie screaming, accusing Louis of kicking her. Peering through a crack in the curtains, she saw the woman standing poised over her husband, a butcher knife in her hand. Laura could tell that he was bracing himself when Mrs. Bouchie turned and took the knife back to the kitchen, continuing her angry mutter-ing. Laura could not sleep for the rest of the night. She never told her parents what transpired, wanting to finish her contract.[134]

Like any fickle sixteen-year-old, Laura cast an eye around her social circle. She was interested in a number of boys, especially Cap Garland; but when Cap asked her to go sleighing one day that winter, she found she didn't want to "make the change."[135] She kept on seeing Manly, as she decided to call him. For his part, Almanzo called her Bessie, to avoid confusion with his eldest sister, Laura Wilder Howard.

In April, Laura somehow found time to participate in the School Exhibition, an extravagant performance of "readings, recitations, declamations, dialogues, personations, songs and choruses" held at the De Smet church building.[136] Laura and her friend Ida (the adopted daughter of Reverend Brown, who had lost her parents in the great Chicago fire) memorized much of American history for the occasion, "dates and names and all important events." These they recited before a paying public, the proceeds going to buy school furnishings. The *De Smet Leader* called it "one of the finest entertainments of the sea-son."[137] Afterwards, Laura's teacher, Ven Owen, told her father that she "had a wonderful mind and memory and ought to be given every chance for an education."[138]

It was an enlightened position for the time. Women in Dakota Territory had been granted the right to vote in school elections just the previous year, and politicians and editorialists were hashing over the question of women's suffrage. The Reverend Brown and his wife were active in the Woman's Christian Temperance Union, a key suffrage supporter in the Territory; Laura was invited to meetings at their house, but disliked the reverend so strongly that she refused to attend, despite her fondness for Ida.[139] She recorded no schoolgirl conversations about the rights of women. But after Ven Owen recognized her ability, she gained a new self-assurance. Her goal was to graduate from high school.

As soon as her two months at the Bouchie school were over, Laura immediately accepted another assignment, taking on the Perry school for the 1884 spring term. With just three very young pupils, it was easy and pleasant compared to her first teaching job. The school was a relaxing walk from her home, taking her past her favorite violet-scented meadow. On Saturdays, she visited Ida, strolling with her across the countryside and enjoying the views of the Wessington Hills.

Almanzo made it a habit that summer to swing by Laura's house in his new buggy, with a pair of fine matched horses. She had a "homelike feeling" when she was with him, after all they had been through: "blizzards, near-murder and danger of death."[140] He drove her around Lakes Henry and Thompson and north to Spirit Lake, dark blue glacial pools that stood out vividly against the green or sere grasses of the high prairie flatlands. They gathered prairie roses by the armful.

In July, Almanzo sped up to her homestead with a wild new team, Barnum and Skip, who tended to bolt and run. She leapt into the buggy as the horses reared before dashing off. They rode in circles around the Fourth of July festivities, Laura dressed in a fine new flowered-lawn dress, pale pink with blue and rose flowers, the horses too rambunctious to risk driving them among the crowd and the fireworks. Cautioned against trusting Almanzo at the reins, she replied, "If the driver fails me, I can do the driving myself."[141]

The courtship was marred only by an interlude in which Almanzo invited another girl, Stella Gilbert, to accompany them on their drives. But Laura soon put a stop to it, managing her beau as handily as she had managed Clarence. She found Gilbert, her final schoolgirl rival, a smug, scheming character who had played on Almanzo's sympathies. After a few shared drives, Laura made him choose: Stella or her. The other girl was not mentioned again.

It was a tumultuous season, the summer of 1884. There were tornadoes, wind storms, electrical storms, and waterspouts. In town, the unfinished Catholic church was lifted off its foundations and dropped on its side. One day, she wrote, "we thought all De Smet was blowing away," and she watched as the wind bent her father's cottonwoods "nearly flat to the ground."[142] They survived.

Almanzo had once told Laura that she was just like her father, ready with a song for every occasion, a compliment she treasured. That fall, the couple attended "singing school," a trend at the time, considered a wholesome way for young people to spend time with each other. They often left early, to keep the frisky horses away from the crowd. Soon, Almanzo had sold Barnum, buying a quieter team and a new buggy. On one long drive home, he fell silent as she sang, "In the starlight, in the starlight, / We will wander gay and free."

He asked whether she might accept an engagement ring, and she said her answer would depend on who was offering. Would she take it from him? he asked, and she said, "Yes!"[143] She was seventeen.

LAURA was wearing Almanzo's pearl and garnet engagement ring when he and Royal set off in November, planning to head south to New Orleans, sell notions out of a wagon, and attend the 1884 World's Fair. They were to return in the spring, in time for planting. Laura found it lonesome with her fiancé gone, but set about studying, hoping to graduate the following year.

Her father sent the Wilder boys a funny, avuncular letter, showing how close they had grown. The specter of the hard winter of 1880 still haunted him. "I wish that I was with you and getting south as far as you are," he wrote, describing a storm on the way:

Last Sunday was a bad day here cold and it blowed so hard that my
back hair is all loose and it looks [tonight] as though it would be
blown clear off. . . . Now boys don't be discouraged . . . I will send a
dispatch by the wind in your direction so you will know what we
poor mortals up here in Dakota are getting.[144]

Look for good land, he urged them, "far enough south to be out of the
blizzards." He was getting tired "of watching the northwest and then
looking every building over to see if it is airtight."

The Ingallses stayed on the homestead that winter, and on a Sunday
night in December, a few days before Christmas, Laura was "feeling
blue."[145] Letters had crossed in the mail, and she had just received one
from her betrothed complaining that she hadn't written. Hearing a
knock at the door, she found Almanzo in the flesh, covered in snow. He
kissed her in front of her family, and told her he couldn't stay away all
winter. He and Royal had only made it as far as their parents' house in
Spring Valley, Minnesota. His romantic surprise return—he gave her a
beautiful gold bar-pin for Christmas—seems to have sealed the bond
between them, a highlight of their courtship.

To her lasting regret, she would never graduate from the new brick
schoolhouse that De Smet dedicated on January 1, 1885. Since she was
ahead of the other students, Ven Owen had held her back, intending
for the class to finish together. But that spring she chose to teach again,
signing up for the Wilkin school, several miles from De Smet.[146] Once
again Almanzo ferried her to and from her parents' house on the weekends. For the first time, she would keep her earnings.

She dreaded going to live with strangers once again, but the term
went smoothly. She boarded with Florence Wilkin, a friend and schoolmate. The most dramatic event occurred when a prairie fire swept past
one evening. Beating the flames with wet gunny sacks, Laura and Florence helped fight throughout the night to keep the house and school
from catching fire, a battle that left Laura exhausted and delirious.[147]

Later that summer, having spent months working on a house for his
bride on his tree claim, Almanzo heard that his mother and Eliza Jane
were planning a church wedding, a large affair that filled him with
unease. He told his betrothed that he couldn't afford such a lavish

affair, and Laura—with what satisfaction at frustrating Eliza Jane's intentions can only be inferred—agreed to a quiet ceremony at her friend Ida Brown's house, presided over by Reverend Brown.

The rough pastor had agreed not to ask Laura to obey her husband. Dressed in her finest, a black cashmere dress buttoned down the front with imitation jet buttons, Laura married Almanzo at eleven o'clock on the morning of August 25, 1885, in the parlor, with Ida and her fiancé standing by as witnesses. The newly married couple returned to her parents' house for a celebratory midday meal. And then—"with good wishes from the folks and a few tears"—they climbed back into Almanzo's buggy and drove away.[148]

Laura Ingalls's childhood was over. Her early life had engendered intense loyalty to her family, a love of the open prairies, and a resentment of authority, tempered by a deep appreciation of kindness and helpfulness in others. Based on her parents' example, she thought she knew how to handle both hard work and hardship.

But the life experience she drew on—the model provided by her parents—was complex, comprised of equal parts recklessness and passivity. While the family had weathered disaster after disaster, their lives never attained true security. Rarely was there foresight or planning. Their lives were balanced on edge, constantly uprooted and often imperiled. At many junctures, catastrophe was barely averted, and the children were often made aware of their poverty. That was hardly unusual for the time, but Laura's response was. She seemed always ready to seize control from parents, siblings, or rivals to right herself, correct injustice, and show others how to behave.

Her memoir of her girlhood would end on a hopeful note. At the freshly constructed house on Almanzo's tree claim, she described herself as "a little awed by my new estate." It was an interesting choice of words, *estate* suggesting a momentary sense of landed property, of wealth. Marriage, in those days, offered women one of their few avenues to prosperity, and it could itself be an expression of ambition. Laura was clearly proud of marrying the town hero, the man who had saved its citizens. Nearing the close of this accounting of her life, she also expressed pride in her work, in the money she had earned, and in her trousseau, fondly remembering each of her four dresses.

She was especially happy, she concluded, at never again having to "go and live with strangers in their houses."[149] Looking back over a childhood of instability, from Indian threats in Kansas to locust plagues in Minnesota to the nightmarish interlude at the Bouchies', she hit upon a final line that summed up a sunny confidence in the future: "I had a house and a home of my own."[150]

But on the back of one of the last pages of her memoir, she wrote two sentences that floated free of the larger text, an allusion to the fact that—unbeknownst to her at the time—there was a heavy debt on the new house. It was "nobody's fault," she wrote, "and is another story anyway."[151] The faintest shadow cast by hindsight, those words offered an ominous hint that perhaps not all would go well with the newlyweds in their hard-won home.

Chapter 5

Don't Leave the Farm, Boys

Two People Thoroughly in Sympathy

By the time she was eighteen, Laura Ingalls had walked away from at least a dozen homes: the house in Wisconsin, the house in Kansas, the house on Plum Creek; hotels, apartments, and rented or borrowed houses in Missouri, Burr Oak, and Walnut Grove; the claim shanty and the surveyors' house on Silver Lake, the buildings Charles built in De Smet, and the shanty on their homestead just south of it.

When she married Almanzo Wilder, she moved into the house he built for her on his tree claim. Barely completed, it was the first she had ever owned. Judging by the effort and expense put into it, it was meant to be permanent. "It was a very bright and shining little house and it was really all [ours]," she wrote.[1] It would be the house she never got over.

Wilder described it on several occasions, with mingled nostalgia, pride, and defeat. From those descriptions, it was nothing like the drafty, cramped, thin-walled, tar-paper-covered shacks that typified homestead dwellings at the time. Handsomely and solidly built, it had three rooms, with a lean-to sheltering the back entrance. The front door opened onto a main room that served as both dining and sitting room, and there were doors to a bedroom and a kitchen. The walls had been finished in white plaster, and the pine floors in the main room and pantry were painted a "bright clean yellow" while freshly oiled wood-work throughout the rest of the house preserved the natural hue.[2] A glass-lamp with "glittering pendants" hung above a sitting area fur-nished with an upholstered armchair, rocking chair, and side table. The moment Laura saw this tableau, she imagined placing her volumes of Scott's and Tennyson's poems on the table, to make it "complete."[3] The bedroom was small, but to her surprise there was a carpet on the floor, with a curtained alcove and cunning hooks for clothes.

The crowning glory was the pantry. Almanzo had hired a skilled elderly carpenter to design and install built-in cabinets against an entire wall. It was a "labor of love," Laura said. The beautifully fitted drawers and shelves were as "well made and fitted as boughten furniture," with separate drawers for white flour, graham flour, and corn meal, white and brown sugar, and a specially sized bin meant to hold a baking of bread.[4] Another drawer held Almanzo's wedding gift: silver knives, forks, and spoons. Laura was proud of them, she wrote later.[5] Oppo-site the cabinets, a wide shelf under the kitchen window would serve as her work space, with a view of a young cottonwood tree and the prai-rie beyond.

In each of the descriptions Wilder wrote, she walked herself through the house as if for the first time, "with all the pride of posses-sion," reliving her delight in the pantry, noting the thoughtful touches that her husband had provided. Even though the house had been fin-ished only days before their wedding, its windows still begrimed with plaster when they moved in, he had decorated the shelves with his dishes and stocked the pantry with bread, pie, and a cake baked by a neighbor, to make it feel like home.

By her account, the young couple's first year together was a magical one, busy but happy. Almanzo finished breaking sod on his land. Laura was learning how to handle on her own all the chores—"cooking, bak-ing, churning, sweeping, washing, ironing and mending"—she had once shared with her mother and sisters.[6]

She was small, standing just under five feet, and found washing clothes particularly exhausting, doubly so when it came to wielding the heavy cast-iron clothes iron that had to be heated on top of the stove. Painstakingly, she had to learn how to cook by herself and, sometimes, for a crowd. On one humiliating occasion, she fixed a noontime dinner for a team of threshers on hand to harvest wheat that first summer. Flustered by her responsibilities, she failed to cook the beans long enough and forgot to put sugar in what turned out to be a very sour rhubarb pie.

Other than such difficulties, it was a blissful time. Almanzo bought a gentle riding pony for Laura and a saddle pony for himself, named Trixy and Fly. Always confident with horses, he told her, "Don't let me hear any more about your father not letting you learn to ride."[7] She ordered a beautiful tan leather saddle with nickel trimmings from the Montgomery Ward's catalogue. When it arrived, Almanzo showed her how to ride side-saddle, setting her to learn on plowed ground, a soft landing if she fell.

Throughout the rest of their first summer, they resumed the buggy rides of their courtship. By fall they were riding horseback across the prairie, teaching the horses to lope, foxtrot, and jump. Sometimes they did twenty miles before breakfast. Laura delighted in racing her husband and beating him: Trixy was the faster pony. "It was a carefree, happy time[,] for two people thoroughly in sympathy can do pretty much as they like," she wrote.[8] It was the closest she ever came to saying they were in love.

IN a later manuscript about her early married life, which she never sought to publish, Wilder allowed a tiny cloud into the picture. She was worried about money.

Though they were only dimly aware of it at the time, the Wilders were facing the same bleak reality as farmers all across the Plains. The economics were punishing, with bankers refusing to lend to bad risks and farmers unable to borrow money at affordable rates to ride out hard times. The Wilders' costs and debts as Laura recorded them may seem vanishingly small from a modern perspective, but those debts were every bit as haunting to them as those that destroyed lives in the Victorian novels of Charles Dickens or Victor Hugo. In the nineteenth century, before government price supports and modern lending practices, ruination was always just around the corner. It took only two or three years of bad crops to bring most homesteaders to the brink of bankruptcy.[9]

Years later, struggling to explain the financial bind that kept him from getting ahead, Almanzo Wilder enumerated as an example the costs he incurred shortly before his marriage. Before he owned a mowing machine, he had to pay threshers and hire workers to cut his hay and wheat. After selling ninety-five bushels of wheat and setting another eighty aside for seed, he had "a little over $40 to live on for another year."[10] At a time when an unskilled laborer could expect to make more than four hundred dollars a year, this was unsustainable.[11]

The Wilders' first wheat crop was worryingly "short."[12] Hay and oats had done well, yielding plenty to feed the horses, but the wheat had come in at only ten bushels to the acre. The weather had been, Laura acknowledged, very dry.

Bills were mounting up. In addition to the saddle ponies, Almanzo had bought another team; he was eager to clear a fifty-acre field, potentially doubling their crop yield for the following year. Four large horses would enable him to handle the "sulky" plow he'd bought, a riding plow capable of turning a wide, sixteen-inch furrow. He paid fifty-five dollars for the plow, half cash down, half to be paid later. He bought a mowing machine and a hay rake, also on credit. Out back of the house, he built a large barn to store hay and house the livestock. Concerned about the bills, Laura gave her husband butter and eggs to sell in town, but with every nearby farm producing their own there was no market for such items. "Why worry," she concluded. "Manly didn't."[13]

And she herself felt "quite rich" once she was paid the remaining thirty dollars owed for teaching her last term at the Wilkin school.[14] On Almanzo's advice, she bought a two-year-old colt, an investment to be sold when he was grown. For their first Christmas together, they chose a gift for themselves from Montgomery Ward, a set of glassware dishes. There was a butter dish, a sugar bowl, a spoon holder, six small plates, and a large oval bread plate inscribed around the rim with the beginning of the Lord's prayer: "Give us this day our daily bread."

They passed their first winter together, much alone, with little visiting due to cold short days and the occasional blizzard. By the spring of

1886, Almanzo was preparing to sow a hundred acres in wheat at the tree claim, as well as fifty acres of oats at the homestead.

He was perhaps basing his expectations on what he knew of his father's successful enterprises in New York and Minnesota, anticipating that a well-run farm, after an investment of hard labor and cash outlay on machinery, could begin to yield dividends almost immediately. After all, the Chicago & North Western promotional brochures told of farmers who paid off debts in the profit earned in a single year.[15] He had good reason to be hopeful: the weather that spring was fine, raining often, and their hundred acres seemed poised to yield forty bushels to the acre of Number 1 hard wheat. At seventy-five cents a bushel, the wheat alone promised to bring in three thousand dollars.

Meanwhile, the notes on farm machinery bought the previous year were coming due. Money was so tight that Almanzo was forced to take out a "chattel mortgage" on his team of working horses, something Laura found deeply distressing. She wrote that she would almost as soon have a mortgage on her husband.

After a mere eight months, their honeymoon was over. In April 1886, at nineteen, Laura became pregnant, suffering considerably from morning sickness. The smell of cooking made her nauseous, and she fainted so often that soon she was merely "creeping" around the house, trying to finish chores while lying down whenever she had the chance. She recalled a proverb her mother used to cite: "They that dance must pay the fiddler."[16] Unable to keep anything down, she lost weight.

By June, however, she was feeling better, able to ride out in the buggy with Almanzo to see the prairie roses in bloom, scenting the air and covering the plains with "glowing masses of color from pale pink to deepest red."[17] Discussing names for the baby on one ride, she told Almanzo that she knew it was a girl, "and we will call her Rose."[18]

The crops looked promising that summer, and they seemed certain to cover their considerable debts. Although precipitation was below average, their spring wheat grew so luxuriant that Almanzo bought a new McCormick binder for two hundred dollars, taking out another chattel mortgage to cover it, this time on their cattle. He planned to pay half the debt when the crop was threshed, the rest the following year. At the time, Dakota farmers were on a spending spree, buying train cars full of plows, seeders, and binders—buoyed by record wheat harvests in 1882, when they'd planted 720,000 acres, and 1884, when a whopping 1.5 million acres had been planted, a feat made possible by the rush to mechanization.[19] The agricultural press urged farmers to be wary of going into debt for machinery, but many believed that the next good harvest would make them whole.

Sometime that summer, Almanzo cut the oats but hesitated on the wheat, not wanting to risk harvesting before the grains fully ripened. The delay proved catastrophic. On one stifling afternoon, the sky darkened. Thunderheads built up, and it began hailing, the lumps of ice so large that Laura compared them to hens' eggs. In twenty minutes, the hail destroyed the wheat, along with the Wilders' hopes and plans.

They were not alone in their difficulties. Farmers had sown a record 2.6 million acres in 1886, but production was down due to fickle weather and localized droughts, which could devastate a farm even while leaving its neighbors unaffected. The governor of Dakota Territory had to admit that "the year has not been altogether as prosperous as desired."[20]

Expecting their first child in December, the Wilders now found themselves in financial straits. Notes on the farm machinery were due, and they needed to buy coal for the winter and seed wheat for next year's crop. It was at this moment that Almanzo revealed to his wife the debt on their new house: an additional five hundred dollars that she had not known about. That was a small fortune to them, worth over thirteen thousand dollars today. Laura was crushed by the news.

The fact that her husband had kept this debt from her—he hadn't wanted to bother her with it, he said—comes up again and again in Wilder's drafts and letters. It affected her deeply and for many years. It still rankled when she was writing her memoir, *Pioneer Girl*, in 1930: "I was to learn that we owed $500 on the house, which we were never able to pay until we sold the farm."[21] In her manuscript from several years later she was even more pointed, squarely placing the blame on her husband, and saying she had started to wonder "how much could she depend on Manly's judgment."[22]

The debts left them little choice but to rent out their new house and move into the much smaller and less comfortable claim shanty on the homestead. They couldn't mortgage the house on the tree claim because they didn't own that land: Almanzo still had to prove up on it. But they did own the homestead. Almanzo mortgaged it for eight hundred dollars, enough to pay for the winter's coal and next year's seed and to cover the interest on the farm machinery loans, extending them by an additional year. On August 25, 1886, their first anniversary, they moved.

They were now living in a single room, twelve by sixteen feet, with their kitchen, bedroom, and sitting room furniture arrayed in different corners. Here, Laura's experience in little-house living stood her in good stead. "It was all very snug and pleasant," she wrote, determinedly cheerful, saying she admired the view from their single window, which looked out on a "sweep of unbroken prairie with the wild grasses waving in the winds."[23]

Knowing she would be confined indoors once the baby arrived she spent as much time as she could outside that fall. She helped Almanzo harvest wild hay, trampling down the grass as he pitched it into the wagon and then standing atop the load until, back at the barn, she slid down the haystack into his arms. When the snow came, he built her a sled and a harness for their sheepdog, Old Shep; she spent her free time outside in the fresh air, sliding down the hill to the road and letting the dog pull the sled back up again. Despite all the sober calculations of money and marriage and debt, she was, after all, a teenager, and loved nothing more than sledding and sleighing and the exhilaration of wild open spaces.

It was at the claim shanty, during a snowstorm on the night of December 5, 1886—or early the following day—that their first child was born.[24] The difficult delivery was attended by her mother, a midwife, and a local physician. Laura's impressionistic account captured hours of listless discomfort, pain, and hazy confusion until the doctor arrived with chloroform or ether. "Borne away on a wave of pain," she recalled a hymn her father used to sing:

Oh, come, angel band,
Come and around me stand;
Oh, bear me away on your snowy wings

To my eternal home;
Oh, bear me away on your snowy wings
To my eternal home.[25]

Her prediction proved correct: the child, a healthy eight-pound baby, was a girl. And they did name her, quite simply, Rose.[26]

One Awful Day

That Christmas, as a gift for his family, Almanzo traded a load of hay in town for a carved walnut clock, its glass door "wreathed with a gilt vine" festooned with four gilt birds.[27] Wilder wrote that she "loved it at once" but wondered at the expense.[28]

In January, two of Laura's "double cousins" arrived, staying with the Ingallses in De Smet. Ella, the eldest offspring of Peter and Eliza Ingalls, was now married, traveling with her husband and two-year-old son, while Peter Franklin Ingalls, only a few months older than Laura, was still single. Ella and her family visited for two weeks, with everyone admiring the children. Grace, who began keeping a diary in a school exercise book for the new year, wrote on January 12 that Rose was just beginning to smile.[29] When Ella left, cousin Peter stayed on, soon becoming an integral part of Laura and Almanzo's household.

The Wilders were barely scraping by. The justice's docket for Kingsbury County recorded a summons issued to A. J. Wilder on February 8, 1887, the day after his wife's birthday.[30] He was being sued by Harthorn & Son, known as the Red Front Store for the color of its façade, for nine dollars owed for goods and merchandise.

The sum may seem minuscule, but when inflation is taken into account it's equivalent to almost two hundred and fifty dollars today. On February 12 Almanzo appeared in court, paying the debt and additional court costs. Whether she was unaware of this, did not recall it, or was merely ashamed, Laura never mentioned the incident. To add to the humiliation, the justice of the peace who recorded the summons was Willard Seelye, the teacher Laura had once tormented. Grace Ingalls recorded that, on the day the summons was delivered, her father was working as deputy sheriff.[31] Whether or not Charles had to summon his son-in-law to court, the suit could only have heightened the tension of the Wilders' debt burden.

Two disturbing events involving Rose took place that winter, which her mother recalled with some chagrin. On one occasion, the Wilders, suffering from cabin fever during a cold snap, decided to take Rose out to see Laura's parents. They stowed their bundled baby behind the dashboard, out of the wind, and rode their sleigh to the Ingallses' house, only to be greeted with dismay by Charles and Caroline, who chided them for venturing abroad with an infant when it was fifteen below zero. "You're crazy!" Laura remembered her father saying.[32] She assured readers that she took care to check on Rose every few minutes to make sure she was warm. But she also admitted: "It seemed there was a good deal to taking care of babies."[33]

The anecdote reflected the harsh reality of Western settlement. The frontier presented grave hazards to all, but especially to children. The record abounds in tales of what one scholar termed "improvisation," if not incompetence, in child-rearing.[34] Babies were kept in drawers and shoeboxes, parked on the open door of ovens to keep warm, and imperiled by all manner of accidents as their mothers tried to cope with competing responsibilities. Parents found it nearly impossible "to give children even minimal care," one historian wrote. "Women worried all the time . . . nearly frantic because it was so difficult."[35]

On a warmer afternoon, the Wilders drove to visit old family friends, the Boasts, who were living alone on their homestead. Wilder never wrote of it, but Ella Boast suffered from severe arthritis and was eventually confined to a wheelchair. Fond of children, she was known for holding parties for the neighborhood.

On this occasion, after their visit, Robert Boast followed Laura and Almanzo to their buggy and made a startling proposition: if the Wilders surrendered their infant, allowing his wife to raise the baby as her own, they could select the finest horse from his stable. He justified the proposal, miserably enough, by saying that the younger couple could have another child, while his wife could not.[36] The Wilders were as shocked as Laura had been years earlier in Burr Oak, when the doctor's wife offered to adopt her. They declined and drove away.

The spring and summer of their second full planting season began with promise. On June 17, 1887, Almanzo finally completed the patent paperwork on his homestead, endorsed in the name of President Cleveland.[37] (He had proved up on the homestead in 1884, but perhaps had not gotten around to attending to the details during his courtship.) The couple enjoyed working outside on their newly secured property, with Rose sleeping in a basket nearby, watched over by a protective Saint Bernard who had arrived unannounced and put himself to work.

But one Sunday in July, when Almanzo went to visit a neighbor, their barn and haystacks caught fire and burned. The blaze was visible all the way from town.[38] It was another setback, and the harvest was a disappointment, with wheat prices lower than expected and the Wilders' wheat field producing less than anticipated. Once again, Wilder wrote, it had been "too dry."[39] Precipitation for the region was actually above average that year, but it could vary over localized areas, and there may have been residual effects from previous years' drought.[40]

Meanwhile, interest kept accruing on their various outstanding debts: the eight-hundred-dollar mortgage on the homestead, five hundred dollars on the tree claim house, and all the farm machinery bought on credit. Along with many others in Dakota Territory, the Wilders were beginning to realize that the paradise promised by the railroads might be a mirage—the kind of cruel, shimmering illusion of water where there is no water that recedes endlessly before those stranded in the desert.

In the summer of 1887, just as the Wilders were reeling at yet another poor harvest, Hamlin Garland came home to Dakota Territory to find his parents mired in the same bleak situation.

Garland's experience parallels the life of Laura Ingalls to an astonishing degree. Born in Wisconsin in 1860, he spent his first years in a "rude little cabin" in a tiny Wisconsin hamlet near the Mississippi River, sixty miles south of Pepin.[41] His mother, too, had wanted to stay in Wisconsin while his father yearned for better land. When he was nine, his family moved to Iowa and cleared a farm in Burr Oak Township. They were living there in 1877, when the Ingalls family spent their own squalid year in Burr Oak. In 1881, after chinch bugs descended on their fields, the Garlands moved to Dakota Territory, lured by the same Chicago & North Western Railway promotions that drew settlers to De Smet. The Garlands filed on homestead land and a tree claim in Ordway, a settlement near Aberdeen, less than a hundred miles north of the Wilders.

Like Laura Ingalls, as a child Garland had been enthralled by his father's stories, "delightful tales of wolves and bears and Indians."[42] He had watched bemused as his mother gave bread and meat to friendly "red neighbor[s]," rejoicing that there was no need to venture farther west, to be "surrounded by Indians who murder by night."[43] He and his siblings loved fiddle tunes: both his mother and uncle played the violin, regaling the family with "Money Musk" and "The Devil's Dream."[44] He read *Godey's Lady's Book* and serials in the *New York World*; he recited the same speech of Regulus from the same readers the Ingalls girls studied. And just as the Ingallses passed through the crucible of Mary's illness, so Hamlin Garland watched as his beloved older sister, Harriet, fell ill of a "wasting fever"—typhoid pneumonia—and died at seventeen.[45]

Nearly grown when his family moved to the Dakotas, Garland also served time as a Plains schoolteacher. And he spent a miserable year, 1883, on his own preemption claim near his parents. "The winds were hot and dry and the grass, baked on the stem, had become as inflammable as hay," he wrote later.[46] "The birds were silent. The sky, absolutely cloudless, began to scare us with its light." He found blizzards equally eerie: "All was unreal, ghastly. No sky but a formless, impenetrable mass of flying snow; no earth except when a sweeping gust laid bare a long streak of blackened sod that had the effect, the terrifying effect, of a hollow, fathomless trough between the hissing waves."[47] Soon he escaped to Boston, determined never again to live on the plains.

But in 1887, worried about his parents, Garland returned for a visit. He was horrified to find his once spirited mother wasting away, "imprisoned in a small cabin on the enormous sunburned, treeless plain, with no expectation of ever living anywhere else."[48] He was powerless to help her or to lift her out of "helpless and sterile poverty"; indeed, he had to work for weeks stacking hay just to earn enough to buy a rail ticket back to Boston. In literary revenge, he bitterly recorded "the ugliness, the endless drudgery, and the loneliness of the farmer's lot."[49] The experience would turn him into a "militant reformer," becoming the raw material of his first work of fiction.

Yet he too was beguiled by the beauty of the land. In thrall to the same infatuation as Willa Cather and Laura Ingalls Wilder, he could not forget "the endless stretches of short, dry grass, the gorgeous colors of the dawn, the marvelous, shifting, phantom lakes and headlands, the violet sunset afterglow."[50] Wherever they went, these troubadours of the prairie carried it with them.

WHEN election time rolled around on November 8, 1887, Charles Ingalls was sworn in as a judge administering the ballot. The seventy-two male voters in De Smet—C. P. Ingalls, A. J. Wilder, and R. G. Wilder among them—could express their opinion on two ballot initiatives. The first asked voters to declare themselves for or against the sale of "intoxicating liquors." The second regarded the division of Dakota Territory into two entities, a political maneuver (the Republican Party was eager to increase its representation in the Senate) that was a prerequisite to application for statehood.

Proud of their home and eager to join the rest of the country on an equal basis, De Smet voters unanimously supported territorial division. Sixty-eight of them opposed liquor sales. Thomas Power—the tailor who once reduced Laura to helpless laughter with his "I'm T. P. Power and I'm drunk" spectacle—did not vote.

On Christmas Eve, Charles Ingalls moved his familiy—Carrie now seventeen, Grace ten—into De Smet. They would never return permanently to the homestead. After seven years of laboring to make the land pay, Charles's lifelong dream of raising a self-sustaining farm out of the prairie soil was at an end. His health may have been a factor: earlier that year, he had been ill for some time, requiring the care of a doctor.[51] He turned his attention to work on the De Smet Township Board of Supervisors and other town affairs.

For the Wilders, Christmas brought fresh expenditures, with Almanzo purchasing a new hard-coal heater for the claim shanty. Again, Laura wondered at the expense, but said nothing. "That was Manly's business," she wrote years later.[52] Rose was beginning to crawl around on the floor, and Laura had noticed that her husband suffered sharply from the cold. It was a condition worsened by his previous brushes with frostbite, including perhaps on the famous 1881 drive with Cap Garland to find wheat for the snowbound town.

On February 7, 1888, Laura turned twenty-one. Almanzo's birthday (his twenty-ninth or thirty-first, depending on which birth date one believes for him) came a few days later. As a birthday treat for him, Laura invited over for dinner her cousin Peter and the neighbors he worked for, the Whiteheads, who lived a few miles north of their homestead. The dinner was a "great success," but afterward Laura fell ill with what she initially thought was a severe cold.[53]

In fact, it was diphtheria, an illness with a deservedly dire reputation at the time, especially when it came to children. The Ingallses' former home, Walnut Grove, Minnesota, suffered a severe outbreak between 1878 and 1884 that left seventy-seven children dead.[54] A bacterial infection, diphtheria usually appears as an upper respiratory illness, with sore throat and low-grade fever, but it can also produce more unusual symptoms. In severe cases, lymph nodes swell, causing difficulty breathing. A white membrane may form in the throat, producing a pronounced barking cough and blocking the airway. In the worst cases, a toxin appears in the blood, spreading throughout the body and potentially causing organ or nerve damage, heart or kidney failure, or paralysis. In the nineteenth century, before effective antibiotics were discovered and a vaccine developed for diphtheria, up to half of those infected died.

The moment Laura was diagnosed, the Wilders sent Rose to stay with Laura's parents in town, hoping she had not been infected. Delighted to play with her young niece, Grace praised her in her diary: "She is the best girl I ever saw. She can now say a good many words such as gramma and grampa and bread and butter and cracker."[55]

Laura's case was severe, and Almanzo cared for her until he too came down with the illness. Royal Wilder arrived to nurse them but grew ill and exhausted himself; eventually he was forced to leave them on their own. Slowly, they began to recover. A month after they fell ill, the local newspaper reported that "Mr. and Mrs. Manly Wilder are doing nicely under the care of Dr. Cushman. Are up and around."[56]

As they recuperated, under strict orders not to overexert themselves, they began to resume their routine. The baby returned to the house. During her time away she had learned how to walk and, her mother recalled, seemed "much older."[57] Fifteen months old at the time, Rose would later claim to recall her brief exile, to remember hearing the word "diff-theer-eeah; a hard word and dreadful . . . big and black and it meant that I might never see my father and mother again."[58]

Their lives appeared to be returning to normal. Then, one cold morning, Almanzo stumbled getting out of bed. His legs were numb to the hips.

After a great deal of massaging, he was able to limp to the wagon with Laura's help, driving into De Smet to see the doctor. The diagnosis was "'a slight stroke of paralysis' . . . from overexertion too soon after the diphtheria."[59] His hands and feet were both seriously affected. Laura's notes on the time fixed on the fact that her young, vigorous, capable husband, the man who once saved the town, could not even hitch up his own horses.

Almanzo never said much about his illness. Existing accounts—by his wife and his daughter—stress his responsibility for it, as if the stroke were his fault. In her manuscript about their early marriage, Wilder bluntly asserted: "Manly—disregarding the doctor's warning— had worked too hard."[60] From that day forward, she wrote, "there was a struggle to keep his legs so that he could use them," hesitating to acknowledge that in fact he could barely walk.[61] She could not quite bring herself to admit it, but their lives would forever after be circumscribed by his condition.

Her matter-of-fact manner concealed what must have been overwhelming fear, dismay, and grief. At the age of twelve, she had been tasked with caring for her blind sister, a responsibility she left behind when she married. Her shock at realizing, if only gradually, that she would have to once again assume the role of caretaker (and even breadwinner) may ultimately have led to a buried sense of bitterness, expressed in a general resentment of those she called "shirkers."

The Wilders were faced with an immediate crisis, an "emergency," as Laura put it.[62] On top of their existing debt, doctors' bills had exhausted whatever cash they had on hand. Almanzo, in his current state, could not manage two properties. The tree claim was not yet theirs to sell, but the homestead was.

They soon found a buyer, who paid them two hundred dollars for it and assumed responsibility for the substantial mortgage. In the spring they moved back to their comfortable house on the tree claim, where Almanzo found it easier to walk across the flatter, more level ground. During the coming months, he would be forced to avoid obstacles as trivial as a board lying in his way, stumbling and falling if he stubbed a toe. His hands remained too clumsy for fine work, and Laura continued to hitch up the horses.

Around that time, Charles and Caroline Ingalls took out a substantial loan from Dakota Loan & Investment against their homestead property, for seven hundred and sixty dollars at 8 percent interest.[63] It must have been a necessity, but it remains unclear why they borrowed it. Did they help their struggling daughter and son-in-law? Or was it earmarked for further medical treatment for Mary? After recovering from the fever that blinded her she continued to suffer severe pain from neuralgia, and from 1887 to 1888 she stayed home from the Iowa College for the Blind, returning to school the following year.

Once again, as it had year after year since the Wilders' marriage, the harvest failed. The previous renter on the tree claim had plowed before he left, and the wheat the Wilders sowed initially looked promising. Laura yearned to be able to pay off the debts, to be free of the interest payments: if they could harvest and sell the crop, she wrote, "it would mean so much."[64] But the only thing reliable about the weather was its destructiveness. Just as they were getting ready to harvest, hot winds blew for days, desiccating the wheat. They were forced to mow it for feed, along with the hay.

They were cheered, however, by another opportunity. Peter Ingalls learned that his employers, the Whiteheads, perhaps fearing a potential change in America's tariff policy, were considering selling their flock of one hundred Shropshire sheep at two dollars a head. On Almanzo's advice, Laura sold the horse she had bought as an investment, earning a hundred dollars, and she and her cousin went in on the sheep. Peter moved in with them and every morning herded the flock south to a neighboring "school section," publicly owned land set aside as a potential school site, where prairie hay was available to whoever cut it first.

The Wilders found time to enjoy themselves once more, riding Fly and Trixy in the moonlight on the road next to their house after Rose was put to bed, circling back to check on her. Gradually, Almanzo was regaining some mobility and feeling in his hands and feet. He was able to tend the struggling young trees he had planted, while working through chores with Peter's help. He planned to plow more land the next year, and bought a team of oxen to break ground that fall.

That November, Laura was pregnant, suffering miserably again from morning sickness. It was allayed, however, by the kindness of a bachelor neighbor, Ole Sheldon, who knocked at her door one day when she was feeling "particularly blue and unhappy" and dumped on her floor a grain sack full of Sir Walter Scott's Waverley novels.[65]

It was an auspicious gift. The series, named for the first volume, published anonymously in 1814, had launched historical fiction, a genre Wilder would one day make her own. For decades, the books were among the most widely read in the English-speaking world, with towns and streets named Waverley from Nebraska to New Zealand. The collected novels, sold in lavishly illustrated sets of forty-eight volumes, including *Rob Roy*, *The Bride of Lammermoor*, and *Ivanhoe*, seethed with Scottish adventures, from the swashbuckling heroics of the Highlanders to the fevered scheming of Jacobites.

In his zeal to burnish the legends of his native land, Scott could hardly have foreseen that his devoted readers would include a queasy young lass on the Great Plains, but her absorption was a testament to his craft. "It was a long way from . . . Scott's glamorous old tales to the little house on the black, wintry prairie," she wrote.[66] But by the time she finished her Highlands sojourn, she felt fully restored.

THE spring of 1889 brought sinister weather. It was exceptionally dry, with the four-month growing season in the De Smet area producing a mere 8.2 inches of rainfall, less than half of the average precipitation.[67] As it turned out, it was not rain that followed the plow. It was drought.[68]

After years of campaigning, Dakota Territory was giddily anticipating its division into North and South, with statehood to be conferred that November. No one, least of all the Wilders, knew that six Biblically lean years were about to come upon them, with devastating consequences not only for the Dakotas but for everyone in the region of the 100th meridian.

On April 2, just as the Wilders were seeding their fields, a terrific dust storm blew up, so powerful that it knocked the sheep off their feet and rolled them like woolly tops along the ground. Peter and Almanzo labored to herd them into their pen, carrying lambs by hand. Afterward they collapsed in the house, where dust filtered through closed doors and windows, sifting across every surface. They heard later that a prairie fire whipped by sixty-five-mile-per-hour winds had jumped firebreaks, burning miles of prairie, houses, barns, and livestock.[69] The wind had also blown away their own work, as wheat was sown just one or two inches deep. The Wilders had to buy more seed to re-sow the crop.

After shearing the sheep that spring, they made a tidy profit off the wool, which was selling for twenty-five cents a pound, but all of that income went to replacing seed. They had so little money that they were buying food on credit, at 2 percent interest, a source of shame to Laura.[70] She deliberately tried to put it from her mind. It was her husband's business, she decided, "and he wasn't worrying."[71]

At this point in her unpublished manuscript, Wilder, somewhat abashedly, recalled a series of anecdotes about hazardous scrapes that Rose got into in the farmyard and barn, humorous incidents nonetheless edged with peril. Going about her chores cooking and cleaning, Laura tried to keep an eye on the toddler's pink sunbonnet through the open door and windows. Once, missing the sound of her daughter, she ran to the barn to find Rose sitting atop one of the prone workhorses, kicking her heels on its stomach. Another time she watched, terrified, as the riding ponies, chasing each other around the house, jumped over Rose's head when she suddenly appeared.

Laura was unable to maintain her mother's unflappable calm and said she felt "sick" when such things happened, helplessly overwhelmed, particularly at the thought of trying to manage everything once her second child was born. At such moments, she wrote, she "hated the farm . . . the smelly lambs, the cooking of food and the dirty dishes."[72] And especially, she added, the debts.

The Wilders watched, day by day, as their crops failed to thrive yet again. During one bad week, the winds blew so hot Laura compared the sensation to the heat in the oven when she baked bread.[73] By the time the windstorm blew itself out, the ten acres of trees Almanzo had planted were dead. So were the wheat and oats, barely worth mowing for feed.

It was a major setback: it had been nearly ten years since Almanzo had filed on the tree claim, and those acres of trees were required for him to prove up on it. The only other way to retain the land—and the improvements made on it—was to buy it outright, by filing on it as a preemption claim. After that filing, the Wilders would have six months to find two hundred dollars to pay for the acreage.[74]

July brought cyclones, and Laura scanned the sky one afternoon as an ominous funnel began forming out of black clouds to the north. The air turned green, filling with debris as the funnel spun toward her over plowed ground and haystacks. Nine months pregnant by this time, she ran to fetch Rose and hid with her in the cellar space under the house, expecting that any minute the house might explode above her. The twister passed by, however, leaving a few tormenting drops of rain in its wake.

One sultry afternoon, she went into labor. Her mother came, but there was not enough time to fetch the doctor. "There was no merciful chlo[ro]form," Laura wrote, "and the baby weighed 10 lbs."[75] A newspaper announcement concurred, reporting the arrival of a ten-pound baby boy on the night of July 11, 1889.[76]

Wilder's memory became hazy and inconsistent at this point. In later years, she believed her son was born not in July but on August 5. She remembered "many painful days in bed for stitches had to be taken by the Dr. and it was so terribly hot that scalded spots came on Laura's back," perhaps bed sores.[77] She was "proud of the baby," she said, but her tone was remote. She was anxious about Rose, cared for by an "indifferent" hired girl while Laura was confined to bed.[78] She was aware of Peter Ingalls singing as he herded the sheep off in the morning and Rose playing with pet lambs abandoned by their mother. She felt guilty about the hired girl's wages.

A few weeks later, she was up and about, but one day—"one awful day," she wrote, the same expression she had used to mark her baby brother Freddy's death—the infant went into spasms and "died so quickly that the doctor was too late."[79] Again the only clear record appeared in the newspaper, which reported that "Mr. and Mrs. A. J. Wilder's little child died Wednesday evening."[80] No cause of death was given. It was August 7; the baby was not quite a month old. He had never been named. No notation was added to the Ingallses' family Bible. He was buried in the De Smet cemetery as "Infant Wilder."

At ten pounds, the baby could not have been premature. Had he been ill? Was the delay in naming him a result of the length and difficulty of Laura's postpartum recovery? There is no way to know. Whatever the circumstances, the loss was so painful that she and Almanzo never spoke of it. Rose did not learn of her brother's brief existence until she was an adult.[81] The twelve-year-old Grace Ingalls wrote sadly in her diary, "He looked just like Manly."[82]

Then, another disaster. On the afternoon of August 23, two weeks after the death of her son, Laura was building a fire in the kitchen stove, preparing to make supper. She was burning dried slough hay for fuel; Almanzo had left an armful near the stove, then gone off with Peter to work with the horses. Waiting for the stove to heat, Laura went into the other room, closing the door behind her. Minutes later, when she opened it again, the kitchen was engulfed in flames—the ceiling, the wall, the floor.

She had only enough time to throw one bucket of water on the flames before she realized it was hopeless: she couldn't pump fast enough. She snatched the deed box from the bedroom and ran outside with Rose. The child was unharmed, but the skin on the top of Laura's head had been blistered by the heat and her eyes affected by the smoke. "Burying her face on her knees," Wilder wrote, "she screamed and sobbed, saying over and over, 'Oh, what will Manly say to me?'"[83]

Running to help, their neighbor, Ole Sheldon, climbed in through a window and was able to throw out a few of their belongings: some clothes, silverware, and part of their set of Christmas dishes, including the oval glass bread plate with the inscription on the rim. Almanzo arrived just as the roof was falling in.

It was the crowning catastrophe of the first years of their marriage, during which crop failures, drought, and debt had conspired to destroy their foundation for a lasting future. "Something in her seemed to break," Wilder wrote of that moment, years later.[84] Whatever was broken would stay broken. Economically and emotionally, coming so soon after their son's death, it was a blow from which no true recovery was possible.

Rose, nearly three, witnessed it all—the fire, her mother's screams and burns, the loss of everything. The child somehow blamed herself, although not a hint of recrimination comes through in her mother's words. Grace's diary, in an entry made a few days after the fact, supported Laura's account, casting no blame. The trauma of the loss of that little house would echo through Laura's and Almanzo's lives, wreaking immediate changes and leaving intangible scars. Rose, too, would never be the same carefree little girl her mother had described.

Over the following week, Laura retreated with Rose to her parents' home in De Smet, where Laura was made to rest and wear dark glasses. The doctor was concerned that nerves in her eyes had been damaged, a grim reminder of her sister's ordeal.[85] Although Wilder did not stress this in her manuscript, there must have been moments of true despair: she had lost her baby, lost her house, and there must have been, if briefly, a fear that she would lose her sight.

She recovered, however, and the family moved in with Ole Sheldon. Laura cooked and cleaned for the farmer and his bachelor brother in exchange for the use of his rooms, while Almanzo and Peter built a tar-paper shanty on the tree claim. They moved back sometime in September.

And there Wilder left them, in her manuscript about her early married life. After describing the fire, she limped on for a few more pages, trying to find something hopeful, something cheerful to say. She closed with a song: "There is gold in the farm, boys / If only you'll shovel it out."[86]

It was not convincing. The manuscript she left conveys an enduring sense of exhaustion, failure, and regret. As a postscript, she appended a few lines of a poem that aptly captured her feeling about that time.

"But for our blunders, Lord in shame / Before the face of Heaven we fall. / —oh Lord be merciful to me a fool."[87]

As for what was to come: never in her life would she attempt to make sense—or fiction—of the next four years.

Don't Be in a Hurry to Go

On November 17, 1889, Grace Ingalls wrote in her diary that Laura had paid a visit on the weekend and that a decision had been made.[88] The following spring, the Wilders would sell up and go to Spring Valley, Minnesota, where they would stay with Almanzo's parents and try to recuperate from their reversals. "I am so sorry," Grace wrote.[89] Everyone was sorry, but there was little to be done. For the next few years, the Wilders would be landless, if not homeless. They were not the only ones.

By 1889, the Great Dakota Boom had imploded. The beginning of the end came in 1887, according to Gilbert C. Fite, whose comprehensive study of the era remains definitive. "If any life remained," Fite wrote, "it was destroyed by the terrible drought of 1889."[90]

The drought was so severe, the wasting of crops so widespread, that people across the Dakotas faced starvation that winter. Kingsbury County, home of De Smet, as well as Clark County to the north and Miner County to the south were all hard hit. The governor of South Dakota reported that at least six hundred families in Clark and Miner counties, along with a third county to the west, were "almost absolutely destitute."[91]

South Dakota's new constitution forbade the appropriation of public money to provide relief. Nonetheless, the newly created state grew rapidly reliant on charity, falling back on neighboring states, railroads, and charitable organizations to fill the gap. Just as Minnesotans had done during the grasshopper years, South Dakotans accepted coal, food, clothing, and other supplies.[92]

The drought was in large part created by the settlers themselves. The Dakota Boom had upended an ecosystem, with dramatic and near-immediate results. After the rapid removal of bison and the interruption of a fire regime eons in the making, more than two and a half million acres of native grasses had been abruptly cleared and plowed within a decade. This stripped out organic matter available to crops, and had profound effects on temperature and climate.

Weather patterns may be among the most complex phenomena to analyze and explain, but studies have conclusively established that agricultural clearing promotes dryness. Indeed, this has been understood for centuries. In 1809, a Vermont scientist compared the temperature in cleared pastures to neighboring woodlots, finding that "the earth and the air, in cultivated parts of the country, are heated in consequence of their cultivation, ten or eleven degrees more, than they were in their uncultivated state."[93] As a consequence, cleared New England fields were "sunnier, windier, hotter, colder, and drier than they had been in their former state."[94]

There were no cool forests on the Great Plains, but a full suite of diverse native grasses—western wheatgrass, buffalo grass, grama grass, little bluestem—had evolved to shade and enrich the topsoil. Their dense, fibrous roots hosted a wealth of microorganisms and insects, from bacteria to dung beetles, an astonishing subterranean ecosystem as complex as it was fragile. Ecologists have estimated that the mass of tiny, invisible organisms on the plains would outweigh all of its larger species—birds, bison, rattlesnakes, pronghorn—combined.[95]

Without knowing it, Charles Ingalls, Almanzo Wilder, and the other settlers who flooded into the Great Plains in the 1870s tore away those protective grasses and their roots, exposing bare soil to intense heat, evaporation, and drying winds. Wheat is a thirsty crop, and every wheat seed they sowed contributed to the desiccation. A few lucky farmers managed a few good harvests, but it could not last. They had changed the climate, the ecology, and the land itself.

The 1871 ditty "Don't Leave the Farm, Boys," popular during the locust years, was suddenly being sung again, with fresh irony. It appeared in *The Conqueror*, the book used at the singing school that Laura Ingalls attended with her beau. The line that Laura pressed into service to end her manuscript about their first four years came from there:

You talk of the mines of Australia,
They're wealthy in gold without doubt,

But ah! there is gold in the farm, boys,
If only you'll shovel it out. . . .
Better risk the old farm awhile longer,
Don't be in a hurry to go.[96]

Given what was coming, the Wilders were fortunate to get out of farming when they did. That Christmas, Almanzo's parents, James and Angeline Wilder, now in their seventies, came to visit, doubtless commiserating with Almanzo and Laura's troubles and discussing the way forward. Laura left little comment on her in-laws but would later portray them as kind, hard-working, and resolute, possessed of boundless energy and common sense.

In the spring of 1890, Laura and her cousin sold their flock of sheep (its size more than doubled under their care) to a butcher, earning five hundred dollars.[97] Much of Laura's share must have gone to settling debts. On April 17, at the Land Office in Watertown, South Dakota, north of De Smet, Almanzo paid the two hundred dollars that he owed the federal government for the tree claim. One month later, the *De Smet Leader* announced that A. J. Wilder was moving his family to Spring Valley.[98]

They left with Peter Ingalls on Friday, May 30, traveling by covered wagon "to more cheaply transfer their twenty head of stock," the *Leader* reported.[99] "They will have it nice," Grace declared, "two a bed set up all the time in the wagon."[100] By day Laura could ride in comfort on her pony, a break from the jolting wagon. Grace, just turning thirteen, seemed envious of her sister's escape, describing a recent "dredful" sandstorm in De Smet. "It blows, and blows, and blows," she wrote.[101]

IN the 1890s, Spring Valley was a well-established railroad town with a population of 1,500, nearly three times the size of De Smet. Founded in the 1850s, it was soon served by two railroads, boasting half a dozen grain elevators.[102] Fillmore County was a key wheat producer, and the town had multiple grocery, hardware, and butcher shops; a roller grain mill, lumberyard, and cigar factory; two newspapers, four doctors, four

lawyers; a two-story brick schoolhouse, and streets lined with fine
Victorian-style homes.[103]

The pride of Spring Valley was a Methodist-Episcopal church of
great physical (if not necessarily spiritual) pretensions, adorned with
flying buttresses, a bell tower, and five matching pairs of stained glass
windows imported from Italy.[104] The cost to build it was so steep that
the congregation nearly foundered after the failure of the 1878 wheat
crop. Among the faithful who helped to lift that burden was James
Wilder, Almanzo's father, who contributed fifty dollars.[105]

James and Angeline Wilder had been drawn to the area in the 1870s,
acquiring a residence and more than ninety acres of land.[106] Their home,
located on the north edge of town, was no little house. It was a substantial L-shaped structure of two stories, with porches along the
front and side, many shuttered windows, and several chimneys. Laura
and Almanzo had their own kitchen and bedroom upstairs, connected
to the large farmhouse kitchen by a steep, enclosed staircase.[107] Nearby
stood a large barn built on a stone foundation. Old burr oaks and evergreen trees shaded the yard.

A tantalizing photograph survives.[108] The Spring Valley Historical
Society believes it was taken around 1890 and shows Almanzo leaning
against a side porch support, hand in pocket, next to his elderly parents.[109] On the front porch sits a young woman in a snowy white apron,
her face in shadow. A girl leans against her, her hand resting in the
woman's lap. Are they Laura and Rose?

Two other female figures in the picture may be Eliza Jane Wilder and
Angelina Howard, one of Almanzo and E.J.'s nieces. The teenage Angelina was living with her grandparents around that time. The image is
too grainy to confidently identify everyone, but it conveys a sense of
peace and prosperity, something the younger Wilders sorely needed.

The peace was somewhat compromised, if only briefly, by the presence of Eliza Jane. She had stuck it out at her homestead until 1885,
with interruptions for the hard winter and other times when she felt
her health failing. In 1887 she traveled to Virginia and Washington,
D.C., where, the following year, she passed the civil service examination and began working as a secretary in the Appointments Division of
the Department of the Interior.[110] During her vacation in 1890, she

stopped in Spring Valley for a time, then boarded the train west, to visit her De Smet property.

Laura felt no more respect for E.J. as a sister-in-law than as a teacher. Years later, she compared her unfavorably to Angeline Wilder, who endeared herself to Laura by rolling her eyes at her daughter. "I never heard the words 'economic independence' on her lips," Wilder wrote of her mother-in-law. "When her daughter, who went to the city and worked in an office came back to talk of these things, she listened with an indulgent smile. She was too busy to bother her head with such notions, she said."[111] Eliza Jane's economic independence must surely have chafed Laura that summer, when she and her family were reliant on their in-laws' hospitality.

The activist rhetoric E.J. was airing that summer can be seen in an editorial she published after returning to the nation's capital. In the *De Smet Leader,* she presented herself as an expert on high tariffs, tight money, and bonds. She expressed devotion to her "brother farmers of Dakota" while suggesting that a few artesian wells might do more to aid "the brave pioneers of Kingsbury than all the stuff and nonsense about farm reform," a reference to populist agitation for measures to ease lending and support cooperative irrigation schemes.[112] She never mentioned her actual brothers, whose Dakota farming experience exceeded her own.

It must have been a busy summer in Spring Valley. In addition to cooking for the extended family, Angeline Wilder, Laura, and Angelina Howard were preparing provisions to outfit an ambitious, even outlandish, expedition. Almanzo's younger brother Perley, twenty-one, was planning to set out in a small sailboat, accompanied by Peter Ingalls and another cousin of Laura's, Joseph Quiner Carpenter, one of Aunt Martha's sons. (Born eight months after the Battle of Shiloh, he was named for the Quiner brother who died there.) The young men proposed to sail the Mississippi and other rivers down to Florida. Angelina later recalled baking "bushels of cookies" for their voyage.[113]

At the time, Florida was experiencing a land boom of its own. Railroads had finally penetrated the dense yellow pine forests of the Panhandle, and promotional brochures, posters, and handbills were doing all they could to whip up appetites for the balmy climate and supposedly rich soils of this "poor man's paradise," said to be ideal for year-round fruit orchards, pecans, and tomatoes.[114] "THESE LANDS ARE NOT ALL SAND AND BARREN," exclaimed one such brochure, with all the typographical force it could muster.[115]

The three young men were persuaded. With the Dakotas crippled by drought and land prices sky-high elsewhere, Joe Carpenter was planning to homestead or purchase woodland in Florida, then cut and sell timber. Perley wanted to go into business with his older brother Royal. Letterhead stationery survives headed "WILDER BROTHERS, Variety and Notions," with an address in Georgiana, Florida.[116]

On October 1, 1890, the tiny craft sailed out into Lake Pepin.[117] In photographs taken on the voyage, the boat appears to be perhaps twelve feet long. In its hold were trinkets or notions from Royal Wilder's inventory, which the men hoped to sell to finance their journey. Crewman Joe kept a log while Captain Peter and Pilot Perley navigated downstream. They camped ashore, cheerfully enduring day after day of rain and supplementing Angelina's cookies with oatmeal, rabbit, and the odd chipmunk. "Ate supper, read stories, told lies, etc.," reads one representative log entry.[118]

On October 23 they camped below Nauvoo, where a mob had killed Mormon leader Joseph Smith nearly half a century earlier. They picked up mail at Hannibal, Missouri, on the 27th, the day Mark Twain's mother, Jane Lampton Clemens, died. Had they stayed a little longer, they would have crossed paths with the celebrated author, who returned to Hannibal to bury her.

By November the small party had reached the Ohio River in Kentucky, sold the sailboat, and boarded a steamer. They spent a short time at Pittsburg Landing in Tennessee, only a mile from the Shiloh battle site, and admired the well-kept cemetery where Joseph Quiner lay.[119] Purchasing another craft, they pressed south, down Alabama's rivers and canals, finally reaching the Florida panhandle on January 14, 1891. There, they began looking for "Government land."[120]

Perley Wilder eventually moved on to Louisiana, but Peter Ingalls filed on a homestead near Westville, Florida, the hamlet near the termination of their voyage, only a few miles from the Alabama border. He spotted a local girl, Mary McGowin, from the prow of his boat and married her within the year.[121] Joe Carpenter also settled nearby.

The crew bragged often about penning letters to their "best girls," but they must also have written to family back in Spring Valley, extolling Florida's charms. At some point that year, after briefly considering emigration to New Zealand—perhaps due to their brief success in raising sheep—Almanzo and Laura Wilder decided to join the adventurous sailors.[122] They, too, would move to Florida.

FIRST, however, the Wilders had to address their finances. On March 19, 1891, the Spring Valley *Mercury* reported that everyone at the Wilder farm had been down with "the grip" but also included a notice by A. J. Wilder, advertising an auction to take place the following Saturday at his father's farm.[123] For sale were one mare with a foal, three additional horses of varying weights, a two-year-old gelding, a colt, and two two-year-old fillies (probably Fly and Trixy, the couple's riding ponies) and their harnesses. Also on offer were "other things too numerous to mention." A couple of weeks later, Almanzo confirmed to the paper that the auction had been "very successful."[124]

During their Spring Valley sojourn, a first photograph was taken of Rose. Three or four years old, she scowls at the camera, the baby fat around her neck cinched in by a tight tatted collar. Rose later recalled the picture-taking, her arguing with the photographer because she wanted the carnelian ring on her left hand to receive prominent placement.[125] She prevailed.

At some point, Laura took her daughter to Pepin, Wisconsin, traveling by train and ferry. We know of it only from a passing reference she made years later, but it must have been a nostalgic journey.[126] They spent time with her Aunt Martha Carpenter, still on the farm near Maiden Rock. Doubtless, she stood with four-year-old Rose on the shores of Lake Pepin one last time, picking up pebbles.

The hot, hazy days of the Minnesota summer would stay in Rose's memory. Alone, she sat under raspberry bushes, eating berries. Years later, she wrote to a relative about her dreamlike memory of neighbors across the way, who kept a beehive. One day the bees swarmed, alighting in a mass on her shoulder—harmlessly, as it turned out. The neighbors rushed to tip the bees back into the hive. The most disturbing thing about it, she said, was that her mother, who by this time she called "Mama Bess," had forbidden her to accept anything from anyone. So when the beekeepers invited her in for cake and milk, she had to refuse.

Rose also recorded another, darker anecdote. One hot day, while her mother, grandmother, and aunts were busy canning preserves in the kitchen, she climbed the stairs and deliberately threw herself down as hard as she could. Her motive, she recalled, was merely to find out what would happen. "I crashed against the door at the bottom, burst it open, rolled out amidst the squawking aunts," she wrote.[127] There were cries of dismay. Her mother wondered how it had happened, while her practical grandmother felt Rose all over to make sure no bones were broken. The child's bruised head was bathed in vinegar.

Rose characterized her action as driven by curiosity rather than self-destruction, but the image she unwittingly conveyed was of a child numb to chaos, impulsively acting out. "All I remember until I was six or seven years old are these incidents of being puzzled, trying to understand and not being able to," she wrote. "WHY did bees fly in a big ball? WHY did they land on _me_?"[128] She may well have had other unanswerable questions: Why did their house burn down? Where would they go?

In September, Almanzo and Laura sold their last piece of property in South Dakota, the tree claim where they had hoped to establish a permanent home. The Dakota Loan & Investment Company acquired it for $200, noting that there was an existing $430 mortgage on the property.[129] The following month, Spring Valley _Mercury_ readers learned that A. J. Wilder and his family had departed Spring Valley on October 5, traveling by train to Florida.[130] There, it reported, they expected to remain.

The move was intended to restore Almanzo's health. In later years, he said he had been "ordered south" by doctors, his constitution nearly ruined by the prairies—reflecting the prevailing medical view that certain climates were injurious, others beneficial. While his mobility had improved marginally, his feet were permanently affected, even deformed, by the paralysis. Throughout the rest of his life, he would cobble his own shoes.[131]

The Wilders rode the Pensacola & Atlantic Railroad to Westville. Railroad boosters for the P. & A. were relentlessly touting the climate not just as ideal for farming but as a panacea for all manner of diseases. *Facts About Florida*, an eighty-four-page advertorial published in the 1880s by William D. Chipley—former Confederate officer and founder of the railroad line—scoffed at the "dry atmospheres" and drought of the Dakotas, promising cool nights and summer temperatures that were never oppressive.[132] Immigrants were assured that yellow fever never penetrated the region, which was "secure from death-dealing diphtheria and typhoids." Benighted souls from the north, accustomed to "hovering over great fires or shivering in great wraps," were promised health "in every breath."[133] Holmes County, where Peter Ingalls had settled, boasted Ponce de Leon's warm springs, the supposed fountain of youth sought by Spanish explorers.[134] Invalids could expect "perfect transformation."[135]

It was nonsense, of course. Malaria occurred in every county in Florida, and the Panhandle had suffered yellow fever outbreaks throughout the 1800s. Recent major epidemics, in 1874 and 1882, left nearly fifteen hundred dead. Unknowingly, the Wilders were taking their lives in their hands.

Laura wrote only a few sentences about their Florida experience, years later, in an autobiographical sketch. Tactfully, she passed over its flaws, touching on the weird natural wonders of the south, its murmuring trees, great butterflies, and "plants that eat insects."[136] Among such oddities, she counted herself: "A Yankee woman was more of a curiosity than any of these."[137]

But judging by her daughter's recollections, Florida was an ordeal. In one of Rose's earliest short stories, "Innocence," written when she was thirty-five, she presented an impressionistic portrait of the trip through the eyes of a four-year-old. There is no knowing how much she fictionalized the material, but the story—an exercise in Southern gothic macabre—suggests that her mother was horrified to learn of "Uncle Charley's" surprise marriage to Molly, the actual name that Mary McGowin, Peter Ingalls's bride, was known by. Aunt Molly is described in "Innocence" as "a black-haired, black-eyed, red-cheeked woman in a beautiful, bright-red dress. . . . Fascinating, like grandfather's big brown horse that lived behind bars and had once killed a man."[138]

In the story, the mother reacts with fastidious disgust to tobacco-chewing, snuff-dipping, toothless southern moonshiners. She alienates her in-laws by urging her brother Charley to leave his wife and return to civilization up north. The child Mary Alice, through innocent outbursts and an inability to comprehend adult fears and prejudices, compounds the conflict, refusing to eat with the "nasty" utensils at her aunt's, only to be hauled from the house and spanked to her "amazement and terror."[139] The family cow turns up, maliciously maimed, and must be killed. Aunt Molly surreptitiously offers the child a ball of spruce gum to chew. Her mother intervenes, confiscating the treat and throwing the gum ball to a hen, who swallows it and dies, indicating poison. Hitching up the horses, the family flees the piney woods that night.

Hardly a factual account, "Innocence" nonetheless introduces a plaintive glimpse of Rose's relationship to her parents, particularly her mother, whose deep unhappiness makes her sharp and punitive, eroding the rapport mother and daughter originally share. In an indelible image, the parents get separated as the family debarks from the train and start anxiously searching for each other. Happily reuniting, they share a glance "as though they were together in a warm little space," leaving the child outside their circle, "chilly and uncomfortable."[140] That moment—that sentiment—was emblematic of Rose's feelings about Laura and Almanzo.

A strange photograph survives of Almanzo planted in a chair in a field of saw palmetto, sporting a handlebar mustache, floppy bow tie, and wide-brimmed hat. His wife stands behind him, one hand hanging limply over his shoulder. Laura is nearly unrecognizable, dwarfed by her clothing, with enormous puffy leg-o'-mutton sleeves nearly as wide as she is tall, an 1890s affectation. A drooping bow tie of her own and a dark cowboy hat lend the impression of a child weighed down by adult castoffs. She looks wan and miserable.[141]

Rose later interviewed her father about their time "Down South," jotting down his responses: "piney woods . . . hummock land . . . poor white trash ... peach-pie."[142] He may have pitched in with Peter's farming, helping him plant peanuts, cotton, or sweet potatoes. But Laura hated the heat, complaining that the "low altitude" did not agree with her.[143] She once tried to help her cousin plant corn while clumsily maneuvering a large black umbrella to shield herself from the sun. He took it away from her and sent her inside.[144]

The Wilders never filed for a homestead in Florida. They stayed less than a year and gave up, taking the train back north. They arrived in De Smet again on their seventh wedding anniversary, in August 1892.

Too Poor to Get Away

1892 was the thirtieth anniversary of the Homestead Act. It would continue to raise the hopes of the land-hungry well into the twentieth century, but it was not an unqualified success. Its failures were caused by a complex combination of human errors and natural disasters, but had the government listened to its own scientists, much adversity could have been avoided.

To be sure, the act did give a start to thousands of solid enterprises. Between 1863 and 1880, nearly 137,000 farms were homesteaded in Minnesota, Dakota Territory, Nebraska, and Kansas, with settlers gaining title to the land after five years.[145] An estimated two-thirds of farms in Minnesota during that period were initially launched by homesteaders.[146] The Brown County Historical Society in New Ulm displays photographs of "Century Farms," each successfully cultivated by a single family for a hundred years or more. By and large, such prosperous farms sprang from the loins of large immigrant families with many sons. Socialism also helped: many century farms improved their chances through cooperative ventures—creameries, grain elevators, and warehouses—in open acknowledgment of the fact that farmers simply could not go it alone.

Overall, less than half of homesteaders succeeded.[147] In the first thirty years of the Homestead Act, more than a million failed to prove up on their claims, and an untold number proved up but then sold out, unable to make a living. Charles Ingalls was one of them.

Aridity was the critical factor, as John Wesley Powell had foreseen. Irrigation had become a hot topic in the 1890s, the *Dakota Farmer* agitating for deep wells to tap into underground aquifers.[148] Congressional attempts to address the act's weaknesses were undertaken in piecemeal fashion and most were outright failures. The Timber Culture Act of 1873 withered along with the trees that settlers planted and tended.

There were other problems, too. Speculation and fraud undermined homesteading from its inception. Bundlers took advantage of the ability to buy claims after half a year for the bargain price of $1.25 an acre, instead of arduously proving up the land. They paid individuals to front for them by signing paperwork and camping out for the required six months (sometimes even using purpose-built shacks on wheels, rolled from one parcel to another), then purchased the land outright. An estimated one hundred million acres were bought in this way.[149]

Lies and omissions on homestead paperwork were not confined to bundlers, of course. Almanzo Wilder probably lied about his age, and he and Royal helped perpetrate a fraud by throwing up a claim shack for a friend and strewing clothing around to make it look occupied. Charles Ingalls lied in a deposition in 1886 when finalizing the patent application for his homestead land near De Smet: asked under oath whether he had ever made a homestead or preemption filing before, he answered "No Sir."[150] That was not true: in Minnesota, he had bought and sold the Plum Creek land under the Preemption Act and had filed for homestead and tree claims nearby, which were eventually abandoned or relinquished.[151]

Still, both Charles and Almanzo were legitimate claimants—farmers who wanted to farm, not speculators—and their dodges and untruths testify mostly to their poverty and desperation. The larger issue is that within a decade after the Civil War, virtually all the land best suited to small-scale agriculture in the United States had been taken, and what was left was marginal. On that leftover land, homesteaders could not succeed, no matter how hard they worked. They were bound to fail.

Yet thousands of American farmers continued to believe that if the government would only lend a helping hand, changing monetary policies and making loans easily available, the way would be clear. Shortly before the Wilders' return to De Smet, two major coalitions of the

Farmers' Alliance, from the Midwest and the South, banded together to create a new political organization: the People's Party, later dubbed the Populists. Charles Ingalls joined up.[152]

In the summer of 1892, the party held a national convention in Omaha, Nebraska, to nominate its own candidates for the White House. Flourishing a "Declaration of Independence" from the other major parties, they demanded, among other things, a government takeover of the railroads, currency reform, and a system of federal warehouses where farmers could stash their crops when prices were low in exchange for paper money issued by the Treasury. They also wanted the government to seize all the excess land owned by railroads and other corporations.[153]

The revolutionary demands reflected the fact that years of drought had concentrated farmers' outrage over a host of issues: wild fluctuations in commodity prices, high rail shipping fees, and price gouging by grain elevators and warehouses. Even farmers who had heeded calls to diversify, raising crops other than wheat and expanding into livestock, were devastated by the wildly changing conditions from season to season. When the price of corn fell in 1888, for instance, farmers stopped selling it, feeding it to their livestock instead. Two years later, when corn failed across the plains, its price rose 300 percent, and every farmer who had fed corn to his cows lost out. If they hadn't realized it before, farmers were increasingly aware that the system was rigged to favor railroads, middlemen, and large operations such as the bonanza farms of the Red River Valley, which could afford to stockpile grain and wait for the market to turn.[154]

At the Omaha convention, Hamlin Garland attended as both land reform activist and invited speaker. His first book, *Main-Travelled Roads*, had been published the year before. Its stories, grounded in the unsparing realism that would characterize later works by Upton Sinclair and Sinclair Lewis, exposed the grim economic laws governing his parents' harsh lives. He dedicated the book to his mother and father, whose "half-century pilgrimage . . . has brought them only toil and deprivation."[155]

Instead of delivering a speech, Garland read aloud one of his most incendiary stories, "Under the Lion's Paw," about a vicious landlord who cheats a tenant farmer out of his labor, selling the man's plowed and improved land out from under him. According to a reporter, the story was greeted with "a whirlwind of applause . . . the whole audience rising and fluttering their handkerchiefs"—surely the only time in American history when a legitimate work of fiction brought a national political convention to its feet.[156] Garland's father, a delegate from South Dakota, was moved to tears.

By the time of the convention, Charles Ingalls's struggles with farming were over. In February 1892, he had sold the De Smet homestead for $1,200 and moved his family to town. The sale, however, did not represent much of a gain; after the mortgage was subtracted from the total, he was left with $400.[157] Like so many thousands of others, he had succeeded on paper, proving up and claiming the land. But he could not make a living as a farmer. For a man who preferred open, unpopulated spaces, it must have felt like defeat.

In town he opened a store—"C. P. Ingalls & Co."—taking over the stock and business of Royal Wilder, who moved back to Spring Valley. When Almanzo and Laura returned to De Smet, they found her parents living a very different life, circumscribed by the limits of town, although Charles ventured out on an occasional "peddling trip" serving outlying communities.[158]

The Wilders' lives, too, would be confined to town. In November, Laura bought a lot, barely a block from her parents, for two hundred dollars.[159] Rose recalled that they lived there in an empty house, furnished only with a cookstove, kitchen table, and chairs; the rest of their furniture was chattel-mortgaged. They slept on pallets on the floor.[160] Laura was determinedly cheerful, saying they were "camping" and "wasn't it fun?" Her daughter was not fooled: "I knew she wanted me to say yes, so I did."[161]

The couple worked diligently. Laura sewed for a dressmaker six days a week, from six in the morning until six at night, making buttonholes for a dollar a day. Almanzo picked up odd jobs: driving a team, painting, filling in at local stores. For one glorious five-week stretch he served on jury duty, earning two dollars a day.[162]

It wasn't all hardship: the families still found camaraderie in church activities, musical performances at the opera house, and meetings of the Masonic community. Charles, Caroline, Laura, and her sister Carrie all joined the local chapter of Eastern Star, a Masonic organization open to men and women, between 1891 and 1893. Within a few years, furthering his business connections, Charles became a Master Mason in De Smet's Lodge, only a few blocks from the Ingalls home.[163]

While her mother worked, Rose spent the days with her grandmother and Aunt Mary. Laura's sister Carrie had graduated from high school in 1888 and was now in her early twenties, working for the *De Smet News* as a printer. Grace, a teenager, was busy with school and her own friends. Rose's memories centered on the two older women cheerfully going about their housework, chatting softly and singing while Rose was set to sewing carpet rags together to make rugs. Within the home, Mary knew her way around confidently, helping with virtually all the chores, washing dishes, sweeping, dusting, making beds, watering plants, sewing clothes. She practiced music and crafts she'd learned in college, quilting, beading, and netting hammocks. On Sundays, when the Ingallses and Wilders were together, she played hymns on her organ.

It may have seemed, Rose wrote later, that calamities had befallen the Ingallses at every turn, but she recalled them as sublimely content with their lot. "The truth is they didn't expect much in this world," she wrote, "and they just shed thankfulness around them for what they had."[164]

It was a characteristic Rose did not inherit. Even at five, she craved novelty, shocking her devout grandmother by saying she wished she had attended Christ's crucifixion so that she could have cursed him and become the Wandering Jew.[165] Her startling ambition was met with wondering silence—"somehow the air sort of crashed, terrifically." On the other hand, Rose's failure to work faithfully on her nine-patch quilt earned only a gentle reproof, a report to her anxious mother who "hated to impose on Grandma by leaving me there."[166]

At six, Rose started school, and the newspaper soon listed her among "pupils perfect in attendance, punctuality, and deportment."[167] She fondly recalled Miss Barrow teaching penmanship, having her students copy twenty times such phrases as "Procrastination is the thief of time" and "Sweet are the uses of adversity."[168]

Walking home from school with friends, Rose sang "O Dakota Land," a favorite of her mother, her Aunt Grace, and, indeed, the whole town. A wicked parody of a gospel song—"Beulah Land," which piously praised a heavenly "land of corn and wine"—the Dakota version raucously denounced the reality:

> We've reached the land of desert sweet,
> Where nothing grows for man to eat,
> The wind it blows with feverish heat
> Across the plains so hard to beat.
> O Dakota land, sweet Dakota land,
> As on thy fiery soil I stand,
> I look across the plains,
> And wonder why it never rains.
> Till Gabriel blows his trumpet sound,
> And says the rain's just gone a round.[169]

Rose omitted some telling verses:

> We have no wheat, we have no oats,
> We have no corn to feed our shoats;
> Our chickens are so very poor
> They beg for crumbs outside our door. . . .
> Our horses are of broncho race;
> Starvation stares them in the face.
> We do not live, we only stay;
> We are too poor to get away.

Songs could say what people could not. For the next two years, from August 1892 until the summer of 1894, the Wilders were only staying, not living, in De Smet. They were too poor to get away.

DURING the Panic of 1893, thousands fled the Dakotas, Nebraska, Kansas, and Colorado. But it was not only the economic depression they were fleeing. It was drought.

"In God we trusted, in Kansas we busted," emigrants painted on their wagons, but the phenomenon was hardly confined to Kansas.[170] Global ecological forces were at work, exacerbating what one historian has termed "folk experimentation with the land."[171] Across every inhabited continent, just as on the Great Plains, mass land clearing and wheat farming had led to significant drying, exhausting the soils and throwing fragile ecosystems out of whack. Combined with the market forces controlling distribution, human-caused climate change joined with natural weather patterns to wreak absolute havoc.

The consequences enveloped the entire globe. During 1890 a strong La Niña ocean temperature anomaly developed, followed by two El Niño years, which warmed Pacific waters and upended normal weather patterns—causing floods in some places, drought in others. In India, monsoons failed, leading to widespread cattle deaths, locust plagues, and grain riots.[172] In Russia, peasants had been pressured to clear huge areas for wheat, with the grain exported as a cash crop; overseers had walked away rich. But by 1891 and 1892, the land was exhausted. Drought, bad harvests, and bitter winters led vast numbers of peasants to burn the thatched roofs of their homes for fuel and eat "famine bread" made out of weeds. Typhus swept in to finish off the emaciated. Worldwide, millions died. It was, as one scholar put it, a "fin de siècle apocalypse."[173]

Weather patterns in the Pacific were not human-driven, but the futures market in Chicago was. The world had shifted so rapidly from subsistence agriculture to a market economy that price fluctuations sent ripples throughout the system, destabilizing entire regions. Traders could now set off starvation halfway across the world with the touch of a telegraph key, sucking up grain supplies in India or the Dakotas and sending them to Europe, where prices were high. It was the dawn of "price famines."[174]

The Panic of 1893 had many proximate causes: a run on gold, collapsing prices for wheat and other commodities that glutted the world market, and overinvestment in railroads, that perennial despoiler of nineteenth-century fortunes. But the 1890s may also count as the first time in human history when market manipulation during a climate crisis crashed the world economy.

Once again, the stock market bottomed out. Railroads began failing one after another: the Philadelphia & Reading, the Erie, the Union Pacific, the Northern Pacific, the Santa Fe.[175] Five hundred banks went bust, over a hundred and fifty of them located in the West.[176] "A panic was nothing new to Grandpa," Rose recalled. "He had seen them before; this one was no worse than usual, he said, and nothing like as bad as the wartime."[177] But if Charles Ingalls did say that, he was wrong. It was worse. It was the worst depression the country had yet known.[178]

On the Great Plains, the curtain was rising on what would culminate in the Dust Bowl of the 1930s. People left in droves, cutting the population in some counties by half.[179] The collapse of the Dakota Boom left so many Victorian mansions deserted that they inspired their own gothic genre, the haunted house story.[180]

Among the ruins of all the promises that had been made—by Horace Greeley, by Abraham Lincoln, by the Homestead Act, by the railroads, by the rain-follows-the-plow fantasists—people were struggling to explain what happened. A new Plains literature began to emerge. One of its first manifestations, unspeakably strange in its combination of a stripped-down style, outlandish daydream, and improbable escapism, was L. Frank Baum's *The Wizard of Oz.*

Baum grew up in New York State, but in 1888—a dozen years before publishing the most famous fantasy in American literature—he moved to Dakota Territory to please his wife, who had relatives in the area. They settled in Aberdeen, near Hamlin Garland's parents and less than a hundred miles north of the Wilders' homestead. While Almanzo Wilder was limping around the tree claim that fall, recovering from diphtheria, Baum, a former chicken breeder and aspiring actor, was opening a novelty store, Baum's Bazaar. It quickly failed when drought dried up discretionary income.[181]

Baum then bought the *Aberdeen Saturday Pioneer*, becoming its editor, writer, and sole proprietor. He wrote most of the editorials, including one calling for the "total extirmination" of the Indians. "Why not annihilation?" he argued. "Their glory has fled, their spirit broken, their manhood effaced; better that they die than live the miserable wretches that they are."[182] That was his response to the death of Sitting Bull and to the 1890 massacre of several hundred men, women, and children at Wounded Knee Creek, which marked the end of the Indian wars that Little Crow had set in motion thirty years earlier. People were still worried about another Minnesota massacre.

An enthusiastic amateur photographer, Baum was captivated by the isolation and stark terror of the plains, and his in-laws' tales of tornadoes. He would set *The Wizard of Oz* in Kansas, but he had never lived there and knew little about the state.[183] His fantasy sprang instead from Dakota Territory. One of his wife's sisters, Julia Gage Carpenter, kept a diary and wrote of being "*franticly* lonely" on the prairie, which she called "a dreadful country . . . *awful country*."[184] She spoke of nearly going blind "looking so hard across the prairie for another human being."[185] Her husband eventually committed suicide, and Julia died in a sanatorium.

Another one of Baum's sisters-in-law, Helen Leslie Gage, wrote an account of "The Dakota Cyclone," published in the *Syracuse Weekly Express* in 1887. She described the same kind of anxious vigil that Wilder would later record in her manuscript about early married life: "Out on this wide prairie, where not a tree or a building obscures the horizon in any direction, we are ever watching its clouds."[186]

Baum himself watched a cyclone forming in 1890 and wrote about the "sensational episode" in the newspaper.[187] Not long after, he fled Dakota Territory, drawn to Chicago, where the World's Columbian Exposition opened in 1893. There he wrote *The Wizard of Oz*, which would be published in 1900.

The first paragraphs of *Oz* describe a little house of the kind Wilder knew well. "There were four walls, a floor and a roof, which made one room; and this room contained a rusty looking cooking stove, a cupboard for the dishes, a table, three or four chairs, and the beds."[188] As in the Wilders' house, a "small, dark hole" led to a crawl space beneath, a place to hide from tornadoes.

Stark and unadorned, Baum's cadence captured the Dakota atmosphere perfectly:

When Dorothy stood in the doorway and looked around, she could see nothing but the great gray prairie on every side. Not a tree nor a house broke the broad sweep of flat country that reached the edge of

the sky in all directions. The sun had baked the plowed land into a
gray mass, with little cracks running through it. Even the grass was
not green, for the sun had burned the tops of the long blades until
they were the same gray color to be seen everywhere.[189]

The tornado that picks up Dorothy's house and drops it in the Land of
Oz is an ideal image of escape, something those trapped in Dakota Territory must have yearned for with all their might. The scarecrow who
becomes Dorothy's guide says that it is a wonderful thing to be made
of straw. He can never be hungry.[190]

OTHER fantasists were also at work in 1893. Next door to the same
Chicago world's fair that attracted Frank Baum to Chicago, Buffalo
Bill Cody and his Wild West show were selling out stadiums seating
eighteen thousand, a banner announcing "PILOT OF THE PRAIRIE,
THE LAST PIONEER." Annie Oakley took aim daily. The show cul-
minated in "Attack on a Settler's Cabin," Buffalo Bill's revenge for the
Minnesota massacre.[191]

Nearby, under a big tent celebrating the four hundredth anniversary of Columbus's journey to the New World, the Exposition hosted
the American Historical Association. There, a young historian stood at
a podium to deliver his thesis on American history at the very moment
when the whole Western experiment was unraveling. Born in Wisconsin six years before Laura Ingalls, only sixty miles from where her
parents were wed, Frederick Jackson Turner was thirty-two. His "The
Significance of the Frontier in American History" would become as
popular, in its way, as Oz itself.

The frontier had by then vanished as if in a tornado. The U.S. Census Bureau had announced in an 1890 bulletin that "up to and including 1880 the country had a frontier."[192] After that, it didn't. The Census
Superintendent found that so many people had populated the West
during the 1880s that the region was thoroughly pervaded by "isolated
bodies of settlement."[193]

Turner argued that it was the frontier that had formed the American character. As pioneers pressed ever westward, losing touch with East Coast centers of elitist or aristocratic traditions, their lonely struggle with the elements (and Indians) shaped their essentially democratic principles. Westerners as he described them were egalitarian, anti-authoritarian, and often violent, the frontier acting as a social safety valve, releasing pent-up tensions of expansion. Without it, he wondered whether Americans would lose "that coarseness and strength combined with acuteness and acquisitiveness . . . that restless, nervous energy" that made them embodiments of self-reliance.[194]

It was not a wholly original point of view. It echoed stereotypes of frontiersmen from James Fenimore Cooper's *Leatherstocking Tales* to Herman Melville's portrait of the "backwoodsman" in *The Confidence-Man*:

> The backwoodsman is a lonely man. He is a thoughtful man. He is a man strong and unsophisticated . . . self-willed. . . . If in straits, there are few to help; he must depend upon himself; he must continually look to himself. Hence self-reliance, to the degree of standing by his own judgment, though it stand alone.[195]

But more than anything written before, Turner's earnest celebration of the pioneer farmer as a "rash prophet," herald of "a better world," would become immensely celebrated and influential.[196] Americans wanted to believe that grit, spunk, and the strength of their own ax-wielding arms had raised a democracy in the wilderness. They wanted to believe that felling forests, breaking sod, and turning "free land" into golden grain had indeed "furnish[ed] the forces dominating American character."[197] Millions of people who never read Turner's thesis nonetheless came to hold it dear, treasuring the fantasy that a fistful of dollars and a plow could magically produce not only a farm but a nation.

Since 1893, scholars have analyzed, deconstructed, and debunked the Frontier Thesis, noting its sentimentality and biases. Turner failed to address key factors, including the role of railroads, banks, and other corporate entities benefiting from the federal government's largesse, in the form of millions of acres of the best farmland. As Turner spoke, he also neglected to take into account the remorseless ecological ravages of American agriculture and the widespread collapse of farms taking place all around him.

But in all the Great Plains literature to come—works as disparate as those by Baum, Hamlin Garland, Willa Cather, Ole Rolvaag, and, eventually, Laura Ingalls Wilder—every writer would be echoing the assumptions of the Turner thesis. It was a manifesto of the country's willful refusal to recognize the limitations of the land.

Land of the Big Red Apples

Quietly persevering in De Smet, the Wilders had not given up. They were working, saving, and waiting until the moment was right. Before long, they had a plan. As with the ill-fated Florida scheme, it was based on railroad boosters and word of mouth. This time, they were going to Missouri.

"Go South," ran notices in newspapers in Kansas, Nebraska, and the Dakotas in the 1890s, advertising the Memphis Route—a rail line from Kansas City to southwest Missouri—alongside ads for cream separators, egg brooders, and threshing machines.[198] The railroad would mail free to anyone who wanted them maps, timetables, and an eight-page illustrated monthly newsletter, the "Missouri and Kansas Farmer." There was also an enticing notice for a lavishly illustrated fifty-three-page book, likewise mailed free: "AMONG THE OZARKS: The Land of Big Red Apples."[199]

No doubt the Wilders perused its mouthwatering paeans to the apricots, pears, plums, cherries, peaches, raspberries, apples, and grapes waiting to spring out of admittedly rocky soil. Rest assured, the railroad promised, this soil was enriched with "crystalized limestone," replete with "Nature's own fertilizers."[200] A full-page illustration of "Mansfield, Mo., on the Memphis Route" showed fine Victorian-style homes on "an avenue to wealth."[201] The land was said to have Biblical properties: "On or about this very spot must have been located the garden of Eden."[202] As with Florida, health claims were prominent, if vague: "The climate is as near perfect for health as can be."[203]

As added inducement, the railroad was giving away free excursion

fares to farmers eager to investigate the real estate. The Wilders had
friends who made the journey, among them Frank Cooley, who caught
the "Missouri fever," as it was known in De Smet.[204] Rose went to school
with the two Cooley boys, Paul and George. Their father returned
from the Ozarks bursting with enthusiasm for the wooded landscape,
the farming, and the fruit.

The Cooleys and Wilders decided to make the 670-mile journey
together, by covered wagon. In May 1894, the Wilders sold their empty
house for $350.[205] A final photograph of the Ingalls family, taken
around this time, reassembled the nuclear family, excepting Almanzo
and Rose. Caroline, Charles, and Mary were seated, while Carrie,
Laura, and Grace stood behind them. Laura's hand rested on her
father's shoulder. Then, on June 16—the wagon packed with all their
possessions, including a crate of chickens—the Wilders went to Laura's
parents' house for the last time.

Laura never wrote about her parting from her family. We know of
it only from Rose. Found among her papers was a story based on fact
but rendered as fiction. Her view of the final parting between the
Ingalls and the Wilder families is impressionistic, and its reliability is
unknown.[206] But if it faithfully reflects reality, the farewell was as
wrenching and painful as anything in Laura's life.[207] For years since
their marriage, she and Almanzo had struggled and failed at every
turn. With drought laying waste to the Dakotas and Almanzo's health
in the balance, they had to leave—to find somewhere with affordable,
arable, easily worked land, where they could eke out some kind of living. For Laura, it was an exile, a banishment from those she had loved
and relied on and endlessly tried to support.

In Rose's version, the painstaking preparations for that final meeting were heavy with sorrow. As if it were a Sunday, the family bathed
and dressed in their best, Almanzo blacking their shoes, Laura donning
her black wool wedding dress. Laura's mother was surprised by their
finery, saying they needn't have bothered, but she too had made special
provisions, spreading a white tablecloth, baking a dried-apple pie, and
even serving Rose her own cup of cambric tea. "I felt as if I were drinking tears," she wrote.[208] In later years, Rose could not recall much of
Charles Ingalls, saying that all she knew of him were his "patched shoes,

and a long beard, and bright blue eyes."[209] But she wrote as if she remembered that night.

Laura asked Charles to play the fiddle, and he did. Long into the night, he spun out all the songs he had played to them across the years in their far-flung houses, in Wisconsin, Kansas, Minnesota, and Dakota Territory. "It was gay and strong and reaching," Rose wrote, "wanting, trying to get to something beyond, and it just lifted up the heart and filled it so full of happiness and pain and longing that it broke your heart open like a bud."[210]

When at last he stopped, Charles laid the fiddle in its box and spoke a final farewell to his daughter:

You've always stood by us, from the time you was a little girl. . . .
Your ma and I never have been able to do as much for you girls as
we'd like to. But there'll be a little something left when we're gone,
and I hope, and I want to say now, I want you all to witness, when
the time comes . . . I want you to have the fiddle.[211]

All she could say in response, was "Oh, Pa." She wept as they walked back to their empty house in the moonlight.

Early the next morning, they were off. Rose would not see her grandparents again and would never return to De Smet. Some years later, her mother retraced the journey, but she could never return to the family that she left behind. After that bittersweet night, it would be many miles down the road and many years into the future before Laura would find a way to ease the ache of hearing her father play for her for the last time.

PART II

THE

EXILE

Chapter 6

A World Made

I Would Have Scalped More White Folks

"Ruin seems to be impending over all," Henry Adams wrote at the start of the Panic of 1893. Returning home from abroad, he advised his friends to consolidate:

> If you owe money, pay it; if you are owed money, get it; if you can economise, do it; and if anyone can be induced to buy anything, sell it. Everyone is in a blue fit of terror, and each individual thinks himself more ruined than his neighbor.[1]

He was thinking of his own social class, but no person in America would instinctively heed that counsel more closely than Laura Wilder. Over the coming years, struggling within the constraints of poverty, she would step by cautious step seize control of their circumstances. She would prove adept not merely at penny-pinching but at finding ingenious ways to generate income, husband their minuscule resources, and protect their assets. As in the schoolyard, she would assume the role of leader, guiding the family on the long and taxing climb to security.

The Gilded Age was collapsing. By 1894, the Panic had set havoc in motion. Fifteen thousand businesses failed, including 156 railroads and 574 banks.[2] The economy came to a standstill, with the unemployment rate topping 18 percent. It would stall above 10 percent for the next four years. Wages plummeted, along with prices for agricultural commodities. Cotton was selling for five cents a pound and wheat for less than fifty cents a bushel.[3] Four million men were looking for work. Soup kitchens opened across the country, while city dwellers planted kitchen gardens in vacant lots. Hobo camps sprang up in Chicago and other major cities.

Riots, thievery, and homelessness set the rich against the poor. During a wildcat strike at Chicago's Pullman factory, workers were ordered to accept a 20 percent wage cut. In response to the outcry that followed, William Howard Taft—later elected president and eventually named chief justice of the Supreme Court—wrote offhandedly to his wife: "It will be necessary for the military to kill some of the mob . . . enough to make an impression."[4] The press encouraged such callousness: the *Chicago Tribune* once urged homeowners pestered by tramps to spike handouts with "a little strychnine or arsenic" and poison men as if they were vermin.[5]

The depression stalked farmers, foreshadowing what was to come in the 1930s. Hunger was prevalent, especially in the West. During the darkest days, a saying took hold in Kansas: "there is no god west of Salina."[6] A farm wife wrote to the governor: "I Take my pen in hand to let you know that we are Starving to death."[7] A Nebraska woman wrote of boiling weeds to feed her grandsons, while a family in Colorado had nothing to eat but squash for six weeks.[8]

Debate broke out—as it would again decades later—over whether federal relief was needed. But national aid programs had never been tried in this country, and politicians in both major parties were dismissive of "paternalistic" charity. In his second inaugural address, delivered just as the economy came crashing down, President Grover Cleveland, a 280-pound Democrat, fond of cigars and tankards of beer, preached self-reliance and frugality. The functions of government, he sonorously pronounced, "do not include the support of the people."[9]

During his first term, Cleveland had vetoed a relief bill that would have provided seed wheat to Texas farmers ruined by drought, and his attitude was shared by other politicians. Colorado's governor similarly vetoed an appropriation of state money to enable farmers to buy seed.[10]

In response to such indifference, the jobless looked to a different kind of leader: a rich man with a populist patois. Jacob S. Coxey was a wealthy and eccentric Ohio quarry owner, rancher, and supporter of monetary reform. He had named his youngest son, born in 1894, Legal Tender.

Coxey was ahead of his time, calling on the government to create public works jobs for the unemployed, to put them to work building and repairing roads. He exhorted men from across the country to hop freight trains, converge on Washington, and lobby for this reform—a "petition in boots." His supporters became known as "Coxey's Army." The march he organized would become the first mass labor demonstration in American history, perturbing the wealthy and emboldening the poor.[11]

In drama and sheer logistical ambition, Coxey's Army has been compared to Sherman's, and its march would become one of the most intensively covered national news stories since the Civil War.[12] Many of the marchers were veterans, reliving former campaigns by camping in their old battlefields.[13] Some were miners, thrown out of work when the price of silver collapsed. And a significant number were farmers. The Populist Party had already begun exposing western anxieties, but Coxey's campaign laid bare farmers' anger on a national scale.

Much of the press describing the march was sympathetic, lamenting Gilded Age inequality. "For years, the rich have been growing richer and the poor poorer," wrote the *Cleveland Plain Dealer*.[14] The *Rocky Mountain News* called the West a "simmering, seething cauldron of discontent."[15] The more discerning recognized that the nation as a whole bore responsibility for urging farmers out onto the plains: one Nebraska editor called the federal government "*particeps criminis*," a criminal accomplice.[16] Meanwhile, the Eastern press sneered, partly because few marchers hailed from the heavily industrialized coast. The *New York Times* described Coxey's recruits as "in the main Huns and Slavs and densely ignorant."[17]

At the head of a column of a hundred souls, Coxey departed Ohio in April 1894. As it neared the capital, the march picked up several

hundred former steelworkers in Homestead, Pennsylvania, who had
recently lost their jobs after a strike at Andrew Carnegie's plant. Other
itinerant "armies" embarked from Seattle, Tacoma, Portland, San
Francisco, Los Angeles, Butte, Salt Lake City, Denver, and Houston. A
Polish army formed in Chicago. Unions and activists, including the
Knights of Labor and the Woman's Christian Temperance Union, lent
their might. Some fifty trains were commandeered by Coxeyites making their way east.[18] Jack London, then a young, unknown socialist sym-
pathizer, joined the march in Iowa, walking as far as the Mississippi. He
peeled off at Hannibal, Missouri, because he was tired of being hungry.
"I can't stand starvation," he wrote.[19]

Marching across the dusty countryside, former factory workers were
resurrecting the evanescent dream of free land even as drought was
exposing the weakness of the Homestead Act, and Coxey's lieutenants
began agitating for public jobs building irrigation ditches. All the arid
West needed was a system of canals, they believed. "When the ditches
are dug and the lands reclaimed we can register homestead claims and
be self-supporting ever after," one argued. The Los Angeles Times concurred, urging Congress to stop "squabbling over the tariff and the
income tax, and spend some weeks devising a plan for irrigating what
is now worthless land . . . settling the labor difficulties which now
confront us."[20]

An 1882 law prohibited public demonstrations at the Capitol, but
Coxey was dismissive of the regulations. "I appreciate as well as anyone else the fact that the preservation of the grass around the Capitol
is of more importance than saving thousands from starvation," he told
the press.[21] On May Day, Coxey's Army marched up to the Capitol
steps in the first mass protest ever held on the National Mall. Joining
the hundreds of marchers, some thirty thousand spectators gathered
to hear Coxey speak. His teenage daughter, dressed in white and riding
a white stallion, accompanied him as the "Goddess of Peace."

As Coxey attempted to speak, police pushed him down the Capitol
steps and arrested him for "trespassing on the grass."[22] A number of
his supporters, many of them black, were beaten by mounted police
armed with billy clubs; the rest soon dispersed. Coxey spent twenty
days in jail. He would later run for office as a Populist, but without

success. His humiliation on the mall essentially brought the march, and his political influence, to an inglorious end.

Nonetheless, the notion of domestic relief programs—something akin to the New Deal—had been planted in the public mind. Populists and the American Federation of Labor took up the call for federal aid. Coxey's march left a lasting impression of the galvanizing power of organized protest and the heartlessness of government.

Voters would long remember the obscene spectacle of Grover Cleveland and his lack of charity in a time of need. No Democrat would be elected president for the next sixteen years; Republicans would hold majorities in Congress for a solid three decades. Not until 1932 would a member of the Democratic party emerge with a different conception of the federal government and what it might do for the American people.

WHILE Coxey's drama was playing out in Washington, in South Dakota there was little excitement and no relief in sight. The drought that had parched the Wilders' crops reached its peak that summer, when high temperatures combined with intensely dry air in a fearsome, parching, punishing cataclysm.

Eighteen ninety-four marked the first year that many states began to compile weather statistics, so there were few points of comparison. But the Iowa Weather and Crop Service regarded conditions as "the most destructive visitation of the kind ever known," withering crops and trees alike.[23] A cartoon on the front page of the *Chicago Sunday Tribune* showed the sun glaring down on a man sweating under an asbestos umbrella. Another depicted the city as a damsel blanching in horror as a devilish figure sprang from a crack in the earth, bearing a box labeled "Condensed Heat."[24] In late July, temperatures at one weather station reached a high of 109 degrees Fahrenheit.[25] That same month, a fire burned most of Chicago's great pride, the fairgrounds of the 1893 Columbia Exposition—the so-called White City—to the ground.

At times, it seemed that the whole West was aflame. Later that summer, superheated air ignited the litter left by Minnesota loggers. It was a repetition of the firestorm that had enveloped Peshtigo twenty-three years earlier, when the Ingallses saw smoke from their little house in the Big Woods. This time, the Great Hinckley Fire consumed another entire town—burning more than 250,000 acres, killing between four hundred and eight hundred people, melting nails, and fusing the wheels of railcars to the tracks.

It was in these torrid temperatures and an atmosphere of national crisis that the Wilders set off on their flight out of South Dakota, headed south to the Ozarks. They were not alone on the exodus. Between 1890 and 1895, some forty thousand people left the state.[26]

In the spirit of Henry Adams, the Wilders had paid their debts, sold everything they could, and economized ferociously. Their covered wagon carried what few possessions they had left. Packed there were the remaining trappings of their domestic life: a bed spring, feather mattress, and hand-pieced quilts; the bread plate and silver saved from the fire; a camp stove, skillet, and coffee pot; and a netted hammock, a last gift from Mary.[27]

Carefully wrapped in the nest of bedding lay an ingenious lap desk Almanzo had made for his wife. A hand-rubbed wooden box, it opened to uncover a red felt surface for writing, a pen tray, and space for an inkwell. The felted surface in turn folded back on hinges, revealing a compartment for writing paper. In that compartment, Laura had concealed bills adding up to $260 or so: money saved from her sewing, Almanzo's odd jobs, and the income from their property sales after the settling of debts. It was their entire life savings.[28] Laura repeatedly counseled Rose never to mention the money to anyone, anywhere. And she carried a revolver.

To support them on the journey, Almanzo Wilder packed a supply of a popular new product, round asbestos fire mats, to sell or trade for food. Placed directly in a fire or atop the cast-iron wood stoves of the day, the mats were meant to keep pots from burning or scorching. They sold for around ten cents.

Like many women who had made covered wagon journeys before her, Laura Wilder kept a travel diary throughout the trip, scrawled in pencil on a small tablet from the Mutual Life Insurance Company of New York. Such diaries ranged from brief notations of mileage covered and complaints about road conditions to detailed descriptions of people met along the way and expansive, lyrical accounts of the beauties and hazards of the rugged landscape. Wilder's fell somewhere in between. Characteristically, she rarely made reference to her feelings. Her emotions were veiled, expressed in reaction to the land as it unspooled before them, inspiring thoughts of penury or promise.

Nearly seventy years later, Rose edited and published her mother's travel notes in *On the Way Home: The Diary of a Trip from South Dakota to Mansfield, Missouri, in 1894*. She also supplied a "setting," a prologue and epilogue retrospectively filling out her mother's observations and recalling the emotions her mother left out.

Waving and calling goodbye, the Wilders left Laura's family behind on the street in De Smet at 8:40 on the morning of July 17, 1894. That day she began her journal, her tone depressed and muted. Laconically, she recorded the sight later that afternoon of a field of grain in hard-hit Miner County, south of De Smet. The stalks were eight inches tall. "Will go about 1½ bushels to the acre," she calculated reflexively, unable to stop her farmer's mind from totting up the yield. The entry concluded with two words: "Hot wind."[29]

The Wilders had a thermometer in the wagon, and the next day it reached 102 degrees, doubtless exacerbated by the black cloth curtains that Almanzo had fitted to the frame. Everywhere they saw crop failure, with grain standing only a few inches high, "worst crops we have seen yet . . . burned brown and dead."[30] Farmers were giving up and mowing the fields for hay. By July 19, a cold front had come through, providing some relief and dropping the temperature to a "cool and pleasant" 92.[31]

The Wilders were traveling, as planned, with Frank and Emma Cooley and their two boys, Paul, nine, and George, eight. To her daughter, Laura emphasized that their party was different from the hordes of other emigrants. Unlike them, the Wilders were not just aimless wanderers who didn't know where they were going, Laura maintained, trying to preserve a sense of purpose and a tentative grasp on social superiority.

According to Rose, Laura even asked Almanzo to take separate roads from the other migrants. He was puzzled by her attitude, suggesting that fellow travelers might make good company. His wife disagreed: "We're not covered wagon folks! . . . We got above that . . . Pa and Ma've got a home of their own, and we had one, and we're going to have one again. We're not just traveling!"[32]

A few days into the trip, as they made their way south, Laura began to take a livelier interest in the oddities they saw and the people they encountered. Her sense of humor began to revive. At one farm, she and Emma went to the house to buy milk. "It was swarming with children and pigs," she wrote; "they looked a good deal alike."[33]

Approaching the James River, the Wilders and Cooleys camped near a Russian settlement, exciting mutual fascinated examination and speculation. Taking a Sunday rest, the travelers went swimming in the Jim and visiting with the Russians, who appeared to be part of one vast family or "commune": Almanzo counted thirty-six children all the same size. Despite the language difficulty, they admired the Russians' well-kept barns, corn cribs, and dairy herd, and gratefully accepted fresh milk and "a great pan of biscuits . . . light and very good." In return, they gave the Russians a fire mat. "They are very kind people," Wilder wrote. She especially admired their huge dog, with a head like a wolf's.[34]

The following day, when they left their comfortable campsite behind to cross the James River, Wilder was struck by the view, looking back across its bluffs:

> We all stopped and looked back at the scene and I wished for an artist's hand or a poet's brain or even to be able to tell in good plain prose how beautiful it was. If I had been the Indians I would have scalped more white folks before I ever would have left it.[35]

She still remembered the Minnesota massacre, identifying with the perpetrators. It was a startling statement for a woman of her day.

For her part, Rose recalled the sight of a long train of emigrant wagons raising a vast cloud of dust as they approached the Missouri River, the border between South Dakota and Nebraska:

> I will never forget that sight—the double line of wagons stretching far back in a strange, dead kind of light, men and women and children

all a confusion along them, and behind them the whole earth rising up and curling in the sky overhead.

The sunset light turned that huge dust-cloud to gold, and Mama said to me, "That's your last sight of Dakota."

She said it in a queer way, hard and tight, and then she sat back on the seat and tears ran down her cheeks. She didn't make a sound, just sat there holding the horses and staring at them, with tears pouring out of her wide-open eyes. I was amazed. I had never seen anything like that before. Staring up at those tears startled me so, I just opened my mouth and bawled. . . .

"Why Laura, what is the matter?" Papa asked and he looked at her in wonderment.

Mama kept her face turned away. She reached across me and blindly gave the lines to Papa and then she put both hands over her face and said, "Let me be. I'll be all right in a minute. Please, just let me be."[36]

In her diary, Wilder wrote nothing of such things. Instead, she praised the "gleaming" water of the James River in contrast to the "very nasty and muddy" Missouri, which they crossed in a dust storm. "The Missouri is nothing like as beautiful as the Jim," she said.[37] She remained true to her roots.

As they rolled along the hard, hot roads of Nebraska and Kansas, Laura anxiously watched the countryside, waiting to come across land where the drought had not taken such an implacable hold. She and Almanzo were constantly assessing the fortunes of fields and crops, looking for alternate sites in case Missouri proved disappointing. This was a real concern, since they had met emigrant wagons coming out of Missouri, including a man who complained about the isolation of the Ozarks. It was the place to go if they wanted to bury themselves and "live on hoecake and clabber," he said, not realizing that he was talking to people who had survived on less.[38]

The Wilders were deeply unimpressed by Nebraska, which appeared, if anything, hotter, drier, and dustier than where they came from. They joked about it, with Almanzo saying that any farmer who wanted to make a go of it would have to throw a fence around the entire state. His wife said it reminded her of a nursery rhyme about Lydia Locket's pocket: "nothing in it, nothing on it, only the binding round it."[39]

Nonetheless, as they drove along the bluffs above the Missouri River, she closely observed natural forces at work. Erosion and flooding were continuously collapsing the bare bluffs, naked except for the shrubs growing in a tangle at the base—plums, black currants, grapes, sweet clover. "What is it about water that always affects a person?" she asked herself. "I never see a great river or lake but I think how I would like to see a world made and watch it through all its changes."[40] They camped in desolate hollows and passed across hills that seemed never to have seen settlement. "I am in a different mood this morning," she wrote on July 25, declaring herself fascinated by the loneliness of the hills, harking back to her embrace of the once-solitary precincts around Silver Lake.[41]

She was relieved, however, when they began to see, farther south, fatter cattle, hogs, and vast fields of corn. On July 27, she underscored her first sighting of "*an orchard with apples*," and Almanzo traded a fire mat for a whole bushel of fruit. By mid-August they were in Kansas, eating their fill of watermelon, marveling over Topeka's smooth "asphaltum" roads, and picking up a stray black-and-white dog they named Fido. They passed some good-looking country near Fort Scott but frowned over ill-kept yards and country places abandoned to a state of nature.[42] Fearing that the locals were "shiftless," they kept going.

Not until they reached Missouri, on August 22, did they find what they were looking for. Wilder chose that moment to send a letter about their travels to the *De Smet News*. She was happy to report on their "very pleasant trip so far," saying that the children had been having "a continual picnic": wading in rivers, playing in the woods, and feasting on plums, melons, and apples. When she wrote about how wonderful it was to satisfy her "Dakota appetite" for such things, a whiff of self-satisfaction crept into her tone. The editor of the *De Smet News* was married to Gussie Masters, eldest daughter of the old Walnut Grove schoolmaster "Uncle Sam," and sister of the reviled George and Genevieve; here was a chance to gloat over former tormentors and rivals.

When the newspaper printed the letter, Laura pasted it into a scrapbook. "First I ever had published," she noted beside it.[43]

A few days later, they entered the Ozarks. "They are beautiful," Wilder wrote, immediately smitten.[44] She loved the wooded hillsides, rock outcroppings, and clear streams. She spent much of one Sunday describing the abundance of the land in a letter to the "home folks," as she called her parents.[45] She also had words of praise for the thriving city of Springfield, unofficial capital of the Ozarks, home to more than 21,000 people. Laura called it "the nicest city we have seen yet . . . simply grand."[46]

The more they saw of the country, the better they liked it. Laura declared the landscape "simply glorious," and Almanzo wholeheartedly agreed.[47] Its open areas reminded Laura of the rolling prairies, but with the welcome addition of beautiful groves sheltering the abundant creeks. Distant vistas of the hills beyond were set off by a soft blue sky. It made her feel, she wrote, "wide awake and alive but somehow contented."[48] A farmer near the Ozark town of Seymour told them that the climate was ideal and said they would never want to leave.

Passing a large fruit farm, Almanzo fell into conversation with the workers and heard about a forty-acre property for sale for four hundred dollars. On their last night camping on the road, just ten and a half miles short of Mansfield after covering close to seven hundred miles, Rose and her mother picked a quart of ripe blackberries in minutes. It wasn't milk and honey, but it was close enough.

Now the great fear was that the best land might be snapped up before they could get to it. Laura noted six emigrant parties camping nearby that night, and the Wilders' wagon joined a line of ten more entering Mansfield the next day—August 30, 1894. That was the last day she wrote in her diary, the last day of their old life. She may have been exiled from everything she knew, but just as her father had done in Kansas, Minnesota, and Dakota Territory, she was determined to start all over again.

Her modest travel journal captured, quietly and without melodrama, her sorrow at leaving the place she had loved, anxiety over their economic future, and delight at discovering a more verdant and forgiving land. It revealed a woman who could be sharp, curious, and wry, given to losing herself in contemplation of nature. When the trip was over, she never wrote another word about it.[49]

But just as the Kansas prairies had been imprinted on the three-year-old Laura, the 1894 trip seared itself into her daughter's memory. In later life, Rose would return again and again to the unforgettable sight of an endless line of emigrant wagons fleeing drought, backed by a cloud of dust and despair. For the rest of her life, she would invoke the Panic of 1893 as a national trial and a badge of pioneering honor, wringing from it every last drop of drama. It marked her induction into the great American tradition of self-reliance, and conferred upon her—or so she felt—unique insight into how her fellow citizens should conduct themselves.

A Violent Fancy

The story of the Wilders settling in the Ozarks is the story of their start on the road back from ruin. Of course, they could not know that at the time. It would be years—decades, in fact—before they would achieve any measure of financial security. After a difficult childhood and the grueling first years of her marriage, the second act of Laura Wilder's life began with a titanic struggle to tame yet another wilderness, alone with her crippled husband and a seven-year-old child.

Rose remembered their days camping in the woods outside Mansfield as joyous ones. The air smelled of sumac and sassafras. Liberated from long days jolting along in the wagon, she and the Cooley boys were free to amuse themselves: climbing trees, stuffing themselves with berries and hazelnuts, wading in creeks shaded by hazel thickets, hunting for rabbits and arrowheads. Meanwhile, Almanzo traversed hills and fields outside of town with a real estate agent, searching for affordable land.

One day, he found it: forty acres of scrub for $400. Returning with the happy news, he took Laura to see the property, leaving Rose with Emma Cooley. They came back ecstatic to have found land they could afford, full of its promise, with a "snug" log cabin near town so Rose could walk to school. There was cold, clear, year-round spring water, and hundreds of apple saplings left by the previous owner, which had only to be planted in cleared land to create a bounteous orchard. After their noon meal, they planned to head into town to the bank, where they would sign the paperwork and buy the land.

Rose remembered, particularly, her father's calm deliberation—"When he was excited, my father always held himself quiet and steady"—and her mother whistling cheerily, as she had not for days. Laura dressed up for the trip to town, brushing out her long brown hair, braiding and pinning it atop her head, and buttoning the black jet buttons of her wedding dress.[50] She crowned her hair with a black sailor hat to match, a jaunty sprig of wheat stuck in its blue ribbon. Thus attired, with kid gloves on, she removed the writing desk to extract the hidden cash. But the money wasn't there.[51]

Rose compared the shock to the sense of falling, of stepping out in darkness onto a missing stair. The terror of that moment inspired a "tight strangeness" in her parents. They turned the lap desk and everything in it inside out, searching desperately. They frantically questioned Rose, asking whether she had told anyone or seen anyone suspicious, whether a stranger had passed through the camp. They wondered even about their friends, the Cooleys, then dismissed the thought. Finally, Laura fixed on Rose herself, asking whether she might have taken the money out to play with it.

Rose's account stresses only her parents' despair, not anger. But there may have been something in her mother's tone, some element of accusation, that turned a bad moment into something worse, something unforgettable or unforgivable. Rose felt "scalded," she remembered nearly seven decades later, "angry, insulted, miserable . . . alone and scared. . . . In the long stillness I sank slowly into nothing but terror, pure terror without cause or object, a nightmare terror."[52] She was plunged into the same hopeless anguish she had felt while watching their De Smet house burning, her mother sobbing on the grass before it. This disaster, too, spelled homelessness, and again she felt blame.

She watched as her mother removed her gloves and set aside her dress and her hopes. The family existed for some days in a numb, demoralized state, unable to speak of the loss and what it meant for the future. The Cooleys had found work in a Mansfield hotel, and

Almanzo looked for odd jobs in town. Their only asset that could be sold for food was the team of horses. Rose said she tried to keep from thinking what would happen on the day when they had nothing left to eat.

Three weeks and a day after arriving in Mansfield, she was outside their campsite, picking the last of the wild blackberries, when her mother impatiently called her to come get in the wagon. The money had been found—it had slipped into a crack in the desk. They had bought the land, and they were leaving, none too soon, having spent their last coins on salt pork and cornmeal.

Wilder herself never wrote about the episode. Years later, Rose brought up those days, only to earn a "fierce" rebuke. "I don't want to *think* of it!" her mother said.[53]

On September 21, 1894, the Wilders took possession of the land. They put $260 down for it, arranging a lien for the rest, $140 at 6 percent interest.[54] The only name on the warranty deed was Laura Wilder. She owned the land.

The likely reason for placing their most important asset in her name would have been to protect it from her husband's creditors, past, present, or future. Back in the early 1800s, married women had not been allowed to enter into contracts or to own personal property or real estate, although single women could do so; upon marriage, a woman became "civilly dead" in the eyes of the law, as Elizabeth Cady Stanton put it in her 1848 Seneca Falls declaration. But in the second half of the century, a series of state statutes had begun the process of reforming property law. Triggered by the potential ruination of families during financial panics, these reforms sought to protect homesteads and homes from seizure or foreclosure by exempting properties placed in women's names from "attachment by creditors of their husbands."[55]

The Wilders appear to have sought such protection in their final dealings in Dakota Territory: their last property in De Smet, the house in town where they lived a block from Laura Wilder's parents, had been bought solely in her name.[56] Missouri, too, had such a protective statute, and they were placing themselves in a position to use it again.[57] Whether the Wilders feared future debt, or whether they had left De Smet under the same kind of cloud that had prompted Charles Ingalls to leave Burr Oak in the middle of the night, remains difficult to determine. But the resolve to avoid loss of the property seems clear.

The prospects of their new land lay more in the imagination than in tangible assets. Only four or five of the forty acres were cleared. Shrubs, trees, and rocks were its only abundant features. The one-room log cabin was perched near a deep ravine, where a spring-fed creek trickled into a pool. It had a wood floor and fireplace but no window. Newspapers had been pasted across the peeled log walls as insulation. Large cracks had been filled with mud. "Light filtered through between the logs where the chinking had fallen out," Wilder wrote later, and "so did wind and rain."[58] The hundreds of apple saplings left by the previous owner had been heeled into a trench, lying on the ground with their roots covered with soil for protection. To plant them, the Wilders would have to clear acres of land. No matter, they thought, since in any case they would need lumber for fuel, and could sell extra firewood to pay for food over the winter.

Years later, in an article attributed to Almanzo Wilder but widely assumed to have been written by his wife, he contended that the land looked "so rough" that he hesitated to buy it.[59] The flat prairies of South Dakota had been "easily farmed," he said; this property, on the other hand, was neither bottomland nor even "second bottom" but rather ridge land, covered by scrub brush, timber, and so many stones that the couple took to calling it "Rocky Ridge." Indeed, it was only because his wife had taken "a violent fancy" to it that he went ahead with the purchase. If she could not have that parcel, she didn't want any, "because it could be made into such a pretty place."

According to Rose, there was a strange coda to the story of the lost cash, one revealing her parents' varying views on charity.[60] Hours after the Wilders arrived on their new land, another family came passing through, in even more desperate straits than the Wilders: homeless, dressed in patched clothes. Rose remembered her mother reaching into

the pocket where she kept the revolver. The man asked humbly for
work, saying his wife and five children had had nothing to eat for several days.

Over his wife's objections, Almanzo unpacked the last of their salt
pork and cornmeal. She cried out, "Manly, *no! We've got Rose*," but he
ignored her, sharing the food and asking the man to return the following day with an ax.[61] He arrived before dawn and cut a full load of
wood, which Almanzo sold for fifty cents in Mansfield. It was a welcome bit of income.

The stranger stayed for some weeks, helping to clear the land and
put a roof on a small barn on the property. After he moved on, Laura
helped her husband with the toil, becoming adept at handling one end
of a cross-cut saw, a skill she often cited with pride in years to come.
Throughout the winter, sales of firewood kept food on the table and
kerosene in the lamp. In the evenings, as Rose lay on the floor before
the fire, her mother sat knitting socks and reading to her family, everything from the *Five Little Peppers and How They Grew*—the 1881
novel that launched a famous series about a poor family of five children
living in a "little brown house"—to books by Jane Austen, Charles
Dickens, and Nathaniel Hawthorne. Historical narratives and novels
were family favorites: James Fenimore Cooper's *Leatherstocking
Tales*, W. H. Prescott's *History of the Conquest of Mexico*, and D. P.
Thompson's tale of pioneering adventure and the settlement of Vermont,
The Green Mountain Boys.[62]

That first winter, Rose walked to school in town. Her parents soon
acquired a donkey to carry her, whom she named Spookendyke. In a
diary entry years later, she wrote about her epic struggles with the recal-
citrant beast: how he loved to tip her over his head when going down-
hill, how she could never fasten the saddle and bridle tight enough to
keep from slipping off, how she ended up walking rather than riding
him.[63] Despite these drawbacks, she grew fond of him, inventing their
own shared language ("Fispooko") and asking to be excused in class
when she heard him braying unhappily, to go speak with him. She carried a lunch pail, in which her mother sometimes supplied treats: raw
carrots, a favorite, or an apple mysteriously split in half inside its unbroken peel, a popular parlor trick performed with needle and thread.[64]

On rare occasions when they could afford sugar, there was a delicious "saucer pie." But most days, Rose ate the same thing, which she concealed from her better-off classmates: brown bread spread with bacon fat. They could not afford butter.

Rose felt their poverty as a burden, ashamed of her peasant food, her clothing, and the donkey. Wealthier children rode horses to school. A photograph of her and Spookendyke captures her wearing an ill-fitting, sack-like dress, a flat beret drooping over her head. Woebegone, shoulders hunched, she stares at the camera unsmiling.

At the imposing two-story redbrick schoolhouse in Mansfield, she did not make friends among the well-dressed town girls and found herself forced to sit next to those she considered social inferiors—"the horrid, snuffling, unwashed, barefooted mountain girls," she called them. Her mother was not the only snob in the family.

She felt superior, as well, to the "professor," a bald man with long whiskers which he grew, he told his pupils, so that he didn't have to put on a tie. He wore a dirty white shirt and, like one of her mother's former teachers in De Smet, had a habit of slipping his pointer down his collar to scratch his back. In the off season, he was an auctioneer.

Rose loathed the institutional green walls of the classroom, to the point of trying to convince her mother that they made her physically ill. She also despised her textbooks, preferring her mother's old grammar. Laura Wilder was only twenty-seven when they arrived in Mansfield, but she assured her daughter that, in the old days, "children had to *work* to learn their lessons." Rose excelled at spelling without much effort, another factor that did not improve her reputation among her fellow students. The only thing she liked about the school, or so she said later, was its small library of cast-off donated books—works by Jane Austen, Charles Dickens, Nathaniel Hawthorne, and the like, which she was allowed to borrow.

Rose would later dwell on her mother's beauty, her hair glistening in the lamplight, her long eyelashes and "very sensitive" mouth, its corners twitching when she heard something amusing. Every night, she recalled, her father would pop a large pan of popcorn, examining the kernels as if they were snowflakes, finding "no two . . . alike and yet they were all pretty." Rose gave every third kernel to their dog, Fido, while Almanzo sat listening to his wife read, soaking his damaged feet in hot water. "Working the hilly, rocky fields hurt his feet cruelly," his daughter wrote; they ached so sharply that he had trouble sleeping at night. Yet she treasured these evenings, recalling later "a cosy, comfortable hour for all of us . . . nothing to worry or hurt us till tomorrow."

The following spring, the Wilders began making improvements to their fledgling farm in earnest. Rose helped plant corn, while her father arduously set out apple trees on twenty acres of newly cleared land. In town, they sold baskets of berries Rose picked. They dug a root cellar out of the hillside. Sometime over the next two summers they were able to save enough to buy a cow and pig, and finally there was butter for the bread. Laura was becoming adept at the trickiest aspects of managing her flock of chickens, feeding them carefully and keeping them laying through the winter.

Having livestock was a boon, but they were still short of ready money. Paying the mortgage while buying food, tools, and other necessities remained a struggle. The Panic peaked in 1894, but unemployment would remain high and money tight for years. During the presidential election of 1896, the arcane issue of the money supply—a debate over maintaining the gold standard versus allowing a standard based on both gold and silver—took center stage. Populists and Democrats argued that farmers and labor needed the infusion of silver, which would lower interest rates and allow them to obtain loans more easily. The Democratic candidate, William Jennings Bryan, galvanized delegates at the party's Chicago convention with his famous plea not to "crucify mankind upon a cross of gold."

Rose remembered the debate in Mansfield, with townsfolk sowing propaganda in their flowerbeds. "To me," she wrote, "a yellow aster still stands for the hated gold standard; the white aster means William Jennings Bryan, whose free coinage . . . would have taken us back to prosperity. But Bryan was defeated by the soulless corporations and our country was forever ruined."[65] Charles Ingalls and Almanzo Wilder were both likely Bryan supporters. Women, of course, would not win the right to vote until nearly a quarter-century later.

For the first few years, the Wilders continued to socialize with the Cooleys, who were running a restaurant and hotel in Mansfield. Paul and George went to school with Rose and loved visiting the Wilders' farm, feasting on persimmons and hazelnuts. "George and I enjoyed the springs and creeks best of all," Paul recalled, "as we didn't have them in Dakota."[66] Their father went into partnership with a drayage firm, hauling water to homes or businesses with no well or pump of their own. He also served as an agent for the Waters-Pierce Oil Company, delivering kerosene.[67]

With a steady income, the Cooleys were on a firmer economic footing than the Wilders, but at the end of 1897 they suffered a terrible misfortune. That December, just after Rose turned eleven, Frank Cooley came down with a virulent case of pneumonia. "He was a big strong man of 37," Paul said, but despite heroic nursing by a local doctor and his wife, his strength could not save him.[68] He died on December 29, leaving Paul and George fatherless.

The loss redounded to the Wilders' benefit. Almanzo's physical struggle with chopping down trees and setting out the apple orchard, which was not expected to begin putting out fruit for several years, made it apparent that even modified farm labor was more than he could bear. He was simply "unable to do a full day's work," his wife would say years later.[69] The couple once again deferred their dream of the independent farm life, opting for Charles Ingalls's solution: move to town and work for wages. In 1898, they leased out their farm and moved into the town of Mansfield. Buying Frank Cooley's team and wagon, Almanzo Wilder took up his friend's job, making kerosene deliveries and hauling passengers and freight from the train depot.

The drayage job allowed Almanzo to sit for periods of time, a welcome relief. Laura went to work as well, keeping account books for the oil company. She also sold butter, ten cents a pound.[70] Eventually, she began cooking meals for railway passengers and taking in boarders.

Mansfield boasted a spacious town square laid out alongside the railroad tracks, and a busy depot. In summer, the square rang with blacksmiths' hammering, the clopping of hooves, and loud, loose talk. It smelled of creosote, horses, and sweat. At first, the Wilders lived on the "wrong" side of the railroad tracks, south of the depot, bunking in a rooming house in what Rose would call "Poverty Flats," a common term at that time. Later that summer, they rented a yellow frame house on Mansfield's main avenue, Commercial Street, only a few blocks from the square. Rent was five dollars a month. The proximity to the train station brought Laura customers, and Rose no longer had to battle with Spookendyke to get to school.

Almanzo's parents, James and Angeline, and his oldest sibling, Laura, spent that summer with them, stopping in Mansfield on their way south. They had sold their farm in Minnesota and were moving to Crowley, Louisiana, to live with Eliza Jane, who had had lasted only a year or so at her government job. In 1893, at the age of forty-two, she had married Thomas Jefferson Thayer, a widower in his sixties with five grown children and a modest fortune gleaned from his Spring Valley grain elevator.[71] The couple promptly moved to Louisiana and went into rice farming there.

Perhaps against his better judgment, the sober and conservative James Wilder had been persuaded to invest much of his wealth—the profits of long years of farming and the proceeds from sales of his Minnesota properties—in the Thayers' rice farming schemes, which collapsed with the first bad harvest. Eighty-five, thin and frail, the elder Wilder realized that most of his investment would be lost. But he had done what he could for Almanzo, buying the Mansfield home that he and Laura were renting and presenting the deed to his son just before leaving town.[72] He died several months later.[73]

In 1900, when the federal census taker enumerated the citizens of the city of Mansfield, he listed the Wilders right after the Cooleys, suggesting that they were now neighbors.[74] A. J. Wilder was described as agent for an oil company. Laura Wilder was noted as the mother of two children, only one of whom was living. As was customary, the line for her occupation was left blank.

The Sweet By and By

James Wilder's gift made all the difference. Without rent to pay, the Wilders could now save some of their earnings, which they invested in adding acreage to the farm. They had already purchased an additional six acres in 1897; in 1899 they added forty more, and a few years after that another twelve, for a spread of nearly a hundred acres.[75] They saw their interval in town as temporary, always intending to return to Rocky Ridge.

Meanwhile, the town was booming around them. Turn-of-the-century Mansfield—the "Gem City of the Ozarks," as it fashioned itself—was the fastest-growing city in Wright County, with a population of more than five hundred.[76] The railroad had arrived in 1882, carrying away lead and zinc from local mines. The depot also served as a major shipping point for fruit, lumber, the U.S. Mail, and livestock—Mansfield was known for its mule breeding.[77]

The town's business district boasted a variety of mercantile, produce, and dry goods stores, Fuson's Drug Store, Freeman's Flour Mill, hardware and furniture dealers, and a livery stable. In 1895, a new city council made the construction of wooden sidewalks in the district its first order of business. The Bank of Mansfield, which gave the Wilders their loan for Rocky Ridge, was a central fixture; founded in 1892, it was run for decades by "Uncle George" Freeman, a legendary power in the town. On one side of the town square, an opera house hosted a lively assortment of Ladies' Aid oyster suppers and traveling entertainment. Rose remembered a visit from John William "Blind" Boone, a nationally known black pianist and composer. Circuses and livestock shows performed in tents and vacant lots, while traveling troupes put on *Uncle Tom's Cabin* or Buffalo Bill's Wild West show.

But for all its growth and glitter, Mansfield had an ominous side, rooted in the slave-owning past. It was a whites-only "sundown town," where blacks were not welcome after dark. They were allowed to camp by day at "Nigger Springs" but were warned not to overstay their welcome: a sign at the public well read "Nigger, don't let the sun set on your ass."[78] There had been around seventy slaves in Wright County at the outbreak of the Civil War, and while Missourians ostensibly supported the Union, local cemeteries were filled with soldiers from both sides.[79] After the war, the Ozark hills—already legendary for bushwhackers, family feuds, and intrigue over backcountry stills—were swept by barn burnings and revenge killings.[80]

Around the time the Wilders arrived, Mansfield was briefly so prosperous that it was even targeted by criminals. The notorious gangster

Jesse James had relatives in the Mansfield area; he was gunned down in 1882, but his brother Frank was said to be picking pockets in town in 1898.[81] The following year, several men boarded a train a few miles east of Mansfield, held the engineer at gunpoint, and blew up the baggage car with dynamite, netting $364.[82] The robbers, caught days later, included at least one former member of the James Gang.[83]

The Wilders relished hearing such stories from friends and neighbors; Rose, who overheard them, would one day weave them into her fiction. But in all other ways, the new arrivals cultivated respectability, becoming absorbed in Mansfield's social scene. They became particularly active in the Order of the Eastern Star, which Laura and her parents had joined back in Dakota Territory.

Meetings of Eastern Star and related fraternal groups served as both diverting social clubs and charitable organizations. The special Masonic dress, including aprons, swords, "jewels," and other ornamentation, and the elaborate ceremonies, with their special knocks, signs, and signals, brought color and drama to lives with little ritual.[84] Once a mainstay of middle American life, Masonic groups organized New Year's parties, plays, celebratory dinners on George Washington's birthday, Easter services, and other patriotic and religious events. They also functioned as a safety net in an era before insurance was commonplace, often paying for needy members' medical care and burial expenses.

The social opportunities offered by Eastern Star proved invaluable to Laura as she sought to gain a foothold in Mansfield. She helped found the Mansfield chapter of Eastern Star in 1897 and would remain active in it for the next forty years, holding many different offices.[85] She also helped launch Mansfield's Methodist church, organizing its first bazaar after the Christmas dedication of a new building in 1899.

Meanwhile, Almanzo kept making deliveries, while Laura hustled to cook and serve meals to train travelers and keep books for the oil company. These responsibilities must have come on top of her daily chores, her life as rigidly defined by them as it had been on the farm: "washing on Monday, ironing on Tuesday, mending on Wednesday, sewing on Thursday, extra cleaning on Friday, baking on Saturday." They were investing every spare dollar in Rocky Ridge.

There had been neither money nor opportunity to go back for a visit to De Smet since the time they left it, almost eight years ago, so it must have come as a blow when alarming news arrived from Laura's family. For some time, all had seemed well there. Caroline Ingalls wrote regularly, even sending the *De Smet News* so that the Wilders could keep up with the community.[86] Mary had continued living at home, helping her mother keep house. Carrie was a working girl: after graduating from high school in 1888 and working for a short stint in a store, she had signed on as an apprentice at the newspaper, learning typesetting and the printing trade. Grace graduated in 1896, attended a small teachers college, and then taught several terms of school near the town of Manchester, some nine miles outside De Smet. She married a Manchester farmer, Nate Dow, in the front parlor of the Ingallses' home on October 16, 1901.

But the following spring, Laura received word that her father was seriously ill. Over the years, since he was a boy, Charles had toiled continuously, as a farmer, homesteader, carpenter, innkeeper, butcher, railroad timekeeper, Justice of the Peace, deputy sheriff, town clerk, shopkeeper, and peddler. He sold farm machinery and twine to bind hay; he sold insurance; he took any work he could get. Long years of acting as his family's principal support, building every one of their little houses and laboring mightily to clear unbroken land, had taken a toll. In 1900, he suffered severely from "congestion of the lungs," and the newspaper reported that he was "in a bad way."[87] By the spring of 1902, at the age of sixty-six, he was dying.

Laura Wilder, now thirty-five, made the long and circuitous journey back: boarding the train north to Kansas City, transferring to go across Minnesota, and finally taking the railway her father had helped build, the Chicago & North Western, which brought her to De Smet. The *Kingsbury Independent* reported that she arrived on the evening of Tuesday, May 27, for a visit planned to last several weeks.[88] The newspaper noted her father's illness, saying he was suffering from heart trouble.[89] Decades later, Rose would say that he had suffered a "coronary thrombosis" caused by what doctors called "tobacco heart," from smoking a pipe.[90]

Wilder never described the vigil at Charles's deathbed, but it must have been the most mournful occasion of her life, as she and her mother and sisters—women who had journeyed with him so long—readied

him for one final departure. He died on June 8, 1902, at three o'clock
on a Sunday afternoon. As far as Laura was concerned, with him went
all of the music and joy of their years together. Gone were the songs
of her childhood, his easygoing ways and cheerful determination, his
adoring gaze.

It had been an extraordinary life. "A Pioneer Gone," the *Kingsbury
Independent* eulogized him. He was the embodiment of what his
daughter would call "the frontier spirit," from his *Mayflower* and
Massachusetts Bay Colony forebears to his far-flung journeys. From
his birth in the burned-over district of New York State to his death in
South Dakota, he had traveled thousands of miles on horseback and
covered wagon, crossed great rivers, hunted in the Big Woods, and
ridden among the last wolves on the Great Plains. He had witnessed
the Osage banished from their prairie home and the grasshoppers
descending upon his. He had seen the rise and fall of homestead hopes,
building house after little house, fighting every prairie fire that sought
to consume them. And he did it with grace, eloquence, and good humor.

Laura would never forget him. Sometime shortly after his death,
she wrote an essay about her earliest memories of him. It seems more
than a mere tribute or homage, attesting rather to a powerful need to
weave her way back into his presence, to find him again through the
art of description. It starts with his eyes, "so clear and sharp and blue"
that could "look unerringly along a rifle barrel in the face of a bear . . .
and yet were so tender as they rested on his Caroline . . . or me." She
recalled his thick brown hair and the strength and endurance he had
had in youth, tramping "all day through the woods without fatigue"
and carrying his infant daughter just as surely and patiently when she
was sick or could not sleep.[91]

His most remarkable gift, as Laura saw it, was a deep and profound
contentment with what he had. Despite all the losses and reversals, the
perils, the hunger, the always disappointed hopes in the next harvest,
he was satisfied in the life he had chosen. He cherished his wife, his
children, and his music:

> All Father needed to make him happy was his family, a new, wild
> country to live in or travel over, good hunting and fishing, some traps,

his gun, two good horses hitched to a rain-proof covered wagon and his violin.

I am not sure but I should have put the violin first and the family second and I know that its place was second only to the family with us all.

It made merry with us when we were glad, it sympathized with us when we were sad, it gave us paeans of praise when we had been good or successful and acted as a father confessor when we had been bad.[92]

She remembered all of the songs he once played, ritually naming them off: "The Blue Juniata" and "Highland Mary," "Bonnie Doon" and "The Devil's Dream," love songs, patriotic songs, dance songs, and beloved old hymns. "Whatever religion, romance and patriotism I have I owe largely to the violin and my Father playing in the twilight," Wilder wrote.[93]

All De Smet grieved his death. "As a citizen he was held in high esteem, being honest and upright in his dealings," the newspaper said.[94] "As a husband and father he was faithful and loving. . . . What better can be said of any man?" It was a fitting judgment. By standards of material success, he may have been an abject failure. But measured by his children's love for him, he was an outstanding man. And through his daughter's remembrance, he would come to achieve a species of American immortality.

His Masonic brothers had helped pay for his medical expenses. They paid, as well, for his funeral and the headstone at the De Smet Cemetery. Somehow, the Lodge's ceremonial compasses—symbols of Masonic dedication to craft—got lost at the gravesite.[95] Perhaps they were buried with him.

There was a final irony to the timing of his death. As if in some preternatural reckoning, a shifting of the scales of justice, the nemesis of Charles Ingalls's life—*Melanoplus spretus*, the Rocky Mountain locust that in its trillions had devoured his crops and rendered him destitute—now abruptly and mysteriously went extinct.[96] The last living specimen was collected in 1902, the year Charles died.

Just as I Am

Though they could not know it at the time, when Laura Wilder left De Smet it was the last time she would see her mother and her sister Mary. They would stay in touch through letters, but for the rest of their lives they would never be in the same place again.

Caroline and Mary faced a precarious financial future. After a lifetime of unrelenting labor, Charles Ingalls had accumulated little to show for it. He left them the house they lived in and not much else.

As they had always done, they simply made do. A notice appeared in one of De Smet's newspapers: "Shirt Making—I am prepared to make men's and boys' shirts to measure on short notice. Satisfaction guaranteed. Mrs. C. P. Ingalls."[97] She also took in washing and rented upstairs rooms to boarders. Mary continued to sell her crafts, including fly nets for horses.[98] For the next few years, Carrie Ingalls's salary at the *De Smet News* helped as well. In 1905, though, she left for a recuperative stay in Boulder, Colorado, to improve her asthma, and then struck out to stake a claim on her own Dakota homestead while managing newspapers in and around the Black Hills.

Back in Mansfield, Laura Wilder's life likewise continued to be filled with odd jobs. But a striking difference in her appeared at this moment, a new determination. Shortly after her father's death, distinct signs of literary ambitions began to emerge. Earlier efforts—childhood poems, the school essay on "Ambition," the 1894 travel journal, the letter from the road to the *De Smet News*—had been casual studies or expressions of a desire to record memories and landmarks. With the death of her father, that desire became a pressing need. The powerful essay about him that survives in her papers may date to this period, shortly after his funeral. In its plaintive tone and passionate longing to capture everything about him—his gaze, his presence, his music, his character—it was unlike anything she had ever written before. It was a beginning.

That was not all. Discovered later among her papers was an envelope with sketches and notes scrawled on stock requisition forms from the Waters-Pierce Oil Company.[99] On one of these scraps she had been writing a ghost story, set on the shores of Silver Lake during her family's isolated winter there. She laid out the scene: "forty miles from our nearest neighbor . . . when the two Dakotas were still one territory."

This too was a beginning, and Wilder would return many times to the vision of the family alone in winter, the wind "howling outside and the snow drifting as only the wind can howl and the snow drift across an unbroken prairie." Another fragment described a frenzied old-time revival meeting, where hymns were sung with extraordinary "lilt and swing and compelling force." Yet another recorded an image of wild purple asters blooming, and thistledown ready to blow away on the next puff of wind.

Wilder was not the only member of the family who was starting to write. Between 1900 and 1902, teenaged Rose had been surreptitiously taking copious personal notes in her textbooks, a disfigurement that her mother, who venerated books, could scarcely have condoned. The scribbled notes recorded classroom exchanges with school friends and reveal a fluent writer capable of capturing a scene. She was quick to eviscerate objects of her contempt, including fellow students, teachers, and even friends. Playing "Truth" with poor Paul Cooley, she extracted a promise that he wouldn't get mad, and then mercilessly listed his faults until he began stammering and turned "purple."

Reminiscent of her mother's sarcastic schoolgirl poems, Rose's schoolbook sorties could be cranky and sardonic. On one page, beneath her name (inscribed in an inky cross-stitch), she recorded a pious maxim of Horace Mann's, then appended her own impatient exclamation: "'Lost, somewhere between sunrise & sunset, two golden hours, each set with sixty diamond minutes. No reward is offered, for they are gone forever.'—& I don't care a continental."[100] Under a paragraph about the Neo-Platonists, she wrote, "Nothing is certain, but if nothing is certain, how can we be certain that nothing is certain?" Expressing such witticisms in class, she was told to go stand in the corner.

On one occasion, asked to paraphrase Tennyson's "Break, break, break! On thy cold gray stones, O Sea!," she told the teacher that it was impossible to summarize poetry: a literal interpretation could not capture the poet's intent. When another student gave a more satisfactory response, the instructor lectured Rose on perseverance. "I stood up," Rose later recalled, "slammed my books on the desk, said in fury, 'I will not stay here to listen to such stupid, stupid . . . !!' and went home."[101] According to her, she did not return for the rest of the school year.

In time, her outbursts may have gotten her expelled. She later boasted that she rarely completed any full year of school, "because for some reason I was 'mad at the teacher.' "[102] She claimed her departures were voluntary, but one wonders whether authorities would have agreed.

Her parents, of course, were veterans of the lackluster education available to rural students. Almanzo had never liked school, and Laura, on one dramatic occasion, had been sent home by Eliza Jane. It was common for older children, particularly boys, to miss school, since they were needed in the fields. But deliberately refusing to attend for months or years on a whim suggests a particularly intractable form of insubordination. Whatever happened, Rose's belief in her superiority, a self-assured rejection of authority and those who wielded it, took hold in her earliest days. It would become deeply ingrained.

How did Rose's parents respond to such behavior? There is no record but Rose's own, in a collection she wrote later, a story cycle about a girl named Ernestine in a town exactly like Mansfield. The book, *Old Home Town*, opened with a map of what was obviously Mansfield, the first-person narrator's house planted on the same spot as the Wilders' own. In the stories, Ernestine was as much Rose as made no difference, and her parents likewise: her father the town drayman, her mother a hot-tempered child bride, married at nineteen and scarcely more mature than her daughter, with long brown hair and "furiously blue" eyes.[103] In that stultifying time, an unmarried girl was thought "ruined" if seen in the wrong company, and the tale's mother and daughter fight bitterly over Ernestine's dalliance with a "traveling man" who rolled into town.

Ernestine's adolescent compulsions, with her fears of being an "old maid," mirrored Rose's own. At fifteen, piqued by the remark of a fellow student, Rose scribbled opposite a textbook exegesis on the decline and fall of the empire of Constantine:

> I wonder why he said that. Did he mean I'd be an old maid because
> he was so conceited as to suppose that if he didn't want me no one
> else would? . . . Or did he suppose that I am naturally adapted for
> an old maid's life? Cats, you know, & knitting, & a fondness for

solitude & a dislike of sweethearts? . . . Do you think he thought I was sentimental or what, that he said an old maid *novelist*? Oh, say, I wish you'd ask him.[104]

The Ernestine of the stories casts an appraising eye on her mother, seeing both a woman who has made her "utterly miserable" and someone touchingly vulnerable, still curling her hair and trying to keep up appearances. "She did look nice; she looked kind and brave and sensible. She was really beautiful."[105] If that captured Rose's own affection, it would rarely be expressed again. The climax of the story cycle caught something of the real dynamic between mother and daughter. Saved from scandal by vigilant parents, Ernestine becomes hysterical, laughing and crying as she confesses a secret tryst, and her mother slaps her across the face.

These tales of precocious sexuality ring true, if only in the sense that Rose had grown so rebellious that her parents scarcely knew how to handle her. In 1903, when Almanzo's sister Eliza Jane, now widowed, came to Mansfield for a summer visit, she left with the Wilders' daughter. Rose had impetuously decided that she must attend her ninth and final year of school in Crowley, Louisiana, to learn Latin, unavailable in backward Mansfield. Deprived of a chance at graduating with her class in De Smet, Wilder may have felt obliged to let her daughter further her education, although seeing her off with Eliza Jane might have cost a pang.

Later, rumors swirled that Rose may have been pregnant, spirited away by her aunt to hide the truth.[106] They can safely be discounted, but the episode was nonetheless tinged with sexual overtones—not least because of Rose's later confession that she spent much of her Louisiana school year, when not studying algebra and Latin, fending off ardent suitors. Among them was "an Older Man, a graduate of the University of Chicago," deploying a sporty phaeton and polished manners.[107]

Eliza Jane turned out to be a less than attentive chaperone. Rose often stayed out until midnight, albeit with her virtue "not at all endangered."[108] Endangered or not, her graduation portrait revealed that the once sullen, unsmiling child had been transformed into a sultry Kewpie doll with rounded cheeks, a sensual pout, and knowing gaze. At the ceremony, while more demure classmates sang songs about the pale moon and recited "The Womanliness of Queen Victoria," Rose chose something darker and more lurid, Edgar Allan Poe's "The Raven."[109]

During the summer, she spent a few days visiting Almanzo's brother Perley Day on the bayou, near the Mermentau River. It was an Old South idyll: "pepper trees, Spanish moss . . . alligators sleeping along the bank, cypress knees. I was 17 . . . and spent afternoons sitting in a boat . . . and reading a novel." The novel was *The Leopard's Spots*, published in 1902, the first volume of Thomas Dixon's admiring trilogy about the Ku Klux Klan, a work that would inspire D. W. Griffith's 1915 film *The Birth of a Nation*.[110]

E.J. had fallen on hard times. Tom Thayer had died at sixty-seven. Louisiana's Napoleonic inheritance law restricted a widow to what had been earned during the marriage, so Thayer's children from his previous wives inherited the bulk of his estate, reportedly going so far as to retrieve E.J.'s wedding ring. Eliza Jane's son with Tom Thayer, Walcott Wilder Thayer, four years old at his father's death, was awarded a small allowance, on which he and his mother subsisted. Whatever satisfaction she may have derived from luring away the only offspring of her once-despised little brother and his wife—the Laura Ingalls who had tormented her in a schoolhouse in De Smet—it was short-lived.

In June 1904, Rose returned to Mansfield, her school days at an end. She had no clue where the future led. Would she be, as her classmate had prophesied, an "old maid *novelist*"?

LAURA Wilder was not idle in her daughter's absence. In September 1903, Carrie Ingalls came to visit. Laura was serving that year as "Worthy Matron" of Mansfield's Eastern Star chapter, and brought her sister—a "Worthy Matron" in De Smet—to meetings with her. It was a sign of Laura's increasing involvement in the Masonic organization, one that would lead to significant responsibilities and, eventually, travel.

The following year, Laura was elected to high office in the Eastern Star, "District Deputy Grand Lecturer," assigned to visit and report on the organization's work in her district, including Mansfield and the surrounding towns of Hartville, Mountain Grove, and Ava. In September of 1905, she traveled to St. Louis to deliver the report at a state meeting. It was brief and plainspoken, though prefaced with wry self-deprecation. "I realize with regret that my report is not as complete as it should be," she wrote, "and had fully intended to do better, but we are told that good intentions make excellent paving stones."[111]

Throughout this period, she and Almanzo continued to live in town while working the farm, using and selling its produce. Apple trees on Rocky Ridge had begun bearing, and Laura was growing adept at hosting summer boarders, tempting city appetites with homemade country fare. "Newly laid eggs, thick sweet cream, new milk, fresh buttermilk and butter, the fruits and vegetables fresh from the garden" were on her menu, she would write later, along with fried chicken and fresh composed salads of "tender lettuce . . . arranged on pretty plates with a hard boiled egg cut in half to show the golden center and a little ball of cottage cheese."[112] Salad dressings were made from scratch, of "homemade cider vinegar, mustard, sugar, an egg, with pepper and salt," and she served fresh fruit—berries or peaches—sprinkled with cream and sugar for dessert.[113]

An impromptu photograph captures her standing on the small porch of the Wilders' house in town, framed by decorative scrollwork above. Dressed in a simple work shift with bell sleeves, covered by a full apron, she smiles shyly, a little diffident. Her hair is still brown, her cheeks as round as her daughter's. Across the back of the photo she has scrawled, "Just as I am, without one plea," a line from a popular hymn.[114]

She was busier than ever. In 1908, the Bluebird Railroad started construction on a sixteen-mile line from Mansfield to Ava, a town in the next county known for scenic streams and lakes. Laura Wilder was one of several women photographed driving a "golden spike" that launched the project, and afterward she cooked for visiting railroad workers and officials.[115]

Proud of turning a profit at cooking and hosting, she pointed out that friends who tried their hand at it often complained of losing money after buying "fancy meats and canned goods" to feed their guests. But those who relied on their own farm produce, she stated, could expect to make "at least $5 a week and often more for each person entertained."[116] She advised fellow country women who took in boarders never to feel inferior to city folk or to harbor a chip on their shoulder. "I think we receive a great deal what we expect in this world," she wrote.[117]

WHILE her mother was refining the art of luring city folks to pay cash money for country food, Rose herself fled to the city. After returning from Louisiana in 1904, aged seventeen, she quickly learned telegraphy at the train depot from the stationmaster's daughter, a former classmate. The stationmaster had also taught telegraphy to Paul Cooley, who had quit school in 1901 and found a job as wire clerk and operator in Osceola, Arkansas, although he still passed through Mansfield on occasion.

Paul retained an affection for Rose and perhaps hopes of something more. She later recalled that at seventeen, "not one young man had actually asked me to marry him, though two had almost done so."[118] With her horror of becoming an old maid, she "did not discourage a possible public belief that they had." Her reputation, however, may have been in jeopardy again. In a later diary entry, she wrote that at seventeen, she went "further to smash in struggling with sex. Not that it was really a struggle; I was a rag-doll in its hands."[119]

Her good friend Blanche Coday went to college in nearby Springfield, but if Rose harbored ambitions to continue her education, she certainly did not have the money.[120] Sometime late in 1904, around her eighteenth birthday, she hopped a train for Kansas City and began working as a telegrapher for $2.50 a week, barely enough to afford a rented room and the handfuls of salted peanuts that sufficed for meals.[121] What her mother and father thought of her departure—leaving the safe confines of Mansfield to join the ranks of working "bachelor girls"—remains unrecorded.

When Rose's musings on her early bachelor days were published in *Cosmopolitan* in 1925, under the title "If I Could Live My Life Over Again," they appeared alongside an advertisement for Corona typewriters. The ad addressed a mother worried about her daughter: "Could she earn her own living? She's your daughter—and perhaps you hate to think of her having to work for a living. But this sort of thing does happen in very nice families."[122] It happened in Wilder's. Laura might

Little Crow, in native dress and holding a feather staff, 1858

Charles and Caroline Ingalls, late 1870s or early 1880s. Caroline is wearing a comb in her hair, perhaps the gift from her daughters described in *Pioneer Girl*.

A dugout on the South Loup River, near
Virge Allen Homestead, Custer County, Nebraska

Grasshoppers stopping a train on the Union Pacific Railroad, from
a sketch by A. P. Smith, *Frank Leslie's Illustrated Newspaper*, August 7, 1875

The first known photograph of the three eldest Ingalls sisters, taken around 1879 or 1880. From left to right: Carrie, Mary, and Laura Ingalls. Carrie is believed to be wearing a string of Indian beads, perhaps those collected by her sisters on the day she was born.

Mary Ingalls, Vinton, Iowa, circa 1880s

Almanzo Wilder as a young man
in De Smet, circa 1880s

Laura Ingalls at seventeen, De Smet, 1884

Laura and Almanzo Wilder in the winter of 1885, shortly after their marriage

Laura and Almanzo Wilder near Westville, Florida, circa 1891–92

Among the Ozarks: The Land of Big Red Apples, an illustrated book promoting the Kansas City, Fort Scott & Memphis Railroad and the "Big Red Apple" region of Missouri, 2nd edition, 1892. The Wilders' daughter, Rose, recalled studying it before the family's journey to the Ozarks in 1894.

The Ingalls family in 1894, shortly before the Wilders left for Missouri. Seated, left to right: Caroline, Charles, and Mary Ingalls. Standing: Carrie Ingalls, Laura Ingalls Wilder, and Grace Ingalls.

not have been as prudish about the need to work for a living, but she must have had concerns about Rose alone in the big city.

In the event, Rose subsisted on peanuts only briefly. She soon graduated to Western Union, first working as a night operator in a branch office in Kansas City's Midland Hotel, then taking a second shift during the day. Told that all wire operators must know touch-typing, she borrowed a machine and learned overnight.

In the fall of 1906, Laura Wilder, on committee assignments for Eastern Star, combined a meeting in Kansas City with a visit to Rose. A fashion plate photograph shows Laura radiating glamor, her face framed by an elaborate feathered hat and a fur collar. In a photo perhaps taken at the same session, Rose is grinning broadly, her head crowned with a jaunty straw bowler, a poster image for carefree bachelor life.

In 1907, during a national telegraphers' strike, Rose came home to Mansfield, and the grinning bachelor girl vanished, the finery set aside to pick apples. The Wilders' orchards were yielding in abundance, and a snapshot finds Rose standing subdued beside her mother, behind barrels of fruit waiting to be shipped off.[123] It remains one of the few images featuring the two women. With the possible exception of the Spring Valley photo, too grainy to identify everyone pictured, there are no existing photographs of Laura, Almanzo, and Rose together.[124]

When the telegraph union caved, in November, Rose moved on to manage a Western Union office several hundred miles east, in Mount Vernon, Indiana, handling duties as "telegraph operator, clerk cashier, janitress, and stern . . . chief of the staff, one messenger boy aged 13."[125] Pulling in $60 a month for what she called a life of leisure—working six days a week, ten hours a day—she was now dining on five-cent fried fish sandwiches. It was in Mount Vernon that she received a forlorn postcard from Paul Cooley: "Say, you might write a fellow [once] in a while, to relieve that lonesome feeling. (On my part, I mean.) Of course you're never lonesome, so long as you hear from . . . Paul."[126]

But if Paul had been expecting something from that quarter, he was to be disappointed. In April 1908, Rose followed one of her beaus to San Francisco. His name was Claire Gillette Lane, and he was one of the notorious traveling men her parents had warned her about. Working in some capacity for the *San Francisco Call*, he was constantly on the move, perhaps selling newspaper advertisements or subscriptions. No one knows where they met—perhaps back at the Midland Hotel in Kansas City—but Rose traveled to San Francisco to be with him. She initially stayed at a hotel, then moved into the same apartment building as Lane, sharing a flat there with Elizabeth "Bessie" Beatty, a rising young reporter for the *San Francisco Bulletin*.

In San Francisco, Rose worked again as a telegrapher, managing the stock market wire from New York. But not for long: her boyfriend's connections proved pivotal. In September and November 1908, Rose Wilder's byline appeared in the *Call*—first above an article about messenger boys, then on a piece about "The Constantly Increasing Wonders in the New Field of Wireless."[127]

As with many newspapers at the turn of the century, the *Call* was enlivened with enormous, eye-catching photos, headlines, and comic strips, the whole package dressed in curling scrolls and wildly inventive typography. Journalistic standards regarding accuracy, attention to detail, and proper sourcing mattered little. Instead, sensational front pages warned of "brutes" threatening "tots" and of other lurid crimes. They used techniques borrowed from fiction, including the colorful depiction of stock characters and the use of dialogue, often invented.

Rose Wilder's first efforts were no departure from that model. Her messenger boys, urchins all, spoke to the reader in a winning working-class manner. Her write-up of the night on Russian Hill when an operator broke the trans-Pacific record by receiving a message from the island of Oahu was highly dramatic, painting the scene as if for the theater, complete with sound effects. "With a deafening roar, a blinding glare, the electric spark leaped out. Crash! crash! crash!"[128] Thus Rose Wilder learned her trade. Her mastery of such techniques would have lifelong consequences for her own work as well as her mother's.

Rose Wilder and Claire Gillette Lane were married in San Francisco on March 24, 1909, the groom's birthday. The bride was twenty-two. Announcements were issued bearing Almanzo's and Laura's names, but they were not in attendance, nor had they met their new son-in-law.

The marriage would be unhappy almost from the start, a chapter in the struggle with sex that Rose later acknowledged, implying that the two had little in common beyond physical attraction. Candid photos taken at the time show her dressed in a loose shift or nightgown, with flying uncombed hair and a postcoital flush, hands splayed across her breasts and fingers spread to show off her wedding ring. Her face bears a triumphant smile.

Her communications had the same glittery-eyed, almost boastful attitude. Graduating to the married state, Lane was no longer in danger of becoming an "old maid." No longer would she have to bow to her mother's instruction or feel the inferiority of being unwanted, "on the shelf." Instead, for the rest of her life she would strive to become her mother's instructor.

Less is known about her husband and their first year of marriage than virtually any other phase of Rose's life. Little survives beyond a few newspaper articles attributed to "C. G. Lane" and the faint shadow of get-rich-quick schemes he cast across her prose. After the wedding, the Lanes visited Rose's parents in Missouri. They then set out across the country on unknown travel presumably related to his work as a salesman.

Soon Rose was pregnant. Aside from the wedding announcement and the marriage certificate, virtually the only documentary evidence of the family's whereabouts at this time comes from a Utah death certificate that only surfaced recently. It records the stillbirth of "Infant Lane" on November 23, 1909, at 2:30 in the morning, at Holy Cross Hospital in Salt Lake City. The baby was a boy, born prematurely at an estimated six months. Gillette Lane supplied information for the form, giving their place of residence as the Colonial Hotel. The baby was buried the following day in Mount Olivet Cemetery.[129]

For a young woman, such a painful and chaotic experience must have been made even more traumatic by the fact that she was miles from home, family, and friends. She may have known her husband for only a year or so. She had probably never seen the inside of a hospital before.

After that loss, under circumstances never explained, Lane underwent a surgical procedure in Kansas City sometime during the winter of 1909–1910. Recovery after a stillbirth can be difficult, and in this case there were apparently complications—perhaps bleeding, infection, or retention of part of the placenta in the uterus, which often results in blood poisoning and can be fatal. Rose would never write about the experience in detail but would later describe her state of mind as "a kind of delirium."[130] She was not physically "normal" between 1909 and 1911, she would say, or mentally fit until 1914. The surgery may have left her unable to have children.

For a time, she went home. In April 1910, the federal census caught Rose living with Almanzo and Laura in the house in Mansfield. But the following month she was back in Kansas City, writing painfully stilted articles for the "Women's Pages" of the *Kansas City Post*. An odd photo shows her sitting on a park lawn, hair hidden under an elaborate hat, eating a cookie. Gone are the rounded cheeks and flushed smile of her newlywed days. She appears thin and nearly unrecognizable. Beside her sits a callow youth in a loud checked suit and newsboy's cap, apparently a photographer, bearing a sandwich in one hand and a piece of twine in the other, disappearing out of the shot. On the back she has written: "Working hard on a Swope Park assignment for *Kansas City Journal*, in an unjustified snapshot taken by Wright with the end of a string."[131] The string pulled the shutter release, an early form of selfie.

Rose kept news clippings in her papers. Few had bylines but some may have been written by her husband, others by herself. "Crowing, Cooing Babies Compete at the Grocers' Pure Food Show" features a wide shot of a beauty pageant: beaming mothers hold plump healthy infants up to the camera, proudly dressed in all manner of finery.[132] What jarring pangs that cost the reporter can only be imagined. Another piece, about the high cost of bread and milk, begins with a nursery rhyme: "By[e] Baby Bunting, Daddy's gone a-hunting, To get some nice, salt, greasy meat, So Babe can have a bite to eat."[133]

Meanwhile, her mother was herself becoming established in her daughter's new profession. Building on the confidence gained delivering reports and speeches for Eastern Star meetings, she delivered an address at a historic "Woman's Land Congress" in May 1910 in Arcadia, a town some 150 miles northeast of Mansfield.[134] The Land Congress, described by an item in the *Country Gentleman* as the first ever in the country, was sponsored by the Woman's Missouri Development Association, of which Wilder was a member. Its aim was to induce people to settle on twelve million undeveloped acres in the state, and it offered exhibits of agricultural products and home weaving.[135]

Wilder's address touched on her efforts to organize auxiliary associations in towns neighboring Mansfield that were working to establish circulating libraries, reading and cooking clubs, and public areas and restrooms. "What a glorious thing it will be," she concluded, "when the women of the entire state, in towns and country, feel themselves united in bonds of friendship & mutual helpfulness, all working together for the best interest of our dear home state—MISSOURI."[136]

Her talk was reprinted in the local newspaper, which touted it as the most enthusiastically received of all the speeches. Wilder carefully pasted it in her scrapbook beside another clipping, a sidebar introducing her to the public. "Several farmers, and particularly those interested in poultry, have inquired who Mrs. A. J. Wilder is," it began.[137] It went on to describe Rocky Ridge as a model poultry farm and Wilder herself as an editor of the *Star Farmer*'s poultry department and a contributor to publications including the *Missouri Ruralist* and the *St. Louis Globe-Democrat*. Whatever Wilder's early newspaper contributions may have been—the earliest yet discovered dates from 1910—this laudatory write-up suggests that she entered the world of journalism just months behind her daughter.[138]

During the winter of 1910–1911, the Lanes took off on a swing through the East Coast, living large at the Waldorf Astoria Hotel on seven dollars a day. (Rose's parents must have blanched at the extravagance.) There they ran into "old" California friends, including the governor-elect, Hiram Johnson. "The hotel itself is on the bum," Rose wrote in her new gushing slang, "not the best of hotels . . . too ostentatious—too much gilt and red," but their room was pleasant, and they were having the "best time."

Somehow they ended up in Maine, with Rose in yet another hotel while her husband traveled. They were pounding the pavement to sell ads, and Rose was already of the opinion that her husband didn't know what he was doing. Sales were not good: the previous day had brought in only nine dollars. "I don't agree with Claire about the sort of ad he is handing them here," she wrote, "and today I'm going to put on an altogether different scheme, and see if I can't wake this town up a little."[139] Whoever Claire Gillette Lane was, he probably had not realized that the fresh-faced young telegrapher he married would turn out to be a relentless competitor.

While ad sales were poor, the young couple pulled off a financial coup, extorting a thousand dollars and expenses from the railroad after Gillette Lane suffered some kind of minor accident. Rose was unabashed about their underhanded tactics, boasting that "we made such a bluff of rolling in wealth and being able to fight the thing." They showed up at the railroad president's office wearing their finest overcoats—and, in Rose's case, a fur hat—and the company paid nearly twice as much as expected.

It was a prophetic incident. Lane's biographer, William Holtz, would attempt to tie it to the prevailing contempt for railroads felt by many Americans at the time. But there was more to it. Throughout her life, Rose Lane would never blanch at exaggerating or telling half-truths and outright lies to gain an advantage, and her journalistic techniques would have more to do with fabulism than with facts. The behavior may have been rooted in her earliest days, when she knew nothing but anxiety about how the family would survive, where they would live, and what they would eat. But as she became an adult, those anxieties sent her on an endless cycle of finagling to make money by any means necessary, then spending it just as frantically.

It was at this time that Rose began hectically advising her mother on money-making newspaper schemes. Fragments of letters that survive suggest a powerful and almost immediate shift in the mother-daughter dynamic dating from Rose's marriage, and here Rose's didactic approach was in full swing. She typed out page after page of editorial advice, leaving nothing to chance, telling Laura exactly what to say to editors, how to approach them, and how to pitch her ideas:

Why don't you write an article for the W.S. Farmer on the possibilities of a five acre farm in Southern Missouri—not a real estate-y sounding one, but just showing the results which can be reaped from the expenditure of say three hundred dollars. Just mention casually—

"There are many so-and-so farms which can be got on time, with a
payment of so-and-so down, and it is quite possible to meet all the
future payments from the profits on the place." And then go on to tell
about how much to spend on a little house, how much for the chicken
houses, how much for the chickens, etc. . . . a sort of "back to the
farm" article.[140]

Her mother was paying attention. Among the first pieces Laura Wilder
would write, in 1911, was just such an article.

Rose also casually suggested that Laura adapt a yet-unpublished
piece that Rose had written for a San Francisco paper about a "certi-
fied milk dairy" and send it out under her own name, perhaps as a "first
story" for a popular regional farmers' newspaper, the *Missouri Ruralist*.[141] Laura apparently asked about newspaper ethics, but Rose dismissed that out of hand, assuring her that they were "the funniest sort
of mixing-up."[142] Like the fast-talking Rosalind Russell in *His Girl
Friday*, she had no patience for her mother's cautious trepidation.
Simply "avoid the appearance of evil," she said. And she sharply advised
her to drop any notion of picking her own cowpeas. Pay someone else
to do it, she advised: far better to write for newspapers.[143]

These early letters establish the new basis of the relationship
between Rose Lane and Laura Wilder: the daughter becoming the often
domineering partner, while the once strict matriarch was forced to
acknowledge her own uncertainties as she launched herself into a new
realm, holding tight to her daughter's hand. This would be their relationship for the next four decades.

For her part, Laura wanted money as well, an impulse rooted every
bit as much as Rose's in a past defined by instability. She was hungry
for security, status, and, increasingly, for a connection to the people
and places she had left behind. Her past had been a struggle to survive,
but thinking of it still gave rise to powerful, inchoate feelings of yearning, loss, and nostalgia.

The first step in dealing with those feelings was to return to the farm.
After years of scrimping and saving—hauling freight from the railroad
depot, cooking for traveling men, and taking in boarders—the Wilders
had put together a financial stake that would take them back to their

land, the dream from their earliest married days. With the five-hundred-dollar inheritance that Almanzo received from his father's estate and another five hundred from the sale of the house in town, they moved back to Rocky Ridge, hiring workers to help them undertake extensive renovations.

The design would overwhelmingly reflect Laura's desires, and for the Ozarks the farmhouse she envisioned was no little house. Almanzo would be called upon for his considerable skill in jury-rigging creative solutions to plumbing difficulties and other practical issues, but the construction process, evolving in stages over the next several years, would leave an indelible impression in the community that the wife "ran the show."[144] It was an impression she would do nothing to discourage in later years, when she related anecdotes about the creation of a home that would be hailed as a local showplace. Almanzo would have been happy with a simple addition, she wrote, but she felt that such a box-like structure wouldn't "look right among the trees, with the everlasting hills around it."[145] She could not distinctly recall his plan, she added, saying, "fact is I didn't listen to it and so, of course, I had my way."

She wanted a home that fit harmoniously on the hillside it commanded, an organic outgrowth of the property, with a beam ceiling hewn from their own oaks and an imposing chimney raised from the rocks "scattered over the fields." Perhaps inspired by the "Prairie style" of Frank Lloyd Wright, whose work had been featured in the *Ladies Home Journal* in 1901, it would bring the outdoors inside by way of large picture windows.[146] Comfortable sitting porches would capture ever-changing views of the woods and fields beyond.

Wright, too, had been born in Wisconsin in 1867. In his prairie houses he made use of raw "unfinished" materials, and now so did Laura. Exhausted by the labor of hauling rocks, Almanzo was at one point ready to abandon the heavy stone fireplace, buying fire bricks instead, but Laura "argued . . . begged" and eventually wept. "For the only time in my life, I made use of a woman's time-honored weapon, tears, and to my surprise it worked," she said, calling upon a hoary gender stereotype that barely concealed the force of her personality.[147] In the end, her living room would be dominated by the fireplace in the north wall, the exterior chimney crafted of "curious rock formations" studded with fossils "which had lain at the bottom of the seas."[148]

By the time they were done, the former mud-chinked shack was gone, and a solid, spacious, and gracious abode, a ten-room home, stood in its place. Compared to the one-room cabins and thin-walled structures Charles Ingalls had built, it embodied solidity and permanence. It was made to last, the culmination of a life's work.

But Laura Wilder was not done. She was forty-four years old. She had been working since she was nine, but she was not ready to retire. After the scourge of the Dakotas, losing virtually everything but the wagon and horses that drew them to Missouri, she had arrived in Mansfield and remade her world—egg by egg, boarder by boarder, step by laborious step. Now she was ready to pronounce on it.

Chapter 7

As a Farm Woman Thinks

That "Story of My Life" Thing

"These whirling times," she would call them.[1] Off in her distant rural nest, Laura Wilder of Mansfield felt things changing. Social forces began a seismic shift in 1910, as Americans began living—and consuming—in ways never before imagined.

A gulf was opening between the city and the countryside, isolating and marginalizing small towns. The country's population was growing, and people were heading to cities, immigrants crowding into urban tenements. In 1890, two-thirds of all Americans had lived in rural communities, but by the turn of the century that proportion started a downward slide that would never be reversed. By 1910, more than half of the population was concentrated in urban areas, lured by jobs and aided by a revolution in transportation that eased rural reliance on the railroads: Henry Ford had introduced his Model T just two years earlier, and would sell fifteen million of them over the next two decades.

But while the citizenry was on the move, massive corporations—"trusts"—seized control of the economy, consolidating the power of banks, railroads, and the oil industry in the hands of two titans, J. P. Morgan and John D. Rockefeller. Farmers fervently believed that these trusts had colluded in keeping crop prices low and costs unbearably high.[2]

They found their champion in Teddy Roosevelt. He ran for president on a promise to contain "predatory wealth," championing "Square Deal" policies: conservation, control of corporations, and consumer protections. New legislation reined in the railroads, trimming sweetheart arrangements and limiting freight prices. He was aided by those he dubbed "muckrakers," early investigative journalists whose leading light, Ida Tarbell, laid the foundation for trust-busting with her meticulously reported *History of the Standard Oil Company*; published in 1904, it sparked public outrage and led to the breakup of Rockefeller's monopoly. The banking and railroad reforms came too late for generations of farmers, including Charles Ingalls and Almanzo Wilder, for whom low-interest loans might have provided a lifeline. But they were a start on progressive legislation that would be taken up, decades later, by Teddy's distant cousin.

Yet the signal accomplishments of the Progressive Era, which hit its stride in the first two decades of the new century, arose not from men at the top but from women at the grassroots. Inspired by the power of labor unions, women began meeting in big-city union halls, small-town church basements, and private parlors, creating a network of loosely linked social organizations, temperance groups, reading clubs, culture clubs, farmers' clubs, and sororities. It was the age of sisterhood, solidarity, and suffrage.

At the same time, women were entering the workforce at a rapid clip, their numbers rising from 2.6 million in 1880 to 7.8 million thirty years later. Around 60 percent were confined to domestic servitude, but others were laboring in garment factories and mills. The Women's Trade Union League was founded in 1903; in 1907, it supported the telegraphers' strike that suspended Rose Wilder's Kansas City job.

The women's suffrage movement, started decades earlier at the 1848 Women's Rights Convention in Seneca Falls, was also gaining ground. Temperance groups promoted "universal suffrage" as a way for women to address alcohol abuse, domestic violence, and exploitative child labor laws. The industrialized East and the South opposed such changes—children provided cheap labor in cotton mills—so the West led the way.

Wyoming Territory, Utah, Colorado, and Idaho gave women the vote before the turn of the century, followed by Washington, California, Arizona, Kansas, and Oregon between 1910 and 1912. Rose Wilder Lane would cast her first vote in California for Woodrow Wilson.[3]

Missouri lagged behind. At a meeting in 1869, St. Louis city councilors had laughed uproariously when women's suffrage was proposed, and during the first decade of the twentieth century no women's rights petitions were presented to the state legislature.[4] One state activist recalled that around 1910, the word "suffragette" was "not even whispered in polite society. . . . It was like throwing a bomb in conservative St. Louis to repeat the new slogan 'Votes for Women!' "[5]

Instead, women's rights were smuggled into Missouri's polite society through the most humble of Trojan horses: farmers' clubs. In 1910, the University of Missouri, eager to attract students to a new College of Agriculture, launched "Farmers' Week" at its Columbia campus, which quickly grew into a highly anticipated annual event. Its legendary parades—featuring a "Corn Queen," girls riding the "Mo-Lasses" wagon, and a "Goddess of Agriculture"—were hardly bastions of liberation, but the event provided a forum for farm women (and men) to gather, confer, and organize.

In 1911, thirteen hundred farmers from ninety-seven Missouri counties came to Columbia. Mingling with cattle growers and swine breeders were the women of the Missouri Home Makers' Conference. In their papers, the word *suffrage* did not appear, but members nonetheless delivered frank talks on issues integral to women's rights and economic independence: the importance of registering births, reducing infant mortality through breast-feeding, promoting food safety, and marketing farm products such as butter and hams. Among the papers read at the conference was one titled "The Small Farm Home," by Mrs. A. J. Wilder of Rocky Ridge Farm, Mansfield, a vice-president of the Missouri Woman's Home Development Association.

Laura Wilder herself apparently did not attend the conference, but someone read her paper into the record. A photograph of the forty-four-year-old author, dark hair piled atop her head and a grave expression on her face, appeared in the Missouri Agricultural Report along with the text of her speech.

It was not her first time in print on agricultural topics. The previous year, Kansas newspapers and the *American Food Journal* had printed remarks by Mrs. A. J. Wilder on the economic benefits of a five-acre farm and poultry operation. She calculated that it cost her eighty-five cents to keep a hen for a year, while the birds averaged 180 eggs each. At twenty cents a dozen, that yielded "a profit of $2.15 for each hen."[6]

"The Small Farm Home," the paper she wrote for the 1911 conference, went far beyond such commercial calculations. It was a manifesto for the philosophy behind the little house:

> There is a movement in the United States today, wide-spread and very far reaching in its consequences. People are seeking after a freer, healthier, happier life. They are tired of the noise and dirt, bad air and crowds of the cities, and are turning longing eyes toward the green slopes, wooded hills, pure running water and health-giving breezes of the country.[7]

Wilder assured readers that a five-acre farm could comfortably support a family through poultry, fruit, and dairy production. She urged them not to be discouraged by the prospect of hard work, citing time- and labor-saving devices from oil stoves—"no carrying in of wood and carrying out of ashes"—to cream separators, sewing machines, gasoline engines, and new methods of piping water into the home from a spring or well. The payoff in space, freedom, and aesthetic beauty, she argued, was more than worth it. "We have a whole five acres for our back yard and all out doors for our conservatory, filled not only with beautiful flowers, but with grand old trees as well, with running water and beautiful birds, with sunshine and fresh air and all wild, free, beautiful things."

As for social life, she argued, a farm was hardly isolated, with rural delivery of newspapers, circulating libraries, and neighbors for company. Country women who believed their "sisters in the city" had it better were advised to "wake up to your opportunities.... Acquire modern appliances, build a social life, and subscribe to the daily paper." In future, she wrote, "the real cultured, social, and intellectual life will be in the country."

From the outset, the essay resounded with Wilder's pronounced optimism, a tendency to emphasize the upbeat, reflecting her lifelong preference for country life. She was also tapping into the national sentiment of the moment. Upton Sinclair's undercover research for his 1906 novel *The Jungle* had exposed the health hazards of meatpacking plants, launching a spate of "pure food" laws that regulated everything from wrapping of bread to tuberculin testing of milk. There was a growing sense that cities were blighted by polluted air, tainted food, and unwholesome influences.

The panacea for such fears was the countryside. Open vistas and wilderness were thought to restore physical and mental health. Champions of nature reserves, for instance, stressed such benefits, the first director of the National Park Service claiming that parks "are national character and health builders . . . giving a new impetus to sane living."[8] For Wilder, farms offered the same restorative qualities, but on a human scale. Beginning with this 1911 essay, her writing would repeatedly compare town and country, magnifying every advantage of life under the open skies, lived as close to the wild as possible.

Her optimistic portrayal of an economic rural utopia was misleading, however. And Wilder knew it: while her family relied on her egg money, as well as livestock, apples, and other produce supplied by Rocky Ridge, the farm never fully supported them, and they regularly had to supplement their income with additional jobs. What's more, the Wilders owned considerably more than five acres, though the extra land did not make the bad years any easier to bear.

Wilder's essay contained its own contradictions, as much of her writing would. But in the audience, listening, was a man who appreciated her bullish message. His name was John Case, and he was an editor at the *Missouri Ruralist*, a new regional farmers' newspaper. Case was exactly the kind of person that Wilder, encouraged by her daughter to pursue writing opportunities, was trying to reach.

The *Missouri Ruralist* was part of the expanding Midwestern publishing empire of Arthur Capper, a Topeka entrepreneur who started as a printer's devil at a small Kansas paper and rose through the ranks to build his holdings until he owned two daily papers, a weekly, a printing company, a farm monthly, five farm papers, and, eventually, radio and television stations.[9] He would later serve as governor of Kansas and as a long-term U.S. senator. In 1910, Capper had acquired the *Ruralist*, the local paper of Sedalia, Missouri, and Case was tasked with consolidating it with another acquisition—the *Breeder's Special* of Kansas City—and expanding it into a regional semimonthly title.[10] His efforts would meet with success: the circulation of the *Missouri Ruralist* would climb steeply in coming years, topping 80,000 by 1915.[11]

At the 1911 Farm Week, Wilder's talk was followed by another, which explored the drawbacks she had minimized. "Inconveniences of the Farm Home" sketched out the bad roads and bad schools, the 7 percent decline in rural population over the past decade, the loneliness of farm life, and the fact that most women had no access to the improvements Wilder touted, including running water, electricity, and oil stoves.[12] Farmers, the author noted, seemed to prefer their backward ways, consistently voting against improvements to roads or schools lest they raise taxes.

But such realism did not impress John Case. He preferred Wilder's idealistic, sunny defense of country life. On February 18, 1911, the *Missouri Ruralist* reprinted her talk, word for word, as "Favors the Small Farm Home."[13] It was her first major publication in the expanding world of agricultural journalism, and it launched a new career.

EVER since Rose Lane's brief 1910 sojourn as a *Kansas City Post* reporter, she had been harrying her mother to write for money. In a few surviving letters written between 1910 and 1914, Lane alluded to an apparently failed effort by Wilder to write for the *Weekly Star Farmer*—"they aren't treating you so very badly," she told her, "just badly enough to make you sore, of course"—and urged her to try the *Kansas City Star*. With typical extravagance, she instructed her to go to Springfield to buy a used typewriter, specifically a fifty-dollar rebuilt Underwood, five dollars a month on the installment plan.[14]

If her mother were to publish an article a week in the *Star*, Lane calculated, she could put aside quite a bit of cash for a trip to San Francisco in 1915. "Why *don't* you write up Mansfield," she enthused, telling her exactly how to do it, while cautioning her not to spend all her earnings on cows but save them for the journey.

The trip to San Francisco had been a mother-daughter dream for some time, intended to coincide with the highly anticipated World's Fair—the Panama-Pacific International Exposition—celebrating the completion of the Panama Canal. The fair was meant to showcase the city's economic rebirth after the 1906 earthquake and fires, which had leveled entire neighborhoods. Built between the Presidio and what is now the Marina District, the Exposition promised dazzling delights. There was to be a model of the canal, as well as a "Tower of Jewels" adorned with cut-glass gems and lit by night with powerful searchlights. There would be exotic international foods and agricultural exhibits from around the world. Laura Wilder had never visited a major city outside Missouri. She had never seen the ocean. It had been years since she'd seen her daughter. Lane had not been able to visit Mansfield between 1911 and 1915, and mentioned being "terribly lonesome."

The problem was money. After returning from Maine, the Lanes had branched out. For Stine & Kendrick, a San Francisco real estate and insurance firm, they sold California farm land to rubes from Oklahoma, running advertisements in small-town newspapers:

CALIFORNIA DAIRYLAND FARMS

in the famous San Joaquin Valley of California: If you are interested in farming where there are no extreme summers or winters; where you have artesian water to irrigate; good land; quick transportation to a market of two million people, write us and we will be glad to send you a descriptive booklet.

STINE & KENDRICK

In October 1914, Lane wrote to her aunt Eliza Jane and to E.J.'s son Wilder on Stine & Kendrick stationery. He, too, wanted to visit the Exposition, but Lane gently discouraged him, saying that she was busy setting up an office in San Jose and that her employers might send her back to Oklahoma at any moment. She sounded listless and discouraged, admitting that she and Claire were living in a studio apartment, with a wall-bed and kitchenette. They had no room for visitors and no money to show them around if they came. Her parents were the "same as ever," she told E.J., "but it has been years since I saw them." At that point, a parental visit seemed impossible:

> No, they are not coming out, I have been hoping for four years to be able to have them come, but guess I won't be able to make it. There have been three very dry years in Missouri, you know, when the crops were nearly complete failures, and now this year, when they get a fair crop, it is impossible to sell anything at a profitable price. I could perhaps manage the fare out, but of course living expenses here are very high in normal times. . . . I think it is going to be about impossible for us to manage at all to get them out. They are on the farm now, you know, and it is fairly profitable, I guess, but it all goes back into the farm.[15]

Lane remarked that her parents seemed so hard up that they could not afford new clothes, an admission that would have horrified her mother.

At times, Lane did not know where her feckless husband was or what he was doing. She appeared to be losing faith in his dealings, referring to vague intrigues in New Zealand and Central America. In one letter, she admitted to her mother that it was "her belief" that Claire had gone to work for "the Carodoc people," an advertising agency that had been—or so he claimed—negotiating for his services. Insulted by a paltry offer, he held out for more, only to be told, "Your wife makes something doesn't she?" She had her doubts about the whole story:

> Claire saw red and I suppose he also talked that way. Anyhow, he left the office in a black rage. And next day they sent for him and offered him forty a week and 20% of the net earnings of the whole company. He said he was going to take it, and he has been going down there ever since, so I believe he has gone to work for them . . . of course there are half a dozen other plans still in the atmosphere, waiting to materialize, such as the Guatemala one. And others.[16]

All these grand plans evaporated. Twenty percent of nothing was still nothing, and the couple was so strapped for cash that they borrowed $250 from Lane's parents. Lane told Wilder that when Claire received a windfall of eighteen dollars, they were ecstatic: "the first real money we have seen for ages and ages, except that you sent. So the rent is no more hanging over us like a piece of black crape."[17] At the same time, she admitted, they were running around with high-rollers, "Claire casually talking millions" with powerful men while she wondered whether their gas would be cut off that night, trying to suppress "the gnawing mad wish for twenty dollar[s] for the rent man."[18]

Thus it was that financial considerations—her wish to visit San Francisco and the Exposition, her daughter's dire straits—drove Laura Wilder's first attempts to write newspaper columns. In other words, it was an economic stopgap, much like her father's carpentry or his civil service jobs. After her "Small Farm Home" article appeared in the *Missouri Ruralist*, she followed up with a more personal piece, "The Story of Rocky Ridge Farm," submitted under the name of A. J. Wilder in response to a farm story contest.[19]

While he may have dictated some details, Almanzo almost certainly did not write the piece. Letters to his daughter reveal how stiff and laborious he found putting pen to paper. The article began by admitting the difficulties the Wilders had faced getting started, acknowledging that Almanzo's "broken health" had made clearing the land and turning it into a farm a "heroic effort," resulting in "short rations at the first." There was no description of the years in town, of supplementing farm income with wages, or of the anxiety engendered by poverty.

Over the following months, Wilder continued journeyman writing efforts under her husband's name, probably utilizing his dictation. A Missouri newspaper article appeared in 1912 with specific instructions, and a diagram, on how to build a sturdy gate that would not sag.[20] A few months later, a *Ruralist* feature with A. J. Wilder's byline explained techniques of apple husbandry. Almanzo criticized the practice of spraying trees with insecticide, recommending an organic method: "As I never allowed hunting on the farm, the quail were thick in the orchard and used to wallow and dust themselves like chickens in this fine dirt close to the tree."[21] Natural pest control, he said, kept his trees free of boring insects. That was indeed Almanzo's methodology, though Laura probably transcribed the material. He would always prohibit hunting on their land.

Soon Wilder was publishing in newspapers all over the state, from Cape Girardeau to Mexico, Missouri. She did not hesitate to step out from behind her husband when offering her own expertise, such as on raising chicks late in the season. Her poultry pieces revealed just how exacting and finicky a business the delicate digestion of young fowl could be. Chicks had to be fed exactly twenty-four hours after hatching, and their diet changed day by day, with the addition of clean sand, fine-chopped bone, and bread crumbs soaked in milk and squeezed, neither too wet nor too dry. The birds required "perfectly clean" coops, adequate ventilation, and constant care, all taking up hours each day.[22] "While they still hover in the coops I dust them with insect powder, rub a drop of oil into the down on their heads, and rub their legs with vaseline," she wrote. The time had to be stolen from other chores, including scalding and skimming milk, churning butter, hauling slop to the pigs, and processing and rendering meat from butchered animals.

Farm work was so labor-intensive that in the fall of 1912, Wilder experienced a health crisis and was hospitalized.[23] She alluded to it in her next *Ruralist* article, "Shorter Hours for Farm Women," published in June 1913 under her own name. "Recovering from a serious illness," Wilder wrote, inspired her discovery that she could do chores—ironing, washing dishes, frying griddle cakes—while seated on a high stool.[24] Beyond tips for reducing the physical and mental strain of housework, though, the article also evoked the suffragist philosophy that was gradually becoming acceptable in Missouri society, albeit in a gentle, nondoctrinaire fashion. "Farm women have been patient and worked very hard," Wilder wrote, but "it has seemed sometimes as though they and their work were overlooked in the march of progress."[25] She was echoing sentiments felt nationwide: a month later, the *Saturday Evening Post* published an editorial proclaiming housework to be "excessively stupid and irksome" and arguing that women "ought to have interests outside the house, as different and as stimulating as possible."[26]

Wilder found those interests on her doorstep. Extolling the latest timesavers, including vacuum cleaners, she elaborated on a favorite topic: finding solace in nature. "I have always found that I did not get so tired, and my day seemed shorter," she wrote, "when I listened to the birds singing or noticed, from the window, the beauties of the trees or clouds."[27]

That same month, Wilder's mother sent a solicitous letter from De Smet, urging her to take it easy. "We are very glad and thankful that you are getting so well and strong again," Caroline Ingalls wrote, "but do not try to stretch those 24 hours you have and make yourself sick again. Take your time for sleep and sleep good. Do you know Laura I sleep so peacefully and soundly all night that I am almost ashamed of myself."[28] Caroline sent news of South Dakota—where it was so hot and dry that the crops would likely be spoiled once again—and detailed instructions on how to make grape juice, a method not improved upon since "old Bible times . . . when Joseph was sold and taken into Egypt." There was, she concluded cheerfully, "nothing new under the sun."

These were prophetic words, for Wilder was coming to this proverbial insight on her own. Sometime in 1914, Lane urged her to retrieve a long reminiscence that Wilder had written and sent to Caroline and Mary Ingalls. Put it "verbatim into that 'story of my life' thing," Lane instructed. The manuscript Wilder had embarked on was apparently substantial, beginning in Mansfield but harking back to the old days.[29] "Just think you are writing a diary that no one anywhere will ever ever see," Rose advised.[30]

For the moment, however, Wilder was concerned with immediate deadlines. The value of women's work would become a prominent theme in her writing for the *Ruralist*. In the summer of 1914, she profiled a Mansfield homemaker much like herself, Mrs. C. A. Durnell, who had left St. Louis seeking a healthier climate for her children in the Ozarks. As the Wilders had done, she rehabilitated an exhausted five-acre farm and log cabin, raised a cow and a flock of Rhode Island Reds, and drew forth from stony fields an abundant fruit orchard and vegetable garden.

Mrs. Durnell, too, had saved up to build a more substantial house, prevailing over stubborn male contractors. The fireplace, Wilder wrote, was "made according to Mrs. Durnell's own plan, with a chimney that draws even though she had to stand by the mason as he was building it and insist that he build it as she directed."[31] Here Wilder began a thread that would run through all of her work and appear in her daughter's as well. Women must assert their authority, she believed; it would pay off in the end.

All True

It was a lesson Rose Lane was learning. In the summer of 1914, after the assassination of Archduke Franz Ferdinand in Sarajevo and the outbreak of war in Europe, sales of California farmland had fallen off. The following January, still managing the faltering business at Stine & Kendrick's San Jose office, Lane received a call from her old roommate, Bessie Beatty, now editor of a woman's page at the *Bulletin* in San Francisco. Mentored by legendary muckraker Fremont Older, editor of the *Bulletin* for the past twenty years, Beatty was looking for an assistant, at $12.50 a week. Lane jumped at the chance, boarding the next San Francisco–bound train. She also chose that moment to free herself of her husband, saying later, without sentiment: "I got rid of Gillette in January, 1915."[32] The marriage had lasted little more than five years, although the couple would not formally divorce until a few years later.

With her new salary, Lane was in a position to make Wilder's trip to San Francisco happen. She wrote to her mother, "I simply can't stand being so homesick for you any more. You must plan to come out here in July or, at latest, August. You've simply GOT to."[33]

She felt relieved at the chance to redeem herself in her mother's eyes. "I know how you felt about being disappointed before," she wrote, "because I felt every bit as bad . . . terribly disappointed for myself and twice as disappointed for you, and sore besides because I could not manage better."[34] A pattern was being laid down. With her parents, Rose would always swing between apologetic and exasperated, begging pardon and then, in the next breath, offering advice on how *they* should manage their affairs. The child who had suffered through all her parents' catastrophes would never establish her own professional or economic independence, always mingling her affairs with theirs.

The trip to San Francisco could happen for only one of her parents. Even combining their finances, the Wilders and Lane did not have enough money to pay the train fare for two, plus wages for a hired man to care for the livestock in their absence. Laura's letters to Almanzo that fall (published later as *West from Home*) express guilt that he remained behind, while she was off to see the world.

She may have been concerned about his disability. Though Almanzo was at Rocky Ridge, arrangements were nevertheless made for the hired man to stay at the farm, to help with work and getting the meals.[35] In advance of the trip and throughout it, both Wilder and Lane were anxiously calculating how long she could afford to stay, and Lane ended up paying her mother five dollars a week to make up for lost egg money. The payments may also have been a sop to the daughter's conscience: she and her soon-to-be-ex-husband had not yet repaid the substantial loan the Wilders had made them, although Gillette had rashly promised to "lift" the Wilders' $500 mortgage if he got a job.[36]

On August 21, Wilder embarked on an exhausting hopscotch of connecting trains: from Mansfield to Springfield to Kansas City and then on to Denver, where she missed a connection and had to stay the night before boarding another train to Salt Lake City. The much-vaunted transcontinentals had not been built with the Ozarks in mind. The journey, covering some two thousand miles, took almost a week. Throughout it, she wrote home from virtually every stop, describing her companions, her first sage brush, and the terrifying spectacle of mountain passes, "huge masses and ramparts of rock, just bare rock in every fantastic shape imaginable." She liked a German from St. Louis and a Frenchman from Baltimore, but gave the cold shoulder to a Harvard lawyer who "talks too much with his mouth and takes much for granted."[37]

The highlight, the "most beautiful sight I've seen yet," occurred the night they crossed the Great Salt Lake by moonlight, "the track so narrow" that the train appeared to be "running on the water."[38] Wilder lay in her berth and watched the moonlight "making a path of silver across the water and the farther shore so dim and indistinct and melting away into the desert as though there was no end."[39]

Her letters home to Almanzo were filled with rich description and moments of spontaneous delight. As she interpreted the sights for him, she tapped into a powerful current from her past, reliving a familiar labor of love. Years before, she had "seen" for Mary, a sacred and sisterly duty, relaying the immediacy and beauty of what had been lost. Now she was doing it again, for her husband. The act of speaking to him directly freed her from the formality of professional efforts, allowing her charm, excitement, and humor to shine through.

When she arrived, she was bewitched by the wonders of San Francisco, the Pacific Ocean, and the Exposition. She had never cared for cities but was smitten by this one on the bay, calling it "simply the most beautiful thing." She delighted in the wind off the Pacific and her first chance to wade in it: "The salt water tingled my feet and made them feel so good all the rest of the day, and just to think, the same water that bathes the shores of China and Japan came clear across the ocean and bathed my feet."[40] At one of the gun emplacements in Golden Gate Park, she kicked a cannon ball to make sure it was real, "and it was."[41]

She learned to love riding streetcars at all hours and discovered a favorite perch on Telegraph Hill, where she counted the boats in the harbor and watched the tide stream in through the Golden Gate. She liked to stand in the prow of ferries and "let the spray and the mist beat into our faces and the wind blow our hair and clothes . . . simply glorious."[42] All her life she had craved fish, and finally she could eat her fill, dining on salmon, sole, and cod. Lane told her father that Wilder stood staring at the glass aquariums at the Fair, longingly.

Wilder threw herself into the Exposition, reveling in fireworks, fountains, and the "Forbidden Garden," a "plant for plant" re-creation of a famous hedged garden, closed to women, that was tended by Franciscans at Mission Santa Barbara.[43] She took pains to describe what was virtually a monument to herself, the statue of "The Pioneer Mother" by Charles Grafly. The figure was standing on a pedestal, she wrote, "in a sunbonnet, of course, pushed back to show her face, with her sleeves pushed up, guiding a boy and girl before her and sheltering and protecting them with her arms and pointing the way westward.

It is wonderful and so true in detail."[44] Peering at the figure's shoe, she could have sworn that it had been resoled, in the frugal frontier fashion.

So entrancing were the exhibits, the food, the ingenious displays and costumes, that she sometimes lost patience with her pen's inability to keep up with "the wonderful beauty, the scope and grandeur." She declared herself disgusted with one letter. But she kept at it, creating indelible descriptions of evanescent events:

> We have had the thickest fog ever for several days. All night and all day we can hear the sirens on the different islands and headlands, and the ferries and ships at anchor on the bay keep their foghorns bellowing. We can not see the bay at all nor any part of San Francisco except the few close houses on Russian Hill. The foghorns sound so mournful and distressed, like lost souls calling to each other through the void. (Of course, no one ever heard a lost soul calling, but that's the way it sounds.)[45]

No matter how excited she was by the city, however, Wilder did not find her head turned by California agriculture. Lane was trying to persuade her mother to move, talking up the fantastic egg market provided by San Francisco and taking her on a daylong excursion through farms in the Santa Clara Valley. But Wilder was not impressed, finding vast orchards of machine-trimmed trees depressing. She thought monoculture "ugly" and pitied the dusty trees, which looked desperate for a drink despite intensive irrigation.[46] The dairy farms were unappealing as well, and the chickens—kept on bare ground in forerunners of today's battery cages—appeared "hot and unhappy."[47] She truly believed, she told Almanzo, that when she came home and they could talk it over, they would decide to "be satisfied where we are."[48] Unlike Charles Ingalls, she was not tempted to start over on the West Coast.

WILDER had never envisioned the trip merely as a vacation. She planned to combine sightseeing with freelance work and intensive study of the writing business. "I am being as careful as I can," she promised

Almanzo. "I am not for a minute losing sight of the difficulties at home or what I came for."[49] During her stay, she intended to model herself on Lane, making a tutor of her daughter and selling travel pieces to the *Ruralist* and other outlets.

In doing so, she was learning from someone who was herself little more than a novice. By the time her mother arrived in August, Lane was being paid thirty dollars a week to produce daily copy for Bessie Beatty's page in the *Bulletin*, under the banner "On the Margin of Life."[50] In light of Lane's approach to the task, the column's subhead carried a certain irony: "Truth is seldom on the written page."[51]

What Lane was writing was far from truth. It straddled a line between fact and fiction, bearing no resemblance to contemporary journalism in terms of accuracy and identification of sources. With no formal education beyond her Louisiana high school, Lane was an apprentice in what was then called the "journalistic kindergarten" of the yellow press.[52] She was learning not to report but to entertain. Her first publications included a romantic serial, "A Jitney Romance," and an as-told-to "autobiography" of an aerial stunt flyer, Art Smith. For her, as for many tabloid journalists of the time, there was little distinction between fact-based reporting and pure invention.

San Francisco was the western headquarters of yellow journalism. William Randolph Hearst's circulation battle with Joseph Pulitzer played out in New York City, but Hearst got his start in his hometown, at the *San Francisco Examiner*, copying Pulitzer's lurid crime reporting and wild headlines. Soon, every other newspaper in the city "fell universally," as one reporter put it, into the same habit, adopting yellow ways in a struggle for survival. The *Bulletin* was no exception, and Older, its editor—a character straight out of Mark Twain, with a handlebar mustache and a cigar clamped in his mouth—was Hearst's disciple. He would eventually be hired by the news titan to edit the *San Francisco Call & Post*, and his wife, Cora Older, would become Hearst's official biographer.[53] Under Older, the *Bulletin* exhibited all the sensational qualities of the golden age of yellow journalism: lurid eye-popping headlines, splashy photographs, and creative use of typefaces. Its inventive reporting refused to be chastened by fact.

One of Lane's first efforts, "Ed Monroe, Man-Hunter," which appeared in installments in August and September 1915, is a case in point. It was loosely based on an actual person, perhaps an ex-convict named Jack Black, a reformed burglar retailing colorful tales about his exploits who happened to be working in the newspaper's circulation department.[54] In Lane's telling, he was transformed into someone altogether different: a heroic "real detective," a crime fighter who had witnessed dramatic incidents during his twenty years on the police force, such as the day when "Three-Fingered Doolan" got out of San Quentin and pumped the "stool pigeon" who'd ratted him out full of lead.[55] Told in the first person, "edited" by Rose Wilder Lane, and illustrated with crude line drawings, the story was a dime novel in miniature, concocted from invented dialogue and comic-book theatrics. An editor's note claimed it bore "the authority of TRUTH, the power of REALITY."[56]

Neither Lane nor her mother saw anything wrong with this. Indeed, Wilder was tremendously excited when the reformed villain who had inspired "Ed Monroe" came to dinner with them one night. She urged Almanzo to read Lane's articles, emphasizing "that all the stories in them, although incidents, are true, and *actually happened*."[57] Yet she acknowledged in the same breath that the real "Ed" was not a detective. Her interpretation demonstrates how elastic the concept of truth and "true stories" was at the time, even in a medium designed to publish factual material. In years to come, she and Lane would cling fast to this notion of "truth," which reflected not objective reality but something closer to felt experience.

Lane was working so frenetically—churning out a first-person "autobiography" of Charlie Chaplin after a few brief interviews, then a similar life of Henry Ford—that even her hard-working mother blanched at her hours. "The more I see of how Rose works," she wrote to Almanzo, "the better satisfied I am to raise chickens. I intend to try to do some writing that will count, but I would not be driven by the work as she is for anything and I do not see how she can stand it."[58] Nonetheless, she found enough time with Rose to "[block] out a story of the Ozarks for me to finish when I get home." She hoped that this professional boost might make a real financial difference: "If I can only get started at that, it will sell for a good deal more than farm stuff."[59]

The two women were already swapping stories for profit. While Wilder was in town, Lane must have inveigled her for tales of the blizzard-bound winter in De Smet, which soon turned up in Lane's "Behind the Headlight," a serialized first-person "memoir" of a railway engineer. The engineer's memories were remarkably similar to events that Wilder would write about in her own memoir, such as an Indian predicting "BIG snows."[60] Without the added depth of Wilder's recollected emotion, the stories seemed flat and false, yet Wilder again told her husband that "every incident . . . is true."[61]

In between days at the office and nights at her typewriter, Lane found time to take her mother to Berkeley to hear Austrian violinist Fritz Kreisler perform at the Greek Theater. (She was interviewing him as well.) Lane also hosted a tea party for her, introducing her to women friends and *Bulletin* colleagues. Among these was Lane's downstairs neighbor, Berta Hoerner, a painter who worked in fashion illustration. Wilder was charmed by Berta, borrowing Lane's phrase to describe her in a letter home as the "little artist girl who lives in the basement."[62]

Lane's readiness to bend facts to her liking was not confined to her work. Although she had apparently split up with Gillette Lane earlier in the year, they were still living together—possibly to share expenses, but also to maintain appearances during her mother's visit. Judging by her letters home, Wilder never realized that the marriage was over. She remained hopeful, she confided to Almanzo, that they might recoup their $250 loan if the man could only lay his hands on deferred commissions owed him by Stine & Kendrick. She would have to be "on the ground" when he received it, she said. If not, it would disappear, since "money runs through his fingers like water."[63] Inevitably, she was disappointed. The perennially unemployed son-in-law spent his time squiring Wilder around the Exposition.

It was on one such excursion, late in Wilder's stay, that Gillette Lane nearly killed her. On October 14 or 15, riding downtown with her on a streetcar, he abruptly jumped off before the car stopped. Surprised, Wilder followed suit, fell to the ground, and struck the back of her head against the paving stones. She was injured badly enough that she would be hospitalized for nearly a week.

Days later, Lane's letter to her father informing him of the accident was remarkably offhand. She assured him that "it was not [Laura's] fault at all," as if blame were the key issue. Only in the fifth paragraph did she get around to telling him that his wife was hospitalized— recovering in "the best hospital in town," Lane said.[64] She expressed regret not for the accident, but for the fact that the streetcar company could not be expected to pay damages.

Wilder spent the last weeks of her stay recovering from her head injury while coping with a busy work schedule. A handful of Wilder's poems about fairies appeared in the children's section of the *Bulletin*, and the *Ruralist* had belatedly come through, asking for two substantial articles about the Exposition. They would be published by the end of the year. One featured recipes of international foods, from French croissants to Chinese almond cakes (Laura privately confided to Almanzo a distaste for Chinese food); the other touted gold medals awarded to Missouri's livestock and its "Palace of Agriculture," which featured a larger-than-life statue of the state's governor rendered entirely in corn.[65]

These published accounts seem flat, in retrospect, and the Missouri article closer to propaganda. It was Wilder's unstudied letters that captured her disarming candor and humor. Her talent lay not in straightforward journalism but in personal writing, the stuff of memoir.

After the novelty of the gaudy Fair had worn off, all she wanted was to go home. Again and again, Wilder assured her husband of her affection and allegiance to the life they had built together after intense struggle. "Believe me," she told him, "there is no place like the country to live and I have not heard of anything so far that would lead me to give up Rocky Ridge."[66]

Here's the Farm Loan Plan

As Mrs. A. J. Wilder was emerging as a columnist for the *Missouri Ruralist*, national farm reform was finally within reach. Back in her father's day, the Populist Party had been agitating for a federal system to ease loans to farmers—the kinds of loans that might have saved Charles Ingalls's homestead or the Wilders' struggling tree claim, allowing access to credit to tide them over hard times. Bogged down in the debate over the gold standard, those ideas had gone nowhere before the turn of the century.

But in 1908, Teddy Roosevelt revived farm credit as part of his Progressive Era reforms, establishing a "Country Life Commission" to study problems faced by rural Americans. While much was left unfinished at the end of Roosevelt's term, his successors, William Howard Taft and Woodrow Wilson, pressed forward with one of the commission's chief recommendations: create a cooperative rural credit system.

The intellectual Wilson, a former president of Princeton armed with a Ph.D. in political science, sent commissioners to Europe to study Germany's *Landschaft* rural credit cooperative system, which dated back to the 1760s. Frederick the Great had permitted landed nobility to band together to form a *Landschaft* bank, mortgage their properties, and borrow a percentage of their value in bonds exchangeable for cash. Wilson's advisers fixed on that system as a model. In the first years of his administration, Wilson had successfully shepherded major progressive legislation through a Democratic Congress, signing the Federal Reserve Act, the Federal Trade Commission Act, and the Clayton Anti-Trust Act. In 1916, during a closely fought reelection campaign, he finally secured what generations of farmers had been calling for: the Federal Farm Loan Act. It would have a profound effect on the Wilders' lives.

Around the time the Farm Loan Act was working its way through Congress, Rose Wilder Lane was walking across California farmland, from Palo Alto through the Santa Clara, Sacramento, San Joaquin, and Napa valleys. She was writing an exhaustive, eighty-eight-part *Bulletin* series, "Soldiers of the Soil," illustrated with large photographs of herself attired in sensible walking dress and floppy hats. An author's note assured readers, as always, that the experiences she described were "strictly true."[67] She interviewed ranchers, dairy farmers, chicken farmers, and the migrant workers who were tending and picking almonds, cherries, apricots, peaches, pears, olives, potatoes, and tomatoes.

With war looming on the American horizon, Lane redefined the seventy thousand farmers serving San Francisco as soldiers, "the real defenders of America . . . the great Continental Army."[68] Farming was portrayed as an epic, heroic national and international project. She ironically invoked a popular song whose refrain proclaimed that "Uncle Sam is rich enough to give us all a farm"; the sentiment had inspired pioneers to settle the West, only to discover, as her parents and grandparents had, that mortgages and natural disasters could ruin even the hardest workers.[69]

After the last installment appeared, Lane was invited to give a talk to the Pomona Grange of Santa Rosa's Patrons of Husbandry. Somehow she gave the audience the impression that she herself owned a farm, hundreds of miles away, which she was "managing" in absentia.[70] She called for farmers to organize, an age-old Grange goal and exactly what the Federal Farm Loan Act was meant to support.

The act allowed for the creation of community-based National Farm Loan Associations, distributing low-interest, long-term loans to farmers who joined them. Farmers could borrow from one hundred to ten thousand dollars, up to half the value of their land and 20 percent of the improvements made on it. Hundreds of associations sprang up nationally. One of them would be in Mansfield, Missouri.

During the Wilders' rooming-house days, a favorite boarder was Jeff Craig, a cashier at the Bank of Mansfield. He became a close friend; when he left his employer to help start a competitor, the Farmers and Merchants Bank, the Wilders had immediately switched their allegiance to that enterprise. In the fall of 1917, they joined Craig and other local farmers in forming a Farm Loan Association in town. Within a few years, a bold announcement appeared in the *Mansfield Mirror*:

Mansfield National Farm Loan Association:

Makes Federal Government Loans at 5½ per cent interest on 34 years time, with privilege of paying sooner if desired. For particulars inquire

John W. Brentlinger, Pres.   Mrs. A. J. Wilder, Secy.[71]

With nineteen members and more than $30,000 to lend, the association was on its way. Wilder would eventually publish the particulars in the *Ruralist*, and her article, "Here's the Farm Loan Plan," was widely distributed as a flyer in Wright County. In terms she would use to counsel hundreds of farmers over the coming years, she laid out the exact cost of a $1,000 loan from the association. At 5.5 percent interest, compared to a standard bank loan at 8 percent, a farmer would save $335.73 over the course of ten years once all the fees were accounted for.[72] It was a good deal, administered by trusted friends and neighbors. In contrast to later federal programs, the association was organized, staffed, and run by the community. Its officers were locals, not outsiders.

To borrow from the association, a farmer was required to become a dues-paying member and to buy a share of stock at $5 for every hundred dollars borrowed. The Wilders themselves applied for a loan from the program in March 1919, the same week that Wilder's article on the plan ran in the *Ruralist*.[73] They borrowed a thousand dollars at 5 percent interest, a slightly more advantageous rate than advertised, with the farm as collateral.[74] They would owe payments of $32.50 every March and September for the next thirty-four years, unless they chose to pay the mortgage off earlier.

Given the disastrous debts that cost them their Dakota homestead and tree claim, it was a notable risk, even though federal land banks were less prone to foreclose than private institutions.[75] The Wilders were in their fifties. Perhaps they wanted to make improvements, or were concerned about future income; or the loan may have been a requirement of association membership and Laura Wilder's position. Whatever the motivation, they placed all ninety-seven acres of their greatest asset, Rocky Ridge Farm, in the hands of the federal government.

For much of the next decade, in the Odd Fellows Hall on Mansfield's town square, Wilder would process loan applications, fill out paperwork, and write to applicants about their progress. She received a small percentage on every loan closed and a flat fee for preparing quarterly and annual reports. Once again, she was following in her father's footsteps, working like he did as a civil servant. In a town every bit as insular as those where he'd worked, she found herself in a position of greater authority, handling what would ultimately amount to nearly a million dollars in loans, managing with discretion the hopes and fears of neighbors, acquaintances, and farmers who were weathering the same financial trials that she and Almanzo had faced. Friends and townsfolk remembered her as a strong promoter of the program. "She wanted everybody to borrow money like they did," one recalled.[76]

Local prejudice did not stand in her way: she shook hands with "our colored member," scandalizing Mansfieldians.[77] She made a joke of it to Lane, referring to rumors that one of President Warren G. Harding's great-grandmothers was an African American: "If we have him for president, why not treat the colored brother kindly?"[78] But she went on in a serious vein, emphasizing her idealism: "I'm a hero worshiper, you know, and likewise a bitter ender and almost all the other foolish things you can think of." She closed by crowing about the 1921 Supreme Court decision that found the Federal Loan Act to be constitutional: "I'll be one busy person then, for I think everyone wants a loan."

The job marked the period of Wilder's greatest engagement in community. Having once found conviviality in spelling bees, singing school, and literary socials in De Smet, she now sought it by joining women's clubs, advancing her Loan Association work at the same time. In 1916, she and Ella Craig, Jeff Craig's wife, were among the founding members of the Athenian Club, a study group devoted to "cultural topics and the exchange of ideas," named in honor of the Greek goddess of wisdom. Its membership consisted mainly of women from Hartville, the nearby town and county seat that Wilder visited on a weekly basis, filing loan paperwork at the courthouse.[79] The club's symbol was the owl, Athena's attribute; its flower, the violet, "sacred to the city of Athens." It would become a local legend.

Wilder was also instrumental in organizing Mansfield's Justamere Club. Groups by that name (often spelled "Just-A-Mere") sprang up across the country at the time, but in Mansfield the Justamere was no mere club. It was a highly exclusive clique, limited to eighteen members, all personal friends dedicated to high-minded talks on "economic world conditions, politics, legislation, inventions, discoveries, new books, poems, drama, music, new fashions, prominent persons, history, religion, art and nature."[80] Each monthly meeting was presided over by a member who led the discussion while plying her fellows with creative refreshments. Wilder herself wrote the words to the club song.

Wake Up and Get Busy

Clubwoman, farm activist, member of a Masonic organization, secretary-treasurer for the Mansfield branch of the federal Farm Loan Association, and columnist for the *Ruralist*: by her fifties, Wilder had become a formidable figure, the embodiment of her teenaged ideal of "ambition." Publishing twenty-one columns in 1916 and twenty-two the year after, she began developing her voice and themes.

She probably had a role model. Among the books in her library was a biography of Fanny Fern, the pen name of Sara Willis, who had risen to fame in the mid-nineteenth century as a popular columnist for the *New York Ledger*, the weekly family journal whose thrilling fictional serials Laura had loved in Walnut Grove.[81] Fern dispensed advice to women on everything from fashion trends to legal rights, becoming the first major woman columnist for a national newspaper, and eventually the highest-paid columnist in the country. Emerging as a regular contributor for the *Ruralist*, Wilder may have modeled her own voice on Fern's relaxed, informal style. She certainly approved of women writers, fondly recalling that the adopted mother of her school friend Ida Brown neglected her housework for days on end in order to write for the newspapers, earning enough money to buy Ida a smart winter outfit.[82]

Tentative at first, growing more relaxed as she got comfortable, Wilder's farm columns contained the genesis of her later novels. Increasingly, she was developing characters, experimenting with scenes and dialogue, and reaching back in her memory for anecdotes from her Dakota days.

The character who emerged most clearly was her husband, whom she referred to not by name but as "The Man of the Place." Quirky, blunt, fond of pie, he wandered in and out of her pieces much as the actual man must have wandered in and out of her sight, going about his business in the barn and fields.

He appeared in her first column of 1916, a meditation on how women were inevitably put in charge of poultry, considered too trivial for men, despite the fact that chickens and turkeys were valuable commodities. She quickly established their economic value, reporting that poultry and eggs brought $97,000 to Mansfield the previous year. Then she dramatized the "spice" of her record-keeping, with The Man of the Place complaining about the empty feed bin: "Those durn hens are eating their heads off!"[83] At that point, she said, she would bring out her account book and quietly point out the bottom line, comparing the price of feed to her profit. Then, she said, a little smugly, "he will feel better about things in general and especially the hens."[84]

The Man played it straight later that year, when Wilder wryly revealed her own bad temper. Trying to please her, he had given her a "patent churn," a newfangled take on the hand-operated model, meant to be attached to a small engine.[85] They had no engine, though, and Wilder struggled to keep the lid on: as the cream thickened, it bucked and kicked. She found herself sitting on a board athwart the lid "in the correct mode for horseback riding," turning the churn's handle with one hand while trying to steady it with the other. What's more, the sharp edges of the tin paddles cut her hands when she washed them. After a painful episode, she flew into a rage and threw the contraption out the side door, "as far as I could"—to her husband's rueful astonishment, she confessed.[86] But he made only the mildest of remonstrations.

Among the most touching of the columns dedicated to him was one she wrote in the summer of 1917, "A Bouquet of Wild Flowers." His habit of bringing her flowers from woods and fields was more welcome than the churn, recalling purple flags she had gathered from creek bottoms when she was a "barefoot child."[87] She remembered the wild Sweet Williams, whose pink hearts she had pressed against a pane of glass with her school friends, and the white daisies with "hearts of gold" that she and "Father and Sister Mary" passed on their walk to Sunday school that long-ago summer when her mother was staying home with their baby brother. "I was only a little girl," she wrote, "but I can still plainly see the grass and the trees and the path winding ahead, flecked with sunshine and shadow and the beautiful golden-hearted daisies scattered all along the way."[88]

At last, she said, she was beginning to learn what mattered in life. Citing the Biblical wisdom her mother had quoted to her a few years earlier—"there is nothing new under the sun"—Wilder made a point that would serve as the moral heart of her later books:

> It is the simple things of life that make living worth while, the sweet fundamental things such as love and duty, work and rest and living close to nature. There are no hothouse blossoms that can compare in beauty and fragrance with my bouquet of wild flowers.[89]

The rest of her family began to crop up in her columns too, with mentions of her father, mother, and Mary. But what began as an exercise in sentimentality and nostalgia soon became something more complex. She began airing unresolved issues, the rivalry and tensions between herself and Mary, left unsettled when Mary went blind and Laura married and left home.

First, she tried to wring a moral from them, recalling that early occasion on Silver Lake when her father went out to shoot a goose for dinner and she and Mary quarreled over whether or not to season the dressing with sage or onion. Their father missed his shot; there was neither goose nor dressing; the girls were abashed. But in this telling, Wilder transposed the goose to Thanksgiving (in her memoir, it had been spring).[90] A touch of fiction reinforced the lesson: be thankful for what you have.

But the moral left her unsatisfied. She returned to the sibling conflict in a column about justice, revisiting an ancient wrong. Resurrecting the childhood spat over whose hair was prettier, Mary's blond curls or her own brown locks, she refashioned it into a parable about nameless girls. For the younger girl, it was "a tragedy in her little life" that her "dark skin, brown hair and snub nose" made her feel homely beside her beautiful sister.[91] Taunted by her bossy sibling, the "little brown girl" lashed out and slapped her. Compounding the injustice, the girl was then "soundly spanked and set in a corner," where she glowered at "the parent who punished her."[92]

The tale revealed resentment suppressed for decades. "I hate to write the end of the story," she said of her punishment and the "sense of injustice" it instilled. What began as a dispassionate exercise turned into an outburst: "No, not the end! No story is ever ended! It goes on and on and the effects of this one followed this little girl all her life."[93] Such primal feelings would compel her to rehearse the family drama yet again, casting herself as the heroine, attempting to wrest from the past the satisfaction life rarely afforded. The story was definitely not ended.

Wilder was not always in full command of her material, but in turning out a column every two weeks she was learning how to tell stories, introduce characters, and craft dialogue. She was becoming comfortable in the public realm, serving up advice to a cohort of women who craved connection, encouragement, and sensible counsel. She was beginning to taste the gratification that came from seizing control of a narrative, summoning beloved figures, settling scores, and addressing grievances.

Among her affectionate portraits and appreciative accounts of fellow farmers, her daughter stood out as a confounding personality. She popped up at frequent intervals but in a fashion invariably abrupt, formal, and distant, as if "Rose Wilder Lane" were a kind of deus ex machina, someone contrived as a plot device, a figure inexplicable and unknowable, liable to descend upon an unsuspecting rural populace and wreak havoc. During these years, at least as far as her mother was concerned, that is exactly what Lane was becoming.

By the time the United States declared war on Germany in April 1917, Rose Wilder Lane was thirty-one, and her burgeoning career as a celebrity biographer was causing friction with virtually every one of her major subjects. After the *Bulletin* released her articles about aerialist Art Smith in a paperbound booklet, she moved on to serialize the lives of Charlie Chaplin, Henry Ford, Jack London, and Herbert Hoover, all of which she attempted to publish in book form.[94] All were controversial.

Ghostwritten memoirs or autobiographies were common enough. After serving an apprenticeship at *McClure's Magazine*, for instance,

Willa Cather was hired by the publisher, S. S. McClure, to write his memoirs. McClure's *My Autobiography* ran in the magazine in eight parts in 1913–1914 and was subsequently published as a book. In a note, McClure thanked Cather for her help "in the preparation," but did not publicly acknowledge her authorship.[95]

Lane, for her part, took a more underhanded approach. In the spring of 1915, she interviewed Charlie Chaplin just as *The Tramp* premiered, securing his global fame. Cobbled together in weeks, her serial—Chaplin in the first person, with no byline—appeared in the *Bulletin* in July, and was syndicated in other newspapers.[96] Soon, the Bobbs-Merrill Company was poised to publish it as a book. A friend of Lane's, the Associated Press reporter Guy Moyston, with whom she would later be involved romantically, acted as her agent in brokering the deal, made without Chaplin's knowledge or consent.[97]

The work's fanciful title—*Charlie Chaplin's Own Story: Being the Faithful Recital of a Romantic Career, Beginning with Early Recollections of Boyhood in London and Closing with the Signing of His Latest Motion-Picture Contract*—suggested a Dickensian novel rather than something that originated in a daily newspaper. (Indeed, it would ultimately be compared to *Oliver Twist*.)[98] Lane was not named as the author. Instead, the copyright page included a note: "The subject of this biography takes great pleasure in expressing his obligations and his thanks to Mrs. Rose Wilder Lane for invaluable editorial assistance."[99] Like the rest of the text, that acknowledgment was a fabrication. Scholars have described the book as a "flagrant autobiographical fake" displaying "great mendacity."[100]

When Chaplin learned of the book's imminent publication, he threatened legal action, charging through his lawyers that it was "purely a work of fiction."[101] He and his brother were particularly disturbed by the portrayal of their father as a vicious drunk. Advance copies had already been distributed, but Bobbs-Merrill recognized that the jig was up and halted distribution rather than risk a lawsuit. Remaining copies were destroyed, although Stan Laurel had a copy, which he lent to another biographer.[102] In this and other ways, Lane's spurious works would continue to mislead the public for decades. (A recent book about the aviator Art Smith, for instance, accepts his "autobiography" as first-person gospel.[103] Those familiar with Lane's style, however, will recognize her voice overlaid upon his.)

Lane urged Chaplin to reconsider, unapologetic about her attempt to capitalize on his fame. Even in a career characterized by audacity, her letter stands out as particularly unprofessional, impertinent, and shameless. "Truly, I don't believe you realize how very well that story was written," she ventured, going on to remark, casually, "You've lived a life which makes a corking book . . . whose popular appeal is greater than that of a book any other hack writer is apt to write."[104] She complained that he had put her in a "perfectly frightful position with the Bobbs Merrill people."[105] His objection to the hijacking of his life must be, she supposed, that he expected "some of the money."[106] She could scarcely offer that, she said, since it would amount to a few hundred dollars at most—a tone all paparazzi would recognize.

In the face of Chaplin's wrath, Lane was neither abashed nor discouraged. Before the Bobbs-Merrill debacle played out, she had already latched on to Henry Ford, interviewing him during his Exposition appearance on a battleship. Her serial on his life appeared in the *Bulletin* in the last months of 1915, and was soon published in book form under an intriguing title: *Henry Ford's Own Story: How a Farmer Boy Rose to the Power That Goes with Many Millions Yet Never Lost Touch with Humanity*.[107] The phrase "Farmer Boy" would be repurposed in one of her mother's titles, years later.

The misadventure with Chaplin did teach her some kind of lesson, perhaps. The byline on the Henry Ford book read "As told to Rose Wilder Lane," and the hagiographic text was cast in the third person. It was still fictionalized, as per her usual fashion. Years later, Lane's own biographer acknowledged that Ford "repudiated the book for its inaccuracies."[108]

Next, she took on Jack London. The author of *The Call of the Wild* and *White Fang* had died suddenly, on November 22, 1916, at the age of forty. Less than six months later, Lane was writing to his widow, Charmian London, pleading for permission to write a biography of him. *Sunset* magazine had commissioned the project, which Lane breezily described to Mrs. London as "a semi-biography . . . a sort of free-hand sketch of his life."[109] Lane presented the project to her as a fait accompli, "my first chance to break into the magazines, and . . . they have given me an advance, and I have spent it!"[110] The widow had already turned away several interested parties but pitied Lane after learning that she needed to "support her family."[111]

The serial, a "Life of Jack London," began appearing in October 1917 and ran for eight monthly installments. Lane told Charmian London she had "verified" the facts, but said it was more important "to get, as nearly as I can, at the truth rather than at the facts."[112] The whole thing was fiction, as London could see from the outset. She and Jack London's stepsister were dismayed right away by the portrayal of his "lonely poverty-cruel childhood" and by depictions of his father as a drunk.

The series opened with an interior point of view of the five-year-old Jack, typical in tone:

> He was unhappy. Although he was so small, so unacquainted with the world outside the farmhouse yard that his imagination could not tell him what he wanted, he was unhappy. A sensation of hunger gnawed at him, but it was not hunger. It was like an ache, but he could not find it anywhere in his little body.

There were many bizarre revelations to come. After wrangling with *Sunset* over an opportunity to examine proofs before the chapters appeared, London was shocked to read an account of how she had lost a child due to the "stresses" of sailing the South Seas. This was "flatly untrue," she said.[113] (Indeed it was.)[114] She rushed corrections to the magazine, but the publication mostly tossed them aside, correcting the miscarriage story but little else. For her part, Lane tried to assuage her by saying that "my own two babies died," a manipulative ploy to play on a bereaved woman's sympathies.[115]

Belatedly, Lane made it clear that she expected to publish the articles as a book. She repeatedly tried to wheedle permission, falsely claiming that she was someone who had never done newspaper work because she had more of a "conscience."[116] She told London, "Surely, you can appreciate that I <u>tried</u> not to be yellow."[117] But London, denouncing the *Sunset* pieces as "an erroneous interpretation" of her husband, was having none of it.[118] "YOU FAILED TO DO WHAT YOU TRIED TO DO," she replied, calling the liberties Lane had taken "NOT NECESSARY TO GOOD WORK."[119] Contemporary scholars concur, describing the serial as having "little value," relying on "fictional devices of imagined conversations, impressionistic descriptions, and tailored atmosphere . . . based on skimpy evidence."[120]

The Lane who emerged during this period had no conscience, was heedless of others' feelings, and possessed little regard for professional courtesy. Past the first flush of youth, without the excuses that can be made for the immature and inexperienced, she was proceeding with her writing career using the same lax standards of behavior she had absorbed from Claire Gillette Lane and the real estate business: make any promise, no matter how misleading; take every advantage in selling a commodity, whether a piece of property or a piece of writing. She appeared to have no qualms or moral compass, no sense of what was fair or appropriate. Her own biographer described her behavior with Jack London's widow as a "subtle and continuing calculation" that skirted outright lies.[121] Actually, it was worse. "Of course the whole thing is fictionized," she wrote to London. "But I hope merely in the matter of color and handling."[122]

MEANWHILE, at the *Ruralist*, her mother's emphasis was on living a moral life. But just as she saw nothing wrong in Lane's fictional reporting, Wilder, too, had little understanding of journalistic ethics. In 1918, in one memorable column, "When Proverbs Get Together," she repurposed under her own name a humor feature Lane had written several years earlier for the *Bulletin*. She expanded it and altered some of the phrasing, yet the two columns—in structure and duplication of material—were much the same.[123] The mother and daughter may have thought it harmless, sharing a humorous yarn the way Wilder's father once swapped whoppers around the stove at the hardware store. But plagiarism had been recognized as unethical since at least the mid-1800s, and a nearby institution—the University of Missouri, which opened the world's first journalism school in 1908—was devoted to promoting strict standards.[124] Neither woman appeared to heed them.

When America was drawn into the First World War, Wilder devoted herself to the war effort and women's role in it. As soon as the U.S. declared war against Germany, her next column explained how country women could contribute, "however much we may regret the necessity." She shared a conversation with a farm neighbor, a woman who had decided to wear overalls in the fields in conscious imitation of women working in the munitions factories. "Isn't the raising of food to preserve life as important as the making of shells to take it?" Wilder quoted her saying. Her description of women's work was patriotic and quietly assertive, assuring her readers that their skills had value:

> Our work is not spectacular and in doing it faithfully we shall win no war medals or decorations, but it is absolutely indispensable. We may feed the field hands, care for the poultry and work in the garden with the full assurance that we are doing as much for our country as any other person. Here in the Hills we have helped plant the potatoes and corn, we help with the milking and feed the calves and hogs and we will be found on the line just behind the trenches, "fighting for Uncle Sam," as I heard one woman say, and every extra dozen eggs, pound of meat or bushel of vegetables we raise will help beat back the enemy, hunger.[125]

She continued the drumbeat in many columns over the following months, urging women to volunteer for the Red Cross and buy Liberty Bonds. She also stepped up herself: buying her own bonds, donating fifteen "thoroughbred" Brown Leghorn eggs and a rooster to a Red Cross auction, and serving on the dinner committee to boot.[126] But she did not engage in mere jingoism, thoughtfully debating America's rush to war in previous conflicts. She criticized founders of a new local farmers' club for failing to include women. She faulted the Women's Trade Union League for working to improve labor conditions and reduce hours solely for urban women and children, while farm women were working fourteen to sixteen hours a day with no representation.

She was becoming a rural rabble-rouser. She called out to her readers: "Write to me and tell me about it!"

They did, and she was thrilled, saying she had feared "no one was listening to me."[127] To hear back from readers, she said, was "truly delightful." She relished, as well, a letter of strong praise from her *Ruralist* editor, George Jordan. "It gives me such a warm, comfortable feeling around in my interior decorations," she told her daughter.[128]

She spread the joy, praising Wright County neighbors for keeping prices low to avoid war profiteering. Ladies in Mansfield churches were lauded for forswearing new hats in favor of Liberty Bond pins and Red Cross buttons. She called out for particular merit A. C. Barton and his "Show You Farm" in nearby Mountain Grove. A former Methodist preacher, Barton had restored his poor soil by practicing crop rotation, eschewing commercial fertilizers, hoeing corn by hand, and condemning the robbery of soil nutrients as "a sin."[129] She praised his "agricultural theology," having long ago taken such advice as gospel: don't go looking for a better place "but MAKE one."[130]

The culmination of this theme of self-reliance came in a column about dreams and their relationship to accomplishment. She joked about gardeners drowsing by the fire over winter seed catalogues, perfect spring produce springing up from the pages. She talked about her own Leghorns and the fantasies she had built on them, a dream punctured by reality. The flock might have made millions, she said, "if the hens had performed according to schedule; if the hawks had loved field mice better than spring chickens; if I had been so constituted that I never became weary."[131] No such excuses sufficed in real life, she knew, but nonetheless it was "necessary that we dream," inspired by an ideal. Then, once the dreaming was over, she told her readers, "wake up and 'get busy.'" That would be her gospel, in life and work.

WILDER'S regular columns were ever more valuable to the *Ruralist*, which elevated her to editor of the paper's Home section in 1917. Lane would one day tell her that her articles stood out in the paper "like a skyscraper on a plain," an apt comparison.[132]

The year after Wilder's promotion, the newspaper's editor, John Case, published a warm profile of her, citing the fact that she had been connected with the *Ruralist* longer than anyone else on the editorial staff. She was characteristically modest, saying her education amounted to "what a girl would get on the frontier," but Case was proud of his star farm columnist, saying she had won recognition "because of ability alone." Wilder's growing reputation was reflected in her work's being given its own column title: it became "The Farm Home" in 1919 and then, in 1921, "As a Farm Woman Thinks."

Her self-assurance would not be undercut until her first article commissioned by a national magazine. That milestone came about through Lane's connections and encouragement, which were indispensable. But her editing of her mother's work also marked their first collaborative clash.

In 1917, Bessie Beatty, Lane's former boss at the *Bulletin*, had achieved national fame as one of the reporters who went to Russia to write about the October Revolution as it unfolded. The next year, she was offered the editorship of *McCall's Magazine*. By that time, Lane had soured on Beatty, but she nonetheless prevailed on her former mentor to secure her mother a prestigious spot in the national publication. The resulting article, "Whom Will You Marry: The Farmer's Wife," was part of a series on the fates awaiting women who married into various professions.

Drafts have not survived to reveal how extensive Lane's changes were, but she wrote to her mother in April 1919 to smooth over Wilder's dismay at the liberties she had taken. "Don't be absurd about my doing the work on your article," Lane wrote.[133] "I didn't rewrite it a bit more than I rewrite Mary Heaton Vorse's articles or Inez Haynes Irwin's stories." (Vorse and Irwin were leftist suffragist writers.) Lane defended at length her decision, supported by the editors of *McCall's*, to cut her mother's discussion of farm economics, and congratulated her on "the size of the check ... really a fairly decent price ... considering that your name has as yet no commercial value." She belittled her mother even as she buoyed her, a dynamic that would continue.

For all her journalistic malfeasance, Lane was a talented and insightful line editor, as she would prove countless times over the years. Often without being asked, she reworked manuscripts not only by her mother but also by friends, acolytes, even mere acquaintances, dispensing reams of professional advice.

In this instance, her advice was accompanied by page after page of suggestions about another project her mother was working on: an extensive memoir. That manuscript, now lost, was apparently also intended for *McCall's*. Judging by Lane's description, it was a tantalizing embryonic version of Wilder's later work, a dry run for her future autobiography. It began by comparing "modern girls" to Wilder's own experience growing up, and ran to at least forty pages.

Going through it section by section, Lane patiently urged her mother to observe time-honored rules of good writing—show rather than tell, stick to a narrative voice, provide colorful details, and pay close attention to transitions:

> If I were you, I would jump directly, after the transition paragraph, into, "when I was a girl—" And draw the contrast clearly. Only one generation ago, Indians and forests and half a continent practically untouched by the white race. Free land, free fuel, food for the hunting it—"Go west, young man, and grow up with the land," "And Uncle Sam is rich enough to give us all a farm." That sort of thing. And do it all concretely—don't say those things were so, show that they were so. Your log cabin in the Great Woods, that is now farming land— your trip through Kansas, across the sites of cities today—the building of the railroad through the Dakotas, now the wheat fields that feed the world during the war—Make it all real, because you saw it with your own eyes.[134]

There, in 1919, was Wilder's autobiography. She had already begun working on it. Even more illuminating: she was writing "children's stories." Lane said she liked them but that they were trivial compared to the memoir. She told her mother: "There is no opportunity to make a name with children's stories."[135]

Diverging Roads

As the nineteen-tens boiled over into the Roaring Twenties, strange manifestations of social ferment began appearing in literature as writers groped toward naturalistic depictions of the complexities of human behavior. In 1919, Sherwood Anderson published *Winesburg, Ohio*, a collection of linked short stories in which small-town lives were warped by conformity into grotesque expressions of despair or deviance. Reviewers blanched at its shocking revelations and frank language, but it quickly became a cornerstone of the emerging Modernist movement. Over the next few years, Lane would herself become so emblematic of a small-town girl turned sophisticate that Anderson would parody her in a novel.[136]

In 1920, Sinclair Lewis's *Main Street* laid bare what he called "the village virus" caught by priggish and prurient denizens of the American small town. The novel's setting, the fictional Minnesota hamlet of Gopher Prairie, was based on the author's own hometown of Sauk Centre, Minnesota. Lewis conceived of the book during a summer home from Yale while reading Hamlin Garland's *Main-Travelled Roads*, which had itself been inspired by Garland's return to the stultifying torpor of a Midwest summer.

After toiling for a time at commercial magazines—including serving as assistant editor of *Adventure*, a pulp title devoted to yarns about cowboys and pirates that was a favorite of the Wilders—Lewis earned world renown with *Main Street*. The book sold three hundred thousand copies in its first year, becoming an instant American classic. Its protagonist, Carol Milford Kennicott, hails from the big city of St. Paul, and when the novel opens, Lewis identifies her as the product of an America that had sped far beyond Wilder's frontier times: "The days of pioneering, of lassies in sunbonnets, and bears killed with axes in piney clearings, are deader now than Camelot."[137] He would be wrong about that, but *Main Street* proved a powerful influence on American fiction, including Lane's.

At the turn of the decade, Lane's life was in turmoil. She had quit the *Bulletin* in the summer of 1918, when Fremont Older left after a dispute with the owner, and moved briefly to Sausalito as a freelance writer. After writing autobiographies of famous men she did not know, she now turned to her own life for material, writing a serial based on her adventures as working girl, telegrapher, and real estate seller. *Sunset* magazine, which had printed her articles on Jack London, published the work in nine parts, advertising it as "A Big, Modern Novel of a Girl's Struggle for Business Success and Happiness."[138] Reminding readers of Lane's "trenchant interpretation" of London, the magazine coyly invited them to speculate about whether the protagonist of this new tale was fictional: "how real a woman we can only guess."[139]

Titled "Diverging Roads: A Story of the Restless Sex," the serial follows young Helen Davies, daughter of a "struggling farmer," on her journey from innocence to experience. After a few months learning the art of telegraphy, Helen moves to San Francisco, where she takes a job sending telegrams in a big hotel. Lane made the parallels with her own life inescapable, naming her small town "Masonville" and her youthful beau "Paul Masters," recalling her Mansfield suitor Paul Cooley.[140] Likewise, Gillette Lane was scarcely concealed by "Gilbert Kennedy," a cad Helen marries and quickly sheds.

Nevertheless, Lane expressed dismay that the piece was read in Mansfield as a roman à clef, with a particularly hurtful portrayal of her mother. At the end of one installment, Helen's mother piteously asks to borrow sixty dollars, saying that the cow died. It must have been aggravating to Lane's actual mother, since money seemed to flow from Mansfield to San Francisco and not the other way around. Lane acknowledged having made things uncomfortable, in a rationalization that showed little self-awareness:

> Everyone will insist that it is my own experience. . . . As a matter of fact, not one iota . . . is my own experience. I simply used the background of parts of my own life, because it was easier than to labor over constructing a purely imaginary one. . . . All the characters, and all the experiences, were purely imaginary, and yet no one will believe it, because I put them in a telegraph office, and I was once a telegrapher, and because I put them in a real-estate office, and I was once a real-estate salesman. . . . I'm sorry you have been hurt by it.[141]

Lane was not distinguishing between reality and fantasy in her writing, even when the subject was herself. The one element of the *Sunset* serial that was clearly supposed to be nonfiction—her author profile—was also "fictionized." She wrote of her parents:

> They were both of the sturdy American pioneer stock that broke the way for the white race westward across the continent. My mother's father was a hunter and trapper; my mother heard in her childhood the long, blood-chilling screams of panthers in the forest around the log-cabin, and saw brown bears in the woods, and knew the Indians. My father's father "slashed and burned" three hundred acres of good hard-wood timber before he drove the plow through the virgin soil of his Minnesota farm, and my father, as a little boy, saw him shoulder his gun and march away with the men who drove back the Indian raiders.[142]

Indian raiders? That was pure invention: there were no tales of Indian raiders in the Wilders' past, either in Minnesota or Malone, New York.[143] As clan mythology, however, it marked a first attempt to write the 1862 Dakota war into the family legend. While Minnesota was on her mind, Lane also threw in a recollection of hurling herself down the stairs in Spring Valley, interpreting the escapade as an occult sign of bravado, a tendency to throw herself into things "headlong."

"Headlong" would be a good description of her behavior over the coming years. She tackled one project after another, at home and then abroad, motivated always by money and without conscious reflection about the development of her career. Accepting a dizzying series of assignments, rarely staying in one place for more than a few months, she began to see herself as a seasoned reporter and world-weary traveler, instructor and mentor to all around her. But as she did so, she never established a separate existence, instead ensuring that her parents' economic lives were inextricably entwined with her own. And she continued incessantly coaching her mother. No matter how far she went—Europe, the Middle East, Russia—binding and constricting ties would remain. Neither mother nor daughter appeared willing or able to free herself.

In 1918, her divorce from Gillette Lane finalized, Lane moved to New York City, rooming with Berta Hoerner in Greenwich Village. While Berta was waiting for her fiancé, Elmer Hader, to return from World War I, Lane accepted an assignment from travel writer Frederick O'Brien to revise and rewrite his book *White Shadows in the South Seas*. The job would become an enduring headache, first in the execution and then, when the book became a bestseller, in an ugly dispute over the sharing of royalties. Having lost her written contract with O'Brien, Lane could never convince him to pay what she believed (probably rightly) she was owed.

Professionally, Lane's New York sojourn would prove critical. For years to come, she would call upon friendships and publishing contacts formed then, measuring herself against the burgeoning careers of her peers, especially women. She signed with a New York literary agency run by the husband-and-wife team of Carl and Zelma Brandt. She fraternized with noted leftists and socialists during the heyday of Bohemian Greenwich Village, including Floyd Dell, playwright, poet, and managing editor of the socialist journal *The Masses*. Like Lane, Dell was from a poor family in the Midwest; he had risen to become editor of a Chicago literary review, publishing Sherwood Anderson, Theodore Dreiser, and Carl Sandburg. Describing Willa Cather's 1913 novel of the Nebraska prairies, *O Pioneers!*, as "touched with genius," he would encourage Lane to move beyond commercial fiction and try for something deeper. In 1918, Cather had published *My Ántonia*, the last of her trilogy of "prairie novels" inspired by her Nebraska childhood and the one bearing the most intriguing resonances with Lane's mother's later work.

Through her friendship with Dell, and a close friend of his, Jane Burr, who lived in Croton-on-Hudson, Lane may have crossed paths with Max Eastman, publisher of *The Masses*, and its most infamous contributor, journalist Jack Reed.[144] Through these circles, she would forge connections with the editors of *Good Housekeeping* and other magazines, as well as friendships with Mary Margaret McBride, a young reporter who also hailed from Missouri, and Clarence Day, a humorist and cartoonist who would eventually write for the *New Yorker* and publish his popular autobiographical *Life with Father*.[145]

In the summer of 1919, she went home to Mansfield for a long vacation. That August, she would appear at the Justamere Club, presenting a talk on New York. It was part of her transformation in the eyes of Mansfield society into a great lady who occasionally descended upon their outpost to share tales of urban extravagance and travel abroad. She was about to go to Europe on an extended, years-long adventure.

Before she did, though, she had one more celebrity biography to write. She spent the first months of 1920 in California researching and writing a life of Herbert Hoover. Eight years away from being elected president, Hoover was already renowned in the state. A graduate of Stanford University, he was a wealthy mining engineer of such avid patriotism that he became known to friends abroad as "Hail Columbia Hoover." Famed for his organizational skills, he had helped repatriate more than a hundred thousand Americans caught overseas at the outbreak of World War I, and had taken on the monumental task of importing and distributing American food aid in Belgium during the fighting. In 1920, as director of the American Relief Administration, he continued aid efforts throughout Europe, harnessing private philanthropies to funnel supplies to Russia and the defeated Germans.

Hoover may have caught Lane's attention when he had published pieces in the *Bulletin* alongside Lane's articles about the state's "embattled farmers."[146] Her serial on his life appeared first in *Sunset* and then, later that year, as a book, *The Making of Herbert Hoover*. Reminiscent of her novelization of the lives of Ford and London, it lingered over Hoover's Iowa farm origins, embroidering on a story she called "stranger than fiction and as real as America."[147] It began with impressionistic scenes of the boy, Bertie, sledding in winter and his encounter with "a live Indian."[148]

This time, however, Lane took pains to justify her approach. "The method used in handling this biographical material is so unusual that a word of explanation is necessary," she wrote. She had taken "meticulous care" with the facts, she assured the reader, but the "interpretation" was her own.[149] Hoover himself may have been embarrassed by the gushing tone and the burnishing of his reputation. But in the years to come, Lane would have the distinction of having written the first biography of the future president.

Hired by the Red Cross to write press releases, she sailed for France in May of 1920. Over the next few years, she would travel incessantly. One of her first stops was Austria, where she was struck by the widespread poverty, malnutrition, and unemployment left in the wake of the war. From a Vienna hotel that June, she sent a twenty-two-page letter to her mother elaborating on her reaction, a missive that revealed as much about Lane herself as about the devastation around her.

She seemed oddly detached from the suffering, casually mentioning that an architect of the opera house had committed suicide in despair over a mistake in the foundation. "Good lord!" she wrote, "if I were an Austrian and saw no possible end to wars I would commit suicide."[150] She spoke of barefoot beggars crowding around the doors of the hotels, with "dying babies in their arms." She couldn't understand German, she wrote, but they had "the whine that is the same in all languages." Perhaps for the first time, she began embroidering on the American exceptionalism that would become a cornerstone of her philosophy in later years, declaring her own countrymen to be "the most humanly decent, and certainly the most physically perfect, of all the peoples I have so far seen." In a disturbed and disturbing letter, her harsh reaction to others' misfortunes hinted at troubled emotional times to come.

She took an apartment in Paris, and then found a nicer one, which she spent much time and effort furnishing. She contemplated adopting a war orphan. She kept company with a new boyfriend from New York, then drifted apart from him.[151] On the Orient Express to Warsaw, she met Helen Boylston, a Red Cross nurse coming off an assignment in Albania, who would become a boon companion. Partying, drinking, staying out all hours, she exhausted herself translating a manuscript about Sarah Bernhardt, writing for both the *Red Cross Bulletin* and the aid group's newsletter for children, and preparing to embark on an extended series of travelogues for the *San Francisco Call & Post*, where Hearst had installed her former mentor Fremont Older as editor.[152] She began to berate herself in her diary for not working hard enough, for bad moods, for "thirty years of blundering."[153]

Back home in Mansfield, her mother was missing her painfully, writing her to say "I'm so hungry to see you," calling her "Honeybug" and "my little Busybee."[154] In December of 1920, Wilder held a party, in absentia, for her daughter's thirty-fourth birthday. It was written up on the front page of the *Mansfield Mirror*:

> Though Rose Wilder Lane is in a foreign land her mother, Mrs. A. J. Wilder, of Rocky Ridge farm, gave a party for her. As the guests entered the spacious living room, though they were not greeted by the living presence of Rose, still, she was very much in evidence, as her smiling countenance greeted one from the den, the mantle, the table and every available place wherein a photograph could be placed. The guests spent the afternoon reading letters Rose had written home, describing her trip across, the visits made to Paris, Poland, etc., the conditions encountered there, the plans of her work, descriptions of places, peoples, and their customs as well as their costumes. After settling around the big, comfortable fire place, eating apples and nuts, each one present wrote a letter to Rose, wishing her a Merry Christmas.[155]

In her daughter's absence, Laura Wilder had re-created the cozy nights before the fire that she and Rose and Almanzo had once shared, snacking and reading. But the texts on this occasion were Lane's adult letters, the guests her former schoolmates from those long-ago, unhappy days. The newspaper captured both the mother's loneliness and the exaggerated reputation that the daughter was acquiring in her hometown, describing her as "a writer of great note, a woman of affairs of the world and numbered among those who are named in the 'Who's Who in America.' " The image of the house decorated on every surface with photographs of the missing daughter summed up the intensity of their relationship.

There was more tangible evidence of that bond in December. Earning a salary from the Red Cross and income as a freelancer, Lane made a commitment to her parents to furnish them with five hundred dollars a year, so that they could retire from farm work. The month before, she had sent them $125, a first payment for 1921.[156]

How badly they needed it is difficult to judge, in the absence of almost any records detailing the Wilders' finances.[157] Wilder was fifty-three, working at two paying jobs. Almanzo, with his disability, was in his sixties, doubtless finding it increasingly arduous to plow, care for livestock, and do the hundred other tasks involved in maintaining farm equipment, fields, and fruit trees. Certainly they needed money, but they may not have required that much. Indeed, they pointed out to Lane that they had a comfortable home and plenty to eat.[158]

During the war, Wilder had written in the *Ruralist* of needing nothing at all, since the farm plentifully supplied wheat, sweet potatoes, Irish potatoes, beans, corn, peas, meat, milk, cream, butter, eggs, and a year's supply of fruit.[159] All the fuel they needed was standing in their woods. Nonetheless, money may have been tight: a severe postwar recession had depressed the average annual farm income, from around a thousand dollars a year in 1920 to between four and five hundred the following year.[160]

Lane was offering to assume responsibility for replacing their income all on her own, while at the same time supporting herself. Over the coming years, she would dutifully continue to supply the sum while at the same time borrowing money from her parents, always recording in her private accounts that the loans came from her mother. She made vague allusions in her diary to "buying her freedom" from her parents, telling friends that as an only child she felt a responsibility for them.[161] Yet in her many diaries and letters of the period, she failed to explain to herself or others why she felt obliged to assume such a specific and extraordinary burden. She may not have known herself.

The five-hundred-dollar-a-year commitment was a complicated gesture and a premature one. As with most acts of generosity, it was undoubtedly born of a complex set of mixed motives, both selfless and self-serving: part love, part duty, part an expression of Lane's desire to attain the accomplishments and financial security that would allow her to bestow munificence on others. "I want a home, love, money, and the envy of others, i.e. 'success,' " she would confide to a diary the following year.[162] Home came first, but these ambitions would often be frustrated by a tendency to squander resources.

Lane's promised gift may also have been a means of expressing to her parents, and especially to her mother, that the tables had been turned. They had not been able to provide the uncomplicated safety and security she craved as a child, but she could provide it for them. She would show them how it was done.

Later in life, children are often reluctant for a host of reasons to assume responsibility over their parents, a reversal of roles that symbolizes impending mortality. But Lane was eager to adopt that position. Whatever role Laura and Almanzo Wilder themselves played in their daughter's largesse remains unclear, but they did not refuse the money. In time, the true cost would be revealed.

Chapter 8

The Absent Ones

Mother's Face, Mother's Touch, Mother's Voice

On August 26, 1920, the Nineteenth Amendment to the Constitution became law, prohibiting denial of the right to vote "on account of sex."[1] To win the vote, women had marched, paraded, picketed, and rioted, been beaten, arrested, jailed, brutalized, and force-fed.

The struggle had taken half a century. Carrie Chapman Catt, president of the National American Woman Suffrage Association, estimated that the long-fought campaign had consumed fifty-seven years and required 480 lobbying campaigns at state legislatures, keeping the pressure on nineteen successive Congresses. The fight for the vote was directly connected to scores of critical issues, including equality in education, employment, wages, working conditions, property ownership, maternal health and infant mortality, contraception, abortion, domestic violence, and child welfare and labor. Winning the vote for half the population was the most important advance in civil rights in America since Lincoln signed the Emancipation Proclamation.

But Laura Ingalls Wilder did not see it that way. In her columns, she neither celebrated nor praised the historic occasion, anxious about the massive social upheaval she saw coming. When newspapers reported on women's refusal to relinquish "mens' jobs" after World War I, she cautioned against "attempted revolution," saying that women should stop "complicating affairs" by trying to hold on to something that did not belong to them. "The commonplace, home work of women is the very foundation upon which everything rests," she wrote.[2]

Her perceptions were circumscribed by the farm. Throughout the war, rural women had stayed at their posts, she argued, unable to be spared, with "no question of our going back or not going back. We are still doing business at the old place, in kitchen and garden and poultry yard and no one seems to be trying to take our job from us."[3] Earnest, wry, she was an agrarian peasant who had seen wars, politicians, and social movements come and go, like seasons or storms. Nothing would surprise us, she seemed to be saying, nothing would shift us. No matter how thrilling it was to see women doing important war work, she argued, small-town women had humbler goals. They dreamed of community kitchens and laundries, not grandiose responsibilities.

In 1919, after Missouri granted women the right to vote in presidential elections, she had wondered whether they would use the ballot "intelligently."[4] Were women "careless" about becoming well informed, she wondered? A note of superiority crept in when she speculated whether "home-loving, home-keeping women" might stay away from the polls, leaving the voting to a "rougher class of women."[5] Overall, Wilder's remarks on suffrage were doubtful, discouraging, and oddly prim. "To my mind the ballot is incidental," she had written dismissively a few years earlier, "only a small thing in the work that is before the women of the nation."[6]

That standpoint contrasted sharply with her more progressive views, her approval of women's organizations and her wholehearted endorsement of abandoning outmoded, time-wasting chores such as ironing, canning vegetables, and twice-yearly housecleaning. In one column she crowed about the growing number of women, more than 200,000, who had joined educational or vocational clubs. "Get the number," she wrote, "two hundred thousand! Quite a little army this."[7] She hailed a study on "The Vocation of Women," which found that "with education and freedom, pursuits of all kinds are open to her."[8]

She liked to think of herself as someone who had long embraced women's independence, boasting about requesting the officiant at her wedding to refrain from asking her to obey her husband.

But as the Roaring Twenties accelerated, Wilder retreated from the abstract to the personal.[9] From her earliest days, she was uncomfortable with public protestations. Moralizing was one thing, but her *Ruralist* columns make it plain that she never developed a taste for pontification.

Indeed, as more and more women accepted a role in public affairs, she was preoccupied not with the behavior of the sex as a whole but with one woman in particular: her mother. Caroline Ingalls was now in her eighties, and while family correspondence has not survived, it was doubtless made clear to Laura by her sisters that their mother's health and strength were waning. In a photograph taken late in life, Caroline Ingalls sits on a chair in front of her house in De Smet, wearing a white blouse and long black skirt, her hair coiled neatly atop her head, her hands clasped in front of her. She had always radiated patience and serenity, but now had begun to look weary.

She was still living quietly with Mary, visited occasionally by a few close friends in town. Carrie Ingalls had married a miner, David Swanzey, in 1912 and moved to the Black Hills town of Keystone, far to the west of De Smet. Grace and her husband, Nate Dow, lived nearby in Manchester. According to a neighbor's recollection, Caroline and Mary Ingalls rarely went out except to go shopping or attend church. "They were never considered to have more than a maintenance income," the neighbor said, and were not outgoing.[10] When townsfolk passed by in fine weather, they might see Mrs. Ingalls sitting "in a plain chair with a severe black dress on," Mary seated on the ground, leaning against her and listening as her mother read aloud.[11]

Again and again, in columns early that decade, Wilder returned to her mother. In the winter of 1920, Wilder recounted a night when she sat beside the fire with her husband as he reminisced about his mother's prodigious feats of spinning and weaving, much of it done by the fireside at night after having spent the daylight hours cooking and cleaning. Wilder fell silent, she said, looking askance at the frivolous magazine in her hands, thinking of all the time she spent engrossed in talking about politics or indulging in clubs and lodge work. "My mother and my mother-in-law had none of these," she noted, recalling how her mother spent the evenings sewing or knitting for her family. It was just a passing reference, but it carried a sense of guilt.[12] She may have been questioning her own ambitions.

An article in the *Springfield Leader* captured the busy, bustling social scene consuming Wilder's time. She was president of the Justamere Club that year, a heady and exalted position. Serving as her vice president was no less a personage than Mrs. George Freeman, whose husband, known colloquially as "Uncle George" Freeman, was a powerful fixer in town, the president of the Bank of Mansfield and owner of both a hardware store and a general store.[13] In a few years, Uncle George would find himself starring in the Ozark fiction of Rose Wilder Lane.[14]

In May of 1922, in compliance with a club rule stipulating that the hostess must prepare recipes she had never tried before, Wilder laid out an unexpected spread at Rocky Ridge Farm, presenting Justamere members with whale meat sandwiches and homemade cheese and strawberry preserves, "served in the French style."[15] For dessert, there was candy from Switzerland. The whale meat, perhaps canned, as well as the candy perhaps originated with Rose Lane, still abroad and visiting Swiss friends.

Absorbed in such activities, as well as her work, Wilder may have had little time or opportunity to return to De Smet. She had found her earlier visit to San Francisco physically draining, telling her husband, "If I had known what a hard trip it would be I don't believe I'd have had the courage."[16] Another trip would also have entailed the same worries: the cost, the care of her hens, and the anxiety of leaving her husband to cope alone.

In addition to the physical and practical stresses, she was overwhelmed by emotional ones. "The older we grow, the more precious become the recollections of childhood's days," she wrote in the fall of 1921. "Especially our memories of our mother . . . mother's face, mother's touch, mother's voice."[17]

Weeks later, she found herself comparing two letters on her desk, one from her mother, the other from her daughter, "far away in Europe."[18] It was her mother's letter that called forth intense feelings. "Reading the message from my mother, I am a child again," she wrote, "and a longing unutterable fills my heart for mother's counsel, for the safe haven of her protection and the relief from responsibility which trusting in her judgement always gave me." Her daughter's letter, on the other hand, reminded her only that Rose would always remain a "little girl" to her. Posing a rather tortured question to her readers, she asked, "What is there in the attitude of your children toward yourself that you wish were different?" She advised readers to "search your heart and learn if your ways toward your own mother could be improved."[19]

Wilder had been away from her mother far longer than Lane from her, nearly twenty years. Originally, it had been spurred by debt and by her husband's physical collapse; eventually, perhaps, the length of time away had itself brought a certain degree of shame. But no matter why Wilder avoided visiting, she felt the yearning for her childhood as an almost physical pressure. In 1923, she wrote:

> Out in the meadow, I picked a wild sunflower and, as I looked into its golden heart such a wave of homesickness came over me that I almost wept. I wanted mother, with her gentle voice and quiet firmness; I longed to hear father's jolly songs and to see his twinkling blue eyes; I was lonesome for the sister with whom I used to play in the meadow picking daisies and wild sunflowers.
>
> Across the years, the old home and its love called to me and memories of sweet words of counsel came flooding back. I realized that all my life the teachings of those early days have influenced me and the example set by father and mother has been something I have tried to follow, with failures here and there, with rebellion at times, but always coming back to it as the compass needle to the star.[20]

Had she returned, of course, she would not have found the family as it once was. The pain of that may also have played a role in keeping her away. She made no move to undertake the trip, although she must have known what was coming.

Caroline Ingalls died on April 20, 1924. She was eighty-four. The *De Smet News* described the death as unexpected, coming after a brief illness, but noted that she had been "feeble all winter."[21] It emphasized her devotion to family and faith, barely hinting at the hardship and upheavals of her life: the loss of her father, the brother killed in the Civil War, the exhaustion and anxiety of repeated journeys across unknown country with a husband whose good intentions were undermined, on occasion, by his recklessness. She had endured the blindness of her eldest child, the premature death of her husband, and the need to provide for herself and Mary as a widow. Unable to attend church in her last years, the obituary reported, she had welcomed visitors, always remaining "interested, bright and happy."

Laura Ingalls Wilder had last seen her mother in 1902, when Caroline Ingalls was sixty-three. She did not return for the funeral, perhaps because she was herself unwell. Family letters attest to an unspecified period of illness or exhaustion in early 1924.[22] Scholars have speculated on the reason for her long absence, surmising a coldness or distance in the relationship.[23]

But there was no distance in what Wilder wrote for the *Ruralist* in June 1924, acknowledging receipt of the telegram announcing that "Mother passed away this morning."[24] Her anguished response— "Memories! We go thru life collecting them whether we will or not!"— was perhaps her most immediate and emotional piece of writing since her brief, unpublished essay about Charles Ingalls penned after his death. "Darkness" and "sadness" were among the words she chose to describe her feelings, and she cried out against memories as "the consuming fires of torment." They may bring joy, she allowed, but only "if we have not given ourselves any cause for regret." They may also leave us abandoned and bereft. "What a sorrow!" she wrote.[25]

We can only speculate about the particular regrets that touched off such exclamations after a lifetime's reticence: the isolation of exile, the sense of shame over past failures, the pain of remembering her parents' love and sacrifice. Whatever the feelings, they would soon drive her to face that torment head-on.

After announcing her mother's death, Wilder would write only two more columns for the *Ruralist*. She resigned with a last piece on December 15, 1924, a retrospective look at her husband's gallantry and fortitude, a blizzard he braved when he was courting her and fetching her every weekend from her lonely post as a schoolteacher in a freezing claim shanty:

When one thinks of 12 miles now, it is in terms of motor cars and means only a few minutes. It was different then, and I'll never forget that ride. The bells made a merry jingle, and the fur robes were warm, but the weather was growing colder. . . . We were facing the strong wind, and every little while he, who later became the "man of the place," must stop the team, get out in the snow, and by putting his hands over each horse's nose in turn, thaw the ice from them where the breath had frozen over their nostrils. Then he would get back into the sleigh and on we'd go until once more the horses could not breathe for the ice.

When we reached the journey's end, it was 40 degrees below zero, the snow was blowing so thickly that we could not see across the street and I was so chilled that I had to be half carried into the house. But I was home for Christmas and cold and danger were forgotten.

Such magic there is in Christmas to draw the absent ones home and if unable to go in the body the thoughts will hover there![26]

She may have thought she was retiring from writing, but her thoughts hovered intently in the past. It wouldn't be long before she would embark on a journey of her own "to draw the absent ones home."

A Match in the Sunshine

During Rose Wilder Lane's far-flung adventures during the early twenties, she met many famous or about-to-be-famous poets, playwrights, novelists, and journalists. She saw the world and wrote prodigiously. But no matter how far she went—the Balkans, Baghdad, Constantinople—she somehow never got far from home. The world kept redepositing her back on her mother's doorstep. Even as she was becoming established as a successful freelance journalist, she did not buy a house, or set up any permanent base for herself. Instead, she kept returning to Rocky Ridge.

While renting an apartment in Paris, she spent much of 1920–1921 traveling in England and western Europe, eventually becoming seriously involved with Guy Moyston, the Associated Press reporter who had helped broker deals for her early biographies. Handsome, bespectacled,

and with a wonderful wry smile, Moyston was a foreign correspondent when Lane reconnected with him in Europe. He had recently been
abducted by the Irish Republican Army while covering the Anglo-Irish
war, and longed to leave the Troubles behind and become a playwright.[27] Even as they fell in love, however, she adamantly resisted
becoming a couple.

Around the same time, in November 1920, she met a fledgling
American reporter, Dorothy Thompson, who was also writing for the
Red Cross. Seven years younger than Lane, Thompson, the daughter of
a Methodist minister, had grown up in New York State, graduated
from Syracuse University, and worked as a suffragist organizer before
coming to Europe with hopes of establishing herself as a journalist.
According to her diary, the serious-minded Thompson was initially
"appalled" by Lane and the shallowness of her friends, who, she
believed, cared for little but bourgeois pursuits. Lane, she wrote, was
"their chiefest writer with her sob stuff"—a reference to her "Diverging Roads" serial, published as a book in 1919, or to commercial pieces
Lane was selling to *Ladies' Home Journal*, *Good Housekeeping*, and
McCall's.[28]

But gradually the two became friends, despite their strongly diver-
gent personal and political beliefs. Over the New Year's weekend of
1921, Lane, Thompson, and another Red Cross writer walked through
the Loire valley, traipsing from village to village in the rain, drying
their clothes before inn fires while wrapped in blankets in rustic kitchens, sharing life stories over strange-tasting soup that they hoped was
not made of cat.[29] The romantic adventure cemented a powerful link
between Lane and Thompson. Throughout that nomadic year, they
were occasionally to be found in Paris, donning elaborate costumes for
all-night bacchanals. In the future, they would rarely be in the same
place at the same time, but their connection would last for decades,
shaping the careers and lives of both women.

In April 1921, Lane embarked on another life-altering journey, this
time to Albania. She had heard Balkan tales from Helen Boylston, the
Red Cross nurse she'd met on the Orient Express, and she had been
enthralled by the lavish embroidery on an Albanian costume at a Mardi
Gras ball in Paris. Initially, her trip was intended to be just a brief visit

to report on Red Cross work. But she had barely arrived in the ancient port city of Scutari when an American in charge of the agency's local activities, Betsy Cleveland, began feverishly promoting "my wonderful Albanians" and urging Lane to trek into the northern mountains with her, on a mission to scout locations for schools. Impulsively, Lane agreed. She had no idea what awaited her.

In addition to Cleveland, the party that crossed the Scutari plains and headed into the snow-covered mountains included Cleveland's partner in social work, Margaret Alexander; a group of gendarmes; and an interpreter from Kosovo, Rrok Perolli, secretary to the Albanian Minister of the Interior and a wanted man in Serbia, just across the border. Rounding out the party was Rexh Meta, an enterprising teenaged orphan in red fez and flannel pajamas who had been learning English from Cleveland. Rexh had taken it upon himself, or so Lane would claim, to organize and oversee the entire journey. In published accounts, Lane gave his age as twelve.[30] He was actually fifteen.

As they set off on a succession of horses and donkeys, Lane was astonished by the extraordinary customs she found in hidden valleys, isolated for centuries. Among those was the blood feud, a rigid tradition of compulsory revenge, which was nonetheless balanced out by a custom known as *besa*, drawn from the Muslim honor code. An Albanian word meaning "to keep the promise," it provided for the absolute safety and protection of guests.

The American women were among the first foreigners to reach some mountain villages, arousing intense curiosity and provoking dramatic celebrations. The terse, clipped notes Lane kept in her diary captured the details, providing the basis for subsequent letters, articles in the *San Francisco Call & Post*, and *The Peaks of Shala*, a travel book that would be published in 1922. On April 14, she wrote: "Washed in the stream. . . . Luncheon on the grassy plateau—Shepherd gives the soup to his pet sheep. . . . Down the cliffs in the rain. The woman with the blue-beaded hair." That night was spent in the company of goats and fleas. The following day, she and Alexander took an alternate route from the rest of the party, and followed a stream bed to a village. They were greeted by an explosion of bell ringing, rifle firing, and gymnastics, treated to baths and mattresses, and presented with the gift of a sheep.

Along the way, Lane learned that the men in the party were constantly at risk of death along the trail due to long-lived internecine feuds, but that she and the other women had the heady power to act as their saviors. In a letter to her mother that may have been intended to be shared with Wilder's *Ruralist* readers, Lane explained the custom:

> There is no law in the mountains, except the ancient tribal laws which are enforced simply and rigorously. . . . All in all, almost everyone is in honor bound to be killing almost everybody else. . . . But a man is safe so long as he is with a woman, for no one can be killed in a woman's presence, and so when I was not otherwise occupied I was usually leaping to someone's side and crying, "May you live long!" to someone else who already was getting his gun in readiness, and then he slung his gun back on his shoulder and passed with averted head, to await a more fitting occasion. Amazing fact, which already seems to me almost incredible, but I did this four times.[31]

The practice had a certain resonance with backcountry justice in the Ozarks, as Lane herself would depict in later fiction, but Wilder apparently judged it too potent for her readers. She shared with them Lane's letters from Paris, Bohemia, and Poland, but not this one.

After days of drenching rain on the trail, Lane came down with a high fever and was forced to return to Scutari. The protective Rexh insisted on accompanying her, despite her protestations that he travel deeper into the mountains with the rest of the party: he had set his heart on seeing the interior, and his sacrifice would instill feelings of guilt and obligation. But with "knives" in her lungs, fearing pneumonia, she gave in and was conveyed along sheer cliffs by mule, seated in a wooden sidesaddle, with one man holding fast to the animal's neck by a chain and another clinging to the tail. Heaved across raging torrents like a bundle of clothes, she marveled at the change the journey had wrought in her after only a few days. She could gaze into cavernous depths "where pine-tree tops looked like a lawn" without shrieking in fear, shrugging at showers of rocks while marveling over "the magnificence of shadow and sunshine on the snow-piled heights."[32]

When the lights of Scutari finally blinked into view late on the evening of April 22, Lane wrote: "One must go across centuries and back, perhaps, to know all the strange things that are at home, all the romances and surprises in one's self."[33] Reaching the city, she collapsed in bed, ending her diary with a note about "the indomitable Rexh." His solicitous nature was rooted in tragedy, she had learned. In Kosovo, his entire family had been killed by Serbs. Left for dead in a pile of bodies, or so she told it, he had crept out, made his way to Scutari, and refashioned himself as an Albanian Oliver Twist, gathering fellow orphans off the street and building a haven in an abandoned hovel.

Recovering from her perilous flight out of the mountains, Lane began to see Albania and Rexh, its representative, through a romantic scrim. Her near-death experience transformed the poor, war-scarred Balkan country and its child into a paradigm of authenticity. On her way back to Paris, she missed the boat to Italy and wound up spending time in the Albanian city of Tirana, which completed her infatuation: the ancient city, believed to have been inhabited since the Paleolithic era, rose fantastically from a valley floor, built into hillsides that faced the Adriatic. Besotted with her veritable paradise, she gushed to friends about "our Albanian spring," its sunsets, minarets, blue skies, and water buffalo.[34]

Quitting the Red Cross, she returned to Albania the following year with a Swiss friend, a photographer named Peggy Marquis, who would repeat Lane's mountain journey all over again to capture images for Lane's book, braving even worse hazards. From Tirana, Lane excitedly reported on the local revolution, catching the eye of an Albanian bey (Turkish for "leader"), who proposed marriage during a pause in the fighting—a touching moment interrupted by a rifle grenade.

In a letter to her parents, an account that rivals a romance novel, she portrayed herself as thrilled to be shot at while standing under a streetlight, dressed in a fur-lined coat over a velvet dinner gown. She was delighted to be inside a revolution, in the thick of the intrigue, just as Bessie Beatty had been in Russia. "It was a night that I shall never forget," she wrote, teasing her parents with her dalliance with "my Bey," implying that she might marry him. "I may do it," she wrote; "there is no use asking . . . whether or not you want an Albanian Bey for a son-in-law, as I shall decide it one way or another in a day or so. . . . I have not the least notion what a Moslem wedding ceremony is like."[35] The Wilders' response, if any, does not survive. In any event, she turned the bey down, having fallen in love not with him but with his country.

She provided a quite different account of the events to Moyston, leaving out her fine wardrobe, the moonlit atmosphere, and all the prattle about her admirer. Instead, she acknowledged that she and Peggy, roused by gunfire in their room, "swore like troopers," and admitted that the bey who proposed already had one wife.[36]

Leaving Albania, she and Peggy Marquis traveled on and on, through Italy, Austria, and Hungary, then back to Albania for more photographs. There she met again with Rexh Meta, now studying at a vocational school through the generosity of Betsy Cleveland. At that point, Lane allowed a fateful fantasy to flourish in her mind: a plan to "adopt" him. On yet another mountain trip, she was gripped by a desire for further dependents, wanting to send a "gifted" mountain boy down to join Rexh at his school. In her diary, she talked herself out of it; but Rexh, whether he knew it or not, was slated for her attentions.

That fall, she and Marquis were forced to stop in Constantinople to recuperate from malaria contracted in the Balkans, but Lane's passion for the country brooked no deterrence. She declared that she would be back someday, this time to stay. "Even the malaria of Albania is superlative," she wrote.[37] She would long claim that *Shala*, her book about the region, was her favorite.

Back in Paris, she became such a bore on the subject of Albania and its politics that she was caricatured in a novel by Dorothy Thompson's new husband, a Hungarian expatriate named Josef Bard. In *Shipwreck in Europe*, Lane plays a cameo role as "Hazel Green," a flirtatious friend of a character based on Thompson, who nurtures the protagonist while his lover is away. Bard substituted Montenegro for Albania:

Hazel Green was near forty, but well-preserved. She was small and not thin, had a very average face, but beautiful expressive grey eyes. She wrote excellently but without much power of discrimination. She hated America for its industrial spirit, and fell in love with the Montenegrins in the far-off Balkans because they had no industrial spirit whatsoever. Of course they had almost no soap either. But Hazel preferred a well-built Montenegrin quite untouched by soap to an industrialized American full of soap. She saved money to build a house on the top of Mount Lovcen in the Bay of Cattaro, and intended to finish her life in the midst of her beloved Montenegrins. She wrote touching stories about their honesty, wisdom and general superiority in manly spirit, and illustrated them by long conversations with these brave mountaineers. How she spoke to her pets remained a riddle, because Hazel did not understand their language.

Catty and mean-spirited, Bard's portrait nonetheless captured the self-dramatizing nature of Lane's fixation, something that would become even more marked before the decade was out.

That fall, Lane began working for the publicity bureau of the Near East Relief Agency, reporting on food aid and refugee programs. Her health remained fragile, but even as she had her tonsils out (in Budapest) and suffered recurrent bouts of malaria (in Armenia), she pushed onward, spinning manically through countries and capitals: Greece, Turkey, Georgia, Armenia, Azerbaijan, Cairo, Jerusalem, Baghdad.

The more misery, poverty, and displacement she saw, the more numb to the experience she became, no matter how shocking or horrific.[38] Confronted with the Armenian genocide, she skirted piles of skeletons: "Skulls grinned among the bones . . . leg bones and rib cages were scattered farther away where hyenas or dogs had dragged them. There were little skulls and tiny backbones." Recording her descent into depression—"Life goes by and nothing comes of it—nothing. No meaning"—she could summon neither perspective nor insight into her despair.[39]

She began to develop a hostility to the very relief work she was supposed to be promoting, a cynical sense that it was all pointless, an exercise in lining the pockets of the exploiting classes. In letters to Fremont Older, who published her accounts in the *San Francisco Call & Post*, she went further, describing dining with Catholic bishops in an Armenian church, feasting on roast flesh while outside "the poor orphans obligingly die all round . . . making wonderful heart-appeals to take back home." A cameraman had wandered by as a child died, and she parodied the delight her fellow relief workers took in his serendipitous capturing of the moment. He "actually got its death on the film!" she wrote.[40]

The massacre of innocents recalled something closer to home. In one of her columns, she reported that a Turkish man had approvingly cited the old American saying, "'The only good Indian is a dead Indian,'" adding that he felt the same way about Armenians. She contemplated it, remarking casually, "We did not kill the Indians because their religion differed from ours. We killed them for economic reasons, because they had the rich continent that we wanted."[41] Yet she criticized the Turk for learning nothing from civilization, comparing the "withering mess" overseas to her own superior country, "clean, happy, innocent and kind America."[42]

In years to come, such experiences would lead her to embrace an uncritical American exceptionalism while issuing blanket denunciations of human pity as a weakness, a "flaw in your defensive armor . . . surface emotion . . . dangerous in itself." She had been made to feel that there was "something extremely unhinged in the universe." Pity had been "dinned" into everyone's heads for eons, she said, by schools, by churches, by the Red Cross and relief organizations. All it accomplished was to "open a door to suffering and suffering is a form of destruction . . . suffering carried far enough is death."[43] Her despairing outbursts of misanthropy, a visceral rejection of hope and charity, were the first expressions of an increasingly vehement and deliberately pitiless outlook. Even the usual pieties were not safe from her cynicism: "I think mother-love is a fiction, myself," she wrote.[44]

As the language in her diaries grew increasingly dark, she stumbled into moments of sheer existential vertigo. One occurred in a market in Tiflis (now Tbilisi), the capital of Georgia, when she stopped to light a cigarette. With the flaring of the match in sunlight, she felt a paroxysm of ecstasy, a rapture at the sudden confluence of sun, flame, and heat. She later called it "the happiest moment of my life . . . the moment I lighted a match in the sunshine, in the Tartar market of Tiflis."[45]

Another day, she ventured out beyond Tiflis and across a grassy plateau, far beyond sight of houses, villages, civilization itself:

It was a clear autumn afternoon. I'd gone out with a car . . . driving
miles across those high, airy plateaus that seem quite deserted, rolling
gently away to interminable distances on every side, covered with
bronzed wild grass. They do not seem to be under the sky, they seem
to be in the sky—lifted, somehow, into that thin blueness. And nothing moves upon them but flights of wild birds. . . . I walked away. . . .
Every few minutes I looked back, to find the car, and the plateau rose
between it and me like the slow swell of a wave. Then I looked back,
and there was no car. Nothing but the thin air that seemed to be the
sky, and the miles of blown grass, red and brown, that faintly rustled
with a dry sound, and a bird that rose and cried and skimmed away
in undulating flight. It was like being quite alone [on] the roof of the
world. I felt that if I were to go to the edge and look over—holding
carefully, not to fall—I would see below all that I had ever known; all
the crowded cities and seas covered with ships, and the clamor of
harbors and traffic of rivers, and farmlands being worked, and herds
of cattle driven in clouds of dust across interminable plains. . . . But
here there was only sky, and a stillness made audible by the brittle
grass. Emptiness was so perfect all around me that I felt a part of it,
empty myself; there was a moment in which I was nothing at all—
almost nothing at all. The only thing left in me was Albania. I said,
I want to go back to Albania.[46]

She did not appear to recognize it, but her description matched,
detail for detail, another high plain under a vast sky, another prairie
covered with brittle grass, far to the west. Once again, she had traveled
thousands of miles, crossed oceans and continents, only to find herself
back at the beginning.

She could not stop. She kept on, crossing the desert sands of Syria,
Beirut, Damascus, Baghdad. By the fall of 1923, she was so exhausted
she could barely push a pen across a page. "Very blue," she wrote.[47] A
few days later, "To think that I'm sitting here in this picturesque dam
town on the Euphrates, when I want to be at home."[48] At a stopover in
Paris, she decided that over the past three years she had lost everything: friends, finances, career. Whatever had been gained was "worthless . . . fading memories." She soon declared the past year "a dead loss."[49]

In that frame of mind she set sail for the United States. She arrived at Rocky Ridge on December 20, 1923, just in time for Christmas. "Like a dream," she wrote, "Mama Bess met me at Mansfield station."[50]

You Must Listen to Me

What Laura Wilder made of the daughter who had returned from Europe is less than clear. We have no account of it in her voice, but she must have seen that something was wrong. The daughter whose pictures adorned the mantel had sailed off to France spirited, ambitious, and eager to see the world. The daughter who came back was devastated and subdued.

Wilder, however, was struggling with her own problems. Continually pushing to do at fifty-seven everything she had demanded of herself as a younger woman, exhausted by housework and farm labor on top of her Farm Loan Association duties and other responsibilities, she was beginning to show the strain. Soon after coming home, Lane described her mother as "old and not very well" to Guy Moyston, then followed it by suggesting that her mother was completely broken down and "should be in a hospital."[51] Even allowing for Lane's tendency to dramatize, it's clear that Wilder was approaching her limits.

The house at Rocky Ridge was comfortable, surrounded by gorgeous seasonal vistas, but the farm required a punishing amount of labor to maintain. Lane moved back into her old bedroom upstairs, making an office out of the sleeping porch and a novel out of her old Jack London articles. (The novelistic veneer would allow her to publish even though Charmian London still disapproved.) She had been homesick in the Middle East but soon found herself overwhelmed by the daily, grinding chores of farm life: hauling water, fetching firewood, peeling potatoes, frying meat, washing dishes, scrubbing floors, ironing, and "waiting on the pigs."[52]

To Moyston, she joked about the daily disruption of having to fetch the cows each afternoon, but it was clearly a genuine irritation. "My people can't see why I shouldn't settle down here for the rest of my life," she complained.[53] Her parents were too old to handle the work themselves, she said, but servants were impossible to find—even if her mother would have welcomed them, which she did not.

No one else wanted to work so hard or live this way, Lane wearily concluded. There were fourteen empty farmhouses for sale in the area, reflecting the economic stagnation of agriculture, once again in a slump. After the tremendous wartime push to ramp up production of wheat, corn, and cotton, crops had once again flooded the market, causing prices to plummet and the farm economy to collapse. People were leaving for cities in droves, and Lane wanted to join them. The constant work and isolation explained why Wilder was so glad to have Rose back home; her mood and health improved dramatically, even if her daughter's did not.

Lane's letters to Moyston recorded lively conversations between mother and daughter, including debates about politics and Prohibition. Nineteen twenty-four was a year of silent movies and bootleggers wielding Thompson submachine guns. Lenin died. J. Edgar Hoover ascended to the Olympian heights of the FBI. Leopold and Loeb attempted to commit their perfect crime. Fascists were on the rise, and a young hysteric named Adolf Hitler spent eight months of the year in jail for shooting off his mouth—and a gun—at the Beer Hall Putsch the previous winter.

The Wilders and their daughter had a chance to chew over these developments with Moyston in person: he came for a three-month stay that spring. It must have made the close quarters of the small farmhouse even closer, and caused talk in town, which Lane acknowledged later, rolling her eyes in letters to her lover.[54] Throughout that year, Moyston was becoming her indispensable foil and confidant. A former Tennessee farm boy, he settled into their routine with relish, going after the cows with Rose, snatching kisses, sitting on the porch in the gloaming and smoking cigarettes as birds settled in the trees and frogs croaked in the ravine.

He was charming, and the Wilders loved him, seeing in him their daughter's last chance for marital happiness and stability. When Wilder's mother died, Moyston dispensed empathy and comfort: his own elderly mother was ailing too. Over the next few years, Wilder would inquire solicitously, through Lane, about his health, thanking him for little gifts of newspaper clippings and magazines. Almanzo, who often complained of sharing the house with multiple women ("there's always a hen on," he grumbled about the facilities), must have cherished having another man around the place.[55] After Moyston left, he tenderly buffed and oiled an old pair of boots that he'd left behind, in case he returned. Lane, for her part, did not hesitate to pass along to the guest the guilt her mother had made her feel, telling him, "There was a large empty space in the house after you left, and my mother said, 'Now can you imagine what it is like when you go, and there is <u>nobody</u>?'"[56]

Politically, it was an unsettled time. Republican Calvin Coolidge had assumed office in 1923 when President Warren G. Harding died suddenly of a heart attack. Harding's popularity had been undercut by posthumous disclosures about the Teapot Dome scandal, in which it emerged that the Secretary of the Interior had accepted gifts and no-interest loans from oil companies in exchange for favorable leases on public lands. The greatest political scandal prior to Watergate, Teapot Dome made cynics out of most Americans when it came to their elected officials. Along with the rest of her community, Wilder subscribed to the widespread assumption that everyone from the president on down was for sale. Lane, for her part, declared that she "never felt much real interest in American politics."[57]

Nonetheless, both of them hung on radio reports of the extraordinarily contentious Democratic National Convention held that summer in New York City. The "Klanbake," as the convention became known, provided unparalleled theater, as Ku Klux Klan delegates attacked effigies of Al Smith, the Catholic governor of New York who was one of the front-runners. The convention would be the longest in American history, with politicians shouting their way through 103 ballots before finally settling on John Davis, a compromise candidate. Wilder had been impressed by Smith, and praised his graceful concession speech, admiring his courage in facing down Klan bullies. There was no hint, as yet, of any swing to the right in either woman's position.[58]

Yet on other topics, her daughter exhibited signs of becoming a reactionary. Lane seemed to approve of California's compulsory sterilization of inmates at insane asylums, and supported Prohibition, declaring alcohol a poison.[59] She also suggested to Moyston that despite Clarence

Darrow's celebrated defense, Leopold and Loeb should be "quietly chloroformed."[60] (Wilder, too, was outraged by the brazen murderers, her daughter wrote, sputtering in her chair while reading newspaper accounts of Darrow's experts, "occasionally exploding, 'Bunk!' ")[61] A few years later, Lane would defend the state's ultimate power at great length in a letter to Fremont Older, again counseling chloroform as the appropriate capital punishment.

Writing long flirtatious letters to Moyston, Lane concealed from him the depth of her depression. Expressions of it had appeared throughout her European travels, feelings that she had bungled her life and career. As soon as she returned to Rocky Ridge, it swamped her. "I am dumb," she wrote in her diary in 1924. "There is an insulation over everything. The unreality of long solitary days. . . . Life goes by, gets away from me, and soon I shall be dead, and everything insulated forever."[62] To Moyston, she merely complained of the monotony, irritably lashing out at him on occasion. Only to her diary did she confess her suicidal leanings, a sense of being buried alive in a stultifying routine, something that applied not only to endless farmhouse chores but to her writing as well.

Her mood lifted a bit when she completed the manuscript for *He Was a Man*, her Jack London novel. Briefly flush with cash, she paid off debts to friends and escaped to the East Coast for five months in the fall and winter of 1924, spending romantic weeks with Moyston in a rooming house in Croton, New York. Moyston wanted to make the relationship permanent, but Lane pulled away, hoping to preserve it as a long-distance affair. She had wanted the kind of love he offered all her life, she said, but she could not stand to be with anyone all the time. "I like loneliness," she told him, not very convincingly. "I DON'T WANT TO BE CLUTCHED."[63] She could never marry him, she said, because "I'm not a wife."[64] She hated the very idea of marriage.[65]

She proved it by returning to Rocky Ridge in 1925, not with Moyston but with her friend Helen Boylston, the Red Cross nurse who had first spoken to her of Albania. Thin, gawky, with a severe pageboy haircut, Boylston, known as "Troub"—a childhood nickname for "Trouble"— provided Rose with undemanding companionship that was laced with caustic humor. Lane, in turn, found Boylston a willing audience for her resentments, as well as an apt pupil; the former nurse was studying to be a writer. Boylston's presence, along with a rotating roster of Lane's other friends passing through Mansfield, contributed to a hothouse writers' colony atmosphere at Rocky Ridge.

Enjoying horseback riding in the bucolic Ozark hills, Boylston took to Almanzo immediately but detested Laura, later calling Rose "her mama's slave."[66] When arguments broke out between Laura and her daughter, she recalled, Almanzo would often seek peace in the convenient haven of the cornfield. "Well, I knew when I married her she had a temper," he said ruefully; "you just get used to those things."[67]

Lane's attitude toward her mother was hardening, perhaps in reaction to the pressure she felt to care for her parents. In a letter from New York, she had lectured her mother, explaining why she had to revise an article Wilder had written about her kitchen for *Country Gentleman*. Gone was the ebullient coaching of previous years, replaced by impatience and irritability. Comparing her mother to a "frolicsome dog that won't stand still to listen," she snapped: "Listen, please, please listen. All I did on your story was an ordinary re-write job. . . . I'm trying to train you as a writer for the big market."[68] She bullied her mother to make more money:

> You must understand that what sold was your article, edited. You must study how it was edited, and why . . . Above all, you must listen to me . . . for years upon years, I have been telling you, "Stop saving money, and make money." . . . Well, now I went out and made you some money, first. To show you it could be done. . . . But God damn it all, you've GOT to go on and make more, now.[69]

Finally, she got to the heart of the matter. "Just because I was once three years old," she wrote, "you honestly oughtn't to think that I'm never going to be anything more than a three-year-old. Sometime you ought to let me grow up."[70] A long-distance tantrum, the letter, if anything, undermined her argument. It marked a moment when everything started to go wrong between them. As if to manifest this inner turmoil, Lane, dissatisfied with her hair, shaved her head. In a photograph taken as it was growing back in, she stares downward, her brow furrowed.

There was blame to go around. Wilder herself had admitted in the

Ruralist that she failed to see her daughter as a grown woman. Playing on Lane's guilt, she heightened her sense of entrapment. At the same time, Lane's insistence on supporting her parents at a level beyond her ability—she was doggedly paying them the promised $500 per year, which she calculated as half their yearly income—and then resenting them for it was beginning to put intolerable strain on the relationship.[71]

"My mother can not learn to have any reliance upon my financial judgment or promises," Lane complained to Moyston. "It's partly, I suppose, because she still thinks of me as a child. She even hesitates to let me have the responsibility of bringing up butter from the spring, for fear I won't do it quite right!"[72] Yet she remained blind to her own grandiosity and impracticality. At a time when her assets amounted to a mere hundred dollars, she told her diary that she needed fifty thousand invested at 8 percent interest.[73] With fantastic optimism, she estimated that she could sell a hundred stories over the next five years at five hundred dollars each, an output scarcely suited to a temperamental writer.

Compared to her own bohemian bravery, Lane found her mother "timorous," unable to believe that the promised $500 a year could be relied upon. As she paraphrased her mother's skepticism, "Suppose I wrote a story, and it didn't sell? Suppose I were suddenly ill, and couldn't write?"[74] Of course, such things would indeed happen, just as Wilder feared.

Deriding her parents' bourgeois devotion to "perseverance, thrift, caution, industry . . . the necessary virtues," Lane could not recognize that her failure to establish a stable and permanent home reinforced her mother's fears. She knew the penury that gave rise to her parents' thrift, yet could be patronizing even while she empathized with their anxiety. "It is really, a sad thing for my parents," she wrote. "They would have had comfort and joy and pride from me, if I had married fairly well, had a good home, been steadily lifted . . . by my husband's efforts, become, let us say, a socially successful woman in Springfield."[75] It was astonishing, she added, that they knew as much of the world as they did, from reading the St. Louis newspapers.

At that moment, Lane was publishing a rhapsodic tribute to her rural farm life in *Country Gentleman*, while declaring privately that her parents should sell the farm and move to England. Supremely confident in this decision, she nonetheless expressed bafflement to Moyston over how they could find a source of income there.[76] The Wilders themselves made no effort to cooperate. In the same article, Lane suggested that her mother adamantly resisted any plans to shift them away from Rocky Ridge, quoting Wilder saying, "I don't see why . . . Why should we move[?]. . . . We already have the farm."[77]

Lane's fevered financial calculations revealed someone motivated not by necessity but by emotion, a desire to make up for the pain she imagined she had caused. In 1924, she had owed her mother $900, noting that her finances were "incredibly and horribly growing worse."[78] In 1925, though, she was telling Moyston that she had already given her mother, that year alone, "$2,600 in 8% bonds and $1,250 besides . . . and her regular $500."[79] No matter how much she gave, her mother never believed in her and never trusted her, or so she felt. Trying to capture her mother's logic, she instead revealed more about her own state of mind:

> Children born of poor people, who all their lives have worked and planned and saved and gone without things they needed, for every painful dollar they've accumulated, just don't suddenly, with no visible means of support—no job, no rich husband, nothing—begin to have bank accounts in four figures. . . . It's incredible. The mind can't stretch large enough to swallow it. . . . I don't save anything. I don't own anything. I take such awful chances. I leave a good job at sixty dollars a month, without a thought for the future. I leave a real estate business which was paying me the enormous unthinkable sum of ten, twelve, fifteen thousand dollars a year, and don't care; am actually glad to get out of it; go to work on a newspaper at $12.50 a week. . . . This unaccountable daughter who roams around the world, borrowing money here and being shot at there . . . is a pride, in a way, but a ceaseless apprehension too.[80]

By this point, the question of who was supporting whom was hopelessly entangled. It was becoming impossible for the Wilders or their daughter to extricate themselves, even if they wanted to.

Pages and Pages of Things You Remember

Practical to the core, Wilder never seemed comfortable relying wholly upon her daughter. She made that abundantly clear in March 1925, when she launched a bold effort to preserve her independence and shore up her finances: she ran for public office.

It was a surprising decision for someone who had recently been touting women's irreplaceable role at home on the farm. "I am not a politician and have no thought of entering politics," she said, almost abashed, as she declared her candidacy for tax collector for Pleasant Valley Township.[81]

She was a late entry in the race, the election happening at the end of that same month.[82] The position paid a handsome salary, three hundred dollars a year for a two-year term. In a statement that ran in the *Mansfield Mirror*, Wilder was quick to claim that she had been "asked to place my name before the voters."[83] Who asked her remains unknown, but she was inspired by confidence gained from her loan work:

> Seven years ago, with eight other farmers, I organized the Mansfield National Farm Loan Association, which I have served ever since as Secretary Treasurer. The Association now has 54 members. . . . I have been entrusted with $102,675 United States Government money, [which] the Association has loaned to farmers in this community at 5 1/2 percent interest. I believe that this amount of money, brought into our community from the government has increased our prosperity by that much, and has been of direct or indirect value to us all.
>
> I have personally handled all the details of these loans and been responsible for the money. Federal Bank Examiners certify that I have attended promptly to the business and that my records are always accurate and in order. I believe the members of the Farm Loan Association who receive an 8 percent dividend on their stock every year, will testify that my work has been satisfactory to them.[84]

Campaigning as an independent, she doubtless worked her Farm Club and women's group connections. Later that month, according to Lane, intrigues broke out, "fast and furious."[85] Lane said that her mother was opposed by "the whiskey element"—the locals who ran stills in the backwoods—as well as by the Woman's Christian Temperance Union and by nearby churches (perhaps Baptists), but she was nonetheless hoping that her mother would triumph.[86] Thinking of her own prospects, Lane predicted that a successful outcome might free her from Mansfield. "This summer will be enough," she told Moyston; "duty to parents or not, I won't stay any longer."[87]

But while the Wilders had long identified as Democrats, Mansfield was heavily Republican, and Laura Wilder's opponents were male. Her chief rival, Charles A. Stephens, had beaten her into the race by a month and boasted considerably more experience, having served as tax assessor for the past eight years.[88] According to results published in the *Mirror*, turnout was low. Although Lane had felt sure of at least a hundred votes for her, Wilder came in last, with only fifty-six.[89] Stephens won with 256.

Lane was aggrieved, though she believed her mother didn't "awfully mind." She told Moyston that Wilder was "apparently elected, but counted out ... The steal was so raw that everyone knows it. And of course will go on letting it happen, over and over again. The dear people don't really care a darn about self-government, in spite of all the Upton Sinclairs."[90]

Wilder probably did mind, more than she let on. For her, the cost in pride and potential income was steep. Had she won, however, the next years of her life might have gone very differently. Serving as tax collector, it is unlikely that she would have had time and energy to devote to writing.

As it was, she turned away from electoral politics and struck out on the only other potential money-making path she could see. On June 22, two months after losing the election, she sat down at a typewriter and wrote to her aunt Martha Carpenter, a task made more urgent by Caroline Ingalls's death the year before.

The letter she composed contained flashes of Lane's hyperbole, but overall it was quintessentially Wilder, folksy and plainspoken, opening with the weather ("very dry") and family news about illness. She described herself as "not very strong," recovering from a "serious sickness, very near to nervous prostration."[91]

Beating about the bush, she first asked her elderly aunt to supply Caroline's "vanity cake" recipe—something Wilder said she wanted for a *Ladies' Home Journal* article on "grandmother's cooking." But then she got to the point, acknowledging her wider ambitions. "There was something I wanted the girls to do for me," she said, referring to her sisters, Carrie and Grace, "but they never got around to it and Mother herself was not able." She had wanted them to take down all the stories their mother could remember from her early days in Wisconsin. Now, she noted sadly, "it is too late to ever get them from her."[92]

Regret, sorrow, and nostalgia pushed her to ask for far more than mere recipes. She wanted everything: "The little everyday happenings and what you and mother and Aunt Eliza and Uncle Tom and Uncle Henry did as children and young folks, going to parties and sleigh rides and spelling schools. . . . About when Grandma was left a widow and the Indians used to share their game with her and the children." She promised to preserve the stories and make copies for all the cousins. She would have liked to come and talk in person, she said, but "I am not able to make such a trip." She asked for "pages and pages of things you remember," offering to pay a stenographer to take it all down. The extravagant idea of hiring a stenographer could only have come from Lane. But the plaintive tone, the longing for lost times and places, was all Wilder's own.

In any event, her aunt needed no prodding. Martha Carpenter was happy to oblige. Confined by age and illness to a spare bedroom of an old farmhouse outside Plainview, Minnesota, the eighty-eight-year-old widow, mother of fourteen, was clearly bored. She had little to do beyond sewing old rags together to make rugs. She complained of having "the blues."[93] She could see out of only one eye and was having trouble walking. Wistfully, she spoke of how hard it was to be dependent on one of her daughters, watching her grandchildren go to school, playing and enjoying themselves. Her childhood had been nothing like theirs, and she was honest enough to admit that it pained her to see what she had missed. "Now I am to[o] old," she wrote. "Life [is] a great deal of work a little sleep a little love then life is over."[94]

But then she got to work, sending two long missives, written in a shaky arthritic hand on the same kind of tablet paper that Wilder herself would use in coming years. Despite her physical frailties including bad eyesight, she recorded pages and pages of things she remembered. There were occasional lapses in her train of thought and abrupt leaps from one topic to the next, but her recollections were full of the rich details that Wilder had asked for.

First, she told her how to make vanity cakes. Nothing much to it, she said. Make a dough with flour and water, then fry spoonfuls in hot lard. The little cakes would puff up, hollow in the middle, and melt on the tongue. She threw in a recipe for cottage cheese pie while she was at it.

Then she carried on, remembering the past until the ink in her bottle ran out. The writing was as rough and raw as the time she described. Her childhood, and that of her sister Caroline and their siblings, had been punctuated by sudden death and periods of extreme privation. The tale that unfolded came with the cold breath of wilderness.

There were also memorable joys along with the hardships. There was the "hot maple sugar party" in Kellogg, where everyone stuffed themselves and danced until morning.[95] There was hilarity on the day the boys stripped to climb trees—to spare their clothes—and were mistaken for "white bears." There were hats to plait out of wheat straw, and corn husking parties, and "plenty of quilting." There were willow branches to strip and weave into baskets. One day a circus had passed by, and Martha saw an elephant crossing a log bridge across the marsh, putting each foot down "so careful."[96]

A neighbor who had survived the same terrible storm that "took" her father was known for his gorgeous flowers. "He had so many pinks," Carpenter recalled, wistfully, of a time starved for beauty.

The wilderness had held remarkable consolations. Domestic pleasures were as nothing to her most treasured memories, all of which focused on the wilds that lay beyond the ragged margins of their stump-studded fields. The woods, she wrote, were full of birds and animals, seen and unseen. "The wolves would howl first at the North then the East the South and last to the west," she wrote, and she and her brothers and sisters listened intently and anxiously to the screaming of panthers at night.[97] As she drew back into those days, she marveled over the glories of that place:

It was beautiful to be out there with birds and other small animals of
the forest and to hear the music of the wilds with the beauty of all the
rest of the landscape it would carry you away and you would forget
[y]ourself and rejoice that you were there to see and have it all.[98]

Bears and mountain lions roamed the woods outside their door. So
did "wild" people, their faces painted, frightening the little Quiner
children just as the Osage would terrify Mary and Laura.

Martha Carpenter died less than two years after writing those letters. She was survived by nine children, twenty-eight grandchildren, and
sixteen great-grandchildren. In the twilight of her life, she had rendered
her niece a remarkable service, reviving for her "the music of the wilds,"
a music that Wilder would soon spend years recapturing in every detail.
But not yet: at the moment, she was still recovering from illness and
exhaustion and grieving over her mother's death. And there was another
trip coming up.

In a characteristic burst of extravagance, Lane had bought her parents a used Buick. Wilder learned quickly, but Lane struggled to teach
her father to drive. During one of their lessons, he nearly killed them
both: accustomed to driving a team of horses, he had braced his foot
on the gas pedal while pulling back on the steering wheel, saying
"Whoa!" Grazing a couple of other cars, the Buick plowed through a
ditch, taking out a barbed wire fence and uprooting a small tree. Lane
went through the windshield, leaving her with glass in her face, a crushed
nose, and two black eyes.[99]

Once she recovered, Lane drove her mother and Helen Boylston
across the west to California. For Wilder, the road trip was by turns
thrilling and exhausting, much like her visit to San Francisco a decade
before. As she always did when leaving home, she felt anxious about
her husband but alert to anything that recalled old times. Crossing
Kansas, she wrote to Almanzo that she had forgotten what it was like
to disappear into the immensity of the plains, "sunset and starlight . . .
on the prairie."[100] Just as she had thirty years earlier, she saw farmers
struggling with dry conditions and lack of irrigation. Only those with
dairy herds seemed successful. "It is strange to see the plains again with

nothing to break the view in any direction as far as we can see," she wrote.[101] "This country is still full of buffalo grass."

But the prairie brought back mixed emotions. She reminded Almanzo, "Please do be careful to remember about the fires."[102]

Fortunately, We Can't Lose

Back home, the turbulent late 1920s passed by Mansfield, barely ruffling the surface. Wilder wrote to friends in Florida, "We are well as usual and have cut down our farming until we really don't do any. Just live on the Ozark climate and views."[103] That was a rosy understatement. Cutting back on chores, Wilder was nonetheless still laboring on the farm loan front, telling her husband that she would rather make money selling cream than processing paperwork. "You don't know how tired I am of the work and responsibility of that secretary business," she said.[104] Yet poverty still haunted her, even when she had such lavish gifts as the Buick. She dreamed at night that there was no car, that it was itself a dream, and occasionally walked out to the garage in the morning to see if it was still there.[105]

But Lane's life would be upended by the economic boom years that came before the fall. Her final, chaotic sojourn in Europe and its aftermath would bring her highs and lows to new extremes, an emotional tumult that paralleled the nation's financial roller-coaster ride. The sheer volatility of her life would make her mother's continued writing career inevitable.

Lane and Helen Boylston spent 1925 at Rocky Ridge. They hoped by the following year to accumulate enough savings to imagine living out Lane's most fervent dream: returning to Albania. In February 1926, Lane received a disappointing settlement from her lawsuit against Frederick O'Brien: seeking royalties for her work on his bestselling *White Shadows in the South Seas*, she got little more than nine hundred dollars. But with earnings from the previous year, she was able to pay off debts and think about investing.

Lane and Boylston had grown tremendously excited about the stock market. Boylston had jumped in earlier, investing the money she had earned from her nursing career with a former employer, George Q. Palmer. His Wall Street firm, Palmer & Co., was bringing her steady returns. Lane soon joined in, asking Moyston whether she could borrow a couple of hundred dollars; she wanted to assemble a thousand-dollar investment, telling him, "I feel like taking the gamble."[106] The rest she planned to borrow from N. J. Craig.[107] In her enthusiasm, she pulled her parents into the market along with her. "Stocks are leaping around like corn in a popper," Rose wrote to them. "Fortunately, we can't lose."[108]

In her embrace of bull market optimism, Lane had plenty of company. After a severe recession in 1920–1921, the economy had come booming back. Americans began to borrow heavily; hundreds of thousands purchased consumer goods such as automobiles and radios "on time." Brokers began lending to small investors, advancing up to two-thirds of their stocks' value, urging ordinary Americans to play the market.

Like most people, Lane saw no potential peril. In 1926, as her annual payment to her parents, Lane transferred five hundred dollars from her Palmer account to their new account with the firm, and the Wilders invested an additional five hundred of their own. Lane assured them that they could anticipate earning 8 percent annually, and she was giddy with the expectation that she could build both accounts to the point where all three could retire and live off the earnings, her parents in Rocky Ridge and she in Albania. "The only proper use for money, for you two now," she told her parents, "is spending." Whatever you want, she told them, "you can have it."[109]

The Wilders, of course, paid no attention to her exuberance, continuing to live a frugal existence among their pigs and hens, entertained by a self-renewing circle of farm cats and their preternaturally gifted Airedale terrier, Nero, who would sit politely at the dinner table like a member of the family, eating off his own plate.[110] They had contemplated driving to the Grand Canyon that summer but could find no one to take care of the livestock.[111] Their daughter, on the other hand, embarked on a spending spree that would not be curbed until the economy crashed.

In March 1926, Lane and Helen Boylston sailed to France, and immediately plunged into language study at the Berlitz School in Paris, devoting themselves to French, Italian, German, and Russian, with plans (unrealized) to branch out into Greek, Serbian, and Albanian. In a note to Moyston, Wilder joked about her daughter's private Babel: "Wouldn't it be funny if Rose and Troub should get their languages mixed? What a confusion of tongues it would be."[112]

Lane paid their Russian tutor, a former architect, to design for her a new home on the Adriatic, in the "pure Arab style." The sketch showed a lavish colonnaded affair with a walled garden, swimming pool, terraces, defensive gun emplacements, open courtyards, and a servants' court.[113] She wrote ecstatically to Moyston, calling it "heaven."

But beneath the ebullience triggered by her escape from the stultifying Missouri farm were other, darker feelings. Two articles she wrote about herself and her parents suggested that her depression ran deep, back to her earliest days in Dakota Territory. Both published in *Hearst's International-Cosmopolitan* (forerunner of the *Cosmopolitan* magazine edited by Helen Gurley Brown), they aimed to shock and to wound.

The first, "If I Could Live My Life Over Again: I Am Successful, Happy and Divorced, But I Wish I Were an Old-Fashioned Wife and Mother," revisited her teenage fears of being an "old maid" and her unhappy marriage. She divorced, she wrote, "as I might have committed suicide," believing she would never be happy again.[114] Painting her single life as selfish, she wrote that if she were twenty again, she would "marry and stay married."[115] It was a bald falsification of her true feelings, since she never regretted leaving Gillette Lane, only having married him in the first place. She also did not acknowledge the fact that she was at that very moment being pursued by an ardent suitor whose strongest desire was to marry her, a desire she continued to discourage.

In Mansfield, the article inspired intense interest. Friends showered copies of it on her parents, she told Moyston. Her mother said not a word about it. "I think she hates it," Lane wrote, and she was probably right.[116]

But it was the second article that provided a blueprint to the emotional breakdown that she was suffering, and would continue to suffer, for the rest of her life. It appeared under a sensational title: "I, Rose Wilder Lane, Am the Only Truly HAPPY Person I Know and I

Discovered the Secret of Happiness on the Day I Tried to Kill Myself."[117]
Her description of her childhood was no less hyperbolic. "All unsus-
pected," she wrote, "I lived through a childhood that was a nightmare."
Although her parents "did their best," she had suffered fear, anxiety,
isolation, malnutrition, torment by peers, and, most startling of all, the
guilt of knowing she had ruined her parents' lives by burning down
their house:

> I was an only child; and I was three years old when the last of seven
> successive years of crop failure on the Dakota prairies ruined my pros-
> perous farmer-father, complications of work, worry and diphtheria
> left him an invalid, and our house burned. My mother was barely
> twenty-one. I stood beside her at the window, my eyes just above the
> sill, on the July harvest day when she watched a hail-storm drive into
> the ground the hundreds of acres of ripe wheat that would have paid
> the mortgages.
>
> I was taken away from home, and told nothing—kind adults
> answering my questions with "Hush!" until I asked no more—during
> those weeks when my father and mother were expected to die of
> diphtheria, and I knew it. And later it was I, alone in the kitchen and
> helpfully trying to put more wood in the stove, who set fire to the
> house. My mother was still ill in bed. She saved herself and me, but
> nothing else. I quite well remember watching the house burn, with
> everything we owned in the world, and knowing that I had done it.
>
> I was always very quiet. No one knew what went on in my mind.
> Because I loved my parents I would not let them suspect that I was
> suffering. I concealed from them how much I felt their poverty, their
> struggles and disappointments. These filled my life, magnified like hor-
> rors in a dream. My father and mother were courageous, even gaily
> so. They did everything possible to make me happy, and I gallantly
> responded with an effort to persuade them they were succeeding. . . .
> I have since seen something of human barbarities, in the Near East
> and elsewhere, but they were no surprise to me.[118]

The article captured the self-dramatizing tendency of her adult years.
One morning, she said, at a difficult moment in her marriage, she

attempted suicide by soaking a rag with chloroform and burying her face in it.[119] She woke later with nothing more than a bad headache. This brush with death, she said, inspired lasting happiness, the joy of being alive. "It is now fifteen years since I began to enjoy living," she claimed, "and I enjoy it more every day." (That assertion of optimism was no more reliable than the rest of her reporting; her diary around this time recorded such reflections as "the leprosy of death, which attacks everyone at about 40.")[120]

Perhaps it is no wonder that Lane had left for Europe before the article appeared. Like so many of her exaggerations, it must have been profoundly disturbing and embarrassing to her parents. According to Wilder's account, her daughter had had nothing to do with the fire. And even if she had tried to add fuel to the stove, Rose was not yet three when the house on the tree claim burned, and no child of that age can be held responsible for such an accident. What made her fabricate that responsibility? Was it something her mother said? Or was Lane, as an adult, acting out a need to assume the central role, casting herself as a tiny angel of destruction?

Whatever the explanation, the articles marked a turning point. From here on out, Lane would repeatedly cause ruination to herself, bringing her life down around her ears. Every time she grasped some semblance of stability, she would burn through it, alienating the people who might have helped her, spending lavishly and frantically until her money was gone.

Rose Wilder Lane's Albanian dream began with a comical road trip in a Model T Ford from Paris to Tirana in August 1926, and ended in an ignominious retreat back to Rocky Ridge seventeen months later. The accounts that Lane produced for friends and family—letters to Moyston, Dorothy Thompson, the humorist Clarence Day, her broker George Palmer, and others, and a travel diary that she and Helen Boylston kept for the Wilders, later published as *Travels with Zenobia*—were self-consciously perky and full of fun, an early Hollywood travel yarn starring two spunky American gals abroad. The commentary she wrote for herself, however, was grim.

In journal entries labeled "My Albanian Garden," she cast back over her life, deploring her youthful "struggling with sex" at seventeen; her naive belief in Gillette Lane; the long recovery after the stillbirth and operation; and lost opportunities in Europe, where she felt she had been "exploited," financially and emotionally, by her travel companions. She seemed to be trying to find a sense of control over her life. But self-analysis only fed her insecurity, and a fixation that began emerging from her time in Albania would become an overwhelming obsession: houses. They would consume her: designing them, building them, renovating them, pouring money into them.

Even before reaching Tirana, she was spending heavily. The new Model T, bought in a Paris showroom, was decidedly not the cheapest means of travel, especially given the various taxes, duties, and fees. Driving to Albania, Lane and Boylston took along with them their French cook, Yvonne. In Tirana, they rented a house, hoping eventually to buy land, but byzantine regulations restricted sales to foreigners.[121] A host of servants was hired: a butler, two gardeners, a houseboy, and an additional cook.

Servants in Albania were affordable enough, but the most extraordinary expenditures came with the rented house. The building and grounds, adorned with courtyards and terraces, fruit trees and flower gardens, were ample for two persons, but within a few months Lane embarked on extensive renovations: taking up floors and cutting archways, installing a full bath (the house had a water closet), and building balconies over the gardens (to be screened in summer, glassed in winter). She also arranged for the construction of no fewer than eight fireplaces.[122]

Over the next few months, with five thousand dollars in her Palmer account, she spent around two thousand on renovations to property she did not own. It recalled her grandfather's fateful decision to build on Kansas land that did not belong to him, and like that decision, it would not end well. At one point, she telegraphed Clarence Day, frantically trying to borrow five hundred dollars: she had run out of money to pay the workers.[123]

Dimly, she recognized that she was creating a financially precarious situation for herself. "I am not a stupid person," she told him, "yet there are . . . times when my grasp on reality goes all to smash, and then I run into such troubles . . . I am forty years old, and should have more sense."[124] She was good for it, she assured him, and if something happened to her, he could expect her mother to cover the debt.

Lane never made the obvious psychological connection between her claim that she had burned down her parents' house and her own incessant house-building, which somehow failed to provide her with a permanent place to live. In a fit of construction fever, she wrote to Dorothy Thompson:

> Days of great excitement, tense and emotional. For the carpenters and the masons have arrived; floors are coming up, foundations are going down . . . studding and rafters mysteriously erect themselves in air. Houses are the abiding joys; they are the most emotion-stirring of all things . . . houses are real, deep, emotional things. . . . Albanians are right in knowing that far worse than to kill the criminal or the enemy is to burn his house.[125]

If she had burned a house, she would now rebuild it, over and over again.

AT the same time as she was renovating the rented house, Lane was sitting at her desk agonizing over her work, trying to churn out Ozark serials to pay the rent. In 1926, she published *Hill-Billy*, a novel cobbled together from pieces she had written for *Country Gentleman* during her year at Rocky Ridge. Its protagonist was transparently modeled on her parents' close friend, the lawyer and banker Noah Jefferson Craig. The book was dedicated to him: "the love and understanding you have for your own hill-folk, who are only by adoption mine, have made a book which never would have been written without you."[126] And Lane named her hero Abimelech Noah Baird, continuing her practice of scarcely concealing the sources of her fictional material. Just like N. J. Craig, A. N. Baird comes down out of a holler to become a lawyer, outwitting the townsfolk who take him for a dumb hillbilly.

Drawing on the legend of Walter Raleigh's lost colony, whose survivors were rumored to have traipsed over to Tennessee and thence to the Ozarks, Lane populated the backwoods with families named Rippee, Garner, and Miller, the names of actual families who lived in Wright County for generations and still do today. Her characters speak in a broad vernacular that strongly recalls denizens of Al Capp's Dogpatch, using expressions such as "woods' colt" for a baby born out of wedlock, and delivering themselves of such remarks as "That thar ornery yellow-livered son of a mangy houn' dawg laid tail betwixt legs an' scringed belly upwards."[127]

Lane dismissed the book in her letters, but nonetheless immediately embarked on another such serial for *Country Gentleman*. It was based on the real-life Ozark blood feud between the Alsups and the Fleetwoods, a local version of the Hatfields and McCoys. Lane made it into a Romeo and Juliet story: Cindy, of the red-gold hair, loves the boy she grew up with, Jefferson Boon, but the star-crossed lovers must survive the animosity between their clans. It was melodramatic hackwork again, to the point where Lane was mortified when *Harper's* insisted on publishing it as a novel, suffering agonies of embarrassment over the gushing, pulpy ad copy.[128]

Not all her writing was quite so mercenary. "The Blue Bead," published in *Harper's* in 1925 and featuring a familiar American woman who travels in the Albanian mountains, hinted at a richer talent, and received an honorable mention in a story contest. "Yarbwoman," published in *Harper's* in 1927, was also a cut above her more commercial efforts. For that story, she borrowed a fable from her grandfather: a tale Charles Ingalls had told Almanzo about Lake Pepin's Maiden Rock, infested with rattlesnakes, and a man mysteriously poisoned by a venom-dripping snake fang piercing a leather boot.[129] It too was a regional tale but quieter and more atmospheric, capturing the grim realities of mountain lives.

Lane admitted to correspondents and her diary that she wanted to write something "worth while," but her cycle of profligate spending kept her tied to commercial production. She linked the "squirrel cage" she was caught in to her early poverty: "I let the money go, as always, in satisfying momentary desires. . . . It seems that I come back, always, to that simple material viewpoint of my childhood."[130]

From here on, she would begin expressing contempt not only for her own work, which she termed "cheap popular success," but for her public, whom she often referred to collectively and sardonically as "Gentle Reader." She demeaned her own constant reading as "little more than a drug habit."[131] She found little to admire in other writers, dismissing the moderns as having nothing to say.[132]

What's more, she told her diary, she was done with men, having realized that her attitude toward them was "essentially exploiting . . . I wanted what they had, not what they were." She had despised all of the men "who said they loved me."[133] Gray-haired and worn-looking at forty, she was through with love affairs. "No affection, poverty, inferiority," she wrote in her diary.[134]

The lower she slipped in her own self-esteem, the more she began playing the grande dame, giving free rein to her imperious impulses. To Dorothy Thompson and others, she wrote condescending descriptions of her servants and neighbors, remarking on their quaint ways: "Their lives go by like the days, without effort or struggle; just naturally passing."[135] One unsatisfactory servant she compared to a "homeless dog," saying, "It must be very difficult to live among human beings, without any kind of human brain."[136] Josef Bard, whose Hazel Green character had viewed Balkans as her pets, had been right.

No dashing Albanian beys were vying for her hand now, but she enjoyed fancying herself as "specially created . . . for the Moslem woman's life," punctuating her letters with "Inshallah!" and "Oh Allah!"[137] At Rocky Ridge, she had been slopping pigs and fetching firewood; in Tirana, she and Troub would have fires built for them. Servants brought them tea and cakes as their gardens were planted and tended, their clothes cleaned and ironed, their meals prepared, and mud cleaned off their shoes. "There is nothing wrong with America but the servant problem," she informed Fremont Older, as if she were to the manor born.[138] To furnish the house, she and Troub planned to adopt a purebred Great Dane puppy from England that cost a lavish fifty pounds.

In keeping with her newfound sense of superiority, she began to express anti-Semitic and racist views, writing to Day to demand why he was outraged by housing restrictions limiting Jews to certain neighborhoods. "We don't like pogroms," she wrote, "so we say that Jews are not only as good as, but the same as, any other people. But we know they aren't."[139] She expounded on the issue for him, in a dogmatic tone she was adopting more and more: "Jewry isn't an abstraction, it's a characteristic something in individuals. . . . If you don't like it, why should you have it in your house?" She recommended that he read *Jud Süss*, a 1925 historical novel by Lion Feuchtwanger, as a "true picture of the Jew."[140] She deplored Americans' sentimentality about "the oppressed negro" and the attitude that interracial marriage might be "admirable."[141]

In the end, Lane could not sustain the intricate fantasy she had been constructing for herself. She felt cut off from magazine editors and the American market. After renovating the rented house, she began fantasizing about a new one to be built at Rocky Ridge. In July 1927, *Country Gentleman* paid her the spectacular sum of ten thousand dollars for her "Cindy" serial, and she and Troub embarked on a victory tour of Europe in their Model T, planning to fetch the Great Dane. When that deal fell through, they adjusted expectations, buying instead a Maltese terrier called Bunting von Sevilla.[142] She told Guy Moyston that she was returning to Rocky Ridge with newfound confidence as a chatelaine, planning "to get servants and boss them."[143] It was either that or buy a house in Albania.

Her mother apparently decided the issue. In January 1928, Wilder sent her daughter a telegram, since lost. It may have asked her to return. Almanzo Wilder was diagnosed with "a beginning cancer"—skin cancer—around that time.[144]

Lane and Boylston sublet their rented house, sold the Ford, and booked passage to New York. She did not bother to report what happened to the servants. In the end, the most remarkable aspect of her Albanian sojourn—the closest emotional attachment she had maintained for years—was the haste with which it was abandoned.

But as she prepared to embark, she had one more grand gesture to make. Rexh Meta, now eighteen and a graduate of the Tirana

Vocational School, had caught the eye of someone at the British embassy, who proposed that he attend Cambridge University in England.[145] He was not often mentioned in Lane's letters or diaries of the period, but the week before she left she gave him five hundred dollars, promising more. In time, he would become her first "adopted" child, another project on which she would lavish time, anguish, and money. Like her houses, however, he would prove a curiously replaceable proposition. After Lane sailed away from Albania on January 27, 1928, she never saw him again.

She was ending a number of things. Back in New York that spring, she broke off her seven-year relationship with Moyston. She fondly recalled their time in Croton and Rocky Ridge, and the night that cows stood around staring "wonderingly" at them. She apologized for hurting him, and quoted Robert Frost's "The Road Not Taken."[146]

On the passage home, she had recorded in her diary that she had around twenty thousand in her Palmer account and intended to spend "no more considerable sums" until she had fifty thousand.[147]

Six months later, she began building a house for her parents.

Chapter 9

Pioneer Girl

Rock House

Laura Ingalls had been born when wheat sold high, and in the late nineteen-twenties the cycle was coming around again. On her 1925 road trip to California and back, she had run her hands through the buffalo grass of Kansas, one of the native grasses of the prairies she had loved. She may have been among the last to do so: all that buffalo grass was soon to go the way of the buffalo.

To the west of Mansfield, the southern Great Plains were about to be stripped bare of topsoil in one of the last land booms in American history. By 1926, buffalo grass was being plowed up by the acre, great swaths of it removed in Kansas, Oklahoma, Colorado, and New Mexico. Within a few years, that ecological rapine would wreak havoc across the prairie.

Wheat had always been an American game of chance, and now the land itself had become a casino. Had anyone been thinking about it, the boom on the southern plains resembled nothing so much as the Dakota Boom of the 1880s. But no one was thinking. Everyone was buying. So-called suitcase farmers—big-city speculators and small-town white-collar workers alike—were arriving by train by the score, buying up a square mile or two or ten and leasing out the land to tenant farmers. Some simply threw seed in the ground and hoped for a big payday.[1]

Charles Ingalls could only have dreamed about such conditions. Wheat prices and exports had reached all-time highs during World War I, when Congress mandated prices at over two dollars a bushel. After the war, prices stayed there for a time, as the United States exported grain to starving countries in Europe: political turmoil in the Soviet Union, once the world leader in wheat exports, allowed America to take the top spot. Gas-powered Ford tractors had eased the backbreaking work of sod-busting, pulling disc plows sharp as knives through virgin turf, grinding the soil to a fine dust. Combines—machines combining a harvester and a thresher—made large teams of men wielding sickles and flails, the laborers Laura Wilder had once dreaded having to feed, obsolete.

Huge factory farms were making unheard-of profits. A woman in Haskell County, Kansas, was christened the "wheat queen" in 1926 after her two thousand acres brought a profit of $75,000.[2] Burgeoning populations nearly burst the seams of sleepy hamlets: in Kansas, Stanton County grew by 137 percent from 1920 to 1930, and Grant County by 184 percent.[3] Dodge City, once a modest village, would become a teeming anthill of ten thousand by 1930, and a building boom taxed contractors and carpenters. There were unforeseen housing shortages in places like Ashland, Kansas, a village of fewer than five hundred at the turn of the century.[4] Inflating along with the wheat boom, a speculative real estate bubble began to expand all across the country. National housing prices rose by around 20 percent, with residential markets heating up from Florida to Chicago.[5]

In a sign of trouble to come, nonfarm foreclosures began rising steeply in 1926, the same year that housing starts peaked. Houses had become almost as easy to buy on credit as cars; they too were now being mass-produced. Alongside Lane's 1925 *Cosmopolitan* article ran an advertisement for a "Five-Room Aladdin," an all-inclusive kit for a wood-frame house, shingles to doorknobs, shipped to the nearest railroad station.[6] Sears, Roebuck—the fantastically successful mail-order firm run by Almanzo's childhood friend from Spring Valley—was the largest manufacturer of such houses. The firm had been selling kits since 1908, but their popularity exploded in the 1920s. By 1930, almost 50,000 of their kits would be sold across the country.

Supplied with pre-milled, precut lumber, the kits represented a miraculous advance in convenience. Ads touted their ease and speed of construction, though Hollywood parodied the misadventures experienced by neophytes. Buster Keaton found inventive ways to hit himself in the face building a kit house in the silent comedy *One Week*. And in *The Cocoanuts*, Groucho Marx, playing a crooked real estate developer, mocked the Florida land boom. "You can have any kind of home you want to, even stucco," he exclaimed, brandishing his cigar. "Oh how you can get stuck-oh! Now is the time to buy while the new boom is on. Remember that old saying, 'A new boom sweeps clean.'"[7]

Lane too was riding the boom, engaging in a clean sweep of her own at Rocky Ridge. Upon her return to the farmhouse in the spring of 1928, finding her father increasingly unable to handle the chores, she urged her parents to retire from farming altogether. As a stopgap measure, Almanzo Wilder brought in a tenant farmer, Bruce Prock, to handle plowing, maintenance, and livestock.

Laura Wilder retired as well from her role as secretary-treasurer for the Mansfield Farm Loan Association, resigning at the age of sixty-one. Her contribution to the community had been substantial. In massive leather-bound volumes recording deeds of trust in the Hartville Courthouse, Wilder had filed document after document throughout the 1920s, painstakingly typing out legal land descriptions, occasionally pasting in revised or corrected wording. Her signature appeared on more than forty such deeds in the volume covering 1922–1926. On occasion, Almanzo filled in for her, signing paperwork as well.[8] Between 1917 and 1928, she had assisted in preparing and closing nearly a million dollars in loans and had earned perhaps several thousand dollars in the process.[9] Notes from her last meeting recorded a "hearty vote of thanks" to her as outgoing secretary.[10]

In what may have been a retirement party, Lane hosted a lavish outing for the Justamere Club, treating ladies to the theater and a luncheon held at the Colonial Hotel in Springfield. The newspapers breathlessly recorded the activities of the "Famous Writer Back to Live in Ozarks."[11] To her mother's chagrin, Lane was already a controversial and much-debated local celebrity.

Ensconced in the crowded farmhouse with Helen Boylston, Lane dedicated the rest of the year to upending her parents' lives. Soon, her fantasies about moving them to England, or even Albania, gave way to a storm of rearrangement, as she began the process of constructing two new houses on the property, one for the tenant farmer and his family and the other for her parents.

No hard evidence survives of the Wilders' reaction to this plan. They had labored for decades to complete the farmhouse to their satisfaction, and by all accounts were comfortable where they were. In retrospect, their ambivalence is clear. On the one hand, they accepted their daughter's gift, just as they accepted her money. On the other, Wilder made it known to her daughter that she wanted nothing to do with the construction, declining even to look at it while it was under way. Lane blithely assured a friend that her mother "wanted a new house, but didn't want to bother with it in the building stages."[12]

Having importuned her daughter to return, Wilder may have felt that relinquishing her house was the price she had to pay to keep Rose down on the farm. But it could not have been easy being relegated to what was, literally, the back forty.[13] The Rock House, as the new dwelling would be called, was to be built nearly a mile away from the original farmhouse, out of its sight. The design was based on a Sears, Roebuck model, "The Mitchell," with two gables and an arched front door with strap hinges, lit by a "quaint English lamp."[14]

Parsimonious to a fault, the Wilders could only have blanched at the excessive spending that ensued. After years of struggling to rise out of extreme poverty, they still lived frugally, wary of expenditures that might revive the specter of the 1890s. Lane had other ideas.

The complete Sears kit was listed for $1,493 to $2,143, depending on finishes. But Lane purchased the design, not the kit, and hired a Springfield architect and a contractor to rework the plans, adding expensive doors, windows, and cabinetry. The architect's final tally climbed to $5,500. And once construction began, Lane showed up daily to supervise it down to the tiniest detail. At one point, she ordered workers to tear out a just-installed ceiling and replace it with a lower one.

She had newly installed floors refinished to her specifications, and altered the architect's design for the bathroom on the fly. The substitutions and changes sent the price ever higher.[15] She wrote wearily that the extra expenditures amounted to "another life wasting mistake that I shall make," but made no effort to stick to a budget.[16] By the time construction was finished, she ended up spending more than $11,000 on the design, construction, and furnishing of Rock House, more than five times the original Sears kit price. She accepted a loan of around $2,500 from her mother to complete the project, signing a note and agreeing to pay interest.[17]

Lane was consumed by the process, writing to an editor at Harper and Brothers, which was publishing her "Cindy" serial as a book that fall, to say that she had not thought about her own work for months. As her spending spun out of control, she found herself increasingly unable to focus. She admitted to the editor, a relative stranger, that her house obsession was an addiction that she could not restrain:

> I am building a house for my father and mother; a really charming little English-type cottage, of field-stone and brick, Johns-Manville asbestos shingles, Truscon steel casements, Rol-screens, made-to-order doors and hardware, and every electrical thing the genius of America has devised.... Houses are my vice; I simply can't take 'em or leave 'em alone. But for houses, I know it well, I'd be much more profitable to everyone, including me. This is my 18th habitation, made or re-made including some apartments. But I can't seem to help it.[18]

As her parents' new house was being built, Lane, like a cuckoo bird, began remaking their old nest, undertaking ambitious renovations by installing electricity and redoing plumbing. At the same time, she was overseeing the completion of the third house on the property, for the Procks. The renovation of the farmhouse seemed to be one final spasmodic effort to assert her adulthood, ascendancy, and authority, and to compensate for earlier losses that she claimed were her fault. But again, she would not truly make her parents' original house her own, choosing to rent it from them once their new house was completed. As in Albania, she had devised a situation that involved spending thousands of dollars on housing that would, inevitably, leave her still without a place of her own.

She could not have chosen a more self-destructive trajectory, a situation perfectly poised to plunge her back into the unhappiness of her previous stay at Rocky Ridge. Flush after the sale of *Cindy*, she could easily have continued to provide income for her parents while locating a New York City apartment or a home for herself in the East, closer to editors, agents, and friends. But she seemed as oblivious to her own needs as to those of others.

Nervous Breakdown

That summer, Lane descended into the most severe depressive period of her life. It was heralded by her destruction of several long and important friendships. Her alienation of friends and colleagues would follow a pattern of aggressive betrayal, one she would inevitably reenact with her mother as well.

That spring, she typed out a three-page, single-spaced letter, most of it a single unbroken paragraph, to Sherwood Anderson, whom she had met casually in Paris years earlier.[19] She had apparently just learned that Anderson had parodied her, as "Rose Frank," in his 1925 novel *Dark Laughter*, capturing the reckless, brassy tone Lane adopted with her friends and in her salacious, gossipy letters.[20]

In the novel's pivotal scene, before an audience that includes an Irish-American journalist clearly based on Guy Moyston, Rose Frank, "a plump strong-looking little American woman of perhaps thirty . . . sending smart Parisian gossip to American newspapers," describes her reaction to playing the voyeur in Paris at a students' ball, watching an orgy take place, "twenty-nine ways of love-making—all done in the life—naked people."[21] In 1921, Lane had indeed witnessed such a scene, graphically recounting it at a garden party Anderson attended. Now she found herself reflected in his prose as a frustrated, sexually repressed bystander who had yearned but feared to join the debauch, her neurotic "dark laughter" supplying the novel's title.

She was furious. "I haven't liked anything else you've written," she told Anderson, "it has all seemed useless and stupid to me." She called *Winesburg, Ohio* "sickening" and "disgusting," lecturing him about his "sex-obsession."[22] She recalled that he had once been to her apartment and she hadn't liked him then. He was, she said, a "poseur" and a "fool."[23]

Lane never sent Anderson the letter. Nonetheless, the fact of writing it underscored her lack of self-awareness, as well as the rages she was prey to. Never once, excoriating Anderson, did she acknowledge that she had written many books caricaturing others, in fiction and fact.

One of those books soon caused a tempest in a teapot. Herbert Hoover ran for president in 1928, and Lane's embroidered 1920 biography of him received renewed attention. An article in the *Saturday Evening Post* claimed that Hoover had asked an aide to buy the plates used to print an embarrassingly adulatory book by a woman journalist from California, planning to destroy them.[24] Recognizing herself, Lane sought to refute what she felt to be the implication—that she had been bribed to suppress the work—but could not reach Hoover. Years later he would suggest, unconvincingly, that it was a matter of mistaken identity: he had been dismayed by another hagiographical work, by another woman in California.[25] But at the time the incident agitated Lane, who was convinced that her reputation had been sullied.

That summer, Lane wrote another unhinged letter that she did not send, this time to Dorothy Thompson. Thompson had divorced Josef Bard the previous year, and Lane had tried—and failed—to talk her friend out of a second marriage, to Sinclair Lewis. She recalled the ex-husband's treachery (Josef Bard having also caricatured her in a novel), comparing him to a "barnyard fowl" and his work to "European slime."[26] She went so far as to say that Thompson's marriage had been "debasing," that the "slime" had rubbed off. And she accused Thompson of becoming unreachable by marrying Lewis. "*You* are gone," she wrote. "Where does the light of the candle go when it is blown out? . . . I know that I won't be able to speak to you."[27]

The letter that Lane did send Thompson, two days later, was less bombastic but scarcely better, suggesting that Thompson was "terribly mistaken" in her decision to remarry and was standing "blindfolded on the chasm's edge."[28] From her honeymoon, Thompson replied with baffled affection.

This loathing of marriage would be at the center of the most remarkable expression of Lane's increasing instability, her break with Clarence Day. He had been one of her closest friends. The relationship was never romantic, but for years she had written him long, confiding letters, discussing every facet of her career and personality. In response, he had offered detailed editorial advice and counsel, and had loaned her money. They had even discussed the idea of publishing a selection of their letters.

But in July 1928, when he wrote with the news that he had just married, Lane was horrified. In yet another letter she did not send, she wrote of receiving his news as Boylston was drawing a bucket of water from the well. She commanded Troub to put the water down, she said, having had a vision of her dropping the bucket "and cold waves lapping my ankles."[29]

The letter she did send to Day was uncharacteristically brief and syntactically tortured:

> It's a little difficult to say anything in response to your news—you will quite understand that. And you know, too, don't you, that it's good news to us, since it means that you're the happier, doing what you want to do, having what you want to have. There's all the warmth of good wishes and good hopes and of happiness for your sake, here, that you can possibly imagine. But I'm sort of dumb; I can't get these emotions down on paper. Because, you see—you of all persons will understand—that the C.D. who embarks on such an adventure isn't quite known to me, and his wife has never been imagined.[30]

Again, as with Thompson, she associated marriage with casting a pall, making Day distant and unknowable, as if he had emigrated to another country or assumed a different identity. Day had been not only her confidant but a fellow sufferer. Like her, he had lived for years with his parents. Like her father, he was a semi-invalid, stricken by disease and struggling with issues of dependency.

When he protested, movingly and at length, against the loss of their friendship, she sent a cold response, telling him, as if someone had died, that he was not the only one who was grieving: "Being married is

like that. . . . It is you who have gone away, have closed a door between."
She concluded with a mystifying image: "None of us can move the
weight of—how many?—centuries."[31]

That was the end, or nearly so. Her files hold a draft of another
long, rambling letter—whether she sent it or not is unclear—in which
she attempted to justify her decision. "As Clarence Day you were an
individual," she said; "as a married man, you are a member of a society
to which I do not belong." She attempted to argue that social conven-
tions prohibited single women from corresponding with married men,
despite the fact that she wrote regularly to Fremont Older, her agent
Carl Brandt, and other such men. "I do not know Mrs. Clarence Day,"
she wrote, "and I'm sorry if this seems rude, but I do not care to know
her. . . . I can't help it that everything changes when a stranger comes
into a conversation between friends. I can't help it that a married man
is not a free and separate individual."[32] Their correspondence and their
friendship stuttered to a halt.

Lane's troubled responses to her friends' marriages reveal something deeper and more profound than her own failed marriage with
Gillette Lane could account for. Whenever she wrote about him, she
was dismissive and offhand, characterizing that union as a youthful
mistake. But her rejection of Guy Moyston, a man she had been in love
with, seemed less a rational choice than an emotional flight. Her response
to close friends who had the temerity to marry without her approval
called up the image of her parents from her story "Innocence"—the
parents who had cleaved together on a railway platform, clutching
each other and shunting her aside, leaving her abandoned. That image
shared something with the exclusionary, even deathly, images in her
letters to Day: cold water lapping her ankles, a great weight descending, a door closing.

Lane's anger and despair over these perceived withdrawals were
signs of a despondency that would persist, in one form or another, for
the rest of her life. "Having something like [a] nervous breakdown,"
she wrote in her diary.[33] Her mother would likewise later admit, in a
letter to a friend in De Smet, that her daughter had had a "nervous
breakdown."[34] But while Lane sometimes counseled others to seek
psychiatric treatment, she would never pursue such care for herself.[35]

WHILE her daughter was incurring self-inflicted losses, Laura Wilder faced a real one. After Caroline Ingalls's death in 1924, Mary Ingalls had been cared for in her De Smet home by Grace and Nate Dow, who moved in with her. In the fall of 1927, Mary traveled to Keystone, South Dakota, for an extended stay with Carrie Ingalls Swanzey. While there, she suffered a paralyzing stroke for the second time in her life, losing the ability to speak.[36] Another stroke followed, and by the following year, the end was at hand. Carrie had written to Laura on October 15, 1928, trying to prepare her sister for what was to come. "Laura," she wrote, "I doubt if she rallies. The trained nurse was up from Rapid [City] . . . she said nothing could be done and the Dr came and said so too."[37] She gently assured Laura that Mary was not suffering, "just sleeping, real quiet." Mary died two days later, on October 17, at sixty-three.

If we are to believe Wilder, Mary Ingalls had always been the favored child. Fair and blond, polite and pious, long-suffering and patient, Mary had been the ideal against which brown-haired, impulsive, sharp-tongued Laura reacted, quick to anger and vengeful to a fault. During her early years, Laura had constantly competed with her, vying for the approval of parents, teachers, and friends.

But when Mary had fallen ill as a teenager, she had become her sister's responsibility, requiring Laura to see for her, care for her, and suppress every rivalrous impulse. Mary's blindness had changed Laura's life. Fearful of public speaking, horrified at the idea of teaching, Laura was forced to adopt those roles, becoming the teacher that Mary was meant to have been, working at sixteen to help the family acquire the resources to send the older girl to college. In doing so, she discovered ambition in herself that she had never recognized before, and gained a sense of what she was capable of when pressed. Mary Ingalls became the first member of the family to graduate from college, but only thanks to her sister's help.

Her death brought up a tumult of conflicting emotions, love and pride as well as Wilder's earlier, never-assuaged feelings of jealousy, of being second best. And the completion of the new house would not lighten the mood.

The Rock House was finished just before Christmas 1928, and Lane brought her mother to see it for the first time. Even the architect appeared nervous about the unveiling, telling Lane that he realized it would be a fateful moment. Several snapshots were taken on the day, the Wilders dressed in their finest, looking uncomfortably formal. Wilder was caught frowning, trying to make Nero, their dog, stand still for the photographer.

The *Springfield Leader* wrote up the occasion, emphasizing the extravagance, the $11,000 price tag, the hiring of architect, builder, and interior decorator.[38] How many homes in the Ozarks in the 1920s had felt the touch of an interior decorator? There were wealthy local families, but the newspaper's praise of the home's wrought-iron fixtures, modern appliances, plaster finishes, and tile fireplace may have caused the Wilders twinges of embarrassment.

Lane recorded contradictory accounts of the event, telling her diary that her mother was "delighted." She relayed a different, more disturbing version of the day to a friend: "Certainly I should have thrilled all over when my mother walked into the new house. I expected to, and would have done, but for a strange but unexpected turn of events."[39] She never explained what she meant by this. Did Wilder compare the new home to the comforts of her old one and find it wanting? Did she criticize the expense out loud? Again, as in 1894, when the money from the lap desk went missing, Lane's anticipated joy—the joy of seeing her parents safe and secure—had turned to ashes.

As her parents settled into the new house, Lane occupied herself with another project: her charge, Rexh Meta, at Cambridge. The epistolary energies once drawn off by Guy Moyston and Clarence Day now played like a fire hose over the young Albanian, who was struggling with an alien culture and studies he was ill-prepared to undertake.

Lane's mentoring took the form of page after page of obsessive, intrusive advice on every imaginable topic, including his digestion ("if the stomach isn't ready for food . . . and you chuck food into it, it struggles along as best it can"), exercise ("walk very fast and vigorously"), and clothing ("English pockets, typically, look a little baggy").[40] Nothing was too small or too vast for her attention: manners, religious observances, Albanian and world politics, marriage and children, and on and on. Replaying her troubled financial relationship with her parents, she stressed her money troubles, at the same time promising to send Meta funds she did not have. He addressed her as "Mother my dear."[41] She signed herself "Much love from your adopted mother."[42] His apologetic replies, as he sought to please and placate her, make for painful reading.

For Lane, the period after her return from Albania was marked by writer's block, and she published less than she had in years, telling Meta, "I have not been able to work very well. . . . It has been the hardest year I remember in regard to my work."[43] She wrote in her diary, "not quite alive and very blue."[44] She was in St. Louis—having dental work, going to the theater, and buying a dozen bath towels—when panic broke out on Wall Street and the market crashed. It was Black Tuesday, October 29, 1929. By December, she was $9,500 in debt.[45] After spending beyond her means—the Rock House, the caretaker's house, extensive renovations in the farmhouse, and assistance for Meta—it was hardly surprising. Nearly three thousand of it she owed to her mother, maintaining the bewildering pattern of supporting her parents even as they continued to support her.[46]

With Lane collapsing under some kind of psychic strain, Wilder took up the slack. As far as the economy went, she had seen it all before. At sixty-two, she had weathered booms and busts all her life, from the Great Depression of 1873 through the Panic twenty years later. She knew—she had to have known—what was coming when the terrifying news of Black Tuesday hit the papers, describing its cataclysmic aftermath, the run on the banks, and the alarming (if fictitious) reports of investors jumping out of windows.

In response, she did what she had always done. She got busy. In this atmosphere of instability—grieving for her sister, distressed for her daughter, anxious about money—Laura Ingalls Wilder decided to write a memoir.

If her daughter could not write, she could. If her daughter could not earn, she would.

Pioneer Girl

Wilder completed "Pioneer Girl," the autobiography covering her first eighteen years of life, in the spring of 1930. On May 7, she brought six handwritten tablets to Lane. We know little about the circumstances of its composition—when she began, how long it took, or whether she was using drafts written years earlier as her starting point.

The memoir began with her earliest memories of crossing the prairies in Kansas, when Wilder was not quite three. It was intended for serialization for an adult readership, but its self-consciously literary opening nonetheless began in the age-old manner of tales for children: "Once upon a time years and years ago, Pa stopped the horses and the wagon they were hauling away out on the prairie in Indian Territory."[47] Instinctively, Wilder had returned to her initial impulse, from years earlier, to write children's stories.

Day after day, seated in the luxury of the pristine new house, free of loans and chickens, she had filled these tablets, pushing the pencil across the page in an expense of will and self-discipline, producing an extraordinary exercise in memory, nostalgia, and yearning for the past. "I lay and looked through the opening in the wagon cover at the campfire and Pa and Ma sitting there," she wrote. "It was lonesome and so still with the stars shining down on the great, flat land where no one lived."

Wilder had once said that she wanted to do some writing that would "count," and in many ways she succeeded. The memoir fairly galloped along, full of lively adventures, fond family recollections, and vivid depictions of frontier scenes—prairie fires, grasshoppers, blizzards, the death of little Freddy. Its pages were studded with strange characters and striking descriptive passages about the wolves on the prairie and the birds on Silver Lake.

Its literary merits lay in its very lack of finesse. Wilder worked best when she was least self-conscious. The writer's voice, her direct address to the reader, and the surprising detail about a way of life already forgotten by 1930 lent it power and promise. Episodes that readers would cherish in the later books were captured in their earliest form in this first manuscript, with much of their charm fully intact:

Pa would run his fingers through his hair standing it all on end; then
he'd get down on all fours and growling would chase us around the
room, trying to corner us so we couldn't get away. We were quick at
dodging him but once he caught us by the woodbox behind the stove.
Then Pa growled so terribly, his hair looked so wild and his eyes so
fierce, that it all seemed real to us instead of just play.

Mary was so frightened she could not move, but I gave a scream
as he started to come nearer and with a wild leap I went over the
woodbox dragging Mary after me.

Then there was no dog at all, only Pa standing there with his blue
eyes so bright and shining looking at me.

"Well," he said, "you may be only a half pint of cider half drank
up, but by jinks you're strong as a little French horse."[48]

Yet in many respects "Pioneer Girl" seemed more a private outpouring than a work for posterity. Wilder had begun with her earliest memories and plowed right on, as if harrowing a field. She scarcely caught a
breath until she got to the final page and married herself off. The manuscript was essentially shapeless, with no chapter headings, no page
numbers, no dramatic pacing, and no identification of obscure figures
who appeared once and then vanished. There was little in the way of
setting or explication placing the reader in the history being covered. In
its later stretches, the narrative grew confusing, doubling back on itself
and covering some things twice. As Wilder reached her most difficult
material—her father's failures, the grasshopper devastation, the dark
days in Burr Oak, the dreadful conditions of the hard winter—she
stood apart from their emotional impact, burying her feelings in dry
facts. Only in the account of Mary's illness did she break through.

The manuscript was intended for Lane's eyes. Several of Wilder's
asides were addressed directly to her daughter. Their casual tone,
almost as if Lane were in the room with her, reveals not only that the
younger woman was meant to be editing and revising from the start
but that Wilder was aware of the tension between truth and fiction. A
passage about her father riding with a wolf pack took the form of an
aside, headed by a note to Lane: "Not to be used. . . . This story would

be called 'nature faking' if anyone read it, but it is true."[49] Early in the century, Teddy Roosevelt had lashed out at the exaggerated anthropomorphism of tales told by Jack London, Ernest Thompson Seton, and others, calling them "nature fakers" and "yellow journalists of the woods" for pretending to know how animals thought or felt; Wilder did not want to be lumped with them.[50] She recognized the distinction between her memory (what "is true") and what is believable.

On other occasions, Wilder included details meant only for her daughter. She was apparently unable to resist recording, for instance, that she and her sisters caught "the itch"—lice or scabies—in Walnut Grove, but marked those sentences off and wrote "Private" above them.[51] This was an explicit elision, but there were also some almost instinctive omissions. Near every little house her father built, for example, he must have built another, smaller structure: an outhouse, the use of which must have posed notable difficulties during Minnesota and Dakota blizzards. But they would never be referred to or included on the subsequent maps or schematics she drew.

Clearly, mother and daughter had a plan. Once the manuscript was in her hands, Lane immediately typed it up. Ten days later, she sent it, largely unrevised, to her agent, Carl Brandt, for his opinion. In her diary, she noted that he found a few sample pages "very fine."[52]

But the following month, Brandt crushed their hopes: he doubted that the work could be sold. Lane then embarked on extensive revisions during a stupefying heat wave, the hottest weather, she told her diary, since 1901.[53] As always, she was laboring under intense financial pressure. Her parents needed funds for a long-anticipated driving trip to De Smet, where the fiftieth anniversary of the founding of the town would be celebrated that summer. "Must have money then," she wrote, noting also that Rexh Meta required $250 and that her mother had mentioned that the paralysis was beginning to creep back up Almanzo's legs.[54] A few days later, her mother decided that they could not afford the De Smet trip. In reaction, Lane castigated herself: "I am a failure and a fool."[55]

Carried out in such a mood, Lane's hasty revisions to the manuscript did not improve matters. In a bizarre move, she decided to veer off in a sensational direction. A few pages into her mother's quietly

powerful depiction of the Ingallses' early days in Kansas, Lane introduced the notorious case of the Benders.

The "Bloody Benders," as they were known, were serial killers on
the Great Plains. Events surrounding their crimes quickly passed into
legend, leaving few verifiable details about their exploits and even their
identities. What seems to be true is that four adults masquerading as a
family, including an alluring young woman called Kate Bender, had
taken a claim seventeen miles northeast of Independence, Kansas. In
the structure they built—half cabin, half inn—they offered meals, lodg-
ing, and store goods on the trail from the frontier town to Fort Scott.[56]

Their business began operating sometime during 1871, and around
the same time travelers on the trail began to vanish. By 1873, enough
individuals had gone missing to spark rumors, and that spring, when a
notable doctor from Independence disappeared, his relatives set out to
search for him. Arriving at the Benders' inn, they found the place abandoned. They soon discovered the doctor buried in a shallow grave
nearby, and eventually uncovered the remains of ten or so additional
victims. Evidence suggested that the killers had preyed on paying customers seated at their table for a meal; one of the perpetrators was said
to attack from behind a curtain, striking the victim in the head with a
hammer. The body was then tipped through a trap door into a squalid
cellar below, stripped of valuables, and concealed until it could be buried
in the orchard or fields.

The murders highlighted the physical and moral isolation of the
prairie, and would remain the most infamous murder case in Kansas
until the 1959 slayings that Truman Capote investigated for *In Cold
Blood*. None of the Benders were ever found, though the governor of
Kansas offered a two-thousand-dollar reward for their capture.[57] The
gruesome discoveries and the mystery of their whereabouts gave rise to
endless flights of fancy in the yellow press. Among the more outlandish
stories was a seaman's tale, attributed to someone named "Fritz,"
explaining that the Benders perished while fleeing across the Gulf of
Mexico in a hot air balloon fueled by natural gas from a Kansas swamp.
They fell from the sky onto a passing vessel, Fritz wrote, with one surviving just long enough to deliver a deathbed confession. Their bodies
were conveniently lost at sea.[58]

The Ingallses did have a glancing proximity to the Benders: they were in residence in Montgomery County, thirteen miles south of Independence, from the fall of 1869 until early 1871. But Lane was not content to merely point that out. Instead, in revising "Pioneer Girl," she injected the murderers into the story, claiming that Charles Ingalls had stopped for a drink at the Benders' inn, nearly entered their house at Kate Bender's invitation, and then rode out as part of a vigilante posse that caught and executed them. A particularly lurid detail of the Bender legend involved a child buried alive, and Lane worked that into the manuscript as well. Her fictional father describes the exhumation: "They found a little girl, no bigger than Laura. They'd thrown her in on top of her father and mother and buried them, while the little girl was still alive."[59] Hearing this tale, the fictional Laura begins to scream.

It was as if Louisa May Alcott had decided to drop Jack the Ripper into the domestic circle of *Little Women* just to see what might happen. What did Wilder make of the Bloody Benders rampaging through her autobiography? Would she accept Lane revising her life story as passively as she had accepted Rock House? The macabre appearance of the Benders set the stage for a clash between mother and daughter over the next decade. More and more, their literary collaboration would become a competition between highly varied styles: Wilder's plain, unadorned, fact-based approach versus Lane's polished, dramatic, and fictionalized one. In Wilder's autobiographical work, "truth" would become a battlefield.

Meanwhile, Lane was growing ever more depressed, despairing over her finances.[60] It was gradually becoming clear that Palmer & Co. was on the brink of folding, taking the Lane and Wilder accounts with it. On August 15, Lane wrote, "no more P. & Co. account. No income. Expenses far more than I can carry and I cannot work."[61] Many days she found herself unable to face her own writing. Sweltering during the "worst drought in U.S. history"—at one point, the thermometer registered 106 degrees—she turned instead to her mother's.

Two days after the bad news from Palmer, she finished work on a brief children's version of "Pioneer Girl," titled "When Grandma Was a Little Girl." Lane would often refer to it as "my mother's 'juvenile.'"[62]

From remarks made in their correspondence, it appeared that Wilder herself initially may not have known of this version's existence. Self-conscious, at times cloying, the retelling seemed to be aimed at four- or five-year-olds. It may have been inspired by Wilder's own early stories for children, now lost. Lane mailed it off to someone, perhaps to Brandt, on August 18.

By mid-October, Lane was in New York City. There she met with Brandt, who again counseled against trying to sell the full version of her mother's memoir.[63] Days later, ignoring this advice, she pitched "Pioneer Girl" to Graeme Lorimer, son of the *Saturday Evening Post*'s legendary editor, George Horace Lorimer. At the same time, Thomas Costain, longtime *Post* fiction editor, told her he "still wants my father's story."[64] It was a reference to Almanzo Wilder's homesteading saga, which Lane was soon to take up in earnest.

Her mother's story languished. In November, Lane wrote to relay the bad news. The *Ladies' Home Journal*, she wrote, had "turned down your manuscript." The *Post*, too, had sent it back, Graeme Lorimer praising its "intelligent writing" but saying that they already had pieces about the same period. She concluded by saying, "I'm awfully sorry. There's nothing to do but try it somewhere else."[65]

There things stood for the rest of the year. Lane was staying with friends in New York, seeing a great deal of Berta Hader (the "little artist girl" who had lived in the basement of Lane's apartment building in San Francisco), her old boss Bessie Beatty, and other acquaintances. December found her house-sitting for Dorothy Thompson at her home in Westport, Connecticut, watching over five-month-old Michael Lewis, Thompson's child with the novelist Lane had advised her not to marry. The couple was off to Stockholm, where Sinclair Lewis would receive his Nobel Prize in Literature.

Casting about for any source of income, Lane kept returning to her mother's manuscript. At some point, she apparently hit upon the idea of showing the juvenile version of "Pioneer Girl" to Hader, who, collaborating with her husband, Elmer, had become a gifted and prolific illustrator of children's picture books. Under contract to Macmillan, the Haders were producing versions of *The Ugly Duckling*, *Hansel and*

Gretel, and *The Little Red Hen*, among others. When Hader received the juvenile "Pioneer Girl," she passed it along to one of her contacts, the editor of Alfred A. Knopf's children's department, Marion Fiery.[66]

A protégé of Anne Carroll Moore, the fabled children's librarian of the New York Public Library, Fiery had launched E. P. Dutton's youth division in the 1920s and was then poached by Knopf for the same purpose.[67] She and her peers at other publishing houses—many of them women—formed the vanguard of a new day in children's books, one dedicated not simply to repackaging classics but finding and launching revolutionary new work.

In February 1931, Fiery read the brief manuscript and immediately wrote to Wilder, asking her to rework the material into a longer story for older children, between eight and twelve. Much as Wilder had done with her aunt, Fiery asked for pages and pages of things that Wilder remembered, requesting twenty-five thousand words about "the everyday life of the pioneers."[68] Awaiting a reply, the editor met with Lane at the Haders' home in Nyack to discuss the project with her.

After the meeting, Lane wrote to her mother elaborating on every aspect of Fiery's instructions, telling her where to find the carbon copy of "Grandma," the juvenile text, in her files on the sleeping porch. There she had kept all her mother's manuscripts, she said, both the long one, of "Pioneer Girl," and "a lot of other manuscripts, various versions of yours."[69]

Get another tablet, she told her mother, and pick up where "Grandma" left off. Write an additional fifteen thousand words, covering a year in the life of the family on the frontier, describing every aspect of their existence, from how the father made bullets to a description of a one-room schoolhouse. "Put in the story of the little boy and the hornets in the harvest field," she told her, "which I did not put in. . . . There is a lovely bit in your tablets, about your big cousin who comes to visit, and your quarrel with Mary about whose hair is the prettier. That should be put back in. . . . Get all the color and feeling of the seasons in. And all from the point of view of the child, just as it is now."[70]

Lane passed along Fiery's praise of Wilder's writing—"she says you make such perfect pictures of everything"—and assured her that, if the sale went through, she would be tremendously fortunate to place her first book with Knopf, "right off the bat." She took pains to let her mother know that she had divulged nothing about "having run the manuscript through my typewriter," since the changes she had made are "so slight that they could not even properly be called editing. It is really your own work, practically word for word."[71] It was a striking passage, confirming that Wilder's writing was both uniquely her own and a product of collaboration with her daughter, a collaboration that Lane was doing her utmost to keep secret.

As always, there was a certain passivity in Wilder's acceptance of her daughter's efforts. She had accepted the five hundred dollars a year; she had accepted the Rock House; she had accepted her daughter's extensive editorial revisions of "Pioneer Girl." Now she took her advice—and Marion Fiery's—about the structure, writing, and disposition of what would become her first published book.

She produced the additional material in two months. Much of the manuscript was relatively tidy, with few crossed-out words or lines. It incorporated some already typed passages, her father's tales, scissored from another version of "Grandma" or perhaps from one of Wilder's earlier attempts at children's stories.[72] As with "Pioneer Girl," she offered no sequential chapter breaks, inserting only a few headings. One of these, "The Dance at Grandpa's," would become the most famous set piece in her first book.

She did exactly as asked, filling out the manuscript with memories, songs, and descriptions, organizing the narrative by season. Here were all the beloved tales: Pa greasing his bear traps, making bullets, and playing "mad dog" with his daughters; the girls helping Ma make butter and cheese; the family going to town, where Laura collected so many pebbles that they tore the pocket out of her dress. Here the family enjoyed relative prosperity, feasting on plentiful game and the bounty of the garden.

Baby Carrie was included in the narrative, because Wilder was beginning her story with the period that followed the family's return from Kansas to Wisconsin. Her manuscript, and the published version of the novel, made no mention of their time in Kansas. So, too, Laura celebrated her fifth birthday in the first novel, just as she had celebrated it in real life after the family's return to the Big Woods. This established a chronological marker that would affect the whole series. Eventually, Wilder would have to fictionalize her family's crucial Kansas interlude, placing it after the events described in the first volume of the series even though it had actually occurred before them.

Included in the manuscript of Wilder's first novel were other stories as well, a shade too grim for children. One described a night when Pa was away and a gang of rough-looking river workers tried to bully their way into the house. In another, a mother sow ate her litter. In a third, Laura cried and dug in her heels because she didn't want to drive Sukey, the old cow, to the butcher. Likewise, the story of the family's visit to Aunt Martha's house—where the children scrapped in the schoolyard and Laura bit a boy and scratched another one and everyone got spanked—was included in the manuscript. At some point before publication, all these jarring notes vanished, everything that smelled of backwoods poverty elided. Exactly who cut them and when remains unknown.

Among the notable deletions was another one of Laura's father's tales, a story about Maiden Rock.[73] Indians had once lived around Lake Pepin, Pa said, fishing, picking berries, and paddling their canoes. They lived happily until a terrible drought, when the berries withered, the creeks dried, and the game went away. Then a starving boy saw a great fish rise out of the water, caught it by the fin, and rode it clear across to the other side of the lake. There, he fell off and found that the water was full of fish. His people were saved.

It was a garbled version of an actual Dakota legend about two Indian boys traveling down the St. Croix River to the point where it enters the Mississippi above Lake Pepin. In one version of the original, a boy turns into a giant fish and blocks the river mouth. He then becomes a sandbar known as *Hogan Wanke Kin*, a Dakota name meaning "where the fish lies."[74]

Wilder's version of the fable captured a raw sense of the history of the place, the shadow cast by its original owners and their fate. It foretold the future of the Ingallses themselves on the frontier—drought, hunger, vanishing game—and hinted at the yearning, felt throughout all of her books, for a land of plenty. The fish tale may have been part of the original ending of Wilder's manuscript, instead of the beautiful dreamlike closing of the published book: "Now is now. It can never be a long time ago."[75] That passage exists nowhere in Wilder's handwriting and may have been added by her daughter. If it was, it represents one of Lane's most extraordinary contributions to the series.

By the time Wilder was done writing the additional material, Lane had returned to Rocky Ridge. Wilder brought her daughter the manuscript on May 8, but Lane was busy finishing something of her own and did not begin examining her mother's work until May 21, when the two women met to discuss it. According to her diary, Lane then spent a week editing, revising, and retyping. Wilder read the manuscript one final time, and Lane sent it off to Marion Fiery on May 27. As others have noted, Lane's turnaround time with the new material was relatively brief, much of it spent retyping.[76] The typescript does not survive, but her own revisions must have been limited. There was as yet no hint of the tendentious working relationship that would evolve between mother and daughter.

In her cover letter to Knopf, Lane again concealed her role, perhaps out of mixed feelings of loyalty to her mother and a desire not to sully her own reputation with "juvenile" work. It was an unnecessary deception that would cause no end of confusion and mischief in decades to come. "I don't know just where or how I come into this," she told Fiery, innocuously. "Do you?"[77]

PART III

THE

DREAM

Chapter 10

A Ruined Country

What a World!

On June 6, 1931, ten days after her manuscript was sent to Marion Fiery at Knopf, Laura Wilder climbed into the passenger seat of the 1923 Buick and she and Almanzo drove off, their dog Nero in the back.[1] It was the trip they had put off the previous year for lack of money. They were returning to De Smet, thirty-seven years after the depression of 1894 had forced them out.

Along the way they battled hot winds, rolling past sere fields and desiccated crops, farmhouses abandoned or about to be foreclosed. Every turn of the journey provided an uncanny reminder of those drought-stricken days of long ago.

Once again, Wilder kept a travel journal, recording her impressions alongside a tally of the trip's expenses, just as she had done nearly four decades earlier. On the first day, she spent ten cents for a tablet and pencil. On the second, she and Almanzo were pleased to recognize a Kansas schoolhouse that had just been completed when they passed years earlier. Rose and the Cooley boys had played there as children. Laura remembered seeing fresh wood shavings beside the door.

Eating at lunch counters, staying at bare-bones cabins next to filling stations or camping beside rivers, they enjoyed cool evenings and pleasant mornings, although the sun blazed hot by midafternoon. Always alert to natural milestones, Wilder recorded the first cottonwood and the song of their first meadowlark. At each community she noted farm conditions, fascinated as always by variations in climate and landscape and in ways of coping with them. She had seen it all before, but she was still shocked by the signs of a collapsing economy as they rolled past acre after acre of fallow dry fields—hay prices were too high to support livestock—and Standard Oil derricks fallen silent due to "overproduction."[2]

Unaware of what was coming, farmers had planted plentifully in 1931, trying to compensate for a declining economy. All the "wheat mad" suitcase farmers who had cleared the southern plains in the late 1920s—plowing more than five million acres of virgin land and stripping away the grass that had kept everything nailed down—flooded the market with grain.[3] Prices began to fall. Before the crash of 1929 wheat had been selling for over a dollar a bushel, but within two years it had plummeted to thirty-eight cents. Grain elevators in 1931 would be packed with wheat that had cost twice as much to grow as it would sell for. Corn dropped to thirteen cents, cheaper than coal. By winter, destitute farmers would be burning corn to heat their homes and cook their meals.[4]

In the Platte River valley of Nebraska, Wilder gloried in a rain shower that settled the dust and in the sight of a few prosperous farmhouses shaded by groves of trees, their fields studded with full corncribs. But down the road, as they neared Yankton, South Dakota, signs of bankruptcy were everywhere:

Gosh, I'd forgotten there was such a farming country in the U.S. And my God it is a ruined country. Being sold out on taxes. Fifty of these wonderful farms now advertised for tax sale. Many already have been sold and the rest just hanging on. Will not be able to last much longer. Haven't made any profit on their farms for 10 years now.[5]

A filling station attendant told them he had lost his two-hundred-acre farm to taxes and interest. With her experience, Wilder recognized that farmers with federal loans were still "hanging on," but couldn't do so for long if crop prices remained low. Hearing news of a paving project, sure to raise local taxes even more, she said crisply, "I suppose there must be a good road for the farmers to walk out of the country on."[6]

At Yankton, where Almanzo, Royal, and Eliza Wilder had limped into town a half-century earlier to file on homesteads, the Wilders were terrified by heavy traffic and fled without stopping. They were back in South Dakota, and it was dry, "trying to rain but can't."[7] Outside town, roads were empty, and they enjoyed the sense of peace, something Wilder said the Ozarks had once possessed but lost.

As they reached De Smet, a certain wariness and distress entered her tone. The town had grown, and the roads were in different places. They drove on to Manchester, where Grace Ingalls Dow lived with her husband, Nate, and Wilder was saddened to find her sister down on her luck. "She is the same old Grace," she wrote, "only not looking very well."[8]

Like her mother and Mary in the years after Charles Ingalls's death, the Dows were barely getting by. Their health was poor: Nate had severe asthma and slept sitting up in a chair. At fifty-four, Grace suffered from diabetes, her feet so swollen that she had difficulty walking. They were welcoming, but temperatures were so hot that the Wilders could barely sleep. Windows and doors had to be kept shut against blowing dust, and the house was an oven. Agitated by heat and the howling wind, Nero stopped eating.

Manchester was so impoverished, Wilder wrote, that it had become a village of scofflaws. No one could afford the fee for a vehicle license plate, so townsfolk shared one, passing it from car to car. Grace said families stole coal off the railroad cars in the winter and drank their troubles away with bootleg liquor at the pool hall.

In De Smet, the sisters sorted through what remained of their mother's and Mary's possessions—furniture, trunks, quilts, clothes, books, photographs, letters—heaped in a spare room while the house was rented.[9] Left to Carrie in exchange for caring for Mary in her final years, the little house had been hard used by its short-term occupants. "Everything of value left there has disappeared," Wilder wrote.[10]

Walking down the street, she enjoyed recognizing old friends,

including her childhood teacher during the hard winter, Florence Garland, now widowed and ailing but "sweet as could be." Wilder and
Almanzo made the nostalgic drive out to their old homestead and tree
claim—"no buildings . . . only a few trees left"—and to her father's
farm, "where Carrie and I walked to school and Manly used to drive
Barnum and Skip as he came dashing out to take me on those long
Sunday afternoon drives when I was seventeen."[11]

She found it amusing that people once formal and distant now hailed
her on the street, calling her "Laurie" and lavishing affection on her.
"In some way I like it," she admitted, but "it all makes me miss those
who are gone, Pa and Ma and Mary and the Boasts and Cap Garland."
De Smet was full of ghosts and memories, her own sister seeming "like
a stranger only now and then something familiar about her face."[12]
The strangeness went deep, and the visit may have been more poignant
than pleasant.

By the time they left for the Black Hills, they were exhausted. Wilder
could barely stay awake on the long drive across South Dakota, finding the landscape "flat and monotonous and *dry*," with fields of withered corn and wilted potatoes.[13] After a night in Pierre and a day so
hot their engine boiled over five times, they reached Carrie Swanzey's
home in Keystone. "She had changed a great deal," Wilder wrote of her
sister, who would be sixty-one that August, "but I knew her."[14] Like
the Dows, the Swanzeys were hard up. Once a miner, David Swanzey
held rights to a handful of tapped-out gold mines and little else. Wilder
was faced with the uncomfortable recognition that compared to her
sisters, she was relatively well off.

The visitors bunked in a cabin across the street from the Swanzeys,
hiring a driver to navigate the twists and turns as they toured the
mountains, Wilder not about to let her husband loose on the precipitous roads. Nearby, Mount Rushmore was slowly yielding presidential
visages; workers chipped away at Washington's chin, a "cloud of granite dust . . . flying." When the Wilders treated Carrie to noon dinner at
a restaurant beside Sylvan Lake—seventy-five cents a plate for "fruit
salad, mountain trout, mashed potatoes, new beets, lettuce and tomato
salad, hot rolls with sweet butter and wild honey," as well as the inevitable pie for Almanzo—she was scandalized at the expense.[15] They fed

the scraps to Nero, and Wilder bought rose quartz pins for Lane and Helen Boylston.

The Wilders reveled in their sightseeing, touring mines and the game lodge where Calvin Coolidge had spent the summer a few years earlier and where he decided not to run for a third term.[16] They wandered through the rebuilt stockade where Wilder's uncle, Tom Quiner, and the renegade miners of the Gordon Party had barricaded themselves against Indian attack during the winter of 1875. It gave Wilder "a queer feeling" to put her eye to peepholes in log walls like those her uncle had once peered through. They spent so long poring over the "beautiful rocks of the hills" that their chauffeur got nervous about driving back in the dark.

They left for home the day after the thermometer topped 105, suffering from altitude headaches (Keystone is 4,331 feet above sea level). Wilder jotted down her parting remark—"The hot wind is blowing us out of Dakota again"—to which her husband shot back, "It's the last time it will ever have the chance."[17] Leaving the high plains gave her a pang, as it had years earlier. As they crossed into Iowa, she paraphrased Lord Byron's parting with his wife: "Farewell Dakota and if forever still forever farewell."[18]

The trip home was sweltering, and they got lost again and again on country roads. Fearing that the dog might die from the heat, they stopped often to pour water over him, and fed him ice cream to cool him off. "What a world!" Wilder wrote in exasperation.[19] They saw more ruined farms, land that had sold during the recent boom for $750 an acre now worth a couple hundred, if that. "Everyone is broke," she wrote, "farms mortgaged for more than they are worth."[20] In today's parlance, the properties were underwater.

They arrived back in Mansfield on June 29, having covered by Wilder's calculation 2,530 miles and spent $120 over four weeks, although she acknowledged having lost track of gas and other expenses. Given what had become of De Smet in the nearly four decades since they left, they were glad they had gone away, despite the heartache of that time.

On the road, they had seen the Great Depression laying waste to farmers' assets, had felt the heat and dust of the Dirty Thirties beginning to stir. Wilder returned more determined than ever to press on with her writing, a bulwark against lost time, lost memories, and lost money.

In September 1931, in the midst of frantic preparations for Children's Book Week, Marion Fiery wrote to Lane, apologizing for the long delay and accepting her mother's "delightful" manuscript for publication. She was "quite keen" on "Little House in the Woods," as it was then called, and would never forget "the picture of the Xhristmas party and the maple sugar celebration."[21] Having taken it up with "Mr. Knopf"— Alfred A. Knopf Sr., founder of the publishing house—she promised that a contract, committing Wilder to produce three books, was on its way.

But as fast as the deal had come together, it unraveled. In November, in the wake of dire Depression forecasts, Knopf decided to close its children's department. By then, Wilder already had the (as yet unsigned) contract in hand, but Fiery, fearing that the book would be orphaned, suggested that she return the contract and seek publication elsewhere. In response, Lane asked the editor to hold off until she could sound out other publishers. While offering regrets that Fiery was about to lose her job, Lane pooh-poohed the Depression, something that would become a perennial theme:

> I don't believe this terror of the future is justified by facts. The more I see of public temper in this depression, the more I'm reluctantly concluding that this country's simply yellow. Our people are behaving like arrant cowards. And it's absurd. Nothing's fundamentally wrong.[22]

At the same time, she was despairing over her own finances, writing on November 10: "Minus nothing in Palmer account. I owe $8200. Have $300 in the bank. . . . Mind still not functioning."[23] The crash had caused her own private ruin but did not inspire in her empathy for others.

Having parted ways with Carl Brandt, Lane had acquired a new agent, George T. Bye, earlier that year. A former reporter for the *Kansas City Star*, he would handle a wide array of political figures and celebrities over his career, including Rebecca West, Charles Lindbergh, Franklin Delano Roosevelt, Eleanor Roosevelt, and Alfred "Al" Smith, presidential hopeful and four-time governor of New York. More vivacious and outgoing than Brandt, Bye was soon exchanging mash notes with Lane, calling a short story of hers—"Immoral Woman," which he quickly sold to *Ladies' Home Journal*—one of the best that had ever come through his office. He felt like taking her on his lap and hugging her after he read it, he said.[24]

He had not thought much of Wilder's "Pioneer Girl" manuscript—it reminded him of an old lady reminiscing in her rocking chair, he wrote, but enthusiastically agreed to represent Wilder's children's work even as Lane denigrated it. "I know you don't really want to spend valuable time and work on that little juvenile," she told him. "It isn't worth your while."[25]

But Bye saw a bird in hand, and the manuscript was sent to Virginia Kirkus at Harper & Brothers.[26] Kirkus had been hired in 1926 to establish Harper's children's department; within a few years, she would depart to create *Kirkus Reviews*. She was unenthusiastic when she first heard of Wilder's project, but met with Fiery at the Biltmore Hotel for tea before catching the train back to her Westport, Connecticut, home. Boarding the train in the dwindling light of a December afternoon, she began reading and was soon so engrossed she missed her stop. The discovery became a highlight of her publishing career. She later wrote:

> At that time I was living a fairly rugged life in a house lighted with kerosene lamps—a house with only the most elementary plumbing, a kitchen pump. Perhaps that was one reason why I was so quickly translated to those Wisconsin woods and small Laura's adventures. But the real magic was in the telling. One felt that one was listening, not reading. And picture after picture—still vivid today, more than twenty years later—flashed before my inward eye. I knew Laura—and the older Laura who was telling her story. Here was the book no depression could stop.[27]

Kirkus wrote to Wilder immediately, accepting the manuscript and asking for permission to make a few editorial changes to ease the

transition between the main narrative and the inset stories told by the
father.[28]

Within days, Kirkus was asking Wilder to clarify the genre of her
story. "We seem to be a little in the dark as to the exact source of your
material," she wrote. "I had understood when your manuscript was
given to me to read, that it was autobiographical and that these were
your own childhood experiences of frontier life. Your letter makes me
feel that perhaps we were wrong in this understanding."[29] Requesting
an autobiographical sketch to clarify matters, Kirkus cut to the heart
of the confusion, doubtless intensified by Wilder's use of her own
name and those of her family. Wilder's reply has been lost, but Kirkus
knew her business. The book would be published as fiction, not autobiography.

The title, too, would undergo revision. Filed with the editorial correspondence is a list of suggested titles, most crossed out. Possibilities
included "Trundle-bed Tales," "Little Pioneer Girl," and "Little Girl in
the Big Woods." The eventual title, "Little House in the Big Woods,"
did not appear on the list but was a portentous choice. In contrast to
another American children's classic, *Little Women*, published in two
volumes in 1868–1869, when Laura Ingalls was an infant, Wilder's final
title turned attention away from the protagonist, emphasizing instead
the security—and insecurity—of home. Over the life of the series, it
would sound a perpetual note of ambiguity, repeatedly employing a
symbol of permanence, the house as a fixed place of abode, to represent the family's incessant wanderings and displacement. It also signaled, in however veiled a fashion, the singular obsession with houses
of the manuscript's original editor, the second-generation product of
all that displacement, Rose Wilder Lane.

Armed with its resonant title and promising to charm young readers at a cheerless moment in the nation's history, the book attracted
attention almost immediately, prior to publication. Before the year was
out, Kirkus was congratulating her new author: the Junior Literary
Guild had adopted the book as an April selection, paying Wilder $350
over and above her contract and agreeing to distribute 3,500 copies.[30]
George Bye sent "Laura Ingalls Lane" a flattering Christmas telegram.[31] It was a slip more telling than he knew.

Little House in the Big Woods was handsomely produced, with fifteen illustrations, including a three-color frontispiece—Ma and Laura confronting the bear in the barnyard—printed on heavy coated stock. The illustrator, Helen Sewell, at the beginning of a long career and with only a few titles as yet to her credit, produced the old-fashioned pen-and-ink drawings, including a title-page rendition of Charles and Caroline Ingalls's wedding; Wilder had sent the wedding daguerreotype to Kirkus in response to her request for period photographic materials. The cover featured a log house, with two small girls peeping out the door. Peering back at them in friendly curiosity from the stylized shrubbery were a bear, a mother deer and fawn, and a rabbit.

The book sold strongly in a market already dampened by the Depression.[32] Its warm critical reception must have been supremely gratifying. The *New York Times Book Review* praised its "refreshingly genuine and lifelike quality," noting that "the portrait of Laura's father, especially, is drawn with loving care and reality."[33] A prominent Wisconsin librarian called it "a delightful, absorbing true story."[34] "Pioneer Girl" had not panned out, but the "story of my life thing" that Wilder and Lane had been trading back and forth for years had finally taken shape, in the genre that Wilder herself had first envisioned.

She was not stopping there. By the time her first book was published, she was hard at work on another. *Farmer Boy*, drawn from Almanzo Wilder's childhood in Malone, New York, was clearly envisioned as a companion to set alongside *Little House in the Big Woods*. It too began in winter, wending its way through the seasons on a working farm; it too captured a child's intensely felt pleasures, satisfactions, dramas, and disappointments.

But it also had significant differences, featuring a new character who was older and male, set in a place Wilder had never seen. It would require more labor, thought, and revision than the first book, and would be undertaken in an atmosphere fraught with tension. For in 1932, after the successful completion and publication of Wilder's first book, Lane began competing with her mother over her material, first in secret and then openly, trying to put her own imprimatur on the family stories and sell them before her mother could.

Hurricane

Lane had dallied with the thought before. On previous occasions, however, she had shrugged at the notion of exploring her roots. In the summer of 1928, when she was casting about for new subjects, she told Clarence Day: "Pioneer America ... I don't care about it. Don't dislike it ... I readily admit all the admirable qualities; I'm simply not interested."[35] During the twenties, she had jotted notes in her diaries, filling one tiny notebook page with ideas for "Pioneer stories" about ponies, including one set in South Dakota. On another page, she wrote: "A series of pioneer stories, featuring the woman."[36] She numbered successive lines from one to ten but filled only two, their titles clearly drawn from her mother's tales: "The Surveyors House" (referring to the Ingallses' stay at Silver Lake) and "The Lotus Eaters" (recalling her mother's fondness for Tennyson, something that would surface later in the Little House books).[37] The rest were left blank.

Lane had also considered writing a novel about her father's life, producing an outline and a few pages of notes for "A Son of the Soil," perhaps inspired by her 1916 *Bulletin* serial, "Soldiers of the Soil."[38] In her outline, the four parts of the book were titled "Back East," "Out West," "Down South," and "The Ozarks," corresponding to her father's periods in New York, Minnesota, Florida, and Missouri. The notes, probably taken down verbatim during discussions with Almanzo, captured his bluff, blunt speech, with descriptions of the joys and terrors of Malone's swimming hole and of his fondness for wintergreen berries: "Never was anything so good. Best time to gather them, on first warm day in spring, when the snow began to run—not to melt, to run."[39] The memories moved him to exclaim, "Gosh! Sure was a happy childhood."

But during the teens and twenties, Lane never sought to utilize this material. Only in the 1930s did she broach the idea of writing about the "hard winter" to Thomas Costain, fiction editor at the *Saturday Evening Post*, who expressed interest.[40] And it was not until January 1932, the month after the flurry of acceptance, congratulations, and praise for her mother's book from Virginia Kirkus and her own agent, George Bye, that Lane suddenly began to write in earnest—not about her own parents, but about her mother's parents, Charles and Caroline Ingalls. She called the story "Courage." Its chief characters were named "Charles" and "Caroline." Wilder, of course, had used her parents' names in *Little House in the Big Woods*, and intended to continue the practice in volumes yet to be written.[41]

But "Courage" borrowed far more than names. Lane's fictional couple were homesteaders, living in a dugout on "Wild Plum Creek." The indomitable, violin-playing Charles sings "Uncle Sam is rich enough to give us all a farm," and works on the railroad to earn money. He and Caroline invest their hopes in a wheat crop that grows magnificently only to be cut down by grasshoppers. Charles then leaves wife and baby to find work. When he is unable to return before the bad weather sets in, Caroline braves blizzards in the dugout until he comes home.

"Courage" also mirrored the Wilders' own early married life. The fictional Charles and Caroline marry young, and have a baby almost immediately; Charles files on a homestead before the legal age of twenty-one, just as Almanzo did. The couple is beset, as the Wilders were, by waves of misfortune but are shown persevering, battling their doubts along with the elements. Yet for all the obvious borrowings and similarities, Lane seems never to have mentioned the project to the person it concerned the most.

The tale had been conceived in the fall of 1931, but Lane worked on "Courage" only sporadically and by her account unsuccessfully through the last months of the year, instead focusing on two stories— "Traveling Man" and "Old Maid"—inspired by her teen years in Mansfield. These would eventually form part of the "Ernestine" story cycle of *Old Home Town*. She took up "Courage" again in January, then discarded it in frustration, before finishing it in the summer of 1932. Meanwhile, her household had undergone significant Depression-related upheaval. Helen Boylston, whose own Palmer account was also wiped out, left at the beginning of the year, returning to New York to take up her old profession, nursing.[42] She would soon be replaced as Lane's companion at Rocky Ridge by Catherine Brody, a struggling writer whose proletarian novel about Detroit autoworkers, *Nobody Starves*, had just been published.

"Courage" was not Lane's only impingement on her mother's

territory. In desperation, she tried to convince Marion Fiery, who had landed at Putnam's, that she intended to launch her own "series of juveniles."[43] (Presumably she did not reveal to the editor how much she despised the genre.)[44] In the face of her mother's success, Lane felt crippled by her limping career, failing health, and especially her finances. Her resentment surfaced in a letter to her old friend Jane Burr, in which she boasted of saving her mother from the foundering of Knopf's children's department even as she adopted a patronizing tone. "My mother is all set up about it," she wrote of Wilder's "little juvenile," adding that the fledgling author in the family was "having all the feelings about HER BOOK, anyway, that it's conventional for writers to have."[45]

In the same letter, Lane also ruefully admitted to Burr that she had gotten herself into a fiscal "tangle" in "building the new house for my mother," comparing the sensation of her myriad obligations to "sticky flypaper."[46] It was a tangle indeed: throughout this period, Lane continued to borrow from her parents even as she helped to support them. A complete account of her financial dealings is difficult to reconstruct from the scattered diary entries and other available sources. But the economic peril engineered by her borrowing may have threatened to take her parents—even Rocky Ridge itself—down with it.

Sometime in the late 1920s, Lane had arranged a loan of more than two thousand dollars from N. J. Craig, a substantial sum that must have been secured by collateral.[47] Lane herself owned no property, not even the Rock House she had built for the Wilders. While she had earned handsomely in the past, she had no job and no salary. Her freelance income was sporadic, irregular, and unsecured; no bank could have accepted it as backing for a loan. Instead, just as she had once assured Clarence Day that her mother would be good for the money she borrowed from him, so her parents may have played a role in securing the loan from Craig. They may well have been co-signers, and as such stood to lose their property if Lane failed to pay.

The stock market crash had wiped out not only Lane's and Boylston's Palmer accounts but her parents' as well, but Lane waited weeks before letting them know. Her diary records her panic throughout the fall of 1931. In December, on the same day that Virginia Kirkus wrote accepting her mother's manuscript for publication, Lane had her parents over for dinner ("spare-ribs and sweet potatoes"). She knew that her mother had not received her Palmer dividend, but was afraid to tell Wilder that the money was gone. Somehow, she had re-created the 1894 nightmare of the lost cash in the writing desk, and once again it was all her fault. The day after the dinner, she noted in her diary: "Too horribly upset about my mothers money to work."[48] Finally, the day after that, she relayed the news, noting that Wilder "took it very well, considering."[49]

The following month, Lane was awoken one January morning by her mother knocking at the door, holding a letter regarding the formation of a "creditors committee"—apparently anticipating the receivership of Palmer & Co., the assets and debts of which were being assumed by Irving Trust.[50] "Couldn't work, feeling ghastly," Lane wrote after the encounter. Her diary increasingly captured feelings of rage she felt toward her mother as the family inched closer to ruin. Night after night, haunted by the "Palmer wreck," she would suffer "a sick panic."[51] "Wish I were dead," she wrote.[52]

As for Wilder, she too was overwhelmed. In February 1932, just before her sixty-fifth birthday, Wilder received a pathetic letter from her sister Grace, pleading for help.[53] Once again she was surrounded by need, with only her own resources to fall back on. When her father's meager fortunes collapsed, when her husband's health failed, she had been forced to lift the family on her own back, pushing through by dint of sheer determination and endless hard work. This time her own daughter—who had assured her that the stock market "could never lose" and told her that from now on money was for spending—had put her at risk.

In April, a week after receiving her author's copies of *Little House in the Big Woods*, Wilder collapsed. There had been a fire at the barns, apparently put out before it did much damage. The memories it must have stirred went unrecorded. A doctor came and diagnosed what Lane termed, unsympathetically, "overexertion & silly eating."[54] She added, "Poor dear will not take care of herself." The exhaustion lingered. John Case, Wilder's former editor at the *Ruralist*, heard of it, writing to Wilder in June to say he was sorry to learn she was unwell.[55]

Lane chose that moment to pen in her journal a merciless dissection of her mother and Laura's friends the Pooles, a neighboring farm couple with an adopted son. Her own self-loathing—the previous day she had dismissed her life as "meaningless"—always called forth a corresponding contempt for others.[56] Mrs. Poole, Lane wrote, was a "cartoon figure of a corseted fat woman," her blunt blond hair cut off at the neck, which was "rough and horribly wrinkled," ornamented by a blue bead necklace from a St. Louis dime store that Wilder had given her as a gift.[57] Lane despised the Pooles' "higgledy-piggledy" flower beds and penchant for "old things," which "they admire & treasure . . . not quite knowing why." The only member of the household she liked was their adopted son, "a thin quick youth with a keen face."

In retrospect, the true source of Lane's rancor was not Mrs. Poole. On the drive home from a visit to them, she grew furious with her mother when Wilder failed to sense her aversion to their lowbrow hosts:

> I remarked thoughtlessly that I had had a nice time. My mother brightened pathetically. "Did you really? You weren't bored?" Before I could collect my idling mind she added, still brightly, "Seeing how the other half lives." Suddenly I was profoundly, coldly angry. I could have killed. But my anger had no focus, no direction. It was not against her or anyone else. "What do you mean?" I said, icy. She looked at me. I could feel the murder in my eyes. Hers seemed expressionless. "Just common ordinary farmers," she said, turning to the road ahead.[58]

Determined to undermine her mother, Lane ignored a request from the *Saturday Evening Post* for a nonfiction article about her parents' pioneer days and instead pressed on with her fiction. She finished "Courage" in July and sent it to George Bye as a three-part serial, retitling it, prophetically, "Let the Hurricane Roar."[59] Having unknowingly provided the material for the story, Wilder also unwittingly supplied that title, remarking during a conversation about the worsening economy: "Well, let the hurricane roar." The phrase, she explained, was from an old hymn: "Then let the hurricane roar, / It will the sooner be o'er; / We will weather the blast, and will land at last, / On Canaan's happy shore."[60] Lane wrote down the lyrics on an undated notebook page scrawled with potential titles.[61]

Buffeted by her moods and sleepless nights, Lane also spent time that spring wrangling with her mother's manuscript for "Farmer Boy," which Wilder had brought to her. She was not happy with the task, bemoaning that she was not "master of my material in writing my mother's second juvenile."[62] At another point, she described her work on the manuscript as "copying." She finished her version of "Farmer Boy" at the same time that she finished "Let the Hurricane Roar."

On August 17, Lane sat writing in her journal, expressing little faith in either project and calling for the annihilation of Rocky Ridge— "If only a tornado would destroy the place and . . ."—when she received a wildly laudatory telegram from George Bye, congratulating her on "Hurricane." He called it "better than money in the bank," predicting that she would be hailed by "millions" of grateful readers.[63] Lane was both thrilled and dismayed, fearful that he was overpraising the piece; he had greeted another story of hers, "Traveling Man," in similar fashion, but it still languished unsold. "Am not really cheered," she wrote, "cold and dull."[64]

Bye did quickly sell "Hurricane," however. It went to the *Saturday Evening Post*, which had also bought the "Old Maid" story earlier that summer. Lane had yearned for years to break into the coveted *Post*; now she had succeeded twice in one year. "Hurricane" was slated to appear as a serial in October.[65] But despite the success, Lane continued to be depressed. And she had still not told her mother about the story.

With these sales, Lane had reversed their roles. Now she was succeeding while her mother failed. Her lack of faith in "Farmer Boy" had been well founded. In September, Harper & Brothers turned down the manuscript, saying that extensive revisions were necessary before it could be accepted.[66] Like many publishers during the Depression, Harper was scaling back its children's titles. Virginia Kirkus left the company that year. Her secretary, Ida Louise Raymond, was tasked with handling the remaining business; the children's department drifted, temporarily in limbo.

Lane had been so consumed with her own depression that she barely seemed to register the greater global collapse, but 1932 was the beginning of the worst of all possible economic times. Every indicator was negative. In the United States, unemployment rose to 24.6 percent, while industrial stocks lost nearly 80 percent of their value. Ten thousand banks failed, and thirteen million people were thrown out of work. Missouri farms lost more than half their value in just a few years.[67]

That fall, Lane had an opportunity to see how the Depression was unfolding firsthand. In October, she took money earned from "Hurricane" and set off on a car trip across the country with a friend from Mansfield, Corinne Murray. While Catherine Brody was up in her bedroom working on her writing, Murray was becoming a fixture in Lane's life, coming over frequently to play bridge or chess. She and her husband, Jack Murray, ran a laundry in Mansfield but had a tempestuous relationship, and she would often seek solace at Rocky Ridge after marital spats. Eventually, Lane hired her as cook, housekeeper, and driver.

Heading for New York to see Lane's agent, publishers, and old friends, the pair took a circuitous route, first heading north to Ottawa, Canada. They wanted to visit Mahlon William Locke, a "toe-twisting" doctor recently written up in *Cosmopolitan*; he was famous for manipulating patients' feet as a cure for fallen arches, a particular complaint of Lane's. On the way they stopped in two of the family's old haunts, Burr Oak, Iowa, and Spring Valley, Minnesota. Lane may have been anticipating that Burr Oak would appear in her mother's novels. A few years later, she herself would set a story in that town, again based on her parents' lives.[68]

Driving south from Canada they also visited Almanzo's hometown of Malone, New York, searching out the county fairgrounds, the church the Wilders had attended, and Franklin Academy, where the children had gone to school. Scouting back roads, Lane found the Wilders' old farmhouse, the original barns, and the sheep pasture leading down to the Trout River—"perfectly lovely"—where her father had fished as a boy and jumped from the slippery banks into the swimming hole.[69] Charming the owners, Lane talked her way into the house, later sending her parents a series of postcards in which she walked them through it room by room, reporting that the pantry was now a bedroom and the stove was missing.[70] All else appeared to be much as it had been when James Wilder built the place. She sent a twig plucked from the balsam tree her father remembered and, by express, wintergreen plants, which she hoped to raise in Missouri for the berries Almanzo had cherished.

Doubtless intended to fill out descriptions for "Farmer Boy," the visit to Malone was also an act of love. Lane's affection for her father shines through the cards she sent. The tender gesture may also have reflected frustration over the rejection of "Farmer Boy," and perhaps guilt over the unpleasant surprises still awaiting Wilder in "Let the Hurricane Roar."

But no matter what Lane saw on her cross-country sojourn, she remained emotionally numb to the Depression, unable to accept the fact that it was real. She admired the fatalism expressed by a young filling station attendant who contended that the catastrophe was "good for us" despite the suffering it caused, saying "that's all life is, anyway."[71] She even urged her mother to send a check for $260 to George Palmer, apparently still doing trades even after his company failed, to purchase more shares of National Industries, potentially throwing good money after bad.[72] "The situation . . . may become disastrous," she wrote, but "I do not really believe it will."[73]

That was not the prevailing view in 1932. Throughout the election year, Hoover had dutifully clung to Republican truisms, insisting that private relief organizations could minister to the millions of Americans thrown out of work and onto the streets. Although he launched a major public works project—the construction of a massive dam on the Colorado River—it was a drop in the ocean of unemployment, so negligible in its effects that his name was initially stricken from the finished product, known as Boulder Dam for more than a decade. He continued to disparage public works programs in general, which he termed as "demoralizing [as a] dole."[74] In desperate retaliation, people living in cardboard shacks named them "Hoovervilles." Newspapers were "Hoover blankets," and empty pockets, turned inside out, "Hoover flags." A hungry nation turned implacably against the president when he told reporters, "No one is actually starving."[75]

Even Lane, Hoover's onetime hagiographer, realized he was a failure. He was "alarming without being arousing," she said, calling his efforts to explain the economic crisis to the public "psychologically bad."[76] His subtlety was his downfall, she told herself. At the moment, she thought that the country "desperately needs one of the good-old slogan-makers, a Roosevelt or a Bryan."[77]

Franklin Roosevelt piled onto his opponent, calling the portly Hoover a "fat, timid capon," a castrated rooster fed for the pot. When FDR won in a landslide that November, carrying all but six states, Hoover, the upright businessman once lionized by Lane, had been reduced to a hated caricature. A rumor went around that he'd been apprehended fleeing the country on Andrew Mellon's yacht, carrying gold looted from Fort Knox.[78]

In an extraordinary reversal, Roosevelt won even conservative Mansfield, in Missouri's predominantly Republican Wright County, 362 to 303. The Senate Democrats also prevailed there, as they would nationally.[79] No one knows how the Wilders and their daughter voted. If they did help to elect FDR, it would be the only time.

WHATEVER their political concerns at that moment, the personal relationship between the two women was poised for upheaval. Lane would claim that her mother didn't care about her writing, not bothering to read it. But Wilder's sharp dismay on the occasion of learning about the progress of "Let the Hurricane Roar" revealed the gravity of the betrayal.

In January 1933, Wilder found out what her daughter had been hiding, in the worst and most public way. Lane had received advance copies of advertisements for the story, scheduled for publication in book form by Longmans, Green and Company that February. She had deliberately hidden them from her mother. But Catherine Brody, unaware of the impact they would have, brought them out, in company, to show off the two full pages of publicity that would run in *The Publishers' Weekly*.

Lane dramatized the scene in her journal, describing her mother studying the ad with "an air of distaste." Wilder interrupted Lane's conversation with friends to question her sharply about it:

"Why do they place it in the Dakotas?"

I: "I don't know."

She: "the names aren't right."

I, alarmed: "What names?"

She: "Caroline and Charles. They don't belong in that place at that time. I don't know—it's all wrong. They've got it all wrong, somehow." Effectively destroying the simple perfection of my pleasure.[80]

Lane's pleasure had been engineered at the cost of Wilder's discomfiture and dismay, and the fact that she fixated on it recalled the worst of her self-serving behavior with Charlie Chaplin and Charmian London. The ad itself was a fanciful portrait of Wilder's parents, a woodcut depicting the windswept couple from behind. Charles, a tall dashing figure with a shapely bottom worthy of that year's screen idol, Clark Gable, clutched his wife's elbow, staring indomitably into the future. The text read:

> A novel that makes you proud of being an American! A novel that moves you deeply, and ends with a "lift"—This is the story of Charles and Caroline, young pioneers in the rich wild Dakotas of the '70s, of hot winds and cyclones, grasshoppers, blizzards, sod shanties; but most of all, of faith and magnificent courage. What these two young heroic pioneers went through dwarfs your present hardships and makes you ashamed to complain. Maybe it can lead America to sing with Charles, "LET THE HURRICANE ROAR!"[81]

Lane could have adopted fictional names for her characters and disguised her borrowings with fresh invention and details. Yet she deliberately chose to trespass on her mother's sacred ground, the reason why Wilder had begun writing in the first place. In that light, Lane's theft appears all the more transgressive, an expression of raw rivalry and jealousy. For both women, it was yet another outbreak of the consuming fires—abandonment, blame, and disappointment—that had been burning through their lives since their earliest days together.

Hurricane sold remarkably well for any book during the Depression, ten thousand copies in four months, and Longmans arranged for a fourth printing only six weeks after it appeared in stores.[82] Lane nonetheless despaired over lost opportunities. Had the book appeared during more auspicious times, it might have been her first major bestseller. As it was, sales quickly fell off, and a possible Hollywood sale that floated into view soon vanished.

Bestseller or no, *Let the Hurricane Roar* was not Lane's best work. She had once stated that "a story too many times told is a dish without salt," and *Hurricane* carried the unconvincing air of something heard secondhand.[83] Compared to her mother's writing about the same experiences, the characters were flat and the language overwrought, the stuff of commercial magazine fare. Lane would call it her "classic," touting it as comparable to *Little Women* "but with much stronger dramatic value and a terrific punch straight to the American heart."[84] It suffered, however, from the fictional equivalent of overacting, its characters ginning up drama by raging, shaking, screaming, and sobbing. Jaws were clenched, and fists pounded on tables. Scholars later dubbed it "stale and formulaic."[85]

Ironically, Lane was writing some of her best stories at the time, the ones that would fill *Old Home Town*, drawn from direct experience of small-town life and enlivened by her adolescent bird's-eye view of Mansfield's scandals. But for someone so gifted at editing the work of others, Lane was her own worst judge.

The story of the falling out between Lane and Wilder over *Hurricane* has survived for decades in Mansfield's memories. Even those who did not know the women at the time eventually learned of it, passing the story along to outsiders. Lane's biographer, William Holtz, who adopted Lane's animus toward her mother, seized on it as an example of the older woman's rancor: "Mama Bess took her chagrin abroad into the community, for there persisted in Mansfield the gossip of her anger and resentment of Rose's use of privileged materials."[86] Longtime Wilder scholar William Anderson reported that as late as the 1980s, "old-timers lounging in Mansfield's town square" were still talking about "a ruckus between the Wilder women" over *Hurricane*.[87] There were even rumors of possible legal action, perhaps arising from the Wilders' association with their old friend N. J. Craig, an attorney as well as a banker.

In her letters, Wilder was clear about her distaste for her daughter's book. A year after the novel appeared, she wrote to Aubrey Sherwood, editor of the *De Smet News*: "In regard to the book 'Let the Hurricane

Roar' I think there is nothing particular to say. It is of course fiction, with incidents and anicdotes gathered here and there and some purely imaginary. But you know what fiction writing is."[88] Nearly two decades later, writing to a librarian in California who had asked about Lane's appropriations, Wilder renounced it completely: "My daughter's book, 'Let the Hurricane Roar,' is fiction with a background of facts as I told her many times when she was a child. The characters in her story have no connection with my family. Her choice of names was unfortunate as it creates confusion."[89] The passage of time had not eased the sting.

Irene Lichty, a friend of Wilder's later in life, would call Lane's betrayal "a rift in the lute," an apt reference to a bond ruined by a seemingly minor blemish. It was a metaphor coined by Wilder's favorite poet, Alfred Tennyson: "Unfaith in aught is want of faith in all. / It is the little rift within the lute, / That by and by will make the music mute, / And ever widening slowly silence all."[90]

But the most remarkable aspect of the quarrel was that it did not bring the women's collaboration to an end. Wilder's initial anger may soon have been overshadowed by concern for her daughter's very survival. In early 1933, Lane grew so desperately depressed that she began weeping inconsolably, day and night.

The precipitating cause of the breakdown was the death of her little dog, Bunting, struck and killed on the road that swung past Rocky Ridge, by then enlarged into a county highway. The Maltese puppy acquired by Lane and Boylston just before they returned from Europe, Bunting had always been an escape artist, constantly running away and being found in the next county. Lane had apparently never thought to curtail his adventures by fencing him in or tying him up. He met his end in early February, just as she was recovering from a severe bout of flu.

Her grief over the loss was boundless, the anguish recorded in a 1933 journal. In February: "I can't stop crying."[91] In March: "Cried most of the night. Still crying."[92] In April: "I really am sick in my head."[93] In May: "I'll be glad to die."[94] An ominous refrain began appearing in her diary: "Dead day."[95] Given what she had just been through with Wilder, it is impossible not to connect the severity of her breakdown with her sense that she had failed both her mother and her beloved pet.

At the same moment, the economic apocalypse was upon them. In the first weeks of 1933, Wilder scraped together all the money she could find and paid off the outstanding balance on the federal farm loan on Rocky Ridge, $811.65.[96] This time, no matter what happened, she would not lose the farm. She was left with around fifty dollars in cash.[97]

Banks were failing all around them, with three hundred shuttered across the state.[98] In January, the Mountain Grove bank, only a few miles from Mansfield, was closed. In February, word came that banks in Arkansas, Kentucky, Ohio, and Pennsylvania were limiting withdrawals. On March 4, the day of Roosevelt's inauguration, they heard that all Missouri banks were to be closed, then that a national "bank holiday" would be in effect for a full week. Roosevelt delivered the first of his fireside chats on March 12, the night before business was to resume, urging "confidence and courage" on a frantic public. "You people must have faith," he concluded. "Let us unite in banishing fear. . . . Together we cannot fail."[99]

Lane had gone to her parents' house to listen to the radio that night, but the receiver was on the fritz. She hurried to a friend's house to listen and called it a "good, plain speech."[100] Wilder, however, began preparing for the worst. Over the next few weeks, doubtless alarmed by her daughter's mental state, she proposed that they sell the Rock House and the forty acres it sat on, telling Lane that she was free to go anytime and need not pay rent for Rocky Ridge. She and Almanzo could manage on their own.[101]

As an interim measure, Wilder suggested turning off electric service at the Rock House.[102] Initially relieved, Lane ultimately flipped these gestures on their head, interpreting them as manipulative and cruel, writing a scathing account of her mother's behavior:

> It's amazing how my mother can make me suffer. Yesterday . . . she was here, and asked to see the electric contract. I must have known, without knowing, what was coming, for I ran upstairs, saying I'd bring it down, telling her—behind me—that she needn't come. Of course she came. She sat at the desk, I in my typewriter-chair. And while she put on her glasses and slowly, very apprehensive, read the contract, I closed my typewriter into the desk as if clearing decks.

Then she began—Cheerful, almost playful, and grave—She has it all
planned. Cut off the electric bill and she can manage indefinitely.
She's doing it to "let me go." . . . After all she didn't have electricity
before; I've given her six "wonderfully easy years." How she hates it,
that I'm her "sole source of support." Implicit in every syllable and
tone, the fact that I've failed, fallen down on the job, been the broken
reed. But never mind, (brightly) she's able to manage nicely, thank
you! And its true enough that to live like a Digger Indian's no esthetic
hardship to her.[103]

In the end, Lane handed over sixty dollars to maintain electricity at
the Rock House; in an act of furious self-sacrifice, she had the electric
service disconnected at the farmhouse instead. She concluded her journal entry by saying that Wilder "made me so miserable when I was a
child that I've never got over it."[104] That statement would find its fictional counterpart in Lane's story "Long Skirts," published in 1935 as
part of *Old Home Town*. In the story, Ernestine says to her mother, a
thinly veiled version of Wilder, "Are you always going to drag me down
and make me miserable? My goodness, mama, I'm not a child! I'm
sixteen! . . . Aren't you ever going to stop making me utterly miserable?"[105] Whether that reflected Rose's views as a teenager, as an adult,
or both, mother and daughter were locked in a cycle of blame and
recrimination. They would never break out.

We do not know Wilder's side of the story. Lane's diaries recorded
small acts of kindness rendered by her mother that year: gifts of strawberries, a surprise pork roast, a high tea. There may have been justification to Lane's complaints, but even in her self-critical state the daughter
never came to grips with her own role in overpromising, overinvesting,
and overbuilding at Rocky Ridge. No one had forced her to pledge
five hundred a year to her parents, move back to Missouri, build a
house that her parents did not want, and go thousands of dollars into
debt. Those were her choices. But she found it easier to locate villains
outside herself. In April 1933, she began denouncing Roosevelt as a
dictator.[106]

Nonetheless, even when she was so distraught she could barely
function, Lane sat dutifully at her desk, revising and copying "Farmer

Boy." Two manuscripts survive. One is a fair copy in Wilder's handwriting, which scholars have argued may be a second or later draft; the other is a typed copy of Lane's.[107] As with *Little House in the Big Woods*, Wilder crafted the bulk of the book, laying out complete scenes and descriptions of the farm and barns of her husband's childhood, capturing Eliza Jane's smug sanctimony and her husband's fondness for the younger, sweeter sister, Alice. She was doubtless aided by Almanzo's recollections—he had helpfully drawn a precise schematic of the house and map of the grounds, using a ruler—as well as her daughter's recent visit to Malone.

For her part, Lane cut extraneous passages, including an ending Wilder had written about the family's move to Minnesota. She was also probably responsible for adding memorable dialogue and details, from the color of Almanzo's mittens ("red as a cherry") to the curious speech pattern of his family, the old-fashioned New England "invariant be," which has James Wilder saying such things as "Be you having a good time, son?"[108] In this and in every other book, it would be the unique combination of their skills that created a transcendent whole: Wilder laying a plain, solid foundation of factual description, holding to simplicity of speech and emotion, while her daughter trimmed, honed, and heightened the drama, adding embellishment and ornamentation.

The finished book betrays no hint of the ongoing economic collapse, Lane's depression, or the animus between mother and daughter. But in its lingering, loving portrayal of the mouthwatering abundance of farmhouse fare, it gestures toward the Depression's straitened circumstances. Rich breakfasts start the farm day, with oatmeal swimming in cream and maple sugar, buckwheat cakes, fried potatoes, sausages and gravy, preserves, jams, jellies, doughnuts, and apple pie, Almanzo's favorite. Likewise, the lavish offerings at the county fair are given pride of place, its communal tables crowded with hams, roasts, chickens, turkeys, ducks, bowls of dressing, pots of boiled and baked beans, dishes of pickles and preserves, and battalions of pies—berry pies, fruit pies, cream pies, custard pies, raisin pies. At a time of the most widespread food insecurity Americans had ever known, *Farmer Boy*'s homely cornucopia delivered comfort as well as a paean to the just rewards of hard work.

In Wilder's series, the book would always be an outlier. Its publisher never quite knew what to do with it, eventually pretending that it was the third, not the second book in the sequence. In March 1933, Harper & Brothers accepted the manuscript, with Ida Louise Raymond describing it as "excellent—different, sincere, authentic" but not quite up to the level of the first.[109] Citing Depression-era strictures, the publisher insisted on a deep royalty cut, offering only 5 percent rather than 10 for the first several thousand copies.[110] Wilder capitulated but never forgot the slight, bringing it up in negotiations years later.[111]

Aimed at boys in a series about girls, *Farmer Boy* never won the popularity of other volumes. But with its companion, *Little House in the Big Woods*, it stands as a timeless fable of familial self-sufficiency. Its farmers are heroes. In a chapter about Malone's Independence Day celebration, Almanzo asks his father why he says that "axes and plows" made America what it is, and his father proudly explains the notion of Manifest Destiny, in what would serve as a thematic declaration of the Little House books:

> We were farmers, son; we wanted the land. It was farmers that went over the mountains, and cleared the land, and settled it, and farmed it, and hung on to their farms.
>
> This country goes three thousand miles west, now. It goes 'way out beyond Kansas, and beyond the Great American Desert, over mountains bigger than these mountains, and down to the Pacific Ocean. It's the biggest country in the world, and it was farmers who took all that country and made it America, son. Don't you ever forget that.[112]

That was probably Lane's high-minded interpolation. By comparison, the Fourth of July scene in Wilder's handwritten manuscript was dry and concise, emphasizing the pomposity, not the patriotism, of the speeches. In her version, Almanzo's father cut a speechifier down to size, saying he "twisted the lion's tail and made the eagle scream."[113]

In Wilder's fictional cosmos, *Farmer Boy* accomplished another critical task, introducing the stalwart and indefatigable character of

Almanzo, who would play a crucial role later. Its portrait of a solid, prosperous farm provided a foil to the struggles the Ingalls family would face after leaving Wisconsin. An abiding tribute to her husband, it eased Wilder into that longer story, giving her breathing room before she took on her next volume, about Kansas and the Indians, the most important book she would ever write.

Indian Country

There was something wrong with the weather. The Wilders had seen it during their trip to South Dakota, when it was so hot and dry and dusty they had to pour water over their dog to keep him alive. But with good rains in the spring of 1933, everyone had taken it for merely a hot spell. No one realized what it was: the beginning of a decade-long drought that would touch off dust storms so dense they would suffocate people, kill children with "dust pneumonia," and decimate animals throughout the southern plains.

Across the high plains of Texas and the Oklahoma panhandle, southwest Kansas and northeast New Mexico, and on into Colorado, normal precipitation fell by 40, 50, and even 60 percent.[114] One Oklahoma county where the annual rainfall usually measured more than seventeen inches received only twelve in 1932 and less than nine in 1934.[115] Ten inches is a desert.

Scientists estimate that it took a thousand years for an inch of topsoil to accumulate on the arid high plains. It was the work of a moment to blow it away. Topsoil exposed by the disc plows turned to dust, and the dust began to eddy, roil, and lift on the wind. "Rolling dusters," they were called, or "black blizzards." There were fourteen of them in 1932. The year after that, thirty-eight. One of them lasted for twenty-four hours. Continental winds powered by the jet stream swept the plains, blowing soil eastward, out of Kansas and Oklahoma into Arkansas and Missouri. The humor was as black as the skies. "Great bargains in real estate," read a sign in a store window. "Bring your own container."[116]

The dusters began rolling into Missouri in 1933. That was the year of the rift between Wilder and her daughter, the year Rose Lane couldn't stop crying, the year Wilder paid off the Federal Farm loan and accepted 5 percent royalties for *Farmer Boy*. It was the year Wilder started working on what she called her "Indian Country" book, at a time when she felt so stretched for cash she was using the backs of letters and pages of her *Little House in the Big Woods* manuscript to begin the new novel. She had pleaded with Ida Louise Raymond to tell her if her books were still selling, "both as a matter of sinful pride and as a hope of addition to an all too small income."[117] Sitting in her daughter's Rock House, a monument to extravagance in a world despoiled by human folly, Wilder embarked on the book she had been waiting her whole life to write.

"Indian Country" was a true departure, celebrating a prelapsarian landscape, a prairie Eden. Her first two books were a hymn to agrarian domesticity and security: cows in the barn, pigs in the pen, and storerooms packed with meats, cheese, and pumpkins. Her third took flight from that safety, reveling in the ecstatic wonders of wilderness and wolves and Indians. In it, fears were transient, subsumed in awe.

Her drafts—three survive—demonstrate a painstaking working process. The first, heavily worked over with revisions and deletions, appears to be a fairly complete rough draft, although the manuscript is not contiguous, perhaps representing the remains of multiple versions.[118] Some pages were written on the reverse of Almanzo's 1909 oil requisition forms and fairy poems she was writing in San Francisco in 1915; some on draft pages from the previous two books. A few initial pages may even come from earlier in her writing career, possibly predating "Pioneer Girl." She also wrote on the backs of letters: messages from schoolchildren who had loved *Little House in the Big Woods* and wanted more, from creditors' committees writing about the Palmer & Co. bust, and from friends, magazine editors, and Raymond at Harper.

Writing and rewriting, she continued polishing, clarifying, adding dialogue and descriptive details. The second draft (missing a few pages) appears to be a fair copy, with extensive revisions from the first. Wilder neatly numbered its pages and provided chapter headings, such as "Prairie Fire," which would turn up in the finished book.[119] The third surviving draft is a partial version, covering roughly the last 30 percent of the book.

Decades later, the women's masking of their editorial relationship would lead to questions about Wilder's authorship. Lane's biographer, William Holtz, would credit all of the books to Lane, asserting that Wilder had no recollection of the events described in her Kansas novel, which was based, he said, "on her father's tales of a time before her memory."[120] But Wilder's drafts demonstrate that nothing could be farther from the truth. The manuscripts exhibit not only her powers of recollection, but her unique ability to transform the raw material of her past into a work of art.

The Dust Bowl was an unspoken presence hovering behind the writing. At the very moment that a maelstrom of dust was blowing across the country, Wilder was summoning a vision of how beautiful the prairies once were. Here and in volumes to come, she would invariably stress that untouched grasslands were sweet and clean, as if the land itself, before the plow, breathed the essence of purity. In her original draft, she described Mary and Laura playing on the prairie, picking wildflowers and trying to catch the elusive picket-pin gophers—so called because they stood up like tethering stakes driven into the ground—then lying down on the grass in the shade of the wagon:

> They watched the clouds in the sky and the wind blowing the grass over the prairie and were happy as they could be, though they didn't know just why. Perhaps it was because the world was so big and everything was so sweet. The very wind smelled good . . . never before had they camped in such a wild beautiful place as this.[121]

As in the first two books, descriptions of process—building a log cabin, crafting a door latch, digging a well—still played a significant role. But rather than emphasizing the family's safety, as Pa's careful gun-cleaning and bullet-making had done in *Big Woods*, the narrative from its first drafts brought difficulties and hazards to the fore. Ma's foot was crushed by a log; Pa was overcome by gases in the well; the door latch failed to keep Indians from walking right in. The making of this little house served a different narrative function, capturing her parents' skills at coping with hazards while revealing their vulnerabilities.

The tension between the ideal of frontier self-determination and

Wilder's captivated preoccupation with anarchic wolves and Indians would never be reconciled, making this the strangest, the most unnerving, original, and profound of all her books. The little house was porous. Malaria entered. Buffalo wolves, the gray wolves of the plains, surrounded Pa on the prairie, then circled the house, howling in the moonlight, terrifying and beautiful. Laura heard them through the chinks in the wall, and Pa held her up to the hole cut for a window, the better to admire them. Prairie fires swept past, and Indians came and went as they pleased, demanding food, filling the house with the smell of skunk skins, commandeering an age-old Indian trail that ran past the cabin.

Indians occupied far more real estate in Wilder's original manuscripts than in the published book, and her identification with them was striking. A pivotal chapter in her first draft described the birth of "Baby Carrie" in high summer, when her father's face was tanned dark brown. "We'll all be Indians together," he told Mary and Laura, drawing them away for a day's outing at an abandoned Indian camp, where they collected colored beads from the ashes of old campfires.[122] Back at home, their mother was in labor, tended by a neighbor, Mrs. Scott, who said, "This sun and wind would make anyone look like an Indian."[123]

Pa and the girls returned to find their mother in bed, and she pulled back the blanket to show them the infant in the crook of her arm. Laura was "fascinated" that the baby's face was "so red and its hair so black."[124] It reminded her of the American children's folk rhyme: "'One little Indian, two little Indians, three little Indian'—'Girls,' Ma finished for her."[125] The family celebrated, Carrie's sisters bestowing upon her their string of Indian beads. With their brown skin and red baby, the family had become native.

In editing, the chapter would be significantly altered. Having appeared in Wilder's first volume, Baby Carrie could not be born in the third. Those changes were a pity. In many ways, the original manuscripts of what would become *Little House on the Prairie* exceed, in raw power and thematic complexity, the finished book.

In later scenes in her first draft, Wilder described the Indians' return to their encampments. When a tall Indian rode by, Laura announced, "I like him . . . his feathers are so pretty."[126] Her admiration, fascination, and yearning led to a climactic final scene. The Indians had spent

nights "screaming" in war council, terrifying the family with their cries
as "wild tribes from the south and west wanted to massacre all the
white settlers."[127] The councils at an end, the Indians rode away, right
past the cabin, and Laura—counting off the colors of their ponies the
way she counted the colors of their beads—stared into the bright black
eyes of an Indian papoose and pleaded with her father, "I want it! Pa,
get me that Indian baby!"[128] In her second draft, Wilder emphasized
her desire with a parenthetical remark, addressed to herself or her
daughter. Encircled in pencil, indicating it was not to be included in the
final copy, it read: "and I've never wanted anything so badly since."[129]

That astonishing statement echoed what she had written in her
diary forty years earlier, expressing a fierce attachment to the landscape that had nothing to do with its farming potential: "If I had been
the Indians I would have scalped more white folks before I ever would
have left it."[130] The wilderness was inherently worth possessing and
protecting. Yet every civilizing impulse described in "Indian Country"
would have destroyed the very qualities that made it desirable. The
genius of the book lay in that tension between its ostensible pioneer
subject—celebrating a destiny made manifest in claiming virgin land,
building a cabin and barn, clearing fields, and establishing a farm—
and its unmistakable appetite for the very opposite.

At the same time, Wilder's treatment of Indians, for all of her admiration for them, had undeniably reductive and racist elements. The
portrait of the Osage did not reflect the desperation of their position
with accuracy or sensitivity. Instead, her depiction of them invoked
stereotypes, and repeated three times a slur that became popular after
the Minnesota massacre: "The only good Indian is a dead Indian."[131]
Eager to invoke the dread and terror associated with the phrase, Wilder
seemed at the same time determined to distance herself from its
condemnation, attributing it to a neighbor. Meanwhile, Pa praised an
Indian chief with a casual backhanded compliment, saying he was "no
common trash." She did not notice the implication.

Wilder was not a historian. Instead, her novels would be created
from a complex tangle of subjective sources: family lore and letters,
old hymnals and songbooks, treasured artifacts of her youth, and her
own recollections. Her depiction of the West was drawn less from

newspapers or encyclopedias than from her inner life. It was a work of pure folk art.

Yet she wanted to get things right. In the first draft, she left blank spaces when she couldn't remember the color of the ground squirrels' stripes, or the name of the Indian chief her father had met. Beginning in the spring of 1933, Wilder and Lane wrote a series of letters to librarians and historical societies in Kansas and Oklahoma, trying to ascertain who the chief might have been, but their queries were hampered by Wilder's indistinct recollections. She believed that her father had built on land forty miles south of Independence, Kansas, a distance that would have placed them in Oklahoma Territory, then known as Indian Territory. It was a misunderstanding that may have arisen from hearing her parents use the term. In fact, Charles Ingalls had built on land fourteen miles from the town, in territory that belonged to the Indians, but was not Indian Territory proper.

The confusion could easily have been cleared up had Wilder consulted her sister Carrie on her birthplace. Surely Carrie knew that she had been born in Montgomery County, Kansas, a fact inscribed by Caroline Ingalls in the family Bible. Instead, Wilder chose to rely on her memory. As for the Indian chief, she accepted the word of R. B. Selvidge, son of a noted Oklahoma pioneer. In reply to her query, Selvidge wrote that "the chief of the Osages at that time was Le-Soldat-du-Chene. This man was very friendly to the white people."[132] A chief named Le Soldat du Chêne had been active in the region decades earlier, but no one by that name was known in 1870.[133] The research was far from rigorous.

In her first draft, Wilder did make one notable deviation from the practice of relying on her memory: she tried to write the story of the Bloody Benders into her family history, with lines saying that her father had taken their cow and calf to sell "at a place half way to Independence, the only house on the way there."[134] Pa then remarked that he found "something queer about that place. They seemed in a mighty hurry to get rid of me." He wondered why they were planting a garden past planting time. Wilder's attempt at the Benders was far more tentative than Lane's earlier effort, and she must have deemed it unconvincing, inappropriate, or in bad taste. She deleted the whole thing.[135]

On the other hand, the resentment of the federal government expressed in Wilder's Dust Bowl travel journal did work its way into the narrative. The Ingallses' expulsion from their Kansas paradise was dramatized in her initial draft by Pa cursing "those durned politicians at Washington" who had led him on, making him believe the land was free for the taking, then sending "soldiers from Fort Gibson to move all settlers off Indian lands in the territory."[136] In that version, he was intemperate, denouncing the government as "worse than the Indians." Ma lamented "a whole year gone" while Pa comforted her, saying, "What's a year anyway! We have all the time there is."[137] In reality, the family had lost—and would lose—much more than just a year, but shifting the blame to the government decisively removed it from Charles Ingalls's shoulders.

Wilder's early drafts of "Indian Country" wove music more and more into the story, with Pa's fiddle playing elevated beyond the rollicking fun and patriotic fervor of the first book. It was more emotional now, a wilder strain, connecting the family to the prairie. For the first time, the words to an entire song appeared: "The Blue Juniata," about an Indian maid who used to wander along the Juniata River. Wilder had found it inscribed in her father's hand in a book made by her mother. Asked where the voice of Alfarata went when it was "borne away" by the years, Ma said, "Oh I suppose she died . . . or went west. That is what they do with Indians, send them west and west and west." To which Laura replied, "But the pretty river stayed . . . Didn't it Ma?"[138]

The scene that closes the house-building chapter finds the family seated under an evening sky as Pa passes a melody back and forth with a nightingale in a tree. Wilder's first draft captured the essence of the moment:

> The nightingale sang on and on. The cool wind moved over the prairie and the nightingale's song was round and clear above the grasses whispering.
>
>   At last the bird was silent. Laura and Mary had not gone to sleep, but they were very quiet. Pa and Ma sat motionless and still. The sky was like a great bowl of soft light overturned on the flat, black land.
>
>   Then Pa lifted his fiddle settled it against his shoulder and touched

the strings softly with the bow. A few liquid notes fell like bright drops of water into the silence, a hesitating, questioning call. A pause and Pa began to play the nightingale's song.

The nightingale answered him, the nightingale began to sing again. It was singing with Pa's fiddle. When the strings were silent the bird went on singing. When the bird paused Pa called to it with his fiddle and it sang again.

The nightingale and the violin were talking to each other in the cool night under the moon.[139]

Another solitary bird appears in the final chapter, as the family packs up to leave the territory. The haunting image of their empty house standing alone on the prairie was underlined by the notes of a mockingbird, singing early in the morning. It was as if Wilder's quintessential American family were abandoning the dream of living at one with nature. They had no other choice. The vision of the prairie she had created was of a wilderness so inviolate no house could tame it.

LANE, as low as she'd ever been in the wake of Bunting's death, deeply resented having to work on *Farmer Boy*. Nineteen thirty-three was one of the worst years of her life. But although she admitted being "sick in my mind," she could not stop working.[140] She began planning a grandiose project, a series of ten novels to rival her mother's. Hers would cover the entire continent, encompassing all classes, from farmers to financiers.

She sketched a broad outline in a notebook, labeling pages with the names of character types who would populate it—clerk, banker, petit bourgeois. Most were left blank. Her sketch of the pioneer was hostile, at odds with the heroic image she had painted in *Hurricane*. The type was irresponsible, "of obscure or debased birth," with little "moral stamina," unable to rise from the lowly, lawless masses. She cast the heroic westward journey as escapism, or running away from debts. She credited settlers only with rendering American life "wholly chaotic."[141] Her early life certainly had been, and her resentment of that was beginning to surface.

That year, she would begin the process, first desultorily and then in earnest, of pulling away from Rocky Ridge for good. Her mother had told her that she was free to leave, but even so she was floundering, unable to decide where to go or what to do.[142] "I <u>know</u> all the time now that I am dying and that it makes no difference at all to anybody," she wrote.[143] As her flowers and vegetables turned to husks, she noted the violent weather that spring, extreme heat, tornadoes, and dust storms. She pledged that "next year I'll get away from here or kill myself."[144]

She spoke to her mother by phone every evening from the old farmhouse, "usually about American politics." She remarked listlessly that whenever Wilder came to see her she seemed eager to get away, never realizing that her own contempt may well have been obvious and unpleasant. Between late July and September, Lane failed to write in her journal, later saying that she had been confined to bed, weeping for days on end, while Catherine Brody and Corinne Murray ran the household.[145]

Then, at the end of September 1933, a chance encounter with a teenage boy would once again change her life. On a cold, rainy day, John Turner, fourteen years old, appeared on the back porch of Rocky Ridge, asking if he could have something to eat. He was around the same age as Rexh Meta when Lane first encountered him.

Tramps were routinely passing the farmhouse door. Its trees had been marked in hobo shorthand to indicate that the household had dogs and was "no good" for handouts.[146] But something about the boy's vulnerability—an air of world-weariness, a pathetic racking cough, and his "beautifully shaped" head—spoke to Lane, and she hired him for fifteen cents an hour to weed the flower beds, letting him sleep in the garage.[147] Before long he was living in the house, dressed in clothes Lane ordered from Montgomery Ward, attending school, playing on the basketball team, and spinning outrageous stories about his previous life, all of which turned out to be lies.

He said he was from Tulsa, describing parents dead of tuberculosis, a run-in with police in El Paso, and a filling station robbery gone bad, weaving tales as if he were himself a fiction writer. He truly was an orphan, but his actual origins were more mundane. Weeks later, Lane would learn that he had been living with an older brother, Al, and an uncle on a dirt-poor farm outside Ava, the next town over from Mansfield. In time, Lane would reluctantly invite Al to join her ragtag family at Rocky Ridge, but only to please John. Al was a "good boy," she thought, but dull. She told a friend she wouldn't "trade John for twenty of him."[148]

From the beginning, her relationship with John Turner was disturbingly intense. Only a few months after they met, she referred to it as "this mother-&-son love affair," admitting that she had an "infatuation for the youngster."[149] Soon she was borrowing more money, planning to renovate the farmhouse, even engaging the architect who had built the Rock House to draw up plans. She threw parties for local teens, and bought John a guitar, a basketball jacket, dance records, radio parts. Eventually, she built the boys their own little house, a clubhouse where they could play the phonograph and invite their friends over. Before long, dance parties were being held regularly, jitterbugging on Friday or Saturday nights. Lane began teaching French to the teenagers, regaling them with tales of how the king of Albania had proposed to her.

Her mother was incensed. According to Lane, Wilder threw "fit after fit after fit," convinced that the boy was trouble, perhaps part of a gang that would "cut our throats."[150] Wilder later took pains to praise the Turner boys, but their sometimes unsupervised presence at the farmhouse inevitably caused friction. Their antics fueled rumors in town about the goings-on, reflecting widespread social disapproval of Lane—a divorced woman living on her own, smoking and dancing with a coterie of unrelated teenage boys. Years later, townspeople would describe Wilder as dignified and well dressed, but spoke harshly of her daughter as "brash" and "a black sheep."[151] In an allusion to loose morals, one would say, "Rose didn't seem that refined."[152] Well aware of her local reputation, Lane rolled her eyes at narrow-minded Mansfield, telling an eastern friend about a matron who confronted her at the Embroidery Club about the number of sheets—linen sheets at that—Rocky Ridge was sending out to be washed. "Who ever heard of changing beds every other day?" Lane wrote, adding, "Anyone can guess that that means—(whisper)—*men*."[153]

Tongues also wagged among the womenfolk when Lane pushed her

way into the decidedly masculine activity of foxhunting, an Ozark tradition that involved men sending their hounds after foxes while they
sat out in the hills past midnight, drinking moonshine and telling tall
tales. Thinking it good material, Lane invited herself along and then
lampooned the hillbillies and their "dawgs" in rollicking accounts to
her friends, in full dialect.[154] Keen for her company, the men attached
a mouthpiece to one of the traditional carved-horn bugles, to make it
easier for her to call the pack in. Meanwhile, their wives sat at home,
fuming about the nerve of the strumpet. To this day, ladies in Mansfield remember it, noting that "Rose was not well-liked here."[155] Into
the 1970s, when her name was mentioned at the Athenian Club, one
member would sit up straight and deliver herself of her opinion: "Rose
was quite the Bohemian."[156]

Lane conducted herself with cool composure despite her notoriety.
In the spring of 1934, she sashayed into N. J. Craig's office to sound
him out about another loan, displaying "all the secure confidence of a
valued, an important client."[157] Her bravado did not carry the day this
time, however, and Craig sidestepped the request, gently saying that he
could barely lend to a tenth of his applicants, even considering just
those with unentailed property and no debt. Lane then appealed to
Fremont Older, who mailed her a check.

In May, despite tooth pain and troubles with her eyesight, Lane
spent days revising her mother's book, which was now being called
"High Prairie." With no surviving draft revisions in Lane's hand, it is
difficult to measure her influence, but echoes of Willa Cather's great
1918 novel of the high prairie offer some clues. *My Ántonia* refers to
"a little town on the prairie," and in Wilder's series some phrases and
images from the novel would recur: straw stacks and Negro minstrel
troupes, "weevily wheat" and women who work alongside men to bring
in the harvest.[158] Cather described the weathered face of a laborer as
"brown as an Indian's," a phrase that appears memorably in the Little
House books, beginning with *Little House on the Prairie*.[159] Both
works feature lyrical encomiums to golden cornfields and America's
farmers. Doubtless some of the overlap arose from common themes
and familiarity with the idiom of the time, but we do know that Lane

knew Cather's writing. She had spoken of Cather during the 1920s, comparing her own work to that of the Nebraska writer and finding it wanting.[160]

The drought continued, unleashing bad dust storms. Temperatures soared so high that month, Lane said, that they eventually topped 135 degrees, an implausible number reflecting either her exaggeration or a faulty instrument.[161] She finished going over Wilder's manuscript and typed a clean copy by the end of June, "all but corrections," her own or her mother's.[162] The only surviving typescript, a carbon, carries a single substantive revision in Wilder's hand. At the end of the critical chapter "Indians Ride Away," she added a final sentence to describe Laura's last look at the vanishing tribe: "She seemed still to see waving feathers and black eyes and to hear the sound of ponies' feet"—just how it reads in the published book.[163]

The manuscript went off to Harper, apparently without indication of whatever editorial role Lane had played. This had become their established practice. On July 13, Wilder heard back from Ida Louise Raymond, who liked it "_very much_ indeed" but wondered whether it had enough "variety of detail" for grade-school children.[164] Still finding her way after the departure of Virginia Kirkus, Raymond then sent it to another reader, a Midwest librarian whose opinion she valued. A few weeks later, she reported that the librarian had greatly enjoyed the book and preferred, among the titles suggested, "Little House on the Prairie."[165] Raymond closed by saying that she considered the book complete, urging Wilder to let the next one "shape itself" in her mind.

By July 11, the county was on its twenty-fourth day of temperatures over one hundred. It was the worst drought in recorded history, Lane noted, worse even than 1931.[166] Two days later, still sweltering, she argued with John Turner and told him to get out of the house, only to change her mind and ask him to stay. At the end of the month, with unexpected _Hurricane_ royalties, Lane fled the Missouri heat for a vacation, taking John to Florida, where she wrote ecstatically of swimming naked in the Gulf of Mexico. John, she said, declined to "go nudist."[167]

Fire—/ Leaving

Sometime in the early to mid-1930s, Wilder wrote another manuscript, one she chose not to revise or publish during her lifetime.[168] On a fresh Fifty-Fifty tablet from the Springfield Grocer Company, she wrote "The First Three Years" at the top of the first page. Beneath, she scrawled an outline of seasons and events in her early married life. Only a few were happy, "Rose in June, born in Dec." among them. The rest tallied distressing, even disastrous, occasions, and the terseness suggested increasing discomfort with the subject matter. "Diptheria" began one line, with only a series of dashes following. The last words on the page were "Fire—" and "Leaving."[169]

Gamely, she persevered. For the second time she wrote about her courtship, with every appearance of enjoying it immensely. "The stars hung luminous and low over the prairie," the scene opened, as "a light buggy drawn by a team of quick stepping dark horses passed swiftly over the road which was only a dim trace across the grass lands."[170] The young couple borne by the buggy were reflected in the waters of Silver Lake and wrapped in the dewy fragrance of "the wild prairie roses that grew in masses beside the way."

It was one of the most romantic passages she ever wrote, more sensuous and lyrical than the matter-of-fact "Pioneer Girl" memoir. She invoked the roses again and again, in the words of a folk song and in her recollection of the evening when she and her beloved were betrothed. "For it was June," she wrote, "the roses were in bloom over the prairie lands and lovers were abroad in the still, sweet evenings, which were so quiet after the winds had hushed at sunset." She was returning to what roses had originally meant in her life: a song, a prairie covered in wildflowers, and falling in love.

Then she put a series of x's under that description and began afresh, recounting Laura and Almanzo's first serious conversation as an engaged couple. It was a negotiation, in which Laura expressed skepticism about the economics of farming. "I've been thinking," she said. "I don't want to marry a farmer. I have always said I never would. I wish you would do something else." When Almanzo asked why she felt that way, she replied:

Because a farm is such a hard place for a woman. There are so many chores for her to do, and harvest help and threshers to cook for. Besides a farmer never has any money. He can never make any because the people in towns tell him what they will pay for what he has to sell and then they charge him what they please for what he has to buy. It is not fair. . . . I don't always want to be poor and work hard while the people in town take it easy and make money off us.[171]

Almanzo tried to laugh it off, anachronistically invoking a twentieth-century saying—"Everything is evened up in this world. The rich have their ice in the summer but the poor get theirs in the winter"—to argue that farmers were enviable because they were independent.[172] Preparing the reader for economic struggles to come, the dialogue set the stage for the harsh reality: the brief honeymoon followed by crop failures, crushing debt, illness, disability, the death of their infant son, and the burning down of their house.

Throughout the manuscript, Almanzo was portrayed with affection but exasperation as a bit of a spendthrift, unconcerned about going deeply into debt and careless with his health. Laura was the anxious spouse, burdened with silent worries over money and so staggered by her duties that she allowed Rose to wander repeatedly into danger, foreshadowing the final, catastrophic fire.

Decades after the fact, Wilder seemed still haunted by trying to make sense of it all, assigning significant blame for their economic morass to her husband. Yet she also, tentatively, criticized herself. In the climactic scene of the fire, Wilder placed Rose nowhere near the stove, saying merely that she herself had lit a fire and left the kitchen, closing the door. Minutes later, she reopened it to find the room ablaze. There was no suggestion that Rose had been responsible.

As was her custom, she addressed several asides in the manuscript to Lane as her editor, including a historical note about railroads. Having perhaps just finished *Little House on the Prairie*, with so much in it about wolves and Indians, she seemed at pains to work them into this manuscript, and admitted that she had fictionalized two episodes. One concerned a pack of wolves prowling around their sheep; the second, an incident when several Indians entered the barn while Laura was alone. The wolves did howl, she acknowledged, but she did not in fact bravely venture out to save the flock. "All true," she wrote, "except that I heard the last howl just before I went out and did not go but why spoil a good story for truth's sake."[173] As for the Indians, in the fictional scene she pluckily confronted them, even slapping one who laid a hand on her. "This is true but happened to a friend of mine," she told Lane.[174]

Lane never mentioned the work in her journals or notebooks. Her only reference to it came in response to a query of her mother's several years later, in 1937. But in the meantime, Lane had published the short story "Long Skirts," with its bitter scene between the girl Ernestine and her mother, expanded for the 1935 publication of *Old Home Town*.[175] In the book version, the scene included a telling line. As Ernestine raged at her mother, accusing her of making her miserable all her life—the same rhetoric Lane employed about her mother in her journal—the narrator said, "Something in me broke; I felt myself go all to pieces."[176] It echoed a heartfelt line in her mother's manuscript, the one describing Laura's horror and despair as she sank to the ground outside their burning house: "Something in her seemed to break."

Who wrote it first? Who was borrowing from whom? Such were the questions that roiled the women after the publication of *Let the Hurricane Roar* and lay uneasily between them as Lane prepared to leave Rocky Ridge Farm for good. For the first time since Wilder had begun writing her children's series, they would be forced out of their long-established routine of editorial conferences masked as teas and social visits. As they took up their consultations by mail, putting all their queries, complaints, and arguments down on paper, the question of how much the daughter would be allowed to influence the mother's work—and how much she could borrow for her own—assumed new urgency.

BY 1935, Rose Wilder Lane, now forty-eight, was beginning to recognize that her once-considerable energies were on the wane. While George Bye was still regularly selling her stories to the *Saturday Evening Post*, her productivity plummeted during the worst of her illness. After her 1933 success with *Hurricane*, she published only three short stories the following year.[177]

Compared to her friends and peers, who were making landmark strides, her career was lagging. In 1932, Dorothy Thompson had published *I Saw Hitler*, based on interviews conducted in Munich. Her subsequent assessment of him in *Harper's* as a "formless, almost faceless man . . . whose framework seems cartilaginous, without bones . . . inconsequent and voluble, ill-poised and insecure . . . the very prototype of the little man" so outraged its subject that in 1934 she became the first foreign reporter to be expelled from Germany. Lane had hailed Hitler privately, the previous year, as "a resurrection of the German people," much as Mussolini was for the Italians.[178]

Thompson was criticized for failing to predict the dictator's ruthless consolidation of power, but she was nonetheless on the cusp of becoming one of the most respected voices in American journalism. In 1936 she began writing "On the Record," a column that appeared three times a week in the *New York Herald Tribune* and in syndication in more than 150 other newspapers, reaching some ten million readers. The same year, hired by NBC, she took to the airwaves as a national radio correspondent and commentator.

Another friend of Lane's was also becoming a household word. Isabel Mary Bowler Paterson, novelist and journalist, was Lane's doppelgänger. Born the same year, in 1886, Paterson grew up on the western prairies and forests of Alberta, Canada, on the Upper Peninsula of Michigan, and in Utah, in a family so poor they were reduced to living in tents.[179] As a child she learned how to ride, hop a freight train, repair a log cabin, cook bear meat, and make butter and her own clothes.[180] As an adult, she remained deeply influenced by her self-reliant pioneer past. An autodidact, she began working at eighteen as a stenographer and bookkeeper, eventually writing for local papers in Washington state and British Columbia. Like Lane, she acquired and quickly shed a faceless husband. By 1917–1918 she was in San Francisco, where the two women likely met.[181] In 1916 she began writing fiction set in the American West, then branched out into historical novels set in Spain and Elizabethan England, producing at least two bestsellers (*The Singing Season* and *Never Ask the End*) during the 1920s and 1930s.

But it was as a regular columnist for the *New York Herald Tribune* that Paterson made a name as a political commentator. For a quarter of a century, beginning in 1924, she wrote the weekly "Turns with a Bookworm" for the *Tribune*, where she praised the best writing of her day—Cather, Ford Madox Ford, Virginia Woolf, and William Carlos Williams—and skewered the pretentious, singling out Gertrude Stein for particular disdain. But literature was not her only concern. As a conservative immersed in the study of social classes, she derided Herbert Hoover as "Fat Boy" and devoted significant space to discussing economics and the evolution of property ownership and financial systems. One of her acolytes was a young Ayn Rand, who described herself as "sitting at the master's feet" on evenings when the column appeared, drinking in Paterson's exegeses.[182] Another friend and follower was Rose Wilder Lane, who subscribed to the *Tribune* at Rocky Ridge.[183]

In December 1934, Lane wrote to "I.M.P.," as Paterson signed herself, to promote her mother's forthcoming book: *Little House on the Prairie* was slated for publication the following September. In a previous piece, Paterson had referred to the Bloody Benders, offhandedly saying their murders were committed in a tent. Lane leapt to put her right, and Paterson obligingly reprinted her remarks:

> "I beg your pardon," [Lane] says, "the Bender family did not commit their murders in a tent. . . . Kate Bender lived in an ordinary house of the times, midway between Independence, Kan., and my grandfather's log cabin on the Verdigris in Indian territory. My grandfather often stopped there, but though he had a good team, a wagon and (on the return trip) a load of supplies amply justifying his murder, he never could afford to buy a meal from the Benders, but frugally ate by his own campfire. The Bender house, completely conventional, had a canvas curtain across the middle, dividing sleeping and living quarters. A bench stood against this curtain, and a table before the bench. Prosperous travelers who could afford to pay for Kate Bender's good home cooking sat on the bench to eat it. . . . My grandfather was one of the volunteer posse that pursued the fleeing Benders. Darkly, he said little about what happened. . . . The ultimate fate of the Bender family is usually reported as shrouded in mystery. . . . But there really was no tent. Kate Bender was the dominant force in that family, and was there ever a woman who would live in a tent if she could help it?"[184]

Claiming to set the record straight, Lane was herself writing fiction, based on the sensational reporting she may first have encountered in Kansas City decades earlier. Having lied in the name of fact-checking, Lane was not satisfied to leave it there. She plugged her mother's book while she was at it:

> This letter was begun as a disinterested service to pure truth; it strikes me suddenly . . . that I am wasting a publicity note. My mother's new juvenile will not be out till next year. It is all about that log cabin on the Verdigris, and the publicity angle would be that it does NOT contain any reference to the Benders. She wouldn't put that in—too gory for her readers of tender age, though I told her they'd love it.[185]

As far as Lane's "disinterested service to pure truth" is concerned, Charlie Chaplin and Charmian London knew all about it. But Lane's offhand comment—"she wouldn't put that in"—suggests that for all of her mother's willingness to fictionalize, there was a line Wilder was unwilling to cross. In coming years, that hesitation would provoke a battle between them over the question of *how* fictionalizing was to be done, and how much of it was permissible.

As the women embarked on writing and editing drafts of the next book, covering the same events Lane had appropriated for *Let the Hurricane Roar*, an eerie visitation from the past arrived to reanimate Wilder's visceral memories of a dark time. The grasshoppers were back.

Chapter 11

Dusty Old Dust

We'll Take the Scarcity and Like It

Nineteen thirty-four saw the worst drought in a thousand years of North American history.[1] Forty-six of the forty-eight states were affected, twenty-seven of them at the most severe levels. The worst of it was in the west. On U.S. government maps, a dark red splotch, denoting "extreme drought," covered eastern Oregon, California, northeastern New Mexico, and virtually the whole of Idaho, Nevada, Colorado, Wyoming, Kansas, Nebraska, the Dakotas, Minnesota, Iowa, and Missouri.[2]

On May 9, a terrific windstorm whipped by high heat swept vast amounts of Great Plains topsoil into the atmosphere and propelled it across the country. Darkness fell as twelve million pounds of it was deposited on Chicago. Over the next two days, everyone in the East got a gritty taste of western distress, as the dust blew from Detroit to Buffalo and beyond. In New York City it obscured the view of the Statue of Liberty; in Washington it drifted down onto the White House. Dirty clouds were seen by mariners hundreds of miles out on the open ocean.

Dust was not the only thing falling from the sky. As with severe droughts of previous years—including the arid 1875, when Charles

Ingalls lost his Plum Creek crops to locusts—the Dust Bowl triggered an invasion of insects. There were record outbreaks of chinch bugs, tiny grass-eating insects that had readily adapted to eating wheat, and localized outbreaks of grasshoppers, who arrived to finish off dried-up stands of corn, alfalfa, and oats. The swarming Rocky Mountain locust was long gone, but hordes of "hoppers" filled the ecological gap left behind. Once again, farmers watched helplessly as insects ate the wooden handles off hoes. Some were struck in the face by the big horny creatures as they drove tractors across the land.

The sheer misery of that time for those living in the worst-affected areas can scarcely be imagined. Intense heat sparked static electricity that made it dangerous to drive, and cars routinely dragged chains to ground them. Men stopped shaking hands. People feared being buried alive in "black blizzards," coughing black phlegm. Conditions were particularly hard on children and the elderly. Caught in a dust storm, a seven-year-old Kansas boy suffocated in a drift.[3] Other children, weakened by malnutrition, died of "dust disease" or "dust pneumonia" similar to silicosis suffered by miners, their lungs overwhelmed.[4]

The conditions were equally horrific for livestock and wild animals. Their forage desiccated, cattle were driven to eat the leaves off trees, and were said to come running if they heard the ringing of an ax.[5] They smothered in dust storms, nostrils packed with dirt. Waves of coyotes and jackrabbits ran amok across the landscape, and towns organized "rabbit drives," where men and boys chased hundreds or thousands of the screaming creatures against fences and bludgeoned them with clubs.[6]

Historian Donald Worster, who interviewed scores of survivors, recorded that nearly all of them had what he called an icebox story, in which they discovered in disbelief that the inside of sealed iceboxes had been sifted over with dust.[7] More ominous was finding fine dust covering a baby's pillow. Women spoke of setting the table by placing plates and glasses upside down to keep them clean, to little avail. There was no help for it: people living through the Dust Bowl inevitably ate dirt.

The world was ending, or so it seemed. If there was any doubt, Black Sunday wiped it out. On April 14, 1935, sixty-mile-per-hour winds in the Oklahoma panhandle whipped up mile-high walls of dust, so massive they were compared to tornadoes lying on their sides. They blotted out the sun, and those caught outside could not see their hands in front of their faces. People cowered indoors, bidding each other farewell.

The next day, an Associated Press reporter, Robert Geiger, gave the catastrophe its lasting name, rechristening the Great Plains as "the dust bowl."[8] A twenty-two-year-old street busker named Woody Guthrie, living in Pampa, Texas, believed as the black wall bore down that he was about to die. He caught the common refrain and wrote it into a song, "Dusty Old Dust," bidding farewell to all he knew. (It would later be recorded as "So Long, It's Been Good to Know You.") It became the anthem for those forced to flee the arid devastation of the plains.

The apocalyptic nature of the times caused widespread self-recrimination and depression. Newspaper editors invoked Pompeii, and the Biblical scale of the plague upon the land was inevitably interpreted as divine wrath.[9] Citing the greed of suitcase farmers, one newspaper quoted Ezekiel 22:13, in which God reached out to smite man's "dishonest gain." Another survivor recalled "lots of talk that God was tormenting us because they plowed up that good sod."[10]

But the Dust Bowl was no act of god or freak accident of nature. It was one of the worst man-made ecological disasters of all time. Farmers had done this, and they had done it to themselves. It was small farmers, in particular, who were responsible, since they were more likely to cultivate intensively and less likely to employ any form of crop rotation or erosion control.[11] As scholars have noted, settlers had boasted of their prowess in dominating the landscape, bragging of "'busting' and 'breaking' the land."[12] Well, now it was broken.

Erosion transformed the southern plains into a desert, peeling off and whisking away two to five inches of topsoil from more than twenty-three million acres.[13] In 1935, some 850 million tons of topsoil blew away.[14] Much of it was blowing straight into Missouri; Lane wrote that "Kansas and Oklahoma dust is so thick in the Ozarks . . . that the sun looks like the moon."[15] Sixty-five percent of the Great Plains, once "so wide and sweet and clean," in Wilder's words, were damaged.[16]

In response, soil scientists and ecologists would aid the federal government in developing a host of sophisticated conservation and reclamation measures, based on the most advanced research of the day.

Experts planned on taking the most marginal land out of production and returning it to grassland, terracing and contouring to reduce erosion, and planting shelter belts. Virtually all the plans, however, relied on fundamentally changing the way farmers thought about their land and their lifestyle. Men and women hitched to the plow of productivity all their lives were being asked to step out of harness and admit the limitations of nature, a shift that felt not only counterintuitive but psychically impossible, even reprehensible. They were being asked to grow not more, but less.[17]

American farmers had long been producing a surfeit of wheat, corn, oats, cattle, pigs, and sheep. At the same time, dozens of other countries were also exporting grain. To make matters worse, the U.S. birth rate during the 1930s was in decline. Somebody had to turn off the spigot.

The Roosevelt administration, passing a raft of New Deal bills in its first hundred days, prided itself on the fact that many of the agricultural programs were crafted by an Iowa farmer. Henry Wallace, FDR's secretary of agriculture, saw his production control plans as a rational response to the national emergency posed by mass foreclosures, low prices, and the desperate need of Dust Bowl–stricken farmers. (Some of them, on the brink of starvation, had resorted to eating pickled tumbleweeds, said to be high in iron.)[18] But in practice, farmers often found his policies as traumatic as the conditions they meant to address.

Using up commodities was one thing, but plans calling for the wholesale disposal of livestock proved radically unpopular, evoking grotesque images that would haunt Wallace for the rest of his tenure and eventually be immortalized in John Steinbeck's *The Grapes of Wrath*.[19] First, over the summer of 1933, farmers were paid $120 million to demolish a quarter of the country's bumper cotton crop, virtually worthless due to overproduction. Then, in September, under orders from the Agricultural Adjustment Administration, two hundred thousand pregnant sows and six million piglets—defined as pigs under a hundred pounds—were slaughtered to kick off price stabilization. Wallace declared that billions of pounds of meat would be distributed to the poor, but many of the piglets were too small to process at packing plants and were instead rendered into grease or fertilizer.[20] Rumor had it that thousands of animals had been dumped in rivers, and radio commentators excoriated the waste. A nation beset by hunger was outraged.

In a speech he delivered, the aggrieved Wallace quoted one of many angry letters he had received, reading a screed from one woman who wrote: "It just makes me sick all over when I think how the government has killed millions and millions of little pigs, and how that has raised pork prices until today we poor people cannot even look at a piece of bacon."[21] Calmly and in painstaking detail, Wallace tried to lay out the rationale, pointing out that the low hog prices of 1933 were "ruinous to farmers" and that government intervention had helped stabilize the market. But he also lapsed into sarcasm, suggested that critics who were so concerned about pig slaughter "perhaps . . . think that farmers should run a sort of old-folks home for hogs and keep them around indefinitely as barnyard pets."[22] The speech captured the breakdown in the relationship between federal bureaucrat and farmer, one that, decades later, has yet to heal.

Roosevelt himself took pains, in a 1935 radio address, to decouple homesteading and "free land" from the nostalgia and lofty expectations surrounding them for so long. "Today we can no longer escape into virgin territory," he said:

> We have been compelled by stark necessity to unlearn the too comfortable superstition that the American soil was mystically blessed with every kind of immunity to grave economic maladjustments, and that the American spirit of individualism—all alone and unhelped by the cooperative efforts of Government—could withstand and repel every form of economic disarrangement or crisis.[23]

To American farmers, who had nothing left but the dreams of their homesteading ancestors, these were fighting words. In response to outrage inspired by the killing of livestock, the Federal Surplus Relief Corporation was quickly organized to funnel commodities to the needy, salvaging everything from apples to pork. But the damage to the New Deal's reputation, particularly in rural areas, had been done.

The public relations disaster was only exacerbated by the creation in 1935 of yet more federal agencies. There was the Resettlement Administration, aimed at moving farmers off the most marginal and depleted land to planned, government-built cooperative communities. Roundly denounced as socialism by its congressional foes, the resettlement program was underfunded and affected relatively few, soon getting folded into another agency. Still, it spread alarm among farmers.[24]

Then there was the Drought Relief Service, designed to buy up cattle in the worst of the drought-stricken areas. Many of these animals were dying anyway, too starved to slaughter for meat. But the process of dealing with them was brutal. Government agents showed up in the worst-affected regions, paid a few dollars a head, then killed the cattle—sometimes beloved family dairy cows—in front of their owners, burning or burying the carcasses in ditches. The experience was so distressing that it lingered for decades in the minds of those who witnessed it. In Ken Burns's recent Dust Bowl documentary, a woman in New Mexico, who had been a child in the 1930s, breaks down weeping when she recalls her father asking permission to butcher his remaining calf for his family. The federal agents said no. One farmer summed up the general feeling: "The average person couldn't stand it."

Laura Ingalls Wilder couldn't stand it. She lamented the arrival of grasshoppers on her land but accepted it as divine retribution for the New Deal:

> The wild hoppers are here. They are eating up my tamarack, eating the bark and cutting off the tender tops with their feather leaves. We are doing what we can to kill them but what's the use fighting a judgement of God. We as a nation would insult Him by wantonly destroying his bounty. Now we'll take the scarcity and like it.[25]

When she wrote that letter to Lane, Wilder was deep into the composition of what would become her fourth volume, *On the Banks of Plum Creek*. Once again, she had taken a Fifty-Fifty tablet; on the cover, beside a line for "Name," she wrote "No One."[26] Then she had plunged in, beginning as Pa stopped the covered wagon near a dugout in the creek bank. If Lane had borrowed the place name for her own purposes in *Hurricane*, that wouldn't stop her mother. Wilder set about taking Plum Creek back.

Her grasshopper letter contained a hand-drawn map of the creek property, which Lane had never seen. It located the dugout on the northern bank, labeling the stable, the swimming hole, the high "table-land" above the banks, her father's fish trap, and the new house he built. For the first time, Wilder was putting down on paper ongoing editorial conversations with her daughter that—aside from brief marginal remarks on manuscripts—had previously taken place in person. "This was and is prairie country," she told Lane, who had been thinking about the gorge on Rocky Ridge as a model. "Get these hills and our gorge out of your mind," she said firmly. "The character of the place was altogether different."[27]

By this time, Lane had left Rocky Ridge for good. She had spent the first two months of 1935 there, writing in her diary in late February, "I can not stand this house, this sunk-in-muck way of living, any more. I must get out."[28] And she did, spending a couple of months in Springfield, then moving into the Tiger Hotel in Columbia, Missouri, where she would stay for much of the next year and a half. She had been commissioned to write the "Missouri" volume for a series of books about the states, and intended to do research at the university and the state historical society.

It was a good time for her to get out of town. *Old Home Town*, her collection of stories set in a barely disguised Mansfield, was to be published that fall, a month after *Little House on the Prairie*, and it got all of Mansfield talking. The town still remembers it. It caused a "huge uproar," says Kathy Short, a volunteer for the local historical society whose family ties to the region date back to before the Civil War.[29] Lane's stories of scandalous doings—girls getting jilted, a married woman running away with a traveling salesman, another woman quietly bumping off her aged husband—were transparently based on real people, just as *Hill-Billy* was clearly based on N. J. Craig. The map printed as a frontispiece might as well have been a scarlet letter pinned to the town square. "People knew exactly who she was talking about," Short says.

No record survives of Wilder's reaction to *Old Home Town*, but her daughter's removal to Columbia may well have been a relief. Although Lane was no longer prostrated by depression, she continued to be buffeted by moods, and she had grown so careless of her reputation and social expectations that Wilder may have felt pained by her presence.

Perhaps most remarkably, Lane was having an affair. During the summer of 1935, she drove off on a two-month trip with Garet Garrett, a twice-married, twice-divorced reporter for the *Saturday Evening Post*. For a three-part piece he was writing for the *Post*, he and Lane were scouting out Midwest farmers chafing under New Deal policies. (Garrett wrote the Wilders anonymously into one of the pieces set in Illinois, saying that he had met "a woman, seventy, who had helped her man clear the ground by taking herself one end of a cross-cut saw.")[30] Like Lane, Garrett had grown up among farmers and fancied himself an expert on American agricultural woes.

Former executive editor of the *New York Tribune* and a star reporter at the conservative *Post*, Garrett was notably eccentric. He had been shot three times at a speakeasy in New York City in 1930, damaging his vocal cords, and spoke afterward in a husky voice.[31] The shooting was rumored to be a romantic dispute, though Garrett believed it might have been a retaliation for his political views.

Whether Lane and Garrett became intimate on that trip or later is unclear, and keeping company might not have raised eyebrows in New York circles at the time. But Mansfield was full of strict Baptists, and the arrangement must have set tongues wagging. Gossips could hardly miss this salacious tidbit, written up in the *Mansfield Mirror*: "Mr. Garet Garrett . . . was in Mansfield over the week end, a guest at the beautiful country home of Rose Wilder Lane."[32] Lane told a friend at this time that her mother "does not much like my stuff," and that it made her "furious" to be the mother of a celebrity.[33] Wilder may have had other reasons to be furious, expressing concern to Lane about becoming "conspicuous" as a result of her daughter's reputation.[34]

The Missouri book, too, would have scandalized Mansfield, had it been published. Lane had never written expository nonfiction before; her biographies were all heavily fictionalized, and even *The Peaks of Shala*, the Albanian travelogue, was composed as a narrative, with fictional touches.[35] Her Missouri history turned out similarly subjective, beginning with a first-person account of the Wilders' 1894 journey, told from the perspective of her seven-year-old self. Taking perfunctory notice of key events on the state's timeline, from Daniel Boone to Mark Twain, Lane filled out the history with long, personal, anecdotal passages about a local Ozark fox hunt, basket supper, and "play-party," revisiting the style of her earlier hillbilly fare. Here, as in *Old Home Town*, she appeared to be writing about actual Mansfield folk, who may have had no idea they were starring in her prose; some names occur in both works.[36] Her portrayal of backwoods society, doubtless meant to supply local color, was nonetheless subtly patronizing. Yet she expected no one to notice, writing resentfully, "Nobody here reads anything of mine. They know vaguely that I rate somewhere . . . below Harold Bell Wright," a well-known author whose 1907 bestseller, *The Shepherd of the Hills*, was set in the Ozarks and drew from local lore.[37]

Judging by diary and journal entries, Lane never fully recovered from the depression she experienced at Rocky Ridge. Even as she moved away from the extreme suicidal thoughts she had so often during 1933 and 1934, she began to indulge in violent bouts of rage expressed toward political figures, especially Franklin D. Roosevelt. She had no compunction about sharing these screeds with those least likely to enjoy them, including George Bye, who was FDR's literary agent and admirer, and Virginia Brastow, an old friend. Brastow had gotten her start in journalism, as Lane had, from Fremont Older, who appointed her city editor of the *Bulletin* in 1900; her book about San Francisco, *The Fantastic City*, had been a bestseller in 1932.

Lane began haranguing Brastow in the mid-1930s in dispatches that would run on, single-spaced, for pages, calling Roosevelt a dictator and comparing him to Lenin.[38] In this, she was doubtless following Hoover's lead. Still smarting from his rough treatment during the election, Hoover marshaled conservatives behind him by comparing Roosevelt's New Deal agencies, many of them created by executive order, to fascist and communist bureaucracies, famously calling on Republicans to mount a "holy crusade" in defense of the freedom of the individual.[39]

Hoover's conviction that the president aspired to attain unprecedented powers during the emergency of the Great Depression received widespread exposure through the dozens of newspapers, magazines, and radio stations owned by William Randolph Hearst, which kept up a drumbeat against Communist infiltration. In Missouri and across the country, newspapers were full of editorials calling FDR a dictator, railing against the "alphabetical bureaus" and bemoaning the ballooning national debt.[40] Lane needed to look no farther than the pages of the *Mansfield Mirror* for the prevailing conservative view. There, the "Modern 'Liberal' " was lampooned as a petty thief plunging his hands into the pockets of the taxpayer.[41]

Lane's rhetoric undeniably aped that of Hoover, Hearst, and other New Deal critics, while her rejection of Roosevelt's economic interventionism was rooted in a long-held distrust of authority. But there was also an emotional undercurrent to her most fervid outbursts. Lane's letters seemed hectic and unhinged, as if she were frantic to change somebody's, anybody's, mind. "What is happening, Virginia, is a death-struggle between The Industrial Revolution and Medievalism," Lane wrote. "Roosevelt is for Medievalism. He has to smash America to get it."[42] She told Brastow she was "moronic" to find Roosevelt sincere and well meaning, a leader doing the best he could:

Doing <u>what</u>? Best for <u>what</u>? You can not speak of the world's most absolute dictator, with this nation in his hands and more power than any former dictator in history, in the same terms you use about the puttering neighbor next door.[43]

She fantasized about taking the president's life, just two years after he survived an assassination attempt in which the mayor of Chicago was killed. "I could kill Roosevelt with pleasure and satisfaction," she wrote to Brastow. "If living got too much for me so that I really wanted to die, I would go to Washington first and kill that traitor."[44]

As in political tirades to follow, Lane argued from authority, contending that what she had seen of Europe and Russia in the 1920s gave her the necessary experience to forecast what FDR's rule was sure to bring about: rampant inflation, collapse of liberty, and the infiltration of the American educational system by Communists. Europe, she said, was a place where children died of rickets, their bodies "soft bits of sick flesh." Soon, she predicted, a book of matches would cost $25,000.[45]

She had sniffed out a Soviet-style "Terror" in Illinois the previous summer, where Garrett interviewed a few of the "millions of human beings" who he claimed the government intended to resettle, a charge so exaggerated that an agricultural expert at the University of Missouri later called the *Post* article "diatribe journalism."[46] Lane told Brastow: "You can smell a Terror . . . I told Garet Garrett ten minutes after we drove into it that it was a Terror, and he would not believe it."[47] The term harked back to the French Revolution, and the Jacobin plotters. During Lane's association with Garrett, her anti–New Deal rhetoric would grow noticeably harsher. Soon even he would not be conservative enough for her. She was outraged that his *Post* articles about their trip were not more pointed.[48]

She saw the Terror spreading to Wright County when a local farmer was discovered with "two pigs more than Wallace permitted," a situation that nearly touched off a riot when federal agents arrived to count the litter. The "unlawful shoats" were ultimately seized and redistributed, she reported, given to "a nest of chicken-thieves and moonshiners who never could be induced to do a day's work in their lives."[49]

Many other outrages were close to home. She knew for a fact, she said, that there were six members of the Communist Party on the University of Missouri faculty.[50] Interviewed by an aspiring journalism student at the university, Norma Lee Browning, Lane encouraged the young woman to drop out of school immediately. Browning declined, but in future years, as she developed into another of Lane's protégés, she would be tutored in an effort to replace what the elder woman termed "all of that trash you learned in college."[51]

There was no form of government "relief" that Lane did not lament, from the modest Mansfield Works Progress Administration sewing room, employing women to mend clothes and stitch pillow cases, to the Tennessee Valley Authority, designed to prevent flooding. She complained to Brastow, who lived in San Francisco, that the top of her beloved Telegraph Hill had been turned into a WPA project. "God damn them," she wrote.[52]

Her preoccupation with houses continued unabated. When she received news that Rexh Meta, "my Albanian son," was engaged, it set off fantasies about "my house" in Albania. Soon she laid plans to have him buy her six acres on a hillside near Tirana on which to build "the Albanian house I really want," with dark-blue gates, cream-colored walls, red-tile coping, walled courtyards, arched passageways, and wall fountains, to create a pleasing sound. "That is what I shall do someday if I live," she wrote. She decided, not for the first time, that "the real me is Moslem and I live in Islam."[53]

WHILE Lane was living in Islam, Laura Ingalls Wilder was working quietly in the Rock House, coping with preoccupations of a different kind. In revisiting Plum Creek, she was confronting the darker chapters of her young life, when the family feared that Caroline Ingalls, stricken with a mysterious illness, was dying, and when the grasshoppers descended and her father was forced to walk hundreds of miles east to find work. The intense heat of the summer of 1936, the ongoing drought, grasshopper outbreaks, and clouds of dust heightened her anxious, pointillist portrait of her childhood: the sensate recollections of the feel of insect claws clinging to her legs, the smell of smudge fires her father set to drive them away, and the numb despair as he walked away in patched boots, looking back from a patch of willows by the creek to wave goodbye.[54]

It is striking that the letters Wilder and Lane exchanged at the time were not more influenced by their shared political concerns, or cognizant of the historical echoes of the current situation. Neither Wilder nor her daughter sought, except in a glancing reference, to include the wider social ramifications of the 1870s locust plague, the fact that thousands, including her father, had been forced to accept government aid to stave off starvation. Instead, their discussions were largely devoted to minutiae: Was the crab in the creek really a crawdad? Are vanity cakes the same as popovers? What kind of birthday cake did Nellie have, and where exactly did the railroad tracks run through town?[55]

By now, Wilder was routinely crafting chapters and scenes within them, but as always, her initial manuscript presented a starker, plainer reality than the finished book. Ironically, given her state at the time, Lane's reworking focused on establishing a sense of safety, emphasizing the cozy confines of home and family. In the peculiar alchemy of literature, the daughter was adept at creating in fiction what she had not known in her own childhood. As the two of them worked through the manuscript, they began paring away grimmer incidents from that time, seeking to impose a narrative arc: from the family's sunny arrival at Plum Creek through the dark times of grasshoppers, crop losses, and blizzards, then back to relative calm and security, something the family in fact never fully achieved. Such an arc was difficult to discern in Wilder's actual experience, and the process involved compression and elision, sparking debates between the women over how to handle the material.

Reading her daughter's expanded scene in which unguarded cattle attack Pa's haystacks and the girls must struggle to drive them off, for instance, Wilder wrote, "I don't like this so well." She added that the story of the runaway oxen that imperil Ma and the younger girls "is excitement enough for one day and better than this . . . I truly think my version best."[56] She also came up with the solution for explaining why small girls had been tasked with such a hazardous responsibility, suggesting that the herd boy had fallen asleep.

For her part, Lane wanted to cut Wilder's recollection of her mother's illness, pointing out that the episode, despite Ma's recovery, seemed excessive. "I am doubtful about Ma's sickness," she wrote. "It is such a wretched miserable time, and in that kind of nasty grasshopper atmosphere. I think the grasshoppers are enough."[57] She advised preserving the bit about Laura's desperate attempt to cross the creek, swollen by rain, to get word to the doctor. (It would appear in chapter 15 of the finished book, "The Footbridge.") Wilder at first resisted and then accepted these editorial suggestions, saying "you know your judgment is better than mine, so what you decide is the one that stands."[58]

But as she perused the drafts, Wilder cautioned her daughter against introducing too much security. Describing the girls' first wide-eyed, solitary walk into town as they looked for the schoolhouse, she said, "We were just two wild Indians . . . on our own and no thought of its being wrong. You <u>must not</u> have us treated like children of today. It would spoil the picture and the interest."[59] Children back then, she wrote, "weren't raised to be helpless cowards."

She was occasionally peremptory, but she could also be grateful and apologetic. "I should think you would be so sick of this darned story, you would gag," she wrote at one point, humbly acknowledging her need for assistance. "I thank you for suggestions on my mistakes. I know they are many."[60] The women were passing manuscripts back and forth, but stages of the work appear to be missing from the record: the finished book does not exactly match either of the draft typescripts that survive.[61]

As they labored, the portrait of Wilder's father that emerged was unvarnished at first, gradually tinged with heroism in later versions. From draft to draft, his grammar improved, as it had in *Little House on the Prairie*. His contributions to the family larder were subject to refinement: early on, he promised to get a "mess of squirrel," a backwoods delight that disappeared before publication.[62] In Wilder's first stab at *Plum Creek*, he curses as he tells the family about spending a blizzard dug into the snow bank beside Plum Creek, eating a pound of oyster crackers that left him as hungry as ever: "The dam things were no bigger than the end of my thumb," he says.[63] In the finished book, curse and complaint have vanished.

The tenderness remained. Writing to her daughter to describe Charles Ingalls's Sunday best, Wilder recalled, "He wore a black silk tie, a coat and vest and pants. . . . Seems as though all I ever saw of Pa was his face especially his eyes, his whiskers and his hair always standing on end. And too his hands on his violin."[64] That vision would become an indelible part of his character throughout the series, and may explain why Wilder so adamantly insisted that her books were "true."[65]

I Find My Heart Is Getting Harder

The Wilders were not done with fires. One night, the electric line behind the Rock House sputtered and sparked, the power went out, and a fire broke out behind the house. Almanzo was already asleep in bed. Alerted by their barking dog, Wilder went to the porch and saw flames. "Believe me, I <u>screamed</u>," she told Lane, thinking that the barn, hay, and sheds were all involved.[66] She dashed out to free the goats, and, not for the first time in her life, ran to fetch buckets of water to throw on the flames. She quickly saw that the fire was confined mainly to the wood lot behind the barn. Dressed only in shirt and shoes, Almanzo came to help, and the two eventually managed to put out the blaze.

Wilder had dropped the phone in her panic, unable to reach anyone over the party line, but at the farmhouse Jack and Corinne Murray heard the dog barking through the receiver and came to help as well. "Nice of them and good to have them," Wilder wrote cautiously to her daughter. But between the lines, it was clear that she did not trust them, and soon she would admit that she found them careless and irresponsible. They were staying in the farmhouse because their own place in town had burned down.[67]

And there were other sources of friction. During their back-and-forth over the Plum Creek manuscript, Lane and Wilder were also squabbling over what was going on in the farmhouse while Lane was away. Corinne Murray had been hired to watch the Turner boys, who were still attending school in Mansfield. But she and her husband often argued with Bruce Prock, the Wilders' tenant farmer and handyman, over how best to take care of the youngsters. Wilder was pulled into adjudicating their arguments.

By this time, Wilder was sixty-nine. Her husband was in his seventies, and they resented having to cope with upheaval on their property. Judging by letters, the Murrays' slovenly housekeeping annoyed them, and with their daughter out of the beloved farmhouse, they may have begun to think about reclaiming it.[68] The situation eventually came to a head in the spring of 1936, when, during the fourth year of a drought, Prock accused Jack Murray—who was still running a laundry service in Mansfield—of stealing water from Lane's well for his business. Prock also claimed that the boys had been running wild because Corinne would not cook for them, and there was a dispute over whether Al Turner had paid a doctor's bill.

Even more aggravating, Wilder found herself wondering how to discipline Al after he was caught, by police, stealing tires off an abandoned car that had been left on the Wilders' property after an accident. Irritated by the officiousness of the patrolman, Wilder said she wanted "to knock his head off," but counseled her daughter against looking the other way on the Murrays' transgressions, as that would give Al the wrong message. She strongly urged Lane not to be defensive on the boy's behalf, saying, "I hope you will not be a crazy nut."[69]

Finally, at her wit's end, she advised Lane to shut down the farmhouse. The Murrays, she felt, should be let go in such a way that they were not angered over their dismissal, lest they steal from the house before they left. Wilder offered to assume responsibility for electric bills and to arrange with Prock to secure the place. She sought to assure Lane that both she and Prock were sympathetic to Al Turner and were supportive of his finishing high school. But she was clearly overwhelmed. "Oh Dam!," wrote the woman taught never to swear, "I don't know what to do." She added, "it seems like I can't stand it."[70]

Years later, Lane would claim that her mother told her to "get out" of the farmhouse.[71] Letters may have gone missing, and on other occasions Wilder did apologize for losing her temper. Nonetheless, Lane's reaction may have been out of proportion. After the argument, she continued to act as if her parents had wounded her unforgivably. She later claimed her mother had ordered her dog killed. (The identity of the animal is unclear, and there was a campaign in Mansfield at the time to rid the town of stray dogs.)[72] In July, she relinquished the farmhouse in a rage, writing in her diary, "This week is all shot to hell by my mother's yowls. I have written to Corinne to take everything on the farm and I will close the place. End 9 years of an utterly idiotic attempt."[73] In the fall, she brought Al Turner to Columbia to live with her and finish high school. John Turner was sent to military school in New Mexico.

Whatever Lane's grievance, her parents seemed unaware of it. Her mother continued to write long confiding letters, addressing her as "Rose Dearest," and apologizing for the Plum Creek "mess."[74] She signed them "Lots of love" and "Still loving you."[75] For all that, Lane only visited her parents twice more, making two quick trips to Mansfield in the spring of 1936.[76] After those, Almanzo Wilder would never see his daughter again. In future years, she would refuse to visit, even when he offered to send money for the train fare.[77]

That same spring, Lane published a political essay in the *Saturday Evening Post*, signaling a shift in her career. "Credo" set forth the pillars of a personal philosophy, a secular religion celebrating "individual liberty" and absolute self-reliance. She argued that the radical form of government created by the Founding Fathers rested upon "a new principle: All power to the individual."[78] Again she rested her case on personal authority, judgments based on her earlier travels in Russia. It was the Russian peasants, she said, oppressed by bureaucrats in Moscow, who had taught her that planned economies were doomed.

Inventing scenes and dialogue, Lane was again writing fiction as if it were fact. She had had a dalliance with socialism, she said, during which she met Jack Reed and witnessed the founding of the American Communist Party. She was insistent on it, though details were hazy: "I forget the precise locale of that historic scene, but I was there."[79] This time, though, she was inserting herself into well-documented events. She may have met Jack Reed in passing, either in New York City or in Croton-on-Hudson. She may even have attended meetings where he spoke in 1919. But in her zeal to assert her authority she went too far. It was in Chicago, not New York, that Jack Reed played his founding role in launching the Communist Labor Party, in a dramatic schism that occurred on August 31, 1919, in a rented basement hall. When it happened, Lane was five hundred miles away, in Mansfield, Missouri, mocking the Bolsheviks in a letter that cast great doubt on her contention that she had once been an ardent fellow traveler. "Dear Comrades," she had then written to the Haders: "Having come so far on my journey back to the people, I am at this moment sitting on the second floor of a plain but comfortable peasant's hut in the Ozark wilderness."[80] She loved New York, she joked, but had given it up for the masses: "No doubt the people will give a tea-party for me soon, and then heaven knows I shall suffer for my convictions!"

Her biographer, William Holtz, acknowledged the fabrications but dismissed their significance. They were not "central to her argument," he wrote, because she was merely "distorting her own personal history a bit."[81] But by this point, Lane's false claims were central to both her argument and her self-image, the two of them increasingly intertwined. After a lifetime of financial insecurity and indebtedness, from which she was still not free, she began to speak as if with a bullhorn, assuming an ever more grandiose tone as an authority on personal and economic responsibility.

Even more troubling, she was beginning to embrace fascism. In "Credo," she wrote that she had seen "the spirit of Italy revive under Mussolini."[82] In concert with a growing isolationist movement, Lane was becoming an apologist for dictatorial regimes. This was in keeping with the politics of George Horace Lorimer's *Saturday Evening Post*, which had been fulminating against the influence of Europe for years, deriding elite intellectuals, foreign immigrants, radicals, and Communists. In the 1920s, the magazine had run a series of lavishly illustrated articles on "race theory," aimed at proving that the "Nordic" type, said to be predominant in America, was superior to Mediterranean and other races.[83] Lorimer had long championed business, industry, and "the silent majority," a term he coined; after Roosevelt's election, virtually every issue of his magazine inveighed against the New Deal as a form of European socialism.[84]

"Credo" was hailed by conservatives far and wide, with the *Post* receiving scores of letters of support. *Reader's Digest* printed an abridged version of Lane's article, and Herbert Hoover wrote to rekindle his relationship with her, urging a reprinting of "millions of copies."[85] Like-minded publishers obliged, issuing it as a pamphlet titled "Give Me Liberty."[86] The pamphlet would become the backbone of an emerging political movement, and a favorite of Wilder's, who kept a supply to send to readers.[87] Their forefather, Samuel Ingalls, the family's standard-bearer in militant broadsides, would have been proud.

But neither "Credo" nor the *Saturday Evening Post* could stop the juggernaut of the Roosevelt administration. To the intense dismay of Lane and her fellow conservatives, Roosevelt was elected for a second term in 1936, winning in a landslide with 60 percent of the popular vote. He lost only two states, Maine and Vermont.

He did not win in Mansfield. There, the New Deal and its "relief" jobs were viewed with suspicion and disdain, despite the fact that, according to one historian, "the relief load was very heavy in the

Ozarks."[88] By 1936, the epochal migration of destitute and broken farmers and their families, forced out of the Great Plains to seek a new life farther west, was well under way. But in remote rural towns like Mansfield, where people had lived in straitened circumstances for decades and somehow made do, government interference was, at least publicly, anathema.

It still is. Ask old-timers who grew up in overwhelmingly Republican Wright County during the Depression, and they will say that few people in the region favored the New Deal. Recently, William Turner, a retired banker who remembers stopping by Rocky Ridge as a teenager to ask for contributions for a pie supper—Wilder donated a poem she'd written on one of her dime-store tablets—described the disapproval of Roosevelt as universal, virtually tribal: "He's a Democrat, so he's a dirty dog, you know?"[89]

In the run-up to the 1936 presidential election, the *Mansfield Mirror* reprinted a popular ditty that was making the rounds that fall, the "New 23rd Psalm":

> Mr. Roosevelt is my shepherd
>> I am in want
> He maketh me to lie down on park benches
>> He leadeth me besides still factories
> He dist[urbeth] my soul
>> He leadeth me in the paths of destruction
> For the parties sake
>> Yea, tho I walk thru the
> Valley of the shadows of depression
>> I anticipate no recovery
> For he is with me
>> He prepareth a reduction in my salary
> And in the presence of mine enemies.
>> He anointeth my small income with taxes
> And my expense runneth over
>> Surely unemployment and poverty shall follow me,
> All the days of my life and
>> I will live in a mortgaged house forever.[90]

In Roosevelt's second inaugural, he spoke of seeing a third of the nation "ill-housed, ill-clad, ill-nourished," and called the country to action, saying that "the test of our progress is not whether we add more to the abundance of those who have much; it is whether we provide enough for those who have too little."[91] It was a humane response to the suffering of those most affected by the Great Depression. In cities, thousands of homeless were still living in shantytowns and shacks cobbled together from scrap lumber, orange crates, or cardboard; others occupied rusted cars. The suicide rate had peaked in 1932, and after dropping briefly was on the rise again.[92] Malnutrition rose among children, leading to rickets. With tax revenue plummeting, schools closed, and some children ended up supporting their parents, working in meatpacking plants or sweatshops—at least until another New Deal law, the Fair Labor Standards Act of 1938, put a stop to it.

But Roosevelt's rhetoric changed nothing about the way Wilder and her daughter defined the nation's priorities. They were political supporters of a local Ozark boy, Dewey Jackson Short, who had been born near Branson, not far from Mansfield. A World War I veteran, former pastor at a Methodist Episcopal church, and an excoriating orator in the tradition of Clarence Darrow, Short had begun serving as a congressman for Missouri's 7th District in 1935. A few weeks after starting his term, he memorably defined the U.S. Congress as a "supine, subservient, soporific, superfluous, supercilious, pusillanimous body of nitwits" who had turned over their powers to the New Dealers—"tax-eating, conceited autocratic bureaucrats, a bunch of theoretical, intellectual, professorial nincompoops out of Columbia University."[93] Wilder and her daughter loved him.

In the spring of 1937, Lane decamped to New York City, permanently removing herself to the East Coast. Almost immediately, her parents began to reclaim their farmhouse, repairing the damage left by former tenants. Airing and disinfecting—Lane and many of her guests were smokers—Almanzo patiently restored the woodwork in the front room, sanding it to remove stains and burned spots. In his humble fashion, he wrote: "I told Bessie I was not a goin to moove till I got the smell out."[94] Sometime that summer, the Wilders moved back to the farmhouse they had built, leaving the Rock House, their daughter's stony gift to them, empty.[95]

In letters in 1937, the two women traded admiring remarks about Dewey Short's wisdom while plotting how to cheat on their taxes. That March, Wilder urged her daughter to continue to claim the "head of the household" exemption at Rocky Ridge, even though she'd moved away.[96] She knew it was wrong, scrawling at the top of the page: "I'll burn your letter and you burn this."[97] During these feverish reckonings, she made a bald admission. "God knows the farm is not self supporting," she told her daughter, who had reason to know. "You have contributed to keeping it up. You don't have to pay rent," she added, in belated acknowledgment of Lane's overgenerous, even self-sacrificial support of the family.

Both women grew markedly more agitated by New Deal social engineering that year, and their rhetoric waxed harsher. "Truman is a liar," Wilder wrote of the new Democratic senator from Missouri, a keen supporter of Roosevelt's programs who had come under fire earlier for accepting a Civil Works Administration patronage job from a Kansas City pol. "People drive me wild. They as a whole are getting just what they deserve," she concluded, before breaking off to thank Lane effusively for sending her a new suit. She had so many new clothes, she said, there was no need to "make over the old ones" in her usual thrifty way. Instead, she would let Almanzo cut them up to braid into rag rugs, a favorite pastime in winter. "As for giving them to anyone," she wrote, the lazy sods "would go on relief before they'd make them over." She was "fed up" with giving things to people, she said, not noticing the irony in her position.

The stress caused by the Depression manifested itself in myriad ways, sparking a preoccupation with frugality that would last a lifetime for many Americans. But for Wilder and Lane, the spectacle of extreme poverty and near-starvation must have triggered their own deep-seated anxieties and shameful memories. They themselves had faced such existential threats before and survived, barely. Wilder had long been intensely frugal; her daughter, on the other hand, exhibited the kind of voracious spending that is another symptom of those who have experienced extreme privation. The two women coped with recurring fears by belittling the needs and anxieties of others.

Wilder had plunged into work on her Silver Lake book that year, expounding to Lane on what drove them to Dakota Territory: the Ingallses' harrowing time in Burr Oak and Walnut Grove, when she worked as a child to help support her parents. She veered from rationalizing her father's financial mistakes to severely criticizing those of her neighbors. Of her father, she wrote that he was always "getting the worst of the bargain," and ended up owing so much money to William Masters in Walnut Grove that he left town in debt, as he had in Burr Oak. He had no choice, she argued: "There were no jobs lying around to go begging while the government hired men as now. Interest was high. A man once in debt would stand no chance of getting out." Ever his defender, she excused his shortcomings, despite knowing full well that farming required sharp business skills. "Pa was no business man," she told Lane, summing up his character. "He was a hunter and trapper, a musician and poet."[98]

She made no such excuses for Bruce Prock, the Rocky Ridge handyman, who had three cows but always seemed short of ready cash:

> If we had such opportunities when we were young we would have been rich. How they can keep from it I can't see, nor what they do with the money they can't prevent themselves from making. . . . And still Bruce is always hard up. . . . But I find my heart is getting harder. I can have no least sympathy for people any more who can do and will only holler that there is no chance any more. I wish they all might have the opportunities we had when I was young and no more. Wouldn't it be fun to watch 'em?[99]

Her own family was not immune to what she called "disgrace."[100] Back in De Smet, Nate and Grace were on relief, she learned, receiving surplus commodity food and payment for leaving their land fallow, part of the New Deal's conservation plan.[101] Carrie wrote asking if Rose could spare any old clothes, and Wilder passed on the request. Knowing how her older sister felt about such matters, Carrie had

insisted: "above all things don't send me any of yours. I can get along."[102]
To her credit, Wilder ignored that.

Such emotionally tangled issues of being beholden, of owing and
being owed, had troubled Wilder all her life. She had helped support
her own family, working since she was nine. She had turned over the
money she made teaching school to her parents, to help send her sister
Mary to college, a chance she never got herself. She was now beholden
to her daughter, and had been for years.

Exhausted by cross-currents of guilt and resentment, she seemed to
have no measure of sympathy left. She could not extend herself further.
Her attitude toward the New Deal was hardly unusual, reflecting the
convictions of Mansfield and rural farmers across the country. But it
was also profoundly, painfully, and ineradicably personal.

All I Have Told Is True

By this time, Wilder was becoming a local celebrity. The publication of
Little House on the Prairie had been applauded on the front page of
the *Mansfield Mirror*: "Every chapter has a thrill."[103] The newspaper
also covered the Wilders' golden anniversary, and an item reported her
finishing the Plum Creek manuscript.

Since their return to the farmhouse, Wilder had been writing in a
nook, "a corner between my bedroom to the east and the living room
at the north," she wrote to a fan. "It is a very small room with a window
to the west and one to the south, looking out into the big trees around
the house. The room is filled with my desk and a table, couch and
small bookcase. It is usually a mess with papers and books and mss.
scattered around."[104] The beautifully carved wooden desk was fitted
with cubbyholes and drawers. The walls were papered in a delicate
floral pattern. The most fanciful element was an old-fashioned fainting
couch under the window: Wilder was accustomed to getting up in the
night, awakened by recollections. "I can't work . . . in the evening," she
told Rose, "because if I do, I can't sleep. My brain goes right on remembering and it's H——."[105]

A train on the track, she was writing continuously, sometimes round the clock. Exhausted or no, she had the look of a woman who was professionally hitting her stride. On Lane's advice, she had publicity photos taken in Springfield to promote *Plum Creek*, and she had grown into the role of sophisticated author: serious but not severe, white hair swept back from her face, long drop earrings accenting the line of her jaw, her customary brooch at her collar. Lane told her she looked like a "lovely [literary] lion," and it was true.

She was asked to give talks to admiring groups, and addressed the Sorosis Club in nearby Mountain Grove, the local chapter of a national women's organization, on "My Work." She spoke of how gratifying it was to hear that schoolchildren across the country devoured each book and called for more, reminding her of her own daughter: "Oh tell me another, Mama Bess! Please tell me another story."[106]

She mentioned trying to nail down facts about Indian chiefs and grasshoppers, and described how concentrating on specific memories could bring long-forgotten details to mind. She concluded with a statement of her philosophy: "Running through all the stories, like a golden thread, is the same thought of the values of life. They were courage, self reliance, independence, integrity and helpfulness. Cheerfulness and humor were handmaids to courage." Describing her parents' travails, she wrote:

> When possible, they turned the bad into good. If not possible, they endured it. Neither they nor their neighbors begged for help. No other person, nor the government, owed them a living. They owed that to themselves and in some way they paid the debt. And they found their own way.
>
> Their old fashioned character values are worth as much today as they ever were to help us over the rough places. We need today courage, self reliance and integrity.[107]

In October 1937, she refined that manifesto. *On the Banks of Plum Creek* was published that month, and Wilder was invited to give a talk at a book fair held at a department store in Detroit. In coming years, she would be invited to ever more illustrious public events, but would invariably turn down the invitations. The Detroit fair was the first and last national stage on which she would appear. She had something to say, and once she said it, that was enough.

It was a long trip to Detroit, but Almanzo had befriended a young garage owner, Silas Seal, who had impressed him by cleaning his windshield and checking the air pressure in the tires without being asked. Worried about the arduous drive, Almanzo hired Seal (who had once lived in Detroit) to ferry the Wilders there and back. It was the beginning of a long friendship.

They arrived at the city's Statler Hotel to find a letter from Lane, offering her mother paragraphs of detailed instructions on how to call the front desk—"You always have to say names slowly and clearly to hotel operators, and spell them after you pronounce them."[108] She spelled out Ida Louise Raymond's name, in capital letters, to drive the point home.

Instead of wishing her mother luck, Lane supplied a passage from the Koran, Sura 99, pleading for the Lord's protection "from the mischief . . . of the night . . . from the mischief of women blowing on knots; from the mischief of the envious."[109] In case Wilder was baffled, Lane insisted that "a lot of people are envying you."

Envy may not have been uppermost in her mind, but Wilder was nonetheless intimidated, telling her editor, "I am just a hillbilly."[110] The massive Statler, eighteen floors tall, stood only a few blocks from the book fair venue, the J.L. Hudson Department Store, an even grander establishment of thirty-two floors. Serving the Motor City at its most posh, Hudson's had once been the tallest emporium in the country. Only Macy's in New York had more floor space.

The book fair, "A Week of Authors," featured events for both adults and children. A star-studded roster included Klaus Mann (son of Thomas) and the bestselling pulp-adventure writer Talbot Mundy, a friend of Lane's. Among the children's authors were Marjorie Flack, promoting *Angus and the Ducks*, a popular picture book about a Scottish terrier, and Kurt Wiese, the German-born illustrator whose titles included the first English version of *Bambi*, translated by Whittaker Chambers.

Wilder was the last speaker on the fair's last day, hailed for harnessing "the experience of her pioneer past to solve the problems of the present day."[111] She had written the speech without assistance from her daughter, and she began where she always had, with her parents: "Many years ago, in the Little House in the Big Woods, Sister Mary and I listened to Father's stories."[112] To an audience of children who had grown up with radios and movies, she stressed that her family had had to be "self-sufficient for its own entertainment as well as its livelihood." She talked about her mother, descended from Scots of legendary thrift, and her father, whose ancestors had arrived on the *Mayflower*. "He was always jolly, inclined to be reckless, and loved his violin," she said.

After her first book was successful and she received pleas from children around the country to continue the story, she said,

I began to think what a wonderful childhood I had had. How I had seen the whole frontier, the woods, the Indian country of the great plains, the frontier towns, the building of railroads in wild, unsettled country, homesteading and farmers coming in to take possession. I realized that I had seen and lived it all—all the successive phases of the frontier, first the frontiersman, then the pioneer, then the farmers and the towns.

Then I understood that in my own life I represented a whole period of American history. That the frontier was gone, and agricultural settlements had taken its place when I married a farmer.

It seemed to me that my childhood had been much richer and more interesting than that of children today, even with all the modern inventions and improvements.[113]

She described the idea of writing a series about her childhood, "a seven-volume historical novel for children covering every aspect of the American frontier," as a unique plan. "Someone has to do a thing first," she said. "I would be the first to write a seven-volume novel for children." (She had not yet realized that the series would stretch to eight.)[114]

She laid out the existing volumes, one by one, and sketched out those to come, adding that her husband, introduced in *Farmer Boy*, would reappear in the fifth volume, which she had already begun. She asserted what she had been saying all along, but with one startling addition:

> Every story in this novel, all the circumstances, each incident are true.
>
> All I have told is true but it is not the whole truth. There were some stories I wanted to tell but would not be responsible for putting in a book for children, even though I knew them as a child.[115]

She then proceeded to relate some of what she had left out—beginning with the story of the Bloody Benders as embellished by Lane, including Charles Ingalls's supposed participation in a vigilante posse that hunted them down. She even put herself into the tale, saying that her family had stopped outside the Benders' tavern on their way to find their own property. "I saw Kate Bender standing in the doorway," she said.[116] Invoking the courtroom oath—"the truth, the whole truth, and nothing but the truth"—she told a story that was embroidered, if not downright false.

Wilder's "truth" was less a matter of fact than of her memories, feelings, and convictions. Her work was based on facts but not factual. It was historical fiction, not history. Its chronology, and certain incidents and characters, were invented, altered, and fictionalized.

Of course, her speech had explicitly described her work as a novel, acknowledging that she was writing fiction. Yet emblazoned on the pale yellow covers of the books she was selling at the fair, above the title and the cover image of Mary and Laura wading in Plum Creek, appeared these words: "The True Story of an American Pioneer Family."[117]

Like Wilder herself, the assertion contained multitudes. It had come about when Wilder pressed her editor the year before to emphasize the autobiographical element. Ida Louise Raymond had immediately agreed: "I think you are quite right in saying we have not sufficiently stressed the fact that these stories are true. We shall do so in the future."[118]

It was this ambiguous relationship to the truth that enabled Wilder to transform her family's lifelong struggles into a sterling portrait of indomitability, security, and success. The freedom she took with the facts was the creative act of a novelist, enabling her to achieve something beyond the flat recitation of the autobiographical "Pioneer Girl." But that fictional freedom jibed oddly with her insistence that "all the circumstances, each incident" were true.

Privately, to friends such as Aubrey Sherwood, editor of the *De Smet News*, she would acknowledge the full extent of her fictionalizing.[119] Publicly, and to children, she hewed to a different line. She seemed ever more invested in presenting her idealized view of her parents as factual, fulfilling a deep longing within herself not only to preserve their legacy but to elevate it, elevating herself in the process. She wanted to have it both ways.

Her ambiguity would become a source of confusion in years to come, exacerbated by Lane's brittle assertions that her mother was not "a liar."[120] The two women's defensiveness would play into the mythology growing up around the series. In years to come, the autobiographical authority of the books would lend considerable power to their influence as chronicles of pioneer triumph.

Wilder would later instruct readers that it was "best to be honest and truthful."[121] But midway through her fictional journey, she found herself in a dark wood. Chronicling her family's frontier days, she was obscuring the truth even as she worked to reveal it.

Chapter 12

We Are All Here

A True Picture

Between 1937 and 1938, Laura Ingalls Wilder and her daughter were immersed in the most editorially incestuous phase of their relationship. Swapping stories, borrowing from each other in ways that left no boundaries between their lives and their writing, they were eradicating any line between them. Economically, their parallel projects would be a success. But emotionally, their tensions, frustrations, and undigested disappointments would destroy much of the remaining bond between them.

Lane's leaving had temporarily eased the strain between the two women, at least on Wilder's side. The mother began doing everything she could to help her daughter with her writing, just as Lane had been helping with hers. Throughout 1937, both Laura and Almanzo penned long letters to their daughter about Almanzo's homesteading experience, recollections that would provide the factual scaffolding for Lane's next and last major serial for the *Saturday Evening Post*, "Free Land." Lane went so far as to ask her father to fill out an ad hoc questionnaire about those days, asking about everything from wind velocity to slang. His replies were terse. "My life has been mostly disappointments," he wrote at one point. She translated this into a portrait of dauntless valor.[1]

Given the rancor between mother and daughter over *Let the Hurricane Roar*, her parents' enthusiastic endorsement of the new project was remarkable. In the same way that *Hurricane* had borrowed from Charles and Caroline Ingalls's Plum Creek years, "Free Land" would reproduce Almanzo Wilder's life and experience, making use of details, incidents, anecdotes, names, and turns of phrase that had occurred or would occur in her mother's memoir and in her novels, those already published and those yet to be written. No letters explain Wilder's change of heart after *Hurricane*, but her acquiescence may have been related to Lane's severe depression after their rift. And having seen *Old Home Town*, she may have preferred that her daughter stick to stories of homesteading.

Money was doubtless also a factor. In 1937, Lane was still "paralyzed" by debt. She was down to her last $104, with taxes coming due, when she heard that *Ladies' Home Journal* had bought her story "Silk Dress" for $2,500.[2] Derived from her parents' lives, "Silk Dress" was a first stab at "Free Land," tracing the lives of a frontier couple named John and Sally. It begins with the couple's marriage in Burr Oak and follows their fortunes on the Great Plains as they settle near a town the spitting image of De Smet, living in a little house just like the one on Almanzo's tree claim. The wind makes Sally "brown as an Indian"; they have a baby right before Christmas, and celebrate among wild prairie roses in June.[3] They lose a wheat crop, nearly freeze in blizzards, dodge fireballs coming down the chimney, and go deeply into debt. After a July hailstorm destroys their next crop, John suggests making ice cream with the hailstones, just as Almanzo does in "The First Three Years."[4] Later, he suffers a crippling injury. It all works out in the end, with Sally singing ecstatically in church, declaring that her cup runneth over. A commercial rewrite of her mother's manuscript, the story's pathos and sentimentality demonstrate the limits of Lane's talents when left to her own.

"Free Land" was more of the same, a virtual Sears, Roebuck catalogue of her parents' lives and her mother's fiction. Borrowing liberally from *Little House on the Prairie*, Lane transferred into her serial the story of settlers driven out of Kansas by the government, describing a family near the Verdigris River building a little house on the high prairie only to be forced out by soldiers after "thousands of Indians were powwowing in the creek bottoms."[5] This family, too, suffered from "fever 'n' ague."[6] They too had a daughter whose face was "as brown as an Indian's."[7]

In "Free Land," Lane again changed the names of the characters based on her parents—Almanzo and Laura Wilder, called John and Sally in "Silk Dress," here became David and Mary Beaton—but otherwise followed her usual practice of using real names. Almanzo may have been bemused to find that David Beaton's father was James; his sisters, Eliza and Alice; his brother, Perley; and that the family hailed from Malone, New York.

The overlaps did not end there. The Minnesota Massacre is mentioned, and the frontier couple twists hay during a "hard winter." The Bloody Benders stagger forth yet again, not very inventively disguised as the "Bordens."[8] Characters sing the same songs as in Wilder's stories—"In the Starlight," "Captain Jinks," and "The Motto for Every Man," the latter two from *Silver Lake*—and attend the same oyster suppers and minstrel shows that would appear in future Little House volumes. A local pastor is "Reverend Brown," the real name of the preacher who married the Wilders. It was as if Margaret Mitchell had a daughter who was selling a magazine serial about Rhett Butler and Scarlett O'Hara while her mother was writing *Gone with the Wind*.

At the same time, "Free Land" was propaganda, something Wilder never aspired to. James Beaton objects to the government giving away "public land to the poor . . . he believed in every man's paying his own way."[9] Including her father's anecdote about lying on the homestead paperwork, Lane pronounces him satisfied, since "a man knew instinctively that Government was his natural enemy."[10] Her anti–New Deal designs on the reader are ever present. Characters denounce eastern trusts and the government's "un-constitutional" tariffs, which, they say, are protecting the railroads and "grinding us down."[11]

Beyond writing detailed letters to Lane, Wilder also offered her daughter free rein to adapt "The First Three Years," and Lane may have seen the manuscript. At some point, Wilder had told Ida Louise Raymond that she had "a grown-up book" in mind, and Raymond expressed delight at the news. On the back of Raymond's letter, Wilder explained to Lane that she had raised her editor's hopes with the idea: "It might wangle a little more advertising for the L.H. Books if I said I would write the grown up one. It was not a promise and if I didn't it wouldn't matter. So I wrote that I had material for one in my head."[12] In fact, of course, she had already written a draft.

Wilder's attempt to manipulate her publisher reveals a startlingly detached attitude toward her own work. She asked if Lane might be planning to "use the framework of The First Three Years," and whether it might be worth it for Lane to write "the one grown-up story of Laura and Almanzo to sort of be the cap sheaf of the 7 volume children's novel. I could write the rough work. You could polish it and put your name to it if that would be better than mine."[13] To some extent, Wilder saw writing as a cottage industry: books were the work of many hands, like quilts at a sewing bee. The notion explains a great deal about her practice of passing manuscripts and raw material back and forth with Lane. She did not always see how powerfully the writer's perspective—an emotional connection to the subject—affects a book.

Lane discouraged her mother from writing for adults, while simultaneously working on just such a manuscript herself. "As to your doing a novel," she wrote, "there is no reason why you shouldn't if you want to, but unless by wild chance you did a best-seller, there is much more money in juveniles. I'd do one myself if I could get time."[14] Harper would give an adult novel scant support, Lane argued, whereas "a juvenile keeps on selling for years as you know." Her advice directly contradicted counsel she had given her mother years earlier, when she had assured her that there was no money in juveniles. She was warning Wilder off her territory and competing with her at the same time.

While less histrionic than Hurricane, "Free Land" would be a similar Frankenstein's monster, assembled from gobbets of her mother's past but without the animating feeling that bound her mother's books together. Given its derivative nature, the most striking aspect of the serial would lie in what it left out. Lane recounted her parents' homesteading experience in virtually every particular: blizzards and hailstorms, debts and droughts. But there is no diphtheria, and no prairie fires. No baby dies.[15] No house burns to the ground. No one loses everything and moves to Missouri. In a work written as propaganda, Lane left out the most salient fact of her parents' lives: their failures.

Lane's strategic omissions left the work rife with contradictions. Intent on proving that there was no such thing as "free land," Lane larded the story with antigovernment statements while glossing over individuals' responsibility for embarking on complex agricultural enterprises without the capital to pay for them or to absorb the risk when they failed. She never questioned the gullibility of those, like her parents, who believed the railroads' huckster promotions during the Dakota Boom. Nor did she comprehend the ecological roots of the Great Plains catastrophe that destroyed their crops and livelihood. In the end, she had James Beaton bail out his son—just as James Wilder bailed out her parents in Mansfield by buying them a house—before the young couple loses everything.

In life, loss was the engine that set Wilder's fiction in motion. Exile propelled the powerful emotional undercurrent of the Little House books, an intensely felt nostalgia for people and places lost to her. That emotion was absent in "Free Land," relegating it to homesteading soap opera. Its loosely linked anecdotes were joined not by familial love but by Lane's, and the *Post*'s, ideology.

In writing about Silver Lake, Wilder was eager to leave things out of *her* story, too. But her reasons were personal, not political. As in the 1920s, dealing with her mother's death and the memories it brought up, she found herself beset by pangs, kept awake at night by the burden of recollection. Searching through her desk one day, she found a homemade, handwritten book of her mother's. "When I put it there," she wrote, "I couldn't bear to read it, but I am having to live over those days with Pa and Ma anyway, so I did."[16] Caroline Ingalls had written her own poems in the book, and copied others she admired. In 1860, the year he married Caroline, Charles Ingalls had written in it the lyrics of two songs Laura would hear him sing throughout her childhood, "The Blue Juniata" and "Mary of the Wild Moor."[17]

Wilder never explicitly addressed why the memories pained her so,

Laura Ingalls Wilder on the porch of her house in town, Mansfield, Missouri, circa early 1900s. On the back of the photo, she has written: "Just as I am without one plea."

Rose Wilder at the time
of her graduation from
high school, Crowley,
Louisiana, 1904

Rose Wilder at
nineteen, when she was
working as a telegrapher,
Kansas City, 1906

Rose Wilder Lane, newly married, in San Francisco, 1909

Rocky Ridge farmhouse and its distinctive fieldstone chimney,
shortly after renovation was completed, 1913

Laura Ingalls Wilder at the
beginning of her career as
a farm columnist for the
Missouri Ruralist, circa 1917

On this undated photo Laura Ingalls Wilder has written, "A J Wilder
making hay on Rocky Ridge farm with horses Buck & Billy."

Laura and Almanzo Wilder visiting neighbors near Mansfield, 1929

Laura Ingalls Wilder in a publicity photo taken in 1937 for the publication of her fourth book, *On the Banks of Plum Creek*

Rose Wilder Lane testifying as a "revolutionist" before a Congressional subcommittee hearing on the Ludlow Resolution, May 10, 1939

Laura and Almanzo Wilder visiting Aubrey Sherwood's newspaper office on Old Settlers' Day, De Smet, South Dakota, June 1939

Laura and Almanzo Wilder greeting visitors at
the Rocky Ridge farmhouse, July 4, 1948

but the degree to which she resisted writing about what happened to Mary suggests how traumatic that experience remained. Her initial manuscripts about Silver Lake opened at the train depot, with Caroline Ingalls and her daughters leaving Minnesota to travel west. Wilder simply presented Mary as blind, as a result of illness, with little in the way of dramatization or explanation.

Wilder wrote to Grace about small details, asking, for instance, which wildflowers grew on the prairie in springtime. At seventy-one, she was losing track of images that had seemed clear even a few years earlier, when she wrote her memoir. "That's why the sooner I write my stuff the better," she told Lane.[18] But she refused to summon the will to probe the most wrenching moments. She did not ask either of her sisters, who cared for Mary in her final years, to recall the exact nature of her illness. Her efforts to describe her feelings about Mary's disability sounded awkward, curt, even indifferent: "Laura was so glad to have Mary well and strong once more that she couldn't feel so very sorrowful even about that."[19] A few pages later she gave it up, writing on a blank page of her tablet, "False Start."[20] Beginning again, she abandoned any attempt to describe her feelings.

At first, Lane was less than helpful. Her advice on these matters took a didactic turn in the fall of 1937, when she counseled her mother, as an exercise, to take one of the previously published Little House books and copy the entire text out longhand, as a means of absorbing its "rhythm."[21] She planned to do something similar herself, she told Wilder, by typing out one of her own favorite novels, W. Somerset Maugham's roman à clef *Cakes and Ale*. Lane went on to parse the "vowel patterns" in one of her mother's sentences, examining it letter by letter. The mystifying discussion veered off into a denunciation of the "damn ignoramuses in publishing houses" who had seen fit to change Wilder's American "plow" to the English "plough."[22] Lane could not bear to look at *On the Banks of Plum Creek*, she said, "without getting so mad I am sick."[23]

A couple of months later, Lane questioned whether, in fiction, Mary needed to be blind at all, then pressed her mother to add a crucial opening scene to provide a transition from the Plum Creek setting of the previous novel and address the circumstances that provoked the family's move.[24] Wilder resisted. Even in private, to her daughter, she fumbled reluctantly in trying to explain that Mary's illness was "spinal meningitis," crossing out the words and writing "some sort of spinal sickness." She could not recall the exact terminology. The family had learned·only years later, when Charles Ingalls took Mary to a specialist in Chicago, "that the nerves of her eyes were paralyzed and there was no hope."[25]

Explaining all this to the reader was another thing entirely, almost too woeful to contemplate. "It seems to me that beginning the story with hard times and sickness and Mary's blindness would be making the story sad," Wilder wrote, "while beginning it with the funny little R.R. journey and touching on the sad part as lightly as I have done makes pleasanter reading."[26] Yet she insisted that Mary must be blind, because otherwise she would have become the schoolteacher that Laura never wanted to be. A little wishfully, she suggested that Lane had been "too tired" when she read the manuscript to appreciate how Wilder had handled the problem.

The debate continued well into 1938. Sensibly enough, Lane pointed out to her mother that "characters in fiction MUST have emotions, I do assure you," only to be greeted by a cry of despair familiar to every editor since the dawn of revision.[27] Buttering her up, Lane praised her mother's fine descriptions, telling her that her writing was "really lovely" and getting "better and better."[28] But Wilder viewed any urging to delve deeper with dismay. "To make the changes you want," she wailed, the manuscript would "have to be practically rewritten."[29] She repeatedly refused the notion of beginning with "a recital of discouragements and calamities such as Mary's sickness & blindness. I don't like it!" At one point, she sharply instructed Lane not to work on the manuscript any more, saying she was going over it carefully and would not be describing Mary's illness or Jack's death. "The reader must know all that but they should not be made to think about it," she said. "I am afraid I am going to insist the story starts as I started it."[30]

Irritable and offended, Lane dared her to go out on her own. She said in a huff that her mother was "one of the few writers in the country who would turn down a collaboration with RWL."[31] Fine, she went on, "go ahead . . . if you don't want this book touched, you're absolutely right not to have it touched." But if she went ahead like that,

Lane warned, there would be consequences. She knew just how to frighten her mother, saying, "you'll lose your audience for future books, and cut your income." Delivering a stinging yet fairly accurate critique, she noted the manuscript's "deadwood," lapses in point of view, wooden dialogue, and poor paragraphing.

In response, Wilder quelled her temper, thanked her daughter for giving her "courage," and humbly acknowledged her heavy debt. "You see, I know the music but I can't think of the words. . . . It is sweet of you to say the nice things you did about my writing and I will try to deserve them more."[32] Expressing a grudging professional respect for each other, trading compliments in a short-lived rapprochement, the two bent to the wheel again.

They began grappling with the chronological complexity of their omissions. Introducing a multiyear gap between Plum Creek and the move to Dakota Territory meant they were eliding years of disaster and calamity: homelessness, the death of Freddy, the dismal and debt-laden months in Burr Oak and the family's flight out of town, as well as the chaotic period in Walnut Grove, when Laura worked for the Masterses and her father tried one thing after another to keep them afloat only to see his eldest daughter fall desperately ill. "It is a story in itself," Wilder acknowledged, "but does not belong in the picture I am making of the family."[33] She was driven to rescue her father from his less-than-flattering past, beginning one Silver Lake draft with the assertion that "Pa was a good farmer, on the banks of Plum Creek, for four years."[34] A bit later she wrote, "Pa paid all his debts."[35]

Again, they were debating what had become a familiar theme, truth versus fiction, this time with Lane waving her hands over the facts the way a magician passes them over a hat, diverting attention while absolving her mother of a reporter's responsibility. "You must take into account the actual distinction between truth and fact," she told her mother:

It is beyond all human power to tell all the facts. . . . Facts are infinite in number. The truth is a meaning underlying them; you tell the truth by selecting the facts which illustrate it. All your travels to Burr Oak and back can be skipped because they do not mean anything except elapsed time. . . . It is not a fact, but it is perfectly true to take them west from the house on Plum Creek, where everything that has happened during this time might as truthfully have occurred as where it did occur.[36]

As a statement of the novelist's prerogative, this was reasonable, but Lane's casual disposal of those years was startling. If anything, the period was among the most consequential in Wilder's young life. Suppressing it would inevitably alter the trajectory of the tale she was telling, transforming the blind alleys and cul-de-sacs of random mischance, and the misfortunes of Charles Ingalls's failed crops and unpaid debts, into an orderly westward progression to homestead and town. It would suppress, as well, any suggestion that Charles had been a less than reliable provider. The less chaotic, more burnished version was the "truth" that Wilder wanted, and her daughter guided her toward it.

As she did, however, the two squabbled over sex, of all things. Silver Lake would be the first of the novels to describe Laura's teenage years, and Wilder had introduced a scene where Laura picked up a knife to ward off a male cousin who tried to kiss her. Lane found it exaggerated, as if Laura were "a slum child" protecting her virginity.[37] On the other hand, Lane argued for a scene in which Laura and Mary might watch the railroad crew at work; Wilder objected, saying that "nice girls" would have never exposed themselves in that fashion. Her daughter countered that workmen were not "degenerate savages."[38] (It turned out that Wilder was alluding to the fact that the workmen relieved themselves in the open air, a topic so indelicate she could barely bring herself to mention it. "The grass was so short it would not hide a thing," she explained to Lane. "If a man wanted to do his jobs he dropped out and did them publicly.")[39] The tension behind the bickering was years in the making, a product of the teenage turmoil Lane had dramatized in Old Home Town as well as Wilder's coldly disparaging response to a steamy scene in Lane's Jack London novel: she had told Lane she would rather read about a bowel movement.[40]

The discussion of propriety evolved into a broader debate over what was "too adult" for the readership. On moral grounds, Lane wanted to leave out any reference to adults (Aunt Docia and her husband) stealing from the railroad, but Wilder argued that this novel should begin to incorporate a grittier sense of realism: "Can't we let the readers see that children were more grown up then? . . . We can't spoil this story by making it childish! Not and keep Laura as the heroine."[41] Wilder cogently assessed herself at that age, saying that she was at once "completely grown up and again just a child," capable of being impetuous or petulant.[42]

In the end, Wilder capitulated, saying, "Change the beginning of the story if you want. Do anything you please with the dam stuff, if you will fix it up."[43] Lane made quick work of it. Her lead has Aunt Docia riding up to the "untidy" Plum Creek house where most everyone has had "scarlet fever." The fever has settled in Mary's eyes, and she has become blind. In a gesture to her mother's wishes, the harrowing events have occurred, offstage, before the novel opens.

Lane transferred the emotional nadir of the family's tribulation to a scene dramatizing the loss of another beloved character, familiar to readers since the first volume. As the family prepares to leave for Dakota Territory, Jack, the faithful old bulldog, dies in his sleep. Simple, affecting, and sorrowful, the scene—perhaps an homage to the late Bunting—acts as a critical linchpin, turning the series to adulthood in a way comparable to the death of Beth in *Little Women*. Laura, who must become her sister's eyes, realizes that she is "not a little girl any more."[44]

It was a fascinating reversal of roles: the daughter only recently bedridden with a mental breakdown was able to deftly handle the difficult emotional material that her mother could not face. Once again, their combined talents overrode their respective weaknesses, producing something that neither one could manage on her own. Lane supplied a powerful transition into the griefs and responsibilities of adulthood, while Wilder prevailed in her larger vision of "a true story" that would capture "a different (almost) civilization."[45] *By the Shores of Silver Lake* faithfully preserves what Wilder emphasized to her daughter: the stoicism of a family "inclined to be fatalistic, to just take things as they came. I know we all hated a fuss, as I still do."[46] To Lane's credit, she followed her mother's lead, and the portrait that emerges in *Silver Lake* stands in marked contrast to the melodrama of her own work.

Silver Lake was Wilder's adolescent book, not only introducing her teenage years but also reflecting her growing pains as a writer. She had been trying to recapture that evanescent time in Dakota Territory her whole adult life. An account of her family's isolated first winter on Silver Lake figures among the earliest surviving fragments of her writing, perhaps dating back to 1903. She had never forgotten the sight and sound of wild birds migrating across its marshes or the image of wolves on its shores. She had felt in her core the last of the wilderness passing into oblivion and mourned its disappearance, making the loss a leitmotif of her books as it had been in her father's life. She labored over her drafts of the "Wings Over Silver Lake" chapter, her farewell to the soul of a place that would be erased by railroads, towns, and agricultural development:

> All those golden, autumn days, the sky was full of wings. Wings beating low over the blue water of Silver Lake! Wings beating high in the blue sky above it! Wings of geese, of ducks, of brant and swan and pellican, and gulls bearing them all away to the green fields of the south. Sometimes Laura dreamed that great wings lifted her and she flew with them.[47]

The ring of wolves surrounding the log house in *Little House on the Prairie* was reduced here to a single pair, backlit by the moon, a melancholy gesture toward nature's impoverishment. The wolves speak across the series to each other, early and late, ghosts of a continent's past.

Stoicism

Early in 1938, Wilder was beginning to sketch out her next book, about the Hard Winter. She was concerned that the mere struggle to survive might not provide enough of a plot.[48] But in a remarkable series of letters that year, she seized hold of her material with a confidence that had heretofore eluded her. She began teaching her daughter the finer points of a kind of spare realism Lane had never attempted, delving into the fortitude shown by those compelled to endure prolonged periods of extreme deprivation.

Reading an initial manuscript, Lane had apparently asked if the townsfolk of De Smet were "monsters" to behave in such hard-bitten fashion, hoarding seed wheat (as the Wilder brothers had done) or urging schoolchildren to walk home in a blizzard.[49] Wilder's reply masterfully captured the extremes of self-sacrifice forced on them, comparing it to scenes in Indian captivity narratives when people went blank-faced, uncomplaining, to face torture and death:

> You know a person can not live at a high pitch of emotion[.] The feelings become dulled by a natural, unconscious effort at self-preservation.
>
> You will read of it in good frontier stories. How the people of a com[m]unity captured by the Indians would hardly turn their heads as one or two at a time were taken away from the main party by their special captors—taken away perhaps to a fate worse than death. . . . Living with danger day after day people become accustomed to it. They take things as they come without much thought about it and no fuss, in a casual way.[50]

Eventually settlers grew to be like the Indians themselves, she remarked. Westerners such as her family, she said, were "frontiersmen," so accustomed to an unrelenting succession of wilderness hazards that it "made us . . . apathetic. I can't get the right word for it. Indians were like that you know and they lived under nearly the same conditions."[51] Those conditions determined the attitude, she seemed to be saying, not culture or color of skin.

Settlers who prevailed, pressing on through grim circumstances, did so without "heroics," Wilder insisted.[52] Depicting such casual bravery was essential to her portrait, giving readers "a feeling of the march westward . . . this feeling that you call apathy and I call stoicism was there and a true picture must show it even to the children if we possibly can. I think neither of us has found the right word for it."[53] Stoicism was indeed the right word. Few works written for children capture it as clearly.

Just as confidently, Wilder flatly refused to include George and Maggie Masters as characters in the family saga, and dismissed as well Lane's suggestion that the Boasts be introduced as dramatic foils. Wilder pointed out that including the Masterses would require an accurate account of their lazy, good-for-nothing ways, which would "spoil the story." To improve their characters would detract from the heroism shown by Almanzo Wilder and Cap Garland, who risked their lives to get wheat for the town.

Time had not lessened her anger, particularly regarding George Masters, who had allowed her father to risk his life venturing out of town to fetch hay for fuel. In language reminiscent of her disdain over New Deal shirkers, she wrote, "He never went with Pa for a load of hay, he never twisted any. He just sat. He would have done differently or I'd have thrown him out, but Pa wouldn't. Sweet charity!"[54] Discussing the novel with Lane, Wilder stuck to her conviction that the Masterses had to be left out of it. "The situation is this," she told her daughter. "Pa is alone."[55]

Instead of bringing in outsiders, Wilder tried to leaven the experience of the hard winter by summoning a scene of sociability, the birthday party at the railroad depot. Lane likely excised that party from the manuscript; it would ultimately show up in the next novel. She also may have renamed the chapter Wilder stoutly called "The Hurricane Roared," titling it instead "We'll Weather the Blast." Lane was hanging on to the hurricane.

But while Wilder still needed her daughter's fine-toothed editing, she was beginning to take a commanding view of the whole tapestry and the minute details that created it. Repeatedly, she corrected the typescript on everything from anachronisms—"Never in the world would Almanzo have said 'What's the big idea?' That . . . would date it somewhere around 1929 or later"—to essential descriptions. "The prairie was not bare," she told her daughter. "Out on the prairie the snow moved over the surface like sand on the desert."[56]

She sketched out detailed maps of De Smet and produced an extensive list of corrections in response to her daughter's first typescript. Get rid of the hymn "Beulah Land," she crisply ordered. "I don't like this song in here." Her mother never sang it, she said, and it was the wrong period. At the same time, she cautioned Lane against trimming thematically important material:

> Don't cut the hymn I had Ma sing to Grace . . . "I will sing you a song
> of that beautiful land the far away home of the soul / Where no
> storms ever beat on that glittering strand / While the years of eternity
> roll." A land where storms never beat would have been thought of
> with longing. It has a wailing tune too. The kind Ma sang when she
> did sing. We must show the effect the winter was having. It nearly
> broke Ma down when she sang of the land where there were no
> storms. And Pa when he shook his fist at the wind. Don't leave that
> out. We have shown that they both were brave let's show what the
> winter nearly did to them.[57]

After the false starts and complications of Plum Creek and Silver Lake, the Hard Winter was Wilder's hard-won, mature masterpiece, in which expertise accumulated over a long apprenticeship was paying off. She occasionally grew exasperated with herself as she wrote, hesitating over alternatives in a parenthetical note: "I have read the darned thing until I don't know which is best."[58] But her manuscript reads as powerfully as the published book, including her recollection of how she grew "stupid and numb" from the continuous sound of the roaring blizzard and how her father, for the first time in their lives, discovered that his fingers were too chapped and stiff to play the fiddle to raise their spirits.[59]

Indeed, some areas of the manuscript are superior to the published version, especially the problematic scene featuring an elderly Indian, the last one to appear in the series. He ventures into the hardware store to warn the town about the coming winter. Both versions traffic in stereotypes, but Wilder's is more naturalistic, struggling to convey the respect accorded the man. "Pretty decent old blanket Indian to give us warning," her father says.[60]

Wilder recognized the novel's difference from anything she had written before, calling it "rather a dark picture, not so much sweetness and light as the other books."[61] She would later admit to George Bye, who praised the book highly, that she had found it a "rather trying" experience to be "living it all over again," and was glad to be done with it.[62]

She was right to insist to Lane on the importance of hymns. In this novel, her evocation of music as a thematic element binding her family together reached its height, as she deployed the hymns they sang a cappella to get them through dark, hungry days. One of them, an old Negro spiritual, "We Are All Here," echoed in her mind with particular force.[63] Revisiting those days, she was enacting a reunion, transcending decades of time and death itself to bring them all together again.

A Strong Feeling of Nostalgia

By the late 1930s, the New Deal was beginning to show its age. The "Second New Deal" round of legislation, between 1935 and 1938, represented the most profound era of governmental reform the country had ever seen. It involved virtually every facet and phase of life: Social Security, agriculture, electric cooperatives, labor reform, housing, federal deposit insurance, national parks, conservation, Indian affairs, art, theater, historic architecture, and national archives. Liberals and labor unions welcomed the programs, but conservatives were appalled by such massive federal interventionism and the deficit spending it entailed. In 1937, when Roosevelt moved to make the Civilian Conservation Corps a permanent agency, Congress failed to approve the measure. That same year, Roosevelt's ill-conceived attempt to pack the Supreme Court was denounced as a "dictator bill," undermining his popularity.

A new element entered Lane's world view during this time: a personal sense of grievance against the federal government, married to the conviction that the income tax system represented an evil to be actively resisted. A few years earlier she had blamed her mother for her financial woes, but now she expanded her sense of victimization to a national scale. In 1937, she was paid a princely twenty-five thousand dollars by the *Post* as an advance on "Free Land," but instead of greeting the payment as just reward for months of hard work, Lane said that tax payments due on the money had "completely sunk" her.[64]

Nevertheless, with that bonanza, she finally paid off her debts— including those to her mother and a substantial, long-running loan from

Helen Boylston—and found herself with four thousand dollars left, most of which was owed in taxes. In her self-aggrandizing way, she reckoned that "I am totally supporting the farm and three persons, and partially supporting six more"—despite the fact that, when it came to her parents, the question of who was supporting whom was hopelessly confused. (In the "partially supporting" category she might have been counting the Turner boys, their tutor, and Rexh Meta and his wife and child.) She listed her parents as dependents on her 1937 tax return, along with an "adopted son."[65]

Yet she continued to treat her rare windfalls with the same reckless abandon she had shown in her twenties. With money advanced by the long-suffering George Bye, she decided that the best way to complete John and Al Turner's education was to send them to Europe, with a paid tutor, for a year.[66] It was an act of extraordinary extravagance. Bicycling through Germany, the boys and their chaperone wrote rapturous post-cards to their benefactor, declaring it the "best place (barring the States) we have ever been in." They sent Lane a portrait of Adolf Hitler, the stamp cancellation a swastika. Above his image, one of the boys had written: "By gosh, you asked for it."[67]

But as Lane spent prodigiously, the country was sliding once again into recession, a depression within the Depression. Divisive rhetoric about the role of government in addressing boom and bust cycles took hold, leading to outsized fears of communism and homegrown dicta-torship. Roosevelt's supporters hailed progress made on creating jobs and managing commodity prices while his critics lashed out at "creep-ing socialism," which they saw as the inevitable result of a government-run "planned economy."

Farmers were still chafing under restrictions. On a fine spring day in 1938, Almanzo Wilder hitched his old Morgan horse, Buck, to the plow and began turning up the earth in a weedy stretch of their old apple orchard, planning to plant oats. (The orchard may have perished by then: tens of thousands of Ozark acres planted in fruit trees were lost during the Dust Bowl, wiped out by drought, disease, and pests.)[68] As he was working, the taciturn Almanzo was roused by the unwelcome intrusion of the federal government. His wife relayed the story to their daughter:

This man came. He asked what Manly was going to sow and Manly told him oats. Thought he was just showing an interest. Then he told Manly how many acres he could sow. He took papers from his pocket and wanted to know how many acres we have in pasture, meadow, corn land, etc., and Manly told him it was none of his business and ordered him off the place. Manly told him he could go to Hell, that he was running this farm and he might write that in his report. Manly came to the house to get his gun and the man left and that was all there was to it.[69]

Like many farmers, the Wilders feared and resented federal meddling. Wilder went on to say that "the woods are full of government men." They had intended to plow a mere twenty acres, but on being informed that the limit was thirty, they talked about going over, "just to see what they could do about it." But the land was in good grass, she told Lane, and "we decided we wouldn't cut off our nose to spite our face." Whatever their political leanings, the Wilders were nothing if not practical.

Ever the agitator, Rose Wilder Lane, an admirer of the *New York Herald Tribune*'s muckraking columnist, Mark Sullivan, wrote to him, embellishing the story and adding dialogue and local color:

This young fellow told him he could put in two acres of oats. . . . Say, my father said, Who are you? I'm a Federal employee, said the young whippersnapper, I represent the Secretary of Agriculture . . . my father asked hmm, you see that house down there? Yes, the Federal man said, he saw it. Well, my father said, there's a shotgun in that house and it's loaded, and it's my house and my shotgun and this is my place. You get off it right now and you stay off it, because if you think I won't use that shotgun you just wait around here and see. Believe it or not that young whelp took out a notebook right while my father was speaking, and began to write in it. . . . You going to make a report of what I say? My father demanded. Sure, said the Federal Man . . . my father said, God damn you, you get to hell off my land and if you're on it when I get to my gun, by God I'll fill you with buckshot. . . . This truly is exactly what happened.[70]

She continued with a long screed against the New Deal, asking the columnist why it was impossible to attack Roosevelt, who she thought was being treated "as sacr[o]sanct as Der Fuhrer or Il Duce" were in their own countries.[71]

In New York City, she had taken up residence in the Grosvenor Hotel on Fifth Avenue, a few blocks north of Washington Square Park. She worked around the clock to finish the serial. When it was completed, she began venturing out to see friends. On the evening of January 24, 1938, one of them took her to a performance of the notorious musical *The Cradle Will Rock,* originally produced by the Federal Theatre Project, one of many arts programs of the Works Progress Administration.

Under fire from congressional critics on the House Un-American Activities Committee, the WPA, months earlier, had shut down the production (directed by a very young Orson Welles) during previews. Its broad allegory of pro-union steelworkers pitted against heartless captains of industry had spurred accusations of Communist influence. Shut out of the theater just as the musical was slated to open, the actors and hundreds of audience members had then marched twenty-one blocks to another venue, where the show went on.

Lane had to have known the play's reputation. Her former beau Garet Garrett had written a piece fulminating against the FTP for the *Post* in 1936. Still, she was so horrified by the play and "the vicious fury of its attack on everything respectable" that she staged a melodramatic protest of her own, walking out during the first act. For years she had inveighed against the hidebound respectability embodied by Mansfield and her mother, but the play's "sneers at America, at liberty, at law" were going too far, she told a friend. When she got home she "burst into tears," sickened to know that "the American government is actually spending hundreds of millions of my money . . . on such propaganda."[72] Weeks later, she was still fulminating: "I knew it was a Red Revolution play," she wrote, but "could only feel as if I were seeing a dog lift his leg at every decent value in this wretched world."[73]

At the moment, Lane's only public outlet for such feelings was "Free Land," which appeared in the *Saturday Evening Post* in eight installments beginning in March 1938.[74] It was a huge success, being published in book form two months later and becoming a bestseller, although *Kirkus* noted "too close a resemblance to *Let the Hurricane Roar* in general pattern and some details."[75] Privately, however, Lane took no joy in it, seething about politics. "Free Land" elevated the self-reliant pioneer to the status of hero, but funneling her anger into fiction was no longer satisfying. To friends, she railed about income taxes, state taxes, and the "destruction" of America.[76] George Bye pleaded with her to set aside these preoccupations and keep writing, saying that he was cross with her for indulging in the politics of paranoia. "I deeply believe you need have no fears of communism, fascism or regimentation," he wrote, adding, "Please, darling, get back in line and do your stuff."[77]

Around the same time, Lane also took the reckless step of sending a significant sum—$2,850 in Albanian gold francs, worth nearly $50,000 today—to Rexh Meta, to purchase undeveloped land on the outskirts of Tirana, Albania.[78] Meta and his wife had named their first child, born in 1937, Borë-Rose, "Snow Rose" in Albanian. The property was intended to provide Meta and his family a place to live and, one day, in Lane's recurring Oriental daydreams, an exotic retirement villa for herself. Beyond the dubious prospect of investing in eastern Europe on the brink of war, the maneuver, according to Lane's biographer, imperiled Meta himself.[79] Due to Albania's laws, the property had to be bought in his name. Working at a government ministry post, unable to afford it on his salary, he was forced to acknowledge to authorities that he was backed by a powerful, wealthy American "mother." In the volatile climate, that exposure could not have served him well.

Alarmed by Lane's improvident spending, an old friend from European days, Isaac Don Levine, a Russian-born journalist and Hearst columnist, urged her not to let all the "Free Land" money slip through her fingers. He and his wife squired her around their neighborhood in Connecticut, showing her likely properties.[80] She ended up buying a Depression bargain startlingly reminiscent of the original Rocky Ridge: a few hilly acres studded with apple trees and an old farmhouse in Danbury, for twenty-six hundred in cash and a nine-hundred-dollar mortgage. It was the first time in her life that she owned her own house.

Tellingly, when she wrote to her mother with the news, she buried it in paragraphs about other matters. It was as if she still felt an ineradicable sense of shame or guilt associated with possessing her own house, having (so she believed) burned down theirs. "I have bought some land in Connecticut," she wrote, "and am going to build a little house on it."[81] Was she sounding out her mother? If so, she quickly moved on, saying she had to live in Connecticut because it had no state income tax. She could not reside in either Missouri or New York State, with their tax burdens. Ironically, the reason she could afford the Danbury house was that it was in foreclosure, its owners unable to pay their taxes or mortgage.[82]

Even then, she could barely bring herself to go through with it. She was so concerned about inheritance taxes that she was going to have the deed made out to both herself and John Turner, or perhaps solely to John. He was now eighteen, and Lane had never formally adopted him.[83] Wiser heads must have prevailed: when the sale went through, hers was the only name on the deed. She was already planning to gut the place. In coming years, she would rebuild and renovate exhaustively.

Her parents continued to be concerned about her mental health and finances. Upon receiving a five-hundred-dollar check Lane sent in early 1938, Wilder gingerly asked if there was anything special she wanted done with it at Rocky Ridge, and whether Lane could really spare the money. "If not," she suggested, "I'll send it back and no one need know."[84] She pressed on to say:

> Neither of us want you to work so hard because you feel you must help us. You are a dear, sweet thing to us all the time. You and your comfort and well being are more to us than anything else. So please take good care of yourself for us.[85]

THE Wilders were gradually reestablishing their own independence. The Little House books were bringing in a small but steady income. On the strength of that, they set off on a monthlong road trip in early May 1938, driving throughout the West—crossing the southern plains of Oklahoma, Texas, and New Mexico, and on through Arizona,

California, Oregon, Washington, Idaho, Montana, Wyoming, Colorado, and South Dakota—before heading back to Missouri. Almanzo would finally see the sights he had missed when his wife visited Lane by train in 1915 and when the women drove to California a decade later. They planned to stop in De Smet on the way home, where his wife could see her sisters and check details about the Hard Winter.

Again, they prevailed on Silas Seal to drive. This time his wife, Neta, came along. Thirty-three years old, Neta Seal was a sweet country girl, who had grown up near Mansfield earning money the way Wilder's father had, trapping rabbits and possums. Despite the age difference, she and Laura recognized each other as kindred spirits, and they sat together in the back seat, singing what Neta called "crazy little songs" to pass the time. Among these were "Waltz Me Around Willy" and a racy, rollicking old-time country blues number, "Ain't Nobody's Business If I Do," recorded in the 1920s by Bessie Smith and in the 1930s by blind country singer Riley Puckett:

> She drives a Ford machine, I buy the gasoline,
> Ain't nobody's business if I do
> It's nobody's business, nobody's business
> Nobody's business if I do
>
> That's where my money goes,
> Buying my baby clothes,
> Nobody's business if I do
>
> She rides a Cadillac,
> Oh boy she makes the jack,
> Nobody's business if I do
>
> That's where my money goes,
> Buying my baby clothes,
> Nobody's business if I do.[86]

"I learned to love her on that trip," Neta would say, and later photographs bear that out, with the taller young woman standing beside

Wilder, a protective arm around her.[87] They had a wonderful time, crossing Oklahoma and the Texas Panhandle, where dust storms had once swept the countryside. They saw the Painted Desert at the Four Corners and the Petrified Forest in Arizona. They celebrated Gold Rush days in Barstow, enjoying a parade and period costumes, and posed in front of a snowdrift at Yellowstone.

The Wilders covered gasoline, and each couple paid fifty cents a night for a cabin along the way, as the Wilders had done in 1931. Almanzo collected branches to whittle into canes and a hunk of Joshua tree to fashion into a lamp. They took in the Grand Canyon, snapping pictures that showed Almanzo as a dignified older gent in sweater and tie, his handlebar mustache now white, his wife peering shyly from beneath a turban or scarf wrapped around her hair, plump and somehow still girlish. Silas drove the Buick through the famous "Chandelier" tree, a 315-foot-tall coast redwood with a passage cut in the trunk. When Neta took the picture, Laura was seated demurely on a root, her pocketbook in her lap.

Wilder kept a travel diary, noting down her favorite vistas, delicious picnics, lousy cabins ("a rotten place to stay!"), and funny road signs: "Honestly now, what's your hurry?"[88] All her life she had loved rivers, and on the way from Grants Pass to Portland she found her heart's desire when they followed the Smith River, a tributary of the Umpqua, up into the mountains "through Big Trees." The vista held some special meaning for her: "Blue water with white riffles. Lovely, never saw anything more beautiful. The dream of blue & white water fulfilled."[89] They drove alongside it until the stream turned into a rivulet high in the Coast Range, and ate lunch perched there, gazing on the snow that fed it.

On the high plains of Montana, between Billings and Sheridan, they encountered a familiar sight: hordes of grasshoppers and crickets. But the Dust Bowl and its horrors were receding. On the same grasslands, Wilder noted, were grazing "lots of fat cattle and pretty horses . . . scattered over the uplands. All fat and shining."[90] In a museum, she was amused to find on display a relic of her own past, a side saddle like the one she had used to ride Trixy.

The trip may have been tied, in part, to Carrie's recent loss: her

husband, David Swanzey, had died a month earlier, in April 1938, at
the age of eighty-four, and the stop in Keystone may have been intended
to pay respects and comfort the widow. Wilder doubtless also used the
opportunity to talk over old times in De Smet, sharpening her recollections, and she helped her sister by paying the taxes owed on Swanzey's
mining claims.[91] Her travel diary concluded in Keystone with four
lines of a song she jotted down "for Prairie Girl," the title she was considering for the book to follow "Hard Winter."[92] It was an old-fashioned
courting song: "Somebody's coming when the twilight falls. / Somebody's coming for a twilight call. / He will be welcome to the best of
all. / And I'll keep a little kiss for him."[93] Once she was finished with
Hard Winter, she would revel in the nostalgia of sleigh rides, parties,
and romance.

In her hometown, she visited Grace and Nathan Dow, earning a
front-page headline in the *De Smet News*: "Mrs. Wilder, Author . . .
Checks Material Here." Basking in the association with the Little
House books, the newspaper reported that Wilder's next book, about
the Hard Winter, was "awaited with interest in the state, following as
it does her daughter's story, *Free Land*."[94] The reporter made it clear
that it was the mother who had "the advantage of first-hand experience in the pioneering of Dakota Territory."[95] Lane had never been
back, an interesting omission given how many of the family's former
haunts she had previously sought out. When it came to De Smet, locus
of the family's own free land and the house lost to fire, she kept clear.
Once burnt, twice shy.

God Help the Poor Taxpayers!

In September of 1938, as Neville Chamberlain met with Adolf Hitler,
American anxieties over whether the United States would be pulled
into another war in Europe ratcheted up. Pacifist organizations such as
World Peaceways ran thousands of radio spots and magazine advertisements that year. One depicted a mother joyfully lifting a baby boy
above her head; scrawled across the child in bloodred letters were the
words "To Be Killed in Action." The America First movement led by

antiwar students and Charles Lindbergh would not be organized until two years later, but editorialists and cartoonists were already promoting isolationism.

Lane, a devoted isolationist, spent significant time that year campaigning for the Ludlow Amendment to the Constitution. Named for Louis Ludlow, the Indiana congressman who introduced it in 1935, the amendment would have required a national referendum to be held before Congress could issue a declaration of war, except in cases of direct attack or invasion. The notion had first been suggested during World War I, but achieved its highest popularity during the mid-1930s, when a Gallup poll showed that 75 percent of Americans were in favor of it.[96]

Roosevelt and his long-serving secretary of state, Cordell Hull, adamantly opposed the measure as a crippling check on presidential powers. When it came up for a procedural vote in the House of Representatives in January 1938, it was narrowly defeated, 209–188. After that—and with increasingly alarming news out of Europe—support for the amendment began to erode, but Lane was not giving up.

On September 26, 1938, four days before Chamberlain would deliver his infamous "peace for our time" proclamation defending the Munich accord that allowed Hitler to annex the Sudetenland, Wilder responded to a letter from her daughter urging her to support the amendment. She enthusiastically took up the cause, although in terms that suggested she was not familiar with the particulars, since she misspelled the amendment's name as "Laidlaw."[97] Nonetheless, she assured Lane that the local Athenian Club was already on the case, planning to send multiple letters to their congressional representatives.

Nannie Davis and her husband, Oliver B. Davis, longtime Ozark newspaper publishers who had owned and edited the *Mansfield Mirror* for years, were among those involved in organizing the local effort.[98] To the Athenian Club's latest meeting, the Davises had brought a letter addressed "To American Mothers," a copy of which, in Wilder's handwriting, survives in her papers. (In that copy, too, Wilder used the "Laidlaw" spelling, and perhaps did not send it out because she noticed the error.)[99] For some years, the letter was believed to have been written by Wilder herself, but her note to Lane casts doubt on that

assumption.[100] Still, it expressed the collective antiwar view, prevalent
at the time.

To American Mothers

<u>Write your candidates for Congress.</u> Tell them you are in favor
of the [Ludlow] Referendum bill. Ask them to let you know before
November election how they expect to vote on this bill making
it necessary to submit to a vote of the people the matter of a
declaration of war, except for defense or invasion of our home-land.

Make copies of this letter and send to ten of your friends,
American Mothers, asking them also to write ten letters to their
friends.

Your failure to do this may bring disaster to your home and your
loved ones and leave the way clear for the War Gods to call your
sons to the trenches, to face the Hell of shot and shell.

Pray that God may save us from another war.[101]

Conceived as a chain letter, a popular form at the time, the missive
was unsigned. That was O. B. Davis's idea, Wilder wrote, as was its
alarmist tone. "That sort of ballyhoo," she told Lane, might "appeal to
lots of people . . . the kind . . . that nothing else would reach."[102] She
had a list of twenty-four people to send it to, rounding up friends and
neighbors to make their own copies, and soliciting her daughter's
praise for her efforts: "Don't you think I have done very well for the
short time since you wrote?"[103]

Wilder's active involvement may have ended there, but Lane stayed
in the fight. She published an opinion piece, "Why I Am for the People's
Vote on War," in *Liberty*, a magazine that calculated the reading time
for its articles. Lane's piece ("9 Minutes, 5 Seconds") employed rhetoric reminiscent of the World Peaceways advertisement: "We know
this is coming. The whole world knows it. . . . Hold your babies in
your arms, see the helpless small things toothlessly laughing."[104] The
article was illustrated with a "war god"—a Viking-like figure with a
dagger at his waist—pounding at the door of an American mother, her
son behind her, their only protection a stout padlock labeled "Ludlow
Amendment." In response, Eleanor Roosevelt ("6 Minutes, 50 Seconds")

criticized the histrionic element of Lane's argument, saying "this does not seem to me a very realistic viewpoint."[105] Wilder thought her daughter's view "plain and fair and true," and gnashed her teeth over Mrs. Roosevelt's perfidy, saying she "evaded the truth."[106]

The same month, in *Woman's Day*, Lane took part in a roundtable feature on "War! What the Women of America Can Do to Prevent It," alongside Eleanor Roosevelt, Dorothy Dix, Norma Shearer, and other prominent figures. She hammered home her message: every woman, she said, should spend three cents to send a postcard to Congress, demanding the Ludlow bill.[107]

As a prominent face of the amendment, Lane appeared before a Senate Judiciary Subcommittee on May 10, 1939. The only other witness testifying in support was a New York attorney, Morris L. Ernst, known for co-founding the American Civil Liberties Union and for successfully defending James Joyce's *Ulysses* against pornography charges. He confined himself to explaining how the Founding Fathers had failed to anticipate the need for such a measure. But Lane took no such temperate route. Looking older and wearier than her fifty-two years, clad in a pinstriped suit, corsage, and shiny black beribboned hat, she declared herself, according to the *New York Times*, "a revolutionist."[108] When a senator tried to convince her to retreat from that radicalism, she refused.

Lane took an equally hard line with her old friend Dorothy Thompson, who appeared on the cover of *Time* magazine a month after Lane's congressional appearance.[109] By now, Thompson was the most famous woman journalist in the world, an expert on the European situation. Once a skeptic when it came to Roosevelt, opposing Social Security and criticizing his Supreme Court ambitions in her column, Thompson had switched her allegiance to him when it became clear that he was no pacifist. She warned continually about the rise of Hitler and the dangers of refusing to take him seriously, calling Charles Lindbergh "America's number one problem child."[110]

Just after the appeasement in Munich, Lane wrote to Thompson, praising it as good diplomacy. Hitler was right, she told her friend, and was "simply stating an obvious fact when he said that . . . defeat of the Chamberlain policy would endanger European peace."[111] As Lane saw it, the true threat to democracy lay in the expansion of Roosevelt's political powers. "A man is free only to the extent that he is NOT governed," she wrote, and "the death-blow to liberty on earth would be America's fighting any war." In such an event, she said, "this country would instantly be a dictatorship, and no matter how the war ended, it would remain a dictatorship."[112] Ruthless as Hitler and Stalin might be, she concluded breezily, they could not "destroy personal freedom on earth . . . Don't be alarmed, darling."[113]

In the spring of 1939, Lane instigated an ugly break with Thompson over a perceived slight to Isaac Don Levine, the anti-Communist Hearst columnist and her neighbor in Connecticut. In a talk at the International PEN Congress at the New York World's Fair, Thompson had warned journalists against becoming propaganda tools in the ongoing "ideological warfare," citing the fact-checking difficulties and ethical dilemmas facing reporters who found themselves relaying accusations that could not be independently verified.[114] As an example, she used the case of Walter Krivitsky, a former intelligence agent and defector from the Soviet Union with ties to Trotsky. Levine and Lane had arranged editorial introductions between Krivitsky and the *Post,* which then published a series of memoirs about his role as an agent in Stalin's secret service. Thompson criticized this, pointing out that the former agent's assertions were "neither provable nor unprovable."[115]

After a phone conversation in which Lane defended Levine's honor while Thompson dismissed him as having an agenda, Lane wrote an excoriating riposte, echoing previous complaints in which she accused her friend of becoming "not the Dorothy I thought I knew":

Once you were a fine person, sensitive, intelligent, witty, poetic, ardent for truth and justice, sure in judgments based on moral and humane values. Now you are coarse and stupid. You surround yourself with sycophants and exploiters who would betray you and vanish at a rumor that the by-line was fading. . . . I see rotten trick after trick, half-truth and propaganda-slant, in your copy. . . . When have I, in the slightest degree, exploited you? Traded on my knowing you? Did I ask you for help in saving my Albanian son and his family, or my Albanian property? In nineteen years, when have I come to you with an axe to grind? Do you no longer know a genuine thing when you see it, or do you no longer value it?[116]

It was an epistolary tantrum, reminiscent of the one Lane had enacted with Clarence Day years earlier. With forbearance, Thompson defended her position and sought to save the friendship, but it would never be the same. Although Thompson had visited her in Missouri, Lane would consistently refuse her friend's repeated invitations to visit her country home in Vermont.

The Levine-Krivitsky affair signaled another major depressive episode for Lane, this one typified by self-pity, professional jealousy, and increasingly unstable rhetoric. It highlighted Lane's lifelong inability to recognize the existence or value of journalistic ethics, something that had hampered her early career as a biographer and would continue to cast a haze of confusion over the "truth" or fiction of the Little House books. As Lane tipped into yet another volatile period, it threatened to destroy the delicate balance in her mother's work, introducing to it an element of propaganda.

WITH delays due to Wilder and Lane's extended debate over its opening, the manuscript for *On the Shores of Silver Lake* was not ready to be turned in to the publisher until May 1939. Earlier that year, abashed by her tardiness, Wilder told Lane she was ignoring Ida Louise Raymond's puzzled queries: "She can think I have gone to Timbuctoo or am sick or mad or just [too] lazy to write."[117] A bout of flu delayed her even further, and she worried that three years might pass between books and "my stories will be forgotten."[118]

She was also worried about her daughter. "I am uneasy about you," she told her in early 1939. If Lane were "short of money," Wilder assured her, she had a couple of hundred dollars she could send.[119]

While continuing to economize by writing on the backs of old letters and burning wood rather than running the furnace, Wilder was finally achieving a sense of security. She told her daughter that she had escaped from the nightmare that once troubled her: "I haven't gone alone down that long, dark road I used to dream of, for a long time," she wrote. "The last time I saw it stretching ahead of me, I said in my dream 'But I don't have to go through those dark woods, I don't have to go that way.' And I turned away from it. We are living inside our income and I don't have to worry about the bills."[120]

At the same time, she acknowledged that Lane must be relieved to be free of her dependents, saying that "it must seem strange to you not to have anyones expenses to pay, except your own, to have everybody, including us, off your hands." She apologized that she still needed Lane's assistance with her books, a "trouble" that would soon, in any case, be over.

When Wilder wrote to George Bye at the end of that month to tell him the manuscript was at the typist, she asked him to get her a good contract, saying that *Plum Creek* had been so successful that Harper should "treat me well."[121] She referred further questions to Lane, since she and her husband were "going wandering." Only a year after their previous visit, they were returning to De Smet for Old Settlers' Day, an annual summer celebration in the town.[122] It would be the last time.

Wilder herself recognized the finality of it. She was nervous about the trip, planning to send Lane the "Hard Winter" manuscript in case anything happened to them.[123] She had been taking stock of her life and reached out to her daughter once again to thank her for the many ways in which she had made their lives easier. She counted over the creature comforts and luxuries their child had thoughtfully provided: dining table and chairs, rose-colored drapes, comfortable mattresses and down quilts, and gifts of jewelry. She thanked her for their financial security, the rent money now coming in from the Rock House and especially the income from the Little House books. "Without your help, I would not have the royalties from my books in the bank to draw on," she acknowledged. It was a genuine outpouring of affection and appreciation that stands out against the women's often querulous exchanges. Signing it, "Very much love, Mama Bess," she wrote as a postscript, "Oh Rose my dear, we do thank you so much for being so good to us."[124]

No reply has survived. Wilder was growing older and may have simply wanted to express the feelings while she had the chance. By withdrawing, her daughter may have triggered the kind of gratitude she had always yearned for, but if so, there is no indication that the words were a balm.

If Wilder noticed her daughter remaining withdrawn, she did not show it, chattering about new curtains, local gossip, and politics. She shook her head over the fact that Mansfield was planning to build a new sewage system with $65,000 in WPA money and a $17,000 bond. "The town is already bonded for more than it is worth," she said. "God help the poor taxpayers!"[125]

The Roosevelts continued to merit caustic remarks. In town, tickets for a celebration of FDR's birthday party, to be held in the Masonic Hall, were twenty-five cents a piece, "and 'they' couldn't sell them."[126] Wilder gloated over the fact that only fifty people showed up, and refreshments took all the ticket money. She wished that "Mrs. Roosevelt would have to scrub her own floors and do her own work," but shrugged her shoulders over foreign news. "We probably are thinking alike about things," she said, adding, "Hitlers word is about as good as Roosevelt's, isn't it." She was sure FDR had already made a secret agreement, and "Elinor knows it."[127]

But unlike her daughter's all-consuming invective, Wilder's politics were more casual, of a piece with rural, conservative, small-town life. She was concerned about communism and dictators, but found the new "Capri blue" curtains she was sewing for the living room a more compelling topic, hoping they would look like "a filmy, misty, blue cloud against the windows."[128] She invested more space and time in relating town gossip and describing how recent rain had filled ditches and made the creek "roar."[129] She kept a distracted eye on the national scene, but her focus was local.

The Wilders left for De Smet on June 6, the mother writing to her daughter with reassurance: "We will be very careful, drive slowly and stop when we please."[130] They pledged not to drive on Sundays, when "every crazy boy is drunk and on the road." As promised, she had sent Lane the "Hard Winter" draft by registered mail. It was the only existing manuscript; she had been unable to finish a fair copy for herself because she had injured her hand. "I expect you will find lots of fault in it, but we can argue it out later," she said.

Despite that anticipation, Wilder's comments suggested that she

was making provisions in case she and Almanzo did not come back. Her
letter to Lane amounted to a kind of last will and testament, telling her
where to find the key to the safety deposit box, the Postal Savings cer-
tificates, and the "little, old writing desk" that had traveled with the
Wilders in 1894. Notes for the next book could be found in an envelope marked "Pioneer Girl," and Wilder suggested that Lane could
"finish the series if you had to do so."[131] Her postscript, too, was a nod
toward the end, begging her daughter never to allow the slovenly Murrays in their farmhouse again. "Do whatever else you please with it but
not that," she wrote.

But the trip was uneventful. Although they encountered heat and
dust returning through Kansas, for the most part the weather offered
"lovely, warm, going-somewhere-days."[132] Wilder wrote a brief account
for the children's section of the *Christian Science Monitor*, chronicling
familiar associations brought on by hearing the Dakota meadowlarks
singing again and feeling the spring wind blowing in her face: "Almost
I seemed to hear Ma say, 'Laura, put your sunbonnet on! You'll look
like an Indian.' So I tilted my wide hat brim to shield my face from sun
and wind."[133]

Mostly, she noted how everything was different. "The little town
we used to know was gone," she said, replaced by sprawling development that reached to what had once been the Big Slough, where she had
walked home from school with Carrie. The schoolhouse was gone, as
were the rickety wooden stores on the main street with their false
fronts. Happily, so was the drought: it rained during their visit, and
after so many dead, dry years, everyone found it refreshing and "nobody
cared."[134]

They were feted as distinguished guests. The publisher and editor of
the *De Smet News*, Aubrey Sherwood—grandson of Sam Masters,
Wilder's old schoolteacher in Walnut Grove—had early on recognized
the importance to De Smet of the historical legacy represented by both
"Free Land" and the Little House books, becoming an ardent promoter
and collector of memorabilia. Sherwood organized the Old Settlers' Day
celebrations, and in coming years he would cover the Ingallses' story so
relentlessly that townsfolk would tire of it. On the Wilders' visit in 1939,
he photographed them seated in his office beneath a wall of historical

images, including the portrait of the Ingalls family taken just before Laura and Almanzo had left town the first time. With "hard winter" commemorative ribbons pinned to their lapels, they show in their determined expressions something of the stoicism that got them through it.[135]

The Wilders drove out to see Charles Ingalls's old homestead, the vanished dream of self-sufficiency, sold soon after he proved up. Wilder's description only hints at what it meant to her, the melancholy of seeing the place for the last time, those who had settled it gone with the prairie wind. "There is a nice farm house in place of the little claim shanty," she wrote wistfully, "but the Cotton Wood trees we set that long ago day when Grace was lost among the violets are still growing—big trees now."[136]

Her memories were already safely preserved, in one of the final chapters of *Silver Lake*, in the scene where Laura finds her baby sister sitting in a shallow concavity full of violets, an old buffalo wallow filled with fragrance and color:

> The whole great plain of the earth was shadow. There was hardly a wind, but the air moved and whispered to itself in the grasses. Laura almost knew what it said. Lonely and wild and eternal were land and water and sky and the air blowing.[137]

Perhaps more than anything that she could say or do in 1939, that was her farewell to the place.

By the Shores of Silver Lake was published in October of that year, earning another Newbery Honor Book nomination and excellent reviews.[138] *Kirkus* called it a "splendidly written contribution to factual frontier material," but conveyed a note of uncertainty about its proper classification.[139] "One always hesitates as to whether these stories of Laura Wilder's childhood belong with fiction or non-fiction," the reviewer said, advising booksellers to "place this where you have found the others sell best."

EVEN after Germany invaded Poland on September 1, 1939, triggering declarations of war by Britain and France, the United States continued to cling to isolation. Roosevelt remained hampered by the 1930s Neutrality Acts. As a way around them, he developed the Lend-Lease policy of providing limited aid in food, fuel, and weapons.

With deep reluctance and foreboding, Americans began to realize the inevitability of war. By July 1940, more than 70 percent supported "compulsory military training for all young men."[140] Asked by *Life* magazine whether, on entering the war, the country should continue to fight "at all costs" as Norway, Finland, and Belgium had, more than half of those polled said yes.[141]

But Lane railed against compulsory government programs of any kind, in ways that became increasingly disturbing to those around her, straining relationships. All her life, she had defied authority. Now, during the run-up to the war and throughout that long conflict, she behaved as if government interference in her life was both a personal affront and a threat to her very existence.

In 1939 she had broken with Dorothy Thompson, and in short order would quarrel with the friends she had fought over with Thompson: Don Levine and his wife, Ruth. On May 10, 1940, a year to the day after her appearance before the Senate subcommittee pleading for isolationism, Lane was at the Levines' home, listening to radio news of the German invasion of Holland and Belgium. The Levines, who were Jewish, were appalled, believing that the United States should declare war immediately, and Don said he would pick up a rifle and fight before ever submitting to Hitler.

Although she had recently published a letter denouncing anti-Semitism, Lane took their reaction personally, writing in her diary "they both . . . turned against me," and recording a lengthy anti-Semitic diatribe:

> I do not know what "the Jew" is. Facts are that he is not a race, a nationality, nor, as an individual, often, the adherent of a religious faith. I do not know what the reality is. I have been unable to see that any [such] reality, The Jew, actually exists. . . . yesterday [Ruth] coldly repulsed my efforts to save what has been a genuine and deep emotional attachment and did this by saying that Hitler's actions probably do not mean to anyone else what they mean to "those of our faith." What does she mean by "our faith"?[142]

Ruth Levine later recalled their discussion differently, and Lane's reaction may well have been tied to instability. Once again, she was suicidal, writing in her journal that month: "Truly I would prefer to die. No argument against suicide has any reality now."[143] In her diary, she described herself as "manic depressive."[144] She had been forced to borrow money from her mother yet again, a circumstance that may have contributed to her worsening mood.[145] Her houseguest, Norma Lee Browning, recalled her ongoing irritation over the continuing demands of editing her mother's work.[146]

A month later, during an argument about politics in the Danbury house, Lane broke with John Turner. To friends who had known them both, their dispute was unclear, and Lane explained little beyond saying that John had "walked out of this house in a towering rage."[147] He took a train to New York City and joined the Coast Guard, later telling Lane that he despised himself for freeloading and wanted to "stand entirely on my own feet."[148] Decades later, Turner said he did not mean to break away entirely but was aware that Lane would be infuriated by his enlistment, telling her biographer, "I knew how she felt about government and that she would feel that I had gone over to the enemy."[149] At the time, Lane said, with finality, "I truly have no interest at all in John Turner."[150] Beyond a brief encounter or two the following year, she would never see him or his brother again. She had been John's "mother" for six years.

Lane also broke with editors at the *Saturday Evening Post*. During the summer of 1939, she had driven across the country gathering material for another *Post* serial, this one attacking the National Recovery Administration. A New Deal agency that regulated working hours and set minimum wages and prices, it was reviled by conservatives for raising the cost of doing business. The fictional protagonist of Lane's piece was a small-scale coal miner in Laramie, Wyoming, who felt oppressed by the government, making bald statements such as "I can't stand no more regulations."[151]

She titled it "Forgotten Man," in an ironic reference to Roosevelt's famous radio address in 1932 recognizing "the forgotten man at the bottom of the economic pyramid."[152] But the magazine's new editor, beginning to shy away from isolationism after the death of George

Horace Lorimer, rejected the manuscript as veiled propaganda, saying Lane's "indignation smothers it."[153] Lane declared herself "stunned."[154] She would never publish another piece of fiction.

Love's Old Sweet Song

While her daughter involved herself in ever more intense arguments, Wilder was wearying of politics. In Danbury, Lane was glued to the radio, feverishly recording European developments in her journal. In Mansfield, Wilder was reveling in her busy teenage self.

Just as her book on the Hard Winter was about to published, a last-minute contretemps over the title broke out, Harper fearing that children would be deterred by anything "hard." Both Wilder and her daughter were annoyed, Lane griping that "there is altogether too much coddling of the mythical tender child."[155] Still, Wilder readily compromised, accepting *The Long Winter* as a substitute. She must have been elated by its reception. Published in June of 1940, it earned high praise, a starred review in *Kirkus*, a Newbery Honor mention, and the *New York Times Book Review*'s imprimatur: "The book is beautifully written, and we could ill spare this picture of a fine pioneer family."[156]

Having pressed through the difficult days of Mary's blindness and that long, hard winter, Wilder was free to relive happier memories. As she worked on the next volume, which she imagined might be her last, she savored delectable moments of teenage glamor: the flowers on her name cards, the styling of her bangs, and her "darling" brown velvet hat.

She wrote to her sister Carrie to ask about the hymns they once sang in Sunday school and details of Mary's college days in Vinton, Iowa. Carrie obliged by sending an old hymnbook, and shared an anecdote about another Laura Ingalls, a well-known pilot and stunt flyer who was passing through South Dakota.[157] Laura Houghtaling Ingalls was a distant relative, her family tracing back to the same Ingallses in England who had given rise to the American branch generations ago. Carrie telephoned the pilot to see if they could meet, but there was no landing field at Keystone.

Wilder later learned that Lane had met this other Laura, and saw a family resemblance. "Adventuring seems to run in the family," Wilder wrote on hearing the news, "and you and she must have a lot in common."[158] True enough: Laura Houghtaling Ingalls was a friend and admirer of Charles Lindbergh and his America First movement. The following year, she would be arrested and charged with acting as a Nazi publicity agent, eventually serving several months in jail.

Wilder's mind remained on "Prairie Girl," as she was calling the new manuscript, and De Smet's lively social scene of decades past. She was reliving the birthday party at the railway station with its oyster soup and frosted cake, the school house "literaries" and spelling bees, the musical evenings and "madcap days" when the town put on a minstrel show. Turning away from the fall of Paris and Rommel's Panzer advance across North Africa, she rushed Laura from party to party with an almost feverish quality, as if she could feel her family slipping away again.

She was also withdrawing from the social clubs she had once attended regularly, finding her circle tedious. "I can't fit in with the crowd someway," she told Lane. "Never could very well and now I am tired of them more than ever."[159] Comparing Mansfield and its surroundings to the frontier town she had once known, she grew derisive, dismissing Ozark hamlets as "these stinking little towns."[160] As for politics, she was fatalistic. "I agree with you about congress," she told Lane, "but what can we expect. This is a representative government we have yet. And I ask you, Does it not represent the majority of the people?"[161]

But Lane chafed at the status quo. Stymied at writing her own political fiction, she looked to her mother's work for an outlet. As a result, the seventh volume in the Little House series—eventually published as *Little Town on the Prairie*, a title originally considered for "Hard Winter"—would be the most overtly political of all.

Wilder's outline of "Prairie Girl" began with a Fourth of July scene.[162] In the manuscript, she devoted an entire chapter to picnic preparations, beating eggs and whipping whites for an iced cake, baking lemon pie, and ironing ruffled dresses.[163] For the day itself, she described the whole Ingalls family trooping into De Smet, sitting with a crowd before a platform alongside the railroad tracks in a cheerful, patriotic scene. "A tall man with a grand manner" read the Declaration of Independence, she said, quoting the famous first sentence.[164] Another speaker described "how our ancestors fought, bled and died that we might be free" and that "a mere handful of ragged patriots had beaten the whole British army."[165] Recalling her original patriotic chapter in *Farmer Boy*, Wilder noted the pomposity of the speakers, who would "wave their arms and shout."[166] She was more interested in describing the horse races afterward than the speeches.

Lane, however, was bent on making a point. She took her mother's straightforward account and transformed it, highlighting Laura's independence, having her attend with only her father and Carrie as companions. Speechifiers were recast into a folksy man of the people delivering an extended address with overtones of New Deal disapproval:

> "Well, boys," he said, "I'm not much good at public speaking, but today's the glorious Fourth. This is the day and date when our fore-fathers cut loose from the despots of Europe. There wasn't many Americans at that time, but they wouldn't stand for any monarch tyrannizing over them. They had to fight the British regulars and their hired Hessians and the murdering scalping red-skinned savages that those fine gold-laced aristocrats turned loose on our settlements and paid for murdering and burning and scalping women and children. A few barefoot Americans had to fight the whole of them and lick 'em, and they did fight them and they did lick them. Yes sir! We licked the British in 1776 and we licked 'em again in 1812, and we backed all the monarchies of Europe out of Mexico and off this continent less than twenty years ago, and by glory! Yessir, by Old Glory right here, waving over my head, any time the despots of Europe try to step on America's toes, we'll lick 'em again!"[167]

The speaker's preoccupations aligned with Lane's:

> "Well, so here we are today . . . Every man Jack of us a free and inde-pendent citizen of God's country, the only country on earth where a man is free and independent. Today's the Fourth of July, when this whole thing was started, and it ought to have a bigger, better cele-

bration than this. We can't do much this year. Most of us are out here trying to pull ourselves up by our own boot straps. By next year, likely some of us will be better off, and able to chip in for a real big rousing celebration of Independence Day. Meantime, here we are. It's Fourth of July, and on this day somebody's got to read the Declaration of Independence."[168]

This would be part of Lane's campaign for Americans' "re-education." She was hammering home what children, in her view, had to learn: that bootstrapping was the only legitimate way to survive a Depression. In letters, she had been railing about the educational system and the stupidity of her fellow citizens. She demanded of Garet Garrett, "How long has it been since the Declaration of Independence was read on the Fourth of July?"[169]

While her mother recalled fidgeting on hard benches, bored by inflated rhetoric, Lane had Laura lapping up selected sections of the Declaration, including what she termed "the long and terrible list of the crimes of the King." Reading as if they were the crimes of Franklin Delano Roosevelt, they included, "He has erected a multitude of new offices, and sent hither swarms of officers to harass our people and to eat out their substance."

Hearing this solemn intonation, Lane's fictional fourteen-year-old Laura forgets to fidget, transfixed by an uncharacteristic interior monologue that has no counterpart, in length or philosophical abstraction, elsewhere in the series:

Laura stood stock still. Suddenly she had a completely new thought. The Declaration and the song came together in her mind, and she thought: God is America's king.

She thought: Americans won't obey any king on earth. Americans are free. That means they have to obey their own consciences. No king bosses Pa; he has to boss himself. Why (she thought), when I am a little older, Pa and Ma will stop telling me what to do, and there isn't anyone else who has a right to give me orders. I will have to make myself be good.

Her whole mind seemed to be lighted up by that thought. This is what it means to be free. It means, you have to be good. "Our father's

God, author of liberty—" The laws of Nature and of Nature's God
endow you with a right to life and liberty. Then you have to keep the
laws of God, for God's law is the only thing that gives you a right to
be free.[170]

The pronounced nationalistic tone and fervor of the passage would
stand out so strongly that Lane's biographer would seize upon it as
evidence that Wilder did not write her own books.[171] That exaggerates
the section's importance, but in letting her daughter's overtly political
revisions stand, Wilder passively accepted her point of view, in the
same way that she had accepted Lane's isolationist agenda.

Virtually no correspondence about *Little Town* and no corrected
typescript have survived. A list of Wilder's final corrections—inserted
in her handwritten manuscript—does make it clear that she remained
devoted to emphasizing her father's success as a breadwinner. She
instructed Lane to delete a reference to his being too poor to buy livestock.[172]

She was also concerned about libel. By now, the Little House books
were reaching so many readers that she was worried about Reverend
Brown's relatives. Although Brown presided over her wedding ceremony, Wilder had never liked him. Now, she dished to Lane about
his peccadilloes—and Reverend Alden's—while omitting the salacious
details from the book:

> I cut about Brown's meanness in taking Rev. Alden's place as preacher.
> It might offend some church people to show up a preacher in such a
> light. Brown has descendants scattered all over the country from his
> first wife's children and foster grandchildren through Ida all over Cali-
> fornia. They would be mad about it and I can't see that it adds to the
> story, so please leave it cut. We didn't make him very attractive as it is.
>
> Did I ever tell you that Rev. Alden deserted his wife and children
> and ran away with a girl just after Mary went to college? Fact.

Wilder also altered her Teacher's Certificate. A reproduction
appeared opposite the last page of *Little Town*, with telling revisions.
The date was changed, from December 10, 1883, on the actual certifi-

cate, to December 24, 1882, in keeping with the fictional assertion that Laura was fifteen when she earned it.[173] While Wilder faithfully reproduced most of her test scores, she awarded herself a better score in history—98 instead of 69—probably because, in the novel, the teaching certificate followed on her triumphant recitation of American history at the school exhibition.[174] In that scene, too, Lane inserted her political views, emphasizing how the "honest United States" had prevailed against "the old oppressions of Europe."[175]

Lane worked over the manuscript during the first months of 1941, and the book was published in November of that year, just in time for Christmas.[176] *Little Town* inspired near-unanimous acclaim, with newspapers urging parents and children to read the entire series. The *New Yorker* called it "a moving and authentic re-creation of American frontier life."[177]

Reviews stressed that these were "true" stories, the *Philadelphia Record* calling them "the finest autobiographical writing for children now being done."[178] Like several of its predecessors, *Little Town* was a Newbery Honor Book. The Newbery Medal winner that year was another work of historical fiction, *The Matchlock Gun*, by Walter D. Edmonds. A tale of "wild America" and tomahawks, it too was inspired by family lore, said to be based on a true story from the days of the French and Indian Wars. Every other runner-up that year was also drawn from American history, summoning the Puritans, George Washington, and an Indian captive, Mary Jemison.[179] Wilder was buoyed by the wave she had set in motion.

SHE was coming to the end. She had done exactly what she set out to do, memorializing her beloved family. All that remained was to write the ending she had promised in Detroit. "My children's novel . . . ends happily, as all good novels should," she had forecast, pronouncing that the series would conclude with the marriage of "Laura of the *Little Houses* and Almanzo of *Farmer Boy*."[180]

But on the way there, Wilder was waylaid by the same feelings that triggered her epic fictional journey in the first place, the sense of the past as "treasure and torment."[181] Her last volume, published as *These*

Happy Golden Years, would be imbued with longing and nostalgia but also marked by the terrifying ordeal of staying with the Bouchies (renamed the "Brewsters"). In a particularly poignant passage, she took her leave of Mary. Ornamented on the surface with charming details of courtship—the sprigged lawn dresses and cream-colored hats of her youth—*Golden Years* would express happiness, but also sorrow.

By now, her battles with Lane had died down to the occasional irritable query.[182] She appeared confident and in control. The surviving original manuscript contains few asides to her daughter. One of the most revealing, a final farewell to her father, comes in her remark near the end, regarding "Love's Old Sweet Song," which Pa plays for her on her last night in the old home before she goes to live with Almanzo. She copied out the lyrics she remembered, in full:

Once in the dear dead days beyond recall
When on the world the mists began to fall,
Out of the dreams that rose in happy throng,
Low to our hearts love sang an old sweet song.
And in the dusk where fell the firelight gleam
Softly it wove itself into our dream.

Just a song at twilight, when the lights are low
And the flickering shadows softly come and go,
Though the heart be weary, sad the day and long,
Still to us at twilight comes love's old song,
Comes love's old sweet song.

Even today we hear of love's song of yore,
Deep in our hearts it swells forever more.
Footsteps may falter and weary grow the way,
Still we can hear it at the close of day,
So to the end when life's dim shadows fall,
Love will be found the sweetest song of all.[183]

She wrote, beneath it, in parentheses: "I don't know if all this song should be used. I love it all but perhaps it is too much. It seems to me to fit right here. The last song Laura hears Pa and the fiddle sing." It did fit, and they used it all.

"Footsteps may falter and weary grow the way": the passage of Laura Ingalls into her married state is among the most melancholy and subdued wedding scenes in children's literature, worthy of the Brontës. The original manuscript skipped the ceremony entirely, in favor of the wedding dinner afterward, when Laura could hardly taste the food for the feeling of finality: "even the wedding cake was dry as sawdust in her mouth for at last she had realized that she was going away for good this time."[184]

In a later draft appeared a description dark with foreshadowing, the young couple waiting for Reverend Brown in his parlor, presided over by a "large colored picture of a woman clinging to a white cross planted on a rock, with lightning streaking the sky above her and huge waves dashing high around her."[185] Wilder would be that woman within a few years of her wedding, battered by storms of ill fortune. But the reader was not to know it; the books would stop before venturing there. Children had to be protected from the truth.

Once more, in her final chapter, Wilder raised her little house from the ashes. "The little gray home in the west," she called it, and for the last time she described its perfect pantry, Almanzo telling her that she needn't build a fire. She left the young couple at home there, sitting on the stoop, bathed in moonlight. She had put everything right that once felt wrong. She was full of happiness, she wrote, because the "old home . . . was so near that she could go to it whenever she liked."[186] The dream was still alive.

These Happy Golden Years brought to a close Wilder's gilded portrait of prairie settlement. Throughout the whole series, her emphasis on her parents' finest qualities built the illusion—the ideal—of the yeoman farmer, able to sustain a family on the homestead, raising something from nothing. "The government bets a man a quarter-section of land, that he can't stay on it five years without starving to death," the fictional Laura explains. There was pride and delight in winning that bet.

Not starving, though, was hardly the same thing as succeeding, if succeeding meant staying on the land. In constructing her autobiographical series, Wilder and her secret editor had skillfully and purposefully left out an exhaustive list of revealing events, details, and characteristics: her brother Freddy's death, her father's persistent debt, his failures as farmer and provider, and the entire span covering the lurid shenanigans of Burr Oak and Walnut Grove, including Laura's servitude under the Masterses. In her Hard Winter, she disposed forever of the horrible George and Maggie, and their ill-timed baby. In *Little Town*, she improved her test scores. In *These Happy Golden Years*, she tidied up her first composition, "Ambition," quoted in full.[187] But nothing was more consequential, more dramatic, and more heartbreaking than what she left out at the end, the grief and penury that were soon to come.

The series would show none of it. Her final novel was her last opportunity to spend time with parents long gone, her last word on a marriage that began with such joy and promise. Secure in the eternal present tense, the last thing Laura says to the reader is, "It is a beautiful world."[188]

Wilder could go no further. Her life story, reimagined as an American tale of progress, was uplifted by authenticity and suffused by an ineffable sorrow. But for the rest of her life, she was done with all that. She had restored the family fortunes, in fiction and fact. She had said goodbye. "We are all here," went the song the family sang in their darkest, coldest hours. In Wilder's re-creation of the past, they still are.

Chapter 13

Sunshine and Shadow

If It Pesters Me Enough

Throughout the last years of her life, Wilder gave every appearance of being done with history. She traveled seldom, refused invitations, saw few people, and remained stubbornly rooted at Rocky Ridge. But at the very moment she wished to retire, it became clear that her audience was not done with her. Librarians, newspapers, and fans of all ages were making ever more pressing demands. Reluctantly, she began tending to the legacy she would leave behind.

She patiently replied to each and every one of her readers, telling her editor at Harper, "I cannot bear to disappoint children."[1] Between letters to young correspondents, she also had to deal with weightier matters.[2] In November 1941, her youngest sister, Grace Ingalls Dow, had died at her home in Manchester, South Dakota, at the age of sixty-four, after a long decline due to diabetes. Growing more reluctant to travel or to leave her husband, Wilder did not return to De Smet for the funeral. The two sisters had not been especially close, and Wilder disapproved of the Dows' reliance on New Deal relief. Nonetheless, Grace's death must have been a sharp loss. To one of her readers,

Wilder said it had "saddened the holidays for me," and noted that "there are only sister Carrie and myself left of our family now."[3]

More and more she relied on her agent, George Bye, to handle professional requests and the institutions vying for her attention. Lane had once acted as go-between, but over the years Wilder grew to welcome Bye's generous response to her books and to rely on his judgment as he fielded requests for a litany of projects, including excerpts, a plan by the state of Ohio to produce a special edition of the Little House books for public school use, a scheme to sell Little House–inspired children's clothing, and a CBS radio show drawn from *The Long Winter*.

Unlike Lane, who could be peremptory with Bye, Wilder was always courteous. Even when he told her that he had shared bits of *Little Town on the Prairie* with Eleanor Roosevelt and her guests at a picnic at Hyde Park, she kept her opinion of the First Lady to herself, saying mildly that she was "flattered that you thought some of my anecdotes good enough to repeat to your friends."[4] If he wanted more such anecdotes, she suggested he ask Lane to tell him one of the amusing stories from her Detroit Book Fair talk, about an Easterner traipsing across the prairie after a mirage. "Like all my stories," she told him, "it is true."[5]

It was with Bye that she shared mixed feelings about coming to the end of her career. "The days of Little Town were great days and at times I have a strong feeling of nostalgia for them," she wrote.[6] But she also felt relief about bringing her work to a close. When she finished reading proofs of *These Happy Golden Years* in the fall of 1942, apologizing for taking so long, she reported to Bye that her children's story was "now complete in eight volumes."[7] That finality would be made clear to readers as well. On the last page of the last book, under a drawing of Laura and Almanzo seated on the stoop of their house, the caption read: "The End of the Little House Books."

Bye offered high praise for the "fundamental decency" of the series, predicting that it would become "an American fixture, something like Little Women and Little Men, but with sounder inspiration for better citizenship."[8] Due to wartime paper shortages, the last book could not be published until March 1943. Shortly after it appeared, Bye sent a telegram congratulating Wilder on winning the *New York Herald Tribune*'s award for "Best Book for Older Children."[9] He urged her to continue writing, suggesting she try a short story, perhaps a wartime colloquy between a woman of her age and a younger woman munitions worker.

Wilder gently discouraged the idea, telling him she had no contact with modern working girls and suggesting Lane as a better prospect.[10] "I don't know what to say about my writing more," she told him. "I have thought that 'Golden Years' was my last; that I would spend what is left of my life in living, not writing about it." But she was tempted to revisit her "adult novel" again: "A story keeps stirring around in my mind and if it pesters me enough I may write it down and send it to you sometime in the future."[11] She promised her editor that she would try to concentrate on a new book, "mostly floating around in disconnected anecdotes," in hopes that it would "jell."[12]

Perhaps she was doing more than thinking about it; perhaps she was researching. That fall, Wilder wrote to the De Smet Cemetery Association, trying to locate the grave of her infant son, whose death was described in her manuscript about the first few years of her marriage. But the deed could not be found.[13]

However tempted to write more, she was tired. In 1943, she turned seventy-six. Almanzo was in his eighties and increasingly frail. In periods of illness, she was his only nurse. Although she continued to do all her own housework, as well as cooking, baking, and churning, she too suffered from bouts of weakness, complaining of breathlessness, possibly from asthma. The couple were divesting themselves of their hard-accumulated acreage, which they could no longer manage. That year, they sold the back forty and the Rock House to a younger couple. The prospect of wrestling with themes of a "grown up novel"—the sorrows and failures of early married life—must gradually have lost its appeal, proving too difficult, too draining, or too sad.

A couple of years later, her editor would try to tempt her again, and Wilder apologized for lacking the time and the energy. "I am sorry too that I cannot see my way clear to writing another book," she wrote. "My mind is filled with what might be written."[14]

LITTLE wonder that Wilder took refuge in her fan mail and farm chores: the world situation was not going the way she and her daughter had hoped. The bombing of Pearl Harbor necessitated an immediate declaration of war, and the country's protracted infatuation with isolationism came to an abrupt end. Culturally, though, Americans continued to turn away from the horrors abroad. What they turned toward was a glorified version of their pioneer past.

The unprecedented savagery of early 1943 made any form of escapism welcome. January saw the culmination of the bitter urban warfare in Stalingrad. In February, Goebbels declared "total war" against the Allies, and Nazi courts beheaded student activists of the White Rose resistance movement. In March, the Germans continued liquidating the Krakow Ghetto in Poland while massacring entire Belarussian villages for collaborating with partisans. In April, the Warsaw Ghetto rebellion was brutally put down, while representatives of the British and American governments met at a resort in Bermuda and agreed that little could be done for the Jews of Europe. The British desultorily proposed that refugees might be sent to north Africa or the Isle of Man, while their American counterparts looked to neutral European countries or the Middle East. Few newspapers covered the failure in either country. "U.S. to Oppose More Refugees," read one headline, far off the front page.[15] "Can Do Nothing Now to Aid Hitler's Victims," was another.[16]

As such barbarities were unfolding in Europe, the musical *Oklahoma!* opened on Broadway on March 31. Rodgers and Hammerstein's show about the romance between a farm girl and a cowboy named Curley became a smash hit, running for more than two thousand performances. In addition to the title tune, many of its songs—"Oh What a Beautiful Mornin'," "People Will Say We're in Love," "The Surrey with the Fringe on Top"—became instantly recognizable classics.

Oklahoma! was based on *Green Grow the Lilacs*, a 1930 play produced by the Federal Theatre Project and written by Lynn Riggs, an Oklahoma writer who was part Cherokee. Both the original play and its musical adaptation were strikingly ahistorical, a singular irony given that Oklahoma had been the dark heart of Andrew Jackson's genocidal Indian Removal policy. Riggs's script set the scene in Indian Territory in glowing terms reminiscent of Wilder's work:

It is a radiant summer morning . . . the kind of morning which, enveloping the shapes of earth—men, cattle in a meadow, blades of the young corn, streams—makes them seem to exist now for the first time, their images giving off a visible golden emanation.[17]

Wilder's *These Happy Golden Years* was published the same month as the musical's premiere, and both provided welcome respite to a harried nation. Both showcased the sunny, unsullied open plains as an American Eden. Both featured horse-drawn carriages as old-fashioned vehicles of romance and song-centered courting rituals of an earlier, more innocent time: box socials, square dances, and singing schools. Both involved dark confrontations and potential knifings, but ended with the laconic Almanzo and the reluctant Curley dedicating themselves to the wholesome pursuit of farming. And both offered wartime America a retreat from the internecine mechanized warfare that was consuming the planet.

These Happy Golden Years was praised extravagantly in the *New York Times Book Review* as a fitting finale to "an invaluable addition to our list of genuinely American stories." The reviewer singled out the "authentic background, sensitive characterization . . . fine integrity and spirit of sturdy independence."[18] *Kirkus* called it "splendid."[19] Wilder herself treasured a more personal reaction, that of her sole surviving sibling, telling a reader, "Sister Carrie writes me that after she read the book it seemed that she was back in those times again and all that had happened since was a dream."[20] As the previous four books had been, the novel was selected for a Newbery Honor. A triumphant conclusion to the series, the book could not help but overshadow Lane's last major work.

The Discovery of Freedom

Rose Wilder Lane, Ayn Rand, and Isabel Mary Paterson each published philosophical works early that year. Lane's *The Discovery of Freedom* appeared in January 1943; Rand's *The Fountainhead* followed in April; Paterson's *The God of the Machine* came out in May. Three weird sisters in an antifeminist trifecta, they each celebrated in their books the strapping male as a hero, and exhibited a striking dissociation from what was happening around the world. Emphasizing free will as essential to liberty, the works laid the foundation for the libertarian political movement in the United States.

Similar themes preoccupied them all. "Collectivism" was the enemy, empowering the group over the individual, an evil taking the form of governments, taxes, planned economies, education, and philanthropy. Free enterprise was invested with mystical Thorlike powers; self-reliance became a commandment, the lone wolf an idol. Howard Roark, Rand's protagonist, was the quintessential individualist, a "prime mover" beholden to no one. Isabel Paterson looked to the past for her hero: "The solitary frontier trapper was an advance guard capitalist," she wrote.[21] Lane likewise hailed the frontier as "the god that created these United States and once made Americans strong and self-reliant."[22]

None of this was a coincidence. They all knew each other or knew of each other. Lane and Rand would not meet in person until a few years later, but they would soon become correspondents. Paterson was their mentor, and already an influential public figure.[23] Since 1924, Paterson had been wielding considerable power with her weekly literary review column in the *Herald Tribune*. Her opinion could sell books or hold them up to ridicule. An author herself, by 1943 she had published eight novels to Lane's five and Rand's two. Ruthless in exercising authority, she could also be witty and entertaining. She illustrated her column with tiny humorous Thurber-esque line drawings, and rolled her own cigarettes. Her highest compliment, bestowed upon an individual who reliably pulled his weight, was "he rolls his own."[24]

Paterson had been working on *The God of the Machine* for years, a closely argued treatise about the historical evolution of power structures and financial systems, intended to demonstrate the machine- or godlike potential of the individual human mind, capable of harnessing and releasing vast economic energies if left unmolested by interfering institutions. During the 1930s she held forth on such topics while acting as Ayn Rand's guru, a singular role: Rand acknowledged no other influence.[25] Beginning with the Greeks and Romans, Paterson worked her way through human history up to the mistakes that led to the Great Depression and federal relief programs, which she condemned as "static" rather than dynamic.[26] Whatever one thought of her conclusions, her work was scholarly and rigorous.

Although Paterson's book was published a few months later than the others, she had been discussing the same ideas and deploying the same images in her column for years. She may well have been startled to see those images and arguments appearing in Lane's book without attribution.

The Discovery of Freedom was profoundly derivative from Paterson. Lane had been reading her column regularly at Rocky Ridge and in New York, and after moving to Danbury she became Paterson's neighbor and frequent companion.[27] Lane's diaries recorded passages of Paterson's conversation, taken down more or less verbatim.[28] "I.M.P. says ... ," she wrote many times, including on November 5, 1940, when the pair spent a disconsolate night at Lane's home listening to election returns as Roosevelt won his unprecedented third term.[29]

Their books were conjoined at many junctures. Both began at the dawn of human history, touching on the Phoenicians.[30] Both warned that important bodies of knowledge could be lost.[31] Both celebrated the power of human energies. In her long-running campaign against philanthropy, Paterson proclaimed that "most of the harm in the world is done by good people."[32] Lane said that "in all history the earnest, sincere, hardworking ruler has done the most harm to his own people."[33]

Paterson's central metaphor for the engine of human creativity was Henry Adams's dynamo. (In *The Education of Henry Adams*, the forty-foot dynamo, or electric generator, displayed at the Paris Exhibition in 1900 was a symbol of new technologies, such as the steam engine and the telegraph, that were replacing older religious beliefs.) Paterson wrote, "Man is the dynamo, in his productive capacity."[34] Lane wrote, "A human being is a dynamo, generating energy."[35]

What was original in *The Discovery of Freedom* sprang from Lane's well-worn personal anecdotes, but she marshaled these haphazardly and with little attention to accuracy. She venerated the American Revolution but never once mentioned the Civil War, overlooking the unfinished business of the country's founding that nearly tore it apart. She was happy to discuss slavery among the Egyptians but not in the American South. It might have tarnished the shine on her golden calf.

Out of a rag bag of historical scraps, she pulled her parents, convenient exemplars of pioneering thrift: "Sixty-five years ago my own mother was living in a creek-bank in Minnesota. . . . Living underground was nothing unusual; less than sixty years ago, American families were living in dugouts all over the prairie States."[36] Given her profound distaste for her mother's parsimony, expressed in letters and journal entries, her celebration of it in the book seems hypocritical.

She returned, as she often did, to the 1894 depression. To her mind, it established her authority on economic failures, proving that depressions were cyclical and could be weathered by anyone willing to work hard. She recalled the Russian community her family met on the journey to Missouri:

> I well remember the incredible abundance of food in the Russian Dukhaber commune in Kansas—or was it southern Nebraska? . . . when I and my parents were traveling among the hundreds of thousands of refugees, walking or riding in covered wagons along all America's dusty or muddy roads, looking for work or food. I can see yet those sleek, unmortgaged cows, those brimming pails of milk, those jars of butter in the spring-house, and the smiling Russian woman with her hair in golden braids, who spoke no known language, but opened the front of her blue blouse and took from next her skin a slab of cold biscuits. That was abundance to most Americans fifty years ago.[37]

The example, however, seemed to prove the opposite of what she intended, suggesting that communal living, rather than being "static" (another echo of Paterson), could in fact yield comfort and security.[38]

Lane attacked taxation as if the government had been caught reaching into her blouse to take her biscuits. Taxes had brought down Rome, she said, and the force brought to bear by the state in collecting them spelled "the swift and violent death of . . . democracy."[39] Compared to Paterson's original argument, Lane's was radically simplified, a punitive version of rules inherited from her grandmother. Caroline Ingalls had always held to a notion of ethical responsibility: no gift, no matter how trivial (a meal, a day's labor, a handful of nails), could be accepted without repaying or returning the favor. But Lane conveniently forgot to mention that the Ingallses did take help when they needed it, gratefully accepting Christmas barrels and donated turkeys, eating the Wilder brothers' seed wheat in the Hard Winter, and receiving state aid to send Mary to the college for the blind. And, of course, there was the land in the Osage Diminished Reserve: they took that without ever paying for it. In Burr Oak, when they had debts they could not cover, they skipped out on them.

Lane's assumption of authority about economies, planned or otherwise, was perhaps the most unconvincing position she had ever taken. Economics begin at home, and as an adult Lane had never shown any mastery of money. She was constantly in debt to family and friends, to banks and her literary agent, frantically borrowing from one to pay the other. Her urge to play Lady Bountiful was so strong that she often gave away money she did not have. Until posthumous royalties from her mother's books finally eased her way, she lived beyond her means. No one was less qualified to pronounce on financial matters.

The only person in her family who could claim financial expertise was her mother, who had responsibly handled federal loan transactions for a decade. But she never chose to stand on a soap box. Lane steadfastly refused to learn from her example.

PATERSON'S book was respectfully reviewed but little read. Lane's attracted less flattering attention. *Kirkus Reviews* wrote that *The Discovery of Freedom* bore "the earmarks of long, long thoughts—and hasty execution . . . choppy, discursive, unorganized, and superficial."[40] After plowing through it, the reviewer concluded, "So what?"

Of the three, the one that proved remarkably successful was, of course, Ayn Rand's. *The Fountainhead* was loosely based on a rejected screenplay she'd written for Cecil B. DeMille in 1928, but the gobbets of turgid argument disgorged by its characters over the course of seven hundred pages showed Paterson's heavy influence, especially in Rand's treatment of philanthropy. Altruism was denounced as an ineffective "sacred cow" and a "weapon of exploitation."[41] Nothing was more loathsome than good intentions.

Praised in future years as the "mothers" of the Libertarian movement, all three women publicly denounced Social Security. Rand nonetheless registered for it and accepted payments, arguing that she had
paid into it and thus deserved the money. Paterson was content to
stash her card in an envelope on which she had scrawled the words
"Social Security's Swindle."[42]

Lane was more militant. Listening to the conservative radio of her
day, she had expressed as early as 1940 her concerns about the FBI's
gaining "Gestapo powers." Refusing Social Security, to her mind, qualified as resisting the secret police, and she leapt at an opportunity to
say so in print.

In the summer of 1943, she sent a postcard to Samuel Grafton, a
radio commentator and liberal supporter of the New Deal who wrote
for the *New Republic*. "All these Social Security laws are German,
instituted by Bismarck and expanded by Hitler," she wrote. "Americans believe in freedom, not in being taxed for their own good and
bought by bureaucrats." Oddly, the card was signed with a name Lane
had not used in decades: "Mrs. C. G. Lane."

Delivered to Grafton, the postcard somehow ended up in the hands
of J. Edgar Hoover's FBI. Authorities dispatched a state trooper to
Lane's home to look into the matter. He found the perpetrator on her
knees, weeding dandelions on her front lawn. When confronted, she
was only too eager to tell him off. According to her account, she told
him, "I am an American citizen. I hire you, I pay you. And you have the
insolence to question *my* attitude? The point is that *I* don't like *your*
attitude. What is this—the Gestapo?" To ensure that the incident received
the widest possible audience, she published a pamphlet titled "What
Is This—The Gestapo?," distributed by the National Economic Council, Inc., an organization that supported the fascist government in
Spain and promoted the idea that Jews were plotting the "complete
destruction" of American constitutional government.[43] She accused the
FBI of interfering with the U.S. Mail. J. Edgar Hoover's flunkies began
compiling a fat file on the whole affair.

Lane claimed that she had used her married name because she
wanted to avoid publicity, but she relished the attention when she got
it. She told the Associated Press: "Social security is National Socialism.

No one could hate the Germans more than I do. I have two boys in the service, one of whom I believe to be in a concentration camp."[44]

That last remark was questionable at best. John Turner had joined the Coast Guard, but she had broken off contact with him around 1940. The concentration camp referred to Rexh Meta, with whom she had lost touch around the same time, having no word where he might be reached. She feared for his life, with good reason. Rebecca West, in her monumental 1941 study of the Balkans, *Black Lamb and Grey Falcon*, closed on a death knell for Lane's beloved country: "I told you it was bad with Albania. It is very bad. It is a massacre."[45] As the war drew to a close, Lane struggled to learn Meta's whereabouts and to aid his family, urging Herbert Hoover to query the State Department for her, to no avail.[46] She feared that her own "vindictive personal enemies among communists" would prove his undoing.[47] Soon she lost all hope of saving him, bitterly remarking to the former president that for Meta's sake, she hoped he was dead. (In fact it appears that he was sentenced to death after the war, possibly on charges of treason, and later had that sentence commuted to twenty-seven years in prison.)[48] Lane was sure he could have been rescued if only she had been a member of the Communist Party.[49]

But as her other adopted sons faded away, Lane found a new protégé. *Reader's Digest* was preparing a condensed version of *Let the Hurricane Roar*, and during the editing process she met with the *Digest*'s senior editor, Burt MacBride, at a restaurant north of Danbury. He brought his fourteen-year-old son, Roger, with him. Over the coming years, as a student at Phillips Exeter Academy and then at Princeton, Roger MacBride would regularly spend evenings and weekends with Lane, imbibing her philosophy.

With others, Lane seemed increasingly incapable of maintaining relationships. Intemperate rhetoric, coupled with acting out, was becoming commonplace. In a New York City apartment she was renovating, she chased a building inspector down the stairs, calling him a "storm trooper."[50] She described herself to Jane Burr, her former landlady in Croton-on-Hudson, as "a hurricane in a teaspoon," digging ditches and canning dozens of jars of string beans, peas, beets, and berries in her pressure cooker, explaining that those who gave in to rationing would "starve to death."[51] Burr would dismiss this as "completely absurd," calling her old friend a "strange, erratic girl."[52] Journalist and editor Ernestine Evans, who had known Lane during her Greenwich Village period, told Berta Hader that she always imagined Lane "floating between sanity and a bedlam of hates."[53]

Increasingly, she was inflating minor issues into major affronts. She railed to George Bye about magazines requesting "all rights" to articles in exchange for payment, saying that this was "undermining . . . the human right of ownership of property" and amounted to an attack on "individual liberty."[54] Her ambitions were grandiose, too: she was planning a sequel to *The Discovery of Freedom*, to be called "The World Is Round."[55] She asked Bye to write to foreign embassies, asking for a "complete set of books" about their history, politics, and economies. "Letter head is very important to foreigners, as you know," she advised.[56]

In 1943, she had started writing a column, "Rose Lane Says," for the *Pittsburgh Courier*, an African-American newspaper that she learned about when her black housekeeper left a copy in the Danbury house.[57] Discovering the "tragic fallacy" of bigotry, she called on Americans to "renounce their race," asserting that the notion of different races was a "fantastic belief." Wartime rationing was "economic slavery," she told her readers, not recognizing that they were the true experts on that topic.[58] Urging insurrection, she assured them that the Founding Fathers wanted citizens to rise up and overthrow the state: that's what the Second Amendment was for.[59] She was fired from the *Courier* in 1945, which she attributed to its pro–New Deal sentiment.

Profiled in the *New York Times* as "on strike against the New Deal," Lane portrayed herself as a Revolutionary War hero, opposing George III's onerous taxation to the end.[60] She spoke of herself as having "two sons in the Army," refusing a ration book, and stockpiling hundreds of pounds of pork and jars of preserved fruits and vegetables, not for the war effort but as a one-woman resistance movement. She had given up writing fiction, she said, to avoid taxation.

Described as a "plump, motherly woman . . . the type that crossed the plains in covered wagon days," she spoke darkly, as if Dust Bowl policies still prevailed, of neighborhood farmers' killing hogs and "burying them in the ground" since there was no feed and they "weren't allowed" to sell them. She knew someone working in a Bridgeport defense plant, she said, who was "penalized for producing." She ushered a reporter down to her cellar to inspect the ranks of home-canned food on her shelves. "That's social security," she declared.

The *New Republic* took up the challenge, fact-checking her accusation about the hogs, among other charges. Danbury representatives of the Department of Agriculture denied that there was a feed shortage in Connecticut. The Bridgeport plant likewise pronounced itself baffled. The magazine concluded that "Unfortunately, to Mrs. Lane the truth seems to be identical with any allegation that will further her own little private revolt against the war effort."[61]

But there was one member of Lane's close circle who was neither perturbed nor alarmed by her politics, who in fact supported her beliefs wholeheartedly. That was her mother.

LAURA Ingalls Wilder rarely commented on her daughter's work. Except for a few disparaging remarks about *Let the Hurricane Roar*, Wilder kept her own counsel about Lane's fiction. She apparently enjoyed the Ozark novel *Cindy*, keeping a copy in her library, but her thoughts on *Old Home Town*, in which she appeared as the waspish mother of the protagonist, went unrecorded.

The Discovery of Freedom was different, however. A month after it was published, Wilder wrote to Aubrey Sherwood in De Smet, to whom she had earlier confided news about Lane's nervous breakdown, saying she found it "the best work [Rose] has ever done . . . fascinating reading."[62] She sent along the name and address of the publisher in case he wanted to order a copy for himself.

In coming years, Wilder would recommend the book widely, along with Lane's pamphlet "Give Me Liberty." In 1945, she sent the booklet to Clarence Kilburn, the conservative Republican congressman from Almanzo's hometown of Malone, New York, and urged him to track down *Discovery*, saying: "Rose stopped writing fiction in 1937 and has done nothing but American propaganda since. She says she doesn't think this is the time for any American to do anything else."[63] Wilder sustained that propaganda in other ways, too, donating generously to the National Economic Council.[64]

Describing the family's difficult early days at Rocky Ridge, she assured Kilburn that "What we accomplished was without help of any kind from any one. There was no alphabetical relief of any description and if there had been we would not have accepted it." She resented the fact that others took advantage of such programs:

> Now here we are at seventy-eight and eighty-eight . . . paying taxes
> for the support of dependent children, so their parents need not work
> at anything else; for old age pensions to take care of those same par-
> ents when the children are grown, thus relieving the children of any
> responsibility and all of them from any incentive to help themselves.[65]

Wilder even went so far as to claim that she had stopped writing to avoid increasing her tax burden, as her daughter had. She told the *Kansas City Star* in 1949: "The more I wrote the bigger my income tax got, so I stopped. Why should I go on at my age? Why, we don't need it here anyway."[66] A Social Security number was never issued to her.[67]

She never sought to explain the contradiction between her denunciation of New Deal programs and her praise of the Federal Farm Loan program she had worked for and borrowed from. Favorable terms on those loans were themselves federal assistance, subsidized by the government. And again, so were the lands given away by the Homestead Act, one of the largest federal handouts in American history.

Why were homesteads and federal loans acceptable, while programs sponsored by the Roosevelt administration were not? Wilder's inconsistency may be explained in part by the stark contrast of ambitions and scale. The Farm Loan program was a model of modest, community-based effort, hiring local bankers and, at least in Mansfield, a secretary-treasurer who was herself a paragon of rural farming. On the other hand, the massive New Deal programs brought in intimidating outsiders intent on inflicting top-down discipline, typified by the officious note-taking bureaucrat whom Almanzo ordered off his property with the threat of his shotgun.

Yet Wilder never came to terms with what FDR saw and explained so clearly: the land had limits, and no solitary, undercapitalized farmer could ever hope to overcome them. She had seen those limits with her own eyes, time and again. But just like her father and his Populist brethren, she clung to the notion that an individual could wrest a living from it nonetheless, without government support.

Her uncompromising, even dogmatic attitude suggests that her abhorrence of dependency was rooted in the humiliations she had worked so hard to leave behind. She herself had been dependent before, on a father forced to accept flour from the state of Minnesota, on a husband forced to sell his land after failing on his homestead. She had borne her own dependent child, someone who claimed to be supportive while actually needing support. For her, the very idea of dependence was wreathed with shame, the most deranging of human emotions.

But a purely psychological explanation may not be adequate. Wilder wrote that her mother was fond of a saying: "What's bred in the bone will come out in the flesh." If anything was bred in her family's Congregationalist bones, it was their exemplary devotion to self-sufficiency. Samuel Ingalls, the "Unlearned Poet," loathed Thomas Jefferson's interference in free trade, every bit as much as his descendants loathed Roosevelt. For generation upon generation, all the way back to Edmund Ingalls—or for that matter to Richard Warren, *Mayflower* ancestor of the Delanos—Puritan identity was based on redemption through mastery of self, and the rigid application of principles including frugality, diligence, and, above all, independence.

Wilder never wavered in reflecting those values. But late in her life, the language in which they were expressed was increasingly shaped by her daughter. Her uncritical acceptance of Lane's most startling conspiracy theories grew more marked as she grew older. Writing to a niece and nephew in 1946, she caught them up on family news:

The New Dealers are in control of most publishing houses in New York and because they think Rose's "Discovery of Freedom" teaches ideas contrary to their plans, they are working against its publication and distribution. Even the publishers of the book are trying to stop it, so I doubt if you can get it from them.[68]

FORTUNATELY, the New Dealers held no sway over Wilder's own readers, who continued to clamor for attention. As if to assuage them, Wilder began to distribute some of the iconographic objects associated with the Little House books. In 1944, she wrote to the South Dakota State Historical Society, which maintained a museum in the state capitol building in Pierre, asking if the state might wish to display her father's violin. It did, arranging the gift.[69] She sent along an inscription of her devising:

Nicolas Amati violin

Owned and played by Charles P. Ingalls before and during the settlement of De Smet Dakota Territory, later De Smet South Dakota from 1879 until his death in June 1902.

Presented to South Dakota Historical Society by his daughters Laura Ingalls Wilder and Caroline Ingalls Swanzey and his granddaughter Rose Wilder Lane.[70]

She requested that the fiddle be played several times a year, to keep it in good shape. (The instrument did have an "Amati" label pasted inside, but examination later showed it to be an inexpensive model, not a work of the famed seventeenth-century Italian violin maker.)[71]

Other things passed out of the family's control. Wilder saw her sister in October 1944, when Carrie Swanzey took the train to Mansfield for a visit. That same year, Carrie had sold, for $800, the last of the little houses their father had built. A room upstairs was still packed full of jumbled Ingalls possessions—books, photographs, and furniture—when the sale was completed.[72]

A year and a half later, the little sister Wilder once fought so hard to protect fell ill. Born on the Kansas prairie, Carrie had modeled her adult life on her parents', working quietly and patiently enduring what could not be changed. In May 1946, she began suffering from pain in the abdomen, perhaps related to the gallbladder. On June 1 she was found unconscious in her Keystone home, wrapped in a blanket on her couch, after worried friends pried open the door.[73] Taken to a hospital in Rapid City, she died the following day.

Like her father, Carrie Ingalls Swanzey had juggled many odd jobs, trying to get by. She had been a pioneering newspaper woman, a homesteader, and a miner's wife. Like her father and husband, she left barely enough to pay her bills. Eastern Star, the Masonic group to which she had belonged throughout her adult life, helped arrange memorial services in both Keystone and her hometown. Her body was sent on the old familiar Chicago & North Western line to De Smet, where she would be laid next to her parents, her sister Mary, and the infant son of the Wilders. Grace and Nate Dow were only steps away.

Wilder offered to pay outstanding expenses from the memorial service, expressing distress and regret that her own health prevented her from attending.[74] The lawyer handling things in Keystone assured her that Carrie's stepdaughter, family, and friends would be present at the Congregational Church in Keystone, from which Mount Rushmore was visible. Both there and in De Smet, he said, the services would be "fittingly and lovingly performed."[75] After the burial, he passed along a report from De Smet of a "lovely" evening ceremony.[76] Wilder's family was now reunited in the town they had helped found, in the wooded cemetery on a rise, with a view of the fields and prairie beyond. She was the only one left.

As time went on, the kindness of Mansfield friends and neighbors, Silas and Neta Seal and others, was becoming increasingly important to the Wilders. Neta was busy with church and volunteer work, but the younger couple visited every Sunday afternoon, and the Wilders stopped by to see them when in town. At their service station on the main street, the Seals had torn down an old building, and—borrowing money interest-free from the Wilders—built a new home, adding a few smart apartments to rent out.[77] Almanzo grew so fond of the idea of living in town that he wanted to leave the farmhouse and move into one of the apartments, until his wife told him to go to his workshop and decide what tools he wanted to get rid of. Wilder told Neta that he silently pondered that for a few hours and never brought it up again.

Indefatigably, Wilder continued responding directly to readers year after year, throughout the 1940s and well into the next decade, fielding requests for autographs or photographs, and answering endless questions, ranging from the innocent and amusing to the offbeat: Did she have pets? Was she interested in insects? What was it like to ride in a covered wagon? Could she come for a visit and bring Almanzo? Some wrote to say that their grandparents remembered the grasshoppers or the blizzards.

She had a significant adult readership, too. Parents, grandparents, teachers, and librarians read the books to children and found themselves drawn into a pioneer world they half-remembered or had heard of from their own elders. Boys as well as girls treasured the novels, responding to the Almanzo of *Farmer Boy* and his adventures and hardships.

Always, readers were interested in whether the characters were real or fictional and whether the stories were true. And everyone wanted to know what had happened next. What became of Nellie Oleson? What became of Mary? Whatever became of Laura and Almanzo? Wilder shared with adult correspondents that some of the names were made up, but kept up the fiction that "Nellie Oleson" was a real person rather than a composite character, saying vaguely that she had moved back east.

Universally, readers wanted her to know how much they loved her books. One child told her she'd wept when she came to the end of the series, so sorry there would be no more.[78] Others offered stories, drawings, and poems of their own. Teachers sent photographs of class projects, such as a replica of the little house on the prairie constructed from orange crates and paper, a real pot hanging before the fireplace and a doll seated beside it.[79] One photo captured children dressed as Pa, Ma, Laura, and Mary, with Ma towering over the rest, and Pa sporting a pasted-on beard.[80] Another class dressed as Little House characters, boys donning Indian headdresses made of construction paper, girls clutching quilts, baskets, and dolls.[81]

Children were homesteading in their basements, hitching their rocking horses to wagons and heading out. Some of their drawings showed bucolic or domestic views: young Laura in a pretty dress or

Ma serving dinner to travelers at Silver Lake. Others zeroed in on the most dramatic or terrifying moments of the series. One child drew burning tumbleweeds threatening haystacks in *Plum Creek*, another the prairie house surrounded by a ring of crayoned orange fire, Ma and Pa beating back the flames.[82] Each figure in the story, including Jack the dog and the horses Pet and Patty, was drawn and clearly labeled, clearly in danger.

Every year, Wilder received a deluge of homemade birthday cards: cut-out cakes with doily frosting, drawings of hearts and the Mansfield farm, a scissored-out telephone bearing the message "HeLLO." An entire autograph album arrived from Grade Five of the Theodore Roosevelt School in Compton, California. The Carson, Pirie, Scott department store in Chicago held a party on her eightieth birthday, February 7, 1947. Unable to attend, she sent two hundred autographs.

Sometimes old school friends or distant relatives got in touch. Replying to a long-lost cousin in Pepin, Wisconsin, Wilder wrote that Almanzo was "rather feeble, being crippled in his feet," and that she sometimes felt lonely after the demise of her South Dakota family.[83] Staying busy helped:

> It does keep me hurrying to do the work and write as much as I must to keep up with the people who write to me after reading my books. The books are selling well. I had more than 200 Christmas cards and letters to answer.[84]

A Mrs. Lena E. Heikes in Dakota City, Nebraska, wrote to say that she had come across a book by Laura Ingalls Wilder, and realized that the author was her cousin when she encountered Charles and Caroline and Mary. "If it tells of Mary's blindness, I'll be sure of it," she'd told her daughter.[85] It was cousin Lena of *Silver Lake*, who had ridden the black ponies with Laura at the railroad camp. As a postscript, Lena recalled a song reminiscent of Wilder's own descriptions of the prairie:

> The sun is now setting in billows
> That arose in the far distant West
> And the morning shall dawn

Through the willows—
And find me forever at rest.

Below, Lena added, "(Do you remember this)—?" Assuredly, Wilder did. It was "My Hopes Have Departed Forever," a popular song composed by Stephen Foster, one of her favorite composers.[86]

Daughter of a man who could play fiddle tunes after hearing them just once, Wilder often jotted down scraps of song or poetry, searching for the source. On one undated sheet of note paper, its addressee unknown, she wrote:

I think the quotation is this
"I thank whatever Gods there be
That even the weariest river
Winds somewhere to the sea."
But I have no idea what it is from or where I read it? Do you know it?[87]

It was from Swinburne's "The Garden of Proserpine," about seeking the underworld:

From too much hope of living,
From hope and fear set free,
We thank with brief thanksgiving
Whatever gods may be
That no life lives for ever;
That dead men rise up never;
That even the weariest river
Winds somewhere safe to sea.[88]

Last things were becoming a preoccupation.

Oh, *I* Would Go!

However much she may have been longing to rest, Wilder was not quite done with the Little House books. Deciding to repackage the series for new generations of readers, her publisher prevailed upon her to meet with a new illustrator and to revisit her family's travels one last time.

Having adopted a child, Ida Louise Raymond left Harper & Brothers in 1940, passing the reins of the modest "Department of Books for Boys and Girls"—with three employees—to Ursula Nordstrom, a lavishly gifted assistant who would become one of the most renowned names in children's literature.[89] Nordstrom had never attended college, taught, or worked in a library, but when the formidable doyenne of the field, New York Public Library's Anne Carroll Moore, asked for her qualifications, she replied, "Well, I am a former child, and I haven't forgotten a thing."[90]

Nordstrom had been handling correspondence with Wilder since *Plum Creek* and greatly admired Wilder's series. She described reading it for the first time "with a big lump in my throat, it was so beautiful." She had seen firsthand the intense relationships children developed with the books, citing the overwhelming volume of mail received from them. Much of it was addressed directly to Laura and conveyed, she said, "great urgency."[91] "Perfectly wonderful letters," she called them, citing one example: "Laura, if I'd been you I would have kicked that mean Nellie Oleson."

But Nordstrom felt that the original design of the series was dated and ill-suited for what she termed "forthright realistic frontier stories."[92] She reached out to a little-known British illustrator who had memorably rendered E. B. White's dauntless mouse child, born of human parents, in *Stuart Little*, published in 1945. Garth Williams's black-and-white drawings had captured a whimsical work of pure imagination, and he was at first hesitant to tackle Wilder's books, which struck him as "very historical, very real."[93] But Nordstrom held firm, ordering him to "go home and read those books thoroughly and don't come back until you have."[94] He did, finding them so compelling that he agreed to a job that would monopolize his time for the next seven years.

Curiously, much like Virginia Kirkus, who had discovered Wilder's Big Woods manuscript while living in a rural home with kerosene lamps and a pump, Williams was also living the little house way, without modern conveniences, on a "very primitive farm in New York State." He had two hundred acres with "a giant" of a barn, a kitchen hand pump, and water fed from a nearby spring, similar to the Wilders' own.[95] Later he wrote of using the first book's lamp-lighting description as a how-to-manual: "I had to clean lamps and trim wicks and I would place little bits of decorative red flannel in the glass bowls of the lamps as Caroline Ingalls had done in the book I had just put down."[96] In years to come, scores of readers, children and adults alike, would follow his lead, employing the books as manuals for churning butter, sewing nine-patch quilts, and twisting hay.

Williams was among the first to make what would become a treasured pilgrimage, retracing the Ingallses' family trail. Living in upstate New York, he felt he had a good handle on the *Farmer Boy* material, but had never been out west and wanted to collect on-the-ground impressions. First, he paid a call on Rose Wilder Lane in Danbury and asked whether her parents might be up for guests, tactfully trying to ascertain whether they still had their wits about them. She assured him they did and in her forceful fashion set about planning the trip for him, routing him through the Shenandoah Valley and the Great Smoky Mountains, where he might see log cabins.

In September 1947, he set out with his wife and daughter. When they reached Mansfield, driving up to the farmhouse, Williams spotted Wilder weeding her garden, and she made an instant impression:

> I found her to be frisky, a person who seemed to be willing to try anything and go anywhere. She was a very cheerful character, very sprightly, very much alive with a very good sense of humor.[97]

She appeared, he said, "a good twenty years younger than her age." Inviting the visitors into the house, she showed them old family photographs, describing people who appeared in the books and offering directions to the various places Williams wanted to see. Although she continued to be in the dark about the Kansas site—believing the little house was in Oklahoma—she gave precise directions to the dugout on Plum Creek, as well as the homestead outside De Smet.

When Williams mentioned driving out to South Dakota, Almanzo grew worried, having heard of heavy snows coming out of the Rockies.

"Those blizzards can blow for weeks," Almanzo cautioned. "I don't think you should risk going to De Smet at that time of year." No one alive knew the danger better. But his wife was sanguine, remarking impetuously, "Oh, *I* would go!"[98] And Garth Williams did.

He never found the little house on the prairie, but he passed through Independence, taking a good look at the Verdigris River, which Mr. Edwards was said to have forded to bring the Ingalls girls their Christmas gifts. Wandering along a rainy, muddy riverbank outside Walnut Grove, Minnesota, he found the exact spot on Plum Creek where the dugout must have been, a hollow in the east bank where the walls had fallen in. He carefully photographed the site.

In De Smet, he was squired around town by Aubrey Sherwood, who took him to the surveyors' house on Silver Lake and then drove him down the main street, pointing out storefronts and landmarks. The newspaper editor introduced him to women who had once played with Carrie and Grace as children, and to another member of the Masters clan (Sherwood himself was the son of Gussie Masters Sherwood, elder sister of Laura Ingalls's old nemeses, George and Genevieve) who told him that Wilder's stories "are more than just stories for us. They are our lives, we lived them."[99]

Finally, Williams drove out to the house south of Silver Lake, now standing empty. He found himself "peering into the windows where Laura, Pa, Ma, Mary, Carrie and Baby Grace once sat. The air was fresh and clear and the sky a quiet blue. I could imagine the children playing in the buffalo grass out on that vast prairie." The photographs he took that day, showing a long, muddy track leading up to a house on a rise, capture the vastness of the sky, the tiny, inconsequential building a mere mote on the horizon. He left for Minnesota just ahead of a snowstorm, feeling the cold wind at his back.

It would be several years before Williams finished the illustrations for the eight books, but the journey had provided a powerful sense of who Wilder was and how she had lived. As much as any reader of the period, he grasped the depth of her vision. "She understood the meaning of hardship and struggle, of joy and work, of shyness and bravery," he wrote later. "She was never overcome by drabness or squalor. She never glamorized anything; yet she saw the loveliness in everything."

AFTER her early isolationist phase, Wilder mentioned the ongoing war only glancingly in surviving letters. Mansfield was subsumed in war news and activities just like any American town, its citizens hanging blackout curtains, rationing, and holding scrap drives for rubber and metal; Neta Seal and others volunteered for the Red Cross. But in the peace of Rocky Ridge, Wilder felt insulated from the maelstrom, telling George Bye in June 1944: "The Ozarks are beautiful now and in our quiet home it seems impossible that such terrible things are happening in the world."[100]

But out in that terrible world, Wilder's books were about to be given an extraordinary role. In postwar Japan, the Supreme Commander for the Allied Powers, five-star general Douglas MacArthur, tasked with rebuilding a nation reduced to rubble, found Wilder's model of cheerful, stoic endurance a useful tool.

Aside from the atomic bombs that destroyed Hiroshima and Nagasaki, sixty-seven additional Japanese cities, including Tokyo, had been firebombed with napalm during the war. Japanese construction before the war had been heavily dependent on wood, paper, and bamboo, and whole cities went up in flames. Roads, bridges, railway lines, and coal and electric plants were destroyed; the country's entire transportation system, industrial capacity, government infrastructure, agriculture, and housing were in ruins. Millions were homeless, and virtually everyone was facing starvation.

During the first years of reconstruction, overseen by General Head Quarters (GHQ), MacArthur's chief priorities were to address food shortages, rebuild housing, and restore basic utilities. But he was also tasked with the "democratization" of a nation steeped in nationalistic and militaristic propaganda. To that end, MacArthur abolished central government control of education, the media, and publishing, outlawing Japanese censorship and replacing it with American control. "I put the Japanese publishing industry on a competitive basis for the first time in the preparation and printing of school textbooks," MacArthur wrote in his *Reminiscences*. "No texts were forced upon them, but the books had to show that the previous . . . propaganda was absent."[101] For the first time, Japan's media were to enjoy a free market, but it was only free to include books, films, and other materials approved by GHQ.

Worried about the potential breakdown of civil society, American authorities cast about for materials to inculcate democratic values. In the aftermath of war, the long, cold winters were exceptionally grim. A thousand people died of starvation in Tokyo alone in the first months after surrender; between 1945 and 1948, more than half a million would perish of cholera, dysentery, typhoid, smallpox, scarlet fever, and diphtheria.[102] Survivors searched through garbage for food, competing with rats or eating them, along with grasshoppers, worms, snails, and snakes.[103] Those suffering such privations, MacArthur believed, needed inspiring role models to stiffen resolve and wipe out anti-American prejudice.

To instill positive views of Japan's former enemies, GHQ launched a "Gift Book Program," asking American librarians and educators to choose titles. Ultimately, more than seven hundred books were put on display in Japanese cities in 1947, drawing curious crowds that topped a quarter of a million in Tokyo in one month alone.[104] The books were later distributed through the new system of public libraries, another American innovation.[105] The collection included children's books, as well as works about the Western frontier. Among them were several of the Little House books.

Seeing the popularity of the exhibit, Aya Ishida, a teacher and translator who had studied at Mount Holyoke College in Massachusetts, asked GHQ for permission to translate Wilder's series.[106] She had first come across *Little House on the Prairie* a decade earlier in a Christian bookstore in Tokyo. In 1948, she was granted permission to translate one of the books, *The Long Winter*. (It was the only Wilder book on the list of the first one hundred English-language titles cleared for translation by GHQ.) The Cosmopolitan Publishing Company won the highly competitive bidding for the rights, and Ishida's translation was published the following year, creating something of a sensation in Japan.

According to Noriko Suzuki, who has studied the book's reception in Japan, *The Long Winter* tapped into the country's anxieties and preoccupations in ways that Douglas MacArthur and authorities at GHQ could never have anticipated. There were obvious parallels between the extended suffering of the Japanese and the Ingalls family in the town of De Smet, Suzuki noted, but also subtler connections that readers in Japan would have recognized, including the value placed on self-sacrifice and the subjugation of individual needs. Citing chapter titles such as "Not Really Hungry" and "It Can't Beat Us," Suzuki pointed to correlations between those sentiments and postwar slogans promoted by Emperor Hirohito, who urged his subjects to "endure the unendurable and bear the unbearable."[107] The book's Japanese title, *Nagai Fuyu*, recalled a native idiom associating winter with hardship and spring with "happiness and a new start."[108]

Wilder immediately began receiving letters from Japanese readers, sharing their powerful identification with *The Long Winter*. One said that the story "brought a soft breeze into my devastated home," offering "a great hope that we could establish a new Japan":

> Everything in the book—the handmade stuff, the family life, and constant hardships—was familiar to me as I survived the same hard life in the ruins of war. The scenes where Laura's family shares scarce food—you'll never understand how hard such a life is unless you experience the war. And the scene where the long-awaited train arrives from the East as the whistle blows! That scene overlapped with my "long winter" and gave me such a restful feeling.[109]

One of Wilder's correspondents in the spring of 1949 was a Tokyo girl named Eiko Matsunawa, whose street had been "burnt by the war."[110] Eiko said that she treasured the photo Wilder sent her, and had read the author's "kind-hearted" letter to her parents and brother who listened "with joy." In thanks, she sent Wilder a children's book with pictures of rice paddies and "country folks," and a postcard of a Japanese farmhouse set against Mount Fuji.[111]

In a message to Japanese readers reproduced on the first page of *The Long Winter*, Suzuki wrote, Wilder had "expressed her sympathy toward Japanese women in the hardship after the war and encouraged them to have courage, honesty, and warm hearts believing in God."[112]

It was a simple formulation that Wilder was beginning to rely upon, one that would eventually be canonized in the standard author's letter sent to readers by her publisher. Wilder used similar wording when a women's journal, *Fujin Asahi*, solicited advice for Japanese women from American authors: "The most valuable thing for life never changes by time or place—it is to be honest and cheerful, to find happiness in what you have, and to have courage in hardships."[113] Japan's embrace of *The Long Winter* heralded an international audience for the Little House books as timeless embodiments of core values.[114]

In the fall of 1949, Wilder would be forced to draw on that courage again, facing one final hardship.

The Pearly Gates

Almanzo Wilder's health had grown more frail. After the couple's retirement from farming, his chores in later years had shrunk to caring for a small herd of goats and a burro. Lover of horses and livestock, he enjoyed milking the goats, training them to hop up on a platform in the barn. Since they grazed on the abundant poison ivy on the Wilders' wooded acreage, he felt that drinking their milk provided immunity. It was common knowledge in town that Almanzo sent the cloths he used in goat-milking out to be laundered because his wife didn't care for the smell.

A lifelong tinkerer, he had always worked with his hands, carving unusual bits of wood, braiding rugs during the winters, and constructing Craftsman-style chairs out of rare woods. Jovial and joking with those he knew well, he was reserved with strangers, especially when it came to religion. The Methodist minister who served in Mansfield in the mid-1940s recalled that whenever he and his wife turned up at Rocky Ridge, Almanzo "skedaddled . . . shy of preachers evidently."[115]

When fans of the Little House books showed up at the front door, he would often make himself scarce as well. On the Fourth of July in 1948, though, he posed with his wife and several beaming child visitors on the lawn in front of the farmhouse. His mustache was completely white, and he held a cane in his right hand. But his back was

straight, and he still possessed the formidable, unbowed demeanor of
the pioneer he once was.

In October of that year, the Wilders negotiated a reverse mortgage on
Rocky Ridge, selling the house and their remaining acreage for eight
thousand dollars to the same couple who had bought the Rock House.
The arrangement allowed the Wilders to continue living in their home
for the rest of their lives. They received a down payment of two thousand dollars, with the remainder due in fifty-dollar monthly installments; the upkeep on the property would be the responsibility of the
new owners.[116]

In December 1948, Wilder received a letter from the Detroit Library
Commission, informing her that the city had decided to name its new
branch library for her. With other branches named for Thomas Jefferson, Benjamin Franklin, and Thomas Edison, it was a singular honor.
The Detroit library director lauded her series, calling it "an invaluable
social history . . . interesting both to children and to adults."[117] Wilder
was deeply pleased, asking George Bye if he was as surprised as she
was by the news. "The Little House Books seem to be getting quite a
bit of publicity," she wrote.[118]

In years past, she might have accepted the invitation to attend the
opening ceremonies in May. But now Wilder declined, saying that her
husband was "ninety two . . . and not strong. It is not safe for him to
be alone and we two are by ourselves in the old farmhouse. . . . I can
not leave him."[119] Instead, she donated to the library the handwritten
manuscripts and revised typescripts of two of her books—*The Long
Winter* and *These Happy Golden Years*—as well as memorabilia: an
old reader and history book from her school days, original Helen
Sewell illustrations, and photographs of herself and friends at Rocky
Ridge. It was a generous gift, and a clear indication that she felt no
qualms about questions that might be raised regarding manuscript
revisions or the books' authorship. She had nothing to hide.

She hesitated, however, to write a dedicatory speech or statement,
sending only a brief, humble letter. Addressed to "Dear Friends," it
declared her "proud and grateful" for the honor and delighted that
children might read her books there. "Unless you have lived, as I did,
where books were scarce and so prized greatly," she wrote, "you can

not realize how wonderful it really is to have a whole library so convenient for your use."[120]

Spurred by news of the library dedication, the *Kansas City Star* published a profile of Wilder in April, in which she candidly admitted that her husband was not the only one with health worries. She could not travel to Detroit, she said, because "I'm too nervous," a symptom she associated with heart problems. The reporter was there when Almanzo walked in, announcing that he had "just finished planting the potatoes," part of their annual kitchen garden.

In late July 1949, Almanzo suffered a heart attack. Neta Seal began spending occasional nights sleeping on the screened porch at Rocky Ridge, and she stayed with him while Wilder ran errands in town. Lane did not come. During the following months, Almanzo appeared to be gradually improving, but in October he lapsed again. On the evening of October 22, Neta dropped by with some goat milk for him, noting in her diary, "He is pretty sick."[121] On the following morning, a Sunday, she received a call summoning her to the Wilders'.[122] Almanzo had died. When she arrived, he was in his usual chair, his wife embracing him. "She just didn't want to let go," Neta said.[123]

They had been married for sixty-four years. He had saved her life and the lives of everyone in De Smet with his daring run for the wheat in 1881. With his Morgan horses, he had courted her. Before their betrothal, he had carefully written an inscription in her autograph book: "Friend Laura No Pearl ever lay under Oman's Green water more pure in its shell than thy spirit in thee," signing it "Yours Truly, A. J. Wilder."[124] Fitting tribute from a man with an Arabic name, the lines were penned by the Romantic poet Thomas Moore, a friend of Lord Byron's, in an Oriental idyll. It was called "The Fire-Worshippers."[125]

No one who reads Wilder's melancholy posthumous book about the first years of their marriage can doubt that the couple were deeply in love or that they clung to each other in their successive sorrows. Compared to his voluble wife, Almanzo said and wrote strikingly little, but the shoes he cobbled for himself offer mute testimony to a life spent in continual, hard physical labor—farming, plowing, building, planting, pruning, delivering fuel, and caring for cows, calves, pigs, goats, and his beloved horses—despite a painful disability.[126]

The illness he suffered and the reversals the couple endured forged a relationship comprised of love, affection, exasperation, disappointment, and—on her part, after learning of their debts—occasional mistrust. But they persevered. At the end of sixty-four years together, they were as tied to each other as two people could be.

Years later, nearing the end of her own life, Helen Boylston, Lane's friend and companion who had spent months living with the family at Rocky Ridge, recalled Almanzo and his generous, tolerant ways with all the effusiveness that Laura herself never displayed. "He was a darling," Boylston exclaimed, "a good, kind, sweet, intelligent, patient man. And why he didn't kill Mama Bess, I don't know. Oh, she nagged him, and yelled at him, howled at him, and adored him. That he knew too."[127]

Almanzo was buried in the Mansfield cemetery on the breast of a hill above town, after services held at the Methodist church his wife attended, presided over by one of the ministers he had studiously avoided in life. No one really knew how old he was, particularly after he admitted to his wife and daughter that he'd lied about his age in applying for a homestead. The birth year inscribed on the tombstone maintained the fiction, if that's what it was: 1857. Rose Lane arrived by train two days before the service and was in attendance, as were his brother Masons, who performed the rites of their office and issued a "Resolutions of Respect" noting his "zeal and fidelity" to their brotherhood.[128]

A few weeks after his death, Wilder wrote to a friend, "This is only a note for my heart is too sore to write more. Almanzo died October 23rd, and I am very lonely. It was his second heart attack. My plans are very uncertain."[129] To another friend in De Smet, recently bereaved herself, she admitted, "It is very lonely without my husband as you so well understand, but there is nothing left but to go on from here alone."[130] She would often mention her loss in the years to come, as if to memorialize the sharply felt and always lamented absence of the Man of the Place.

Almanzo Wilder had sworn out a final will and testament a few years before he died, a document as straightforward as he was. He left his sassafras chair and cypress table to Silas Seal, the monthly payments from Rocky Ridge to his wife and daughter, and everything else to "Bessie."[131]

NINETEEN forty-nine was a year of legacies. That summer, Wilder had written to George Bye, asking him to transfer 10 percent of her royalties to her daughter. It was a step she should have taken "long ago," she said. She was also beginning to consider turning her home at Rocky Ridge into a museum, thinking about her reputation and posterity.

Lane stayed only a week with her mother after Almanzo's death. She was eager to get back to Danbury, where she had spent much of the previous year completely overhauling her house. In early 1949, she picked up her journal for the first time in many years to record the sense of accomplishment it gave her: "Fireplaces are built in living room and study, bay window in my bedroom, new closets, new furnace room, new porch . . . new front door . . . new ceilings, paint and paper throughout, floors refinished, and shutters." The house was not in Albania, but clearly fulfilled the same proprietary need.

While apart, Wilder and her daughter were doubtless still writing to each other, although most later correspondence has been lost. In one of the last surviving letters, Lane advised her mother on how to make hairpin lace and how best to poison mice. She described an incident in her kitchen, a minor explosion sparked when she brought a match to the hissing gas jet in her oven a moment too late. And she weighed in on what appeared to be an extended discussion regarding what it meant to know the difference between right and wrong. "Forty or fifty years ago I used to be bothered, trying to figure out what people meant by conscience, what is it, why don't I have one, whatever it is?" Lane wrote.[132] What her mother made of this confession, we do not know.

In letters after her husband's death, Wilder was undecided about staying at Rocky Ridge, and friends urged her to consider living in town. She seems never to have entertained the thought of moving east to be near her daughter. "I'm not sure they got along too well," one Mansfield neighbor recalled.[133] The town had not forgotten Lane's portrait of them and continued to shake their collective heads over her. A story circulated that Lane had watched her mother take a hard fall outside a restaurant and stood by, coldly, not helping her up.[134]

In the end, Wilder stayed right where she was. She reassured those who were concerned about her, writing to one friend:

> There are neighbors just across the road and just a short distance to the side. Groceries are delivered to the door; mail every morning to the box by the road; my fuel oil tank for my heater is kept filled with no trouble to me and electricity and telephone ready to my touch. The house is warm and comfortable.
>
> Two boys from the neighbors on the East come every day to see if there is anything they can do for me and a taxi from town is on call to take me wherever I wish to go. Friends from town, only 1/4 mile away, come often to see me.[135]

Her last years were comfortable, secured by her profitable books. No longer confined by the need to stay with Almanzo, she resumed Sunday trips to church. The neighbors nearby were Iola and Marvin Jones, who had built a house near the Wilders after the war. Wilder befriended their boys, Sheldon and Roscoe, who performed seasonal chores, carrying her mail up the steep drive, mowing her yard, raking gravel, and moving heavy things.

She paid them a quarter for such chores, "big money for a kid," as they recalled, and fed them chocolates, "a rare thing for us at that time."[136] At school, the boys had listened to Wilder's books, chapter by chapter. Sitting with the author in her dining room, they heard the same stories directly, with embellishment. "She'd say, 'Well . . . this is the way this story actually happened,'" assuring them that the real Nellie was meaner than her fictional counterpart.[137] One Christmas, she gave Sheldon his favorite book, *Farmer Boy*, and Roscoe, *The Long Winter*, autographing both. Soon the boys were running interference for her, protectively heading off the many unannounced visitors who trooped up to the door, wanting to meet the author.

She retained her love of wild things. The Jones family recalled how she doted on pets that had the run of her house, a big cat and an old boxer dog, "the greatest thing that walked around on four legs."[138]

But Iola Jones was particularly struck by the sight of Wilder feeding terrapins, turtles that would venture up from the spring in the ravine below the farmhouse. Arriving at the back porch, the turtles "got so that they would line up and look in" through the screen door. Wilder soaked bread in milk and fed them "as they stretched out their necks," Iola said, adding, "I've never seen anything like it."[139] As a child, Laura had loved nothing more than playing in the creek. Decades later, she had the creek's denizens eating out of her hand.

As always, Wilder kept intently busy with correspondence, fielding reports about the progress of the Little House uniform edition and yet more ceremonial invitations. Another library sought to honor her: Clara Webber, the head of the children's department at a library in Pomona, California, was a devoted Little House fan. In 1950 she proposed renaming the Pomona children's room after Wilder. The dedication would happen in May.

Once again, Wilder begged off from attending the ceremony. Asked for a statement, she supplied only the briefest of remarks, once more stressing the eternal verities as her mother had interpreted them: "courage and kindness, loyalty, truth and helpfulness."[140] To Webber, she apologized, saying, "It is not very good but since Mr. Wilder's death my thoughts do not flow freely. I am still rather stunned from the shock."[141]

She declined to make a recording to be played at the event, but she sent another treasure: the handwritten manuscript of *Little Town on the Prairie*. That would be augmented by a full set of autographed Little House first editions Webber had secured in the 1940s. Over the years, the librarian created a folksy Wilder shrine, of a type that would be widely imitated by others, adding two sets of "character dolls," a replica of Ma's china shepherdess, copies of family photographs, and translations of the books.

Other accolades poured in, local, national, and international. In August 1950 she was the honored guest at an Athenian Club event—a "Laura Ingalls Wilder Day" tea—at the Wright County Library in Hartville. A hundred and thirty-five people turned out from clubs and towns nearby, each handed a souvenir booklet bearing the titles of Wilder's books. A reporter who wrote up the event remarked on the

"Americanism of this little town; the gaiety, freedom and friendliness."[142] Already, Wilder was a watchword for the country's values.

On her eighty-fourth birthday, in February 1951, she received more than nine hundred cards and messages, the fruits of a "birthday card shower" organized by Florence Williams, librarian of the Mansfield branch. Williams even wrote to General Douglas MacArthur, asking if he could spread the news to Wilder's Japanese readers, so that they might participate.[143] In lieu of that, a lieutenant colonel in the U.S. Marine Corps informed Williams that a "joint radiogram" would be sent to Wilder by the Japanese translators of *The Long Winter*, *Little House in the Big Woods*, and *Little House on the Prairie*.[144] This may have given rise to the persistent rumor that Wilder received a cablegram from the illustrious general himself, though no evidence of such a message exists.[145]

Later that year, Mansfield paid Wilder a high honor, naming its branch library for her at a dedicatory ceremony held in the high school gymnasium. In years past, she had complained of being treated as an outsider by the insular Ozark community, despite having arrived in 1894, so she was thrilled by the gesture. She wore her Sunday best, a dark red velvet dress, an orchid corsage pinned to her shoulder, listening as a violinist played her father's favorite songs.

In gratitude, she would give to the library a number of heirlooms, including Almanzo's handcrafted walking canes, her teenage autograph album, a set of the "character dolls" given to her by California librarians, a set of her books, and the trove of birthday cards she had received earlier that year. She would also include the Mansfield branch library in her will, a bequest that would become a source of controversy decades later.

The honors and tributes must constantly have reminded her of encroaching mortality. On July 30, 1952, she sat down to address a letter to her daughter, to be read upon her death. An ambiguous message, it encapsulated the tensions of their relationship, warm and chiding by turns. To the end, Wilder's affection for her daughter retained an edge.

"Rose Dearest," it began, "When you read this I will be gone and you will have inherited all I have."[146] She directed Lane, once she had selected volumes she wished to keep, to donate her personal collection of books to the Mansfield library. Rather imperiously, she went to say, "My jewelry is unique and should not be carelessly scattered . . . preserve it in some way if you can."

Lane was to "do as you please" with the household's treasured china, but her mother hoped she would use the dishes, remarking, "We were proud of my Havalind . . . but loved best the English made blue Willow-ware." As with many of Wilder's remarks, this may have grated on her daughter's ear: it was Lane who had given them the French Limoges Haviland.[147] Wilder did not mention another set of dishware, a pink one that had been Lane's somewhat odd gift to her father for his birthday.[148] Wilder signed the letter, "My love will be with you always / Mama Bess (Laura Ingalls Wilder)."

MEANWHILE, in New York City, the process of transforming the Little House books with fresh illustrations, covers, typeface, and a uniform design across all the volumes continued. In the annals of children's literature, it was a revolutionary undertaking, incorporating the latest thinking about how to create attractive, accessible books for young readers. It heralded a new age, reevaluating the needs and capacities of children in light of the realization that style, format, and artwork were integral to the reading experience, especially at a tender age.

Helen Sewell's old-fashioned originals had featured a color frontispiece and a few full-page black-and-white illustrations, with a dozen or so smaller line drawings throughout. Reminiscent of woodcuts, the style, which Nordstrom would characterize as "extremely decorative and stylized," embodied a timeless, fairytale quality: human figures were simple and blocky, with rounded faces and indistinct features.[149] After Sewell was injured in a car accident, another artist was brought in to assist with later volumes, and the quality had suffered; the full-page illustrations, each bearing a formal caption, appeared stiff and stagy. The books had never been issued in paperback or as a boxed set.

For the new uniform edition, Nordstrom hired an outside consultant, Helen Gentry, trained in the art of fine bookmaking in San Francisco. In 1935, Gentry had founded her own press, Holiday House, the first American publishing company devoted entirely to children's

books, but she continued to consult for larger houses. Working with
Garth Williams, whose carbon pencil drawings had far greater naturalistic detail, Gentry created a design that let his images span the gutter,
covering both pages with text wrapped around them.[150] Commonplace
now, such techniques found an exciting and inventive first expression
in the Little House books.

Williams's illustrations, widely recognized as among the finest of a
stellar career, brilliantly conveyed moments of tenderness—Pa cradling
Laura in his arms, Mary balancing a kitten on her palm. But they also
captured joyous play and dramatic threats—Laura running across the
prairie, the girls sliding down haystacks, Lena and Laura racing their
ponies, the prairie fire roaring toward Ma and Pa as they run toward
it to set the backfire, Mrs. Brewster raising her knife in the dark. The
pencil drawings brought out the individuality of each character: Ma's
patience, Pa's humor, Mary's serenity, Laura's intent determination,
Carrie's frailty, the fierceness of Jack, and the hauteur of Eliza Jane
Wilder. His detailed drawings would be termed "a visual encyclopedia
of the things of everyday life."[151]

The text received attention, too, although a few things were overlooked. Earlier, Wilder had declared her intention to correct the spelling
of the town of Brookings (misspelled in *Silver Lake* as "Brookins"), and
wrote to Nordstrom asking her to do so.[152] Lane had raged over the
British spelling of "plough" in *Plum Creek*.[153] Neither would be altered
in the 1953 edition.

It fell to Nordstrom to correct a more grievous error, although
Wilder quickly accepted responsibility. In October 1952, the mother of
a seven-year-old girl wrote to Wilder, care of her publisher, to object to
a passage at the beginning of *Little House on the Prairie*. It read:

> In the West the land was level, and there were no trees. The grass
> grew thick and high. There the wild animals wandered and fed as
> though they were in a pasture that stretched much farther than a man
> could see, and there were no people. Only Indians lived there.[154]

After consulting with Wilder, Nordstrom apologized with characteristic frankness, assuring the mother that her complaint was "very

reasonable."[155] "We were indeed disturbed by your letter," Nordstrom
went on:

> I must admit to you that no one here realized that those words read
> as they did. Reading them now it seems unbelievable to me that you
> are the only person who has picked them up and written to us about
> them in the twenty years since the book was published. . . . Perhaps it
> is a hopeful sign that though such a statement could have passed
> unquestioned twenty years ago it would never have appeared in
> anything published in recent years.[156]

Nordstrom also passed along the author's response. Wilder told her
editor, "You are perfectly right about the fault . . . and have my permission to make the correction you suggest. It was a stupid blunder of
mine. Of course Indians are people and I did not mean to imply they
were not."[157] The passage would be revised in the 1953 edition to read,
"There were no settlers."[158]

The complaint foreshadowed other troubles to come. Nordstrom
asked Wilder to reconsider the minstrel scene in *Little Town* in which
Pa and others put on blackface and sing "Skidmore Guard," referenc-
ing "coons" and "darkies." Wilder suggested cutting the entire song or
the offensive "coons," a slur popularized by another minstrel song of
that time.[159] "Do as you think best," Wilder told her editor, "it seems
no one should be offended at the term 'darkies.' "[160] But the entire scene
rested upon stereotypes recognized as offensive long before Wilder
wrote her book. Frederick Douglass had denounced blackface perform-
ers as "the filthy scum of white society" a century earlier, in 1848.[161]
Nordstrom's editorial intervention, like the reader's distress over the
Indian passage, signaled that new generations would be more attentive
to such issues.

Now eighty-five, Wilder may not have been well enough to expend
much energy responding to queries or studying proofs for the new edition. In a note to schoolchildren in the spring of 1951, she apologized
for taking so long to answer, saying, "I have been very sick."[162] The
following year, she thanked a reader for an invitation but said her traveling days were done: "At 85 one loses the desire and the ability to

wander far."[163] She suffered intermittently from heart palpitations and shortness of breath.[164] At some point, she suffered a heart attack.

Her last public appearance came before the new edition was completed. During Children's Book Week in November 1952, she autographed books for two hours at the Brown Brothers Bookstore in Springfield, Missouri, signing hundreds, including one for a soldier in uniform buying it for his kid sister.[165] In the line of children waiting that Saturday afternoon was also a ten-year-old Missouri girl named Ann Romines, who had traveled a hundred miles from her own small town for the privilege.

Forty years later, as a scholar writing on Wilder, Romines recalled that her grandmother had taken "great pains to give me my first look at an actual woman writer," an experience that changed her life.[166] At the time, standing in line with girls from the big city of Springfield, Romines was struck dumb with awe but remembered the author as a tiny figure with "pure white" wavy hair. Wilder again wore her favorite dress, "a rich dark red with a matching velvet hat."[167]

A photo taken that day shows Wilder seated at a broad table before shelves laden with her books, smiling and surrounded by girls dressed in their finest.[168] Behind her hovers a proud and protective face, Irene V. Lichty, who had driven her to the event. Lichty was a relatively new friend of Wilder's, having moved to the nearby town of Ava in the 1940s. The two had bonded over a shared past: Lichty hailed from Kansas, daughter of Great Plains pioneers. In years to come, she would be instrumental in promoting Wilder's legacy to a new generation of readers.

They were ready and waiting. The public would be galvanized by Harper and Brothers' uniform edition of the Little House books, which appeared in the fall of 1953, in plenty of time for holiday shopping. In June, after sending Wilder early copies of *Little House in the Big Woods* and *Plum Creek*, Garth Williams and Ursula Nordstrom had awaited Wilder's response with some trepidation, but they needn't have worried. "The books are beautiful and I am so pleased with them," Wilder wrote.[169] In August, she sent a telegram praising the whole set: "Mary Laura and their folks live again in these illustrations."[170]

In December, *The Horn Book*, America's premier publication on children's literature for teachers, librarians, and fans, devoted an entire issue to the Little House books. It featured tributes by Virginia Kirkus, Nordstrom, and Williams, and included the artist's documentary photographs of the Little House sites. Also included was a long biographical piece about Wilder, emphasizing the books' "incorruptible decency" and "steadfast morality" as emblematic of American pioneer values.[171]

Inspired by these events, members of the American Library Association began reassessing the nature of Wilder's work. Suspicious of down-market, mass-produced "series" books—the Bobbsey Twins, the Hardy Boys, and their like—librarians had long been reluctant to recognize sequels or series with their highest accolade, the Newbery Medal, awarded annually to an author who had made the "most distinguished" contribution to children's literature in America. Five times, the ALA had included Wilder's books on its honor roll, but never had she won the medal.

Now, many librarians came to feel that Wilder's achievement warranted special recognition. In 1954, the ALA devised an entirely new prize: the Laura Ingalls Wilder Award, a bronze medal to be awarded to authors who had made a "substantial and lasting" career contribution to American children's letters. Its first recipient was its namesake.

Williams designed the medal, which showed the child Laura cradling her doll, Charlotte. The sweet image nonetheless reflected the ambiguity over the autobiographical nature of Wilder's work, conflating character with author. (The Theodore Seuss Geisel Award, another medal awarded by the ALA, features an image of the adult Geisel.) Wilder was thrilled by the award but declined the invitation to attend the ceremony in Minneapolis. "Being 87 years old with a tired heart," she wrote, "I have to avoid excitement even if pleasant."[172]

"IT is a long story, filled with sunshine and shadow," Wilder had written in her letter to children, the standard reply Harper began sending out when the rheumatism in her hands made it too difficult to answer mail personally.[173] It was a phrase that held special meaning for her. Her sister Mary had used it in her own tribute to their father, a poem titled "My Father's Violin": "Long years have passed since childhood's happy day / Sorrow and joy have fallen in my way / Sunshine and shadow along my pathway lay."[174]

The words were a romantic commonplace in the nineteenth century, cropping up in a late Edgar Allan Poe poem, "Eldorado," and in the title of a work by a Congregationalist minister.[175] For Wilder, the phrase served as shorthand covering a multitude of joys and sorrows. It alluded to everything she forbore to mention after her experiment in trying to write about her marriage. That manuscript lay untouched in her papers.

Her last journey was to visit her daughter's home. Lane had been coming to see her mother fairly regularly since her father's death, and in 1954 she convinced her to fly back to Danbury. From covered wagons, Wilder had graduated to the aviation age, but little is known of the trip aside from its brevity.[176] She apparently met friends and neighbors of Lane's, writing to one Danbury acquaintance in June to thank her for news that her daughter had recovered from a back strain. She remarked on her own health: "I am quite well usually but must be slow and careful to keep that way. There are days when I lie down most of the time to let my tired, old heart rest."[177]

On other days, she ventured forth. In 1954, she splashed out on a new pastel green Oldsmobile 98, a car that retailed for close to three thousand dollars. She made friends with the local taxi driver, Jim Hartley, who chauffeured her to town on Wednesdays for grocery shopping, and took her on Sunday drives to Ava or Mountain Grove, where she frequented local restaurants. She craved company on these excursions, dining with Hartley or asking Nava Austin, a young Mansfield librarian she had befriended, to join her. She had always loved dining out, and now she was flush with cash from royalty checks.

Wilder was heartbroken when Hartley died suddenly later that year, but found comfort in his daughter-in-law, Virginia Hartley, who took his place. Neta Seal, Irene Lichty, and other ladies continued to help with chores and cleaning, calling her every morning and evening to check on her. Yet Wilder often remarked on her isolation. To a De Smet friend, she wrote that she found it so lonely without her husband "that at times I can hardly bear it, but one has to bear what comes."[178]

Early in 1955 she fell and cut her head badly. Seal spent night after night sleeping at Rocky Ridge to care for her. Wilder's notes dwindled to a few words but captured her gratitude. One invited the Seals to dinner, saying it was her turn to treat. Another on a torn piece of notebook paper read, "Dear Neta How about taking me to town."[179] She scrawled out instructions in case "anything happens to me," asking Neta to "take charge of my house and its contents until Rose can do so. . . . Better keep this with the key."[180] One scrap read simply, "This is just to say Thank you."[181] As a mark of gratitude, she began distributing treasured keepsakes, giving the Ingalls family Bible to Nava Austin, the Mansfield librarian, and an old typewriter to her teenage neighbor Roscoe Jones.[182]

Still, she spent considerable time alone. When a *Kansas City Star* reporter, Fred Kiewit, turned up unannounced to knock at her front door one May evening in 1955, Wilder appeared at the window, waving him around to the latched screen door at the side of the house. "I'm not afraid to be living here by myself, just cautious," she told him later, having ascertained his bona fides. "I have a little gun in a cabinet by the screen door," she said, and "I've got a shotgun in my bedroom and I know how to use them both."[183] The little gun was the revolver she had kept in her pocket during the 1894 journey to Missouri.

For Kiewit's benefit, she reprised her experiences and career in cadences that recalled her writing, explaining how she came to the task late in life. It was the last time she would cover this well-worn territory, and once again she reached back to her father and his gift for regaling his children with unforgettable tales. "When my daughter was grown and gone and my husband and I were taking things a little easier I used to think about the stories my father used to tell us four girls when we were little," she said. He was still alive to her:

> He was a trapper and a frontiersman. He liked the wide-open spaces. When neighbors got too thick he just up and moved mother and us girls. . . . It seemed a shame to let die those stories that father told us of his boyhood on a New York farm before the Civil War. I hated to see them lost.[184]

Her final summing-up was frank and straightforward. She had begun her career by penning several stories "just as I would tell you," she said, sending them to her daughter, who felt "they might be the basis of a picture book but nothing else. . . . She told me to put some meat on the bones and then send the stories back and she would see what she could do."

Intending to write only that first book, she was astonished to hear from children begging for more. "I was amazed," she said, "because I didn't know how to write. I went to little red schoolhouses all over the West and I never was graduated from anything." The only way she could account for it, she explained, was to credit her parents: "Both mother and father were great readers, and I read a lot at home with them. I just had those stories to tell and I wrote them like I would tell them to you." Her process was simple. "After I would write something I would set it back for a month or so and let it cool," she said, as if it were a pie. "Then I would read it back and maybe change it a little before I sent it in."[185] Like most writers, she did not mention the unseen presence or influence of her editor.

Emphatically, she declared herself done. "I wrote all seven after the first one trying to stop and not being allowed to," she said, hurriedly adding, in case readers harbored any illusions: "Now I'm 88 and I'm tired and no one is going to get me to write any more." That was her final word on the subject.

She stoutly told the reporter that she was alone but not lonely, mentioning a cat in the barn who was keeping the mice down and the turtles that "come up out of the holler to see how I am doing." But aside from the succor of turtles, she was indeed lonely. Reading was one of her few remaining pastimes. She enjoyed westerns that Nava Austin loaned her at the library and the yarns in *Adventure* magazine. She kept her Bible next to her chair, with a list of verses to consult in times of trouble, when "facing a crisis" or "sick or in pain." One admonitory passage held special meaning. "To avoid misfortune," she looked to Matthew 7:24–27:

Therefore whosoever heareth these sayings of mine, and doeth them, I will liken him unto a wise man, which built his house upon a rock:

And the rain descended, and the floods came, and the winds blew, and beat upon that house; and it fell not: for it was founded upon a rock.

And everyone that heareth these sayings of mine, and doeth them
not, shall be likened unto a foolish man, which built his house upon
the sand:

And the rain descended, and the floods came, and the winds blew,
and beat upon that house; and it fell: and great was the fall of it.[186]

Lane arrived for another visit around Thanksgiving in 1956 to find
that her mother's health had deteriorated. Wilder was taken to the
hospital in Springfield and diagnosed with diabetes. She remained
there for several weeks, the Seals visiting often. She disliked the hospital water, so they brought water from her spring at Rocky Ridge. They
drove Lane there and back, Neta Seal learning that "Rose was more
rough" than her mother.[187] A twelve-foot-long "Get Well" scroll arrived,
crafted by the children of Springfield. Wilder returned home on the day
after Christmas and seemed to be recovering some strength.

On January 20, 1957, Rose Lane wrote to a conservative friend,
Jasper Crane, a former vice president of the DuPont chemical company.
She described herself as "frantically busy" with housework, cooking,
and nursing chores as she consulted with a Springfield doctor by phone,
trying to cope with her patient's new diabetic diet. Lane wished that
her mother would come with her to Danbury, she told another friend,
"but of course I understand her attachment to home."[188]

Ten days later, Lane wrote to Crane again, thanking him for com-
forting her with a box of libertarian books, including Ludwig von
Mises's *Anti-Capitalist Mentality.* Reminded fondly of her first flush of
anti–New Deal ardor, she regaled him with a nostalgic tour of her
glory days with Garet Garrett, confronting the "Terror" as "Government men" tore through the countryside condemning private property
against the wishes of "frantic and furious" farmers.[189] She closed with
more reflections on the perfidy of the publishing world: "The truth
about this country never does get into print."[190] She did not mention
her mother.

In early February, Neta Seal, newly released from the hospital herself after a knee surgery, visited Wilder at Rocky Ridge, noting how ill
the older woman seemed. The Seals returned the next evening, after
supper, and again on Wilder's ninetieth birthday, on February 7. The

occasion must have been somber. By this point, Virginia Hartley and Neta were taking turns staying by Wilder's side throughout the night, spelling Lane, who tended her mother during the day. Three days after her birthday, on Sunday evening, February 10, 1957, Laura Ingalls Wilder at last came to the end of the long road that had begun in Wisconsin so many years before.

She was buried beside her husband on February 13, in the cemetery on the hill, after a two o'clock service in the Mansfield Methodist Church. It was a simple ceremony, friends recalled, but the church was full.[191] At the end of her life, Wilder still may have felt like an outsider, but the pallbearers who carried her to rest were a litany of old Mansfield family names: Tarbutton, Craig, Coday, Freeman, Tripp, and Marvin Jones, father of Sheldon and Roscoe.[192] Families of original Ozark folk—homesteaders who had arrived before the Civil War—remembered her with awe and respect, recalling her fine clothes, her formal manner, and her reserve.

Several of those who attended later remarked that Mrs. Wilder wasn't really famous then. That was the perception locally, but nationally she was already a notable figure. Her fame was beginning to eclipse that of her bestselling daughter. The New York Times ran a prominent obituary, citing Wilder's American Library Association medal and other honors.[193]

As the eulogies recognized, Laura Ingalls Wilder had traveled an extraordinary distance in her lifetime, and not just in hard miles in covered wagons. Culturally, intellectually, socially, and economically, she had risen far beyond any dreams she may have had as a child. The pioneer girl with bare feet and a rudimentary education had become a respected journalist and prominent author. The impoverished country girl who gazed with envy at classmates' books and toys had amassed a small fortune, the equivalent of more than half a million dollars today. The wife of a broken farmer, who watched her home burn to the ground, had, step by step, reestablished security for herself and her family. The daughter who lived through the ruination of her beloved parents had raised them up, idealizing and immortalizing them, relegating their failures to oblivion. And the writer whose memoir was rejected by publishers had persevered, finding the perfect vessel for her father's tales and her own most treasured memories.

It was only in her role as a mother that she had appeared, at times, at a loss. She had loved her only child, the Rose born in December, weathering the breakdowns and betrayals while swallowing her pride and relying on the younger woman's superior proficiency and professional competence. But somehow the bond with her daughter had proved the most difficult trial of all, despite Wilder's storied closeness to her own parents.

Wilder's first memories had been of her father, him gazing at her as he carried her in the first little house he had built.[194] The comfort of looking up at him, listening to his soothing voice, and watching the flickering wash of candlelight on log walls had created, she said, "a picture that will never fade."[195] Perhaps her last thoughts rested upon him too. Years earlier, in the dark days after losing that beloved man, she had reflected on her own ending. "I am sure that when I come to die," she wrote, "if Father might only be playing for me I should be wafted straight to heaven on the strains of 'The Sweet By and By,' for the pearly gates would surely open."[196]

Chapter 14

There Is Gold in the Farm

The Truth and Only the Truth

When her mother died, Lane was herself an old woman. She turned seventy while caring for Wilder in her final illness. By her own account, she was deeply distraught after Wilder's death. Trying to clean house, she began burning her mother's papers in the stove.[1] Less than a month later, leaving the task incomplete, she fled Mansfield, heading out with friends on a trip through the Southwest.[2] From the road, she sent apologetic letters to Neta Seal, saying she felt "ashamed" of departing so hastily, leaving Neta, still on crutches, to finish straightening up. She said she was not in her "right mind," and she may not have been.[3] Back in Danbury, she embarked on yet more house renovations.

Memorials to her mother were already being discussed in De Smet and Mansfield. Within weeks of Wilder's death, Irene Lichty had written to Lane proposing that the Rocky Ridge farmhouse become a museum. A few months later, Lichty filed papers to incorporate the "Laura Ingalls Wilder Home Association," and arrangements were made to purchase the house from its new owners. That spring, a headline in Wilder's hometown newspaper announced that Mansfield would "Make Shrine of Wilder Home."[4] A shrine is what it would become.

In accordance with Wilder's wishes, the Seals had been given whatever possessions of Wilder's Lane did not want, but now Lane urged them to sell back the furniture, either to herself or to the Home Association.[5] The couple might not care for it anyway, she said, since they already had "nice things." Or, she suggested, Neta could loan the items. Lane supplied text to be affixed to cards in the museum: "Laura's rocking chair in their first little house, in Happy Golden Years. Brought in a covered wagon to Mansfield in 1893, always Laura's favorite chair."[6] The Seals went along, selling much of the furniture—including the clock Almanzo had bought his bride for their first Christmas in 1885, Wilder's writing desk, and the fainting couch she rested on while working on her manuscripts—to the Home Association for a dollar.[7]

As for Wilder's books, her will bequeathed to her daughter "all my Copyrighted Literary property and the income from same for and during her natural life." Upon Lane's death, Wilder directed, those assets should go elsewhere, instructing that "said Copyrighted Literary property and the income from same be given to the Laura Ingalls Library of Mansfield, Missouri."[8]

It would not take long for Wilder's literary estate to become embroiled in controversy. George Bye died in November 1957, nine months after Wilder. For twenty-six years, he had served her and her daughter as literary agent, handling contracts for each of the Little House books, furthering Lane's career by easing her way into the *Saturday Evening Post*, and shepherding *Let the Hurricane Roar*, *Old Home Town*, *Free Land*, and *The Discovery of Freedom* through book publication. Lane had long considered Bye and his wife close friends, using her agent as her banker, borrowing money from him against future earnings, even instructing the agency's accountant to pay the premiums on Rexh Meta's life insurance when he disappeared during World War II. Throughout the years, as scores of letters and telegrams bear out, Bye proved unfailingly cheerful, courteous, and competent.

In 1949, the Bye agency had been acquired by James Oliver Brown, whose James Brown Associates managed a roster of respected writers, including Erskine Caldwell, Jessica Mitford, Katherine Anne Porter, and Jean Stafford. To handle queries regarding perennial earners such as Wilder and Eleanor Roosevelt, Brown kept Bye's agency open for business under its original name.[9] It was one such query that touched off the first explosive dispute in the vexed afterlife of the Little House books. The Canadian Broadcasting Corporation sought permission to adapt a scene from *Little House on the Prairie* for a ten-minute live televised segment. The fee was minimal, just fifteen dollars.[10] But after Brown sent a contract to Lane for her approval, he received an ominous reply from Roger MacBride in January 1959. Lane no longer wished to retain an agent, MacBride said, requesting copies of all Wilder and Lane contracts in Brown's possession.

MacBride—the son of an editor of *Reader's Digest* who had been sitting at Lane's knee, as he put it, since the age of fourteen—was increasingly an integral part of Lane's life. He referred to himself as Lane's "adopted grandson." In her own will, written a few months before her mother's death, Lane had named him her sole executor and beneficiary.[11] He was now twenty-seven, two years out of Harvard Law School. He had never met Laura Ingalls Wilder.

With the young and inexperienced MacBride as her financial advisor, Lane staged an old-fashioned showdown between herself and several agitated parties: attorneys representing Bye's estate; Wilder's publisher, Harper & Brothers, now instructed by MacBride to no longer pay Bye's 10 percent commission; and James Oliver Brown himself.[12] Legally speaking, Lane may have been within her rights. Depending on wording, the agency clause—defining the relationship between agent and author in the book contract—may or may not have terminated with the death of both parties. Whatever the case, Lane and MacBride appeared determined to wrest away the disputed 10 percent from Brown and Arlene Bye, George Bye's ailing widow.[13]

On Lane's behalf, MacBride derided Bye's work for the Little House books, suggesting that Lane had negotiated her mother's contracts with Harper herself.[14] While Lane and her mother had maintained "a deep and abiding affection" toward Bye, he said, they did not think that "he gave much service." MacBride later claimed that he knew of no agreement "between George Bye & Company and Mrs. Lane entitling the former to an agent's commission."[15] In fact, every contract Bye negotiated for Lane and her mother involved such an agreement. Notably, MacBride not only presented himself as a "family friend" of

Rose Wilder Lane's—which was true enough—but falsely suggested that he had been a friend of her mother's as well.[16]

MacBride urged a private settlement, saying that Lane would be reluctant to malign the deceased Bye. With his future relationship with a major publisher on the line, Brown could hardly afford a public lawsuit, and the dispute was resolved out of court.[17] In correspondence, he labeled Lane's behavior "blackmail."[18]

THE contretemps revealed how valuable the Wilder properties had become. At her death, annual income from royalties was estimated at $18,000.[19] By the summer of 1959, *Little House in the Big Woods*, the top seller, had gone through thirty-one printings in the original edition and seven in the uniform edition. *Little House on the Prairie*, second in popularity, had reached twenty-four printings in the old edition, four in the new. In total, the series had sold close to a million copies in the original edition, and the new edition was moving briskly, having already exceeded more than 420,000.[20]

Foreign editions were popular as well. The entire series had been translated into German, and there were Japanese versions of *Big Woods*, *Little House on the Prairie*, *The Long Winter*, *Little Town*, and *These Happy Golden Years*. *Big Woods* had been translated into Danish, Dutch, Chinese, Korean, Burmese, Bengali, Hindi, Telugu, Gujarati, and Slovenian. Finnish parents were reading *Little House on the Prairie* to their offspring while Filipino children thrilled to Nellie Oleson's outrages and Laura's revenge in the Tagalog version of *Plum Creek*. International in their appeal, the Little House books offered everyone, no matter what language they spoke or where they lived, a taste of the American pioneer experience.

It turned out there was indeed gold in the farm—but in books, not crops. During the six-month period from December 1957 to June of the following year, Lane's royalties amounted to $8,716 (less James O. Brown's $968 commission), the equivalent of close to $75,000 today.[21] For the first time in her life, Lane found herself comfortably off. Having refurbished her house, she turned to her protégé. He would be her next renovation.

For her purposes—promoting a conservative antigovernment agenda—Roger MacBride was perfect. Like Lane, he had been an unhappy loner as a child, confident in little except his own superiority. Round-faced and chubby-cheeked, he bore a slightly unfinished juvenile air well into adulthood. A fourth-grade teacher recalled that he was sidelined by his profound nearsightedness, standing on the playground in thick glasses "with a secret, ironic smile," occasionally struck by wayward balls.[22]

Under Lane's tutelage, MacBride rapidly developed into a libertarian activist. While still at Harvard Law, he had published a brief study, *The American Electoral College*, suggesting not an abandonment of the complex system but a policy of greater flexibility, empowering electors to ignore the popular vote and elevate third-party candidates.[23] It was published by Caxton Printers, a publisher in Idaho with a conservative bent. Anyone who had been paying attention—not many were—might have seen it as a sign of things to come. Lane boasted to her friend Jasper Crane that MacBride was "one of SIXTEEN young Princeton alumni" who were dedicated to "combating socialism" at their alma mater. She was deeply proud that MacBride had dressed down his high school, Phillips Exeter, grandly informing fund-raisers that they could expect nothing from him until they stopped "indoctrinating boys with socialism."[24]

After law school, MacBride worked for a time at a Wall Street firm, then left to open a private practice. In 1960, having studied political prospects in various states, he moved to Halifax, Vermont. The following year, he married Susan Ford, a debutante with a Connecticut pedigree, who held that a lady should never go out in public without wearing gloves.[25] The couple sent Lane a telegram shortly after their wedding, signing it, "Love from your grandchildren, Susan and Roger."[26]

If Lane was grooming MacBride, it often appeared that he was assiduously grooming her back, lavishing her with greeting cards, postcards, gifts, and long chatty letters addressed to "Gramma." Susie joined the effort and was warmly embraced by Lane. She gave the MacBrides money and other gifts, continuing a generosity that had preceded the marriage. In 1959, young Roger had fulsomely thanked her for 220 shares in the General Reinsurance Corporation, a gift worth several tens of thousands of dollars, which allowed him, he said, the luxury of feeling the "solidity of capital" under his feet.[27] He compared the moment to what David Beaton in *Free Land* must have felt surveying his homestead. "It's MINE," he declared of his windfall, and no government would ever take it away from him while he had breath in his body.[28] He promised to use it to further their shared beliefs. Finally, Lane had the scion of her dreams.

A few years after her mother's death, Lane took the first step in shaping the legacy that had passed to her. In 1962, she published *On the Way Home*, her mother's record of their journey to Missouri, amplified by her own autobiographical essays at the beginning and end of the volume. It would be the first of several crucial posthumous additions to the Wilder canon.

On the Way Home was familiar territory for Lane. In one form or another, she had returned repeatedly to the 1894 economic depression, to Coxey's Army and the family's *Grapes of Wrath*–style escape from South Dakota. She had written it into her biography of Jack London, into drafts of her unpublished Missouri book, into "Credo" and *The Discovery of Freedom*. In interviews and articles, she often cited those events as the basis of her expertise on the Great Depression, saying "we've had crises in this country before and we've come out of them." She'd been "a malnutrition child in the panic of 1893," she said, but they had all survived "without governmental help."[29]

The version of events that Lane presented in her "setting" for *On the Way Home* differed markedly from her earlier accounts. She was settling scores. In *The Discovery of Freedom* her parents had been stalwart pioneer folk, surmounting every hardship, thoroughly admirable. Now, she gleefully talked of her mother's harsh temper, claiming that Wilder had lashed out at her over the legendary lost writing-desk cash meant to pay for the Missouri land. Her father's solicitous concern for her mother, meanwhile, was exposed as coming at the daughter's expense, in a scene where Lane described his reaction to her blurting out to her mother the good news of his sale of a load of firewood. "Oh, why did you tell her?," she has her father say. "'I wanted to surprise her.' You do such things, little things, horrible, cruel, without thinking, not meaning to. . . . This is a thing you can never forget."[30] Lane had never forgotten it, and nobody else would be allowed to either.

At the same time, she touted the diary to her friend Jasper Crane as an example of the political value of "real Americana," presenting her mother's books as subterranean conservative propaganda.[31] "How much good my mother's books have been—and are—doing in their quiet way," she wrote. "And this diary is more of the same." She urged him to read the Little House books. They were, she said, "true autobiography in the third person."[32]

Lane continued to insist that her mother's books were accurate in every detail, even as scholars were beginning to note their departures from the truth. They found census information, for instance, proving that Laura Ingalls was only three when the family left Wisconsin, though her character celebrates her fifth birthday in *Little House in the Big Woods*. Lane responded by blaming the publisher, claiming that Harper & Brothers "refused" to publish her mother's first book without altering her age, insisting that "no child younger than five has a memory."[33] (There is no evidence that this happened.) Confronted with this, Lane said, she and her mother had waged a heroic but losing battle: "She and I fought for the truth, futilely. To save her father's stories, she finally consented."

Lane refused to admit that the books were novels, as they had been published. Instead, echoing the words Wilder once used in Detroit, she insisted on their absolute veracity: "It has been charged that my mother's books are fiction. They are the truth, and only the truth. . . . She added nothing and 'fictionized' nothing."[34] Not long afterward, she delivered a stiff lecture to Roger MacBride on the importance of differentiating fiction and nonfiction: "You may be unable to distinguish a novel from a political treatise or a historical work . . . but I am not."[35]

She was alert to the tiniest hint of doubt. When William Anderson, a thirteen-year-old boy in Michigan, wrote a pamphlet about the Ingallses' lives, he politely sent a copy to Lane for her approval. He planned to sell it as a fund-raiser at the home sites, which were becoming tourist attractions; it was a model of the free enterprise Lane claimed to love. But his offhand description of the Ingallses living in the vicinity of Silver Lake in 1879 "with a few settlers as neighbors" provoked a scathing response.

The Ingallses had lived "approximately sixty miles from any neighbor," Lane wrote, and any suggestion to the contrary was an insult:

> I object to your publishing a statement that my mother was a liar. . . .
> You will please correct your proposed publication to accord with my
> mother's published statement in her books. . . . I cannot permit publication of a slander of my mother's character, and I shall not do so.[36]

But Anderson was right about the neighbors. Lane's defense of her mother's truthfulness was itself untrue.

In Lane's last book, an expanded collection of articles about needlework that she had written for *Woman's Day*, she again tried to convince the American multitudes to be responsible for their own loaves and fishes. Reaching back to the Massachusetts Bay colony, she wrote of pioneers who had survived in a "savage wilderness," where they had proved that "each must survive by his own effort or perish."[37] Readers enjoying crewelwork patterns of a bygone age may have been startled to find that the flowers embellishing aprons or chair covers harbored the seeds of "world revolution."[38]

Fans, however, appeared indifferent to Lane's philosophy. Many of the letters regarding both the articles and the book instead eagerly inquired as to how they might visit the Wilder Home Museum, where crocheted tablecloths and knitted afghans pictured in the photographs were said to be on display.[39]

Lane should have been proud of the publication. Despite its eccentricities, the *Woman's Day Book of American Needlework* was (and remains) an important historical resource on American fabric arts. But she resented the project, at one point threatening to take her name off it.[40] Perhaps the reason was this: no matter what she did, it all came back to her mother.

An Army of Principles

In 1962, Roger MacBride ran for a seat in the Vermont State House of Representatives and won. He was thirty-four. By this time, his mentor

was being hailed by other libertarian-minded conservatives. The Freedom School near Colorado Springs, where Milton Friedman and Ludwig
von Mises would lecture, named a building for her that year.[41]

Lane cautioned her protégé against having high expectations of
elected office. At the start of the session, from a rented home in
Montpelier, he lamented sorrowfully that he found it much as she had
told him.[42] Disgusted by backslapping colleagues and their "socialist-
interventionist" bills, he began plotting to convince Vermont to ratify
the "Liberty Amendment" to the U.S. Constitution: a favorite of the
John Birch Society, it was aimed at repealing the personal income tax,
along with estate and gift taxes. He also sponsored bills designed to
reduce Vermont's state income tax by 10 percent, claiming its citizens
were the most heavily taxed in the country.[43]

The state's governor accused MacBride of trying to "eliminate Vermont."[44] Indeed, his cuts would have demolished subsidies to the state
symphony, the Vermont Recreation Board, the Arts and Crafts commission, *Vermont Life* magazine, and Middlebury College's forestry
department, as well as the Morgan Horse Farm, serving the state animal that was the darling of Almanzo Wilder's heart. He did not prevail,
but told a local paper he was delighted to have caused a stir. An article
reported that he was being talked up as a "GOP gubernatorial candidate."[45] MacBride cut out the clipping and sent it to Lane, scrawling
across it, "Your grandson Strikes Again!"[46]

In November 1963, eight days before John F. Kennedy's assassination, MacBride delivered a blistering address to Citizens for Goldwater
attacking the president's civil rights bill. The landmark legislation,
which would be passed the following year, outlawed discrimination on
the basis of race, color, religion, sex, or national origin. MacBride saw
it as evidence of a "Communist shadow," representing "forces of darkness."[47] He may have been angling for further recognition within the
Republican party, or even a vice presidential nod.

While politicking, he found time to reopen hostilities on the Little
House front, excoriating Ursula Nordstrom for failing to place advertisements of Wilder's books during the Christmas season and Children's
Book Week. He regretted to inform her, he said (not sounding in the
least regretful), that this constituted a breach of contract, which meant

the reversion of all rights to his client, Rose Wilder Lane. Harper was not to print any further copies of the books.

Lane applauded the action, praising MacBride's chilling tone and urging him to hold out for high cash penalties. The issue wasn't the money, she said; it was publishers' contemptuous treatment of authors. She herself knew a book designer who could do a far better job than Harper had done.

By telegram, Nordstrom hastened to assure them that large advertisements had in fact been placed in the *Herald Tribune*'s Christmas issue, among others. The whole affair blew over, with MacBride smoothly attributing the accusations to his "enraged" client.[48] But the exchange showcased the kind of bullying invective of which Lane and her attorney were proud. Her mother had never expressed anything but appreciation toward her publisher.

In the spring of 1964, MacBride announced he was running for governor of Vermont, as a Republican. Lane was supportive, heartily denouncing his rivals. In one of her last major editing jobs, she revised his rough draft of a pamphlet on taxes, and donated the money to print it. MacBride's rhetoric mirrored his mentor's. "Not since King George III" had rulers been pushing Americans around so officiously, he said of a personage who served as a favorite whipping boy in *Discovery of Freedom* and Lane's angry New Deal interviews.[49] In another homage, he singled out farmers as the constituents he hoped to win over.[50]

But as his heavy campaign schedule ate into the time available for her, Lane grew pettish, complaining that he had no time to spare for his clients. She urgently needed advice on the copyright of *The Discovery of Freedom*, she told him—could he refer her to another attorney?[51] As Rexh Meta and John Turner had learned, Lane's maternal favor came at a price.

Soon she found the whole political process distasteful, suggesting that even if MacBride were elected governor he would have limited exposure and little access to real power. She had told him before: joining a gang was no way to defeat gangsters. She felt that the only way to cripple socialist enemies was to attack them by force, as the American Revolutionists had attacked the British.[52] Those she most admired, she said, were the members of the John Birch Society, which promoted

limited government and opposed socialism and collectivism with an
ardor matching her own.

At times, she seemed to be wearying of the fight. Her letters to the
MacBrides kept reverting to domestic pursuits: the exploits of her
dogs, the baking of cupcakes, the excitement of new Teflon pans. Occasionally she lectured Susie on topics she considered her expertise, revisiting her admiration for Islam and her conviction that powerful Jews
had manipulated the world wars.[53] Youthful musings that verged on
anti-Semitism had hardened into something nastier. She told another
friend that *Fountainhead* had become a bestseller because Ayn Rand
was a Jew, and "that makes a difference in New York."[54]

MacBride's gubernatorial campaign turned into something of a
farce as he committed neophyte blunders. He sent postcards to potential supporters showing disquieting cartoon figures of himself and
Susie wielding knives in their backyard, pursuing rabbits labeled
"Income tax," "Gas tax," and the like. He criticized economic excess
while offering free liquor and sandwiches at campaign events; newspapers sneered that the new "golden boy" of Vermont politics was "no
penny pincher."[55] In a three-way Republican primary, he predicted he
would win by a landslide but instead came in last.[56] Only a minority
found his anti-tax, anti-government message appealing.

In a final effort to put the world right, Lane set domestic politics
aside and embarked in 1965 on a trip to Vietnam, sent by *Woman's
Day*. She was seventy-nine, scowling in her passport photo, hair covered by a lofty turban. In the lounge of Saigon's Caravelle Hotel, she
ran into the son of her old friend and neighbor Isaac Don Levine, as
she surprised a crowd of swaggering male war reporters who were
astonished that "somebody's grandmother" had turned up to do their
job.[57] The article she wrote for *Woman's Day* promoted the domino
theory, warning that the evils of Communism, left unchecked, would
soon wash up on the shores of Hawaii.[58]

Back home, she painted a gory little portrait for the town newspaper of what Danbury might look like once the approximately one
thousand Communists she estimated were already in residence rose up
and murdered the mayor, local ministers, teachers, and the editor of
that very paper.[59] Foretelling roadblocks and sniper attacks on Route

6, she compared Dien Bien Phu to Yorktown, returning to her favorite war, the American Revolution. She saw no contradiction in her call for the elimination of taxation and her support for a tax-funded controversial war half a world away.[60]

While in Vietnam, she had located another needy recipient for her charity: the sister of her interpreter, a young woman named Nguyen Tho Hong Phan. Lane would support Phan's attendance at a college in Illinois, and host her at Harlingen, Texas, where she had acquired a second home near the Gulf of Mexico. She enjoyed Harlingen's warm climate and southern neighbors, whose politics and values matched her own.

Once again, she was spending money nearly as fast as it came in. For the past several years, she and the MacBrides had been planning the construction of an elaborate, two-story fireproof library at the MacBrides' Vermont home, designed to house Lane's ten thousand books. She wanted custom-built shelves, sending sketches of them to her puzzled acolyte, as well as an elevator, powder room, coat closet, and a handsome view.[61] She planned to spend time there, studying her volumes.

But she was not content to stay in Vermont, Texas, or Connecticut. Soon she was planning another ambitious travel itinerary, this time across Europe and beyond. To drive her on the continent she had adopted yet another youth, the twenty-three-year-old son of a neighbor in Harlingen, asking him to pose as her "grandson" in order "to avoid questions as to why an elderly lady would be in the company of a very young man."[62] Lane and her new companion were preparing to embark in November 1968.[63]

She was about to turn eighty-two but had long neglected her health. Despite having had a face lift and cosmetic surgery on her hands, she distrusted doctors, preferring fad diets such as those promoted by Adelle Davis, an advocate of dangerously massive vitamin supplementation.[64] She resisted being tested for diabetes, which ran in the family. She ordered MacBride never to let her die in a hospital, asking for a provision in her will that would redirect her wealth to homeless dogs should he dare to allow it.

On the journey from Texas, she stopped in Danbury, planning to rest for a few days before her trip across the Atlantic. On the night of

October 30, 1968, she baked some bread, then went to bed. She never woke up.

Among the many papers Lane left behind was an unpublished story about her childhood, titled "Grandpa's Fiddle."[65] Written in the first person, it appeared to contain recollections of her grandparents, recounting the night the Wilders took their leave from the Ingalls family and De Smet before their long, sad 1894 journey. It was, however, yet another one of Lane's many conflations of truth and fiction. Laura was called "Carrie," Carrie was called "Aunt Susan," and Grace was dispensed with entirely. Mary remained Mary. Little Freddy died in Wisconsin.

After Lane died, as if channeling her spirit, William Anderson—the former teen pamphleteer, who had become a leading researcher and writer on Wilder—found the story, split it in two, restored the actual names, tweaked some of the details, and published it in a university press anthology, *A Little House Sampler*, as if it were an autobiographical, nonfiction "account" in which "Rose graphically recalled her childish memories."[66] He did not explain what he had done.

Notwithstanding all that dissembling, the story is among the finest Lane wrote, unsparing of herself and accepting of her parents' frailties. Perhaps only in fiction could she achieve that equilibrium. In the end it was her life, more than her father's, that seemed to be "mostly disappointments": her fears and frustrations, her anguish and suicidal depressions, her struggles with money and inability to carve out a creative life that could yield lasting joy or satisfaction. But all of that was washed away in the heartfelt words she summoned to describe her mother's beautiful brown braids and high forehead, "curving innocently, like a baby's," and her father's cheerful blue eyes and "capable" hands: "He knew how to handle anything, and how to meet people and circumstances . . . he had a kind of gaiety in his independence."[67] The story formed a fitting epitaph to Lane's once rich talents, buried somewhere under all her windy rage.

But it would not be her epitaph. She was laid next to her parents, in the Mansfield cemetery, and the marker on her grave contrasts sharply with the spare silence of her parents' stones. It is covered in militant verbiage, shouting capitals chosen by Roger MacBride. The inscription reads, after Thomas Paine:

> AN ARMY OF PRINCIPLES
> WILL PENETRATE WHERE
> AN ARMY OF SOLDIERS
> CANNOT. NEITHER THE
> CHANNEL NOR THE RHINE
> WILL ARREST ITS PROGRESS.
> IT WILL MARCH ON THE
> HORIZON OF THE WORLD
> AND IT WILL CONQUER.[68]

The irony cannot be overstated. MacBride chose a quotation much bandied about by conservatives like himself, who had not read the original. Paine's "Agrarian Justice," a pamphlet issued in 1797, argued that those who owned private property should be taxed to create "a national fund" benefiting the blind, lame, and elderly, as well as young persons just starting out in life. It was the first argument for Social Security.

How Affluent Is My Prairie?

Wilder's will seemed straightforward: after Lane's death, the copyrights to Wilder's books were to pass to the Mansfield branch library, which bore Wilder's name. But despite the apparent clarity of those instructions, they would not be carried out.

During her lifetime, Lane had renewed copyright in the first six Little House books in her own name. The law at the time required copyright to be renewed within twenty-eight years of a book's publication, so Lane's renewals were prudent: without them, the copyright to *Little House in the Big Woods*, for instance, would have expired in 1960. But wittingly or unwittingly, they also set in motion a legal sleight of hand. By renewing the copyrights in her own name, she effectively made them part of her estate. And Lane's will left her entire estate "to my friend Roger Lea MacBride."[69]

By 1972, acting as executor of Lane's estate, MacBride had transferred the copyrights to Wilder's first six books to himself. He had also convinced the Wright County probate court to let him renew the copyrights for the last two books in the series, which he transferred to himself as well. And by 1974, he had registered in his own name the copyrights to her posthumously published work as well. His literary takeover of the Wilder estate was complete.[70]

One of those posthumously published books would be Wilder's abortive attempt at "one grown-up story of Laura and Almanzo." Five months after Lane died, on April 1, 1969, MacBride arrived at Ursula Nordstrom's office with news of Wilder's handwritten manuscript of "The First Three Years." Nordstrom was exultant: "A voice from the grave! . . . How thrilling it would be to have a new Wilder book!"[71] She wrote to Zena Sutherland, a pioneering scholar in children's literature studies at the University of Chicago, saying that MacBride

> casually mentioned that there is, among Mrs. Lane's papers, THE MANUSCRIPT OF A NINTH WILDER BOOK IN LAURA'S OWN HANDWRITING!!!!!! At first I thought wildly Oh he is playing an April Fool joke on me. But no, it IS TRUE!!!!! Mrs. Lane hadn't wanted to send it in to us because it covers the first year of the marriage of Almanzo and Laura and "there is a faint note of disillusion in it that Mrs. Lane thought didn't fit in with the eight published books."[72]

MacBride, she surmised, was open to Harper's publishing the manuscript. He was having his secretary type it.

When Nordstrom read the manuscript, however, she was taken aback by its unfinished nature and somber subject matter. She was determined to publish, but agonized over the question of editing, revising, or adding to it. She noted that the only manuscripts in her entire career that had required no editing, "no repeat absolutely no editorial suggestions from me or anyone else," were Wilder's and E. B. White's.[73]

In the end she opted to make only a few changes, most of them superficial. Among substantive cuts was MacBride's deletion of

THERE IS GOLD IN THE FARM

Wilder's account of the pain she suffered in childbirth, deemed too graphic for children. Removed as well was the highly suggestive question Wilder had posed to herself: "How much could she depend on Manly's judgment, she wondered."[74]

Published in February 1971 as *The First Four Years*, the book inspired in its audience a reaction similar to Nordstrom's own. Initially there was excitement and anticipation, then confusion and in some cases dismay. Readers were struck by both its similarity to the previous novels and its divergence from them. It opened with a beautiful lyrical passage describing Laura and her beau taking a buggy ride in the gloaming; but the Wilders' engagement, wedding ceremony, and the little house on Almanzo's tree claim were described in terms notably different from passages covering the same material in *These Happy Golden Years*. (Neither Nordstrom nor MacBride realized that the book had been composed before *Golden Years*; in his brief introduction, Mac-Bride speculated that it was written in the late 1940s.)[75]

Astute readers immediately noticed the gulf between the polished series and the harsher adult perspective of the new volume. This Laura was initially joyful in her marriage, then fearful, doubtful, haunted, on occasion even petulant. During her pregnancies and the couple's disastrous bout with diphtheria she endured terrible suffering without the cheerful moral uplift reliably provided in the prose of previous volumes. The once stalwart and reassuring Almanzo appeared reticent to a fault, his wife stung into mistrust upon learning of his undisclosed debts.

The gauzy scrim placed before pioneer life by the collective efforts of Wilder and Lane was beginning to dissolve. Beyond it, questions loomed about the autobiographical sources of Wilder's fiction and the creative process that had transformed her life into an American success story. But as if to obscure things again—erecting a phantasmagorical display to distract from what was coming into focus—Roger MacBride made a fateful move. He decided to bring the Little House to television.

BACK in 1959, when the Canadian Broadcasting Corporation's request to adapt a scene from *Little House on the Prairie* prompted a dispute over agent commissions with George Bye's estate, Lane and MacBride had claimed that "the family" had a policy of never licensing television rights for Wilder's work.[76] There was too much potential for "distortion of the context of the books," they said. But by 1971, when Ed Friendly approached MacBride about TV rights, MacBride's earlier objection was long forgotten.

Friendly, producer of the counterculture hit *Rowan & Martin's Laugh-In*, was searching for a new project for his Los Angeles production company. His wife, who had read the Little House books to their children, had once urged him to construct a series around them. When Friendly caught his teenage daughter rereading the novels—something she did every year—he realized the devotion they inspired. On a flight to New York, he took one of his daughter's Little House books with him, concealed inside a *Time* magazine. By the time he crossed the country, his mind was made up.[77]

MacBride told Friendly he was already in negotiation with a major studio, but later flew to California to hear the full pitch. Friendly laid out a pilot and a weekly series to follow, and soon convinced MacBride to allow him to option the rights.

Friendly then worked through the nine books, hiring a writer to craft a two-hour pilot based on *Little House on the Prairie*. The script was delivered to Michael Landon, a star of the western hit *Bonanza* whose directing Friendly admired. Landon wanted in immediately, and Friendly negotiated a deal with NBC allowing Landon to produce, direct, and star as Charles Ingalls. MacBride was given a coproducer credit.

The culturally convulsive sixties and the crime- and scandal-ridden seventies were propitious for entertainment that embodied "traditional" family values. Disgraced by Vietnam and Watergate, the country was once again turning to old-fashioned, heartwarming rural tales. In the second half of the 1960s, *Petticoat Junction*, loosely set in the Ozarks, and its spinoff, *Green Acres*, wrested humor from America's farm past. *The Waltons*, a gentle family drama about three generations abiding in rural Virginia during the Great Depression—poor in funds but rich in spirit—debuted in 1972 to high ratings.

The three commercial networks were cringing away from the consequences of what was thought to be an excess of violence in programming. In 1972, the Surgeon General had issued a report investigating a causal link between televised mayhem and crime. Two years later, after congressional hearings, the Federal Communications Commission released guidelines on children's programming, sharply urging networks to move beyond Saturday-morning cartoons advertising sugary cereals and to serve families in prime time. *Little House on the Prairie* was tailor-made to address those concerns and that constituency.

When the pilot of *Little House on the Prairie* premiered in 1974, it earned the highest Nielsen ratings of any made-for-television movie that year, and the series was immediately approved. Initial plots were derived from the original books, following the Ingalls family as they left the Big Woods for Indian country and then established themselves in Walnut Grove. But Landon seized control early on, assuming the role of head writer, and the show quickly branched out into ever more ahistorical directions.

Pet raccoons, birth defects, hybrid corn, and a massive typhus outbreak: the first season was padded with distractions. It ended with a log-splitting competition, showing off Landon's pectoral muscles to advantage. His chest would become a primary visual motif, as the television Charles Ingalls frequently found cause to remove his shirt, baring a clean-shaven and well-oiled expanse. As for Pa's beard, Landon sloughed that off as well, a publicity release solemnly announcing that he "just did not look good" with facial hair.[78] When Landon had starred as Little Joe Cartwright in *Bonanza*, his hindquarters had been a staple of the teen fan magazine *Tiger Beat*, so he wore no underwear under Pa's tight trousers.[79]

Ratings were high even if critics found the series dull, calling it "a sort of Sweet 'n Low *Waltons*." Ed Friendly was forced out during the first season, though he retained his share of the royalties. The producer did not go quietly, telling the media he was dismayed that the show revolved around Landon, pushing Laura's character into worshipful orbit. He derided the star as a "mediocre writer . . . not up to the task of adaptation." Landon shrugged off the barbs, boasting that librarians and bookstore owners had thanked him for reigniting interest in Wilder's books.[80] He had a point: sales of the Little House books rose sharply during the nine-year run of the series.

But while television spiked sales, it also caused confusion. The show was not so much an adaptation as a hyperbolic fantasy spin-off, wildly exaggerating the family's well-being. In place of the flimsy tar-paper shanties that served real homesteaders, Landon erected a luxurious two-story frame house with a baronial stone fireplace and sixteen-pane windows. Friendly griped that Landon found it "depressing to live in a sod house."[81] If the actual Laura had yearned for a china doll she could never attain, Landon's Laura would get that doll, only to see it broken by a vengeful Mary. Walking to school, his Mary and Laura wore shoes rather than going barefoot, because Landon didn't want his show-children to be "the poorest kids in town." Friendly joked that the series should be renamed "How Affluent Is My Prairie?"[82]

The prairie was affluent enough to launch Roger MacBride's last bid for political power. By 1972 he was serving as treasurer of the Republican Party of Virginia, and was a member of the electoral college when Nixon won his landslide victory against George McGovern. True to his treatise, he acted as a "faithless elector," casting his vote not for Nixon but for the nominee of the Libertarians, John Hospers. He earned the wrath of the Republicans but did not care. His defiance secured his position within the Libertarian party, granting them their first—and to this date only—electoral vote in history.

In 1975, he won a three-way contest at the Libertarian convention and became a presidential candidate himself, running against Jimmy Carter and Gerald Ford as the nominee of the Libertarian Party. He embarked on the race with fifty thousand dollars of his own and a quarter million raised by the party.

MacBride was endorsed by Charles Koch, heir to Koch Industries and a multibillion-dollar fortune built on oil refineries, who called him "far better fitted to be President than any candidate of any party has been in my lifetime."[83] (Koch's brother David would go on to serve as the Libertarian vice presidential candidate in 1980.) Long before the Koch brothers became nationally known for trying to sway elections, the endorsement of MacBride marked the beginning of their deep investment, first in Libertarian politics and ultimately in attacking all government regulation of big business.

To garner local press attention, MacBride relied on flying himself into towns and airfields in a vintage red-white-and-blue DC-3 prop plane. Many newspapers hailed his connection to *Little House on the Prairie*, weirdly calling him a "self-made millionaire."[84] At least one said that the television show was based on "stories written by his grandmother."[85]

The *Atlantic Monthly* sent a freelancer to profile the long-shot campaign. Witheringly, the article outlined everything that the Libertarians wanted to do away with, a list taking up many column inches and including Medicare, Medicaid, Social Security, OSHA, the FBI, the CIA, the EPA, the Federal Reserve, farm subsidies, anti-gun laws, child labor laws, safety belts, public schools, overseas military bases, and federal control of the Post Office. Startlingly, given his preferred mode of travel, MacBride also wanted to dispense with the Federal Aviation Administration.[86]

He confided to the reporter that he knew he'd lose three-quarters of the country—East, South, and Midwest—but expected the West to be another matter. There, he said, he was taken seriously: "People out there . . . went to get away from authority. It's close to the surface out there . . . this feeling that, God damn it, it's *my* life. Let *me* live it."[87] Ultimately, though, he tallied just 172,553 votes, coming in fourth after Eugene McCarthy, who had over 740,000. That was the end of his political career.

He turned back to his mentor and her mother. Walking in Lane's footsteps, he concocted a biography of her based on details from her 1919 *Sunset* serial, *Diverging Roads*. He called it a "perfectly genuine fictional autobiography."[88] It begins with the assertion that "Rose Wilder Lane was a great person."[89]

When that received little attention, MacBride aided the research of William Holtz, a University of Missouri professor at work on a comprehensive biography of Lane. He was bitterly disappointed, however, with the resulting work, *The Ghost in the Little House*, which portrayed Lane as the true author of her mother's books. Holtz had shown MacBride early versions of the text, but he seems to have kept in reserve the full force of his argument, presented almost entirely in a seven-page appendix.[90] MacBride decried it as "sensationalist" and complained that "the book can only serve to disappoint children who read the 'Little House' volumes."[91]

Holtz may have been influenced by Lane's most apt pupil, Norma Lee Browning, who had herself become a journalist, columnist, and ghostwriter, and who also believed that her mentor had written all of Wilder's books.[92] Over the years, Browning regaled Holtz with fond aggrandizements, claiming in a memoir of her Danbury days that Lane was the "highest paid woman writer in America," and more valued by editors for her short fiction than any writer since Somerset Maugham.[93]

As if he had contracted a severe biographical strain of Stockholm syndrome, Holtz uncritically adopted Lane's harsh view of her mother, treating Wilder with contempt throughout *The Ghost in the Little House*. He referred to her by Lane's own nickname, "Mama Bess," in belittling references that grew more and more cutting. She was portrayed as shrill, grasping, and talentless, a "pedestrian" parasite on her daughter's far superior talents.[94] Denouncing the biographer's perfidy in letters to the Wilder home sites, MacBride urged them not to sell the book.

Eventually, though, MacBride sought to leave his own mark on Wilder's canonical works, planning an extensive series of sequels. The first, *Little House on Rocky Ridge*, purported to tell the story of Rose's childhood, and peddled Lane's political philosophy in a form unmediated by her mother's restraint. When Rose traps a rabbit during their first year in Missouri, Almanzo says: "That rabbit you caught is helping to keep us free and independent, Rose. So long as we can live off our land, we will never be beholden to others."[95] Other sequels, such as *Little Farm in the Ozarks* and *In the Land of the Big Red Apple*, would quickly follow.[96]

But before he could complete his Rose saga, MacBride died suddenly, of a heart attack, on March 5, 1995, at the age of sixty-five. His death would reopen questions about Wilder's will, exposing the machinations he had engaged in to secure Little House copyrights in his own name. Within a few years, a lawsuit would be filed by the Wright County library in Missouri, seeking to re-register Wilder's copyrights and claim the royalties Wilder left to the library in her will. It would be joined by the Missouri Attorney General on behalf of the people of that state, sparking headlines such as "Little Uproar on the Prairie."[97] The litigation would be settled out of court in 2001, for a one-time payment of $875,000.[98] The copyrights stayed with MacBride's estate.[99]

ANACHRONISTIC though it was, the television show remained popular. In the summer of 1980, *New York Magazine* profiled Ronald Reagan, then campaigning for the presidency, as "a nice, well-intentioned man who loves his family, likes to consult his horoscope before making major decisions, and cries when he watches *Little House on the Prairie.*"[100] Michael Landon, a longtime Republican and Reagan supporter, must have been pleased. Denying that his show bore any political message, Landon nonetheless connected its popularity to the "optimism" Reagan inspired.[101]

According to costars, Landon maintained his own optimism by smoking heavily and swigging from a bottle of Wild Turkey between takes.[102] He was hardly the first Hollywood star to promote clean living while indulging his vices. Still, his take on the *Little House* grew darker and more baroque as the years ticked by. Having exhausted Wilder's material, he recycled story lines from *Bonanza* and took up contemporary concerns, including rape, drug addiction, and Caroline Ingalls's menopause. Mary got married and had a kid. Carrie fell down a mine shaft, and Rose was kidnapped.

Whether Landon admitted it or not, his show was indeed political. It reinforced a powerfully simplistic reading of Wilder's work, extending her portrait of Charles Ingalls's stoicism to absurdly heroic lengths. Its audiences were led to believe, among other things, that small-scale farming had reliably and sustainably fed American families on the Great Plains.

The show's crowning incongruity was that it aired during the most explosive period of protest and resistance for American Indians since the nineteenth century, beginning with the 1973 occupation of the Pine Ridge reservation in South Dakota. Across the country, Indian scholars and activists, confronted by the ubiquitous popularity of *Little House on the Prairie* in all its manifestations, challenged the novel's presence in elementary schools and libraries, arguing that it was little more than a justification for American colonialism. The questions they raised were far more urgent, anguished, and critically complex than the reader's query Ursula Nordstrom had fielded years earlier.[103]

Inevitably, cultural tastes shifted over time, and ratings for the television series declined near the end of its run, in 1983. Landon ended his opus with a literal bang: in a final made-for-TV movie, broadcast in 1984, the people of Walnut Grove rebel against the railroad by dynamiting the town, leaving it a smoking ruin. Melissa Gilbert, who played Laura, later said that Landon wanted to destroy the sets so that no future productions could poach them.[104] The little house itself—the only one of the buildings to be preserved—burned down in a wildfire in 2004.

The show continues to enjoy a perpetual life in syndication, popular around the world. In her memoir, Alison Arngrim, the child actor who played Nellie Oleson, recalled an occasion in a bar in New York City "where the bartender was from Israel, the waitress was from Argentina, and the manager was from Iran."[105] They were all comparing favorite *Little House* episodes. However silly or saccharine, the show was transmuted by fans' love for it into a touchstone: Arthurian legends rendered in braids, calico, and suspenders.

But if Landon's production was frivolous, Wilder's great novel, *Little House on the Prairie*, endures as a classic work. Over the years, the perception of it has deepened and broadened. Beloved at first as a simple adventure story for children, it has become a cultural monument, open to question, interpretation, derision, satire, adaptation, and analysis. With the cryptic statement "I can't forget the Minnesota massacre," the novel has continued to keep before the public, perhaps more than any other single work, one of the most haunting chapters of the Plains Indian wars.

Critical or adoring scholars and readers might agree about one thing: the Little House books are not history. They are not, as Wilder and her daughter had claimed, true in every particular. Yet the truth about our history is in them. The truth about settlement, about homesteading, about farming is there, if we look for it—embedded in the novels' conflicted, nostalgic portrayal of transient joys and satisfactions, their astonishing feats of survival and jarring acts of dispossession, their deep yearning for security. Anyone who would ask where we came from, and why, must reckon with them.

Epilogue

What were Wilder's dreams? She told us, again and again. She wanted to save her father's stories from being lost. She wanted to promote her parents' values, which were her own: "courage, self reliance, independence, integrity and helpfulness." They ran through all her stories, she said, "like a golden thread." They still do.

In the decades after her death, heirs, editors, directors, and publishers sought to steer her legacy in directions of their own choosing. Lane worked to tie the books ever closer to the American jeremiad that she and Isabel Paterson and Ayn Rand had preached. MacBride's dream was to be president. Landon's, to perpetuate his fame.

The efforts of those curators and caretakers often strongly diverged from the purity of Wilder's vision, and there is no denying their impact—especially the powerful influence of the television series. But for all its syndicated popularity, it is the books that endure. The Little House world belongs to the readers.

The reach and stature of Wilder's books have grown over decades, inspiring a level of devotion usually reserved for baseball statistics or comic-book superheroes. Fans don sunbonnets and prairie dresses, festooning their children in like fashion. They sew nine-patch quilts in Wilder's honor, travel thousands of miles to visit her home sites, and

attend pageants based on the books. A biennial Midwestern conference, LauraPalooza, celebrates her legacy. The books have inspired other
novels, how-to manuals, and memoirs, including Wendy McClure's
bestselling *The Wilder Life*, exploring her obsession with the Little
House lifestyle. Readers have claimed that "Laura" saved their lives.
Mothers have named their daughters for her.[1]

Aside from children themselves, teachers and librarians have always
been the books' most enthusiastic adopters. In a 2008 study, Anita
Clair Fellman painstakingly traced the widespread practice of excerpt-
ing the Little House books in "basal readers," the basic textbooks used
to teach reading. Across the decades, beginning in the forties and fifties, such textbooks saturated young minds with Wilder's values.

Some of the teachers Fellman described went well beyond excerpts,
reading the entire series to their spellbound classes. A third-grade teacher
organized a "weeklong blitz" around the books, using them to teach
every subject: history, social studies, art, math, and music. She even
prevailed upon the gym teacher to organize games of "Pussy in the
corner" from *Plum Creek*.[2]

It was in one such third-grade class that William Anderson, who
later so annoyed Lane with his pamphlet and eventually became a
leading Wilder scholar himself, entered the Little House universe in the
1960s. He and his classmates drew maps, made cornbread, constructed
a reading tepee, and put up Little House dioramas on the walls. "Almost
everybody has a Wilder story," he says, and "when you meet them they
have a memory of it." Much Wilder scholarship, he suggests, was inspired
by such memories.[3]

Across the country, countless students have learned about pioneer
life from *Little House in the Big Woods*: shaking cream in mason jars
to make butter, building cabins out of cardboard, and putting on plays.
Writing students have compiled their own "autobiographies" based on
Wilder's example. "No other books equaled them in popularity," a
teacher testified.[4]

Like the coyotes outside the surveyors' house at Silver Lake, readers
have followed a trail of breadcrumbs to all of Wilder's little houses. It
is there, at the home sites devoted to her memory, that what lives on
of Wilder's dreams can best be seen. The relics of her life form the

economic heart of Pepin, Wisconsin; Spring Valley and Walnut Grove, Minnesota; Burr Oak, Iowa; De Smet, South Dakota; and Mansfield, Missouri. They are the embodiment of small-town American austerity. To reach them involves hours of driving: De Smet is four and a half hours west of Minneapolis, two and a half hours east of Pierre.

The home sites celebrate the generally accepted moral of Wilder's life, which many have emblazoned on their walls, newsletters, and fund-raising pamphlets. Their improving text is taken not from any book that Wilder wrote, but from the form letter distributed by Harper when she became too frail to answer her voluminous mail. The nostrum is treated as if it constitutes a commandment: "It is still best to be honest and truthful; to make the most of what we have; to be happy with simple pleasures and to be cheerful and have courage when things go wrong."[5]

But nostrums have a way of papering over contradictions. The *New York Times* asked recently, "Why Do People Who Need Help from the Government Hate It So Much?"[6] It was no mystery to Wilder. As she knew too well, people who are poor are ashamed. It's easier to blame the government than to blame yourself. Wrestling with shame was one of the reasons she wrote her books—Nellie Oleson was the devil she put behind her—but she also labored to lift that feeling out of her stories and out of her past, setting aside her father's debts and her own grubby days working for the Masterses. She said she made the changes for children, but she did it for herself too.

Wilder's hometowns are a mute witness to what has happened to small-town farming and self-reliance, lost to taxes, to banks, to big business. We know, or should know, that Independence, Kansas, is now more closely associated with oil wells than wheat. Yards behind the quaint replica of the "little house on the prairie," built in the 1970s to celebrate the television show, lies a buried Enbridge petroleum pipeline that can carry more than half a million barrels of crude a day from Illinois to Oklahoma, a "quiet clone" of the controversial Keystone XL.[7] Visible off the county road, like a disgruntled dipper on the land the Osage once patrolled, an oil derrick pumps slowly, day in and day out. In the former Indian Territory, the Osage made a fortune off oil, becoming for a time the richest people per capita in the world, in one of the few instances of poetic justice in Native American history. Yet that story, too, reminiscent of Wilder's image of the Indians riding away, would not end happily.[8]

De Smet is still a pretty little town, and the house that Charles Ingalls built abides humbly on Third Street, where Laura and Almanzo and Rose waved goodbye in 1894. Its nostalgic charm is very much intact. Yet around the corner, in the church building that had once hosted Congregational services, a pastor puts up folding chairs for people who never come.[9] Calumet Avenue, once the little town's hive of activity, where the Ingallses lived cheek by jowl with Fuller's hardware and T. P. Power's tailor shop, is now studded with empty storefronts. By the shores of Silver Lake, there is a cement factory.

South Dakota Highway 25 runs past the homestead and the tree claim, and the wind still blows where a pregnant young woman once slid down the hill on the snow. But these gusts are coming off the big rigs speeding past, the lifeline of industrial agriculture and the boom-and-bust cycles of hydraulic fracking across the Northern Plains. Crisscrossed by barbed wire fences, pockmarked by cell towers, the prairies where Laura and Almanzo rode their ponies beside the heart-stopping blue of pothole lakes are cut to pieces. The cottonwoods that Charles Ingalls planted one afternoon in the 1880s still stand, next to "Laura's Living Prairie"—a tourist site with RV parking, a lookout tower, and ten acres of commemorative cropland planted in wheat, corn, and oats.

Mansfield is one of the hundred poorest towns in the country.[10] Median household income is $17,750. Stay long enough, and a pickup truck flying a Confederate flag will drive by. Stand around in the newspaper office, the library, or the gas station, which sells Subway sandwiches and fried catfish, and you'll hear people lamenting the few jobs, the loss of a Walmart to another town, the prevalence of drugs. One of the few enterprises still open on the main street is the Bank of Mansfield, where the Wilders borrowed money to buy Rocky Ridge in 1894. For many years, it held Wilder's handwritten tablets in its vault. A new visitor center has been constructed at the base of the farmhouse on the hill; to build it, the Laura Ingalls Wilder Home & Museum took stimulus money from the federal government. Presumably its previous owner would have disapproved. Even so, it was a mere pittance, scarcely more than all their mortgages put together.[11]

Parts of the Great Plains were never successfully farmed, except by heavily subsidized agribusiness and operators with the kind of deep pockets that bonanza farmers brought to Dakota Territory's Red River Valley in the 1870s.[12] Ranches run into the tens of thousands of acres, and much of the West is now a vast feedlot given over to the livestock industry.[13]

Monoculture has always been with us, and it has always been the model that pays. But it too has its limits. Even the richest, most productive land has been relentlessly strip-mined for resources—from the central valleys of California, with their massive fruit orchards trimmed to a fare-thee-well, to the cruel crowded egg sheds that made Wilder turn away in horror. The depletion of rivers, ground water, and aquifers, drained by intensive irrigation, continues apace. Thanks to the abandonment of conservation practices, sparked by short-lived booms in ethanol, the specter of the Dirty Thirties looms again on the horizon. Suitcase farmers manage enormous spreads from distant towns and cities. Dust is eddying in Oklahoma, and during recent droughts parts of some plains states were said to be "drier than the Dust Bowl."[14]

According to the USDA, many small farms cannot turn a profit even during the best years. In 2015, median farm income was negative $765.[15] Ninety-one percent of farmers are dependent on multiple sources of "off farm" income, just as Laura Ingalls Wilder was, and her father before her.

In something like despair, a small-scale farmer, part of the ostensible boom in sustainability and trendy organic micro-crops, wrote an op-ed in the *New York Times*, "Don't Let Your Children Grow Up to Be Farmers." In it, he outlined exhausting strategies to make ends meet that Wilder herself would have instantly recognized:

> The dirty secret of the food movement is that the much-celebrated small-scale farmer isn't making a living. After the tools are put away, we head out to second and third jobs to keep our farms afloat.... I've hustled wooden crafts to tourists on the streets of New York, driven lumber trucks, and worked part time.... Laden with college

debt and only intermittently able to afford health care, my partner
and I have acquired a favorite pastime in our house: dreaming about
having kids. It's cheaper than the real thing.[16]

Echoing generations past, he called for farmers to organize the way
they did in the 1880s, another elusive and perhaps impossible dream.

COMMENTING on a campaign for a postage stamp honoring her
mother, Rose Wilder Lane wrote that if the effort failed in 1967, on the
occasion of Wilder's hundredth birthday, fans would need to try again
fifty years later, in 2017. "I hardly expect to be here in 2017," she
wrote, "but my mother's books will be."[17] She was right about that.

There would indeed be a stamp, honoring not the life but the work.
In 1993, the U.S. Postal Service issued a block of twenty-nine-cent
stamps celebrating four American children's classics: *Little Women*,
The Adventures of Huckleberry Finn, *Rebecca of Sunnybrook Farm*,
and *Little House on the Prairie*. The image chosen to depict Wilder's
book showed a windswept girl beside a log cabin, her face hidden by
an enormous sunbonnet.

By now, the work and the life have become inextricable. Visitors to
the home sites do not particularly distinguish between what belonged
to the Ingalls family and what's a replica, between what is real and
what is fiction. The children shout and point, but the adults walk softly,
whispering, taking each other's elbow to point out the precious objects:
There's Pa's fiddle. There's the china shepherdess. There's the parlor
organ. That must have belonged to Mary.

There is something moving in these murmurings, something that
speaks of veneration and awe. The home sites are so humble, so homelike in their modest Americana, filled with the flotsam washed up by
the past—old quilts, faded tea cups, blurry black-and-white photographs,
impossibly tiny shoes, a chipped bread plate with the Lord's Prayer on
it. These are the contents of everyone's grandmother's attic. This is the
detritus of our complicated history, residue of all the tears and broken
promises and unpaid debts everyone left behind.

If Wilder's life was triumphant—and it was—it was a different kind of triumph than we are accustomed to recognizing. She wrote no laws, led no one into battle, waged no campaigns. If we listen to her, we can hear what she was telling us. Life in frontier times was a perpetual hard winter. There was joy—riding ponies, singing hymns, eating Christmas candy—but it was fleeting. There was heroism, but it was the heroism of daily perseverance, the unprized tenacity of unending labor. It was the heroism of chores, repetitive tasks defined by drudgery. Cooking and eating the same fried potatoes, day in and day out. Washing dishes in dirty water. Twisting hay with hands so cracked they bled. Writing with a blunt pencil on a cheap tablet.

Laura Ingalls Wilder was a real person. Not only a fictional character, although she lives on in that guise. When you stand in the small town cemeteries where she and her people are buried, you know that they were real. In the silence on the rise in De Smet, on the hill in Mansfield, covered by grass and gray markers, there are real bodies buried in the ground, not images or icons or fantasies.

Her voice speaks to us of those people and their feeling for the land. It speaks not about policy or politics but about her parents, her sisters, her husband, and her love for them. It speaks of her delight in nature, those glorious moments on untouched open prairies, watching the geese fly overhead. "Our family was De Smet," she said simply, of those days when they were alone on Silver Lake.[18] She always remembered that place, that moment, "a wild, beautiful little body of water, a resting place for the wild water birds of all kinds, many varieties of ducks, wild geese, swans, and pelicans."

Wilder's family was every family that came to the frontier and crossed it, looking for something better, something beyond, no matter the cost to themselves or others. But however emblematic her portrait, it was also achingly specific, down to the lilt of the songs they sang and their last glimpse of an intact prairie: the grasses waving and blowing in the wind, the violets blooming in the buffalo wallows, the setting sun sending streamers through the sky. In the end, being there was all she ever wanted.

NOTES

Names of Individuals
Laura Ingalls Wilder: **LIW**
Almanzo James Wilder: **AJW**
Rose Wilder Lane: **RWL**
George Bye: **Bye**

The Little House Books
Little House in the Big Woods: **LHBW**
Farmer Boy: **FB**
Little House on the Prairie: **LHOP**
On the Banks of Plum Creek: **PC**
By the Shores of Silver Lake: **SL**
The Long Winter: **LW**
Little Town on the Prairie: **LTOP**
These Happy Golden Years: **THGY**
The First Four Years: **TFFY**

Unless otherwise indicated, citations from the texts of the published works refer to *Laura Ingalls Wilder: The Little House Books*, volumes 1 and 2, ed. Caroline Fraser (New York: Library of America, 2012). Citations from the manuscripts of the books, some of which bear titles different from the published work, use the original title. For example, "Little House in the Woods" refers to the manuscript of *Little House in the Big Woods*; "The First Three Years" refers to the manuscript of *The First Four Years*.

Other Frequently Cited Works

Pioneer Girl: The Annotated Autobiography: **PG**

The Selected Letters of Laura Ingalls Wilder: **SL LIW**

A Little House Sampler: Laura Ingalls Wilder and Rose Wilder Lane: **Sampler**

A Little House Reader: A Collection of Writings by Laura Ingalls Wilder: **Reader**

Libraries and Archives

Herbert Hoover Presidential Library, Rose Wilder Lane Papers: **HHPL**

Herbert Hoover Presidential Library, William Holtz Collection: **HHPL, WHC**

Western Historical Manuscript Collection and State Historical Society of Missouri: **SHSM**

James O. Brown Associates Records, 1927–1992, Butler Rare Book and Manuscript Library, Columbia University: **JOB**

Burton Historical Collection, Detroit Public Library: **Burton Collection**

Laura Ingalls Wilder Memorial Society, De Smet, South Dakota: **De Smet Collection**

Laura Ingalls Wilder Home and Museum, Mansfield, Missouri: **Mansfield Collection**

Almanzo and Laura Ingalls Wilder Association, Malone, New York: **Malone Collection**

Pomona Public Library, Pomona, California: **Pomona Collection**

Wisconsin Historical Society: **WHS**

The Herbert Hoover Presidential Library holds many of the letters, diaries, manuscripts, typescripts, and photographs of Laura Ingalls Wilder and Rose Wilder Lane in its Rose Wilder Lane Papers: 1804–1986. Additional materials regarding Lane are held in the Hoover's William Holtz Collection, 1887–1996, and Isabel M. Paterson Papers, 1857–1998.

Unless otherwise indicated, letters, diaries, manuscripts, typescripts, and other materials referred to in the notes can be found at the Herbert Hoover Presidential Library. Items held by other collections are identified separately.

One additional bibliographical note regarding Rose Wilder Lane's diaries: during the 1920s and 1930s, Lane kept multiple diaries, journals, and notebooks in any given year. For ease of reference, while I do not provide box and file number for materials in the Rose Wilder Lane Papers, I do supply the archival names and item numbers for her diaries and journals, keyed to the "Diaries and Notes" section of HHPL's folder list of the Rose Wilder Lane Papers.

Original manuscripts of *Pioneer Girl*, *Little House in the Big Woods*, *Farmer Boy*, *Little House on the Prairie*, *On the Banks of Plum Creek*, *By the Shores of Silver Lake*, and *On the Way Home*, as well as some correspondence between Wilder and Lane, 1933–1936, are the property of the Laura Ingalls Wilder Home and Museum in Mansfield, Missouri. Microfilm versions of those manuscripts are loaned by the joint collection of the Western Historical Manuscript Collection of the University of Missouri and the State Historical Society of Missouri. When referring to manuscripts in this joint collection, I use the name assigned to them there (for example, "'Little House on the Prairie,' fragmentary draft").

In citing page numbers of unpaginated manuscripts, diaries, and other materials, I have included numbers in parentheses.

Aside from the manuscripts and correspondence microfilmed by SHSM, the remainder of the Mansfield holdings have not been catalogued or made available for research. References to materials in the Mansfield Collection are to those that have been on display in the Laura Ingalls Wilder Home and Museum.

The Burton Historical Collection of the Detroit Public Library holds original manuscripts and typescripts of *The Long Winter* and *These Happy Golden Years*.

The Pomona Public Library in Pomona, California, holds an original manuscript of *Little Town on the Prairie*.

The Wisconsin Historical Society holds a collection of letters by Ingalls relatives in the Laura Ingalls Wilder Family Correspondence, 1861–1919, as well as relevant Civil War records, tax records, and other materials.

INTRODUCTION

1. Laura Ingalls Wilder, "As a Farm Woman Thinks," *Missouri Ruralist*, June 1, 1924.
2. Ibid.
3. Ibid.
4. LIW to RWL, March 17, 1939. William Anderson, ed., *The Selected Letters of LIW* (New York: Harper, 2016), p. 194.
5. Ibid., February 5, 1937, p. 110.
6. RWL Papers, HHPL, Diaries and Notes Series, Item #6, unpaginated.
7. LIW, "Speech at the Book Fair, Detroit, Michigan, October 16, 1937," in *LIW: The Little House Books*, vol. 1, Appendix, p. 588.
8. Hilary Mantel, "Royal Bodies," *London Review of Books*, vol. 35, no. 4 (February 21, 2013), p. 6.
9. Michael Kramer, "When Reagan Spoke from the Heart," *New York Magazine*, July 21, 1980, p. 18.
10. Monica Davey, "Little-Noticed College Student to Star Politician," *New York Times*, October 23, 2008.
11. Alison Arngrim, *Confessions of a Prairie Bitch: How I Survived Nellie Oleson and Learned to Love Being Hated* (New York: HarperCollins It Books, 2010), p. xii. Arngrim heard of Hussein's fandom from actress Jayne Meadows, wife of comedian Steve Allen; see Gayle MacDonald, "Whoa Nellie," *Globe and Mail*, June 16, 2010.
12. See, for example, "All-Time Bestselling Children's Books," ed. Diane Roback, compiled by Debbie Hochman, *Publishers Weekly*, December 17, 2001. All nine of Wilder's titles appear on the paperback list, seven within the top fifty. The top seller, *Little House on the Prairie* (New York: Harper & Brothers, 1935), appeared as number 12, with sales of 6,172,525; *Little House in the Big Woods* as number 13, with 6,140,525. According to *PW*'s 2001 calculations, Wilder's total sales, in paperback, amounted to 37,615,483. Hardcover sales were dominated by illustrated books, such as those by Dr. Seuss, as well as the works of J. K. Rowling.
13. Mrs. Dean Helwig, "The Helwigs' First Hundred Years in Buffalo County," *Mondovi Herald News*, undated.

ON THE FRONTIER

1. LIW, *LHBW* (New York: Harper & Brothers, 1932), p. 1.

2. Donald Zochert offers a similar description of the Big Woods ("it was a real place, dark and deep") in the first Wilder biography, but does not address issues of Indian land ownership or population in the region. See Zochert, *Laura: The Life of Laura Ingalls Wilder* (New York: Avon Books, 1976), p. 14.

3. "Big Woods" is enshrined in place names (the township of Big Woods in Marshall County, Minnesota) and appears on historical maps, in paintings ("In the Big Woods, Between Carver and Glencoe," landscape watercolor by Edwin White-field, circa 1856–1859, collection of Minnesota Historical Society), and in period books. See, for example, *The New American Cyclopaedia: A Popular Dictionary of General Knowledge*, vol. 11, ed. G. Ripley and C. A. Dana (New York: D. Appleton, 1861), entry on "Minnesota," p. 546.

4. Gwen Westerman and Bruce White, *Mni Sota Makoce: The Land of the Dakota* (St. Paul: Minnesota Historical Society Press, 2012), p. 13.

5. Ibid., p. 22. Westerman and White list seven bands, or "seven fires of the Dakota."

6. See entry on "Oglala Sioux," *The Encyclopedia of North American Indian Wars, 1607–1890: A Political, Social, and Military History*, vol. 1, ed. Spencer C. Tucker (Santa Barbara: ABC CLIO, 2011), p. 579.

7. See Westerman and White, pp. 85–111.

8. George Catlin, *Letters and Notes on the Manners, Customs, and Conditions of North American Indians*, vol. 2 (New York: Dover, 1973), p. 3.

9. Ibid., p. 16.

10. Ibid., p. 156.

11. For a breakdown of Dakota population at the time, see Table 1.1, "Dakota Indian Bands, 1805–1846," in *They Chose Minnesota: A Survey of the State's Ethnic Groups*, ed. June Drenning Holmquist (St. Paul: Minnesota Historical Society, 1981), p. 20.

12. *Through Dakota Eyes: Narrative Accounts of the Minnesota Indian War of 1862*, ed. Gary Clayton Anderson and Alan R. Woolworth (St. Paul: Minnesota Historical Society Press, 1988), p. 12.

13. See Hiram M. Drache, *The Day of the Bonanza: A History of Bonanza Farming in the Red River Valley of the North* (Fargo: North Dakota Institute for Regional Studies, 1964), p. 17.

14. Westerman and White, p. 163; Historic Context Study of Minnesota Farms, 1820–1960, by Susan Granger and Scott Kelly, prepared for the Minnesota Department of Transportation, June 2005, section 3.5.

15. See Barbara T. Newcombe, "'A Portion of the American People': The Sioux Sign a Treaty in Washington in 1858," *Minnesota History*, vol. 45, no. 3 (Fall 1976), p. 96.

16. See Jonathan H. Earle, *Jacksonian Antislavery and the Politics of Free Soil, 1824–1854* (Chapel Hill and London: University of North Carolina Press, 2004), p. 36.

17. Ibid., p. 37. For an example of presidential opposition to the distribution of free land, see James Buchanan, Veto Message, June 22, 1860.

18. Abraham Lincoln, "Sixth Lincoln-Douglas Debate, Quincy, Illinois," October 13, 1858, in *Abraham Lincoln: Speeches and Writings, 1832–1858* (New York: Library of America, 1989), p. 740.

19. Abraham Lincoln, "Speech to Germans at Cincinnati, Ohio," *Abraham Lincoln: Speeches and Writings 1859–1865* (New York: Library of America, 1989), p. 203.

Two printed versions of the speech exist; this follows the text from the *Cincinnati Daily Commercial,* February 13, 1861.

20. Beginning with the signing of the act, some 75,000 would enter Minnesota over the next few years. See "Homestead Act: May 20, 1862," in "U.S.-Dakota War of 1862: Timeline," Minnesota Historical Society: http://www.usdakotawar.org /timeline.

21. Among those who warned Lincoln about the perils of Indian poverty and agency corruption in Minnesota were George E. H. Day, an attorney and special commissioner assigned to investigate the problem, and the Episcopal Bishop of Minnesota, Henry Benjamin Whipple. See David A. Nichols, *Lincoln and the Indians: Civil War Policy and Politics* (Urbana: University of Illinois Press, 1978; 2000), pp. 70–74.

22. Display panel, "Milford, Summer 1862," in "Never Shall I Forget: Brown County and the U.S.-Dakota War," Brown County Historical Society, New Ulm, Minnesota.

23. Henry David Thoreau, *The Journal: 1837–1861*, edited by Damion Searls (New York: New York Review Books, 2009), p. 661.

24. Ibid.

25. The Upper Sioux Agency was known to Indians as Yellow Medicine Agency, the Lower as Redwood Agency. The two sets of names are used interchangeably in many historic accounts.

26. Ibid., p. 662.

27. Ibid., p. 372.

28. Ibid., p. 662.

29. Minnie Buce Carrigan, *Captured by the Indians: Reminiscences of Pioneer Life in Minnesota* (Buffalo Lake: The Newsprint, 1912), pp. 9–10.

30. Sarah F. Wakefield, "Six Weeks in the Sioux Teepees," in *Women's Indian Captivity Narratives,* edited by Kathryn Zabelle Derounian-Stodola (New York: Penguin, 1998), p. 250.

31. See Scott W. Berg, *38 Nooses: Lincoln, Little Crow, and the Beginning of the Frontier's End* (New York: Knopf Doubleday, 2013), p. 26.

32. Ibid., p. 28.

33. Ibid., p. 29.

34. Ibid.

35. Representative accounts of the war's legendary opening act include that of Kenneth Carley, *The Dakota War of 1862: Minnesota's Other Civil War* (St. Paul: Minnesota Historical Society Press, 1961, rev. ed. 1976), pp. 7–9.

36. See Berg, p. 3.

37. This was Paul Mazakutemani, who had converted to Christianity; see ibid., p. 106.

38. Ibid., pp. 13–14. Berg's source for Little Crow's speech is the "literal transcription" in H. L. Gordon, *The Feast of the Virgins and Other Poems* (Chicago: Laird & Lee, 1891), pp. 343–44. As Berg notes, "this version of Little Crow's speech cannot be taken at face value," but its resonance with the Ingallses' subsequent plains experience makes it a crucial text in this discussion.

39. Berg, p. 9, quoting Gordon, *The Feast of the Virgins.*

40. Carrigan, p. 11.

41. Ibid., p. 12.

42. Ibid., p. 14.

43. Ibid., p. 16.

44. The account of Justina Boelter is taken from Augustus Lynch Mason, *The Romance and Tragedy of Pioneer Life: A Popular Account of the Heroes and Adventurers Who, By Their Valor and War-Craft, Beat Back the Savages from the Borders of Civilization and Gave the American Forests to the Plow and Sickle* (Cincinnati: Jones Brothers, 1883), pp. 814, 817–18.

45. Documentary evidence of the Jedediah Hibbard Ingalls family includes the 1860 United States Federal Census for Hawk River and Vicinity, County of Renville, Minnesota, which enumerates "Dedediah Ingalls" and his four children, Elizabeth J., Amanda, Melvina, and Geo. W. See also the Will and Guardianship Papers filed in the Estate of J. Hibbard Ingalls in the Probate Court of Nicollet County, October 23, 1863, Probate Case Files, No. 74-122.

46. The encounter of Elizabeth (known as Jenny) and Amanda Ingalls with Cut Nose is described in "Samuel J. Brown's Recollections," in *Through Dakota Eyes*, pp. 75–76. Modern accounts have been compiled by Rochelle Sjolseth, a great-granddaughter of George Washington Ingalls: "Blood Relatives on Both Sides," The U.S. Dakota War of 1862, Minnesota Historical Society: http://www.usdakotawar.org/stories/share-your-story/2763; and "George Washington Ingalls," http://www.dakotavictims1862.com/descendants-stories-of/descendants-stories-of/george-washington-ingalls.pdf.

47. See, for example, "A Wisconsin Boy Rescued from Captivity," *Semi-Weekly Wisconsin* (Milwaukee), July 3, 1863, p. 2; Harriet E. Bishop McConkey, *Dakota War Whoop: or, Indian Massacres and War in Minnesota, of 1862–'3*, rev. ed. (St. Paul: Wm. J. Moses' Press, 1864), pp. 349–50.

48. At the time, historians were confident that all Ingallses in the U.S. were descendants of Edmund Ingalls, an Englishman who arrived in Massachusetts in 1628. See, for example, the entry on George A. Ingalls (1820–1885), *Magazine of Western History*, vol. 14 (May 1891–October 1891), p. 511: "It is said that all who bear the family name of Ingalls, in America, are descended from Edmund Ingalls." According to a much-reproduced chart of the "Posterity of Edmund Ingalls," Charles Ingalls was a ninth-generation descendant; see William Anderson, *The Pepin Story of the Ingalls Family* (Pepin, MN: Laura Ingalls Wilder Memorial Society, 1981), unpaginated.

49. Display panel, "The War Begins," in "Never Shall I Forget: Brown County and the U.S.-Dakota War," Brown County Historical Society, New Ulm, Minnesota. Quotation attributed to Samuel Brown, Yellow Medicine Agency.

50. Charles E. Flandrau, *The History of Minnesota and Tales of the Frontier* (St. Paul: E. W. Porter, 1900), p. 157.

51. Carley, p. 21.

52. Ibid., pp. 40–41.

53. Curtis Dahlin, *Victims of the Dakota Uprising: Killed, Wounded, and Captured* (Roseville, MN: Curtis Dahlin, 2012), pp. 199–200.

54. Carley, p. 24.

55. The full text of Ramsey's speech, addressed to a special session of the Minnesota legislature on September 9, 1862, is held by the Minnesota Historical Society Manuscript Collection in the "Alexander Ramsey and family personal papers and governor's records, 1829–1965." Scans of the document can be seen online at usdakotawar.org.

56. The first governor of California, Peter Burnett, called for Indian extermination; see his State of the State address, January 6, 1851. In the first days of the 1862

war, John G. Nicolay, Lincoln's private secretary, proposed mass killing to the Secretary of War, Edwin Stanton: "As against the Sioux, it must be a war of extermination." See Berg, p. 97.

57. Thomas J. Galbraith, "Northern Superintendency," in *Report of the Commissioner of Indian Affairs for the Year 1863* (Washington, DC: Government Printing Office, 1864), p. 294.

58. See Berg, p. 225.

59. A drawing by W. H. Childs appeared in *Leslie's Illustrated Newspaper*, January 24, 1863, based on a hand-colored lithograph, "Execution of the 38 Dakota at Mankato, Minnesota, December 26, 1862," in the collection of the Minnesota Historical Society.

60. See Berg, pp. 194–95.

61. See Westerman and White, p. 201. See also Robert J. Werner, "Dakota Diaspora After 1862," *Minnesota's Heritage*, no. 6 (July 2012), pp. 38–56.

62. This was accomplished through the Forfeiture Act of February 16, 1863. See Guy Gibbon, *The Sioux: The Dakota and Lakota Nations* (Malden, MA: Blackwell, 2003), p. 111.

63. William E. Lass, "The Removal from Minnesota of the Sioux and Winnebago Indians," *Minnesota History* (December 1963), pp. 353–64.

64. Curt Brown, "Little Crow's Legacy," *Star Tribune* (Minneapolis), April 24, 2015.

65. Massacres at Sand Creek, Washita River, and Wounded Knee targeted other tribes, but whites may not have noted the distinction. See, for example, the report of Major General S. R. Curtis to Headquarters, Department of Kansas, January 12, 1865, in the aftermath of Sand Creek: "the popular cry of settlers and soldiers on the frontier favors an indiscriminate slaughter, which is very difficult to restrain. . . . So it goes from Minnesota to Texas."

66. For a definitive account of the origins of the proverb and its connections to the 1862 Dakota War, see Wolfgang Mieder, "'The Only Good Indian Is a Dead Indian': History and Meaning of a Proverbial Stereotype," *Journal of American Folklore*, vol. 106, no. 419 (Winter 1993), pp. 38–60.

67. Gibbon, p. 111.

1. MAIDEN ROCK

1. John F. Case, "Let's Visit Mrs. Wilder," interview with Laura Ingalls Wilder, *Missouri Ruralist*, February 20, 1918, p. 15. The fifth article in the *Ruralist*'s "Get Acquainted" series, this was reprinted in *A Little House Sampler: Laura Ingalls Wilder and Rose Wilder Lane*, ed. William Anderson (Lincoln: University of Nebraska Press, 1988), p. 9.

2. Mark Twain, *Life on the Mississippi*, in *Mark Twain: Mississippi Writings*, ed. Guy Cardwell (New York: Library of America, 1982), p. 573.

3. Catlin, *Letters and Notes*, vol. 2, p. 143.

4. William Cullen Bryant memorialized the lake in *Picturesque America* (1874). For a full discussion of sources on the legend of Maiden Rock, see G. Hubert Smith, "The Winona Legend," *Minnesota History*, vol. 13, no. 4 (December 1932), pp. 367–76.

5. LIW, LHBW in *LIW: The Little House Books*, vol. 1, pp. 69–79.

6. LIW, undated fragment in *A Little House Reader: A Collection of Writings by*

Laura Ingalls Wilder, ed. William Anderson (New York: HarperCollins, 1998), p. 160.

7. LIW, THGY in *LIW: The Little House Books*, vol. 2, p. 635.
8. LIW, *Pioneer Girl: The Annotated Autobiography*, ed. Pamela Smith Hill (Pierre: South Dakota Historical Society Press, 2014), pp. 36–39. In Wilder's text, she identifies the brothers as "James" and "George." Lansford Whiting Ingalls (1812–1896) did have a brother James Ingalls (1798–1868), who was fourteen years older. Given their respective ages, the brothers who joined in the sledding caper may have been those closer in age to him, perhaps Aaron Ingalls (1802–1886), Benjamin Ingalls (1804–1894), or John W. Ingalls (1806–1892). The identity of "George" remains a mystery, since Lansford had no sibling by that name. See "Laura Ingalls Wilder Genealogy Chart," compiled by Ellen Charbo, 1977. Malone Collection.
9. See Alice Morse Earle, *The Sabbath in Puritan New England* (New York: Charles Scribner's Sons, 1891), pp. 245–58. Morse notes that so-called blue laws, or Sunday laws, were most closely associated with New England, particularly Massachusetts, Connecticut, and New Hampshire; Samuel Ingalls, Charles Ingalls's grandfather, was born in New Hampshire.
10. Charles Burleigh, *The Genealogy and History of the Ingalls Family in America* (Malden, MA: Geo. E. Dunbar, 1903), p. 17. My assessment of the difficulties faced by the first Ingalls is based on standard accounts of harsh conditions faced by early colonial settlers in New England, who struggled with inadequate housing, poor soil, and severe weather. See, for example, William Babcock Weeden, *Economic and Social History of New England, 1620–1789*, vol. 1 (Boston and New York: Houghton, Mifflin, 1891), pp. 18, 89, 427, et cetera.
11. Edmund Ingalls drowned in March 1648, when he and his horse fell through the Saugus River bridge. Sources on his will include: Alonzo Lewis and James R. Newhall, *History of Lynn, Essex County, Massachusetts* (Boston: John L. Shorey, 1865), pp. 111–12; Weeden, *Economic and Social History of New England, 1620–1789*, vol. 1, p. 186; and "Will of Edmund Ingalls," in *The Essex Antiquarian*, vol. 3–4 (Salem, MA, 1899), p. 120. Edmund Ingalls's estate was appraised at 135 pounds, but according to experts, the value of colonial currency cannot be accurately converted or evaluated (see http://www.history.org/foundation/journal/Summer02/money2.cfm). Compared to other prominent men of the time, however, Ingalls's estate contained relatively small plots of land, the largest, of sixty acres, valued at 50 or 60 pounds. By comparison, John Endecott, who led the Salem expedition and died two years before Ingalls, left more substantial farms, one consisting of several hundred acres, and a quarter of Block Island, yet his biographer considered him "more or less land-poor." If Endecott was poor, Edmund Ingalls was poorer still. See Lawrence Shaw Mayo, *John Endecott: A Biography* (Cambridge: Harvard University Press, 1936), p. 282.
12. See Philip Alexander Bruce, *Economic History of Virginia in the Seventeenth Century: An Inquiry into the Material Condition of the People, Based upon Original and Contemporaneous Records*, vol. 1 (New York: Macmillan, 1896), p. 333.
13. Mark Fiege, *The Republic of Nature: An Environmental History of the United States* (Seattle: University of Washington Press, 2012), pp. 50–51.
14. Samuel Ingalls's birthday, July 11, 1770, is occasionally given as 1771, but a birth certificate, produced in 1906, has surfaced bearing this date. Burleigh, *Genealogy and History of the Ingalls Family*, provides no birthdate, p. 93.

15. Thomas Jefferson, "Query XIX," in *Notes on the State of Virginia* (Richmond, VA: J. W. Randolph, 1853), p. 176.

16. Lacking a local assembly, Congregationalists numbered among the founders of the Presbyterian Church in Cuba, New York, records of which date to 1827. Ingallses were not among its early members, according to Reverend John Woodring, current curator of those records. The only occurrence of the name is of a Mrs. Fred Ingalls, a church member in 1899.

17. Wilder wrote two versions of this tale, the first in PG, pp. 36–39; the second in LHBW, in *LIW: The Little House Books*, vol. 1, pp. 36–39.

18. Samuel Ingalls, "A Dream, or Vision, by Samuel Ingalls, of Dunham, in the Province of Lower Canada, on the night of Sept. 2, 1809," in John J. Duffy, "Broadside Illustrations of the Jeffersonian Federalist Conflict in Vermont, 1809–1816," *Vermont History*, vol. 49, no. 4 (Fall 1981), fig. 1, p. 211. Ingalls's use of the term "wicked club" suggests to historians that he was a Federalist, opposed to Jefferson's party, the Democratic-Republicans, who were supported by several dozen state political "clubs." Federalists rallied around Alexander Hamilton's plan for a strong federal government, charging that Jefferson's "clubs" bore a dangerous semblance to the French revolutionary Jacobin Club, whose members fomented the Reign of Terror.

19. Samuel Ingalls, *Rhymes of "The Unlearned Poet"* (Angelica, NY: publisher unknown, 1825), no extant copies known. Modern version compiled by Robert L. Middlestead and Barb Klecker, Ellsworth, WI, 2011.

20. Ibid., "The Difference of Time," pp. 19–21.

21. Ibid., "Lines Written on the Great Hail and Wind Storm That Passed Through the Counties of Cattarraugus and Allegany in the Spring of 1834," pp. 46–47.

22. Ibid., "A Ditty on Poverty," pp. 61–62.

23. See Proverbs 24:33–34.

24. Ingalls, untitled poem in *Rhymes of "The Unlearned Poet,"* pp. 48–49.

25. This was before the turnpike to Olean was completed, when Lansford was ten: See John S. Minard, Esq., *History of Cuba, New York: A Centennial Memorial History of Allegany County, New York*, ed. Georgia Drew Andrews (Alfred, NY: W. A. Fergusson, 1896), pp. 816, 826.

26. Samuel Rezneck, "The Social History of an American Depression: 1837–1843," *American Historical Review*, vol. 40, no. 4 (July 1935), p. 676.

27. Ibid., p. 665.

28. The brothers who left for the west were James and Samuel Worthen Ingalls (known as Worthen). James Ingalls appears on the 1840 U.S. Federal Census for Kane County, Illinois. Those who stayed in Cuba were John W. Ingalls and Aaron Franklin Ingalls: "Aaron Ingals," age fifty-seven, and "John W. Ingals," age fifty-four, appear on the 1860 U.S. Federal Census for Cuba, New York, described as farmers. An 1869 atlas shows J. Ingalls owning plot 55 in District 5, near Oil Creek Reservoir (now Cuba Lake), north of Cuba Village. Adjoining the southeast corner of his land appears a plot owned by Aaron Ingalls: see *Atlas of Allegany County, New York* (New York: D. G. Beers, 1869), pp. 51, 55.

29. Daniel Pingree to Samuel Rowell, April 10, 1840, published on the website of Pingree Grove, Illinois: http://www.villageofpingreegrove.org/about-pingree-grove/history-of-pingree-grove/.

30. U.S. Federal Census, Campton, Kane County, Illinois, October 2, 1850.

31. John Russell Ghrist, *Plato Center Memories: A History of Plato Center, Illinois and Surrounding Areas of Kane County* (Dundee, IL: JRG Communications, 1999), vol. 1, p. 6.

32. Ibid., p. 13. See also "Plato Township," *History of Kane County*, ed. John S. Wilcox (Chicago: Munsell, 1904), pp. 715–16.

33. According to town records in Concord, Wisconsin, Lansford Ingalls purchased land on December 31, 1853; see www.concordwisconsin.org/history.

34. After Charles, the surviving children born to Lansford and Laura Ingalls in New York were Lydia Louise (1838), Polly Melona (1840), and Lansford James (known as James, b. 1842). The two children born in Kane County, Illinois, were Laura Ladocia (known as Docia, b. 1845) and Hiram Lemuel (1848). In Wisconsin were born George Whiting (1851), Ruby Celestia (1855), and Lafayette (1858).

35. Martha Quiner Carpenter to LIW, July 18, 1925. HHPL.

36. The brother-in-law was Garrett McGregor. For more on the accident, see "Daily Gazette," *Milwaukee Daily Sentinel*, November 12, 1845, p. 2.

37. Carpenter to LIW, September 2, 1925.

38. Ibid., October 9, 1925.

39. Joanna L. Stratton, *Pioneer Women: Voices from the Kansas Frontier* (New York: Simon & Schuster, 1981), p. 68.

40. Carpenter to LIW, July 18, 1925.

41. Ibid.

42. Charlotte Holbrook, known as "Lotty" or "Lottie," was born in 1854.

43. See *Laura's Album: A Remembrance Scrapbook of Laura Ingalls Wilder*, compiled by William Anderson (New York: Scholastic, 1998), p. 9. Original in De Smet Collection.

44. Ibid.

45. Carpenter to LIW, September 2, 1925.

46. See Nancy Cleaveland and Penny Linsenmayer, *Charles Ingalls and the U.S. Public Land Laws* (privately printed: Seventh Winter Press, 2001), pp. 8, 13.

47. 1860 U.S. Census, Jefferson County, Wisconsin.

48. Frank L. Klement, *Wisconsin in the Civil War: The Home Front and the Battle Front, 1861–1865* (Madison: State Historical Society of Wisconsin, 1997), p. 3.

49. Ibid., p. 20.

50. Caroline Ingalls to Martha Quiner Carpenter, October 6, 1861. WHS.

51. Ibid. Ingalls's 1861 letter contains hints of their whereabouts at that time. She was still in Concord; Martha was up north, in Pepin.

52. Ibid. According to this letter, in 1861, Lansford and Laura Ingalls had gone north to the headwaters of the Baraboo River, a tributary of the Wisconsin River northwest of Concord. "They felt very bad about leaving their place and it was too bad," Caroline Ingalls wrote to Martha. Her in-laws were "too old to be moving," Caroline mourned: Lansford had done his best, but it could not be helped. The newlyweds, Peter and Eliza Ingalls, were traveling with them.

53. Donald Zochert, Wilder's first biographer, claimed that family lore held that the entire Ingalls clan traveled together by covered wagon to Pepin, where "Pa and Uncle Peter and no doubt Uncle Henry swam across Lake Pepin to work as harvest-hands in the Minnesota Territory during the summertime." He supplies no year for the exodus, and his source appears to have been a written recollection associated with Gertrude Yanisch, granddaughter of Lansford Whiting Ingalls.

His work contains no notes, however, and no corroborating documents have surfaced to support the account. See Zochert, pp. 14–15.

54. Nancy Frank Quiner to Martha Quiner Carpenter, April 16, 1862. WHS.

55. Eliza and Peter Ingalls to Martha and Charles Carpenter, June 29, 1862. WHS.

56. Caroline Quiner Ingalls, undated fragment, De Smet Collection. Reprinted in William Anderson, "The Uncle Laura Never Knew," *The Best of the Lore* (De Smet, SD: Laura Ingalls Wilder Memorial Society, 2007), p. 2.

57. Richard Current, *The History of Wisconsin: The Civil War Era, 1848–1873* (Madison: State Historical Society of Wisconsin, 1976), p. 317.

58. Klement, p. 27.

59. State Historical Society of Wisconsin, Series 1137. Lists of Persons Liable for Military Duty, Autumn, 1862 (Manitowoc-Racine, reel 2 of 3). Medical complaints cited in this paragraph can be found in the "Remarks" column of men interviewed in Outagamie, Ozaukee, Pepin, Pierce, and Prescott Counties.

60. Current, p. 313.

61. Klement, pp. 30–31.

62. No records survive of Jefferson County's 1862 militia draft. Neither Charles Ingalls nor his brothers or brothers-in-law appear on Pepin County's 1862 draft list; of them Charles and Peter Ingalls and Henry Quiner fell within the "first class" of recruits, men between the ages of 25–30. See State Historical Society of Wisconsin, Series 1137. Lists of Persons Liable for Military Duty, Autumn, 1862 (Manitowoc-Racine, reel 2 of 3). In Pierce County, neighbor to Pepin County, a "Charles Ingli" presented himself, but he was thirty years old and unmarried, while Charles Ingalls was twenty-six and married. In Pepin, a significant number of men paid others to take their place, a common practice, enshrined into law the following year in the Enrollment Act of 1863, but it is doubtful that Charles could have supplied the cost, three hundred dollars, and a willing substitute.

63. Existing letters cast little light on the Ingallses' whereabouts after mid-1862. When Eliza Ingalls wrote to her sister Martha Carpenter on June 29, 1862, she said that there "has been a great change in Concord since you left it," referring to their brother Joseph's death: Joseph and Nancy Quiner had been living in Concord. She said that Caroline had been among the family members caring for Nancy Quiner in her bereavement and indicated that Caroline and Charles Ingalls had recently been "up here" to make a visit of some days; Eliza had just given birth to the couple's first child, Alice. That would suggest that Peter and Eliza Ingalls may have been living somewhere north of Concord, perhaps in Waterloo, Wisconsin, twenty-five miles northwest. Civil War Draft Registration Records, 2nd Congressional District, place a Peter Ingalls (age 28) and a James Ingalls (age 21) in Waterloo, Wisconsin, in June 1863. Later in the letter, Eliza refers to having made a recent visit, which lasted several days, to the town of Concord.

64. Klement, p. 29.

65. Current, p. 333.

66. *History of Buffalo and Pepin Counties, Wisconsin*, compiled by Franklyn Curtiss-Wedge, vol. 2 (Winona, MN: H. C. Cooper Jr., 1919), p. 868.

67. See Menomonie's newspaper, the *Dunn County Lumberman*, September 6, 1862.

68. M. M. Quaife, "The Panic of 1862 in Wisconsin," *Wisconsin Magazine of History*, vol. 4 (1920–1921), p. 181.

69. Ibid., p. 178.

70. Ibid.

71. In LHOP, the character Mrs. Scott makes this statement; see LIW: *The Little House Books*, vol. 1, p. 356.

72. Warranty deed given to Charles Ingalls and Henry Quiner by Charles and Abbie Nunn for southern quarter of Section 27 in Twp. 24 R. 15, 160 acres, September 23, 1863. Pepin Collection.

73. By January, 1865, Henry and Polly Quiner's children included Louisa (b. 1860) and Charles (b. 1863); Peter and Eliza Ingalls had Alice (b. 1862) and were expecting Ella (born January 25, 1865); Charles and Martha Carpenter had Willie (b. 1861), Joseph (1863), and Lettie (1864).

74. LIW, "'My Work': Speech to the Sorosis Club, Mountain Grove, Missouri, Winter 1935–36," in *LIW: The Little House Books*, vol. 1, p. 583.

2. INDIAN SUMMERS

1. Deed given to Gustaf Ryinholt Gustafson by Charles and Caroline Ingalls for South ½ of SW ¼ of Sec. 27, Twp. 24N., R15W, April 28, 1868; Deed given to Gustaf Ryinholt Gustafson by Henry O. Quiner and Polly M. Quiner for North ½ of SW ¼ of Sec. 27, Twp 24N., R15W, April 28, 1868. Pepin, Book G, pp. 162, 164. The question of where Charles Ingalls and his family were living between the April 1868 sale of this property and the fall of the following year, when he and his wife sign paperwork in Chariton County, Missouri, remains unanswered; perhaps the Ingalls and Quiner families continued to live in one of the purchased cabins or with other family members. Town voting records seem to confirm that the family remained in the Pepin area during 1868. Charles, his father, Lansford Ingalls, and Henry Quiner all voted to elect town officers on April 7, 1868; Charles Ingalls served as treasurer for the local school district that year; and Charles Ingalls and his brother-in-law Thomas Quiner voted in the General Election of November 3, 1868. See Town Records of Pepin, 1857–1878, pp. 251, 257.

2. 1870 U.S. Census, Pepin County, Wisconsin, schedule 3, Production of Agriculture, cited in Catherine H. Latané and Martha Kuhlman, *The Village of Pepin at the Time of Laura Ingalls Wilder* (Pepin: T&C Latané, 2004), p. 17.

3. LIW, "On the Banks of Plum Creek," manuscript, p. 67 (her pagination).

4. See Appendix: Tables of Prices of Wheat and Other Articles, Table I.—Prices in Chicago, in Thorstein Veblen, "The Price of Wheat Since 1867," *Journal of Political Economy*, vol. 1, no. 1 (December 1892), p. 157.

5. E. W. Stephens, "The Grand River Country," *Missouri Historical Review*, vol. 17, no. 1 (October, 1922), pp. 24–25.

6. 1860 U.S. Census, Chariton County, Missouri, Slave Schedule.

7. Deed of Trust, Chariton County, May 28, 1868, Book D, pp. 121–22. Robert H. Cabell, Adamantine's father-in-law, also appears in the paperwork.

8. District Treasurer's Bond, October 15, 1868, signed by Charles Ingalls, treasurer of School District Six of the Town of Pepin, Thomas P. Huleatt, his surety. Witnessed by Henry Quiner.

9. Town Records of Pepin, 1857–1878, pp. 264–66. Henry Quiner was the only member of the extended Ingalls-Quiner clan to vote in the April 1869 election. In a town meeting held on May 3, 1869, ninety-nine voters turned up to address bylaws; none of the family voted (except for an "Isaac Ingalls," whose relationship to Lansford Ingalls and his family, if any, remains unknown).

10. Linda Peavy and Ursula Smith, *Pioneer Women: The Lives of Women on the Frontier* (New York: Smithmark, 1996), p. 20.

11. "Letter of Louisiana Stretzel," *Covered Wagon Women: Diaries and Letters from the Western Trails, 1840–1849*, vol. 1, ed. Kenneth L. Holmes (Lincoln and London: University of Nebraska Press, 1983), p. 266.

12. Peavy and Smith, p. 28.

13. Laura Ingalls Wilder, PG, p. 1.

14. Dale L. Morgan, cited in Marc Simmons, "Public Discussion of the Privy, a Historically Private Matter," *Santa Fe New Mexican*, April 18, 2015.

15. Randolph B. Marcy, *The Prairie Traveler: The 1859 Handbook for Westbound Pioneers* (New York: Dover, 2006 reprint), p. 59.

16. Martha Gay Masterson, quoted in Peavy and Smith, p. 42.

17. Power of Attorney, signed and sealed in Chariton County, Missouri, August 26, 1869, Miscellaneous Records, Pepin County Courthouse, Durand, Wisconsin, vol. A, p. 342.

18. Power of Attorney, signed and sealed in Chariton County, Missouri, September 1, 1869, Miscellaneous Records, Pepin County Courthouse, Durand, Wisconsin, vol. A, pp. 342–43.

19. "A Record of Bloody Deeds," Chariton County Historical Society, State Historical Society of Missouri.

20. Sandy Gladbach, interview with the author, February 10, 2015.

21. Quiner reappears in the Pepin voting record on September 14, 1869: Town Records of Pepin, 1857–1878, p. 279.

22. PG, p. 1.

23. The Preemption Act of 1841, 27th Congress, Ch. 16, 5 Stat. 453 (1841), Section 10.

24. See Penny T. Linsenmayer, "A Study of Laura Ingalls Wilder's *Little House on the Prairie*," *Kansas History*, vol. 24, no. 3 (Autumn 2001), p. 174; see also U.S. Federal Census, 1870, Montgomery County, Kansas.

25. See "Following the Frontier Line, 1790–1890," U.S. Census Bureau: https://www.census.gov/dataviz/visualizations/001/.

26. D. C. Krone to "Charley," March 17, 1870. Independence Historical Society.

27. Thomas Jefferson to Albert Gallatin, July 12, 1804. National Archives, Papers of Albert Gallatin.

28. Watercolor by Charles Balthazar Julien Févrét de Saint-Mémin, 1807. Winterthur Museum, Winterthur, Delaware.

29. Louis F. Burns, *A History of the Osage People* (Tuscaloosa and London: University of Alabama Press, 2004), pp. 18–19.

30. Ibid., pp. 263–64.

31. See Linsenmayer, p. 173.

32. Charles Ingalls's cabin is believed to have been built in Montgomery County's Rutland Township on the southwest quarter of Section 36, Township 13, Range 14. See Margaret Gray Clement, "Research on 'Little House on the Prairie'" (Independence, KS: Chamber of Commerce, December 1972). For a description of how Clement found the location, see Zochert, pp. 31–33. For maps, see Linsenmayer, pp. 178, 180.

33. Burns, pp. 173, 308.

34. Ibid., p. 308.

35. See Linsenmayer, p. 174; see also U.S. Federal Census, 1870, Montgomery County, Kansas.

36. Isaac T. Gibson, United States Indian Agent, Osage Agency, Kansas, to Enoch Hoag, Superintendent of Indian Affairs, Lawrence, February 19, 1870, in "Encroachments Upon Osage Indian Lands: Letter from the Secretary of the Interior," 41st Congress, 2nd Session, House of Representatives, Ex. Doc. No. 179.

37. D. C. Krone to "Charley," March 17, 1870. Independence Historical Society.

38. Gibson to Hoag, January 8, 1870, in "Encroachments."

39. Ibid.

40. Linsenmayer, p. 179.

41. Gibson to Hoag, January 13, 1870.

42. Ibid., January 10, 1870.

43. Many of these have been collected in the eleven volumes of *Covered Wagon Women* and in other anthologies.

44. PG, p. 5.

45. Chariton County, Missouri, Register of Deeds, Book 11, p. 381. The deed is dated February 25, 1870.

46. Everett Dick, *The Sod-House Frontier, 1854–1890* (Lincoln and London: University of Nebraska Press, 1979), p. 438.

47. PG, p. 5.

48. Ibid.

49. Susan Thurlow, "Dr. George Tann: Black Frontier Physician," self-published essay, 2013.

50. PG, p. 7.

51. Ibid., p. 11.

52. Ibid. The editors of *Pioneer Girl* note that Wilder's account of the Osage comings and goings may not have been chronologically accurate; their "nightly debates" may well have occurred earlier in 1870, at the period when tensions were at a high. See PG, p. 11n.

53. PG, p. 14.

54. U.S. Census, Rutland Township, Montgomery County, Kansas, August 13, 1870, pp. 9–10.

55. Ibid., p. 13.

56. PG, pp. 14, 16.

57. Ibid., p. 16.

58. See PG, p. 16n36; Wilder refers to him as "Mr. Brown." In LHOP, he would become the memorable fictional character Mr. Edwards.

59. Ibid.

60. Ibid., p. 18.

61. Ibid.

62. Ibid.

63. Enoch Hoag, Superintendent of Indian Affairs to Hon. E. S. Parker, Commissioner of Indian Affairs, February 25, 1870, in "Encroachments Upon Indian Lands, Letter from the Secretary of the Interior," 41st Congress, 2nd Session, Ex. Doc. No. 179.

64. See Linsenmayer, p. 181.

65. Ibid., p. 185.

66. PG, p. 18.

67. Ibid., p. 21.

68. Ibid., p. 22.

69. Ibid., p. 15.

70. While never disparaging her father, Wilder felt free to acknowledge his shortcomings in letters to her daughter, suggesting that he was "no businessman" and was occasionally taken advantage of by unscrupulous parties. She also admitted that he owned no land in Kansas. See LIW to RWL, March 23, 1937. See also LIW to RWL, January 25, 1938: "In L.H. on Prairie Pa was a *squatter*. He had no title whatever." Italics in original.

71. PG, p. 47.

72. "Aunt Polly Visited Barry Corners School," *Notes from Laura Ingalls Wilder Memorial Society, Inc.*, vol. 2, no. 2 (December 1977), p. 4.

73. PG, p. 49.

74. LIW, manuscript of PC, microfilm image 133.

75. See LIW, "Let Us Be Just," *Missouri Ruralist*, September 5, 1917, in *Laura Ingalls Wilder: Farm Journalist*, ed. Stephen W. Hines (Columbia: University of Missouri Press, 2007), pp. 121–23.

76. PG, p. 27.

77. Ibid., p. 41.

78. Ibid., p. 45.

79. See Adina Popescu, "Casting Bread Upon the Waters: American Farming and the International Wheat Market, 1880–1920," doctoral thesis, Columbia University, 2014, p. 29.

80. Richard White, *"It's Your Misfortune and None of My Own": A New History of the American West* (Norman: University of Oklahoma Press, 1991), p. 246. White cites C. Knick Harley, "Western Settlement and the Price of Wheat, 1872–1913," *Journal of Economic History*, vol. 38, no. 4 (December 1978), p. 878.

81. Richard White, *Railroaded: The Transcontinentals and the Making of Modern America* (New York: Norton, 2011), p. 79.

82. Ibid., pp. 78–81.

83. Deed given to Horace Richards by Charles and Caroline Ingalls for Section 27, Twp. 24N., Range 15W, April 15, 1873, for $250. Pepin, Book H, p. 611.

84. Warranty deed given to Andrew Anderson by Charles and Caroline Ingalls for Sec. 27, Twp., 24N., Range 15W for $1000, October 28, 1873. Pepin, Book J, p. 150.

85. Latané and Kuhlman, p. 7.

3. CRYING HARD TIMES

1. Anna Maria Wells, *The Floweret: A Gift of Love* (Boston: William Crosby, 1842). See also PG, p. 59.

2. Eliza and Peter Ingalls to Martha and Charles Carpenter, June 28, 1862. Wisconsin Historical Society.

3. De Smet Collection.

4. PG, p. 59.

5. Ibid., p. 61.

6. Ibid., p. 62.

7. Ibid., pp. 62, 64.

8. Redwood County's northern border is formed by the Minnesota River. The Lower Sioux Agency, where the uprising began, was on the southern bank.

9. Cleaveland and Linsenmayer, p. 8.

10. Ibid., p. 2.

11. *The History of Redwood County, Minnesota*, compiled by Franklyn Curtiss-Wedge, vol. 1 (Chicago: H. C. Cooper Jr., 1916), pp. 550–51.
12. PG, p. 64.
13. Dick, p. 112.
14. Ibid., p. 111.
15. In 1873, wheat prices reached 102.9 cents a bushel; see Table I.—Prices in Chicago in Veblen, "The Price of Wheat Since 1867," p. 157.
16. There is some confusion concerning when Charles Ingalls built on this land; the preemption claim paperwork filed in 1876 suggested that the house was built soon after the family settled there, in 1874. Wilder's memoir, on the other hand, described the family living in the dugout for a year and the house being built in the spring of 1875; see PG, p. 68n26.
17. PG, p. 72n34.
18. Ibid.
19. Ibid., p. 74.
20. Ibid., p. 71.
21. Ibid., p. 75n39.
22. Both of the previous claims were made under the Preemption Act. See Cleaveland and Linsenmayer, p. 8.
23. *Murray County Pioneer,* July 19, 1888, cited in Daniel D. Peterson, *The Grasshopper Years, 1873–1877* (Walnut Grove, self-published, undated), p. 5.
24. Ibid., p. 19.
25. Annette Atkins, *Harvest of Grief: Grasshopper Plagues and Public Assistance in Minnesota, 1873–1878* (St. Paul: Minnesota Historical Society Press, 1984), p. 17.
26. Ibid., pp. 20–21.
27. Jeffrey A. Lockwood, *Locust: The Devastating Rise and Mysterious Disappearance of the Insect That Shaped the American Frontier* (New York: Basic Books, 2004), p. 8.
28. Atkins, see chart, p. 22.
29. Gilbert C. Fite, *The Farmers' Frontier, 1865–1900* (New York: Holt, Rinehart and Winston, 1966), p. 63.
30. Ibid., 60.
31. Walter N. Trenerry, "The Minnesota Legislator and the Grasshopper, 1873–77," *Minnesota History*, vol. 36, no. 2, p. 55.
32. Fite, pp. 69–70.
33. Lockwood, *Locust*, p. 26.
34. Ibid., p. 21.
35. Ibid., p. 27.
36. See Mike Davis, *Late Victorian Holocausts: El Niño Famines and the Making of the Third World* (London: Verso, 2002), p. 110.
37. Lockwood, p. 22.
38. Susan Proffitt, quoted in Stratton, p. 105.
39. Ibid.
40. Lockwood, p. 22.
41. See the account of Charles Nelson in Gales township, in Peterson, p. 9; Atkins, p. 39.
42. *The Grange Advocate*, Red Wing, Minnesota, May 25, 1875.
43. See PG, p. 65.

44. See Chapter 16, "The Wonderful House," in PC in *LIW: The Little House Books*, vol. 1, pp. 467–71.

45. The Timber Culture Act of 1873, an adjunct to homestead legislation, granted settlers the opportunity to acquire 160 acres at no cost in exchange for planting forty acres in trees and keeping them alive for eight years. It was envisioned as a means of providing timber for fuel and as building material, but also served the larger goal of altering the Great Plains environment, reducing wind and increasing rainfall. An abject failure, it was repealed after twenty years.

46. Ingalls also filed on a homestead nearby; for information on Charles Ingalls's land claims in Minnesota, I am indebted to Cleaveland and Linsenmayer, pp. 8–9.

47. PG, 79.

48. Ibid.

49. Cited in Lockwood, p. 20; see also the 1880 U.S. Entomological Commission report.

50. Lockwood, pp. 19–20.

51. See Atkins, epigraph.

52. Charles V. Riley, *The Locust Plague in the United States: Being More Particularly a Treatise on the Rocky Mountain Locust* (Chicago: Rand, McNally, 1877), p. 87.

53. Lockwood, p. 27.

54. Mary Lyon, in Stratton, p. 103.

55. Stratton, p. 104; Peterson, p. 5.

56. Adelheit Viets, in Stratton, p. 105.

57. See Atkins, pp. 30–31, 66.

58. PG, 79.

59. Ibid., 81.

60. Ibid.

61. See Lockwood, p. xix; the calculation covered the years 1874–1877 and first appeared in the U.S. Entomological Commission report of 1880.

62. Atkins, see chart, p. 22.

63. Fite, p. 68.

64. See ibid., p. 68; Atkins, p. 65.

65. Fite, p. 68.

66. Atkins, p. 51.

67. "Grasshopper Notice," June 9, 1875. Burr Oak Collection.

68. *The Grange Advance*, Red Wing, Minnesota, May 25, 1875.

69. A number of maps exist showing the extent of locust damage. See, for example, "Area of Grasshopper Damage in the United States, 1876," in Atkins, p. 14; "Locust Egg Map of Minnesota, 1877," Minnesota Historical Society.

70. PG, p. 83.

71. State of Minnesota, County of Redwood, town of North Hero, November 30, 1875, signed C. P. Ingalls. Collection of the Minnesota Historical Society. Copy on display in Masters Hotel, Burr Oak, Iowa.

72. LIW to RWL, August 6, 1936.

73. Charlotte Quiner Holbrook to Martha and Charles Carpenter, December 24, [1875]. There is some question as to whether the date is 1875 or 1876. WHS.

74. PG, p. 76.

75. See Chapter 29, "The Darkest Hour Is Just Before the Dawn," in PC in *LIW: The Little House Books*, vol. 1, pp. 526–31. The doll story occurs in *Pioneer Girl*

and the published novel; it does not appear in the surviving handwritten manuscript of *Plum Creek*.

76. PG, p. 87.
77. Ibid.
78. Ibid., p. 94.
79. Ibid.
80. Ibid., p. 85.
81. Ibid., p. 94.
82. *Annual Report of the Auditor of State, to the Legislature of Minnesota for the Fiscal Year Ending Nov. 30, 1876* (St. Paul: Pioneer Press, 1877), p. 139; Atkins, p. 84.
83. Atkins, p. 84.
84. Ibid., p. 86.
85. PG, p. 94.
86. See Cleaveland and Linsenmayer, p. 8.
87. PG, p. 97.
88. Ibid.
89. Allen L. Whipple, personal interview, September 20, 2014. See also "Dale Pleasant Prairie Cemetery," compiled by Whipple as president of the Cemetery Association.
90. PG, p. 101.
91. Hamlin Garland, *A Son of the Middle Border* (New York: Grosset & Dunlap, 1914 and 1917), p. 205.
92. PG, p. 103.
93. As the editors of PG note, this was an era when pregnancy or other aspects of reproduction were not discussed openly; see PG, p. 84n64. Viable and safe forms of contraception did not become available until late in the nineteenth century and would have been difficult for rural women, in particular, to access. According to one study of the 1840 census, women in one representative Indiana county "had an average of eight children during their lifetime." See Timothy Crumrin, "'Her Daily Concern': Women's Health Issues in Early 19th-Century Indiana," *Civil War Rx: The Source Guide to Civil War Medicine*: http://civilwarrx.blogspot .com/2014/11/her-daily-concern-womens-health-issues.html#comment-form.
94. PG, p. 104n15.
95. Ibid., p. 105.
96. Ibid., p. 106.
97. Ibid., p. 112.
98. Ibid., p. 110.
99. Ibid., p. 111n34.
100. Ibid., p. 112; the editors of PG also supplied the correct spelling and identification of Mr. Bisby; see PG, p. 103n12.
101. Ibid., p. 113.
102. Ibid., p. 120.
103. Ibid., p. 131.
104. Ibid., p. 125. Walnut Grove's temperance phase, tied to the movement for prohibition, did not last long; see PG, p. 125n32; and Daniel D. Peterson, *Wet or Dry? The Temperance Movement to Prohibition: Walnut Grove, Minnesota* (privately printed, 2013), p. 20.
105. Ibid., p. 122.
106. See ibid., p. 124.

107. Ibid., p. 137.

108. Ibid., p. 123. I have corrected the spelling of "villians."

109. See ibid., pp. 140–41.

110. See ibid., pp. 127–28, no. 43. Rose Wilder Lane would later weave this into a story, "Object Matrimony," published in the *Saturday Evening Post*, September 1, 1934.

111. PG, p. 137.

112. Ibid., p. 139n71. The editors of PG were unable to locate any such family or incident in the historical record. As with the story of the Benders, who appear in the more fictionalized versions of *Pioneer Girl* as revised by Lane (known as the Brandt Revised and Bye versions), the anecdote may have been heard second-hand, with Charles Ingalls inserted.

113. Records of the Walnut Grove Union Congregational Church are reproduced on displays at the Laura Ingalls Wilder Museum, Walnut Grove, Minnesota.

114. *Redwood Falls Gazette*, April 10, 1879.

115. Ibid., May 15, 1879. See William Anderson, *Laura Ingalls Wilder's Walnut Grove* (Walnut Grove, MN: Laura Ingalls Wilder Museum, 2013), p. 47.

116. *Redwood Falls Gazette*, June 26, 1879.

117. PG, p. 142; see nn. 80–82. In a letter, LIW to RWL, March 23, 1937, Wilder recalled that her sister's illness was attributed to spinal meningitis, but then crossed that diagnosis out. A contemporary study conjectured that the illness may have been viral meningoencephalitis: see Sarah S. Allexan, Carrie L. Byington, Jerome I. Finkelstein, and Beth A. Tarini, "Blindness in Walnut Grove: How Did Mary Ingalls Lose Her Sight?" *Pediatrics* 131 (March 2013), pp. 1–3.

118. See *Reader*, pp. 10–18.

119. PG, pp. 141–42; note my correction of punctuation.

120. PG, p. 142.

121. Grace Ingalls Dow to Aubrey Sherwood, October 20, 1939, reprinted in "Two Readers Recall Earliest Issues; Sisters Revive Memories in Reading Diary," *De Smet News*, November 9, 1939.

122. In her novel *By the Shores of Silver Lake*, Wilder suggests that her father asked her to "see" for Mary (p. 17), but this is not spelled out in Wilder's letters, essays, or memoir.

123. LIW to RWL, undated fragment, 1937. This letter, of which only p. 5 appears to exist, recounts the circumstances behind Docia Forbes's first marriage, to Augustin Eugene Waldvogel; Lena and Eugene were his children. Wilder remarks of the scandal, "Oh yes! There are skeletons in our family closet." For more, see *LIW: The Little House Books*, vol. 2, no. 6.21, p. 832.

124. PG, p. 145.

125. Ibid., p. 145.

126. Ibid., p. 153.

4. GOD HATES A COWARD

1. Fite, p. 100.

2. Annie D. Tallent, *The Black Hills; or, The Last Hunting Ground of the Dakotahs* (St. Louis: Nixon-Jones Printing, 1899), p. 39. Tallent, the sole woman in the Gordon Party, lists Thomas Quiner as a member on p. 24 but does not mention him again.

3. George Kingsbury, *The History of Dakota Territory*, vol. 1 (Chicago: S. J. Clarke, 1915), p. 152.

4. George N. Lamphere, "History of Wheat Raising in the Red River Valley," in *History of Red River Valley: Past and Present*, vol. 1 (Chicago: C. F. Cooper, 1909), p. 218.

5. Kingsbury, p. 344.

6. See Candace Savage, *Prairie: A Natural History* (Vancouver, BC: Greystone Books, 2004), p. 72.

7. See ibid.: "Over the Great Plains as a whole, precipitation is more variable than it is almost anywhere else on the continent. . . . Only 'normal' values were truly abnormal."

8. Thomas Jefferson, *An Account of Louisiana, Laid Before Congress by Direction of the President of the United States of America, November 14, 1803* (Providence: Heaton & Williams, [1803]), p. 6.

9. See separate entries of Meriwether Lewis and William Clark, May 26, 1805, *The Journals of Lewis and Clark*, ed. Frank Bergon (New York: Penguin, 1989), p. 139. See also Major Z. M. Pike, Appendix to Part II, *An Account of Expeditions to the Sources of the Mississippi* (Philadelphia: C. & A. Conrad, 1810), p. 8.

10. Gail Geo. Homes, *The Chiefs of Council Bluffs: Five Leaders of the Missouri Valley Tribes* (Charleston: The History Press, 2012), p. 15.

11. Donald Worster, *A River Running West: The Life of John Wesley Powell* (New York: Oxford University Press, 2001), p. 349. See also Drache, p. 41.

12. See Charles A. Schott, "Rain Chart of the United States," from J. W. Powell, *Report on the Arid Lands of the United States*, 1878.

13. Worster, *A River*, p. 366.

14. Ibid., p. 350.

15. Fite, p. 95.

16. Worster, *A River*, p. 352.

17. John Wesley Powell, *Report on the Lands of the Arid Region of the United States*, 2nd ed. (Washington DC: Government Printing Office, 1879), p. vii.

18. Fite, p. 82.

19. J. H. Sheppard, "History of Agriculture in the Red River Valley," in *History of the Red River Valley: Past and Present*, vol. 1 (Chicago: C. F. Cooper, 1909), p. 194.

20. Fite, p. 82.

21. Kevin Burkman, "John Wesley Powell and the Arid Empire of the American West," *Bloustein Review*, May 16, 2014 (http://blousteinreview.rutgers.edu/john-wesley-powell-arid-empire-of-the-american-west/).

22. Fite, p. 96.

23. Drache, p. 42.

24. Kenneth M. Hammer, "Come to God's Country: Promotional Efforts in Dakota Territory, 1861–1889," *South Dakota History*, vol. 10, no. 4 (Winter 2000), p. 295.

25. Fite, p. 96.

26. Hammer, "Come to God's Country," p. 292.

27. Fite, p. 97.

28. See White, *Railroaded*, p. 487. The presidents were Sidney Dillon and Charles Francis Adams; the USGS employee was Ferdinand Vandeveer Hayden.

29. See Powell, *Report*, 2nd ed., pp. 70–71.

30. Chicago & North Western Railway poster, National Park Service website.

31. H. Roger Grant, *The North Western: A History of the Chicago & North Western Railway System* (DeKalb: Northern Illinois University Press, 1996), p. 41.

32. Fite, pp. 98–99.

33. Ibid., p. 100.

34. James F. Hamburg, "Railroads and the Settlement of South Dakota during the Great Dakota Boom," *South Dakota History*, vol. 5, no. 2 (1975), pp. 165, 168.

35. PG, p. 158.

36. Dick, pp. 388–89.

37. LIW to RWL, undated letter from early 1937; see SL LIW, pp. 115–16.

38. PG, p. 160.

39. Ibid., p. 165.

40. Ibid., p. 172.

41. Ibid., p. 174. See also, LIW to RWL, February 5, 1937.

42. PG, p. 178.

43. In addition to the account of Charles Ingalls cited below, see Carrie Ingalls Swanzey to Mr. Mallery, April 11, 1930. De Smet Collection. Caroline Ingalls also wrote a historical note describing Silver Lake on the back of a 1914 postcard; see Aubrey Sherwood, "I Remember Silver Lake," *The Best of the Lore* (De Smet: Laura Ingalls Wilder Memorial Society, 2007), pp. 29–30.

44. Charles Ingalls, "The Settlement of De Smet," reprinted under a different title in *Reader*, pp. 3–4.

45. PG, p. 181.

46. Ibid., see p. 187n87.

47. Ibid. See also, "Swindling at the Agencies," *New York Times*, August 15, 1878.

48. PG, p. 192.

49. Ibid., p. 181.

50. See ibid., p. 178n67; see also LIW to RWL, undated early 1938 draft, beginning "Silver Lake / Laura was impatient on the train." See SL LIW, p. 156.

51. Charles Ingalls, "The Settlement of De Smet."

52. Letter signed "C.S.I.," *Brookings County Press*, February 2, 1880. In 2014, the Pioneer Girl Project of the South Dakota Historical Society Press discovered this letter; the initials of the signature are believed to be a typographical error for "C.P.I." or "C. P. Ingalls," as he often signed himself. See Nancy Tystad Koupal, "Rare Charles Ingalls Letter Discovered," blog post, Pioneer Girl Project, August 5, 2014. https://pioneergirlproject.org/2014/08/05/rare-charles-ingalls-letter-discovered/.

53. See PG, p. 189n94; a plat map of De Smet appears on p. 190.

54. Ibid., p. 191.

55. See Nancy S. Cleaveland, "History of the Ingalls Building in De Smet," and Richard B. Kurz Jr., "How the Store Was Recreated," in *Pa Ingalls' Store* (self-published scale model, 2013).

56. Pierre-Jean De Smet, "Observations upon America," in *Life, Letters and Travels of Father De Smet among the North American Indians*, vol. 4, ed. Hiram Martin Chittenden and Alfred Talbot Richardson, chap. 6, p. 1430.

57. "First Letter of Father Christian Hoeken to Father De Smet, Sioux Country, Fort Vermilion, Dec. 11, 1850," in ibid., chap. 2, p. 1251.

58. PG, p. 194.

59. No exact date can be supplied for this photograph, and there has been speculation about whether it was taken before Mary's illness or following it.

60. PG, p. 198.

61. Ibid., p. 201.

62. George Kingsbury, *The History of Dakota Territory*, vol. 2 (Chicago: S. J. Clarke, 1915), p. 1148.

63. "Fall Blizzard 42 Years Ago Began 'Winter of the Big Snow,'" *Milwaukee Journal*, October 15, 1922. Wisconsin Historical Society.

64. PG, p. 203; see also Barbara E. Boustead, "The Hard Winter of 1880–1881: Climatological Context and Communication via a Laura Ingalls Wilder Narrative," doctoral dissertation, University of Nebraska, 2014, p. 127.

65. See PG, p. 204n8, and Nancy S. Cleaveland, *Laura Ingalls Wilder and Education in Kingsbury County, Dakota Territory: 1880–1885* (De Smet: Laura Ingalls Wilder Memorial Society, 2015), p. 5. See also *The Revised Codes for the Territory of Dakota, A.D. 1877*, ed. Geo H. Hand, Secretary of Dakota, Chapter 24, section 44 (Yankton: Bowen & Kingsbury, 1877), p. 91; chapter 40, section 62, p. 209.

66. See PG, p. 204n9, pp. 204–205n10; p. 207n18.

67. LIW to RWL, March 7, 1938.

68. PG, pp. 203, 207.

69. Ibid., p. 207.

70. LIW to RWL, March 7, 1938.

71. See PG, p. 209.

72. Ibid., p. 210.

73. Ibid.

74. See Dick, pp. 258–59.

75. Ibid., p. 259.

76. PG, p. 215.

77. Ibid., p. 213.

78. Ibid., p. 220.

79. "Kolapoor Mission, India: Summary of Work Done," in Royal Gould Wilder papers. Malone Collection.

80. See LIW, "Speech at the Book Fair, Detroit, Michigan, October 16, 1937," *The Little House Books*, vol. 1, p. 587. Genealogical sources have not yet turned up additional uses of the name "Almanzo" in the Wilder family record: See Rev. Moses H. Wilder, *Book of the Wilders: A Contribution to the History of the Wilders* (Brooklyn, NY: Edward O. Jenkins, 1878).

81. Other literary sources include tales of valor inspired by the eighteenth-century Battle of Almansa, named for a Spanish town, which gave rise to a popular ballad by the same name; see "The Battle of Almanza" in *A Pedlar's Pack of Ballads and Songs*, collected by W. H. Logan (Edinburgh: William Paterson, 1868), pp. 82–84. The introduction to the volume and the headnote indicate that the source of the poem was a broadside dated "somewhere about 1760." Another potential source might be *Almanzor and Almahide, or the Conquest of Granada by the Spaniards, a Tragedy* in *The Works of John Dryden, Now First Collected In Eighteen Volumes*, ed. Walter Scott, vol. 4 (London: William Miller, 1808), p. 1. Dryden's Restoration tragedy was satirized for bombast but given new life by Scott's reverent edition.

82. Edward Maturin, "Inez: A Tale of Grenada," *Ladies' Companion and Literary Expositor: A Monthly Magazine*, new series, vol. 1 (1844), p. 237. Maturin

penned another serial containing the name "Almanzor": see his "Alonzo and Zamora," *Ladies Companion*, new series, vol. 1, pp. 87–88. These serials were reprinted in New York State newspapers: see, for example, *The Corrector* (Sag Harbor, NY), October 17, 1846, p. 1.

83. U.S. Census, Schedule 4, Production of Agriculture in Burke, in the County of Franklin, New York, July 23, 1860, p. 49.

84. An assumption derived from the description in *Farmer Boy* in *LIW: The Little House Books*, vol. 1, pp. 204–205.

85. See LIW to RWL, March 23, 1937.

86. See AJW to RWL, March, 1937.

87. No birth certificate documented Almanzo Wilder's date of birth, but three census records in a row document his year of birth as 1859. The U.S. Census, Schedule 1, Burke, Franklin County, New York, July 24, 1860, listed the child as one year old; the 1870 U.S. Census gave his age as eleven; the 1875 New York State Census gave his age as sixteen.

88. See LIW to RWL, undated letter, 1937 (probably March): "Manly was supposed to be 21 years old. To enter a homestead a man must be 21 or the head of a household . . . E.J. told later (she would) that he was only 18. Manly has never admitted it but as near as I can figure E.J. was right."

89. Ruth A. Alexander, Introduction to *A Wilder in the West: The Story of Eliza Jane Wilder*, ed. William Anderson (privately printed: Anderson Publications, 1971; 1985), p. iii, citing Mary W. M. Hargreaves, "Women in the Agricultural Settlement of the Northern Plains," *Agricultural History*, vol. 50, no. 1 (January 1976), p. 182.

90. Eliza Jane Wilder left a lengthy account of her Dakota homesteading experience, apparently intended to be filed with claim paperwork, addressed to the "Department of the Interior." It is reprinted in *A Wilder in the West*, p. 8.

91. See letter from AJW to RWL, March 20, 1937.

92. Ibid.

93. See LIW to RWL, March 22?, 1937, letter beginning "Monday P.M."

94. See LIW to RWL, March 20, 1937.

95. PG, p. 221.

96. Ibid., p. 223.

97. *The New York Public Library American History Desk Reference* (New York: Macmillan, 1997), p. 282.

98. White, *It's Your Misfortune*, pp. 372–73.

99. "Populism in the Plains and Midwest," *Encyclopedia of Populism in America*, pp. 528–29.

100. PG, p. 231.

101. Ibid., p. 237.

102. Ibid., p. 231.

103. James Woodress, *Willa Cather: A Literary Life* (Lincoln and London: University of Nebraska Press, 1987), p. 36.

104. Ibid.

105. PG, pp. 239–41.

106. Ibid., p. 241.

107. Ibid., p. 243.

108. See LIW to RWL, December 29, 1937, see attached sheets, in SL LIW, p. 142. The story of the goose is told first in *Pioneer Girl*, p. 189.

109. Wilder retold the goose story as a Thanksgiving parable; see Wilder, "Thanksgiving Time," *Missouri Ruralist*, November 20, 1916, in *LIW, Farm Journalist*, pp. 90–91.

110. PG, p. 251.

111. Ibid., p. 243.

112. Ibid., p. 246.

113. Ibid., p. 248.

114. Ibid.

115. Ibid., p. 247.

116. Anderson, *A Wilder in the West*, p. 17.

117. Ibid., p. 259.

118. Ibid., p. 285.

119. Ibid., p. 287.

120. Ibid.

121. Ibid., p. 288n34.

122. LIW, "Ambition," in *Reader*, pp. 32–33. Original on display in Mansfield Collection.

123. LIW, "Do It with All Your Might," in *Reader*, p. 42.

124. LIW, "The Difference," in *Reader*, p. 39.

125. LIW, "My Sister Mary," in *Reader*, p. 43.

126. Ibid., p. 36.

127. See PG, p. 260n81. Wilder would later claim to have begun teaching at fifteen, perhaps having initially misremembered the chronology. Notably, she would remain insistent on the error long after she must have realized the confusion. Having cast herself as a trailblazer, she valued that persona. Her first teaching certificate would be reproduced in *Little Town on the Prairie* with some telling revisions, including its date. She also gave herself higher marks in history and geography and omitted her results for orthography (70 out of 100).

128. See Michael Lesy, "1900," in *Wisconsin Death Trip* (New York: Doubleday, 1973), unpaginated.

129. Hamlin Garland, "Up the Coolly," in *Main-Travelled Roads* (New York: Harper & Row, 1899), p. 79.

130. See PG, p. 262n84. The editors of PG found no children corresponding to Wilder's description of "Martha" and "Charles."

131. Ibid., p. 267.

132. Ibid., p. 266.

133. Ibid., p. 269.

134. When Wilder wrote her memoir, she may or may not have been aware that a killing was committed among the Bouchies only months after her departure. Clarence Bouchie, a half brother of Louis Bouchie and likely the difficult student Wilder identified as Clarence, threw a bone at another of his siblings, hitting him in the face and causing lockjaw, which led to his death. Clarence Bouchie and his mother, Elizabeth, would be convicted of second-degree manslaughter in 1887. See PG, p. 272n98.

135. PG, p. 279.

136. "School Exhibition," *De Smet Leader*, March 29, 1884.

137. Ibid. See also *De Smet Leader*, April 12, 1884.

138. PG, p. 292.

139. Ibid., p. 256.

140. Ibid., p. 297.
141. Ibid., p. 305.
142. Ibid., p. 308.
143. Ibid., p. 307.
144. C. P. Ingalls to Royal Wilder and AJW, November 19, 1884. Mansfield Collection.
145. PG, p. 314.
146. Ibid., p. 317n93.
147. See ibid., p. 319; see also LIW, "Prairie Fire," a brief unpublished essay. Typescript, De Smet Collection.
148. Ibid., p. 322.
149. Ibid.
150. Ibid., p. 324.
151. Ibid.

5. DON'T LEAVE THE FARM, BOYS

1. LIW, "The First Three Years," undated manuscript, c. 1930s, unpaginated (p. 21).
2. Ibid.
3. Ibid. (p. 22).
4. Ibid. (p. 18).
5. Ibid.
6. Ibid. (p. 29).
7. Ibid. (p. 31).
8. Ibid. (p. 35).
9. Owing to differences in regional prices and other factors, the cost of living is difficult to calculate for specific areas of the United States in the nineteenth century, but for a summary of the economic hazards facing pioneers, see Fite, pp. 40–42.
10. AJW to RWL, March 25, 1937. SL LIW, p. 130.
11. See Table 43, "Average Wage-Rates of Laborers and of Five Skilled Occupations," in Clarence D. Long, *Wages and Earnings in the United States, 1860–1890* (Princeton: Princeton University Press, 1960), p. 99.
12. LIW, "The First Three Years" (p. 35).
13. Ibid.
14. See PG, p. 319; LIW, "The First Three Years" (p. 37).
15. Fite, p. 98.
16. LIW, "The First Three Years" (p. 57).
17. Ibid.
18. Ibid. (p. 58).
19. Fite., p. 105.
20. Ibid., p. 106.
21. PG, p. 324.
22. LIW, "The First Three Years" (p. 159). See also *The First Four Years* in *LIW: The Little House Books*, vol. 2, no. 795.28, p. 854.
23. LIW, "The First Three Years" (p. 73).
24. RWL would always celebrate her birthday on December 5, but two newspapers supply the date of her birth as December 6. The *De Smet Leader*, December 11, 1886, reported: "At the home of Mr. and Mrs. A. J. Wilder, on Monday last, a daughter came." Monday was December 6. See also John Miller, *Becoming*

Laura Ingalls Wilder: The Woman Behind the Legend, Missouri Biography Series (University of Missouri Press, 1998), p. 79.

25. See LIW, "The First Three Years" (p. 83); the folk song was "Angel Band."

26. I am indebted to Sharon Jahn, a genealogist and historian at the Spring Valley Methodist Church Museum, in Spring Valley, Minnesota, for raising the question of Rose's lack of a middle name, a striking omission given that middle names were bestowed on all the Ingalls girls, a pattern seen also with Caroline Ingalls's and Charles Ingalls's siblings. In later years, lacking a middle name, Rose would adopt her maiden name along with her married name.

27. LIW, "The First Three Years" (p. 85).

28. Ibid. (p. 86).

29. See Grace Ingalls, Diary, January 12, 1887. Original manuscript, De Smet Collection. Reprinted in William Anderson, *The Story of the Ingalls* (privately printed, Anderson Publications, 1967; 1993), p. 34. Excerpts were also reproduced in *Reader*, p. 24.

30. Justice's Docket, Kingsbury County, "E. M. Harthorn & Son vs. A. J. Wilder," February 8, 1887, p. 328. De Smet Collection.

31. Grace Ingalls, February 9, 1887. Charles Ingalls's election to the post of deputy sheriff took place two months later, but he may have been serving on an ad hoc basis.

32. LIW, "The First Three Years" (p. 88).

33. Ibid. (p. 89).

34. Elizabeth Hampsten, *Settlers' Children: Growing Up on the Great Plains* (Norman and London: University of Oklahoma Press, 1991), pp. 76–77.

35. Ibid., p. 76.

36. LIW, "The First Three Years" (p. 89).

37. Homestead patent granted by the United States of America to Almanzo J. Wilder, June 17, 1887, Homestead Certificate No. 1490, Application 3610.

38. Grace Ingalls, July 23, 1887.

39. LIW, "The First Three Years" (p. 99).

40. Wayne L. Decker, "Weather During Wilders' Homestead Years," *Best of the Lore*, p. 52.

41. Hamlin Garland, *A Pioneer Mother* (Chicago: Bookfellows, 1922), p. 5.

42. Garland, *A Son of the Middle Border*, p. 9.

43. Ibid., p. 45.

44. Ibid., p. 65. Both of these songs appear in PG and LHBW.

45. Ibid., p. 170.

46. Ibid., p. 308.

47. Hamlin Garland, "Holding Down a Claim in a Blizzard," cited in Keith Newlin, *Hamlin Garland: A Life* (Lincoln and London: University of Nebraska Press, 2008), p. 59.

48. Hamlin Garland, Foreword to *Main-Travelled Roads* (New York: Harper & Brothers, 1899), p. xii.

49. Ibid., p. xi.

50. Garland, *A Son of the Middle Border,* p. 248.

51. Grace Ingalls, March 26, 1887.

52. LIW, "The First Three Years" (p. 102).

53. Ibid. (p. 105).

54. The outbreak was chronicled in Daniel D. Peterson, *The Diphtheria Epidemic of 1880: Walnut Grove, Minnesota* (Walnut Grove: self-published, undated), pp. 10–12.

55. Grace Ingalls, March 5, 1888.

56. *Kingsbury County News*, March 9, 1888.

57. LIW, "The First Three Years" (p. 106).

58. See the prologue to Laura Ingalls Wilder, *On the Way Home: The Diary of a Trip from South Dakota to Mansfield, Missouri, in 1894*, ed. Rose Wilder Lane (New York: Harper & Row, 1962), p. 2. Lane implies that she was seven when her parents contracted diphtheria; she was actually not yet two.

59. LIW, "The First Three Years" (p. 107).

60. Ibid.

61. Ibid.

62. Ibid. (p. 106).

63. A chronology of homestead transactions compiled by researchers in De Smet lists a $760 loan, borrowed by Charles and Caroline Ingalls from the Dakota Loan and Investment Company in April 1888; see "Ingalls Homestead," De Smet Collection. The loan also appears on the Deed Record documenting the Ingallses' sale of the homestead in 1892, as a "mortgage and note . . . from April 30, 1891."

64. LIW, "The First Three Years" (p. 116).

65. Ibid. (p. 129). Ole Sheldon was probably Oliver Sheldon; Oliver C., Alfred J., and Uri Sheldon served as witnesses to the final proof filed on Almanzo Wilder's preemption claim on January 21, 1890.

66. Ibid. (p. 130).

67. Decker, p. 52.

68. I am indebted for this phrase—"Drought follows the plow"—to Mike Davis, *Late Victorian Holocausts*, p. 121.

69. LIW, "The First Three Years" (p. 137).

70. Ibid. (p. 144).

71. Ibid.

72. Ibid. (p. 141).

73. Ibid. (p. 146).

74. See Land Office receipt, Almanzo J. Wilder, Watertown, South Dakota, dated April 17, 1890, six months after filing for preemption.

75. LIW, "The First Three Years" (p. 150).

76. *De Smet Leader*, July 13, 1889.

77. LIW, "The First Three Years" (p. 150).

78. Ibid.

79. Ibid. (p. 153).

80. *De Smet Leader*, August 10, 1889. Decades later, Wilder may have mistaken the date of his birth with the approximate date of his death.

81. Circumstances regarding Lane's discovery of her infant brother are murky. Holtz claims she did not learn of it until after her mother's death: see William Holtz, *The Ghost in the Little House: A Life of RWL*, Missouri Biography Series (University of Missouri Press, 1993), p. 414n6. He cites RWL to Aubrey Sherwood, October 23, 1958, and argues that Lane had not yet read her mother's "First Three Years" manuscript.

82. Grace Ingalls, August 27, 1889.

83. LIW, "The First Three Years" (p. 155).

84. Ibid.

85. Ibid. (p. 156).

86. Ibid. (p. 160).

87. Probably quoting from memory, she misremembered these lines: "But for our blunders—oh, in shame / Before the eyes of heaven we fall.... But Thou, O Lord, / Be merciful to me, a fool!" See Edward Rowland Sill, "The Fool's Prayer," in *American Poetry: The Nineteenth Century*, vol. 2 (New York: Library of America, 1993), p. 398. Wilder also wrote about the poem in "A Few Minutes with a Poet," *Missouri Ruralist*, January 5, 1919; *Farm Journalist*, p. 169.

88. Grace Ingalls, November 17, 1889.

89. Ibid.

90. Fite, p. 108.

91. Ibid.

92. Ibid., p. 109.

93. William Cronon, *Changes in the Land: Indians, Colonists, and the Ecology of New England* (New York: Hill and Wang, 1983), p. 122.

94. Ibid., p. 123.

95. Savage, p. 85.

96. C. E. Leslie and R. H. Randall, *The Conqueror* (Chicago: Chicago Music Company, 1880), pp. 24–25.

97. Grace Ingalls, May 18, 1890.

98. *De Smet Leader*, May 17, 1890.

99. *De Smet Leader*, May 31, 1890.

100. Grace Ingalls, May 18, 1890.

101. Ibid.

102. See Mary Jo Dathe, "Looking Back at the 'Wheat Era': Glimpses of Yesteryear," *Spring Valley Tribune*, October 3, 2012.

103. Mary Jo Dathe, *Spring Valley: The Laura Ingalls Wilder "Connection," 1890* (Spring Valley: Spring Valley Tribune, 1992), rev. ed., pp. 20, 24.

104. Ibid.

105. Ibid., pp. 6–8.

106. Dorothy Smith, *The Wilder Family Story* (Malone, NY: Almanzo and Laura Ingalls Wilder Association, 1972), p. 21.

107. RWL to Gladys Wilder, March 14, 1962. Spring Valley Collection.

108. See William Anderson, *The Little House Guidebook* (New York: HarperCollins, 1996), p. 90.

109. Sharon Jahn, interview with the author, January 19, 2015.

110. Anderson, *A Wilder in the West*, p. 26.

111. LIW to RWL, undated letter. Quotation in Anderson, *A Wilder in the West*, p. 28.

112. *De Smet Leader*, July 29, 1890, cited in Anderson, *A Wilder in the West*, p. 28.

113. I am indebted throughout to Dorothy Smith, *The Log Book of the Sailing Craft "Edith": An 1890 Trip Down the Mississippi Made by Three Relatives of Laura Ingalls Wilder*, settings and editing by Dorothy Smith (Malone, NY: Industrial Press, 1984). See p. 11.

114. W. D. Chipley, *Facts About Florida* (Louisville, KY: Courier-Journal Press, 188?), p. 18.

115. Ibid., p. 6.

116. Malone Collection.

117. Smith, *Log Book*, p. 11.

118. Ibid., p. 15.

119. See Smith's "Interlude About the Battle of Shiloh and the Crew," *Log Book*, p. 30.
120. Ibid., p. 40
121. Peter Ingalls married Mary McGowin in September 1891. Alene M. Warnock, *Laura Ingalls Wilder: The Westville Florida Years* (Glen Burnie, MD: self-published, 1979), p. 8.
122. See LIW to AJW, October 14, 1915, in LIW, *West from Home: Letters of Laura Ingalls Wilder, San Francisco 1915*, ed. Roger Lea MacBride (New York: HarperCollins, 1974), p. 149.
123. *Spring Valley Mercury*, March 19, 1891.
124. *Spring Valley Mercury*, April 2, 1891.
125. Holtz, *Ghost*, p. 23.
126. LIW to Miss Alfarata Allen, September 26, 1933, Burr Oak Collection.
127. RWL to Gladys Wilder, March 14, 1962, Spring Valley Collection.
128. Ibid. Lane retold the story in "Rose Wilder Lane By Herself," *Sunset*, November 1918.
129. Deed Record from Almanzo J. Wilder and Laura E. Wilder to Dakota Loan and Investment, September 16, 1891, Kingsbury County, South Dakota, Book 11, p. 283. The Wilders were in Fillmore County, Minnesota, when they filled out the paperwork, but the deed was ultimately filed in Kingsbury County.
130. *Spring Valley Mercury*, October 8, 1891.
131. Hines, "The Story of Rocky Ridge Farm," pp. 17–18.
132. Chipley, pp. 7, 19.
133. Ibid., p. 43.
134. Warnock, p. 20, citing another Chipley publication.
135. Chipley, p. 43.
136. LIW, "Autobiographical Sketch for 'The Junior Book of Authors,'" in *LIW: The Little House Books*, vol. 2, p. 799.
137. Ibid.
138. RWL, "Innocence," *Sampler*, p. 45.
139. Ibid., p. 49.
140. Ibid., p. 43. For more on the psychological and cultural pressures affecting Rose's relationship to her mother, see Anita Clair Fellman, "Laura Ingalls Wilder and Rose Wilder Lane: The Politics of a Mother-Daughter Relationship," *Signs: Journal of Women in Culture and Society*, vol. 15, no. 3 (1990), pp. 535–61.
141. *Sampler*, p. 41.
142. RWL, Notes on "A Son of the Soil." HHPL. Lane intended to write a series of articles for the *Bulletin* or perhaps a novel on her father. It was never completed, but she ultimately used some of the material as the basis for *Free Land*.
143. See Case in *Sampler*, p. 9.
144. Warnock, p. 8.
145. Fite, p. 23.
146. Ibid.
147. "The Homestead Act 1862–2012," U.S. Department of the Interior, Bureau of Land Management (BLM website).
148. Fite, p. 134.
149. Ibid., p. 31.
150. See "Homestead Proof—Testimony of Claimant" in Homestead file for Final Certificate, No. 2708, Application No. 4091, Charles P. Ingalls, at Watertown, Dakota Territory, May 11, 1886; see also handwritten questions and answers in file.

151. Cleaveland and Linsenmayer, p. 9.
152. See the entry for Charles Ingalls in *Memorial and Biographical Record: An Illustrated Compendium of Biography*, South Dakota edition (Chicago: Geo. A. Ogle, 1898), pp. 1028–1029.
153. Frank B. Latham, *The Panic of 1893* (New York: Franklin Watts, 1971), pp. 35–36.
154. Ibid.
155. Garland, *Main-Travelled Roads*, p. iii.
156. Newlin, p. 164.
157. Warranty Deed from Charles P. Ingalls and Caroline L. Ingalls to George Elderkin, February 18, 1892, Deeds, Book 15, p. 97. Kingsbury County, De Smet, South Dakota. De Smet Collection. See also Cleaveland and Linsenmayer, p. 12.
158. *Kingsbury County Independent*, August 17, 1894, and September 28, 1894.
159. Warranty Deed from Emil A. Syverson and Inga Syverson to Mrs. Laura E. Wilder, November 14, 1892, Deeds, Book 18, p. 24, Kingsbury County, South Dakota. De Smet Collection.
160. RWL, "Grandpa's Fiddle I," *Sampler*, p. 65.
161. RWL, *On the Way Home*, p. 4.
162. Ibid., p. 6.
163. Teresa Lynn, *Little Lodges on the Prairie: Freemasonry and Laura Ingalls Wilder* (Austin: Tranquility Press, 2014), pp. 150–51.
164. RWL, "Grandpa's Fiddle I," p. 64.
165. RWL, "Memories of Grandma's House," *Sampler,* p. 58.
166. RWL, "Grandpa's Fiddle I," p. 65.
167. *Kingsbury County Independent*, May 4, 1894.
168. RWL, *On the Way Home*, p. 4.
169. This version of "Dakota Land" is taken from Carl Sandburg, *The American Songbag* (New York: Harcourt, Brace, 1927), pp. 280–81. RWL's version is somewhat truncated: see *On the Way Home*, p. 6.
170. Pamela Riney-Kehrberg, *Rooted in Dust: Surviving Drought and Depression in Southwestern Kansas* (Lawrence: University Press of Kansas, 1994), p. 8.
171. Davis, p. 121.
172. Ibid., p. 122.
173. See ibid., pp. 126, 138. See also Richard G. Robbins, *Famine in Russia, 1891–1892: The Imperial Government Responds to a Crisis* (New York and London: Columbia University Press, 1975), pp. 9–10.
174. See Davis, pp. 121–23.
175. Latham, p. 4.
176. Ibid.
177. Lane, *On the Way Home*, p. 1.
178. See David Whitten, "Depression of 1893," EH.Net Encyclopedia, ed. Robert Whaples, August 14, 2001. URL http://eh.net/encyclopedia/the-depression-of-1893/.
179. White, *It's Your Misfortune*, p. 230.
180. Charles Hoffman, *The Depression of the Nineties: An Economic History* (Westport, CT: Greenwood Publishing, 1970), p. 109.
181. L. Frank Baum, *The Annotated Wizard of Oz*, ed. Michael Patrick Hearn (New York: W. W. Norton, 2000), p. xxii.
182. *Saturday Pioneer*, Aberdeen, South Dakota, January 31, 1891; December 20, 1890.
183. *Annotated Oz*, p. 15n2.

184. Katharine M. Rogers, *L. Frank Baum: Creator of Oz* (New York: St. Martin's Press, 2002), p. 19.

185. *Annotated Oz*, p. 16n3.

186. Ibid., p. 21n9.

187. Ibid., p. 23n10.

188. Ibid., p. 11.

189. Ibid., p. 18.

190. Ibid., p. 75.

191. See Erik Larson, *The Devil in the White City: Murder, Magic, and Madness at the Fair That Changed America* (New York: Random House, 2003), pp. 222–23.

192. U.S. Census Office, Extra Census Bulletin No. 2, "Distribution of Population According to Density: 1890" (1891). Text reproduced in Compendium of the Eleventh Census: 1890, Part 1. Population (1892), p. xlviii.

193. Ibid.

194. Frederick Jackson Turner, "The Significance of the Frontier in American History," in *The Frontier in American History* (New York: Henry Holt, 1920), p. 37.

195. Herman Melville, *The Confidence-Man: His Masquerade* (New York: Grove Press, 1949), pp. 172–73.

196. Turner, p. 37.

197. Turner, p. 3.

198. See, for example, "Go South," *Council Grove Republican* (Council Grove, Kansas), September 28, 1888, p. 2.

199. *Among the Ozarks: The Land of "Big Red Apples"* (Kansas City: Hudson-Kimberly, 1894), ninth edition.

200. Ibid., p. 12.

201. Ibid., p. 41.

202. Ibid., p. 42.

203. Ibid., p. 41.

204. See *Sampler*, p. 75.

205. Warranty Deed from Laura E. Wilder and Almanzo J. Wilder to Clara A. Abel, May 25, 1894, Book 18, p. 326, Kingsbury County, South Dakota. De Smet Collection.

206. According to those who knew her, Lane related this as a true story. Norma Lee Browning, longtime friend of Lane's, wrote: "She often told us the story—and always with gentle laughter and a far-away look in her eyes—of how Pa played the violin as they all sat on the porch of that house the night before they left for Missouri in 1894, when she was seven." See Browning, "Rose and Laura," draft manuscript of an article written for Waldenbooks Kids Club, p. 12. De Smet Collection. An edited version of Browning's memoir, with this sentence elided, appeared as "Little House in Danbury," *Rose Wilder Lane Lore* (A special issue of *Laura Ingalls Wilder Lore*), vol. 12, no. 2 (December 5, 1986), pp. 8–11.

207. Found among Lane's papers, the undated manuscript of "Grandpa's Fiddle" was written as fiction but clearly based on fact, with depictions of "Aunt Mary," who was blind, and Lane's parents, grandparents, and aunts. In the original manuscript, the family name is "Clayton," and Laura is "Carrie," Carrie is "Aunt Susan," and the first person narrator is "Molly." When the story was published, for the first time, in the anthology *A Little House Sampler*, its editor, William Anderson, implied that "the account" was nonfiction and made a number of

editorial changes, including switching the names of the characters back to their real-life counterparts. He did not indicate the changes he made. See RWL, "Grandpa's Fiddle I," in *Sampler*, pp. 59–75.

208. The image of "drinking tears" bears a striking resemblance to the image of tears in a teacup developed in Elizabeth Bishop's "Sestina," a poem published in her 1965 volume, *Questions of Travel*; it may suggest a possible dating of the story. The fictional story is not referred to in Lane's 1930s or 1940s diaries or journals, where she commonly recorded progress on her work.

209. RWL, "Grandpa's Fiddle," manuscript, p. 4.

210. Ibid., p. 7: The sentence in the manuscript, as revised by Lane, reads as follows: ". . . it just lifted up the heart and filled it so full of happiness and pain and longing that it broke, your heart broke open like a bud."

211. Ibid., p. 8.

6. A WORLD MADE

1. Henry Adams to Sir John Clark, July 30, 1893, and Henry Adams to Elizabeth Cameron, August, 8, 1893. In *The Letters of Henry Adams, Vol. IV: 1892–1899*, ed. Jacob Clavner Levenson, Jayne Newcomer Samuels, et al. (Cambridge: Belknap Press of Harvard University Press, 1988), p. 117.

2. Latham, p. 4.

3. Ibid., p. 50.

4. These phrases are drawn from two letters to Taft's wife, dated July 6 and July 8, 1894; see Jonathan Lurie, *William Howard Taft: The Travails of a Progressive Conservative* (New York: Cambridge University Press, 2012), p. 31.

5. *Chicago Tribune*, "Class Warfare in Chicago," online feature, July 27, 2014. According to this source, the strychnine article dates from 1877.

6. See Donald Worster, *Dust Bowl: The Southern Plains in the 1930s* (Oxford: Oxford University, Press, 1979; 2004), p. 84. Vance Johnson provides a slightly different version of the saying in *Heaven's Tableland: The Dust Bowl Story* (New York: Da Capo Press, 1974), p. 63: "West of Junction City there is no Sunday, and west of Salina there is no God."

7. James L. Roark, Michael P. Johnson, Patricia Cline Cohen, Sarah Stage, Alan Lawson, and Susan M. Hartmann, *Understanding The American Promise, A Brief History, Volume 2: From 1865* (Boston: Bedford/St. Martin's, 2011), p. 550.

8. Fite, p. 130. Also see Worster, *Dust Bowl*, p. 84. The fifth chapter of his classic contains an extensive description of the 1890s as a precipitating event of the Dust Bowl.

9. Grover Cleveland, Second Inaugural Address, March 4, 1893.

10. Fite, p. 130.

11. Carlos A. Schwantes, *Coxey's Army: An American Odyssey* (Lincoln and London: University of Nebraska Press, 1985), p. 1.

12. Ibid., p. 2.

13. Ibid., p. 141.

14. Ibid., p. 19, from *Cleveland Plain Dealer*, April 1, 1894.

15. Ibid., p. 59, from *Rocky Mountain News*, June 1, 1894.

16. Fite, p. 130.

17. Unsigned, "Coxey Has a New Commissary," *New York Times*, April 6, 1894.

18. For the estimate of fifty trains, see Schwantes, p. 195.

19. See Schwantes, p. 194. See also *Jack London on the Road: The Tramp Diary and Other Hobo Writings*, ed. Richard W. Etulain (Logan: Utah State University Press, 1979), p. 54.

20. Ibid., pp. 276–77.

21. Schwantes, p. 168.

22. Ibid., p. 179.

23. United States Department of Agriculture, Weather Bureau, "Annual Report of the Iowa Weather and Crop Service, in Co-operation with the United States Weather Bureau, for the Year 1901" (Des Moines: Bernard Murphy, State Printer, 1902), p. 25.

24. Cartoons by "HRH," *Chicago Sunday Tribune*, July 22, 1894, p. 1.

25. "Annual Report of the Iowa Weather and Crop Service," p. 25.

26. John R. Milton, *South Dakota: A History* (New York: Norton, 1988), p. 95.

27. For RWL's recollections of the wagon's contents, see *On the Way Home*, p. 11. Wilder herself later recalled the possessions they brought with them in a newspaper interview; see Dorothy O. Moore, "Ozark Author of Children's Books Recalls Hardships in Pioneer Days," *St. Louis Post-Dispatch*, January 14, 1952.

28. For a description of the writing desk and the money concealed within, see *On the Way Home*, pp. 8–9.

29. Ibid., p. 15.

30. Ibid.

31. Ibid., p. 16.

32. Lane, "Grandpa's Fiddle I," p. 74.

33. *On the Way Home*, p. 17.

34. Ibid., p. 23.

35. Ibid., pp. 23–24.

36. RWL, "Grandpa's Fiddle II," *Sampler*, p. 78.

37. *On the Way Home*, p. 28.

38. Ibid., p. 59. Hoecake, or johnnycake, is a flat bread baked from cornmeal, similar to a pancake; clabber refers to a yogurt-like food made from curdled, unpasteurized milk.

39. *On the Way Home*, p. 29.

40. Ibid., p. 28.

41. See original manuscript of Wilder's notebook, July 25, 1894 (unpaginated). SHSM.

42. *On the Way Home*, p. 59.

43. *De Smet News*, August 23, 1894, reprinted in *Sampler*, pp. 87–88.

44. *On the Way Home*, p. 65.

45. Ibid., p. 66.

46. Ibid., p. 67.

47. Ibid., p. 68.

48. Ibid., p. 69.

49. Wilder did mention the trip in interviews; see note 27.

50. RWL, *On the Way Home*, p. 77.

51. In *On the Way Home*, Lane wrote that all the money they had left was a hundred-dollar bill, and it was that bill that went missing.

52. Ibid., p. 81. Compare Lane's account in *On the Way Home*, however, to her earlier account of the purchase of the property, written in 1935 in her unpublished nonfiction manuscript, commissioned by Robert M. McBride & Co. about Missouri state history, "The Name Is Mizzoury," in which she states that there were seven pieces of folding money in the writing desk. In that version, there is no reference to the missing bill. See RWL, "The Name Is Mizzoury," version 2, HHPL.

53. RWL, *On the Way Home*, p. 75.
54. Wright County, Missouri, Warranty Deeds, Book 28, p. 178, Grantor, Thomas M. White; Grantee, Laura E. Wilder. The indenture, made on September 21, 1894, includes the names of Thomas M. White and Charlotte White, husband and wife, as parties of the first part, and Laura E. Wilder, party of the second part. Almanzo Wilder's name does not appear.
55. Richard H. Chuset, "Married Women's Property Law: Reception of the Early Married Women's Property Acts by Courts and Legislatures," *American Journal of Legal History*, vol. 29, no. 1 (January 1985), p. 3.
56. See Deed Record, from Emil A. Syverson and Inga Syverson to Laura E. Wilder, November 14, 1892, Book 18, p. 24, Kingsbury County, South Dakota. De Smet Collection.
57. See *The Revised Statutes of the State of Missouri, 1909* (Jefferson City: Hugh Stephens Printing Co., 1909), vol. 2, Chapter 77, Section 8309, "Married woman to hold her personal property and her real estate as her separate property." The historical note appended to this section suggests that the statute was first enacted in 1875.
58. Dorothy Moore, "Ozark Author."
59. A. J. Wilder, "The Story of Rocky Ridge Farm," *Missouri Ruralist*, July 22, 1911, reprinted in *Sampler*, pp. 104–105.
60. The encounter is described in Lane's coda to *On the Way Home*, p. 91. It differs from an earlier account Lane wrote about the family's first days on Rocky Ridge; see RWL, "The Name Is Mizzoury," version 2, pp. 1–10, HHPL. In "Mizzoury," the homeless man is described as a neighbor.
61. RWL, *On the Way Home*, p. 92.
62. RWL Diaries and Notes, Item #4, 1920, September 22–25. During a 1920 journey from Paris to Poland, Lane wrote an extended diary entry about her childhood from which these details and those in the next few paragraphs are drawn. It was addressed to Arthur Griggs, her boyfriend at the time. Unpaginated, HHPL. Excerpts were published as "The Ozark Years," in *Sampler*, pp. 88–96.
63. Ibid.
64. See "To Cut an Apple Without Breaking the Skin," *American Thresherman*, vol. 10, no. 9 (January 1908), p. 50.
65. RWL, *Old Home Town* (Lincoln and London: University of Nebraska Press, 1935; 1963), p. 9.
66. Paul E. Cooley, "Some Recollections of Parts of the 19th and 20th Centuries," unpublished memoir, p. 2. De Smet Collection.
67. Ibid.
68. Ibid., p. 3.
69. Case, "Let's Visit Mrs. Wilder," *Missouri Ruralist*, February 20, 1918, in *Sampler*, p. 9.
70. William Anderson, *Laura Wilder of Mansfield* (Mansfield, MO: Laura Ingalls Wilder Museum, 1974; rev. ed. 2012), p. 7.
71. See Anderson, *A Wilder in the West*, p. 31.
72. William Anderson, *Laura Ingalls Wilder: A Biography* (New York: HarperCollins, 1992; 2007), p. 165. Although Anderson's book contains no endnotes, his source may be an August 30, 1963, letter from RWL to Irene V. Lichty. A transcript of the letter prepared by William Holtz is kept in HHPL, WHC.
73. James Wilder died on February 1, 1899, at the age of 86, at the Mermentau, Louisiana, home of his son Perley Wilder; his obituary stated that he had arrived

in the state only four months earlier. See "Death of James Wilder," *Daily Signal* (Crowley, Louisiana), February 2, 1899, p. 1.

74. On the 1900 Federal Census, Almanzo Wilder reported the year of his birth as 1861; see U.S. Census, Mansfield, Pleasant Valley Township, Wright County, Missouri, June 1, 1900. If 1861 was correct, that would have made him six years older than his wife rather than ten, as has been assumed.

75. Anderson, *Laura Wilder of Mansfield*, pp. 4, 7; see also Miller, p. 99.

76. See City of Mansfield website: http://mansfieldcityhall.org/info.html.

77. Mansfield Area Historical Society, *Images of America: Around Mansfield* (Charleston, SC: Arcadia, 2013), p. 15.

78. Gloria Bogart Carter, interview with the author, October 30, 2015. This description was confirmed by members of the Mansfield Historical Society.

79. *Black Families of the Ozarks*, vol. 1, Greene County Archives Bulletin Number Forty-Five (Springfield, MO, n.d.), p. 108. See also *History of Laclede, Camden, Dallas, Webster, Wright, Texas, Pulaski, Phelps, and Dent Counties, Missouri* (Chicago: Goodspeed, 1889), p. 370.

80. See, for example, *A Reminiscent History of Douglas County, Missouri, 1857–1957*, compiled and written by J. E. Curry (Douglas County Herald, 1957), p. 163.

81. See *Sketches of Wright County: Part Two, Towns and Hamlets*, compiled by Vearl Rowe (Hartville, MO: Wright County Historical Society, n.d.), p. 55.

82. Mansfield Area Historical Society, *Images of America: Around Mansfield* (Charleston, SC: Arcadia, 2013), p. 19.

83. Ibid.

84. Lynn, pp. 53, 68, 114.

85. Ibid., p. 212.

86. Grace Ingalls to Aubrey Sherwood, October 20, 1939, reprinted in "Two Readers Recall Earliest Issues; Sisters Revive Memories in Reading Diary," *De Smet News*, November 9, 1939.

87. *De Smet News*, August 31, 1900.

88. *Kingsbury Independent*, May 30, 1902.

89. Ibid.

90. RWL to Clara Webber, October 24, 1961. Pomona Collection.

91. LIW, "First Memories of Father," *Reader*, p. 160.

92. Ibid.

93. Ibid., pp. 161–62.

94. "A Pioneer Gone," *Kingsbury County Independent*, June 13, 1902.

95. Lynn, p. 163.

96. Lockwood, p. 128.

97. Undated clipping from *De Smet News*. De Smet Collection.

98. Anderson, *Story of the Ingalls*, p. 17.

99. The stock requisition forms are dated 1903, but the envelope itself—addressed to Mrs. A. J. Wilder at Rocky Ridge Farm from the editor's office of *The Farm World*, a publication in Chicago—appears to date to 1912, based on the postmark and date of issue of the four one-cent stamps. Whether the fragments and sketches were written in 1903 or a decade later remains unknown.

100. Rose Wilder, "Notes to School Friends Written on Textbooks, 1900–1902." HHPL, WHC.

101. Lane to Jasper Crane, December 13, 1961, in *The Lady and the Tycoon: The*

Best of Letters Between Rose Wilder Lane and Jasper Crane, ed. Roger Lea Mac-Bride (Caldwell, ID: Caxton Printers, 1973), p. 278.

102. Ibid.

103. RWL, "Old Maid," in *Old Home Town*, p. 38.

104. Rose Wilder, "Notes to School Friends."

105. RWL, "Long Skirts," *Old Home Town*, p. 157.

106. Holtz reported these rumors in an endnote in *Ghost*, p. 391, no. 28. He concluded that Rose's attendance at the Crowley school would surely have been impossible if she had been pregnant. Lane herself, while acknowledging the stillbirth of a baby early in her marriage, never hinted at such a traumatic event in her teenage years.

107. RWL to Norma Lee Browning, May 17, 1964.

108. Ibid.

109. "Class Exercises at High School," *Crowley Signal*, May 7, 1904, p. 1.

110. RWL to Gladys Wilder, February 12, 1962. Spring Valley Historical Society. Lane later wrote a profile of Griffith; see "Mars in the Movies," *Sunset*, February 1918.

111. Lynn, p. 225.

112. LIW, "Summer Boarders," in *Reader*, p. 66.

113. Ibid.

114. Photograph, HHPL. The hymn, "Just as I Am," with lyrics by Charlotte Elliott, begins, "Just as I am, without one plea, / But that thy blood was shed for me."

115. Anderson, *Laura Wilder of Mansfield*, p. 7.

116. "Summer Boarders," *Reader*, p. 67.

117. Ibid., p. 68.

118. Lane, "If I Could Live My Life Over Again," *Hearst's International, Combined with Cosmopolitan*, vol. 78, no. 3 (March 1925), p. 32.

119. RWL, Journal, "My Albanian Garden," November 3, 1926, p. 2.

120. 1903 Drury College Yearbook, Springfield, Missouri, p. 85.

121. See Holtz, *Ghost*, p. 46. The identity of Rose Wilder's first employer appears to be unclear.

122. Lane, "If I Could Live My Life Over Again," p. 178.

123. See Anderson, *Laura Wilder of Mansfield*, p. 10.

124. No such photograph exists in the archives of the Herbert Hoover Presidential Library or in the De Smet Collection; nor have images of the Wilder family appeared in previous biographies or in the copiously illustrated volumes of Wilder photographs, such as William Anderson, *LIW Country* (New York: HarperCollins, 1990) or *Laura's Album*.

125. RWL, "Faces at the Window" (published privately, 1972), p. 7.

126. Paul Cooley to Rose Wilder, postcard in Mansfield Collection.

127. See Rose Wilder, "Ups and Downs of Modern Mercury," *San Francisco Call*, September 20, 1908, p. 4, and Rose Wilder, "The Constantly Increasing Wonders in the New Field of Wireless," *San Francisco Call*, November 22, 1908, p. 4.

128. Wilder, "The Constantly Increasing Wonders . . ." Compare Rose Wilder's impressionistic copy with the more factually based report that ran on the front page of the same newspaper the previous month: "Gap to Hawaii Is Bridged by Wireless Men," *San Francisco Call*, vol. 104, no. 134 (October 12, 1908), p. 1.

129. State of Utah, Death Certificate, Infant Lane, November 23, 1909; first reported in Sallie Ketcham, *LIW: American Writer on the Prairie* (New York: Routledge, 2015), pp. 91, 93n41.

130. RWL, "My Albanian Garden," November 3, 1926, p. 2.

131. RWL Photographs, Kansas City, 1910. HHPL.

132. "Crowing, Cooing Babies Compete at the Grocers' Pure Food Show," *Kansas City Post*, May 20, 1910, p. 8. HHPL.

133. "Bread and Milk May Become High Luxury in Future," *Kansas City Post*, May 5, 1910, p. 5. HHPL.

134. Wilder's talk was titled "District Organization"; the women's association meeting was held as part of a larger event, the Arcadia Land Congress, held May 24–25, 1910, sponsored by the Missouri Immigration Board; see "Ozarks' Praise to Be Sung at Land Congress," *St. Louis Post-Dispatch*, May 15, 1910, p. 18.

135. "A Woman's Land Congress," *Country Gentleman*, Albany, NY, July 7, 1910, vol. 75, p. 646.

136. Undated newspaper clippings, c. 1910, Mansfield Collection. See "Laura's Land Congress Speech," *Sampler*, pp. 96–99.

137. Ibid.

138. Among Wilder's earliest publications was "Profits of the Good Fat Hen: Missouri Woman Offers Statistics to Prove It a Money Maker," *Coffeyville Daily Journal* (Coffeyville, Kansas), September 12, 1910, p. 4. This unsigned report quoted extensively from an article by or interview with Mrs. A. J. Wilder said to have run in *Woman's National Daily*, a short-lived turn of the century newspaper owned by the Lewis Publishing Company of St. Louis, which also printed *Woman's Magazine* and *Woman's Farm Journal*. Edward Gardner Lewis, the company's owner and a notable real estate developer, would eventually face charges of mail fraud arising from the heavy advertising content of the publications.

139. RWL to LIW, letter fragment beginning "answers to poultry raisers," no date. References to Maine later in the letter suggest that the letter dates from the winter of 1910–1911.

140. Ibid.

141. RWL to LIW, pre-1915 letter, beginning "Muvver dear."

142. RWL to LIW, undated letter fragment, beginning "Newspaper ethics."

143. RWL to LIW, undated letter fragment, beginning "you'll be astonished at the different looking copy you'll turn out."

144. See Stephen W. Hines, introduction to *Laura Ingalls Wilder: Farm Journalist*, pp. 5–6.

145. LIW, "The Building of a Farm House," in *Reader*, p. 53. The conversational tone of the essay recalls Wilder's *Missouri Ruralist* columns, with its references to "The-Man-Of-The-Place," but Anderson provides no date or place of publication.

146. See Anderson, *Laura Wilder of Mansfield*, p. 13.

147. "The Building of a Farm House," p. 58.

148. Ibid., p. 57.

7. AS A FARM WOMAN THINKS

1. LIW, "Who'll Do the Women's Work?," *Missouri Ruralist*, April 5, 1919, in *LIW: Farm Journalist*, ed. Stephen W. Hines (Columbia and London: University of Missouri Press, 2007), p. 181.

2. Some scholars argue that farmers' post–Civil War complaints about "greedy railroads, creditors, and industrialists" may have been misplaced or exaggerated,

but at least one skeptic of those complaints notes nonetheless that the charges against railroads "appear to have the most merit." See James I. Stewart, "The Economics of American Farm Unrest, 1865–1900," at EH.net, an online source operated by the Economic History Association: https://eh.net/encyclopedia/the -economics-of-american-farm-unrest-1865-1900/.

3. RWL to Jasper Crane, April 19, 1966, in *The Lady and the Tycoon*, p. 386. Lane refers to Wilson's campaign slogan for his second term, in 1916: "He Kept Us Out of War." It's unclear if she voted for Wilson for his first term, in 1912.

4. Karen Graves, *Girls' Schooling During the Progressive Era: From Female Scholar to Domesticated Citizen* (New York: Garland, 1998), p. 76.

5. Ibid., pp. 78–79.

6. "Poultry Raising as an Occupation for Women," *American Food Journal*, September 15, 1910, p. 27. The article may have been reprinted from *The Woman's National Daily*, a short-lived newspaper published in St. Louis, Missouri. The article appeared previously as "Profits of the Good Fat Hen," in the *Coffeyville Daily Journal* (Coffeyville, Kansas), September 12, 1910, p. 4; and in the *Parsons Daily Sun* (Parsons, Kansas), September 13, 1910, p. 4.

7. Mrs. A. J. Wilder, "The Small Farm Home," Missouri State Board of Agriculture, *43rd Annual Report of the Missouri State Board of Agriculture* (Jefferson City: Hugh Stephens Printing, 1911), p. 252.

8. Stephen Mather, as quoted in Dayton Duncan and Ken Burns, *The National Parks: America's Best Idea* (New York: Knopf, 2009), p. 174.

9. Homer E. Socolofsky, "The Evolution of a Home Grown Product, Capper Publications," *Kansas Historical Quarterly*, vol. 24, no. 2 (Summer 1958), p. 151.

10. Ibid., p. 156.

11. Ibid., see chart tracking circulation growth, p. 165.

12. Mrs. W. T. Flournoy, "Inconveniences of the Farm Home," *43rd Annual Report of the Missouri State Board*, p. 255.

13. Mrs. A. J. Wilder, "Favors the Small Farm Home," *Missouri Ruralist*, February 18, 1911, in *LIW: Farm Journalist*, pp. 13–16.

14. RWL to LIW, undated pre-1915 letter fragment, beginning "I have taken the tail from the new blue serge dress."

15. RWL to Eliza Jane Wilder Thayer and Wilder Thayer, October 3, 1914. Malone Collection. Weather records reveal that 1911 and 1913 were years of "extreme drought" in southwest Missouri; 1912 was also dry. See Claude Burton Hutchison and T. R. Douglass, *University of Missouri College of Agriculture Agricultural Experiment Station Bulletin No. 123: Experiments with Farm Crops in Southwest Missouri* (Columbia: University of Missouri College of Agriculture, January 1915), p. 169.

16. RWL to LIW, undated letter fragment, beginning "perceived a real basis."

17. RWL to LIW, undated pre-1915 letter, beginning "Muvver dear."

18. Ibid.

19. A. J. Wilder, "The Story of Rocky Ridge Farm," *Missouri Ruralist*, July 22, 1911, in *LIW: Farm Journalist*, pp. 17–19.

20. A. J. Wilder, "Substantial Gates on Farm," *Cape County Herald* (Cape Girardeau, Missouri), March 29, 1912, p. 7.

21. A. J. Wilder, "My Apple Orchard," *Missouri Ruralist*, June 1, 1912, in *LIW: Farm Journalist*, p. 21.

22. Mrs. A. J. Wilder, "Judgment Needed with Late Chicks," *Mexico Missouri Message* (Mexico, Missouri), July 24, 1913, p. 3.

23. See Anderson, *Laura Wilder of Mansfield*, p. 14. No records survive to indicate the nature of the surgery.

24. "Shorter Hours for Farm Women," *Missouri Ruralist*, June 28, 1913; *LIW: Farm Journalist*, p. 24.

25. Ibid., p. 23.

26. Editorial, "A Woman's Sphere," *Saturday Evening Post*, July 19, 1913. As quoted in Jan Cohn, *Creating America: George Horace Lorimer and the Saturday Evening Post* (Pittsburgh: University of Pittsburgh Press, 1989), pp. 78–79. Cohn suggests that the author of this editorial may have been Adelaide Neall, who would later edit Rose Wilder Lane's *Post* fiction.

27. "Shorter Hours for Farm Women," *LIW: Farm Journalist*, p. 26.

28. Caroline Ingalls to Laura Wilder, June 18, 1913. Mansfield Collection.

29. RWL to LIW, undated letter fragment, beginning "I have taken the tail from the new blue serge dress."

30. Ibid.

31. "A Homemaker of the Ozarks," in *LIW: Farm Journalist*, p. 30.

32. RWL, "My Albanian Garden," p. 2.

33. RWL to LIW, undated letter on *San Francisco Bulletin* stationery, spring of 1915, reprinted in *West from Home*, p. 3.

34. Ibid.

35. Wilder's guilt may also have been exacerbated by the fact that this was the second World's Fair her husband was missing on her account, having abandoned a planned trip with his brother Royal to New Orleans for the 1884 World's Fair in order to get back to his fiancée.

36. LIW to AJW, September 21, 1915, and September 23, 1915, in *West from Home*, pp. 103–104, 112–13.

37. LIW to AJW, August 22, 1915, and August 23, 1915, in ibid., pp. 11–14.

38. LIW to AJW, August 26, 1915, in ibid., p. 23.

39. Ibid., p. 24.

40. LIW to AJW, August 29, 1915, in ibid., pp. 32–33.

41. Ibid., p. 32.

42. LIW to AJW, September 21, 1915, in ibid., p. 97.

43. *Official Guide of the Panama-Pacific International Exposition—1915* (San Francisco: Wahlgreen, 1915), p. 29.

44. LIW to AJW, September 4, 1915, in *West from Home*, pp. 43–44. Grafly's "Pioneer Mother" was originally displayed in the Exposition at the main entrance to the Palace of Fine Arts; it was later moved to Golden Gate Park; see Sam Whiting, "Panama-Pacific International Expo: Tracking Down the Artifacts," *San Francisco Chronicle*, February 14, 2015.

45. LIW to AJW, October 6, 1915, in *West from Home*, pp. 137–38.

46. LIW to AJW, September 23, 1915, in ibid., p. 109.

47. Ibid.

48. Ibid., p. 111.

49. LIW to AJW, September 21, 1915, in ibid., p. 104.

50. Holtz, *Ghost*, p. 66.

51. See "On the Margin of Life," *Bulletin*, March 27, 1915.

52. See W. Joseph Campbell, *Yellow Journalism: Puncturing the Myths, Defining the*

Legacies (Westport, CT: Praeger, 2001), p. 20n81. The phrase appeared in an article for a trade journal: "Journalistic Kindergarten," *Fourth Estate* (May 5, 1900), p. 6.

53. See Cora Older, *William Randolph Hearst, American* (New York: Appleton-Century, 1936).

54. See Holtz, *Ghost*, p. 66. Holtz theorizes that "Ed Monroe" was Jack Black, an ex-convict befriended by Fremont Older. Black's 1926 memoir was dedicated to Older, and the author mentions working in the *Bulletin*'s circulation department and later as librarian for the *Call*: See Jack Black, *You Can't Win* (New York: Macmillan, 1926), pp. v, 368, 391.

55. "Ed Monroe, Man-Hunter" ran in the *Bulletin* from August 11, 1915, through September 15, 1915.

56. "Real Detective to Tell Story: 'Ed Monroe, Man-Hunter,'" *Bulletin*, August 5, 1915.

57. LIW to AJW, September 11, 1915, in *West from Home*, p. 81.

58. LIW to AJW, October 4, 1915, labeled "Private," in ibid., pp. 134–35.

59. LIW to AJW, September 21, 1915, in ibid., p. 104.

60. See "Behind the Headlight," chapter 2, *Bulletin*, October 11, 1915, and chapter 3, October 12, 1915. The serial appeared in twenty-four installments, from October 9 to November 5, 1915. For related material in Wilder's memoir, see PG, p. 203.

61. LIW to AJW, October 22, 1915, in *West from Home*, p. 162.

62. Ibid., p. 119.

63. LIW to AJW, September 23, 1915, in ibid., p. 113.

64. RWL to AJW, October 20, 1915, in ibid., p. 155.

65. Wilder's *Ruralist* articles about the Exposition were "Magic in Plain Foods," November 20, 1915, and "And Missouri 'Showed' Them," December 5, 1915; see *LIW: Farm Journalist*, pp. 37–47. Wilder expressed her true feelings about Chinese food to her husband in a letter dated September 7, 1915; see *West from Home*, p. 49.

66. LIW to AJW, September 13, 1915, in *West from Home*, p. 89.

67. Rose Wilder Lane, "Author's Note" published alongside "Soldiers of the Soil, Chapter 1: The Couple Who Made Chicken Raising Pay," *Bulletin*, February 24, 1916.

68. "Soldiers of the Soil: Rose Wilder Lane to Make Tour Among Farms of California," *Bulletin*, February 1916.

69. RWL, "Man Struggling with Man," Chapter LXXXVII [87] of "Soldiers of the Soil," *Bulletin*, June 2, 1916.

70. Two newspaper clippings documenting Lane's talk survived in her papers, the first from an unidentified Santa Rosa newspaper, "Farm Writer Tells Grange of Her Work" (no date), and the other, "Rose Wilder Lane Greeted by Grangers," *Bulletin*, April 28, 1916. The first of these articles claims that "Mrs. Lane said she was raised on a farm and that she was a long distance farmer, directing operations on her own farm 300 miles away."

71. See Lynn, p. 246; the advertisement, and others like it, appeared regularly in the *Mansfield Mirror*; see, for example, August 23, 1917.

72. See Wilder, "Here's the Farm Loan Plan," *Missouri Ruralist*, March 20, 1919.

73. Judging by Wilder's explanation, the couple's role in founding the association, as well as their membership, entailed their applying for a loan. The delay between

Laura Wilder's assumption of the position in August 1917 and their loan application, in March 1919, may be accounted for by legal notices regarding property owned by Laura E. Wilder, plaintiff, published in the *Mansfield Mirror*, July 11, 1918, addressing what appear to have been errors or discrepancies in the title paperwork of the land that went back to previous owners in the 1870s and 1859. While Laura was listed as the sole owner of the land in 1894, the names of both Laura and Almanzo Wilder would appear in the Federal Farm Loan paperwork.

74. Wright County, Missouri, Deeds of Trust, Book 39, p. 619. The grantor was Laura E. Wilder; the grantee, the Federal Land Bank. Date of Instrument was March 21, 1919; date of filing instrument was March 26, 1919. A perusal of loans in Wright County at the time suggests that a few of the Wilders' neighbors borrowed considerably more than they did, in amounts equal to or exceeding eight thousand dollars, while many others borrowed less, with loans as low as four hundred.

75. See Lee J. Alston, "Farm Foreclosure Moratorium Legislation: A Lesson from the Past," *American Economic Review*, vol. 74, no. 3 (June 1984), p. 448.

76. Anna Gutschke, in Dan L. White and Robert F. White, *Laura Ingalls' Friends Remember: Close Friends Recall Laura Ingalls Wilder* (Hartville, MO: Ashley-Preston, 1992), p. 33.

77. LIW to RWL, c. April 1921: See SL LIW, pp. 28–29.

78. Ibid.

79. "Athenian Club," *History and Families, Wright County, Missouri*, ed. Clyde A. Rowen (Morley, MO: Wright County Historical Society, 1993), p. 132.

80. "Mansfield Justamere Club Stages Unusual Programs," *Springfield Daily Leader*, May 8, 1922, p. 6.

81. See PG, p. 123. In Wilder's library at Rocky Ridge is a copy of *Fanny Fern*, an 1874 biography by James Parton, Willis's third husband.

82. LIW, "If We Only Understood," December 5, 1917, in *LIW: Farm Journalist*, pp. 129–30.

83. Wilder, "All in the Day's Work," February 5, 1916, in *LIW: Farm Journalist*, p. 49.

84. Ibid., p. 50.

85. LIW, "All the World Is Queer," *Missouri Ruralist*, September 20, 1916, in *LIW: Farm Journalist*, p. 84.

86. Ibid., p. 85.

87. LIW, "A Bouquet of Wild Flowers," *Missouri Ruralist*, July 20, 1917, in *LIW: Farm Journalist*, p. 118.

88. Ibid., p. 119.

89. Ibid.

90. Wilder, "Thanksgiving Time," *Missouri Ruralist*, November 20, 1916, in *LIW: Farm Journalist*, pp. 90–91. See also PG, p. 189.

91. LIW, "Let Us Be Just," *Missouri Ruralist*, September 5, 1917, in *LIW: Farm Journalist*, p. 121.

92. Ibid., p. 122.

93. Ibid.

94. *Art Smith's Story: The Autobiography of the Boy Aviator Which Appeared as a Serial in the Bulletin*, ed. by Rose Wilder Lane (San Francisco: Bulletin, 1915).

95. "My Autobiography, by S. S. McClure," article at Willa Cather Archive, editor Andrew Jewell, http://cather.unl.edu/index.mcclure.html.

96. "Charlie Chaplin's Story: The Life History of the Funniest Man in Filmland Told by Himself," in the *Bulletin*, appeared in twenty-nine installments from July 3 to August 5, 1915.

97. See David Robinson, *Chaplin: His Life and Art* (New York: McGraw-Hill, 1985), pp. 180–85. Published prior to William Holtz's biography of Lane with its identification of Guy Moyston, Robinson reproduced Moyston's name as "Mayston," an error introduced by the 1915 telegrams. According to archival records of the Associated Press, Moyston joined the news service in January 1910. Francesca Pitaro, email to the author, August 24, 2015.

98. David Robinson, "An Imposture Revived," review of the reprint of *Charlie Chaplin's Own Story*, *Times Literary Supplement*, June 27, 1986, p. 716.

99. The suppressed book was republished as *Charlie Chaplin's Own Story*, ed. Harry M. Geduld (Bloomington: Indiana University Press, 1985).

100. See Robinson, "An Imposture Revived."

101. Robinson, *Chaplin: His Life and Art*, p. 182.

102. Ibid., p. 185.

103. See Rachel Sherwood Roberts, *Art Smith: Pioneer Aviator* (Jefferson, NC: McFarland, 2003), pp. 78–79. For similarities between Lane's *Art Smith's Story* and her later work, compare her description of Smith's mother ("Mother was a little, quick woman, all nerve and energy," p. 9) to her description of her own mother's "surface quickness and sparkle" in a publicity sketch reprinted in *Reader*, p. 171.

104. Robinson, *Chaplin: His Life and Art*, p. 183. According to Robinson, Lane's letter to Chaplin and all correspondence relating to *Charlie Chaplin's Own Story* are held in the Charlie Chaplin Archive in Vevey, Switzerland: Robinson, *Charlie Chaplin: His Life and Art*, p. 637n15.

105. See Robinson, *Chaplin: His Life and Art*, pp. 183–84.

106. Ibid.

107. RWL, *Henry Ford's Own Story: How a Farmer Boy Rose to the Power That Goes with Many Millions Yet Never Lost Touch with Humanity* (Forest Hills, NY: Ellis O. Jones, 1917). "Henry Ford's Story" appeared in the *Bulletin* in thirty installments from November 2 to December 6, 1915.

108. Holtz, *Ghost*, p. 394n14.

109. RWL to Charmian London, May 22, 1917. Utah State University Special Collections and Archives. Lane had already met with London once before this letter was written.

110. RWL to Charmian London, May 31, 1917.

111. Richard W. Etulain, "The Lives of Jack London," *Western American Literature*, vol. 11, no. 2 (Summer 1976), p. 151.

112. RWL to Charmian London, September 22, 1917.

113. Charmian London to RWL, April 28, 1918.

114. See Earle Labor, *Jack London: An American Life* (New York: Farrar, Straus & Giroux, 2013), pp. 326–27. Lane claimed that Charmian London suffered a miscarriage after an ocean voyage. According to Jack London's biographer, the event took place after the couple traveled from New York to Seattle by freighter. But according to London's doctor, the miscarriage was caused not by the voyage but by injuries she had sustained during the birth of her baby girl a year earlier, a child who lived only hours due to trauma caused by a mishandled delivery.

115. RWL to Charmian London, May 2, 1918. In later letters, Lane would acknowl-

edge having had one child who died (likely the 1910 stillbirth in Utah); she would never again make the claim of losing two.

116. RWL to Charmian London, May 2, 1918.
117. Ibid.
118. Charmian London to RWL, May 6, 1918.
119. Ibid.
120. Etulain, p. 152.
121. Holtz, *Ghost*, p. 69.
122. RWL to Charmian London, September 22, 1917.
123. For example, Lane's piece, "Quarrels of the Proverbs," had the following passage:

> "A rolling stone gathers no moss," one of them—the one with the long gray beard—says sententiously.

> "A setting hen never grows fat," one of the others will retort immediately, in the meanest way.

Wilder ran it through her typewriter as follows:

> "A rolling stone gathers no moss," said a rather disagreeable voice and I caught a shadowy glimpse of a hoary old proverb with a long, gray beard.

> "But a setting hen never grows fat," retorted his companion in a sprightly tone.

Lane, "Quarrels of the Proverbs," *Bulletin*, February 12, 1915; Wilder, "When Proverbs Get Together," *Missouri Ruralist*, September 5, 1918, reprinted in *LIW: Farm Journalist*, p. 158. Parallels between the two pieces have been noted previously: see Susan Wittig Albert, "A Reader's Companion to *A Wilder Rose*," pp. 29–30, available at www.awilderrosethenovel.com.

124. See Norman P. Lewis, "Plagiarism," *Encyclopedia of Journalism*, ed. Christopher H. Sterling (Los Angeles: Sage Publications, 2009), p. 1074.
125. LIW, "Each in His Place," *Missouri Ruralist*, May 5, 1917; *LIW: Farm Journalist*, pp. 108–109.
126. See coverage of the Red Cross Auction and Dinner, *Mansfield Mirror*, vol. 10, no. 11 (May 2, 1918), p. 8; see also "Over the Top: Mansfield Oversubscribes Her Quota of Third Liberty Loan Bonds," *Mansfield Mirror*, vol. 10, no. 9 (April 18, 1918), p. 1.
127. Wilder, "Dear Farm Women," *Missouri Ruralist*, January 5, 1921, in *LIW: Farm Journalist*, p. 241.
128. LIW to RWL, April 1921, SL LIW, p. 27.
129. Wilder, "Visit 'Show You' Farm," *Missouri Ruralist*, March 20, 1918, in *LIW: Farm Journalist*, pp. 141–42.
130. Ibid., p. 142.
131. Wilder, "Make Your Dreams Come True," *Missouri Ruralist*, February 5, 1918, in *LIW: Farm Journalist*, p. 134.
132. RWL to LIW, undated (November 1924).
133. RWL to LIW, April 11, 1919, p. 1.
134. Ibid., p. 3.
135. Ibid.
136. The novel was Anderson's *Dark Laughter* (1925); see William Holtz, "Sherwood Anderson and Rose Wilder Lane: Source and Method in *Dark Laughter*," *Journal of Modern Literature*, vol. 12, no. 1 (March 1985), pp. 131–52.

137. Sinclair Lewis, *Main Street* (New York: Grosset & Dunlap, 1920), p. 1.

138. RWL, "Diverging Roads." The series appeared in *Sunset* between October 1918 and June 1919; for the tag line, see part 3, "Diverging Roads," *Sunset*, vol. 42, no. 6 (January 1918), p. 33.

139. Editors' note, "Beginning Mrs. Lane's New Serial," *Sunset*, vol. 41, no. 10 (October 1918), p. 17.

140. RWL, "Diverging Roads," *Sunset*, vol. 41, no. 11 (November 1918). The name "Paul Masters" also recalled the name of her mother's close connection to the Masters family of Walnut Grove and De Smet, while "Gilbert Kennedy" adopted another name from her mother's past, that of the Kennedy family in Walnut Grove.

141. RWL to LIW, April 11, 1919.

142. RWL, "Rose Wilder Lane *By Herself*," *Sunset*, vol. 41, no. 11 (November 1918), p. 26.

143. Neither of the two published accounts of the Wilder family includes stories of James Wilder encountering Indians: See Smith, *The Wilder Family Story*, and William T. Anderson, *The Story of the Wilders* (self-published, 1973).

144. "Jane Burr" was the pen name of Rosalind Mae Guggenheim.

145. For details about Clarence Day, see Holtz, *Ghost*, pp. 92–93. For more on Day's life, see the biographical note published by the New York Public Library Archives and Manuscripts department and "Clarence Day, 61, Author, Is Dead," *New York Times*, December 29, 1935.

146. See Holtz, *Ghost*, p. 89; Lane's "Embattled Farmers" ran in the *Bulletin* from May to July 1918.

147. See "Editors' Introduction" in "The Making of Herbert Hoover: A Biography," by RWL, in collaboration with Charles K. Field, *Sunset*, vol. 44, no. 4 (April 1920), p. 24. The six-part Hoover series ran from April to September 1920. Editor of *Sunset*, Charles Kellogg Field was a friend and classmate of Hoover's; the two were members of Stanford's first graduating class. Field's name does not appear in the byline of Lane's book, but he is credited in her preface with having "inspired" the work, collected material, and assisted "day by day in the writing and edited the whole." See RWL, *The Making of Herbert Hoover* (New York: Century, 1920), pp. v–vi.

148. RWL, *The Making of Herbert Hoover*, p. 36.

149. Ibid., p. v.

150. RWL to LIW, June 27, 1920.

151. See RWL to Berta Hader, September 7, 1920; see also Holtz, pp. 100, 103.

152. Lane wrote four articles for the *Junior Red Cross News* between 1920 and 1922 and a series of signed and unsigned reports for the *Red Cross Bulletin* between October 1920 and November 1921; see HHPL, American Red Cross file. First announced in October 1918 (based on news of an earlier Red Cross assignment that fell through), her series of travelogues for the *San Francisco Call & Post* began appearing in 1921 and would run throughout the next two years.

153. RWL Notebook 1921–36, entry for January 22, 1921. HHPL, RWL Diaries and Notes, item #12.

154. LIW to RWL, c. April 1921; see Anderson, *Selected Letters*, p. 29.

155. *Mansfield Mirror*, December 2, 1920, p. 1.

156. RWL Diary and accounts—California, Washington D.C., New York, and Europe, March–December 1920, entry for November 23, 1920. HHPL, RWL Diaries and Notes, item #2.

157. Aside from a few years of RWL's tax returns, which include sporadic notations on some of her parents' expenses, the holdings at HHPL provide little detail on the Wilders' financial situation. Miscellaneous holdings in the Mansfield Collection have not been catalogued or made available to researchers.

158. See RWL to Guy Moyston, February 9, 1924.

159. See Wilder, "Are We Too Busy?," *Missouri Ruralist*, October 5, 1917, in *LIW: Farm Journalist*, p. 125.

160. See Gene Smiley, "The U.S. Economy in the 1920s," EH.net: https://eh.net /encyclopedia/the-u-s-economy-in-the-1920s/. See also L. C. Gray, "Accumulation of Wealth by Farmers," *Annual Economic Review: Papers and Proceedings of the Thirty-fifth Annual Meeting of the American Economic Association*, vol. 35 (New Haven, CT: American Economic Association, 1923), p. 177.

161. See RWL Notebook 1921–36, entry for August 15, 1929. HHPL, RWL Diaries and Notes, item #12 (p. 78). See also, RWL to Guy Moyston, February 9, 1924.

162. RWL Notebook 1921–36, entry for January 22, 1921. HHPL, RWL Diaries and Notes, item #12 (p. 3).

8. THE ABSENT ONES

1. Joint Resolution of Congress proposing a constitutional amendment extending the right of suffrage to women, approved June 4, 1919; Ratified Amendments, 1795–1992; General Records of the United States Government; Record Group 11; National Archives.

2. LIW, "Who'll Do the Women's Work," *Missouri Ruralist,* April 5, 1919; *Farm Journalist*, p. 179.

3. LIW, "Who'll Do the Women's Work"; *Farm Journalist*, pp. 180–81.

4. LIW, "Women's Duty at the Polls," *Missouri Ruralist*, April 20, 1919; *Farm Journalist*, p. 182.

5. *Farm Journalist*, p. 182.

6. LIW, "Look for Fairies Now," *Missouri Ruralist*, April 5, 1916; *Farm Journalist*, p. 64.

7. LIW, "Folks Are 'Just Folks,'" *Missouri Ruralist*, May 5, 1916; *Farm Journalist*, p. 70.

8. *Farm Journalist*, p. 70.

9. Ibid., p. 181.

10. Alice Johns Myers, "My Roots Are Very Deep Here," *The Best of the LORE* (De Smet: Laura Ingalls Wilder Memorial Society, 2007), p. 56.

11. Ibid.

12. LIW, "The Farm Home," *Missouri Ruralist*, January 5, 1920; *Farm Journalist*, p. 210.

13. *Who's Who in Finance, Banking, and Insurance: A Biographical Dictionary of Contemporaries, 1920–1922*, ed. John William Leonard, vol. 2 (New York: Who's Who in Finance, 1922), p. 251.

14. See RWL, *Hill-Billy* (New York: Harper & Brothers, 1926). The character of "Uncle George Haswell" is clearly based on Freeman.

15. "Mansfield Justamere Club Stages Unusual Programs," *Springfield Daily Leader,* May 8, 1922, p. 6. "In the French style" presumably referred to serving a cheese course for dessert accompanied by preserves.

16. LIW, *West from Home*, p. 20.

17. LIW, "Mother, a Magic Word," *Missouri Ruralist*, September 1, 1921; *Farm Journalist*, p. 259.

18. LIW, "A Homey Chat for Mothers," *Missouri Ruralist*, September 15, 1921; *Farm Journalist*, p. 260.

19. *Farm Journalist*, p. 260.

20. LIW, "As a Farm Woman Thinks," *Missouri Ruralist*, August 1, 1923; *Farm Journalist*, p. 290.

21. "Mrs. C. P. Ingalls, Pioneer of County, Dies at 84," *De Smet News*, April 25, 1924.

22. See RWL to Guy Moyston, January 19 and February 9, 1924.

23. See Fellman, p. 26.

24. LIW, "As a Farm Woman Thinks," *Missouri Ruralist*, June 1, 1924; *Farm Journalist*, p. 309.

25. *Farm Journalist*, p. 310.

26. LIW, "As a Farm Woman Thinks," *Missouri Ruralist*, December 15, 1924; *Farm Journalist*, p. 311. Wilder wrote one last article for the *Ruralist* in 1931, but it was not a continuation of her column.

27. Moyston and Lane would work on at least one play together, *Fanutza*, a one-act adaptation of a short story by Konrad Bercovici, produced at London's Grand Guignol. See "Books and Authors," *New York Times Book Review and Magazine*, December 11, 1921, p. 20.

28. Dorothy Thompson, November 27, 1920, as quoted in the introduction to *Dorothy Thompson and Rose Wilder Lane: Forty Years of Friendship, Letters, 1921–1960*, ed. William Holtz (Columbia and London: University of Missouri Press, 1991), p. 4.

29. See ibid., pp. 4, 189.

30. See RWL, *The Peaks of Shala: Being the Record of Certain Wanderings Among the Hill-Tribes of Albania* (London: Chapman & Dodd, 1922), p. 24. See also RWL Diary, April 1921. HHPL, RWL Diaries and Notes, item #9.

31. RWL to LIW, April 27, 1921, p. 3. I have corrected a typographical error ("rigosouly") in the first sentence of the quotation.

32. RWL, *The Peaks of Shala*, p. 207.

33. Ibid., p. 223.

34. See, for example, RWL to Dorothy Thompson, February 16, 1927, in *Dorothy Thompson and Rose Wilder Lane*, pp. 42–49.

35. RWL to LIW and AJW, March 21, 1922.

36. RWL to Guy Moyston, March 15, 1922.

37. RWL to Guy Moyston, September 12, 1922.

38. See Holtz, *Ghost*, pp. 124, 128.

39. RWL Diary, October 23, 1922.

40. RWL to Fremont Older, February 23, 1927, p. 5.

41. RWL, "America's Guiding Spirit," part of "Where the World Is Topsy-Turvy," a series of World Travelogues, *San Francisco Call & Post*, August 20, 1923.

42. Ibid.

43. RWL to Fremont Older, February 23, 1927, p. 4.

44. Ibid., p. 2.

45. RWL Journal 1929, "Little Review Questionnaire," unpaginated, HHPL, p. 76.

46. RWL to Clarence Day, June 19, 1926, p. 2.

47. RWL Diary, 1923, entry for October 3, 1923. HHPL, RWL Diaries and Notes, item #17.

48. Ibid., October 9, 1923.

49. Ibid., December 31, 1923.

50. Ibid., December 20, 1923.

51. RWL to Guy Moyston, January 19 and February 9, 1924.

52. RWL to Moyston, February 9, 1924.

53. Ibid.

54. See RWL to Guy Moyston, August 6, 1924, writing about their plans to take rooms at Jane Burr's house in Croton, New York, that fall: "if we were to stay at Jane's, in that transplanted Greenwich Village, the Villagers would put the same construction on it that the Mansfield villagers put upon your being here."

55. William Anderson, interview with Helen Boylston, August 4, 1981, p. 28. Transcript, HHPL, WHC.

56. RWL to Guy Moyston, undated letter, circa June 1924, beginning "Dear Guy, It's good to hear that the cool weather followed you eastward."

57. RWL to Guy Moyston, undated letter, circa 1924, beginning "Wishing for something to write about's a useless expenditure of good wishing."

58. RWL to Guy Moyston, undated letter, circa June 1924, beginning "Dear Guy, It's good to hear that the cool weather followed you eastward."

59. RWL to Guy Moyston, undated letter, circa summer, 1924, beginning "The clipping about English folk songs."

60. RWL to Guy Moyston, undated 1924 letter, beginning "Dear Guy, The serial has gone to you and to Brandt's . . ."

61. Ibid.

62. RWL Diary, 1924, entries for January 15 and February 2, 1924. HHPL, RWL Diaries and Notes, item #21.

63. RWL to Guy Moyston, January 17, 1925, p. 2.

64. RWL to Guy Moyston, February 9, 1925.

65. Ibid.

66. William Anderson, interview with Helen Boylston, August 4, 1981, p. 3. The interview was conducted when Boylston, age 86, was suffering from memory loss. At one point in the interview, she exclaimed that "Mama Bess had red hair and the temper of an angry boa constrictor." HHPL, WHC.

67. Ibid., pp. 35, 37. HHPL, WHC.

68. RWL to LIW, undated (November 1924).

69. Ibid., p. 3.

70. Ibid.

71. See RWL to Guy Moyston, August 30, 1925; in this letter, Lane calculates her parents' annual income as one thousand dollars, half of it derived from her yearly contribution.

72. RWL to Guy Moyston, July 27, 1925.

73. RWL Notebook, 1921–36, entry for March 31, 1925. HHPL, RWL Diaries and Notes, item #12 (p. 45).

74. RWL to Moyston, July 27, 1925.

75. Ibid.

76. See RWL to Guy Moyston, August 30, 1925.

77. RWL, "A Place in the Country," *Country Gentleman*, vol. 90, no. 11 (March 14, 1925), p. 4.

78. See RWL Notebook, 1921–36, entry for May 4, 1924. HHPL, item #12 (p. 30).

79. RWL to Guy Moyston, July 27, 1925.

80. Ibid.

81. LIW, "A Few Words to the Voters," *Mansfield Mirror*, March 19, 1925. The statement ran throughout that month.

82. Wilder's late entry in the race can be seen from the Announcements column running in the *Mansfield Mirror*. Both of her opponents announced in February, with C. A. Stephens running his statement "To the Voters of Pleasant Valley Township" on February 12, 1925.

83. Ibid.

84. Ibid.

85. RWL to Guy Moyston, March 9, 1925.

86. Ibid., March 22, 1925.

87. Ibid., March 31, 1925.

88. C. A. Stephens, "To the Voters of Pleasant Valley Township," *Mansfield Mirror*, February 12, 1925, p. 4.

89. "The Election," *Mansfield Mirror*, April 2, 1925, p. 3. According to these results, Stephens received 256 votes, Hugh Williams 84, and Wilder 56. See also RWL to Guy Moyston, April 1, 1925.

90. RWL to Guy Moyston, April 1, 1925.

91. LIW to Martha Carpenter, June 22, 1925.

92. Ibid.

93. Martha Carpenter to LIW, October 9, 1925.

94. Ibid. September 2, 1925.

95. Ibid.

96. Ibid., October 9, 1925.

97. Ibid., September 2, 1925.

98. Ibid.

99. RWL to Guy Moyston, undated mid-April 1925 letter beginning "I'm awfully lonesome . . ."; RWL to Fremont Older, November 25, 1926.

100. LIW to AJW, September 18, 1925.

101. Ibid., September 21, 1925, p. 2.

102. Ibid., p. 3.

103. LIW to Meroe Andrews, December 17, 1924, in SL LIW, p. 30.

104. LIW to AJW, October 6, 1925, in SL LIW, p. 48.

105. See RWL to Guy Moyston, July 27, 1925.

106. Ibid.

107. See RWL to Guy Moyston, May 30, 1925.

108. RWL to AJW and LIW, October 7, 1926.

109. Ibid.

110. This story was told by Don Brazeal and Imogene Green in Stephen W. Hines, *"I Remember Laura"* (Nashville: Thomas Nelson, 1994), p. 228. Brazeal and Green, brother and sister, recalled that their father, Pete Brazeal, worked for the Wilders in the mid-1920s, at a time when the Wilders' Airedale dog ate at the table with them. Although they remembered the dog's name as "Ring," their description matches that of Nero.

111. See LIW to Guy Moyston, June 28, 1926.

112. Ibid.

113. The sketch was included in RWL to Guy Moyston, July 4, 1926.

114. RWL, "If I Could Live My Life Over Again," *Cosmopolitan*, March 1925, p. 33.

115. Ibid., p. 179.

116. RWL to Guy Moyston, February 25, 1925.

117. RWL, "I, Rose Wilder Lane, Am the Only Truly Happy Person I Know . . . ," *Hearst's International, combined with Cosmopolitan*, June, 1926, pp. 42–43, 140.

118. Ibid., p. 42.

119. There is no way to verify Lane's story, but chloroform figured prominently in detective fiction of the time.

120. Holtz, *Ghost*, p. 170.

121. See William Holtz, ed., *Travels with Zenobia: Paris to Albania by Model T Ford* (Columbia and London: University of Missouri Press, 1983), pp. 111–12.

122. RWL to Guy Moyston, March 5, 1927, p. 2; see also RWL to Clarence Day, March 5, [1927], and RWL to Clarence Day, undated fragment following her letter to him of March 5, beginning "Do you ever have times . . ."

123. RWL to Clarence Day, March 5, [1927].

124. Ibid., undated fragment beginning "Do you ever have times . . ."

125. RWL to Dorothy Thompson, March 11, 1927, in Holtz, *Dorothy Thompson and Rose Wilder Lane*, pp. 54–55.

126. RWL, *Hill-Billy*, unpaginated dedication.

127. Ibid., p. 19.

128. See RWL to Carl Brandt, May 26, 1928.

129. RWL, "Yarbwoman," *Harper's Magazine* (July 1927), pp. 210–21.

130. RWL, "My Albanian Garden," November 3, 1926, p. 4.

131. RWL Notes and Analysis, Books Read, 1928–33, entry c. June 1930. HHPL, RWL Diaries and Notes, item #35.

132. RWL, "My Albanian Garden," November 3, 1926, p. 4.

133. RWL Notebook 1921–36, entry for October 17, 1927. HHPL, RWL Diaries and Notes, item #12 (pp. 55, 56).

134. Ibid., p. 58.

135. RWL to Dorothy Thompson, March 11, 1927, in Holtz, *Dorothy Thompson and Rose Wilder Lane*, p. 54.

136. "My Albanian Garden," February 7, 1927; November 16, 1926.

137. RWL to Guy Moyston, March 5, 1927; RWL to Dorothy Thompson, March 11, 1927, in Holtz, *Dorothy Thompson and Rose Wilder Lane*, p. 52; and RWL to Clarence Day, July 10, 1927.

138. RWL to Fremont Older, July 14, 1927.

139. RWL to Clarence Day, July 10, 1927.

140. Ibid. Lane referred to the novel by its English title, *Jew Süss*; Feuchtwanger's novel was not anti-Semitic, but in 1939 it was transformed by Josef Goebbels into the notorious Nazi propaganda film by the same name.

141. RWL to Clarence Day, July 10, 1927.

142. RWL to Fremont Older, January 23, 1929.

143. RWL to Guy Moyston, September 6, 1927.

144. RWL to Mary Margaret McBride, April 1930. Lane alluded to her father being diagnosed with cancer "last summer," but may have mistaken the time.

145. Holtz, *Ghost*, p. 184.

146. RWL to Guy Moyston, March 6, 1928.

147. RWL Notebook 1921–36, entry for February 26, 1928. HHPL, RWL Diaries and Notes, item #12 (p. 45).

9. PIONEER GIRL

1. Donald Worster, *Dust Bowl: The Southern Plains in the 1930s* (New York: Oxford University Press, 1979; 2004), p. 93.

2. Ibid., p. 92.

3. Riney-Kehrberg, Map 1.2 on p. 13.

4. Ibid., p. 14.

5. Eugene N. White, "Lessons from the Great American Real Estate Boom and Bust of the 1920s," National Bureau of Economic Research, December 2009, p. 8.

6. See RWL, "If I Could Live My Life Over Again," p. 179.

7. See White, "Lessons from the Great American Real Estate Boom," p. 1.

8. Wright County, Deeds of Trust, vol. 48.

9. In a profile of her mother for Harper & Brothers, Lane wrote that her mother had handled "nearly a million dollars of government money"; see "My Mother, Laura Ingalls Wilder," in *Reader*, p. 170. My estimate is based on this and on information given in the minutes of the last Farm Loan Association meeting in which Wilder served as secretary, on February 25, 1928. Mansfield Collection.

10. Mansfield Farm Loan Association minutes, February 25, 1928.

11. "Famous Writer Back to Live in Ozarks," *Springfield Leader*, May 23, 1928.

12. RWL to Fremont Older, October 31, 1928.

13. The Rock House was built on what the Wilders called "the Newell forty," part of the acreage that had been added to their farm in years past. See RWL Diary, 1926–30, entry for August 1, 1928. HHPL, RWL Diaries and Notes, item #25.

14. Katherine Cole Stevenson and H. Ward Jandl, *Houses by Mail: A Guide to Houses from Sears, Roebuck and Company* (New York: John Wiley & Sons, 1986), p. 212.

15. See RWL Diary, 1926–30, October 11, 1928. HHPL, RWL Diaries and Notes, item #25.

16. Ibid., April 17, 1928.

17. See Holtz, *Ghost*, p. 244. Holtz provides no source for this information, but Lane's sporadic financial accounts, kept in a notebook, record the ongoing debt to her mother, calculated as $900 in 1924, $2,700 in 1929, and $2,800 in 1931. See RWL Notebook 1921–36, entries for multiple dates. HHPL, RWL Diaries and Notes, item #12 (pp. 30, 59, 62, 78).

18. RWL to Mr. Briggs, October 15, 1928.

19. Lane's meeting with Anderson is recorded in RWL Diary and accounts—Europe, 1921, entry for May 26, 1921. HHPL, RWL Diaries and Notes, item #7. See also RWL to Sherwood Anderson, May 11, 1929.

20. Holtz, "Sherwood Anderson and Rose Wilder Lane," pp. 131–52.

21. Sherwood Anderson, *Dark Laughter* (New York: Boni & Liveright, 1925), p. 183.

22. RWL to Sherwood Anderson, May 11, 1929, labeled by Lane, "Not Sent."

23. Ibid.

24. See Garet Garrett, "Hoover of Iowa and California," *Saturday Evening Post*, June 2, 1928, p. 18. Queried about the contretemps, Garrett told a *Post* editor that his source for the anecdote had been Hoover himself; see Bruce Ramsay, *Unsanctioned Voice: Garet Garrett, Journalist of the Old Right* (Caldwell, ID: Caxton Press, 2008), p. 181.

25. See RWL to Herbert Hoover, April 12, 1936; Herbert Hoover to RWL, April 16, 1936.

26. Unsent letter from RWL to Dorothy Thompson, July 11, 1928, in Holtz, *Dorothy Thompson and Rose Wilder Lane*, p. 84.

27. Ibid., p. 82.

28. Ibid., RWL to Dorothy Thompson, July 13, 1928, pp. 87–88.

29. RWL to Clarence Day, July 19, 1928, labeled by Lane, "Not sent."

30. Ibid., July 20, 1928.

31. Ibid., undated, beginning "Dear C.D. I know."

32. Ibid., undated letter beginning, "My dear Clarence Day, Floyd Dell is bringing out a new book this spring."

33. RWL Diary, 1926–30, entry for May 16, 1928. HHPL, RWL Diaries and Notes, item #25.

34. LIW to Aubrey Sherwood, January 15, 1934.

35. In a series of letters, Lane had recommended that Guy Moyston see a psychiatrist Boylston had once worked for, Dr. Foster Kennedy. See RWL to Moyston, March 10 and March 23, 1925.

36. The sequence of events was laid out in Mary Ingalls's obituary; see "Mary Ingalls Was a Real Pioneer," *De Smet News*, October 26, 1928, reprinted in *The Ingalls Family of De Smet* (De Smet: Laura Ingalls Wilder Memorial Society, 2001), p. 16.

37. Caroline Ingalls Swanzey to LIW, undated, beginning "Saturday morning." Mansfield Collection.

38. "Rose Wilder Lane Builds Fine Home for Her Parents," *Springfield Leader,* January 4, 1929.

39. RWL to Fremont Older, January 23, 1929.

40. RWL to Rexh Meta, October 24 and July 19, 1928.

41. Rexh Meta to RWL, January 11, 1929.

42. RWL to Rexh Meta, February 11, 1929.

43. Ibid., July 19, 1928.

44. RWL Diary, 1926–30, entry for October 21, 1929. HHPL, RWL Diaries and Notes, item #25.

45. RWL Notebook 1921–36, multiple dates. HHPL, RWL Diaries and Notes, item #12 (p. 62).

46. Ibid. (p. 78), page headed August 15, 1929.

47. See the first page of Wilder's manuscript, "Pioneer Girl," HHPL; LIW, PG, p. 1.

48. PG, p. 32.

49. Ibid., p. 8. The passage occurs on page 5 of the original manuscript.

50. See Theodore Roosevelt, "Nature Fakers," *Everybody's Magazine*, vol. 17 (September 1907), pp. 427–30. As Roosevelt noted, naturalist John Burroughs originated the charge of "yellow journalism of the woods" in "Real and Sham Natural History," *Atlantic Monthly*, vol. 91, no. 545 (March 1903), pp. 298–310. See also Sue Walsh, "Nature Faking and the Problem of the 'Real,'" *ISLE: Interdisciplinary Studies in Literature and Environment*, vol. 22, no. 1 (Winter 2015), pp. 132–53.

51. See PG, p. 83, and note 65, p. 84.

52. RWL Diary, 1926–30, entry for May 17, 1930. HHPL, RWL Diaries and Notes, item #25.

53. Ibid., July 11, 1930.

54. Ibid., July 16, July 28, and June 26, 1930.

55. Ibid., July 29, 1930.

56. For more on Lane and Wilder's adaptation of the Bender legend, see Caroline Fraser, "The Strange Case of the Bloody Benders: LIW, RWL, and Yellow Journalism,"

in *Pioneer Girl Perspectives: Exploring LIW*, ed. by Nancy Tystad Koupal (Pierre: South Dakota Historical Society Press, 2017), pp. 20–51.

57. "Governor's Proclamation," *Atchison Daily Champion* (Atchison, Kansas), May 23, 1873, p. 4. See also "Bender Knife," Kansas Historical Society, https://www.kshs.org/kansapedia/bender-knife/10106.

58. "The Benders," *Fort Scott Daily Monitor*, August 7, 1877, p. 4.

59. "Pioneer Girl," Brandt revised, p. 6a; see also, "The Benders of Kansas," Appendix B in PG, pp. 353–55.

60. RWL Diary, 1926–30, entry for August 5, 1930. HHPL, RWL Diaries and Notes, item #25.

61. Ibid., August 15, 1930.

62. Ibid., August 17, 1930.

63. Ibid., October 17, 1930.

64. Ibid., October 28, 1930.

65. RWL to LIW, November 12, 1930.

66. A page of one of Wilder's handwritten drafts of *Little House on the Prairie* was written on the back of the first page of the juvenile "Pioneer Girl" bearing the return address of the Haders. See "Little House on the Prairie," fragmentary draft, p. 77 of 217. Hader herself remembered the sequence of events differently, believing she had received the manuscript from Wilder: "One day, years after Elmer and I had been married, Laura sent me a manuscript to look at. . . . I read it and liked it because of the story's simplicity and homespun quality. I showed it to my agent and to several publishers, but everyone said the same thing—'No hope in such a story.' One day an editor friend from Alfred A. Knopf visited with me. She told me that the company was looking for some exciting materials about early days in America, written by people who had lived it." Lee Bennett Hopkins, *Books Are by People: Interviews with 104 Authors and Illustrators of Books for Young Children* (Citation Press, 1969), p. 99. Cited in William T. Anderson, "The Literary Apprenticeship of Laura Ingalls Wilder," *South Dakota History*, vol. 13, no. 4 (Winter 1983), p. 323.

67. Leonard Marcus, *Minders of Make-Believe: Idealists, Entrepreneurs, and the Shapers of Children's Literature* (New York: Houghton Mifflin, 2008), p. 104.

68. Marion Fiery to LIW, February 12, 1931.

69. RWL to LIW, February 16, 1931.

70. Ibid.

71. Ibid.

72. The typewritten passages do not exactly correspond to either the juvenile "Pioneer Girl" or to the finished book.

73. "The Indian Boy and the Big Fish," in "Little House in the Woods" manuscript, unpaginated (images 170–71).

74. Antecedents of the legend are discussed in Westerman and White, pp. 73–74.

75. LIW, LHBW in *LIW: The Little House Books*, vol. 1, p. 95.

76. See, for example, John E. Miller, *Becoming LIW: The Woman Behind the Legend* (Columbia and London: University of Missouri Press, 1998), p. 184.

77. RWL to Marion Fiery, May 27, 1931. The version of this letter that survives appears to be Lane's draft, with words crossed out, but the fact that Fiery received such a letter is documented by her reply; see Marion Fiery to RWL, September 17, 1931.

10. A RUINED COUNTRY

1. In his biography, William Anderson writes that the Wilders' dog Nero rode on the running board of the Buick, a claim repeated in John Miller's biography; see Anderson, *LIW: A Biography*, p. 197; Miller, *Becoming Laura Ingalls Wilder*, p. 192. That may have been the Wilders' practice near home, but a close reading of the travel diary suggests that the dog was riding inside the vehicle on this longer journey. See LIW, "The Road Back," *A Little House Traveler: Writings from Laura Ingalls Wilder's Journeys Across America* (New York: HarperCollins, 2006), pp. 294, 336.

2. Ibid., p. 294.

3. "The Great Plow-Up," part 1, *The Dust Bowl*, PBS documentary, directed by Ken Burns, November 18–19, 2012.

4. "Farming in the 1930s: Burning Corn for Fuel," Wessels Living History Farm, York, Nebraska: http://www.livinghistoryfarm.org/farminginthe30s/money_05 .html.

5. LIW, "The Road Back," *A Little House Traveler*, p. 301.

6. Ibid., p. 302.

7. Ibid., p. 304.

8. Ibid., p. 307.

9. For a detailed account of the fate of the Ingallses' De Smet house over the years, see "Not Such a Big House," *Laura Ingalls Wilder Lore*, vol. 4, no. 2 (Fall–Winter 1978), pp. 4–6.

10. LIW, "The Road Back," *A Little House Traveler*, p. 310.

11. Ibid., p. 311.

12. Ibid., p. 307.

13. Ibid., p. 317.

14. Ibid., p. 320.

15. Ibid., p. 325.

16. Coolidge's decision took place before the Twenty-Second Amendment, limiting an elected president to two terms in office, came into being. It would be passed by Congress in 1947 and ratified by the states in 1951.

17. LIW, "The Road Back," *A Little House Traveler*, p. 337.

18. Lord Byron's "Parting and Absence: Farewell to His Wife" reads "Fare thee well! and if forever, / Still forever, fare thee well; Even though unforgiving, never / 'Gainst thee shall my heart rebel."

19. LIW, "The Road Back," *A Little House Traveler*, p. 342.

20. Ibid., p. 340.

21. Marion Fiery to RWL, September 17, 1931.

22. RWL to Marion Fiery, undated [ca. November 1931].

23. RWL Notebook 1921–36, entry for November 10, 1931. HHPL, RWL Diaries and Notes, item #12 (p. 78).

24. Bye to RWL, October 1, 1931.

25. RWL to Bye, November 9, 1931. JOB.

26. Marion Fiery to RWL, December 4, 1931. Fiery says in the letter that the manuscript had been returned to George Bye and "sent to Harpers already." Kirkus remembered it differently but may have been at pains to conceal Fiery's role in passing the manuscript along to her, something that could have been seen as disloyal to Fiery's soon-to-be ex-employer, Knopf. Hence, Kirkus says, "It is an odd story and one that cannot all be told." Kirkus's meeting with Fiery and reading of

the manuscript probably took place on December 4, the same date as Fiery's note to Lane, a Friday; Kirkus wrote to Wilder accepting the manuscript on December 8, the following Tuesday.

27. Virginia Kirkus, "The Discovery of Laura Ingalls Wilder," *The Horn Book's Laura Ingalls Wilder,* ed. William Anderson (Boston: The Horn Book, 1987), p. 39.

28. Virginia Kirkus to LIW, December 8, 1931.

29. Ibid., December 15, 1931.

30. See Virginia Kirkus to LIW, December 18, 1931. In this letter, Kirkus explained that the Junior Literary Guild would "pay for the manufacturing costs and a flat author royalty of $350.00 for the 3500 books they use."

31. Bye to LIW, December 24, 1931.

32. See royalty statement for June 30, 1932, attached to Ida Louise Raymond to LIW, July 22, 1932. HHPL. The statement reports that 1,004 copies of LHBW had sold since the book's publication in April.

33. Anne T. Eaton, "Books for Children," *New York Times Book Review,* April 24, 1932, p. 9.

34. Marion E. Sharp, "The Bookman's Corner," *Green Bay Press-Gazette,* November 15, 1932, p. 20.

35. RWL to Clarence Day, June 26, 1928.

36. RWL Notebook 1921–36, multiple dates. HHPL, RWL Diaries and Notes, item #12 (pp. 30, 64).

37. Ibid. (p. 64). Tennyson's poem "The Lotus-Eaters" (1832) would appear in Chapter 12 of LTOP.

38. Both the *Bulletin* serial and the notes for "A Son of the Soil" are contained in Lane's papers at the HHPL. See also William T. Anderson, "Laura Ingalls Wilder and Rose Wilder Lane: The Continuing Collaboration," *South Dakota History,* vol. 16, no. 2 (Summer 1986), pp. 121–22.

39. RWL, "A Son of the Soil," Outline and Notes (Story of Almanzo Wilder). HHPL.

40. RWL Diary, 1926–30, entry for October 28, 1930. HHPL, RWL Diaries and Notes, item #25.

41. In LHBW, Wilder most often refers to her parents as "Ma" and "Pa," but the name "Charles" occurs nine times, "Caroline," five.

42. Helen Boylston had published a memoir, *Sister: War Diary of a Nurse,* in 1927; her popular fictional series for children, *Sue Barton: Student Nurse,* began appearing in 1936. Reminiscent of Wilder's work, the first books in the series were based on Boylston's experience and employed the names of real people for several characters. An author's note in one edition claimed that "every single incident . . . actually happened."

43. RWL to Bye, May 8, 1932.

44. Lane's attitude toward what she invariably called "juveniles" can be seen in apologetic and belittling references she made to her agent and others; see, for example, her letter to Bye on October 5, 1931, regarding Wilder's Knopf contract: "I have known nothing about juvenile publications for thirty years or so, but imagine they don't pay enough to bother with. . . . It's really awfully decent of you to bother with this small fry . . . I don't expect you really to bother."

45. See RWL to Jane Burr, January 7, 1932. Smith College Special Collections.

46. Ibid.

47. References to this loan appear in several diary entries: See RWL Notebook 1921–36, entry for 1928. HHPL, RWL Diaries and Notes, item #12 (p. 59). It reads in

part, "I O Craig $2[0]60." The notation of the amount is unclear, reading either $2060 or $2660. See also RWL Diary, 1931–35, entry for April 28, 1932. HHPL, RWL Diaries and Notes, item #37. That entry records "mail notification note due at bank, $1,500." There appears to be no record of such a loan in the Abstract and Index volumes kept in the Wright County Courthouse in Hartville, but Craig may have arranged a personal loan or promissory note.

48. RWL Diary, 1931–35, entry for December 9, 1931. HHPL, RWL Diaries and Notes, item #37.

49. Ibid., December 10, 1931.

50. Ibid., January 15, 1932. The letter from Percival E. Jackson, addressed to creditors of Palmer & Co., dated January 21, 1932, appears in the LHOP manuscript; see Wilder's "fragmentary draft," microfilm image 22 or the reverse of the page Wilder numbered as p. 4.

51. RWL Diary, 1931–35, entries for January 15 and 28, 1932. HHPL, RWL Diaries and Notes, item #37.

52. Ibid., January 22, 1932.

53. See ibid., February 5 and 6, 1932.

54. Ibid., April 11, 1932.

55. John Case to LIW, June 8, 1932. Letter appears in "fragmentary draft" of LHOP, microfilm image 98.

56. RWL Journal, May 1932–January 1933, entry for June 5, 1932. HHPL, RWL Diaries and Notes, item #45.

57. Ibid., June 6, 1932.

58. Ibid.

59. See Graeme Lorimer to Bye, April 15, 1932, and RWL Journal, August 17, 1932.

60. See Anderson, "LIW and RWL: The Continuing Collaboration," p. 104. This chorus from "The Evergreen Shore," with lyrics by William Hunter, an Irish immigrant who became a minister in the United States (1811–1877), differs from many published versions, whose last line reads, "We will weather the blast and will land at last, / Safe on the evergreen shore."

61. RWL Notebook, 1921–36, undated entry. HHPL, RWL Diaries and Notes, item #12 (p. 32).

62. RWL Journal, May 1932–January 1933, entry for June 8, 1932. HHPL, RWL Diaries and Notes, item #45.

63. Ibid., August 17, 1932.

64. Ibid.

65. Lane's "Let the Hurricane Roar" appeared in the Saturday Evening Post, October 22 and 29, 1932; "Old Maid" appeared in the Post on July 23, 1932.

66. See RWL Diary, 1931–35, entry for September 22, 1932. HHPL, RWL Diaries and Notes, item #37.

67. See Richard S. Kirkendall, A History of Missouri, vol. 5 (Columbia and London: University of Missouri Press, 1986), p. 131.

68. RWL, "Silk Dress," Ladies' Home Journal, August 1937.

69. RWL to AJW, October 7, 1932.

70. Lane's postcards to her parents from Malone are dated October 7, 1932, and include views of Upper Main Street, the Hotel Franklin, the Franklin Academy, and the Northern New York Deaf-Mute Institute. HHPL, LIW Files, Correspondence, 1908–40.

71. RWL, Itinerary and Expenses, Canada and New York Trip, September 1932, unpaginated. HHPL, RWL Notes and Diaries, item #46.

72. RWL Journal, May 1932–January 1933, June 2, 1932. HHPL, RWL Diaries and Notes, item #45. In 1932, "National Industries" appears on published lists of "Investment Trusts"; see, for example, *Indianapolis News*, January 20, 1932, p. 20.

73. RWL Journal, May 1932–January 1933, June 2, 1932. HHPL, RWL Diaries and Notes, item #45.

74. Vincent H. Gaddis, *Herbert Hoover, Unemployment, and the Public Sphere: A Conceptual History: 1919–1933* (Lanham, MD: University Press of America, 2005), p. 112.

75. See Richard Norton Smith and Timothy Walch, "The Ordeal of Herbert Hoover," part 2 *Prologue*, vol. 36, no. 2 (Summer 2004): https://www.archives.gov/publications/prologue/2004/summer/hoover-2.html.

76. RWL Journal, May 1932–January 1933, entry for June 2, 1932. HHPL, RWL Diaries and Notes, item #45.

77. Ibid.

78. "From Hero to Scapegoat," permanent exhibit at HHPL.

79. See Miller, *Becoming LIW*, p. 197.

80. RWL Journal, 1933–34, January 25, 1933. HHPL, RWL Diaries and Notes, item #47, pp. 11–12.

81. *Publishers' Weekly*, February 11, 1933, vol. 123, no. 6, p. 184.

82. See Anderson, "LIW and RWL: The Continuing Collaboration," p. 112.

83. RWL, "The Blue Bead: A Story," *Harper's Monthly Magazine*, June 1925, p. 35.

84. RWL to Bye, October 14, 1934.

85. Ann Romines, *Constructing the Little House: Gender, Culture, and Laura Ingalls Wilder* (Amherst: University of Massachusetts Press, 1997), p. 49.

86. Holtz, *Ghost*, p. 239. Throughout his biography, Holtz utilizes Lane's nickname for her mother, "Mama Bess."

87. See Anderson, "The Literary Apprenticeship of LIW," pp. 109–10.

88. LIW to Aubrey Sherwood, January 15, 1934.

89. LIW to Clara J. Webber, February 11, 1952.

90. See the letter from Irene Lichty to Holtz, December 27, 1982, HHPL. See also Alfred, Lord Tennyson, "Vivien's Song," in "Merlin and Vivien," *Idylls of the King*.

91. RWL, Diary, 1931–35, entry for February 13, 1933. HHPL, RWL Diaries and Notes, item #37.

92. Ibid., March 9, 1933.

93. Ibid., April 28, 1933.

94. Ibid., May 4, 1933.

95. Ibid., March 26, 27, 31, and April 2, 1933.

96. Wright County, Missouri, Deeds of Trust, Book 39, p. 619. The grantor was Laura E. Wilder; the grantee, the Federal Land Bank; the date of instrument, March 21, 1919. The loan was "fully paid and discharged . . . this 19 day of May 1933."

97. RWL Diary, 1931–35, entry for January 11, 1933: "Mother sends $811.65 to F. F. L. Bank, clearing this farm & leaving her about $50." HHPL, RWL Diaries and Notes, item #37.

98. Kirkendall, p. 133.

99. President Franklin Delano Roosevelt, radio address, March 12, 1933.

100. RWL Diary, 1931–35, entry for March 12, 1933. HHPL, RWL Diaries and Notes, item #37.

101. Ibid., March 28 and 31, 1933.

102. Ibid., April 9, 1933.

103. RWL Journal, 1933–34, entry for April 10, 1933, p. 63. HHPL, RWL Diaries and Notes, item #47, pp. 63–64.

104. Ibid., p. 67.

105. "Long Skirts" was originally published in shorter form in *Ladies' Home Journal* in April 1933, vol. 50, no. 4; that initial version does not contain these lines. See "Long Skirts," *Old Home Town*, p. 139.

106. RWL Diary, 1931–35, memoranda page opposite April 1, 1933. HHPL, RWL Diaries and Notes, item #37.

107. For more on the composition of *Farmer Boy*, see Anderson, "LIW and RWL: The Continuing Collaboration," pp. 89–141.

108. LIW, FB, in *LIW: The Little House Books*, p. 125; see also p. 624, no.101.16. Wilder's handwritten manuscript contains relatively little dialogue and does not reproduce the "invariant be" speech pattern. A typescript survives with a few corrections in Lane's hand, but the text does not exactly correspond to that of the published book.

109. RWL quotes from Raymond's letter in her own to George Bye, March 20, 1933.

110. Judging by Wilder's and Lane's contracts, 10 percent for the first several thousand copies was standard at the time, rising to 15 percent thereafter. See Agreement regarding "Little House in the Woods," signed by Laura Ingalls Wilder and Harper & Brothers, December 8, 1931; and Agreement regarding "Farmer Boy," signed by Laura Ingalls Wilder and Harper & Brothers, May 9, 1933. JOB.

111. See, for example, LIW to Bye, July 3, 1941; Bye to LIW, July 25, 1941.

112. LIW, FB, in *LIW: The Little House Books*, vol. 1, p. 183.

113. Wilder, FB manuscript, microfilm image 115. Since colonial times, the idiom referred to the practice of taunting England (the British lion) while inciting American fervor (the eagle). Around the turn of the century, it became associated with Independence Day celebrations and fireworks displays: See "The Glorious Fourth," in the *Medical Times*, vol. 37, July 1909, p. 211.

114. "Comparison of Dust Bowl Regional Precipitation in 1930s vs. 2000s," National Weather Service Forecast Office, Amarillo, TX [online], Figure 2.

115. This was Cimarron County, Oklahoma. See Worster, *Dust Bowl*, p. 106.

116. Donald Worster uses this as the epigraph to his section on Cimarron County, Oklahoma, in *Dust Bowl*, p. 99.

117. LIW to Ida Louise Raymond, March 16, 1934, in *Selected Letters*, pp. 73–74.

118. The roughest extant draft of the LHOP manuscript, perhaps the first or among the first created by Wilder, was designated as the "fragmentary draft" by the University of Missouri Western Historical Manuscript Collection of the State Historical Society of Missouri, the organization that preserved the manuscripts and created the microfilm copies available to researchers. Wilder numbered earlier pages of this draft but dropped the practice at page 39; for ease of reference, I am supplying the number of the microfilm image.

119. The fair copy draft, which begins on page 3 and contains some missing pages, has been designated as the "Little House on the Prairie manuscript" by SHSM.

For purposes of this discussion, I refer to it as the second draft. This draft has been paginated by LIW; see her p. 148 or microfilm image 168. The chapter heading also appears in the third, or "partial draft," image 36.

120. Holtz, *Ghost*, p. 253.
121. LIW, LHOP, "fragmentary draft," microfilm 42.
122. Ibid., microfilm image 141.
123. Ibid.
124. Ibid., microfilm image 144.
125. Ibid. In the published book, the folk rhyme would be transposed to Chapter 10, "A Roof and a Floor," LHOP in *LIW: The Little House Books*, vol. 1, p. 320.
126. Wilder, "fragmentary draft," microfilm image 190.
127. Ibid., image 196.
128. Ibid., image 199.
129. This passage occurs in the second draft (the 198-page "manuscript"), paginated in Wilder's hand, p. 162.
130. LIW travel diary, July 23, 1894; see *On the Way Home*, p. 24.
131. The slur had often been attributed to General Philip Sheridan, but folklore scholar Wolfgang Mieder has demonstrated that it was established in American usage in the aftermath of the Dakota War of 1862, first appearing in print in the *Congressional Globe*, a forerunner of the *Congressional Record*, in a transcript of remarks made in the House of Representatives by James Michael Cavanaugh, congressman from Montana. On May 28, 1868, Cavanaugh said, "I will say that I like an Indian better dead than living. I have never in my life seen a good Indian (and I have seen thousands) except when I have seen a dead Indian. . . . I believe in the policy that exterminates the Indians, drives them outside the boundaries of civilization, because you cannot civilize them." He justified extermination policy by citing inflammatory anecdotes of atrocities attributed to the Dakota during the War, saying, "In Minnesota the almost living babe has been torn from its mother's womb; and I have seen the child, with its young heart palpitating, nailed to the window-sill. I have seen women who were scalped, disfigured, outraged." See Mieder, "'The Only Good Indian Is a Dead Indian': History and Meaning of a Proverbial Stereotype," *Journal of American Folklore*, vol. 106, no. 419 (Winter 1993), p. 42.
132. R. B. Selvidge, Muskogee, OK, to LIW, July 5, 1933. Selvidge was the son of William H. Selvidge (1842–1920), described in his obituary as a "pioneer in the Indian country"; later in life he served as a deputy U.S. marshal. It remains unclear how Wilder located Selvidge; her original query does not survive.
133. See Penny T. Linsenmayer, "Kansas Settlers on the Osage Diminished Reserve: A Study of Laura Ingalls Wilder's *Little House on the Prairie*," *Kansas History*, vol. 24, no. 3 (Autumn 2001), p. 184. Another independent researcher has theorized that Wilder may have confused the name Soldat du Chêne with the term "soldat du chien," or "dog soldier," although this seems unlikely given that "dog soldier" refers to one of the military societies of the Cheyenne. See Stephanie A. Vavra, "Who Really Saved Laura Ingalls: Soldat du Chêne or a Soldat du Chien?" (Morrison, IL: Quill Works, 2001), p. 5.
134. LIW, LHOP, "fragmentary draft," microfilm image 212.
135. Ibid. Lines crossing out the passage are in pencil, Wilder's preference.
136. LIW, "fragmentary draft," microfilm images 203–204.
137. Ibid., image 205.

138. LIW, LHOP, second draft manuscript (198-p. version), microfilm images 138–39.

139. LIW, LHOP, "fragmentary draft," microfilm images 63–65. At the bottom of image 65, Wilder aims remarks to her daughter about the phase of the moon.

140. RWL Journal, 1933–34, entry for April 29, 1933. HHPL, RWL Diaries and Notes, item #47, p. 70.

141. RWL American Novel Outline. HHPL, RWL Diaries and Notes, item #51 (pp. 11, 13).

142. See RWL Journal, 1933–34, entry for April 29, 1933. HHPL, RWL Diaries and Notes, item #47, p. 70.

143. Ibid., May 23, 1933, p. 79.

144. Ibid., June 23, 1933, p. 102.

145. Ibid., September 25, 1933, p. 115.

146. RWL to Virginia Brastow, undated, labeled in Lane's hand "late 1935 or early 1936, Rocky Ridge Farm," p. 1.

147. Ibid., p. 2.

148. Ibid., p. 10.

149. RWL Journal, 1933–34, entries for March 1 and April 8, 1934. HHPL, RWL Diaries and Notes, item #47, pp. 135, 145.

150. RWL to Virginia Brastow, undated, p. 6.

151. Roscoe Jones, quoted in "I Remember Laura," p. 145; ibid., Don Brazeal and Imogene Green, p. 229.

152. Ibid., Iola Jones, p. 137.

153. RWL to Mary Margaret McBride, undated (April 1930), HHPL.

154. Ibid.

155. Kathy Short, interview with the author, October 28, 2015.

156. Ibid.

157. RWL Journal, 1933–34, entry for March 1, 1934. HHPL, RWL Diaries and Notes, item #47, p. 136.

158. Willa Sibert Cather, *My Ántonia* (Boston and New York: Houghton Mifflin, 1918). For Negro minstrels, see p. 180; "weevily wheat," p. 181; "little town on the prairie," p. 197; "sliding down straw-stacks," p. 256.

159. See *My Ántonia*, p. 7; LHOP in *LIW: The Little House Books*, vol. 1, p. 336.

160. RWL to Carl Brandt, May 26, 1928.

161. RWL Diary, 1931–35, entry for May 31, 1934. HHPL, RWL Diaries and Notes, item #37.

162. Ibid., June 25, 1934.

163. LHOP Typescript—Final (Carbon), p. 164, HHPL. Despite the typescript's designation as "final," it is apparent that minor editorial corrections were made subsequently, perhaps by Ida Louise Raymond at Harper & Brothers. For example, the "final" contained two chapters designated as chapter 4. Harper & Brothers retains some correspondence with Wilder, but whatever manuscripts of hers they once possessed are rumored to have been lost. In response to the author's queries, HarperCollins has repeatedly asserted that "we typically do not allow outsiders access to our archives." See Tzofit Goldfarb, Director, Information Center/Archives, HarperCollins, email to author, May 23 and June 10, 2011.

164. Ida Louise Raymond to LIW, July 13, 1934.

165. Ibid., August 27, 1934.

166. RWL Diary, 1931–35, entry for July 11, 1934. HHPL, RWL Diaries and Notes, item #37.

167. Ibid., July 28, 1934.

168. The scholar William T. Anderson, who examined the manuscript decades later, pointed to clues that it had been written in the early 1930s; see Anderson, "The Literary Apprenticeship of LIW," pp. 285–331. Most significantly, Wilder wrote one page on the back of an unfinished letter addressed to the Federal Land Bank in St. Louis, requesting an updated statement. The letter, dated January 20, 1933, probably concerned the Wilders' Federal Farm loan, paid off a few months later.

169. LIW, "The First Three Years," outline on first page of tablet.

170. Ibid., unpaginated (p. 3, HHPL numbering).

171. Ibid. (p. 7).

172. Ibid. The rich getting their ice in the summer, the poor in winter originated with Bat Masterson in 1921: See LIW: The Little House Books, vol. 2 (Library of America), p. 737, note 737.27–29.

173. Ibid. (p. 128).

174. Ibid. (p. 39).

175. See RWL, "Long Skirts," Ladies' Home Journal, vol. 50, no. 4 (April 1933).

176. RWL, "Long Skirts," in Old Home Town, p. 139. The version of the story that appears in the book was heavily revised; the magazine version does not include this phrase.

177. The three stories were "Vengeance," Liberty, February 17, 1934; "Object Matrimony," Saturday Evening Post, September 1, 1934; and "Pie Supper," American Magazine, October 1934.

178. RWL to Virginia Brastow, December 16, 1933.

179. See Stephen Cox, Introduction to the Transaction Edition, The God of the Machine, by Isabel Paterson (New Brunswick: Transaction Publishers, 1993), p. x.

180. Stephen Cox, The Woman and the Dynamo: Isabel Paterson and the Idea of America (New Brunswick and London: Transaction Publishers, 2004), p. 18.

181. Ibid., p. 216.

182. Cox, Introduction, The God of the Machine, p. xix. Cox cites Barbara Branden, The Passion of Ayn Rand (Garden City, NY: Doubleday, 1986), p. 133.

183. Lane mentions receiving a gift subscription to the Herald Tribune Books section in RWL to Virginia Brastow, February 13, 1935; she also thanks Brastow for sending her copies of the review.

184. Isabel M. Paterson, "Turns with a Bookworm," New York Herald Tribune Books, December 23, 1934, p. 7. Except for the first, ellipses appear as in the original column; the letter itself may not survive. Paterson's original reference to the Benders, which inspired Lane's retort, appeared in "Turns with a Bookworm," New York Herald Tribune Books, September 30, 1934, p. 26. HHPL, Isabel M. Paterson Papers, 1857–1998, "Turns with a Bookworm," September 1932–August 1939.

185. Paterson, "Turns with a Bookworm," December 23, 1934. Ellipsis mine.

11. DUSTY OLD DUST

1. "NASA Study Finds 1934 Had Worst Drought of Last Thousand Years," NASA press release, October 14, 2014; Benjamin I. Cook, Richard Seager, and Jason E. Smerdon, "The Worst North American Drought Year of the Last Millennium: 1934," *Geophysical Research Letters*, 41 (2014), pp. 7298–7305.

2. National Oceanic and Atmospheric Administration, Palmer Drought Severity Index map, August 1934.

3. Worster, *Dust Bowl*, p. 16.

4. "Reaping the Whirlwind," part 2, *The Dust Bowl*, PBS documentary, directed by Ken Burns, November 18–19, 2012.

5. Christopher Lowe, "Farming in the Great Depression," *Chariton Collector*, Spring 1986.

6. "The Great Plow-Up," part 1, *The Dust Bowl*, PBS documentary, directed by Ken Burns, November 18–19, 2012.

7. "Interview: Donald Worster, On Dust Bowl Roots," American Experience website: http://amextbg2.wgbhdigital.org/wgbh/americanexperience/features/interview /dustbowl-worster//?flavour=mobile.

8. Worster, *Dust Bowl*, p. 28.

9. Ibid., p. 17.

10. "Reaping the Whirlwind," part 2, *The Dust Bowl*, PBS documentary.

11. Zeynep K. Hansen and Gary D. Libecap, "Small Farms, Externalities, and the Dust Bowl of the 1930s," *Journal of Political Economy*, vol. 112, no. 3 (June 2004), p. 667.

12. Worster, *Dust Bowl*, p. 4.

13. Ibid., p. 29.

14. Vance Johnson, *Heaven's Tableland: The Dust Bowl Story* (New York: Da Capo Press, 1974), pp. 194–95.

15. RWL to Bye, March 6, 1935.

16. LIW, *Little House on the Prairie* in *LIW: The Little House Books*, vol. 1, p. 316; Hansen and Libecap, "Small Farms, Externalities, and the Dust Bowl of the 1930s," p. 668.

17. For an extended discussion of farmers' reaction to reduced productivity, see Worster, *Dust Bowl*, pp. 182–97.

18. See Timothy Egan, *The Worst Hard Time: The Untold Story of Those Who Survived the Great American Dust Bowl* (New York: Houghton Mifflin, 2005), p. 163.

19. The pigs slaughtered due to this policy appear in the paragraph that gives Steinbeck's novel its title; see John Steinbeck, *The Grapes of Wrath* (New York: Penguin, 1976), p. 385.

20. See Michael Hiltzik, *The New Deal: A Modern History* (New York: Free Press, 2011), pp. 108–10.

21. Henry A. Wallace, "Pigs and Pig Iron," delivered November 12, 1935. From Henry A. Wallace, *Democracy Reborn* (New York: Reynal & Hitchcock, 1944), ed. Russell Lord, p. 103.

22. Ibid.

23. Franklin Delano Roosevelt, *Radio Address to the Young Democratic Clubs of America*, August 24, 1935. Reprinted in *The Public Papers and Addresses of Franklin D. Roosevelt*, vol. 4, 1935 (New York: Random House, 1938), p. 336.

24. See "Resettlement Administration" at the Living New Deal: https://livingnewdeal.org/glossary/resettlement-administration-ra-1935/.

25. LIW to RWL, undated (in a group of letters, probably 1935 or 1936).

26. LIW, PC.

27. LIW to RWL, undated.

28. RWL Diary, 1931–35, entry for February 26, 1935. HHPL, RWL Diaries and Notes, item #37.

29. Kathy Short, interview with the author, October 28, 2015.

30. Garet Garrett, "Plowing Up Freedom," *Saturday Evening Post,* vol. 208, no. 20 (November 16, 1935), p. 69.

31. Ramsey, *Unsanctioned Voice,* pp. 139–42.

32. "Writer for Saturday Evening Post Here," *Mansfield Mirror,* August 1, 1935.

33. RWL to Virginia Brastow, July 5, 1935.

34. See RWL to Mark Sullivan, October 11, 1938.

35. Perhaps in homage to the exaggeration of Mark Twain's early travelogues, Lane included an introductory note in *The Peaks of Shala* hinting at liberties she may have taken, saying, "I would not have this book considered too seriously." See RWL, *The Peaks of Shala* (New York: Harper & Brothers, 1923), frontispiece. In another note, opposite the title page, she wrote that photographer Annette Marquis had "accompanied the author on her trip through Albania"; in fact, Marquis had retraced Lane's initial journey, unaccompanied by her, a year later. See Holtz, *Ghost,* pp. 121–23.

36. "Ab" and "Minty," for example, appear in RWL, "The Name Is Mizzoury," version 2, p. 342; "Ab Whitty" is a character in *Old Home Town*'s "Country Jake" and "Minty Bates" appears in "Long Skirts."

37. RWL to Virginia Brastow, July 5, 1935.

38. RWL's letter to Brastow of June 16, 1935, for example, is eleven single-spaced pages. As a postscript she writes, "How about writing me as much as I write you?!?"

39. See Arthur Krock, "Hoover Excoriates New Deal as Fascism, Demanding a 'Holy Crusade for Freedom'; Currency Plank Pledges Stabilization," *New York Times,* June 11, 1936.

40. See, for example, "Political Observations," *Republican Tribune* (Union, Missouri), March 9, 1934, p. 6.

41. See "The Modern 'Liberal,'" cartoon, *Mansfield Mirror,* November 4, 1937, p. 6.

42. RWL to Virginia Brastow, July 5, 1935.

43. Ibid.

44. RWL to Virginia Brastow, June 16, 1935.

45. Ibid., July 5, 1935.

46. See Garrett, "Plowing Up Freedom," p. 69. William Holtz, together with his copy of Garrett's article, preserved a letter from Harold Breimyer, a professor emeritus at the University of Missouri–Columbia's College of Agriculture, consulted for his expertise on the New Deal. Breimyer also categorized Lane's later recollection of the trip, sent to Jasper Crane, as "what we used to call yellow journalism." See RWL to Jasper Crane, January 30, 1957, in *The Lady and the Tycoon,* pp. 168–70; Harold F. Breimyer to William Holtz, April 24, 1991, in HHPL, WHC.

47. RWL to Virginia Brastow, March 8, 1936.

48. See RWL to Jasper Crane, January 30, 1957, in *The Lady and the Tycoon*, pp. 169–170; Lane tells Crane that *Post* editor George Horace Lorimer refused to print the story of a "Communist Terror in Illinois" because the manager of the resettlement project was a Communist. She was probably referring to Rexford Tugwell, one of FDR's "Brain Trust," an economist at Columbia University, and head of the short-lived Resettlement Administration; he was commonly denounced as a Communist.

49. RWL to Virginia Brastow, March 8, 1936.

50. Ibid., April 16, 1936.

51. Norma Lee Browning, "Rose and Laura," draft of a memoir written for Waldenbooks Kids Club Magazine (De Smet Collection); see also Browning to William Holtz, undated postscript beginning "PS—later—Bill, I've decided to send you . . ." HHPL.

52. RWL to Virginia Brastow, April 16, 1935.

53. Ibid., March 8, 1936.

54. See Wilder's holograph manuscript version of PC, chapters 6 and 7, "Grasshoppers" and "Pa Goes Away."

55. See RWL to LIW, undated 1936 letter beginning "Look Mama Bess"; Laura Ingalls Wilder Papers, 1894–1943, Correspondence 1933–1936, microfilm image 20, SHSM.

56. See unpaginated insertion in Wilder's handwriting, PC, Draft A typescript, following page 49.

57. RWL to LIW, June 13, 1936.

58. LIW to RWL, undated letter ca. 1936, beginning "School began in the spring"; LIW Papers, 1894–1943, Correspondence 1933–1936, microfilm image 26, SHSM. Wilder's resistance is expressed earlier in the same letter: "I do think the picture of two little girls doing what they did while Ma was sick and the fact that it was nothing for a Dr to be 40 miles away and no auto, would make a great impression on children who are so carefully doctored in schools and all. I think if you can better leave it."

59. Ibid.

60. LIW to RWL, undated letter beginning "Potatoes, carrots, onions, etc.," and LIW to RWL, undated letter beginning "School began in the spring"; Correspondence 1933–1936, microfilm images 23, 31, SHSM.

61. Compare, for example, the chapter titled "The Glittering Cloud" in the "Draft B typescript" to the published book: clearly additions, deletions, and editorial changes have been made in the interim. Note as well that Wilder's original holograph manuscript is tidy, with few revisions or deletions; this may indicate that it was not her first draft.

62. Fragmentary draft of LHOP, p. 124.

63. See LIW's holograph manuscript, p. 136 (her page number).

64. LIW to RWL, undated letter beginning "School began in the spring"; Correspondence 1933–1936, microfilm image 28, SHSM.

65. See, for example, LIW, "Speech at the Book Fair, Detroit, Michigan, October 16, 1937," *LIW: The Little House Books*, vol. 1, p. 588.

66. LIW to RWL, undated, probably June 1936, Correspondence 1933–1936, microfilm images 33–34, SHSM.

67. See RWL Diary, 1936–38, entry for January 15, 1936. HHPL, RWL Diaries and Notes, item #59.

68. Wilder's attitude toward the Murrays can be gleaned in a couple of letters; see LIW to RWL, March 12, 1937, and June 3, 1939, to which she added a postscript pleading with her daughter, should something happen to her, never to let the Murrays, "either one or both, back on the place. Do whatever else you please with it but not that."

69. LIW to RWL, June 25, 1936; Correspondence 1933–1936, microfilm images 38–39.

70. Ibid., images 41, 43.

71. RWL Journal, 1933–34, entry for August 10, 1940. HHPL, RWL Diaries and Notes, item #47, p. 151.

72. "'Licencing' of Dogs Planned: City Council Discusses High Costs of Riddance of Strays," *Mansfield Mirror*, April 15, 1937, p. 1.

73. RWL Diary, 1931–35, entries for July 15 and 16, 1936. HHPL, RWL Diaries and Notes, item #37.

74. LIW to RWL, July 2, 1936.

75. See, for example, LIW to RWL, July 2, 1936, and undated 1937 letter beginning "Tuesday Morning."

76. RWL Diary, 1931–35, entries for April 10 and 19, 1936. HHPL, RWL Diaries and Notes, item #37.

77. RWL Diary, 1942–43, entry for April 10, 1942. HHPL, RWL Diaries and Notes, item #68. Lane note, "Wrote in reply to fathers offer to pay R.R. fare that I do not want to go to Mansfield."

78. RWL, "Credo," *Saturday Evening Post*, vol. 280, no. 36 (March 7, 1936), p. 31.

79. Ibid., p. 5.

80. RWL to Berta and Elmer Hader, undated; Holtz believes it was 1919 based on internal evidence. See Holtz, *Ghost*, p. 90n15.

81. Ibid., p. 261.

82. RWL, "Credo," p. 30.

83. See Jan Cohn, *Creating America: George Horace Lorimer and* The Saturday Evening Post (Pittsburgh: University of Pittsburgh Press, 1989), pp. 195–96.

84. Ibid., p. 169.

85. See RWL, "Credo: Condensed from the Saturday Evening Post," *Reader's Digest*, vol. 28, no. 169 (May 1936), pp. 1–6; Herbert Hoover to RWL, April 16, 1936.

86. "Give Me Liberty" was first printed and distributed by Longmans, Green, then by the Patriot's Bookshop and Liberty Library.

87. See, for example, LIW to Hon. Clarence E. Kilburn, March 9, 1945. Kilburn was a Republican member of the U.S. House of Representatives, born in Malone, NY.

88. Kirkendall, p. 165.

89. William V. Turner, interview with the author, July 23, 2015.

90. "New 23rd Psalm," *Mansfield Mirror,* October 1, 1936. A typographical error in the fifth line of the poem has been corrected.

91. Franklin Delano Roosevelt, Inaugural Address, January 20, 1937.

92. José A. Tapia Granados and Ana V. Diez Roux, "Life and Death During the Great Depression," *Proceedings of the National Academy of Sciences*, vol. 106, no. 41 (2009), pp. 17290–95.

93. Dewey Short, U.S. Congress, January 23, 1935; admiring citations of this example of Short's oratory are many, including "Long and Short," *Los Angeles Times*, June 17, 1935, p. 28.

94. AJW to RWL, May 12, 1937.

95. The Wilders eventually rented out the Rock House, but it remained empty for a time; see Miller, *Becoming LIW*, p. 213.

96. LIW to RWL, March 12, 1937; see also Wilder's reference to taxes the following year, in LIW to RWL, February 15, 1938. At that time, "Head of Household" appeared under "Personal Exemption" on both federal and state tax returns. Those claiming the credit for care of elderly parents were required to live in the same household as those they were supporting. On her 1936 federal return, despite having spent most of the year living off the farm, Lane claimed a personal exemption as head of family of $2,500, and credit for dependents of $1,400, listing four, the Turner boys and "Mother and Father, who are incapable of self-support." Of herself, she noted, "Provides a home for aged parents who are totally dependent." At the end of 1936, Wilder would negotiate the contract for PC, receiving an advance of $500 in early 1937. See "Explanation of Personal Exemption and Credit for Dependents" in "Schedules for 1936 Return of Rose Wilder Lane," attached to Individual Income Tax Return, Calendar Year 1936, for Rose Wilder Lane. HHPL.

97. LIW to RWL, March 12, 1937.

98. Ibid.

99. Ibid.

100. See LIW to RWL, undated fragment, 1937, numbered page 5, beginning "to her husband to shoot." In the letter, just before divulging the details about Nate and Grace accepting "relief," she writes, "Oh yes! There are skeletons in our family closet, but I never felt disgraced by them until lately and this is it."

101. Ibid.

102. Carrie Ingalls Swanzey to LIW, undated letter of 1939, perhaps included in LIW to RWL, May 24, 1939.

103. "Little House on the Prairie," *Mansfield Mirror*, October 3, 1935.

104. LIW to Miss Crawford, September 16, 1940, in SL LIW, p. 225.

105. LIW to RWL, February 5, 1937, in SL LIW, p. 110.

106. Wilder, "My Work": Speech to the Sorosis Club, Mountain Grove, Missouri, Winter 1935–36 in *LIW: The Little House Books*, vol. 1, p. 581. The text of this speech was derived from the only known source, Irene Lichty Le Count, *Laura Ingalls Wilder Family, Home and Friends (Potpourri)* (privately printed, 1980), pp. 43–47. The original manuscript was presumably once the property of the Mansfield Collection, where Lichty Le Count served as director for many years, but has apparently been lost.

107. Ibid., p. 584.

108. RWL to LIW, October 11, 1937.

109. Ibid.

110. LIW to Ida Louise Raymond, October 8, 1937, in SL LIW, p. 134.

111. Program for "The Book Fair: 'A Week of Authors,' October 11 through 16, 1937" (Detroit: J. L. Hudson, 1937), p. 19. Collection of the author.

112. LIW, "Speech at the Book Fair, Detroit, Michigan, October 16, 1937," in *LIW: The Little House Books*, vol. 1, p. 585.

113. Ibid., pp. 585–86.

114. Ibid., pp. 586.

115. Ibid., p. 588.

116. Ibid.

117. See LIW, PC.

118. Ida Louise Raymond to LIW, December 22, 1936.
119. See LIW to Aubrey Sherwood, February 23, 1943.
120. RWL to William T. Anderson, June 30, 1966, cited in Anderson, "The Literary Apprenticeship of LIW," p. 288.
121. LIW, "'Dear Children': A Letter from Laura Ingalls Wilder," in *LIW: The Little House Books*, vol. 2, p. 802.

12. WE ARE ALL HERE

1. See RWL, "Questionnaire for Almanzo Wilder on Dakota Territory," HHPL; and "Rose Wilder Lane, interview with Almanzo Wilder," *Sampler,* p. 213.
2. RWL Diary, 1936–38, entries for January 20 and 21, 1937. HHPL, RWL Diaries and Notes, item #59.
3. RWL, "Silk Dress," *Ladies' Home Journal,* August 1937, p. 46.
4. Ibid., p. 50. See also LIW, "The First Three Years," p. 65 (HHPL pagination).
5. RWL, *Free Land* (Lincoln and London: University of Nebraska Press, 1938; 1966), p. 25. For ease of reference I have provided page numbers for the novel rather than the *Saturday Evening Post* serial.
6. Ibid., p. 26.
7. Ibid., p. 23.
8. Ibid., pp. 94–96.
9. Ibid., p. 7.
10. Ibid., p. 29.
11. Ibid., p. 230.
12. LIW to RWL, letter beginning "Perhaps you don't know about the 'Horn Book'" on reverse of letter from Ida Louise Raymond to LIW, December 18, 1937.
13. Ibid.
14. RWL to LIW, December 20, 1937.
15. The serial, as well as the novel, did contain a fictionalized account of an anecdote Wilder and Lane had been trading back and forth for years, the story of the desecration of an Indian graveyard by a doctor who stole the body of an infant. Wilder described the incident in her memoir; see PG, pp. 227, 229. For Lane's version, see *Free Land*, p. 104.
16. LIW to RWL, February 5, 1937.
17. The former appeared in LHOP, the latter would be included in SL.
18. LIW to RWL, February 5, 1937.
19. SL, manuscript version 2, p. 2, HHPL.
20. Ibid., following p. 5.
21. RWL to LIW, undated, late October 1937.
22. Ibid.
23. Ibid.
24. RWL to LIW, December 20, 1937.
25. LIW to RWL, March 22, 1937.
26. LIW to RWL, undated letter with "Plum Creek" inscribed across the top. In sequence at the HHPL, this letter appears to follow and respond to Lane's letter of December 20, 1937.
27. RWL to LIW, January 21, 1938.
28. Ibid., December 19, 1937.
29. LIW to RWL, January 25, 1938.

30. Ibid., January 28, 1938.
31. RWL to LIW, February 3, 1938, in *Selected Letters*, p. 160. Anderson was given a transcript of the letter by Roger MacBride.
32. LIW to RWL, February 19, 1938.
33. Ibid., undated letter with "Plum Creek" inscribed across the top.
34. See page 1 of "The Shores of Silver Lake," SL manuscript (version 2). SHSM.
35. Ibid.
36. RWL to LIW, January 21, 1938.
37. Ibid.
38. See LIW to RWL, January 25, 1938; and RWL to LIW, January 21, 1938.
39. LIW to RWL, January 25, 1938. See also Rosa Ann Moore, "Laura Ingalls Wilder and Rose Wilder Lane: The Chemistry of Collaboration," *Children's Literature in Education*, vol. 11, no. 3 (Autumn 1980), p. 106.
40. RWL to Guy Moyston, May 30, 1925; "movement of the bowels" was Lane's term, although she implies that it was the language used by her mother. According to Lane's letter, Wilder "hate[d] anything at all that has to do in any way with sex." See also RWL, *He Was a Man* (New York: Harper & Brothers, 1925), pp. 93–94. The racy scene that Wilder objected to depicted the novel's protagonist, Gordon Blake (based on Jack London), losing his virginity to an older, experienced woman who lived with a colorful friend, Frisco Jack. Wilder apparently stopped reading the novel at that point; Lane expressed relief that her mother quit before reaching the scene in which Blake seduces "Spanish Mary," a teenaged refugee, in suggestive but hardly explicit terms: "Her body was firm and yielding, pressed against him by his masterful arms." See *He Was a Man*, p. 99.
41. LIW to RWL, January 26, 1938.
42. Ibid., undated letter headed "Plum Creek"; see also LIW to RWL, January 26, 1938.
43. LIW to RWL, undated letter headed "Silver Lake," in 1938 correspondence.
44. LIW, SL in *LIW: The Little House Books*, vol. 2, p. 12.
45. LIW to RWL, January 25, 1938.
46. Ibid., undated letter headed "Silver Lake," in 1938 correspondence.
47. LIW, manuscript (version 2), of SL, p. 95.
48. LIW to RWL, February 19, 1938.
49. Ibid., March 7, 1938.
50. Ibid.
51. Ibid.
52. Ibid.
53. Ibid.
54. Ibid.
55. Ibid.
56. LIW, "The Hard Winter," List of Corrections to typescript, see corrections to p. 107, p. 104. HHPL.
57. LIW, "The Hard Winter," List of Corrections and Map of De Smet. HHPL. See corrections to p. 86.
58. LIW, "Hard Winter" draft manuscript, p. 199. Burton Collection.
59. Ibid., p. 206.
60. Ibid., p. 52. Often repeated in Wilder's work and in her daughter's, the anecdote of the Indian predicting the hard winter must have been among her enduring

memories of that winter. It appeared in *Pioneer Girl*; in Lane's quasi-fictional series for the *Bulletin*, "Behind the Headlight"; in drafts of "Hard Winter"; and in the published novel. See PG, pp. 203, 204n7; chapter 3 of "Behind the Headlight: The Life Story of a Railway Engineer," *Bulletin*, October 12, 1915, p. 8; and chapter 7, "Indian Warning," of LW in *LIW: The Little House Books*, vol. 2, pp. 207–208.

61. LIW to RWL, June 3, 1939.

62. LIW to Bye, May 7, 1940.

63. "We Are All Here" appears in *The Conqueror*, the songbook used at the singing school attended by Laura Ingalls and Almanzo Wilder during their courting days; see "We Are All Here," in C. E. Leslie and R. H. Randall, *The Conqueror* (Chicago: Chicago Music Company, 1880), p. 22. See also notes on "We Are All Here," in *The Ingalls Wilder Family Songbook*, ed. Dale Cockrell (Middleton, WI: A-R Editions, 2011), p. 399.

64. RWL to Mary Paxton Keeley, February 14, 1938.

65. Ibid. See also Lane's 1040 Federal Tax Return and Missouri State Tax Returns for 1937, HHPL.

66. See RWL Diary, 1936–38, entry for January 17–18, 1937: "I have $189 in bank, besides $600 cushion reserve, & $1000. put aside for boys' trip to Europe this summer." HHPL, RWL Diaries and Notes, item #59. See also Holtz, *Ghost*, p. 272.

67. See John Turner and Charlie Clark to RWL, August 26, 1937 (postcard). The Hitler postcard is undated and the date of cancellation on the reverse is illegible; it too probably dates from August 1937.

68. I am indebted to Kathy Short, of the Mansfield Historical Society, for alerting me to this information; personal interview, October 28, 2015. See also Susan Dolan, *Fruitful Legacy: A Historic Context of Orchards in the United States* (Washington, DC: National Park Service, 2009), p. 101.

69. RWL quotes from her mother's letter in her own to Mark Sullivan, October 11, 1938. Wilder's original letter has not surfaced.

70. RWL to Mark Sullivan, August 16, 1938.

71. Ibid.

72. RWL to Mary Paxton Keeley, February 14, 1938.

73. Ibid.

74. See RWL, "Free Land," *Saturday Evening Post*, March 5 to April 23, 1938.

75. Kirkus Reviews, *Free Land*, May 4, 1938.

76. RWL to Mary Paxton Keeley, January 25, 1938.

77. Bye to RWL, October 11, 1936.

78. Rexh Meta to RWL, February 28, 1938. The cable transfer from Guaranty Trust Company of New York, dated January 28, 1938, is in Lane's papers at HHPL.

79. See Holtz, *Ghost*, p. 277.

80. RWL Diary, 1936–38, entry for February 5, 1938. HHPL, RWL Diaries and Notes, item #59. See also Holtz, *Ghost*, p. 284.

81. RWL to LIW, December 20, 1937.

82. See RWL, "My House in the Country," *Woman's Day*, May 1942, pp. 12–13.

83. RWL to Mary Paxton Keeley, February 14, 1938.

84. LIW to RWL, February 19, 1938.

85. Ibid.

86. "Friends and Travelers: The Personal Recollections of Neta Seal," in Hines, *"I Remember Laura,"* p. 108.

87. White, *Laura's Friends Remember,* p. 20.

88. Portions of LIW's 1938 travel diary, including a photograph of one page, appear in Helen Burkhiser, *Neta, Laura's Friend* (privately printed, 1989). The location of the diary is currently unknown.

89. Burkhiser, p. 15.

90. Ibid., p. 17.

91. See William Anderson, *Story of the Ingalls* (Mansfield, MO: LIW Home Association, 1967; 1993), p. 31.

92. Ibid.

93. "Somebody's Coming When the Dew Drops Fall," music and lyrics by James C. Macy (Cleveland: S. Brainard's Sons, 1878).

94. *De Smet News*, June 3, 1938.

95. Ibid.

96. Ole R. Holsti, *Public Opinion and American Foreign Policy*, rev. ed. (Ann Arbor: University of Michigan Press, 2004), p. 17.

97. LIW to RWL, September 26, 1938.

98. See the history of the *Mansfield Mirror* in *History and Families, Wright County, Missouri*, ed. Clyde A. Rowen (Morley, MO: Acclaim Press, 1993), p. 76.

99. Nannie Davis was a member of both the Athenian Club and the Justamere Club. See "Rose Wilder Lane Is Luncheon Hostess," *Springfield Leader*, May 23, 1928, p. 17.

100. See Miller, *Becoming LIW*, p. 227, and LIW to RWL, September 26, 1938.

101. A copy of "To American Mothers" was found in Wilder's papers. See also LIW to RWL, September 26, 1938.

102. LIW to RWL, September 26, 1938.

103. Ibid.

104. RWL, "Why I Am for the People's Vote on War," *Liberty*, April 1, 1939, pp. 11–12.

105. Eleanor Roosevelt, "Why I Am Against the People's Vote on War," *Liberty*, April 8, 1939, p. 7.

106. LIW to RWL, April 2, 1939.

107. RWL, "War! What the Women of America Can Do to Prevent It," *Woman's Day*, April 1939, p. 4.

108. For Lane's appearance that day, see the photograph held in the Library of Congress. "Neutrality Snags Plague Congress," *New York Times*, May 11, 1939, p. 12.

109. See *Time*, June 12, 1939.

110. Peter Kurth, *American Cassandra: The Life of Dorothy Thompson* (New York: Little, Brown, 1991), p. 312.

111. RWL to Dorothy Thompson, October 15, 1938, in Holtz, *Dorothy Thompson and Rose Wilder Lane*, p. 147.

112. Ibid.

113. Ibid., p. 148.

114. For an extensive discussion of the spat, see Holtz, *Dorothy Thompson and Rose Wilder Lane*, pp. 149–52. See also Holtz, *Ghost*, pp. 295–96.

115. Ruth Levine to William Holtz, April 22, 1991, HHPL. Dorothy Thompson to RWL, June 6, 1939, in Holtz, *Dorothy Thompson and Rose Wilder Lane*, p. 161. Thompson is quoting from a speech she had recently given at the PEN Congress.

116. RWL to Dorothy Thompson, June 1, 1939.

117. LIW to RWL, January 26, 1939.

118. Ibid., April 2, 1939.

119. Ibid., January 10, 1939.

120. LIW to RWL, March 17, 1939.

121. LIW to Bye, May 29, 1939.

122. Ibid.

123. LIW to RWL, May 23, 1939.

124. Ibid., January 27, 1939.

125. Ibid., February 20, 1939.

126. Ibid.

127. Ibid., April 2, 1939.

128. Ibid., January 27, 1939; see the extended postscript.

129. Ibid., February 20, 1939.

130. Ibid., May 23, 1939.

131. Ibid., June 3, 1939.

132. For the weather on their trip home, see "Local Residents Distinguished Visitors Old Settlers' Day," *De Smet News*, June 29, 1939. Wilder's article, "In the Land of Used-to-Be," appeared in the *Christian Science Monitor* on April 4, 1940; it is reprinted in *Sampler*, p. 226.

133. Ibid., p. 228.

134. Ibid., p. 230.

135. *De Smet News*, June 29, 1939.

136. LIW, "The Land of Used-to-Be," in *Sampler*, p. 230.

137. LIW, SL in *LIW: The Little House Books*, vol. 2, p. 164.

138. See, for example, Anne T. Eaton, "The New Books for Younger Readers," *New York Times Book Review*, February 11, 1940, p. 96.

139. "By the Shores of Silver Lake," *Kirkus Reviews*, October 1, 1939.

140. "What the U.S.A. Thinks: A Picture of the U.S. Mind, Summer of 1940," *Life*, July 29, 1940, p. 20.

141. Ibid.

142. See Lane, "American Jews," *American Mercury*, December 1938, pp. 501–502; RWL Diary/Journal—War News, May–June 15, 1940, entries for May 10 and 11, 1940, including typed insertion. HHPL, RWL Diaries and Notes, item #65.

143. Ibid., May 9, 1940.

144. RWL Diary, August 1939–April 1940, entry for November 1, 1939. HHPL, RWL Diaries and Notes, item #64.

145. Ibid., March 9, 1940, "Check for $500 received from mother. Working on Hard Winter."

146. See Norma Lee Browning, "Rose and Laura," draft of a memoir written for a publication of Waldenbooks, p. 4. De Smet Collection.

147. RWL to Charlie Clark, August 11, 1943.

148. John Turner to RWL, undated. In the letter, Turner expresses a wish to "break completely," which appears to refer to his financial dependence on Lane. Decades later, Turner wrote to William Holtz to suggest that he did not consider it a "good bye" letter.

149. John Turner to William Holtz, undated letter, circa early 1990s. HHPL, WHC.

150. RWL to Charlie Clark, August 11, 1943.

151. Several manuscript versions of "Forgotten Man" survive in Lane's papers at HHPL. The quotation is taken from one labeled in Lane's handwriting, on the first page, "Last copy"; see p. 10.

152. Franklin D. Roosevelt, Radio Address, Albany, NY, April 7, 1932. See *The Public Papers and Addresses of Franklin D. Roosevelt*, vol. 1 (New York: Random House, 1938), p. 648.

153. See RWL to Ruth Levine, September 15, 1939. In this letter, held in the Isaac Don Levine Papers at Emory University's Manuscript, Archives and Rare Book Library, Lane quotes extensively from the *Post*'s rejection letter, written by its new editor, Wesley Stout.

154. Ibid., September 15, 1939.

155. RWL to Bye, June 5, 1940.

156. "The Long Winter," *Kirkus Reviews*, June 15, 1940; Anne T. Eaton, "The New Books for Younger Readers," *New York Times Book Review*, January 26, 1941, p. 52.

157. See Carrie Ingalls to LIW, August 6, 1940.

158. LIW to RWL, March 17, 1939.

159. Ibid., January 27, 1939.

160. Ibid., January 25, 1938.

161. Ibid., May 24, 1939.

162. LIW, "Prairie Girl" outline, HHPL.

163. See Chapter 3, "Getting Ready for the Fourth," in LIW, manuscript for LTOP, pp. 18–24. Pomona Collection.

164. LIW, manuscript for LTOP, p. 28. Pomona Collection.

165. Ibid.

166. Ibid., p. 29.

167. LIW, LTOP in *LIW: The Little House Books*, vol. 2, pp. 409–10.

168. Ibid., p. 410.

169. RWL to Garet Garrett, undated partial letter, late 1930s, beginning "P.S. Besides, it is not a question merely of the New Deal."

170. LIW, LTOP in *LIW: The Little House Books*, vol. 2, p. 412.

171. See Holtz, Appendix A, *Ghost*, pp. 379–85.

172. See LIW, "List of Corrections," p. 1, correction to p. 23.

173. Wilder's teaching certificate is on display in the Mansfield Collection. It is reproduced in *Laura's Album*, p. 25.

174. See LIW, LTOP in *LIW: The Little House Books*, vol. 2, p. 543.

175. Ibid., p. 536.

176. Lane did not keep a diary in 1941; either she did not record her work on LTOP or the relevant records or letters have been lost. Miller surmised that Lane must have done her work between January and July of that year; see Miller, *Becoming LIW*, p. 239. Wilder submitted three copies of the typed manuscript to Bye in early July; see LIW to Bye, July 3, 1941.

177. "Briefly Noted," *New Yorker*, December 6, 1941, p. 143.

178. *Philadelphia Record*, December 21, 1941.

179. In addition to *Little Town*, the 1942 Newbery Honor Books were *George Washington's World*, by Genevieve Foster, *Indian Captive: The Story of Mary Jemison*, by Lois Lenski, and *Down Ryton Water*, by Eva Roe Gaggin.

180. LIW, "Speech at the Book Fair," in *LIW: The Little House Books*, vol. 1, pp. 587–88.

181. LIW, "As a Farm Woman Thinks," *Missouri Ruralist*, June 1, 1924.

182. As with LTOP, correspondence regarding Wilder's final volume does not survive. In addition to Wilder's holograph manuscript, two typescripts survive: an earlier typescript, with editorial remarks typewritten by Lane and holograph changes by both Wilder and her daughter, as well as a near-final typescript. Wilder's draft manuscript and the later typescript are held at the Burton Collection; the earlier typescript is in the HHPL.

183. LIW, THGY, manuscript, p. 303. Burton Collection.

184. Ibid., p. 305.

185. LIW, THGY, in *LIW: The Little House Books*, vol. 2, p. 724.

186. LIW, THGY, manuscript, p. 313.

187. LIW, "Ambition." Mansfield Collection. A reproduction appears in Anderson, *Laura's Album*, p. 24. Wilder misspelled Alexander (as "Elaxander") in her original, which begins with an opening—"Ambition is, like other good things, a good only when used in moderation"—that differs from the version she wrote in her handwritten draft and in the first typewritten manuscript. See LIW, THGY, draft manuscript in the Burton Collection, p. 89 (microfilm image 93). In an editorial note, Lane encouraged her mother to dramatize the essay's success to heighten the drama of the scene; see THGY, HHPL typescript manuscript with holograph changes, p. 75.

188. LIW, THGY in *LIW: The Little House Books*, vol. 2, p. 730.

13. SUNSHINE AND SHADOW

1. LIW to Ursula Nordstrom, May 7, 1945, in SL LIW, p. 272.

2. *Kirkus Reviews* gives the publication date of *Little Town* as November 20, 1941.

3. LIW to Alvilda Sorenson, December 29, 1941, in SL LIW, p. 236.

4. Bye to LIW, July 25, 1941; LIW to Bye, August 1, 1941.

5. LIW to Bye, August 1, 1941.

6. Ibid.

7. Ibid., September 28, 1942.

8. Bye to LIW, September 29, 1942; May 5, 1943.

9. Ibid., May 6, 1943.

10. LIW to Bye, May 10, 1943.

11. Ibid.

12. LIW to Ursula Nordstrom, March 1, 1943, in SL LIW, p. 243.

13. Martha A. Green to LIW, September 10, 1943.

14. LIW to Ursula Nordstrom, May 7, 1945, in SL LIW, p. 271.

15. *Evening News* (Harrisburg, Pennsylvania), April 19, 1943, p. 5.

16. *Ottawa Journal*, May 19, 1943, p. 12.

17. Lynn Riggs, *Green Grow the Lilacs: A Play* (New York: Samuel French, 1930), scene 1, p. 3.

18. Anne T. Eaton, "New Books for Younger Readers," *New York Times Book Review*, April 4, 1943, p. 58.

19. "These Happy Golden Years," *Kirkus Reviews*, March 1, 1943.

20. LIW to Mrs. Phraner, May 10, 1943, in SL LIW, p. 248.

21. Isabel Paterson, *The God of the Machine* (New Brunswick: Transaction Publishers, 1993), p. 167.

22. RWL, *The Discovery of Freedom* (New York: John Day, 1943), p. 12.

23. Lane and Rand met in person in 1947; see Rand to RWL, December 13, 1947, in *Letters of Ayn Rand*, ed. Michael S. Berliner (New York: Dutton, 1995), p. 383.

24. Stephen Cox, Introduction, *The God of the Machine*, p. xxiv.

25. See Cox, *The Woman and the Dynamo*, pp. 220–21. Rand may have had other influences; Garet Garrett's 1922 novel *The Driver* featured a steely individualist by the name of "Galt," a name shared with the protagonist of Rand's fourth and final novel, *Atlas Shrugged*, published in 1957.

26. See, for example, Paterson, p. 50 and pp. 155–56.

27. Lane was reading the *New York Herald Tribune* Books section regularly, from at least the 1920s on. Living in Albania, she thanked Clarence Day for a gift subscription in 1927; see Lane to Clarence Day, July 10, 1927. She mentioned another gift subscription to the publication in Lane to Virginia Brastow, February 13, 1935; she also thanked Brastow for sending copies of the review. Years later, she quarreled with Paterson over who had paid for the subscription; see Lane to Paterson, March 26, 1942 (a letter misdated as 1932 but originating from McAllen, Texas, where Lane stayed briefly in 1942). Clippings from Paterson's "Turns with a Bookworm" column were also found in Lane's papers; see HHPL, Lane Papers, Correspondence & Subject Series, Paterson, Isabel, 1933–1945.

28. RWL Journal, June 28, 1939.

29. See RWL 1940 Journal, including May 29 and November 5, 1940.

30. See Paterson, pp. 3–5; RWL, *Discovery of Freedom*, p. 14.

31. Regarding bodies of knowledge, see Paterson, pp. 290–91; RWL, *Discovery of Freedom*, pp. 13–14 and p. 148.

32. Paterson, p. 235.

33. RWL, *Discovery of Freedom*, p. 32.

34. Paterson, p. 82.

35. RWL, *Discovery of Freedom*, p. x.

36. Ibid., p. 26.

37. Ibid.

38. Ibid.

39. Ibid., p. 180.

40. *Kirkus* review of *The Discovery of Freedom*, January 8, 1942.

41. Ayn Rand, *The Fountainhead* (New York: New American Library, 1952), pp. 624, 680.

42. Cox, Introduction, *God of the Machine*, p. xxix.

43. RWL, "What Is This—The Gestapo?" (New York: National Economic Council, Inc., 1943). In 1945, Lane would become the editor of the N.E.C's book review, a publication with an unsavory background; for more on the National Economic Council and its leader, Merwin K. Hart, see Joseph W. Bendersky, *The "Jewish Threat": Anti-Semitic Politics of the U.S. Army* (New York: Basic Books, 2001), p. 412; and Max Wallace, *The American Axis: Henry Ford, Charles Lindbergh, and the Rise of the Third Reich* (New York: St. Martin's Press, 2003), p. 252.

44. "Author's Criticism of Social Security Brings F.B.I. Probe," *Washington Star*, August 9, 1943. This Associated Press article appears in Lane's FBI file, declassified in 1984; versions of the piece, datelined Danbury, Conn., appeared across the country. See, for example, "'What's This? Gestapo?' Asks Novelist in Security Quiz," *Oakland Tribune*, August 10, 1943.

45. Rebecca West, *Black Lamb and Grey Falcon* (New York: Penguin Classics, 1941; 2007), p. 1070.

46. See RWL to Herbert Hoover, June 12, 1945. During 1945 and 1946, Lane wrote repeatedly to Hoover regarding Rexh Meta; she also asked Bye to consult his contacts and her friend Mary Paxton Keeley, who knew Truman, to intervene on Meta's behalf. See HHPL, Herbert Hoover, Post-Presidential Individual Correspondence, Box 119, Rose Wilder Lane, 1945–1963.

47. RWL to Hoover, June 12, 1945.

48. Sources on Meta's fate during and after the war are few, contradictory, and perhaps unreliable. He was interned in Italy during the early part of the war, according to Lane; see RWL to Herbert Hoover, May 30, 1945. An online Albanian source suggests that Meta returned to Albania in 1943 where he took part in the founding of the Second League of Prizren, a fascist organization bent on preserving the unification of Kosovo and Albania. After the war he was arrested by the Communist regime of Enver Hoxha, tried (for treason or perhaps for "anti-communist activities," as Lane believed), and given a death sentence, later commuted to twenty-seven years. Lane received news through an intermediary suggesting that he may have been released in the mid-1960s; see Roger MacBride to RWL, July 1, 1966. He died in Tirana in 1985. For more, see RWL to Herbert Hoover, June 27, 1945; see also the Albanian Wikipedia entry on Rexh Meta, which may include material from an online magazine, www.panorama.com. That source was translated by a specialist in Albanian studies; Dr. Robert Elsie, email message to the author, January 6, 2016.

49. RWL to Herbert Hoover, October 25, 1946.

50. See Holtz, "Ghost," p. 290.

51. RWL to Jane Burr, January 18, 1945.

52. See ibid.; this letter, held in the Jane Burr Papers at the Sophia Smith Collection at Smith College, contains Burr's penciled responses in the margins. See also Holtz, "Ghost," p. 305; Holtz cites Jane Burr to Floyd Dell, November 9, 1949.

53. Ernestine Evans to Berta Hader, August 3, 1953. Copy in HHPL, reproduced from original, Berta and Elmer Hader Correspondence, Special Collections Knight Library, University of Oregon.

54. RWL to Bye, February 28, 1942.

55. Ibid., August 25, 1942. Lane worked on but apparently never completed the sequel.

56. Ibid.

57. David T. Beito and Linda Royster Beito, "Selling Laissez-Faire Antiracism to the Black Masses: Rose Wilder Lane and the *Pittsburgh Courier*," *Independent Review*, vol. 15, no. 2 (Fall 2010), p. 282.

58. RWL, "Rose Lane Says," *Pittsburgh Courier*, March 27, 1943, and February 3, 1945; the latter column, which included Lane's critique of rationing, was written in response to remarks made by an unnamed "Communist fellow-traveler acquaintance." That acquaintance was Jane Burr; see RWL to Jane Burr, January 18, 1945. Jane Burr Papers, Smith College.

59. See RWL, "Rose Lane Says," *Pittsburgh Courier*, November 11, 1944.

60. "Novelist, on Strike Against the New Deal, Retires to Farm with Food-Stocked Cellar," *New York Times*, April 4, 1944, p. 23.

61. "Mrs. Lane's Sitdown Strike," *New Republic*, April 24, 1944, p. 553.

62. LIW to Aubrey Sherwood, February 23, 1943. De Smet Collection.

63. LIW to Hon. Clarence E. Kilburn, March 9, 1945. Franklin County Historical and Museum Society, Malone, New York.

64. Merwin K. Hart to RWL, November 3, 1960. In this fund-raising note, Hart asks Lane for a donation, adding, "Your mother, over quite a period of years, gave us a fairly substantial amount, and we deeply appreciated it." HHPL.

65. LIW to Kilburn, March 9, 1945.

66. Chester Bradley, "Mansfield Woman's Books Favored Both by Children and Grown-Ups," *Kansas City Star*, April 10, 1949.

67. Keisha Mahoney-Jones, Acting Freedom of Information Officer, Social Security Administration, to the author, November 9, 2015.

68. LIW to Dorothy Wilder Pittman and Carl Pittman, June 9, 1946. Spring Valley Historical Society & Museum.

69. See Lawrence K. Fox to LIW, April 20, 1944, and May 22, 1944, as well as two undated drafts of letters in Wilder's hand. HHPL.

70. Addendum to undated letter, LIW to South Dakota State Historical Society.

71. See PG, pp. 32–33, no. 29.

72. For details about the sale of the Ingallses' Third Street house and the disposition of the family's belongings, see "The House Is Sold," *Laura Ingalls Wilder Lore*, vol. 4, no. 2 (Fall–Winter 1978), pp. 5–6.

73. See Walter G. Miser to LIW, June 3, 1946. De Smet Collection.

74. Ibid., June 5, 1946.

75. Ibid.

76. Ibid., June 10, 1946.

77. See Burkhiser, p. 18.

78. Many of these were later collected in *Dear Laura: Letters from Children to Laura Ingalls Wilder* (New York: HarperCollins, 1996); see Pat to LIW, September 3, 1943, p. 61.

79. Ibid., p. 29.

80. Ibid.

81. Ibid., p. 55.

82. Ibid., pp. 93–92.

83. LIW to Millicent Carpenter Axtell, January 20, 1948. De Smet Collection.

84. Ibid.

85. Mrs. Lena E. Heikes to LIW, undated, HHPL.

86. See Ken Emerson, *Doo-dah!: Stephen Foster and the Rise of American Popular Culture* (New York: Simon & Schuster, 1997), p. 168; and Timothy E. Scheurer, *American Popular Music: The Nineteenth Century and Tin Pan Alley*, vol. I (Bowling Green: Bowling Green State University Popular Press, 1989), p. 57.

87. Undated fragment in LIW's hand. De Smet Collection.

88. Algernon Charles Swinburne, "The Garden of Proserpine," *The Norton Anthology of English Literature*, ed. M. H. Abrams et al., 4th ed., vol. 2 (New York: Norton, 1979), p. 1564.

89. See Leonard S. Marcus, *Minders of Make-Believe: Idealists, Entrepreneurs, and the Shaping of American Children's Literature* (Boston: Houghton Mifflin, 2008), p. 159.

90. Ursula Nordstrom, quoted in the introduction to *Dear Genius: The Letters of Ursula Nordstrom*, collected and edited by Leonard S. Marcus (New York: HarperCollins, 1998), p. xxii.

91. Ursula Nordstrom, "Re-Issuing the Wilder Books," *Top of the News*, American Library Association newsletter (April 1967), unpaginated reprint.
92. Ibid.
93. William T. Anderson, Introduction to *The Horn Book's Laura Ingalls Wilder* (Boston: Horn Book, 1987), p. 4.
94. Ibid.
95. Garth Williams, "Illustrating the Little House Books," in Anderson, *Horn Book*, p. 27.
96. Ibid., p. 28.
97. Ibid.
98. Ibid.
99. Ibid., p. 34.
100. LIW to Bye, June 10, 1944.
101. Douglas MacArthur, *Reminiscences* (Annapolis: Naval Institute Press, 1964), p. 312.
102. John W. Dower, *Embracing Defeat: Japan in the Wake of World War II* (New York: W. W. Norton, 1999), pp. 93, 103.
103. Ibid., p. 91.
104. For details about the Gift Book Program, see Tsuyoshi Ishihara, *Mark Twain in Japan: The Cultural Reception of an American Icon* (Columbia and London: University of Missouri Press, 2005), p. 63.
105. See Noriko Suzuki, "Japanese Democratization and the Little House Books: The Relation between General Head Quarters and *The Long Winter* in Japan after World War II," *Children's Literature Association Quarterly*, vol. 31, no. 1 (Spring 2006), p. 66.
106. Ibid., p. 67.
107. Ibid., p. 71.
108. Ibid.
109. Ibid., p. 72.
110. Eiko Matsunawa to LIW, May 27, 1949. HHPL.
111. Ibid., May 8, 1949, HHPL, and July 1, 1949. De Smet Collection.
112. Suzuki, p83n41.
113. Ibid., p. 76.
114. Just as *The Long Winter* was distributed in Japan in the aftermath of the war, so copies of *Little House on the Prairie*, translated into Persian, were distributed to newly reinstated women members of a literary society in Herat, Afghanistan, after the Taliban fled the region in 2001. See Amy Waldman, "A Nation Challenged: Culture; Afghan Poets Revive a Literary Tradition," *New York Times*, December 16, 2001.
115. See the recollections of Rev. and Mrs. Carleton Knight in Hines, *"I Remember Laura,"* p. 224.
116. See Anderson, *Laura Wilder of Mansfield*, pp. 34–35.
117. Ralph Ulveling, quoted in Chester Bradley, "Mansfield Woman's Books Favored Both by Children and Grown-Ups," *Kansas City Star*, April 10, 1949.
118. LIW to Bye, July 16, 1949.
119. LIW to Ralph A. Ulveling, Director, Detroit Public Library, May 3, 1949, reprinted in "Detroit Honors Laura," *Top of the News* (American Library Association newsletter), April 1967.

120. LIW, Letter sent to be read at the May 12, 1949, dedication of the Laura Ingalls Wilder Branch of the Detroit Public Library. Reprinted in *Top of the News*, April 1967.

121. Neta Seal, diary, quoted in Burkhiser, p. 22.

122. Ibid.

123. Interview with Neta Seal in Dan L. White and Robert F. White, *Laura's Friends Remember: Close Friends Recall Laura Ingalls Wilder* (Hartville, MO: Ashley-Preston, 1992), p. 30.

124. Autograph book, circa 1880s. Wright County Library Collection, Mansfield, MO.

125. Thomas Moore, "The Fire-Worshippers," *Lalla Rookh: An Oriental Romance* (New York: Thomas Y. Crowell, 1888), p. 196.

126. Almanzo Wilder's shoes and the tools he used to craft them are on display in the Mansfield Collection.

127. William Anderson, interview with Helen Boylston, August 4, 1981. Transcript, HHPL, WHC.

128. The original "Resolutions of Respect" is held at the Mansfield Collection; it is reproduced in Teresa Lynn, *Little Lodges on the Prairie: Freemasonry and Laura Ingalls Wilder* (Austin: Tranquility Press, 2014), p. 267.

129. LIW to an unnamed "friend," November 19, 1949. Mansfield Collection.

130. LIW to Mrs. E. F. Green, November 18, 1949. De Smet Collection.

131. Almanzo Wilder's Last Will and Testament, dated October 21, 1944. De Smet Collection.

132. RWL to LIW, July 9, 1951. De Smet Collection.

133. Roscoe Jones, as quoted in Hines, *"I Remember Laura,"* p. 145.

134. Holtz, *Ghost*, p. 337.

135. LIW to Ida Carson, February 1, 1950, in SL LIW, pp. 316–17. Carson, who had taught in South Dakota and Iowa, kept up a correspondence with Wilder in the 1940s; see ibid., p. 275.

136. Sheldon Jones and Roscoe Jones in Hines, *"I Remember Laura,"* pp. 139, 144.

137. Roscoe Jones, ibid., p. 144.

138. Sheldon Jones, ibid., p. 142.

139. Iola Jones, ibid., p. 135.

140. LIW, Letter sent to be read at the May 1, 1950, dedication of the Laura Ingalls Wilder Room. Pomona Collection.

141. LIW to Clara J. Webber, May 20, 1950. Wilder's exchange of letters with Webber is reproduced at the end of the microfilm copy of LTOP. Pomona Collection.

142. "Mrs. Peggy Brown Tells of Meeting Famous Writer, Laura Ingalls Wilder," undated clipping. Private Collection.

143. Florence G. Williams, Librarian, Mansfield Branch, to General Douglas MacArthur, Commander in Chief, Far East Command, November 16, 1950. MacArthur Memorial, Norfolk, Virginia.

144. D. R. Nugent, Lt. Col., USMC, Chief, CIE Section to Florence G. Williams, January 29, 1951. MacArthur Memorial.

145. The rumor was passed along by William Anderson; see his *LIW: A Biography*, p. 224. Noriko Suzuki repeated it in her essay on "Japanese Democratization," adding that "MacArthur and Wilder knew each other, and MacArthur sent Wilder a congratulatory cablegram for her birthday in 1951"; see Suzuki, "Japanese Democratization," p. 69, and p. 80n18. Suzuki also suggested that Jean

MacArthur, the general's wife, "loved the Little House books" and encouraged her husband to select the series for publication; Suzuki gave as her source Jean Coday, the longtime head of the Laura Ingalls Wilder Home and Museum in Mansfield, who recalled hearing the anecdote; see Suzuki, pp. 67 and 78n8. Archivists at the MacArthur Memorial have found no evidence of a cablegram from MacArthur to Wilder. To date, their only findings are the two letters cited above. Personal communication, James W. Zobel, MacArthur Memorial, to author, October 14, 2015.

146. LIW to RWL, July 30, 1952.

147. See commentary by William Anderson, *The Laura Ingalls Wilder Country Cookbook* (New York: HarperCollins, 1995), p. 126; the Haviland china is pictured on p. 58.

148. Lane's 1931 gift set is on display at the Rocky Ridge Farmhouse and is often pointed out by tour guides, who remark on the oddity of a daughter giving a set of pink dishes to her father.

149. For the woodcut comparison, I am indebted to Sallie Ketcham, "Fairy Tale, Folklore, and the Little House in the Deep Dark Woods," *Pioneer Girl Perspectives: Exploring Laura Ingalls Wilder* (Pierre: South Dakota Historical Society Press, 2017), p. 228.

150. The lead of a carbon pencil is a combination of graphite and carbon, producing more intense blacks than a standard graphite pencil.

151. Elizabeth K. Wallace and James D. Wallace, *Garth Williams, American Illustrator: A Life* (New York: Beaufort Books, 2016), p. 85. It should be noted that the uniform edition would not be entirely uniform. In later volumes, Gentry and Williams apparently hit upon the idea of using miniature embellishments to set off the enlarged capital letter at the beginning of chapters, introducing a gorgeous panoply of snowflakes, plum boughs, milking stools, lamps, stoves, tools, trees, grasses, and flowers, each unique. Some volumes developed a theme for these miniatures: *Plum Creek* favored tree limbs; *The Long Winter*, garlands of snowflakes; and *Little Town*, a succession of storefronts and buildings. Early volumes—*Little House in the Big Woods*, *Farmer Boy*, and *Little House on the Prairie*—lack these. So does *Silver Lake*, which in many ways appears to be the least adorned of the 1953 volumes, perhaps reflecting an adaptation to older readers. *These Happy Golden Years* includes tiny drawings at the beginnings and ends of chapters, but the placement differs.

152. See LIW to Ursula Nordstrom, November 24, 1947, in SL LIW, p. 292. See also LIW to Aubrey Sherwood, November 18, 1939, in ibid., pp. 210–11.

153. RWL to LIW, undated, late 1937.

154. LHOP, p. 1.

155. Ursula Nordstrom to unidentified reader, October 14, 1952, in Marcus, *Dear Genius*, p. 55.

156. Ibid., p. 54.

157. Ibid.

158. LHOP in *LIW: The Little House Books*, vol. 1, p. 2.

159. See LIW, LTOP, 1941 edition, p. 243. The passage deleted was this: "With the left foot first, / The right foot following, / The HEEL down MIGHTy HARD, / It's ten platoons of dandy coons, / March in the Skidamore Guard!" For the other minstrel song, "Old Zip Coon," see PG, p. 35.

160. LIW to Ursula Nordstrom, May 21, 1953, in SL LIW, p. 352.

161. Frederick Douglass, "The Hutchinson Family.—Hunkerism," *North Star*, October 27, 1848.

162. LIW to the children of Santiam School, Lebanon, Oregon, March 8, 1951. De Smet Collection.

163. LIW to Mrs. Helmboldt, April 25, 1952. De Smet Collection.

164. See the recollections of Peggy Dennis in Hines, "*I Remember Laura*," p. 221.

165. See the Brown Brothers Book Store advertisement in the *Springfield Leader and Press*, November 14, 1952, and "Ozarks Author Meets Admirer," *Springfield Daily News*, November 16, 1952.

166. Romines, p. ix.

167. Ibid., p. 3.

168. "Mrs. Wilder's Day," *Springfield Leader and Press*, November 17, 1952.

169. LIW to Ursula Nordstrom, June 6, 1953, in SL LIW, p. 353.

170. Ibid., August 13, 1953. The telegram is reproduced in Anderson, *The Horn Book*, p. 7.

171. Anderson, *The Horn Book,* pp. 19–20.

172. LIW to Dr. Irvin Kerlan, May 31, 1954, in SL LIW, p. 364.

173. Versions of Harper's composite letter are included in *Dear Laura*, pp. 149–51; and *LIW: The Little House Books*, vol. 2, pp. 801–802.

174. Mary Amelia Ingalls, "My Father's Violin," in *Reader*, p. 13.

175. Edgar Allan Poe, "Eldorado," *Selected Poetry and Prose of Edgar Allan Poe* (New York: Modern Library, 1951), p. 45; William Benton Clulow, *Sunshine and Shadows, Or, Sketches of Thought—Philosophic and Religious* (London: T. Fisher Unwin, 1883).

176. See Anderson, *LIW: A Biography*, p. 230.

177. LIW to Lydia Morgan, June 13, 1954. De Smet Collection.

178. LIW to Mrs. Ada Keating, February 26, 1951. De Smet Collection.

179. LIW to Neta Seal, undated. De Smet Collection.

180. LIW to Neta Seal, August 3, 1951. De Smet Collection.

181. Undated. De Smet Collection.

182. Nava Austin, interview with the author, April 29, 2014. See also White and White, *Laura's Friends Remember,* p. 9, and Roscoe Jones in Hines, "*I Remember Laura*," p. 143.

183. Fred Kiewit, "Stories That Had to Be Told: Laura Ingalls Wilder Wrote Eight Books After She Was 65, But Now, at 88 and in Poor Health, She's Quitting," *Kansas City Star,* May 22, 1955.

184. Ibid.

185. Ibid.

186. List of Bible references, Mansfield Collection; Matthew 7:24–27.

187. Neta Seal in White and White, *Laura's Friends Remember*, p. 29.

188. RWL to Jasper Crane, January 20, 1957.

189. RWL to Jasper Crane, January 30, 1957, in *The Lady and the Tycoon*, p. 169.

190. Ibid., p. 170.

191. Carl Hartley Sr., in White and White, *Laura's Friends Remember*, p. 40.

192. Program from Wilder's funeral. Malone Collection.

193. "Laura I. Wilder, Author, Dies at 90," *New York Times*, February 12, 1957.

194. LIW, "First Memories of Father," *Reader,* p. 160.

195. Ibid.

196. Ibid., pp. 161–62.

14. THERE IS GOLD IN THE FARM

1. William Anderson, interview with the author, February 12, 2016. Anderson was recalling Irene Lichty's description of Lane's behavior in the aftermath of her mother's death. An edited version of the interview was published as "The Wilder Women," in *Slate Book Review*, March 7, 2016: http://www.slate.com/articles /arts/books/2016/03/the_selected_letters_of_laura_ingalls_wilder_interview _with_editor_william.html.

2. See Holtz, *Ghost*, p. 338.

3. RWL to Neta Seal, March 2, 1957. De Smet Collection.

4. *Mansfield Mirror*, May 2, 1957.

5. See RWL to Neta Seal, April 30, 1957. Wilder's wishes regarding her belongings were not spelled out in her will, but she had instructed Lane to give to the Seals all of the household "furnishings" that she herself did not wish to keep. De Smet Collection.

6. RWL to Neta Seal, January 1, 1958. De Smet Collection.

7. See Bill of Sale between Mr. and Mrs. Silas Seal and the Laura Ingalls Wilder Home Association, August 15, 1958. De Smet Collection.

8. LIW Last Will and Testament, State of Missouri, County of Wright, February 6, 1952.

9. See James O. Brown to Roger MacBride, April 16, 1959, in which Brown explains that payments under the Wilder contracts are being made to George T. Bye and Company, "which is still in existence and functioning." JOB.

10. See Peter Paterson, Canadian Broadcasting Corporation, to James Oliver Brown, January 29, 1959. JOB.

11. See timeline in complaint filed in U.S. District Court, Western District of Missouri, Southern Division, Jeremiah W. (Jay) Nixon, Attorney General of Missouri, Plaintiff v. Abigail MacBride Allen, Joe B. Cox, personal representative of the estate of Roger Lea MacBride, and HarperCollins Publishers, Inc., case no. 99-3368-CV-S-3-ECF.

12. See Louis V. Haynie, Harper & Brothers, to James Oliver Brown, March 6, 1959. JOB.

13. See James Oliver Brown to Roger MacBride, April 16, 1959, in which Brown urges MacBride to consider that his actions will deny money to "the helpless and incompetent widow of a man who for years served Mrs. Wilder and Mrs. Lane faithfully and well." JOB.

14. Memorandum of meeting between Roger MacBride and F. Richard Ford III, Esquire, Cummings & Lockwood, August 20, 1959. Ford was the attorney representing Brown; subsequent to the meeting a legal memorandum was produced by Ford's office covering major points made by MacBride on Lane's behalf. JOB.

15. Roger MacBride to F. Richard Ford, III, Esq., Cummings and Lockwood, September 24, 1959. JOB.

16. Memorandum of meeting between Roger MacBride and F. Richard Ford III, Esquire, August 20, 1959. JOB.

17. See James Oliver Brown to Frank S. MacGregor, Esq., Harper and Brothers, September 28, 1959; see also "Agreement Between: James Brown Associates, Inc. as Successor to George T. Bye and Company, James Oliver Brown, and Rose Wilder Lane, Relative to Certain Works of Laura Ingalls Wilder." JOB.

18. James Oliver Brown to Nannine Joseph, September 8, 1959. JOB.

19. See "Royalties from Wilder Books Left to Local Library," *Mansfield Mirror,* February 21, 1957. HHPL.

20. See chart attached to Mary Russell to Roger MacBride, June 23, 1959. HHPL.

21. See James Oliver Brown to RWL, October 3, 1958. JOB.

22. Andrew Ward, "Campaigning II: The Libertarian Party," *Atlantic Monthly*, vol. 238, no. 5 (November 1976), p. 26.

23. See Roger Lea MacBride, *The American Electoral College* (Caldwell, ID: Caxton Printers, 1963).

24. RWL to Jasper Crane, June 30, 1953, in *The Lady and the Tycoon*, p. 83.

25. "Miss Susan Ford of Southport Fiancee of Roger L. MacBride," *Bridgeport Post*, June 25, 1961. Ford's engagement to MacBride was her second; the first, to an Air Force veteran, had been publicly announced in 1959 but subsequently broken. See "Miss Susan Ford Is Fiancee of Douglas S. McClenahan," *Bridgeport Post*, October 28, 1959. McClenahan would go on to found Charter Arms, a gun manufacturer known for its .38 and .44 Specials. See also RWL to Susie MacBride, March 1, 1962.

26. Susan and Roger MacBride to RWL, September 23, 1961.

27. Roger MacBride to RWL, November 30, 1959. This is one of the few letters from MacBride to Lane that are addressed to "Rose."

28. Ibid.

29. Julia Shawell, "Fireside Chat with Rose Wilder Lane," *Woman's World*, September 1939, p. 16.

30. RWL, *On the Way Home*, p. 94.

31. RWL to Jasper Crane, March 20, 1962, in *The Lady and the Tycoon*, p. 287. All quotations in this paragraph are from the same letter.

32. Ibid., p. 288.

33. RWL to Louise Hovde Mortenson, December 31, 1963, in "Idea Inventory," *Elementary English* (April 1964), p. 428.

34. Ibid. See also Anderson, "LIW and RWL: The Continuing Collaboration," *South Dakota State Historical Society Quarterly*, vol. 16, no. 2 (Summer 1986), pp. 287–88.

35. RWL to Roger MacBride, June 2, 1967.

36. RWL to William T. Anderson, June 30, 1966, in Anderson, "LIW and RWL: The Continuing Collaboration," p. 288. Lane's assertion about the distance of the nearest neighbor was contradicted by Wilder's own memoir; see PG, p. 181n73.

37. RWL, *Woman's Day Book of American Needlework* (New York: Simon & Schuster, 1963), p. 41.

38. Ibid., p. 45.

39. See RWL to Neta Seal, February 1, 1962. Lane writes that "thousands" of readers of her *Woman's Day* needlework articles had expressed interest in the Wilder Museum in response to a caption appearing beneath a sample of crochet, identifying the piece as the property of the Laura Ingalls Wilder Home. See also RWL, *American Needlework*, pp. 147, 149, 160–61.

40. See Roger MacBride to RWL, February 25, 1963.

41. Following a flood at the Colorado campus, the Freedom School moved to California, and the Rose Wilder Lane Building was eventually abandoned. For more on the history of the campus, see Noel Black and Jake Brownell, "Liberty's Pitchman—Robert LeFevre and The Freedom School," KRCC, June 17, 2016:

http://krcc.org/post/wish-we-were-here-episode-16-libertys-pitchman-robert-lefevre-freedom-school.

42. Roger MacBride to RWL, January 22, 1963.

43. See "Two Topics Lively at Valley Forum," *Brattleboro Daily Reformer,* March 4, 1963; and Roger MacBride, "Let's Lower Taxes," campaign pamphlet. HHPL.

44. Tyler Resch and Ernest A. Ostro, "Roger MacBride: The Only Real Liberal in Montpelier," *Bennington Banner,* May 16, 1963; "Two Topics Lively at Valley Forum," *Brattleboro Daily Reformer,* March 4, 1963.

45. "Spending Scored by MacBride," *Brattleboro Daily Reformer*, November 5, 1963.

46. Ibid.

47. Pamphlet, "Excerpts from an Address by Roger Lea MacBride Before the Central NY Citizens for Goldwater, November 14, 1963, Syracuse, NY." HHPL.

48. Roger MacBride to Ursula Nordstrom, December 9, 1963.

49. See, for example, RWL, *The Discovery of Freedom,* pp. 51 and 172; "New Deal Can't Expect Much Help from Rose Wilder Lane," Danbury newspaper (no title), April 4, 1944. HHPL.

50. See syndicated column by John Chamberlain, "A Goldwater Man in Vermont," which appeared in a number of newspapers just prior to the September 1964 primary, including the *Daily Republican* (Monongahela, Pennsylvania), September 2, 1964.

51. RWL to Roger MacBride, July 11, 1964.

52. RWL to Susie MacBride, June 14, 1963.

53. Ibid., January 28, 1965.

54. RWL to Norma Lee Browning, June 26, 1963.

55. "Roger MacBride's Political Image," *Bennington Banner,* May 16, 1964.

56. The primary took place on September 8, 1964. For results, see Ronald E. Cohen, "Now It's Hoff Versus Foote," *Bennington Banner,* September 9, 1964, p. 1.

57. Holtz, *Ghost,* p. 356.

58. RWL, "August in Viet Nam," *Woman's Day,* December 1965, pp. 33–35, 89–94.

59. Robina C. Clark, "Rose Wilder Lane Tells About Viet Nam: Author Gives Views on Communist Threat," *Danbury News-Times,* September 21, 1965. HHPL.

60. If Lane could not eliminate taxes, she would evade them. She had Roger MacBride inform the editor of *Woman's Day* that the Vietnam article was somehow "owned" by him, a fiction she also tried to maintain with her needlework book. She wanted no trace of the money she made from them to appear on her tax returns. See Roger MacBride to RWL, January 22, 1963.

61. See RWL to Roger MacBride, February 16, 1964, and June 19, September 2, and December 3, 1965, as well as Roger MacBride to RWL, December 8, 1965. A schematic drawing is attached to Susie MacBride to RWL, November 21, 1965.

62. Susan Wittig Albert, "Rose Wilder Lane in Texas," online interview with Carol Giffen Mayfield, posted September 7, 2014. http://susanalbert.typepad.com/lifescapes/2014/09/rose-wilder-lane-in-texas.html.

63. Donald Giffen to Roger MacBride, January 6, 1969. HHPL. Throughout this letter, Giffen refers to RWL as "Grandma," and he and his parents were included in codicils to RWL's will. They would become the caretakers of Lane's dogs.

64. See Holtz, *Ghost,* p. 348; for Lane's distrust of doctors and devotion to Adelle Davis, see, for example, RWL to Susie MacBride, December 20, 1963, and January 8, 1964; Susie MacBride to RWL, January 4, 1964; and Roger MacBride to RWL, April 25, 1967.

65. The original, undated manuscript of "Grandpa's Fiddle" is held in HHPL. Thirty pages long, the manuscript contains no breaks.

66. *Sampler*, p. 60. The anthology was originally published by the University of Nebraska Press in 1988. For Anderson's changes, see, for example, p. 2 of the manuscript of "Grandpa's Fiddle," and the paragraph beginning, "There were only the two other children, both girls, mama and Aunt Susan." Lane's retelling of the 1894 trip and her portrayal of the Cooley family are more melodramatic than Anderson's version or Wilder's account in her diary. The mother slaps the daughter after bursting into tears after the river crossing; see "Grandpa's Fiddle," p. 19.

67. RWL, "Grandpa's Fiddle," ibid., pp. 70–71.

68. Thomas Paine, "Agrarian Justice, Opposed to Agrarian Law, and to Agrarian Monopoly, Being a Plan for Meliorating the Condition of Man, by Creating in every Nation, A National Fund, to Pay to every Person, when arrived at the Age of Twenty-One Years, the Sum of Fifteen Pounds Sterling, to enable Him or Her to begin the World! And Also, Ten Pounds Sterling per Annum during life to every Person now living of the Age of Fifty Years, and to all others when they shall arrive at that Age, to enable them to live in Old Age without Wretchedness, and go decently out of the World" (Philadelphia: Printed by R. Folwell, for Benjamin Franklin Bache, 1797), p. 29. MacBride misquoted the closing passage, which reads, "An army of principles will penetrate where an army of soldiers cannot—It will succeed where diplomatic management would fail—It is neither the Rhine, the Channel, nor the Ocean, that can arrest its progress—It will march on the horizon of the world, and it will conquer."

69. See complaint filed in U.S. District Court, Western District of Missouri, Southern Division, Jeremiah W. (Jay) Nixon, Attorney General of Missouri, Plaintiff v. Abigail MacBride Allen, Joe B. Cox, personal representative of the estate of Roger Lea MacBride, and HarperCollins Publishers, Inc., case no. 99-3368-CV-S-3-ECF.

70. Ibid. According to the above filing, in preparing the accounting of Lane's estate after her death, MacBride did not disclose the fact that she had been left only a life interest in her mother's copyrighted literary works. Less than four months after she died, he wrote to a Wright County Probate judge, requesting that Wilder's estate be reopened because it had created a "power" that needed to be exercised in order to close Lane's estate. He asked that a local attorney be appointed as administrator. The "power" referred to was the power to renew copyrights to *Little Town on the Prairie* and *These Happy Golden Years*, and the Wright County Probate court complied, allowing MacBride to renew the rights in the name of the administrator. Not long after, in closing the Wilder estate, it was determined by the same court that the Laura Ingalls Wilder Library was entitled to a single payment of $28,011.05, which represented the royalties paid on the last two novels from Lane's death to the end of the original copyright term. In 1972 the Library received a check in this amount, the entirety of what they would inherit during MacBride's lifetime.

71. Ursula Nordstrom to Virginia Haviland, April 8, 1969, in Marcus, *Dear Genius*, p. 268.

72. Ursula Nordstrom to Zena Sutherland, April 1, 1969. University of Chicago, Zena Bailey Sutherland Papers, 1953–2003.

73. Ursula Nordstrom to Zena Sutherland, November 18, 1969, in Marcus, *Dear Genius*, p. 289.

74. See LIW, "The First Three Years" manuscript, unpaginated (p. 159); see also TFFY in *LIW: The Little House Books*, vol. 2, note 795.28, p. 854.

75. See "Introduction," by Roger Lea MacBride in TFFY (New York: HarperCollins, 1971), p. xiv.

76. Memorandum of meeting between Roger MacBride and F. Richard Ford III, Esquire, Cummings & Lockwood, August 20, 1959.

77. Valerie J. Nelson, "Ed Friendly, 85; helped bring 'Laugh-In' and 'Little House' to TV," Los Angeles Times, June 20, 2007; for additional details, see: "The Creation of Little House on the Prairie," at the website maintained by Friendly Family Productions: http://littlehouseontheprairie.com/ed-friendlys-life-and-legacy/.

78. "Premier TV Show Saturday May Lead to Series Based on 'Banks of Plum Creek,'" Walnut Grove Tribune, vol. 83, no. 32 (March 28, 1974), p. 1.

79. See Arngrim, Confessions of a Prairie Bitch, p. 121.

80. Barbara Wilkins, "Little Joe in 'Little House' Is a Big Man Now," People, October 14, 1974, p. 34.

81. Ibid.

82. Ibid.

83. Nicholas Confessore, "Quixotic '80 Campaign Gave Rise to Kochs' Powerful Network," New York Times, May 17, 2014.

84. Tom Eckhardt, "Libertarians' Presidential Candidate Interviewed Here," Daily Herald (Provo, Utah), July 9, 1976, p. 1.

85. Editorial, "Every Man for His Libertarian Self," Daily Times-News (Burlington, North Carolina), March 29, 1976, p. 4.

86. This is only a partial list; see Andrew Ward, "Campaigning II: The Libertarian Party," Atlantic Monthly, vol. 238, no. 5 (November 1976), pp. 24–25.

87. Ibid., p. 33.

88. Rose Wilder Lane and Roger Lea MacBride, Rose Wilder Lane: The Daughter of Laura Ingalls Wilder (Briarcliff Manor, NY: Stein and Day, 1977), p. 10.

89. Ibid., p. 9.

90. "Appendix: The Ghost in the Little House Books," in Holtz, Ghost, pp. 379–85.

91. Nancy Watzman, "Little Fraud on the Prairie?," Washington Post, July 11, 1993.

92. Norma Lee Browning to William Holtz, November 5, 1979: "Yes, RWL really wrote them. As for that lovely Laura, she was lucky to have such a daughter." Browning met Lane in the winter of 1937 and probably never met Wilder; she described their editorial process more accurately in the draft of her memoir than she did in this letter.

93. See Norma Lee Browning, "Rose and Laura," draft of a memoir written for a publication of Waldenbooks, p. 1. De Smet Collection. Roger MacBride made the same claim regarding Lane and Maugham in his foreword to "Faces at the Window," self-published booklet, 1972. HHPL. Browning's notion of Lane's earning power was exaggerated. Of Lane's peers, Dorothy Thompson earned more over her career than Lane, while many women publishing literary and commercial fiction earned top dollar from magazine publishers, including Edna Ferber, Mary Roberts Rinehart, Zona Gale, Marjorie Kinnan Rawlings, Pearl S. Buck, Rebecca West, and Daphne du Maurier.

94. Holtz, Ghost, p. 334. For further examples of Holtz's attitude toward Wilder, see pp. 65, 148, 153, 244–45, and 306.

95. Roger Lea MacBride, Little House on Rocky Ridge (New York: HarperCollins, 1993), p. 302.

96. In addition to MacBride's Rose series, HarperCollins—after the model of Marvel Comics—would extend prequels far into the past, following Caroline Ingalls's grandmother and great-grandmother all the way back to Scotland.

97. Paula Chin, Hayes Ferguson, Margery Sellinger, and Edmund Newton, "Little Uproar on the Prairie," *People*, November 1, 1999, pp. 73–77.

98. "Library to Get $875,000 in Wilder Copyright Suit," *American Libraries Magazine*, April 16, 2001: https://americanlibrariesmagazine.org/library-to-get-875000-in-wilder-copyright-suit/.

99. In 1995, MacBride's heir, his daughter Abigail Adams MacBride, assigned the copyrighted literary property she had inherited to the Little House Heritage Trust.

100. Kramer, "When Reagan Spoke from the Heart," p. 18.

101. Michael Leahy, "Michael Landon Opens Up: There've Been Painful Detours Along His Highway to Heaven," *TV Guide*, March 2, 1985, p. 13.

102. See Arngrim, p. 113.

103. For contemporary Indian scholarship examining the Little House books, see Waziyatawin Angela Cavender Wilson, "Burning Down the House: Laura Ingalls Wilder and American Colonialism," in *Unlearning the Language of Conquest: Scholars Expose Anti-Indianism in America*, ed. Four Arrows (Don Trent Jacobs) (Austin: University of Texas Press, 2006), pp. 66–80. See also Frances W. Kaye, "Little Squatter on the Osage Diminished Reserve," *Great Plains Quarterly*, vol. 20, no. 2 (Spring 2000), pp. 123–40.

104. Melissa Gilbert, Archive of American Television, Academy of Television Arts and Sciences: http://emmytvlegends.org/interviews/people/melissa-gilbert.

105. Arngrim, p. xii.

EPILOGUE

1. See Anita Clair Fellman, *Little House, Long Shadow: Laura Ingalls Wilder's Impact on American Culture* (Columbia: University of Missouri Press, 2008), p. 186.

2. Ibid., pp. 119–20.

3. William Anderson, interview with the author, February 12, 2016.

4. Fellman, p. 121.

5. LIW, "'Dear Children': A Letter from Laura Ingalls Wilder," *LIW: The Little House Books*, vol. 2, Appendix, p. 802. Examples of home sites using this quotation include the Laura Ingalls Wilder Home Association, the entity behind the Laura Ingalls Wilder Historic Home & Museum in Mansfield. See: http://www.lauraingallswilderhome.com/?page_id=64. Parts of the quotation are inscribed on placards on the walls of the Masters Hotel in Burr Oak, Iowa, as "Laura's Virtues."

6. Jason DeParle, "Why Do People Who Need Help from the Government Hate It So Much?," *New York Times*, September 19, 2016, p. BR16.

7. Enbridge's "Great Lakes to Gulf Coast Series (Part 11)," published January 15, 2015. http://www.enbridge.com/stories/great-lakes-to-gulf-coast-part-11. See also Steve Horn, "Silent Coup: How Enbridge Is Quietly Cloning the Keystone XL Tar Sands Pipeline," Desmog, June 19, 2014.

8. The discovery of oil on the Osage reservation led to an infamous series of murders in the 1920s; for more, see David Grann, *Killers of the Flower Moon: Oil, Money, Murder and the Birth of the F.B.I.* (New York: Simon & Schuster, 2017).

9. The former Congregational Church, which Charles Ingalls and other townsfolk helped to build in De Smet in 1882, is now the De Smet Alliance Church.

10. U.S. Census Bureau, American Community Survey, 2008–2012. Mansfield is number 55 on the list of 100 poorest towns. Figures on median income are included in this study.

11. The Laura Ingalls Wilder Home Association of Mansfield received $200,000 from Community Facilities Loans and Grants, Rural Housing Service, Wright County, Missouri, September 30, 2010, Department of Agriculture: https://projects .propublica.org/recovery/locale/missouri/wright/dept/1200.

12. See John C. Hudson, "Agriculture," *Encyclopedia of the Great Plains*, http:// plainshumanities.unl.edu/encyclopedia/doc/egp.ag.001.

13. As John Wesley Powell predicted, average farm size in the United States has grown, to around 440 acres in 2015, while the number of farms has dropped by half, from more than four million in 1880 to just over two million currently. "Farms and Land in Farms: 2015 Summary," U.S. Department of Agriculture, February 2016, p. 4; http://usda.mannlib.cornell.edu/usda/current/FarmLandIn /FarmLandIn-02-18-2016.pdf. For the total number of farms in the U.S. in 1880, see "Statistics of Agriculture," in *Report on the Productions of Agriculture*, Tenth Census, June 1, 1880, p. ix.

14. Betsy Blaney, "Parts of Some Plains States Drier Than Dust Bowl," *Santa Fe New Mexican* (AP), May 11, 2014, p. C-5. Scientific studies predict "megadrought" due to climate change, which is expected to affect southern California, the American southwest, and the Plains states within the next few decades; see, for example, Benjamin I. Cook, Toby R. Ault, and Jason Smerdon, "Unprecedented 21st Century Drought Risk in American Southwest and Central Plains," *Science Advances*, vol. 1, no. 1 (February 12, 2015).

15. USDA Economic Research Service, "Farm Household Income (Historical)," https://www.ers.usda.gov/topics/farm-economy/farm-household-well-being/farm -household-income-historical/.

16. Bren Smith, "Don't Let Your Children Grow Up to Be Farmers," *New York Times*, August 9, 2014.

17. RWL to Mrs. Davis, February 10, 1966. De Smet Collection.

18. LIW to G. E. Mallery, March 12, 1930. De Smet Collection.

ACKNOWLEDGEMENTS

In 1993, I had the great good fortune to meet Barbara Epstein, co-editor of *The New York Review of Books*, and it was she who first encouraged me to examine the authorship of the Little House books. Two years and many rolls of microfilm later, the NYRB published my first article for them, "The Prairie Queen," which led to other opportunities. I doubt that this book would ever have been imagined, much less written, without Barbara. She died in 2006, leaving behind scores of writers who cherished her curiosity, dry wit, and cheery if remorseless editorial acumen. I will always be grateful to her.

In 2011, Max Rudin, publisher of the Library of America, asked me to edit Wilder's Little House books for the nonprofit organization that, for the past thirty-five years, has been re-issuing classic works of American literature in authoritative editions. It was an honor, and in preparing the first new edition of Wilder's novels since 1953, I discovered her anew, uncovering historical nuggets with the greedy delight that Laura knew, searching for colored beads in the ashes of Osage fires.

Writing a chronology of Wilder's life was a revelation that always left me wanting more. In preparing the texts and notes, I was aided and inspired by the Library of America's tireless contributing editor, Chris Carduff, and by an exceptional editorial staff including G. Thomas Tanselle, textual advisor; Brian McCarthy, associate publisher; Stefanie Peters, associate editor (who among other finds helped us track down the elusive "Little Dickie Dilver"); and managing editor Trish Hoard.

I thank Chris as well for recommending me for a travel grant to the Herbert Hoover Presidential Library in 2014. On repeat visits, I've grown to depend on the archival expertise of Matthew Schaefer, Spencer Howard, and Craig Wright. Photo archivist Lynn Smith kindly tracked down additional items, as did audio-visual specialist Jim Detlefsen. Thanks are due as well to Delene McConnaha of the Herbert Hoover Presidential Library Association for handling details of the grant. On several occasions, beginning in the 1990s, I benefited from discussions with Dwight M. Miller, now retired senior archivist, about the Library's acquisition of the Rose Wilder Lane Papers and his pivotal early visit to Wilder's Rocky Ridge farmhouse.

Over the past year, it has been a real pleasure to work with Nancy Tystad Koupal, editor of the South Dakota Historical Society Press and leader of the Pioneer Girl Project, the venture that published the revelatory annotated edition of Wilder's *Pioneer Girl* in 2014. I thoroughly enjoyed working with Nancy on an essay for *Pioneer Girl Perspectives*, published earlier this year in celebration of Wilder's 150th birthday, and participating in the related conference, "Laura Ingalls Wilder: A 150-Year Legacy." There I learned a great deal from fellow contributors William Anderson, Michael Patrick Hearn, Elizabeth Jameson, Sallie Ketcham, Amy Mattson Lauters, John Miller, Paula Nelson, and Ann Romines, all of them specialists in history, literature, and Wilder herself.

Of those Wilder specialists, Bill Anderson deserves a special vote of thanks from scholars for his work over the decades, and he has kindly spoken with me at length on several occasions. John Miller, too, author of a fine biography of Wilder for the University of Missouri, has answered questions and offered valuable suggestions.

Librarians close to home have been generous with their time and assistance. Barbara Messer, who handles the interlibrary loan program at the Santa Fe Public Library, tracked down exotic and obscure items, including Samuel Ingalls's broadside, newspaper microfilm, and many other works. It may be a small-town library, but under the able direction of Patricia Hoddap, herself a noted Laura Ingalls Wilder fan, it is also mighty. In addition, two private libraries in Santa Fe allowed me to use their collections: the Fogelson Library at the Santa Fe University of Art & Design and the Meem Library at St. John's College.

Farther afield, Dawn Eurich, Archivist at the Burton Historical Collection of the Detroit Public Library, helped arrange for scanning of their Wilder manuscripts. I'm grateful as well to Dale Ann Stieber, Special Collections Librarian and Archivist at the Occidental College Library, which holds the papers of Bessie Beatty; Evelyn Parker, who helped locate letters in the Jane

Burr Papers of the Sophia Smith Collection of Smith College; Clint Pumphrey, at Utah State University, for supplying Charmian London's correspondence with Rose Wilder Lane; and Kathy Shoemaker, at Emory University's Manuscript, Archives, and Rare Book Library, which holds the papers of Isaac Don Levine and Ruth Levine. Lee Grady, reference archivist, and other staff at the Wisconsin Historical Society aided in navigating their rich collections, and Heather Stecklein and Robin Melland at the University of Wisconsin, Stout, arranged for me to examine WHS materials at their campus research center in Menomonie, Wisconsin. Reference librarians Nancy Robinson at the Cuba Circulating Library in Cuba, New York, and Kelly Sheahan at the Ella Johnson Memorial Public Library in Kane County, Illinois, diligently searched through rare items in their collections. The public library in Durand, Wisconsin; the Wright County Library in Hartville, Missouri; and especially the Laura Ingalls Wilder Public Library in Mansfield, Missouri, were also enormously helpful.

Two professional researchers supplied welcome assistance. Kevin Leonard, of the Leonard Group, charted a path through the byzantine halls of the National Archives, providing important background on the Federal Farm Loan program. David Williams patiently unfurled Civil War records and searched other materials at the Wisconsin Historical Society. In addition, Sarah Miller generously bestowed digitized materials; Jeff Nillson, archivist & historian at the *Saturday Evening Post*, compiled a list of Lane's contributions to the *Post* and spoke to me about the strange career of Garet Garrett; and Dr. Robert Elsie gave his insight into Albanian history and the sad case of Rexh Meta.

Everyone writing about Wilder is obliged to the home sites that maintain her legacy, and I have found their guides, staff, and local researchers endlessly knowledgeable, engaging, and helpful. I'm indebted to Cheryl Palmlund, former director of the Laura Ingalls Wilder Memorial Society in De Smet, for allowing me to spend a week examining their collection, including items on display and their extensive newspaper files, which I examined on Rose Wilder Lane's Harlingen patio furniture, a gift from Roger MacBride. The Society's current executive director, Tessa Flak, has also lent a hand, offering timely help with photo research.

I thank Roland Rydstrom, guide at the nearby Ingalls Homestead, for an enlightening personal tour of Silver Lake, the family homesteads, and other landmarks. On the same trip, Marie Tschopp graciously invited me to join her on her visit to De Smet's First Congregational Church and the town cemetery with Craig and Bonnie Munger, whose knowledge of the town goes back decades.

In Malone, New York, Anne Smallman, of the Almanzo and Laura Ingalls Wilder Association, opened the archives for me during the off-season. In Pepin, Wisconsin, Catherine Latané joined me on a Sunday morning to discuss years of research. Nicole Elzenga, collections manager at the Laura Ingalls Wilder Museum in Walnut Grove, Minnesota, explained their significant holdings, and in Spring Valley, Sharon Jahn stole time from farming duties to describe her genealogical research, sending key documents and photos. Allen Whipple pored over historical records with me at the Dale Pleasant Prairie cemetery in Zumbro Falls, Minnesota, where Frederick Ingalls may be buried; at the Masters Hotel in Burr Oak, Iowa, curator Bonnie Tieskoetter displayed plat maps and other records. Researchers Sarah Uthoff and John Bass have also provided valuable insight and information. I'm grateful to them all.

In Mansfield, Missouri, I was overwhelmed by the kind hospitality of everyone at the Historical Society, but especially Kathy Short and Donna Brame Climer. Publisher Larry Dennis and staff at the *Mansfield Mirror* allowed me to look through fragile back issues. "Everyone looks in the *Mirror*" used to be their slogan, and it's still true today.

Up in Hartville, I must thank Kathy Garrison, Recorder of Deeds at the Wright County Assessor's Office, who arranged for an assistant to handle her duties one morning so that she could lead me up to the second floor of a dark, abandoned building where she shifted what appeared to be several tons of leather-bound volumes, helping to locate deeds Wilder had recorded during her tenure as secretary/treasurer of the Mansfield Federal Farm Loan program.

I'm obliged as well to Wanda Cope, the Mayor of Hartville, and her husband Darrell Cope. Over the course of an afternoon and on little advance notice, they unspooled for me decades of Wright County political history and their recollections of local hardships during the Great Depression. I'll never forget Darrell Cope's story about a dark day during the Depression when his father set off to confess to the tax collector that he lacked money to pay the bill, expecting to lose his family's home. On the way to town, however, he found and unearthed a nest of skunks and sold their skins for a quarter each, saving the day. It's one thing to read about history, another entirely to hear it firsthand.

In that same vein, I spent a riveting afternoon with Gloria Bogart Carter, who grew up in Mansfield and had astonishing stories to tell about the history of the region. As a teenager, she waited on the Wilders at Winslow's Cafe; as an adult she became a genealogist and historian, acquiring and maintaining a trove of materials documenting local Ozarks lore and lives. I am deeply grateful as well to Nava Austin, for speaking with me about her memories of Wilder. Gloria and Nava remain highlights of my time in that part of the country, and I thank them both.

It remains something of a national shame that this country does not support its literary heritage as well as it might. All of the Wilder home sites have struggled to secure adequate funding, but Mansfield merits particular mention in this regard. While its Wilder manuscripts were microfilmed and made available in the 1980s, the Wilder Home and Museum has never hired a full-time archivist or librarian and its holdings have not been properly catalogued or made available for research, a problem that still awaits a solution. I'm grateful, however, to the tour guides and staff at Rocky Ridge for sharing their abundant knowledge of the Ozarks and of the Wilders' remarkable farm.

AT Metropolitan Books, I have been extremely fortunate to work with the superlative publisher and editor Sara Bershtel. She has, as always, seen exactly what was needed. I benefited as well from the gifted and meticulous line editing of Grigory Tovbis, who patiently pruned and untangled overgrown passages. Prudence Crowther supplied her discerning skills in copyediting, maintaining her good cheer in a pinch.

I'm also grateful to Don Fehr, of Trident Media, who reached out to me in 2013 and has since delivered fine literary representation and clear, calm advice at every turn.

I'd like to thank my friend James McGrath Morris, an accomplished biographer and a founder and past president of the Biographers International Organization, who was kind enough to take time from his own work to supply a recommendation and offer invaluable tips about historical research in Missouri.

My friends Jeff Dreiblatt, William Walker, and the lovely Bess provided a warm Brooklyn haven during Hurricane Sandy, which struck hours after I gave a Wilder talk at the Bank Street BookFest, hosting me as well while I was doing research at Columbia University's Rare Book and Manuscript Library. Though deeply troubled by the episode of the pig's bladder, Jeff, a vegetarian, persevered in reading *Little House in the Big Woods*, a mark of true devotion.

My close friend Harbour Fraser Hodder has always been an indefatigable supporter of my work, generously organizing a book event for my last work. As always, she listened to my hopes and plans for this one, asking important questions, and from her Massachusetts home she sent me on my way to Malone. I value her more than I can say.

While I was working on this project, my brother, Christopher Fraser, and sister-in-law, Linda Warner, discovered and passed along the article describing our Wisconsin past, inspiring the description in the introduction. For that and for so much else, I thank them. My sister Katie Wheatley has likewise uncovered startling details of our ancestry, and she and her exceptional offspring, Sarah Wheatley and Colin Wheatley, have long buoyed my spirits and spurred me on.

Hal Espen, my husband, has put up not only with my actual absences, but with years of Wilder-related absorption. In the early 1990s, he drove me through miles of sunflowers, across half the west to reach De Smet. In addition to dispensing sage editorial advice, he has read untold drafts, pitching in with suggestions for titles, subtitles, photos, and other matters. If books, like quilts, are the work of many hands, his are all over this one. Along with the essential canine comfort of Huck Fraser and Alice Espen, he is my life, and I'm thankful for him every day.

Finally, my preoccupation with western settlement began long ago, with my maternal grandmother telling me about her own labors on a Minnesota farm, where she baked bread before dawn to feed a multitude of brothers and sisters. Her education went only through the fourth grade, and she was supremely unsentimental about the rigors of pioneer life. But she remembered Longfellow's poem, "The Village Blacksmith," and when prodded would dreamily recite it at bedtime to help a little granddaughter go to sleep. This all goes back to her.

My mother, her only child, would grow up to become a public school teacher who would spend her professional life teaching children to read. Then she would come home and read to her own, and I owe to her my sense that the books we discover as children shape our lives. She helped me make books with crayons and bind them with yarn. She took me to libraries and bookstores, gave me every book I ever asked for, and my first typewriter. I promised that if I ever wrote a book I would dedicate it to her, and I regret that this comes too late for her to see it. Memories are our treasures and torments, as Wilder once said, and somehow it is only in books that it can all be set right in the end.

INDEX